Time Out

Dubai

www.timeout.com/dubai

Time Out Digital Ltd
4th Floor
125 Shaftesbury Avenue
London WC2H 8AD
United Kingdom
Tel: +44 (0)20 7813 3000
Fax: +44 (0)20 7813 6001
Email: guides@timeout.com
www.timeout.com

Published by Time Out Digital Ltd, a wholly owned subsidiary of Time Out Group Ltd. Time Out and the Time Out logo are trademarks of Time Out Group Ltd.

Previous editions 2003, 2005, 2007, 2009.

10 9 8 7 6 5 4 3 2 1

This edition first published in Great Britain in 2015 by Ebury Publishing.
20 Vauxhall Bridge Road, London SW1V 2SA

Ebury Publishing is part of the Penguin Random House group of companies whose addresses can be found at global.penguinrandomhouse.com

Distributed in the US and Latin America by Publishers Group West (1-510-809-3700)

For further distribution details, see www.timeout.com.

ISBN: 978-1-84670-716-2

A CIP catalogue record for this book is available from the British Library.

Printed and bound in China by Leo Paper Products Ltd.

MIX
Paper from responsible sources
FSC® C018179

Contents

60

112

240

282

Time Out Dubai

Editorial
Editor Paul Clifford
Copy Editor Ros Sales
Proofreader Tamsin Shelton
Indexer Patrick Davis

Editorial Director Sarah Guy
Group Finance Manager Margaret Wright

Design
Art Editor Christie Webster
Group Commercial Senior Designer Jason Tansley

Picture Desk
Picture Editor Jael Marschner
Deputy Picture Editor Ben Rowe
Picture Researcher Lizzy Owen

Advertising
Managing Director St John Betteridge
Advertising Sales Claude El Feghali, Michael Smith, Christian Kachacha, Rami Akawi, Louise Sweeney, Farrah Taylor

Marketing
Senior Publishing Brand Manager Luthfa Begum
Head of Circulation Dan Collins

Production
Production Controller Katie Mulhern-Bhudia

Time Out Group
Founder Tony Elliott
Chief Executive Officer Tim Arthur
Managing Director Europe Noel Penzer
Publisher Alex Batho

Contributors
Top 20 Paul Clifford. **Dubai Today** Sofia Fernandez-Vyas. **Itineraries** Paul Clifford. **Diary** Paul Clifford. **Dubai's Best** Paul Clifford. **Explore** Paul Clifford, Sofia Fernandez-Vyas, Christopher Hough. **Children** Christopher Hough. **Film** Sofia Fernandez-Vyas. **Outdoors** Sofia Fernandez-Vyas. **Performing Arts** Christopher Hough. **Nightlife** Sofia Fernandez-Vyas. **Spas** Holly Sands. **Escapes & Excursions** Christopher Hough. **Hotels** Christopher Hough. **Directory** Christopher Hough.

Maps JS Graphics Ltd (john@jsgraphics.co.uk). Maps are based on material supplied by Netmaps and updated using OpenStreetMap contributors.

Cover Photography © Robert Harding Images/Masterfile

Back Cover Photography Clockwise from top left: Francesco Dazzi/Shutterstock.com; Patryk Kosmider/Shutterstock.com; Maksym Poriechkin/Shutterstock.com; S-F/Shutterstock.com; slava296/Shutterstock.com

Photography pages 2/3, 26/27 (top), 32 (top), 160/161 Sophie James/Shutterstock.com; 4, 10/11, 12 (top), 16 (top), 17, 26, 29 (bottom), 31 (bottom), 32 (bottom), 33 (top), 39, 40/41 (bottom), 42/43, 43, 54, 64, 65, 71, 73, 76, 77, 88, 95, 96, 102, 106/107, 112, 116, 120, 122, 135, 138, 139, 142, 146, 154 (bottom), 160, 168/169, 170, 179, 180, 189, 190, 200, 201, 202, 204/205, 216, pull-out map ITP Images; 5 (bottom right), 154 (top), 244/245, 284, 285 Nicolas Dumont; 11, 49, 136, 237, 305 Philip Lange/Shutterstock.com; 12 (bottom), 258, 264, pull-out map Laborant/Shutterstock.com; 16 (bottom), 42 TheAkkaas; 18/19 © Maggie Steber/National Geographic Creative/Corbis; 25 Sheikh Mohammed Center for Cultural Understanding; 26/27 (bottom), 78, 132, 133, 256/257 S-F/Shutterstock.com; 34/35 (top) Ross Kinnaird/Getty Images; 34/35 (bottom) Jonathan Walley; 46/47, 48, pull-out map Patryk Kosmider/Shutterstock.com; 53 Mosh Lafuente/ITP Images; 55 Zhukov Oleg/Shutterstock.com; 58, 174 Naiyyer/Shutterstock.com; 78/79 Sorbis/Shutterstock.com; 82 THE-COOL-BOX; 91 momentaryawe.com; 98/99, 261, 262 (top) Rus S/Shutterstock.com; 128/129, 197 Chris Cypert; 137 GTS Productions/Shutterstock.com; 140 (top) Russ Kientsch; 145 Neil Scott Corder; 153 Kiev.Victor/Shutterstock.com; 172, 212, 230/231 Lester Ali/ITP Images; 175 Thor Jorgen Udvang/Shutterstock.com; 176/177 Alisdair Miller; 182/183 © The MusicHall, Dubai; 195 Universal Pictures/The Kobal Collection; 206 Dan Martensen; 207 TO Dubai; 208, 210 PHISHFOTOZ; 217, 263 Emaar Properties; 231 Leisa Tyler/LightRocket/Getty Images; 244/245 Paul Popper/Popperfoto/Getty Images; 246 Look Bellow/Wikimedia Commons; 249 AP Photo/Roy Essoyan/Press Association Images; 250 PA Archive/Press Association Images; 259 Tux the penguin/Wikimedia Commons; 262 (bottom) Goran Bogicevic/Shutterstock.com; 265 mohamed alwerdany/Shutterstock.com; 268 Eric Cuvillier; 304 Ilona Ignatova/Shutterstock.com

The following images were supplied by the featured establishments: 5 (left), 16 (middle), 27, 29 (top), 38, 40/41 (top), 46, 60, 61, 84, 85, 86, 92, 98, 105, 108, 109, 111, 121, 124/125, 127, 140 (bottom), 143, 158, 159, 164, 167, 172/173, 184, 185, 186, 192, 193, 194, 196, 198/199, 209, 214, 218, 219, 222, 223, 239, 260, 266/267, 271, 274, 275, 277, 280, 283, 286

About the Guide

GETTING AROUND

Each sightseeing chapter contains a street map of the area marked with the locations of sights and museums (❶), restaurants (❶), cafés and bars (❶) and shops (❶). There are also street maps of Dubai at the back of the book, along with an overview map of the city. In addition, there is a detachable fold-out street map.

THE ESSENTIALS

For practical information, including visas, disabled access, emergency numbers, lost property, websites and local transport, see the Essential Information section. It begins on page 266.

THE LISTINGS

Addresses, phone numbers, websites, transport information, hours and prices are all included in our listings, as are selected other facilities. All were checked and correct at press time. However, business owners can alter their arrangements at any time, and fluctuating economic conditions can cause prices to change rapidly.

The very best venues in the city, the must-sees and must-dos in every category, have been marked with a red star (★). In the sightseeing chapters, we've also marked venues with free admission with a FREE symbol.

THE LANGUAGE

Many Emiratis speak English as well as Arabic, especially those working in tourism. There is a short Arabic primer on page 299.

PHONE NUMBERS

The area code for Dubai is 04. When calling within Dubai people generally dial the area code even if they are calling from the same area. So, to make a local call within Dubai, it is usual, though not essential, to dial 04. From outside Dubai, dial your country's access code (00 from the UK, 011 from the US) or a plus symbol, followed by the United Arab Emirates country code (971), then 04 for Dubai (dropping the initial zero) and the number. So, to reach the Dubai Museum dial +971 4 353 1862.

FEEDBACK

We welcome feedback on this guide, both on the venues we've included and on any other locations that you'd like to see featured in future editions. Please email us at guides@timeout.com.

© Copyright Time Out Group 2015

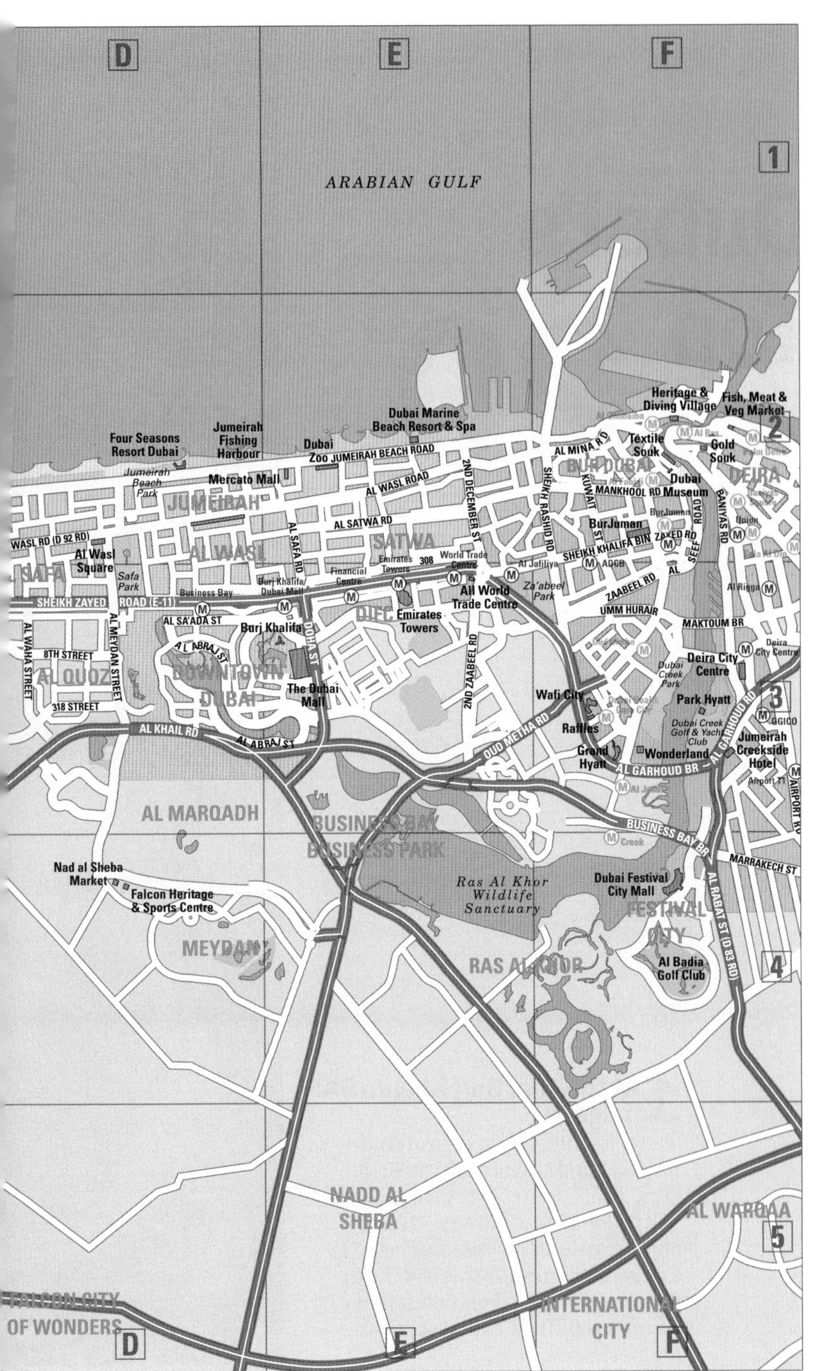
D
E
F
1
2
3
4
5
ARABIAN GULF
Heritage & Diving Village
Fish, Meat & Veg Market
Dubai Marine Beach Resort & Spa
Four Seasons Resort Dubai
Jumeirah Fishing Harbour
Dubai Zoo
JUMEIRAH BEACH ROAD
Textile Souk
Gold Souk
AL MINA RD
BUR DUBAI
DEIRA
Jumeirah Beach Park
Mercato Mall
JUMEIRAH
AL WASL ROAD
2ND DECEMBER ST
SHEIKH RASHID RD
KUWAIT ST
MANKHOOL RD
Dubai Museum
BANIYAS RD
AL SATWA RD
BurJuman
SEEF ROAD
WASL RD (D 92 RD)
AL SAFA RD
SATWA
SHEIKH KHALIFA BIN ZAYED RD
Al Wasl Square
AL WASL
Emirates Towers
308
World Trade Centre
Al Jafiliya
ADCB
SAFA
Safa Park
Financial Centre
Burj Khalifa/ Dubai Mall
Business Bay
All World Trade Centre
Za'abeel Park
ZAABEEL RD
Al Rigga
SHEIKH ZAYED ROAD (E-11)
AL SA'ADA ST
Burj Khalifa
DIFC
Emirates Towers
UMM HURAIR
MAKTOUM BR
AL WAHA STREET
AL MEYDAN STREET
8TH STREET
AL ABRAJ ST
DOHA ST
2ND ZAABEEL RD
Dubai Creek Park
Deira City Centre
AL QUOZ
DOWNTOWN DUBAI
The Dubai Mall
Wafi City
Park Hyatt
318 STREET
Raffles
Dubai Creek Golf & Yacht Club
AL GARHOUD RD
Jumeirah Creekside Hotel
AL KHAIL RD
AL ABRAJ ST
OUD METHA RD
Grand Hyatt
Wonderland
AL GARHOUD BR
Airport T1
AIRPORT RD
AL MARQADH
BUSINESS BAY BUSINESS PARK
BUSINESS BAY BR
Creek
MARRAKECH ST
Nad al Sheba Market
Falcon Heritage & Sports Centre
Ras Al Khor Wildlife Sanctuary
Dubai Festival City Mall
FESTIVAL CITY
AL RABAT ST (D 83 RD)
MEYDAN
RAS AL KHOR
Al Badia Golf Club
NADD AL SHEBA
AL WARQAA
FALCON CITY OF WONDERS
INTERNATIONAL CITY

Dubai's Top 20

From the world's tallest building to a fish shack by the sea, we count down the city's finest.

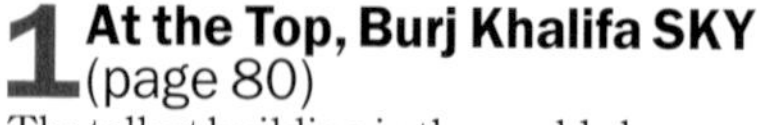

1 At the Top, Burj Khalifa SKY (page 80)

The tallest building in the world also has the world's highest observation deck. At 555 metres (1,820 feet), the view will take your breath away – and not only because the air is thinner here. On a clear day you can see beyond Dubai and, disorientingly, helicopters flying beneath you. Try it just before dusk for the clearest view.

2 Abra ride across the Creek (page 55)

Once the hub of Dubai, the Creek (which runs between Deira and Bur Dubai) remains busy. The waterway is packed with multicoloured dhows piled high with cargo bound for the Indian subcontinent and *abras* carrying passengers from one side of the Creek to the other. An *abra* ride costs Dhs1 per person one-way and only lasts a few minutes, but there's nothing like it elsewhere in Dubai. If you're on the Creek as the sun is setting, the views are intoxicating.

2

3 Gold, spice & textile souks (pages 49, 53, 72)

No visit to the old part of Dubai would be complete without taking in the souks. From Al Fahidi in Bur Dubai, wander through the textile souk with its myriad coloured fabrics. Then get an *abra* over to Deira for the spice souk, which adds smell to the sensory load. It's not huge but there are stores crammed with aromatic powders, most noticeably saffron and cumin. The gold souk is nearby and positively drips with the stuff.

4 Al Fahidi Historical Neighbourhood
(page 64)

This neighbourhood, in Bur Dubai, takes visitors back to the early 1900s. The oldest part of Dubai – a piece of the original wall – is here. Today, the areas has been regenerated and its alleyways are lined with art galleries, cafés and restaurants in old-style flat-roofed buildings, while the distinctive wind towers atop the buildings are a traditional form of air-conditioning. The nearby Dubai Museum, within the old Al Fahidi Fort, is excellent.

5 Dubai Mall
(page 88)

Consumer heaven: the world's largest shopping mall has just about every major store and brand you could ever hope to find, as well as a luxury hotel, a 22-screen cinema, and more than 100 restaurants and cafés. It's also home to the Dubai Ice Rink, Dubai Aquarium and Underwater Zoo, Sega Republic and KidZania, where children work in adult jobs in exchange for pay. Topping out the bizarre factor is the DubaiDino – a 155-million-year-old relative of the diplodocus.

6 Jumeirah Corniche
(page 117)

Much of the coast is broken up by private beaches, making for small, patchy public areas. The Jumeirah Corniche is a new 14-kilometre (nine-mile) strand completed in October 2014 that allows uninterrupted walks between Dubai Marine Beach Resort & Spa and the

Burj Al Arab on a five-metre-wide (16-foot) boardwalk. There are plenty of kiosks along the way, plus a jogging track and shaded benches overlooking the sea.

7 Aquaventure at Atlantis The Palm

(page 153)

The imposing Atlantis Hotel and Resort is home to many restaurants and beach clubs, but perhaps the most fun can be had at Aquaventure. A 1.6-kilometre (one-mile) river with rapids runs through the park, with tributaries flowing to the Tower of Neptune – three slides including a near-vertical drop into a 'shark-infested' lagoon – and the Tower of Poseidon, with the world's longest waterpark slide.

8 Desert Safari

(page 215)

There's a lot of empty sand around Dubai. Explore it with Arabian Adventures' Sundowner tour. Trained guides drive 4x4s over sand dunes deep into the desert to a Bedouin-style camp, for an Arabic buffet, belly dancing, falcon viewing and camel rides.

9 Ski Dubai

(page 130)

Yes, snow. Lots of it. Enough to ski, snowboard, sledge or just play about. Outside it could be over 40 degrees, but indoors, at Al Barsha's Mall of the Emirates, it's minus five. The penguins – gentoo and king – that are kept here for tourist photo opportunities (at extra cost) are probably most relieved.

10 Dubai Fountain

(page 80)

Yes, it's the world's biggest. The Dubai Fountain was designed by the team behind the fountains at Las Vegas's Bellagio Hotel. Lit by 6,600 lights and 26 colour projectors, water is sprayed up to 150 metres (500 feet) into the air during the show. The promenade around the lake gets very busy on weekend evenings, so grab some food or a drink at one of the many restaurants or cafés nearby, listen to the music (including Michael Jackson's 'Thriller' and 'I Will Always Love You' by Whitney Houston, plus classical and Arabic pieces) and soak up the performance.

11 Skydive Dubai
(page 209)

There aren't many ways to get higher than the Burj Khalifa, but one of them is to jump out of a plane at 4,000 metres (13,000 feet). Skydive Dubai provides tandem parachute jumps from its base on Dubai Marina. From that height there are about 40 or 50 seconds of freefall and a few minutes dangling from a parachute – plenty of time to take in the sights.

12 Ravi Restaurant
(page 125)

When it's time for a change from five-star dining, Ravi is the answer. It serves simple Pakistani food on plastic plates, the water comes in paper cups and the tables are adorned with wipe-down tablecloths. It's popular with the local Pakistani community, but less well known among Westerners. One of the best (and cheapest) meals you'll get in Dubai.

13 High tea at the Burj Al Arab
(page 279)

Now 15 years old, the Burj Al Arab stands on an artificial island off Jumeirah Beach. It had the chutzpah to proclaim itself the world's first seven-star hotel and the label has stuck. The interior is as impressive as its boast suggests and is best enjoyed while taking a champagne afternoon tea at Sahn Eddar. Just don't expect a bargain.

14 Jumeirah Mosque
(page 117)

To get a feel for the deep-rooted religion that's the backbone of Dubai, make sure you plan a visit to Jumeirah Mosque, the only mosque in the emirate that's open to non-Muslims. Universally known as 'the big mosque' to taxi drivers, it's easy to find and is open to visitors from Saturday to Thursday at 10am.

15 Barasti beach bar

(page 154)

At the other end of the spectrum from the sobriety of the big mosque is Barasti, winner of *Time Out Dubai*'s Best Bar award in 2015. It attracts a fairly rowdy crowd who want to enjoy the beach setting, live music and party atmosphere, but there's plenty of space to spread out, watch sports on the big screen or chill out with some food.

16 The Beach

(page 164)

This being Dubai, the Beach is a development that comes complete with accompanying shops, cafés and restaurants. There aren't many places suitable for a stroll in the emirate, so its open-air plan is a welcome addition to the city. No bars, but there's a waterpark and outdoor gym. Oh, and there's a beach too.

17 Bu Qtair
(page 138)

It looks fairly unassuming, a white Portakabin by the beach with an old sign and a few tables outside. Just a stone's throw from the Burj Al Arab, the difference couldn't be more stark. However, this is an experience like no other in Dubai. There's little choice this is a fish restaurant specialising in Keralan food, serving whatever's caught that day – but it really is as good as everyone says it is.

18 Madinat Jumeirah
(page 137)

Madinat Jumeirah is a huge resort, chock full of bars, restaurants and shops as well as two of Dubai's most luxurious hotels. It was designed to resemble a traditional Arabian town and is roughly the size of one. Inside there's the souk, as well as an American-style smokehouse and bar, an incarnation of Ibizan nightclub Pacha, a theatre and an amphitheatre. Some of the restaurants require an *abra* ride on the Madinat's waterways to get to them, adding a little romance to a night out here.

19 Food tour of Old Dubai
(page 77)

Discover the culinary delights of Dubai on this unique and insightful walking tour. Foodies can experience the diverse flavours of all of the nationalities in the city, as well the emirate's heritage, on these tasty trails. Led by sisters Arva and Farida Ahmed, who are passionate about what they do, tours take visitors away from the five-star haunts to discover some secret culinary stars.

20 Dubai Moving Image Museum
(page 144)

A hidden gem, the Dubai Moving Image Museum houses the private collection of Akram Miknas. He accumulated the collection of artefacts – which showcases the progression of moving images up to the birth of cinema – over 25 years, and wanted to share it with the world. The museum is the only one of its kind in the Middle East and is off the beaten track in the mostly residential area of TECOM. It's accessible by metro, though, and well worth the trip to see pieces dating back to the 1700s.

Dubai Today

'Dubai is back' – Sheikh Mohammed bin Rashid Al Maktoum.

TEXT: SOFIA FERNANDEZ VYAS

Stroll along the Beach at JBR and you could be in LA; step off the metro at Al Fahidi and it's another world. Here, you'll find yourself in the microcosm of Asia that is Old Dubai, the area that grew up around the original 19th-century Creek-side settlement and is now home to thousands of expats from countries such as India, Pakistan, the Phillipines and Sri Lanka. It's a distinctive divide and one that can't be ignored. There are few places in the world where that overused phrase 'city of contrasts' rings as true as in this cosmopolitan desert city, where locals are vastly outnumbered by expats, from both East and West. It's a contrast that's a crucial part of the city's identity – and a cause of controversy.

A TALE OF TWO CITIES

Spend a few minutes scrolling through Google and you'll find countless articles similar to Johann Hari's notorious 'The Dark Side of Dubai' in *The Independent*, a 2009 piece that highlighted, among other issues, bad conditions for migrant workers. It's certainly true that the city owes its almost impossibly fast expansion to foreign labour, and that a sizeable portion of the city's economy is propped up by low-income expats from across Asia. In fact, remove them and the city would quite literally grind to a halt – left without public transport and taxis, as well as construction workers, shop assistants, cashiers, customer service agents and teachers. These issues began making international news around 2006, almost ten years ago, a time when the country was just beginning to become the metropolis that it is today.

Not long ago, however, Sheikh Mohammed bin Rashid Al Maktoum, vice-president and prime minister of the UAE and ruler of Dubai, began opening up to the foreign press and answering frank questions about these concerns and his visions for a tolerant, vibrant and modern Middle Eastern city. In an interview with the BBC's Jon Sopel, he admitted that – as with many of the world's biggest cities – there are issues that still need attention. He agreed that in the past poor practice had occurred with the treatment of the migrant workforce, but argued that policies had been put in place to hold companies accountable for their treatment of workers, to raise standards of living and ensure correct salary payment. He stated that the human rights record of Dubai was not satisfactory, but as an imperfect country it would continue to strive to fix its problems and rectify mistakes.

THE MAKTOUM FAMILY

Support for the UAE government, led by the royal families of its seven emirates, is extremely high, especially when compared to the Arab countries affected by the Arab Spring.

The Nayhan family rules over Abu Dhabi and the UAE. Sheikh Zayed bin Sultan Al Nayhan became president following the UAE's official formation in 1971, a post he kept until his death in November 2004. The Maktoum family rules over Dubai, and has done since 1833. The UAE system also features a half-elected federal assembly with a consultative role, but there are no political parties.

The Maktoum family's popularity in Dubai is partly down to the approachability of Sheikh Mohammed bin Rashid Al Maktoum. His son, Sheikh Hamdan bin Mohammed bin Rashid Al Maktoum, affectionately known as Fazza, is the crown prince of Dubai and just as popular with much of the country's young population.

Evidence of this admiration can be seen in the photographs of the royal family on billboards by the side of the city's highways or hanging in office buildings. When Dubai won the bid for the World Expo 2020 in 2013, one proclaimed, 'Whoever said winning isn't everything doesn't know Dubai,' beside photographs of Sheikh Mohammed and Sheikh Zayed, while another pictured Fazza sitting atop the spire of the Burj Khalifa, showing Sheikh Mohammed's three-fingered 'Win, Victory and Love' symbol.

'OPEN DOORS, OPEN MINDS'

Although respect for Dubai's royal family is common among local Emiratis and expats, assimilation between the two communities isn't. Dubai is notably more Westernised and liberal than neighbouring emirate Sharjah, or the capital Abu Dhabi, and peaceful coexistence has never been an issue, but integration in a social sense is minimal.

It's difficult to pinpoint the root of this failing. Emiratis are warm, generous and hospitable people who are eager to share their traditions with visitors, and the government makes consistent efforts to preserve the culture of the UAE and promote better understanding between the many cultures that inhabit it. Arabic, for example, is compulsory in schools for non-Arab students up to the end of Year 9, and the evaluation of students' 'understanding of Islamic values and awareness of Emirati and world cultures' is a key component of school inspections made by the Education Authority.

Initiatives like the Sheikh Mohammed Centre for Cultural Understanding, which was set up in 1999, aim to promote the local culture under the motto 'Open doors, open minds', giving visitors the chance to enjoy a traditional Emirati meal with a volunteer who answers questions about local culture. The Al Marmoon Heritage Festival takes place over 12 days each year and sees thousands of camels compete in

races and events and, just an hour away in Abu Dhabi, the Qasr Al Hosn Festival promotes all aspects of Emirati culture, from the traditions of *ghawa* – Arabic coffee – to falconry and traditional performance.

EMIRATISATION EFFORTS

Initiatives are being put in place to increase Emirati employment levels in the private sector. Emiratis make up less than 20 per cent of the country's population – in 2010 there were only 900,000 to more than seven million expatriates – but their employment levels remain low, at just 2.7 per cent of the county's total workforce.

'Bulldozers and cranes are moving again.'

Emirati youth unemployment in the UAE was eight per cent in 2012, following which 2013 was declared the year of Emiratisation, aiming to tackle the unemployment rate of UAE nationals and double their numbers in the private sector. Compulsory national military service was introduced in 2014 for Emirati men between the ages of 18 and 30: nine months for those who have completed secondary school, and two years for those who have not, in an attempt to lower unemployment and encourage young Emiratis to continue with education.

ROLLING WITH THE WORLD ECONOMY

The Dubai Strategic Plan 2015 – a ten-year plan drawn up in 2005 – pinpointed aims for the emirate's social and economic development. It also called for Emiratisation, along with the preservation of national identity and community cohesion, and prompted the Dubai initiatives to improve Arabic language proficiency, get locals into jobs and develop the city's cultural environment. But the main focus was on how to continue the city's economic success.

Although the basis of Dubai's initial economic boom was the discovery of oil, by 2005 the oil and gas industry accounted for just 5.1 per cent of its GDP and the government was channelling money into building its tourism and construction sectors. But the city didn't manage to evade the world financial crisis and recession, and there was a lull in the rate of building for a few years from 2008, when a number of large-scale projects were halted. These included the second Palm Island in Jebel Ali and Dubailand. This ambitious development had included plans for a Universal Studios; more than 20 theme parks, one of which was the flagship Six Flags Dubai; seven markets and malls as part of a Retail World; and 20 other developments taking in leisure, sport and tourism, eco-tourism, plus a downtown area. However, depite the problems, Dubai emerged relatively unscathed, and the government continued to work towards the Strategic Plan's aim to sustain an 11 per cent growth in GDP up to 2015.

Now, the Strategic Plan has been replaced with Vision 2021 and the perhaps more realistic goal of five per cent GDP growth each year by that date. The rest of the plan illustrates the wider goals that the UAE's leaders have set for the country, including being listed as one of the top five countries in the world for happiness, and to have 20 Olympic medals.

Meanwhile, the bulldozers and cranes are moving again. The Dubai tram is now running, public areas such as the waterfront have been developed and construction has begun on the Dubai Canal project and Dubai Design District (d3), with its planned complex of retail, leisure and office buildings.

THE FUTURE

Dubai is no stranger to criticism, but there is something to be said for its wacky, weird and uninhibited development; after all, how many other cities have made such a splash in so short a time? And it's not just flash and ostentation. Cultures from across Asia have left their mark in 'Old Dubai', even though, in Jumeirah, there are more than enough mansions and Lamborghinis to go round for the most avid collector of outrageous bling. Meanwhile, Downtown is dominated by the unexpectedly beautiful feat of engineering that is the world's tallest building.

There are few cities in the world which have been influenced by so many cultures as Dubai. As it continues to add to its competitive, anything-you-can-do-I-can-do-better portfolio of skyscrapers, malls, hotels and theme parks, a genuine identity is also emerging.

LIFE IN DUBAI

The low-down on Emirati culture.

ISLAM

Islam plays an integral and public role in Emirati society and visitors soon become accustomed to the sound of the call to prayer on mosque loudspeakers. Observant Muslims fulfill the requirements for five-times daily prayer, facing Mecca, and its not uncommon to see people praying in office corridors or by the side of the road, although there are prayer rooms at most shopping centres and at the airport. As for other faiths, the UAE allows temples and churches, though active proselytisation is not allowed.

RAMADAN

Ramadan is a particularly important time for Muslims, who are required to abstain from eating, drinking and smoking between sunrise and sunset – and visitors are asked to refrain from the above in public or else cop a fine and possible jail sentence. During the Holy Month, cafés and restaurants close or lower their blinds during the day, while some shops will open at sunset. Live music and dancing are also banned. However, the evening festivities for *iftar* – when Muslims break their fast – and on into the night can be enjoyed by locals and visitors, with most hotels erecting special Ramadan tents for feasting, socialising and traditional games.

THE WEEKEND

The official weekend is Friday and Saturday. Friday is the Islamic holy day, and Emiratis like to spend it with loved ones at parks, beaches or in their homes. Many shops and souks don't open until late afternoon.

THE FAMILY

The extended family is of crucial importance to Emiratis. Names tend to define someone within their immediate family – such as *bin* ('son of') or *bint* ('daughter of') – and within their tribe or extended family by the prefix *Al* (the). The existence of *wasta* (connections) – the 'old boys' network' giving favours to those with family and friends in high places – still exists alongside a new meritocracy.

NATIONAL DRESS

Most Emiratis wear their national dress in public, though at home many tend to wear Western clothing. Men wear the white full-length robe known as a *dishdasha*, with a white or red head dress called a *ghutra*. The black cord that wraps around the *ghutra* is known as an *agal*, which Bedouins once used to secure camels. Women wear the black robe called an *abaya* with a head scarf known as a *shayla*; these days it's becoming increasingly rare to see a plain *abaya* – many are embroidered and embellished with beads or even Swarovski crystals. Though it's less common, you may also spot more traditional Arab women wearing a *burka* – a tough fabric mask covering their faces.

WOMEN

Emirati women are free to drive and pursue studies and hobbies. Generally, unmarried men and women tend to lead separate lives – at weddings women usually hold separate celebrations to the men. Some areas of life are still off-limits to women. At public events, such as the horse races, it's rare to see Emirati wives accompanying their husbands. These traditions extend to ladies' days in parks, female-only beaches and to women being served first or separately in banks or other queues. If a woman offers her hand to you, a shake is OK. If not, a smile and a nod are appropriate.

TIPS FOR VISITORS

Alcohol There are plenty of restaurants and bars serving alcohol, mostly inside hotels, although there are a few standalone establishments, mostly in the free zones such as DIFC. The law states that everyone drinking in the bar should be a guest of that hotel, but this is a grey area and enforcement is rare. Residents are free to drink in their own home providing they hold an alcohol licence issued by the municipality. There are two main alcohol distributors, a+e and MMI, which distribute alcohol to bars and also sell it through their own shops to licence holders. Tourists are free to bring limited amounts of alcohol into the country (*see p292*). It is illegal to drink in the streets or in public places.

Clothes Sunbathing in swimwear on the beach is fine, but you must don more substantial clothes over your swimsuit before stepping off the beach. In all public places (streets, shopping malls and restaurants), shorts and skirts must be of a reasonable length – avoid miniskirts or short shorts. Avoid wearing clothing that is low-cut, transparent, or that displays obscene or potentially offensive pictures or slogans.

Drugs The UEA takes a hard line on drug use, dealing and importing. *See p293*.

Hotel rooms Strictly speaking, it's illegal for an unmarried couple to share a hotel room. However, very few establishments will actually ask to see a marriage certificate – particularly if you are a Western couple.

Language Dubai is effectively bilingual – road signs, maps and daily newspapers are in English, and most Emiratis speak the language well. However, some public-sector staff and other officials don't have the same language skills and as a result can sound quite brusque. But this has more to do with the imprecise art of translating Arabic into English than rudeness. It is also worth tuning your ear to the mix of Hindi or Urdu and English that you'll commonly hear around town. Dubai's ethnic majority comes from the subcontinent and often mixes this unique blend of English with a smattering of Arabic.

Mosque tour Non-Muslims aren't normally allowed inside Dubai mosques, but visitors can join the Sheikh Mohammed bin Rashid Centre for Cultural Understanding on a guided tour of Jumeirah Mosque every day except Friday. It's a unique opportunity to learn about Emirati culture and religion in a relaxed and open atmosphere. Tours start at 10am; reservations aren't required, although you should arrive at the mosque's main entrance at 9.45am. Tours last around 75 minutes and you are asked to wear modest clothing (traditional attire can be borrowed, if needed). Visit www.cultures.ae or call 04 353 6666 for more information.

Pork Most supermarkets have specific non-Muslim sections selling otherwise forbidden meat products, and numerous restaurants also have licences to serve pork.

Public displays of affection Despite the scare stories, you won't end up in jail for holding hands in Dubai. But this isn't to say you should throw all caution to the wind; displays of affection with someone to whom you are not married are illegal under the UAE penal law of 1987. You will see plenty of married couples holding hands in the malls and our advice would be, if you're married, to be respectful of local customs and not go any further than that.

Itineraries

Plan your perfect trip with our step-by-step Dubai planner.

Clockwise from left: **Tom & Serg**; **Burj Khalifa**; **Gramercy**; **Dubai Aquarium**.

Day 1

9AM Begin the day at the 2015 winner of *Time Out Dubai*'s best café award, **Tom & Serg** (*p135*). The cool space, just off Sheikh Zayed Road in the upcoming, arty Al Quoz district, kickstarted a coffee scene in the city and was one of the first places to have an open-plan, warehouse feel. It does good breakfasts too. From there it's a short walk to Alserkal Avenue (if you can stand the heat, if not it will be a very cheap taxi). Since 2007, the cluster of units in the industrial area have been transformed into an arts hub, with more than 20 creative and artistic spaces now occupying the warehouses.

NOON After Alserkal Avenue everything is sunny, sandy or shiny. Take a taxi to **Dubai Mall** (*p88*) in Downtown. There are more than 1,200 stores, selling almost everything you could wish for, and distractions ranging from the aquatic – **Dubai**

Aquarium (*p88*) – to the arctic – **Dubai Ice Rink** (*p187*) – to the downright bizarre – **DubaiDino**. You'll find food from every cuisine here, but for an extra touch of class, make your way to **Armani/ Dubai Caffè** (*p87*) in the mall's Fashion Avenue. There's no question of style over substance here, and the food is great, though you might want to look the part – it's a place to see and be seen.

5PM Depending on the time of year, the sun will set some time between 5pm and 7pm – which is also the best time to visit At the Top at **Burj Khalifa** (*p80*). As the haze in the air begins to disappear the view improves. There are often queues, so it's best to book in advance (the tickets will also be cheaper). The At the Top viewing platform is either 456 metres (1,495 feet) or 555 metres (1,820 feet) high (the latter if you choose the SKY option) on the world's tallest building. Learn about its construction and sip a cofffee in the café before heading down.

7PM Once the sun has gone down, the **Dubai Fountain** (*p80*) outside the Dubai Mall really comes to life. Squeeze in with the crowds and watch as the fountains dance to classical, Arabic and pop music every 15 minutes. After the show, walk over the footbridge to **Souk Al Bahar** (*p93*) and its bars and restaurants. Favourites are cool hangout Karma Kafé, Cuban-themed Café Habana, or the more low-key bar Left Bank.

9PM Time to eat. **Zuma** (*p103*) is the place. This Japanese restaurant is a multiple *Time Out Dubai* award winner. After dinner stay in Zuma's lounge bar for some post-food drinks, or head to the **Gramercy** (*p103*) for a pint in a proper pub (or as close as you'll get in this part of town), a short walk away.

Mall of the Emirates
Shopping is just the beginning

Day 2

9AM After a day seeing the dizzying heights of Downtown Dubai, it's time for the more traditional Deira and Bur Dubai. Begin in Deira, at the **Fish Market** on Al Khaleej Road, watching as fishermen bring in and sell their catch. (Its days may be numbered, as a new market on the other side of the Creek was in the works at the time of writing.) From here, take a short walk to the **Gold Souk** (*p49*), where you can barter for jewellery if you've got the cash and the inclination, and then move on to the **Spice Souk** (*p53*), where sacks filled with aromatic cinnamon, sumac, cloves and other spices line the streets; you can also buy boxes of saffron. Walk the short distance to the Creek, past the dhows loading cargo, to the *abra* stations for the ride across Dubai Creek.

NOON On the Bur Dubai side of the water visit **Creekside** (*p69*), the café, bistro and cultural centre perched on the water's edge. Walk along the Creek, past the Ruler's Court, to **Al Fahidi Historical Neighbourhood** (*p71*), a re-creation of the original settlement that stood here, dating from 1859. Get lost in its narrow alleyways and stumble upon art galleries, including the **XVA Art Gallery** (*p72*), which also does a mean line in vegetarian food and ice teas. The **Textile Souk** (*p72*) is close by, down the tiny alleyway which also leads to the city's only **Hindu Temple**. The souk takes you to **Bayt Al Wakeel** (*p68*), an Arabic restaurant in one of the city's oldest buildings, perched out over the Creek.

7PM With the unrelenting heat of the sun gone, stroll further along the Creek towards the coast, to **Shindagha Tower** (*p64*), one of Dubai's original defensive watchtowers, before reaching the **Saeed Al Maktoum House** (*p68*), dating from 1896, with its fascinating collection of stamps, coins and illuminating photographs of Dubai. Further along the waterfront is the **Heritage & Diving Village** (*p65*), a re-creation of the fishing village that once stood there. The Creekside restaurants, amid twinkling lights, are a good place to stop for dinner. Try **Al Bandar** for a fine selection of seafood, freshly caught that day.

11PM It's night, and if you've still got energy, it's time to play. For a night to remember, head for **Cirque le Soir** (*p200*) at the Fairmont Hotel, a nightclub and circus with its own troupe of performance artists and dancers, as well as visiting DJs.

Above: **Spice Souk**.
Below: **XVA Art Gallery**.

Day 3

10AM There are guided tours of the **Jumeirah Mosque** (*p117*) on Tuesday, Thursday, Saturday and Sunday. Phone ahead to book a tour and come in modest clothing; the tour lasts around 75 minutes.The mosque is on **Jumeirah Beach Road**, a long stretch taking you from the old town towards 'new Dubai', with lots of cafés and malls. Running parallel to Beach Road is Al Wasl, home to **BoxPark** (*p122*), a new shopping centre made up of shipping containers (much in the style of the venue in London's Shoreditch). It hosts stores for the likes of Adidas and Nike as well as places to eat and have a (non-alcoholic) drink. Try **Bianca Mozzarella & Co** (*p122*) for a light Italian lunch.

2PM After refuelling, head back towards the coast for an afternoon at **Kite Beach** (*p114*) for beach volleyball and football, stand-up paddling and kitesurfing (hence the name). There are changing and showering facilities here, and the beach is lined with cool places to grab a snack, including Dubai's first food truck, **SALT** (*p115*). If the heat gets too much, though, grab a taxi to **Mall of the Emirates** (*p136*) and indoor ski venue **Ski Dubai** (*p130*). If you don't fancy taking on the slopes, take a seat at **Après** (*p134*) and consider the incongruity of watching people ski from the vantage point of a desert mall.

9PM The **Burj Al Arab** (*p283*) is the landmark that really put Dubai on the map. There are some restaurants inside the seven-star hotel, but they're expensive and, of course, you miss the view, so head to **Madinat Jumeirah** (*p137*) instead. Walk around the mall's souk-style interior, stopping for refreshments at the **Belgian Beer Café** (*p60*) or the **Agency** (*p143*). For a romantic meal try **Pierchic** (*p141*), then work off the last ergs of energy at super-club **Pacha** (*p198*).

Above: **Jumeirah Mosque**. Below: **SALT**.

20 THINGS TO DO FOR LESS THAN DHS1

You don't have to splash the cash to enjoy Dubai.

Thought Dubai was the city of excess? Well, you're not wrong. Nevertheless, there are plenty of ways to pass the time without having to splash the cash.

1 CROSS THE CREEK

Hop on a motorised wooden *abra* and travel between Bur Dubai and Deira for just a dirham. It's one of the best experiences in the city. Board at Deira Old Souk or Bur Dubai Abra stations. *See p55.*

2 GET MAKE-UP TIPS

Brush up on your application methods and skills with a free lesson taught by make-up artists at Bobbi Brown stores. *Bobbi Brown stores, various locations including Dubai Mall, Downtown (04 330 8151). Metro Burj Khalifa/Dubai Mall.*

3 VISIT A TRADITIONAL SUMMER HOUSE

Majlis Al Ghorfat Um Al Sheif was built in 1955 as a summer residence for the late Sheikh Rashid Bin Saeed Al Maktoum. It's made of gypsum and coral rock, with a date palm frond roof and wind tower. *See p117.*

4 WATCH MOVIES ON A ROOFTOP

Head to Wafi's Movies Under the Stars screenings every Sunday evening to relax on huge beanbags and watch films on a giant screen. *See p194.*

5 FIND YOUR ZEN

Join a free community yoga session at Al Barsha Pond Park every Saturday evening. *Al Barsha Pond Park, Al Barsha (050 873 8109, www.lakshya yoga.com). Metro Mall of the Emirates.*

6 VISIT DUBAI'S OLDEST SCHOOL

Al Ahmadiya School is the oldest school in Dubai and now houses an interesting museum of education. *See p187.*

7 BOOK IN FOR A HAIR CUT

Get your tresses trimmed by students at French hairdressing academy Formul'A. Trainees are supervised by experienced instructors as they chop away. *Block 11, Knowledge Village, Al Sufou (800 380 623, www.formula-academy.net). Tram Knowledge Village.*

8 POUND THE PAVEMENTS
Join the Dubai Road Runners for training sessions every Sunday and Tuesday evening. *Al Barsha Park, Al Barsha (www.dubairoadrunners.com). Metro Mall of the Emirates.*

9 DINNER FOR A DIRHAM
Ladies can head to SoHo Bar & Grill to enjoy its 'Dinner for a Dirham' promotion every Tuesday evening. *Century Village, Garhoud (next to Dubai Tennis Stadium) (04 286 8520, www.sohobarandgrill.ae). Metro GGICO.*

10 WATCH WATER
The largest choreographed fountain show in the world, the Dubai Fountain shoots water 150 metres (500 feet) in the air; its beams of light are visible from space. *See p80.*

11 A DAY ON THE BEACH
With its white sand and ample changing facilities, the beach at JBR is the perfect spot for sun-seekers on a budget. *The Beach, JBR (04 431 0190, www.thebeach.ae). Tram Jumeirah Beach Residence 2.*

12 STEP BACK IN TIME
Head to the Heritage and Diving Village to see potters and weavers practising traditional crafts, as well as pearl-diving demonstrations. *See p65.*

13 TREAT THE CHILDREN
Entertain the kids at Fun City, with its Fun Day Monday promotion, which lets them play for a dirham a game. *Fun City, various locations including Oasis Centre (04 339 7783). Metro Noor Bank.*

14 WATCH STREET WRESTLING
Make your way to Deira on a Friday afternoon to join the crowds watching the south Asian sport of *pehlwani*. *Near Deira Fish Market, Deira. Metro Palm Deira 2.*

15 SEE FLAMINGOES
Stand at the flamingo roost at Ras Al Khor Wildlife Sanctuary to watch the pink birds against a spectacular cityscape. *Ras Al Khor Wildlife Sanctuary, off the junction of Al Wasl and Oud Metha roads (04 606 6822, www.wildlife.ae).*

16 GET A SWEET FIX
Enjoy Tim Hortons' Timbits – bite-sized doughnuts – for a dirham each. *Tim Hortons, various locations including Dubai Mall, Downtown (05 5213 6678, www.timhortons.com). Metro Burj Khalifa/Dubai Mall.*

17 ENJOY PARK LIFE
Most parks in Dubai charge entrance fees, but Al Barsha Pond Park bucks the trend with free admission. *See p130.*

18 VISIT AN ART GALLERY
Art Sawa Gallery is dedicated to contemporary art from the Middle East, North Africa, and neighbouring countries. *Street 14, Al Quoz, Sheikh Zayed Road (04 340 8660, www.artsawa.com). Metro Noor Bank.*

19 ENJOY PAKISTANI FOOD
Head to legendary Pakistani eaterie Ravi Restaurant in Satwa to enjoy delicious parathas, naans and rotis for a dirham a pop. *See p125.*

20 STROLL THE OLD TOWN
Spend a morning or afternoon exploring the narrow passageways and wind tower houses in Al Fahidi Historical Neighbourhood, formerly known as Bastakiya. *See p71.*

Diary

Our year-round guide to what's on when.

Omega Dubai Desert Classic.

Standard Chartered Dubai Marathon.

Outside the summer months – when pretty much everything shuts down – barely a weekend goes by in Dubai without some kind of music festival, religious celebration or sporting event. Some are announced just days beforehand, leaving little time for preparation or planning. Others, however, are more established, such as the world's richest horse race, the Dubai World Cup, the celebration of all things retail that is the Dubai Shopping Festival and the crowd-pleasing Emirates Dubai Rugby Sevens.

Before setting out or planning a trip around an event, it's best to call or check online as dates, times and locations are subject to change. For more festivals and events, check out the chapters in the Arts & Entertainment section. For the latest listings, consult *Time Out Dubai* magazine or www.timeoutdubai.com.

Jan-Mar

Standard Chartered Dubai Marathon

Umm Suqeim Road, Jumeirah Beach Road, Dubai Marina (04 433 5669, www.dubaimarathon.org). **Date** late Jan.

From fun-runners and fundraisers to running club members and elite athletes, you'll find competitors of every type in this event – which includes a 3K charity run and a 10K road race, as well as the full 42K marathon. Some of the biggest names in long-distance running take part every year.

Dubai Shopping Festival

Various locations (www.mydsf.ae).
Date Jan-early Feb.

The Dubai Shopping Festival is ten years old in 2016, an event that will no doubt be celebrated with even more bargains than usual. It's one of the best times to be in the city, with events and activities in every mall: competitions, performances and giveaways alongside colourful street displays, fireworks and fashion shows.

Omega Dubai Desert Classic

Emirates Golf Club, Emirates Hills (04 380 1234, www.dubaidesertclassic.com). **Date** late Jan-early Feb.

Watch some of the finest golfers in the world hit little white balls down the fairways of this luxury golf course. This longstanding PGA European Tour fixture has been won by legends including Ernie Els and Tiger Woods. The 2015 winner was Northern Irishman Rory McIlroy.

Emirates Airline International Jazz Festival

Media City Amphitheatre, Dubai Media City (04 391 1196, www.dubaijazzfest.com). **Date** mid-Feb.

A favourite in the Dubai calendar, the annual Jazz Festival manages to attract some big international performers. The line-up isn't solely jazz, though, with James Blunt, Sting and Christina Perri all performing at the 2015 event.

IN THE KNOW FORMULA ONE

There are many events in the UAE capital Abu Dhabi throughout the year, including huge concerts and its own food festival. However, the main attraction is when F1 rolls into town. The **Formula One Etihad Abu Dhabi Grand Prix** takes place in November at Yas Marina Circuit. As well as the on-track action, there's a whole host of events for petrolheads, as well as concerts by the likes of Pharrell Williams, Prince and the Who. For more information, visit www.yasmarinacircuit.com.

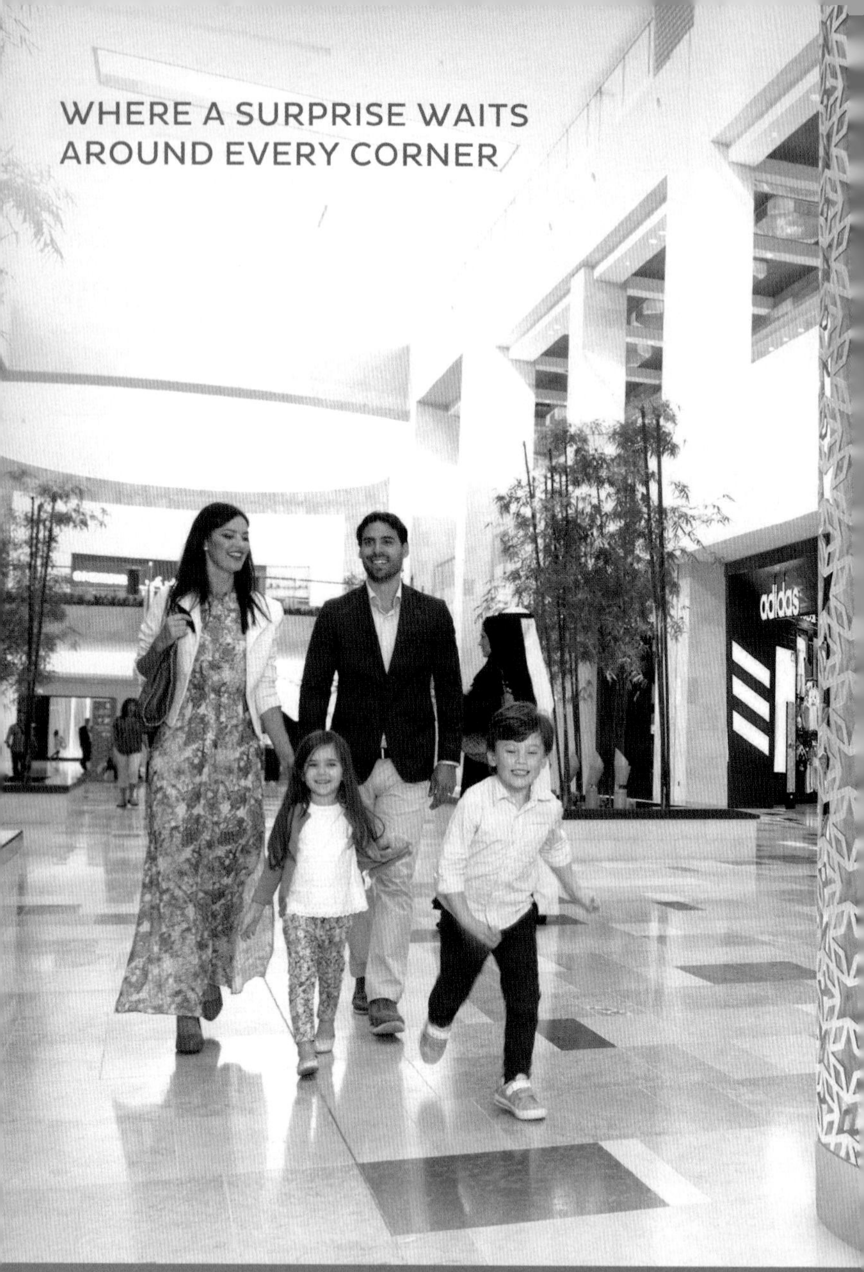
WHERE A SURPRISE WAITS
AROUND EVERY CORNER
adidas

Dubai Duty Free Tennis Championships

Dubai Tennis Stadium, Garhoud (04 417 2415, www.dubaidutyfreetennischampionships.com). **Date** late Feb-early Mar.
The top seeds in the world meet at the Dubai Tennis Stadium for this ATP and WTP World Tour tournament to battle it out for the title and more than $2.5 million. In 2015, Roger Federer beat rival Novak Djokovic in the men's competition, while Romanian Simona Halep won the ladies' week.

Emirates Airline Festival of Literature

InterContinental Hotel, Dubai Festival City (04 355 9844, www.emirateslitfest.com). **Date** early Mar.
The Middle East's largest celebration of the written and spoken word includes workshops and competitions as well as attracting big-name authors such as Michael Morpurgo, Alexander McCall Smith and David Mitchell.

Dubai International Boat Show

Dubai International Marine Club, Mina Seyahi (04 308 6430, www.boatshowdubai.com). **Date** mid-Mar.
Gawp at the floating palaces at the largest marine industry exhibition in the Middle East. You might not be able to afford the yachts on offer, but you can still enjoy the spectacle.

Taste of Dubai

Media City Amphitheatre, Dubai Media City (04 800 4669, www.tasteofdubaifestival.com). **Date** mid Mar.
This foodie fair has grown into a huge event that sprawls throughout the Media City Amphitheatre. As well as food demonstrations from celebrity chefs and displays of the latest kitchen gadgets, there are dozens of food stalls and pop-up bars, plus a beer garden and stage for live music.

Dubai World Cup

Meydan Racecourse, Nad Al Sheba (04 327 0077, www.dubairacingclub.com). **Date** late Mar.
The world's richest horse race takes place at the stunning, state-of-the-art Meydan Racecourse. The prizes are immense (in 2015 they amounted to more than $30 million) and the atmosphere inside the stadium matches the big money. Celebs from the UK come to be photographed, while most of Dubai buys a new hat for the occasion.

Art Season

Various locations (600 56 0000, www.dubaiculture.gov.ae). **Date** Mar-mid Apr.
A catch-all banner that includes headline events such as Sikka Art Fair, which supports emerging Dubai artists, Art Dubai, showcasing global artists, and Design Days Dubai, which exhibits objects from innovative designers from around the world. There is also Middle East Film and Comic Con, World Art Dubai and pop-up events throughout the city.

PUBLIC HOLIDAYS

New Year's Day
1 January

UAE National Day
2 December

Islamic Holidays

The main Muslim festivals during the year are *Eid Al Fitr* (which marks the end of Ramadan and is the festival of the breaking of the fast) and *Eid Al Adha* (the festival of sacrifice, which marks the end of the pilgrimage to Mecca). *Mawlid Al Nabi* is the holiday celebrating the Prophet Muhammad's birthday and *Lailat Al Mi'raj* is the celebration of the Prophet's ascension into heaven. *Al Hijara* is the Islamic new year.

Islamic holidays are based on the lunar calendar, meaning dates vary from year to year, and can only be finally determined when a new moon phase is seen by the UAE's moon-sighting committee. This often means that a public holiday is only decided the day before it is due. Therefore the dates given below are estimates. Public sector workers will be given some time off for each holiday (three days for the *eids*), while private sector workers will have time off at their company's discretion.

	2016	2017
Lailat Al Mi'raj	5 May	23 April
Ramadan	6 June-5 July	27 May-25 June
Eid Al Fitr	6-8 July	26-28 June
Eid Al Adha	11-13 Sept	1-3 Sept
Al Hijara	2 Oct	21 Sept
Moulid Al Nabi	12 Dec	1 Dec

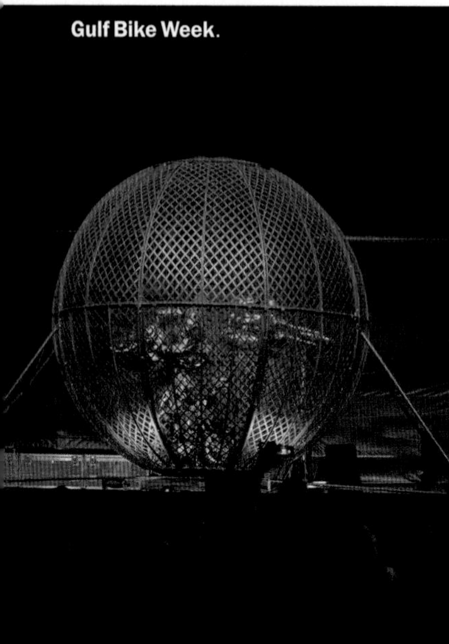

Gulf Bike Week.

June-Sept

Not much goes on during the summer months as temperatures reach a sweltering 50°C. Many expats return home for the holidays.

Dubai Summer Surprises

Various locations (www.dubaievents.ae).
Date late June-July.
Held in shopping malls around the city, Summer Surprises offers a chance to take advantage of air-conditioning in the summer heat. Retailers offer discounts and special offers as well as putting on fun performances and activities for families.

Oct-Dec

GITEX Technology Week

Dubai World Trade Centre, Sheikh Zayed Road (www.gitex.com). **Date** late Oct.
A huge event showcasing the latest technological innovations and gadgets for industries and governments. The GITEX Shopper gives you the chance to buy some of the goods on show at discount prices.

Gulf Bike Week

Media City Amphitheatre, Dubai Media City (04 435 6101, www.gulfbikeweek.com). **Date** late Oct-early Nov.
Thousands of visitors descend on the amphitheatre to enjoy stunt shows and motorbike displays and listen to rock bands on the big stage.

UAE National Day

Around the city. **Date** 2 Dec.
Every 2 December, the country is awash with the colours of the flag. Green, black, red and white flags are flown from apartment windows, cars, vans and trucks, with pictures of the country's rulers. Formed in 1971, the UAE will turn 44 in 2015. The National Day Downtown Dubai Parade features performers, animals, floats and more, and brings the area around the Burj Khalifa to life in colourful fashion.

Emirates Airline Dubai Rugby Sevens

Sevens Stadium, Dubai to Al Ain Road (04 321 0008, www.dubairugby7s.com). **Date** early Dec.
More than 100,000 spectators/revellers make the fairly long trip to the Sevens Stadium to drink and be merry, and perhaps watch international teams battle it out for the Sevens trophy. It's as much about the occasion (and dressing up in fancy dress) as the sport.

Dubai International Film Festival

Various venues (04 363 3456, www.dubaifilmfest.com). **Date** early Dec.
A showcase of new Hollywood, Middle Eastern and international films – all uncensored. Premières are generally held at Madinat Jumeirah while screenings take place in cinemas across the city.

RAMADAN

Make the most of the holy month.

Ramadan is one of the most important and contemplative times in the Islamic calendar. Dated by the lunar calendar, each year it starts roughly 11 days earlier than the year before. Observers fast from all food, drink and nicotine during daylight hours. The sundown meal that breaks the fast is called *iftar*, and is generally a family or social affair, and evenings following it are often spent enjoying the company of family and friends. Before dawn and another day of fasting, Muslims have another meal, *suhour*. Though everyone in Dubai is expected to be respectful of Ramadan, those who aren't observing the fast are able to eat and drink behind closed doors. Here are a few tips for a happy Ramadan, UAE-style.

DO... make the most of the festive atmosphere and community spirit you'll find at this time of year. Enjoy the food and entertainment put on in Ramadan tents at the city's hotels – many will have Arabic *oud* players, whirling dervishes and other traditional entertainment.

DO... get into the Ramadan spirit of giving. *Zakat*, the practice of charitable giving in Islam, is significant during this time.

DO... if you're driving, be careful as many people hurry home for *iftar*, or drive while tired and hungry. Be even more vigilant than usual.

DO... Enjoy late-night shopping. Many malls and shops stay open until the small hours.

DO... mind your language. Obviously, swearing is never a good idea, but it's especially unwelcome at this time of year.

DON'T... smoke, drink, chew gum or eat in public during daylight hours. Not only will it offend people, but you could get into trouble with the law in the UAE. Public places include offices and workplaces (check the rules here as they vary), lifts, hallways and cars.

DON'T... expect to go clubbing. And if you're tempted to break out into song or dance in public, restrain yourself. Dubai doesn't have live performances during Ramadan (traditional music aside). Loud music blaring out of cars (or anywhere else) isn't allowed either.

DON'T... wear revealing or tight clothes in public. Both men and women should make sure that at least their shoulders and knees are covered.

Dubai's Best

A handy guide to the city's must-sees and must-dos.

XVA Gallery.

Sightseeing

VIEWS

Burj Khalifa p80
You can marvel at the whole of Dubai from this iconic tower – the world's highest building, of course.

Alta Badia p104
Superb Italian restaurant in Emirates Towers, with stunning views over Sheikh Zayed Road and the Jumeirah coastline.

The Observatory p171
On the Dubai Marriott Harbour Hotel's 52nd floor, this bar looks out over the Al Sufouh shoreline and gives a new perspective on the Palm Jumeirah.

Tomo p76
This restaurant in the Raffles Hotel has a terrace bar on one side with Creek views, and a terrace restaurant on the other with Downtown views.

ART

Alserkal Avenue p130
A hub for the arts and creativity in Al Quoz, which is otherwise a dusty industrial estate.

XVA Gallery p72
Courtyard gallery in the Al Fahidi neighbourhood, with work from local artists. It's also a cool café and hotel.

DIFC p100
The financial district has some great art galleries in its Gate Village area.

Al Fahidi Historical Neighbourhood.

HISTORY

Dubai Museum p65
Find out the history of the city in its oldest building.

Heritage & Diving Village p65
Check out this 'living museum' and see how Dubai's early inhabitants existed.

Al Fahidi Historical Neighbourhood p71
Walk around a recreation of one of the first settlements in Dubai. The homes have now been turned into cafés, restaurants and galleries.

Heritage House p49
A traditional Dubai home, which dates back to 1890.

OUTDOORS

Skydive Dubai p209
For the fearless – jump out of a plane and see stunning views of the Palm Jumeirah and Marina coastline.

Desert Safari p215
Visit camel farms, go dune bashing and stop for sandboarding or quad biking.

Boat trips p167
Board at the Marina and take a trip into the Arabian Gulf.

Dinner in the desert p215
Hop in a vintage Land Rover and get driven into the desert for a traditional Arabic feast.

Camel trek p208
Take a more relaxed approach to seeing the Dubai desert by joining a camel trek.

CHILDREN

Dubai Aquarium & Underwater Zoo p184
Aquarium with a tunnel in Dubai Mall filled with all manner of marine life, including sharks and rays – and a 750kg crocodile.

Snow penguins p185
It may seem slightly crazy being in the desert and going to see penguins,

Barasti.

but kids will love meeting the colony at Ski Dubai.

KidZania p189
The place where kids are in charge – little ones get jobs, earn money and live the life of a working adult, with no adults allowed.

Aquaventure p190
Lots of slides and activities to keep kids busy, and plenty of options for parents as well.

Eating & drinking

CAFÉS

Tom & Serg p135
Coffee is king in this cool café, but the food (especially breakfast) is also worth tucking into.

Bystro p144
Gem of a café, with great coffee, cracking breakfasts and unbeatable cakes.

Comptoir 102 p120
A health-food café near the beach in Jumeirah, with a boutique selling jewellery, clothes and furniture.

Omnia Gourmet p116
Silvena Rowe's Fishing Harbour outlet uses local produce to create great food.

XVA Café p71
In a courtyard in Bur Dubai's historic area, this vegetarian café is an oasis of calm.

BLOWOUTS

Pierchic p141
Dubai's most romantic restaurant – delectable seafood on a pier perched over the Arabian Gulf.

Solo p76
The place looks good and oozes charm; it also serves some brilliant Italian food.

At.mosphere p82
The highest restaurant in the world, with amazing views and amazing food.

Pierchic.

La Petite Maison p102
Some of the finest French food in town.

Zuma p103
Impeccable setting, service and food at this Japanese restaurant.

BARS

Barasti p154
More people will tell you to go to this buzzing bar than

Irish Village.

anywhere else in Dubai. It's an institution – everyone must go at least once.

TR!BECA Kitchen + Bar p166
Trendy New York loft-style bar with great music (courtesy of resident DJ Stu Todd) and a laid-back vibe.

Zero Gravity p171
Another bar with a view, and a great line-up of international DJs playing regularly.

40 Kong p108
This is a cracking bar, 40 floors up, looking over the Sheikh Zayed Road.

Irish Village p59
A few beers in the Irish Village is a rite of passage for everyone visiting Dubai. A brilliant beer garden, decent pub food and reasonable prices.

Shopping

MALLS

Dubai Mall p88
The daddy of them all. Bigger than all the others.

Mall of the Emirates p136
It has its own ski slope – what else do you need to know?

FASHION

Bloomingdale's p91
The first outpost for this New York giant. You want fashion? They've got it.

Level Shoe District p92
The place to get your Louboutins on – as well as dozens of other designer shoes.

Nightlife

CLUBS

Pacha p198
The Ibizan import, with live shows and music running from soulful house to nu disco and more mainstream house.

Mahiki p197
Polynesian-themed club with a wide-ranging music policy; it's always busy.

Cirque Le Soir p200
A cabaret club with burlesque dancers and fairies, jugglers and clowns.

Societe p199
The party never ends at Societe – a club where the emphasis is on fun.

MUSIC

The Music Room p205
Impressive venue in Dubai's old town, where you'll find local talent as well as visiting bands.

Irish Village p204
If they're Irish (and sometimes Scottish) they're on here. Previous gigs have included Sinead O'Connor, Bob Geldof and Deacon Blue.

Arts

FESTIVALS

Dubai Jazz Festival p35
Not just covering jazz, this three-night festival is a hit with music-lovers.

Emirates Airline Festival of Literature p37
The Middle East's largest celebration of the written and spoken word.

Explore

Deira, Garhoud & Festival City

It's surprising how little evidence there is in Dubai to suggest that it's ever been anything other than the entertainment playground it is today – more surprising still when you consider that UAE nationals value tradition and history very highly. However, the government's drive to protect the handful of landmarks that remain has given visitors a chance to experience Old Dubai. Deira, alongside the Creek, is home to a number of the city's best-preserved heritage sites, including its atmospheric souks. Beyond Deira is Garhoud, best known as the home of Dubai International Airport, but also for its casual restaurants and bars. Festival City, meanwhile, is a relatively new dining, drinking and shopping hub.

Reflets par Pierre Gagnaire.

Don't Miss

1 **Abra ride** Cross the Creek by boat (p55).

2 **The souks** Explore Deira's traditional marketplaces (p48).

3 **Dinner cruise** High-end dining aboard Bateaux Dubai (p53).

4 **Go Irish in Garhoud** Try the Irish Village or the Dubliner's (p59).

5 **Reflets par Pierre Gagnaire** Indulge at this standout French restaurant (p60).

نزل ميراج
MIRAGE
GUEST HOUSE
MZTCO
SPEEDEX
TRADING LLC
DIABLO
MAX
QUALIT

DEIRA

Broadly speaking, the term Deira is used to describe everything north of the Creek, but in reality it is an amalgam of sub-districts. For anyone on the history trail however, the most exciting part is the original Deira alongside the Creek – the heart and soul of old Dubai. It's a bustling, chaotic, dusty commercial hub where plate glass office blocks tower over old souks.

Five-star hotels such as the Sheraton Dubai Creek (*see p269*) and Radisson Blu (*see p270*) are just yards away from wharfs that haven't changed in 60 years. On the roads, limousines and 4x4s jostle for space with rickety, multi-coloured pickup trucks, while sharp-suited business folk wait at zebra crossings alongside sarong-clad workers pushing handcarts, and fishermen in work-stained *khanduras*. Traditional dhows still line the wharf and, day and night, goods are unloaded, destined for the many tiny shops that make up Dubai's oldest trading area.

What Deira lacks in refinement it makes up for in atmosphere and character. And to experience it at first hand, all you have to do is walk along the corniche. Go far enough and you'll stumble across Deira's souks. The area is best explored during late afternoon or evening, when temperatures are lower and the traders are at their busiest. The entrance to the souk area stands under renovated buildings with traditional wind towers. Like most markets, it has evolved into sections defined by the goods sold in each, and criss-crossed by alleys.

Step into the **spice souk** and you instantly breathe in the scents of Arabia and the East. Chillies, cardamom and saffron are piled high outside shops; ornately decorated bottles line shelves in traditional perfume stores; the sweet aroma of frankincense fills the air. At one time more valuable than gold, frankincense remains one of Arabia's most prized perfumes. The souk's original coral-stone shops have been renovated, and much of the dusty charm has been lost these days, but it is now a far cleaner place to visit.

Take the time to make your way through the myriad alleyways to explore the shops selling antiques. Once you reach them you know that you're approaching the **gold souk**. Its centre is a wide alley covered by a roof and supported by carved wooden pillars, but the souk extends into the adjoining streets. It's worth venturing beyond the main plaza-like area to explore the outer alleys, where many specialist shops trade in silver, pearls and semi-precious stones. Bargaining or haggling is expected in all souks; don't be afraid to leave a shop to try the competition next door. Some shopkeepers will offer tea, coffee or cold drinks while a deal is being struck.

Sights & Attractions

FREE Al Ahmadiya School

Al Ahmadiya Street, Al Ras (04 226 0286, www.dubaiculture.gov.ae). Metro Al Ras.
Open 8am-7.30pm Mon-Thur, Sat, Sun; 2.30-7.30pm Fri. **Admission** free. **Map** p50 A2 ❶

EXPLORE

Established in 1912, this was the first school in Dubai, and was renovated as a museum in 1995. It now showcases examples of school life before Dubai was transformed by the discovery of oil. It's one of the city's oldest buildings.

★ Dhow Wharfage

Off Baniyas Road, next to the National Bank of Dubai building. **Map** p50 D3 ❷

Set along the Creek, the Dhow Wharfage is a nod to the city's past. The many dhows that dock alongside each other here, bringing in spices, textiles and other goods from neighbouring countries, are more than just vessels. In many cases, the seafarers who brave the Gulf and the Indian Ocean live in these colourful wooden beauties.

★ Gold Souk

Off Al Khor Street. Metro Al Ras. **Open** times vary. **Map** p50 A2 ❸

Dubai's most famous souk sells everything from bangles to tiaras, elaborate rings to bespoke name-plate necklaces in English or Arabic script. Trading is mainly in 24-carat gold, so don't expect to find the cheap stuff here. Do be prepared to haggle, though – prices are set to gold-market levels twice daily, but there's always room to negotiate a discount.

FREE Heritage House

Al Khor Street, Al Ras (04 226 0286, www.dubaiculture.gov.ae). Metro Al Ras. **Open** 8.30am-7.30pm Mon-Thur, Sat, Sun; 2.30-7.30pm Fri. **Admission** free. **Map** p50 A2 ❹

Next door to Al Ahmadiya School is Heritage House, a traditional home with original interiors from 1890. Guides and touch screens take you through the tour of the two small museum halls. This is one of the only original houses to have survived Dubai's construction boom, and is considered one of the city's best examples of a traditional Emirati home.

FREE Museum of the Poet Al Oqaili

Sikka 21B, off Al Ras Road (04 234 2385, www.dubaiculture.gov.ae). Metro Al Ras. **Open** 8am-2pm Mon-Thur, Sun. **Admission** free. **Map** p50 A2 ❺

This museum only opened in 2012, but the building dates back to 1923. As the name suggests, it was the home of the poet Mubarak Al Oqaili, who settled in Dubai after travelling around Bahrain, Oman, Iraq and other places within the UAE. The two-floor museum contains examples of his poetry and details about his life.

FREE Naif Museum

Deira Corniche, next to Hyatt Regency Dubai (no phone, www.dubaiculture.gov.ae). Metro Palm Deira. **Open** 8am-2pm Mon-Thur, Sun. **Admission** free. **Map** p50 A3 ❻

This building was originally constructed in 1939 as a fort to protect the business district in Deira. It later become the first headquarters of the Dubai Police, and also served as public offices. The museum features exhibitions displaying old weapons, uniforms and photographs documenting the history of the police force.

Gold Souk.

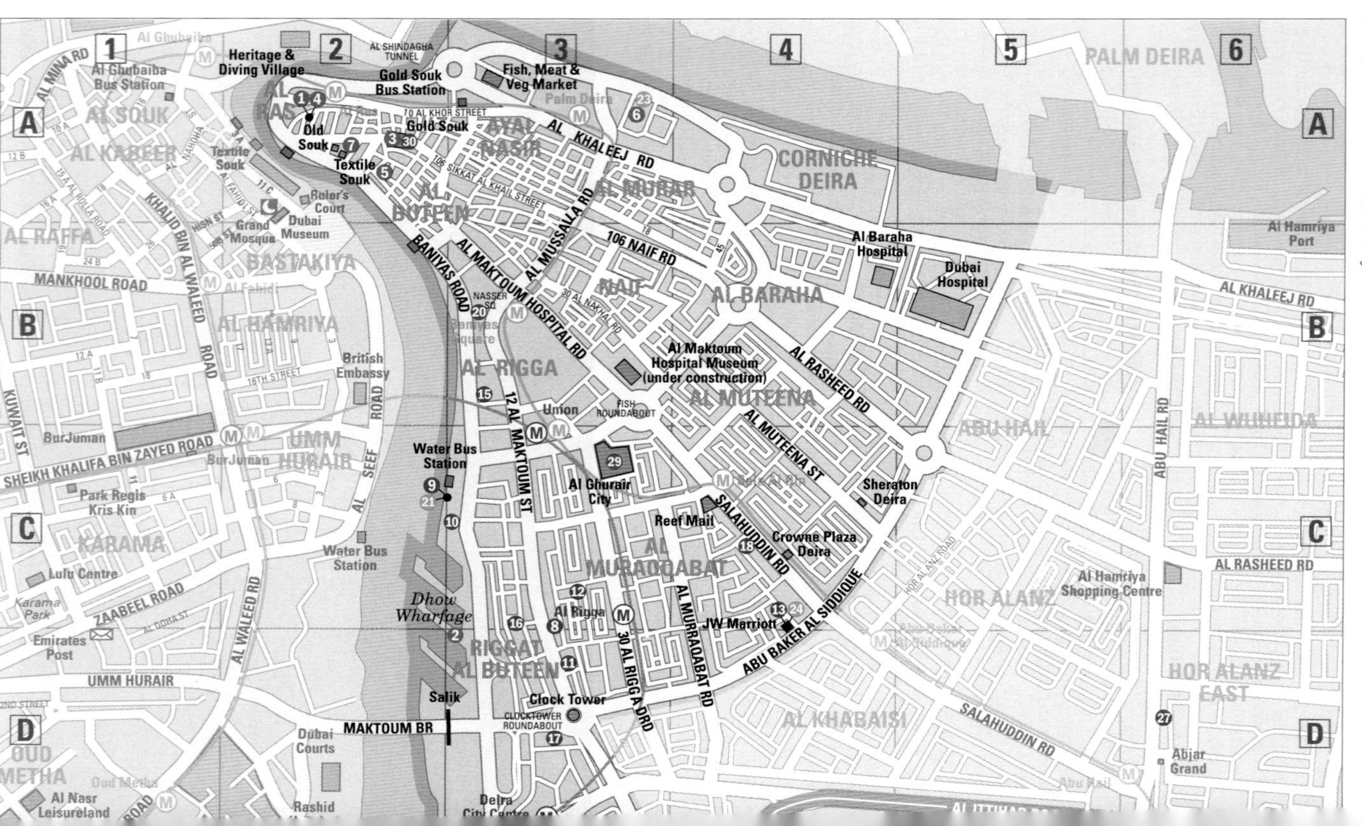

PALM DEIRA
Al Hamriya Port
CORNICHE DEIRA
AL BARAHA
AL MUTEENA
ABU HAIL
AL WUHEIDA
HOR AL ANZ
HOR AL ANZ EAST
AL KHABAISI
AL MURAQQABAT
RIGGAT AL BUTEEN
AL RIGGA
NAIF
AL MURAR
AYAL NASIR
AL BUTEEN
AL RAS
AL SOUK AL KABEER
AL RAFFA
BASTAKIYA
AL HAMRIYA
UMM HURAIR
KARAMA
OUD METHA
AL KHALEEJ RD
AL RASHEED RD
ABU HAIL RD
SALAHUDDIN RD
AL MUTEENA ST
SALAHUDDIN RD
ABU BAKER AL SIDDIQUE
AL MURRAQABAT RD
30 AL RIGGA RD
12 AL MAKTOUM ST
AL MAKTOUM HOSPITAL RD
BANIYAS ROAD
AL MUSSALLA RD
106 NAIF RD
30 AL NAKHAL RD
106 SIKKAT AL KHAIL STREET
10 AL KHOR STREET
AL SEEF ROAD
AL WALEED RD
KHALID BIN AL WALEED ROAD
SHEIKH KHALIFA BIN ZAYED ROAD
MANKHOOL ROAD
ZAABEEL ROAD
UMM HURAIR
KUWAIT ST
AL MINA RD
16TH STREET
MAKTOUM BR
AL SHINDAGHA TUNNEL
Dubai Hospital
Al Baraha Hospital
Al Maktoum Hospital Museum (under construction)
Sheraton Deira
Crowne Plaza Deira
JW Marriott
Reef Mall
Al Ghurair City
Al Hamriya Shopping Centre
Abjar Grand
Fish, Meat & Veg Market
Gold Souk Bus Station
Gold Souk
Textile Souk
Old Souk
Heritage & Diving Village
Ruler's Court
Dubai Museum
Grand Mosque
Textile Souk
British Embassy
Water Bus Station
Water Bus Station
Dhow Wharfage
Salik
Clock Tower
CLOCKTOWER ROUNDABOUT
FISH ROUNDABOUT
NASSER SQ
Union
Dubai Courts
Rashid
Al Ghubaiba Bus Station
BurJuman
Park Regis Kris Kin
Lulu Centre
Karama Park
Emirates Post
Al Nasr Leisureland
Deira City Centre

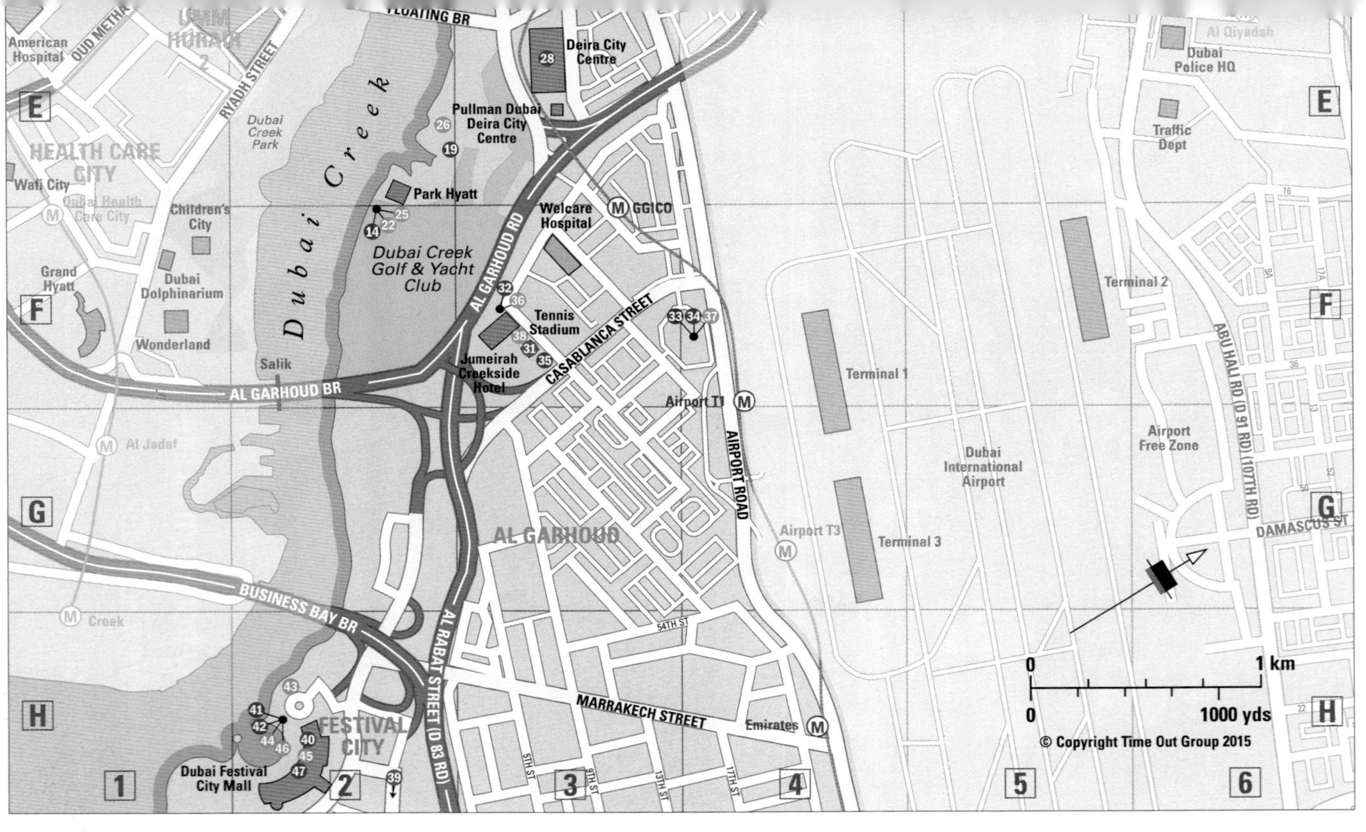
FLOATING BR
American Hospital
OUD METHA
UMM HURAIR 2
RYADH STREET
Deira City Centre
Pullman Dubai Deira City Centre
Dubai Creek Park
Dubai Creek
HEALTH CARE CITY
Wafi City
Dubai Health Care City
Children's City
Park Hyatt
Dubai Creek Golf & Yacht Club
AL GARHOUD RD
Welcare Hospital
GGICO
Grand Hyatt
Dubai Dolphinarium
Wonderland
Tennis Stadium
CASABLANCA STREET
Jumeirah Creekside Hotel
Salik
AL GARHOUD BR
Airport T1
AIRPORT ROAD
Al Jadaf
AL GARHOUD
Airport T3
BUSINESS BAY BR
AL RABAT STREET (D 83 RD)
Creek
54TH ST
MARRAKECH STREET
Emirates
FESTIVAL CITY
Dubai Festival City Mall
5TH ST
9TH ST
13TH ST
17TH ST
Al Qiyadah
Dubai Police HQ
Traffic Dept
Terminal 2
Terminal 1
Terminal 3
Dubai International Airport
Airport Free Zone
ABU HALI RD (D 91 RD) (107TH RD)
DAMASCUS ST
1 km
1000 yds
© Copyright Time Out Group 2015

EXPLORE

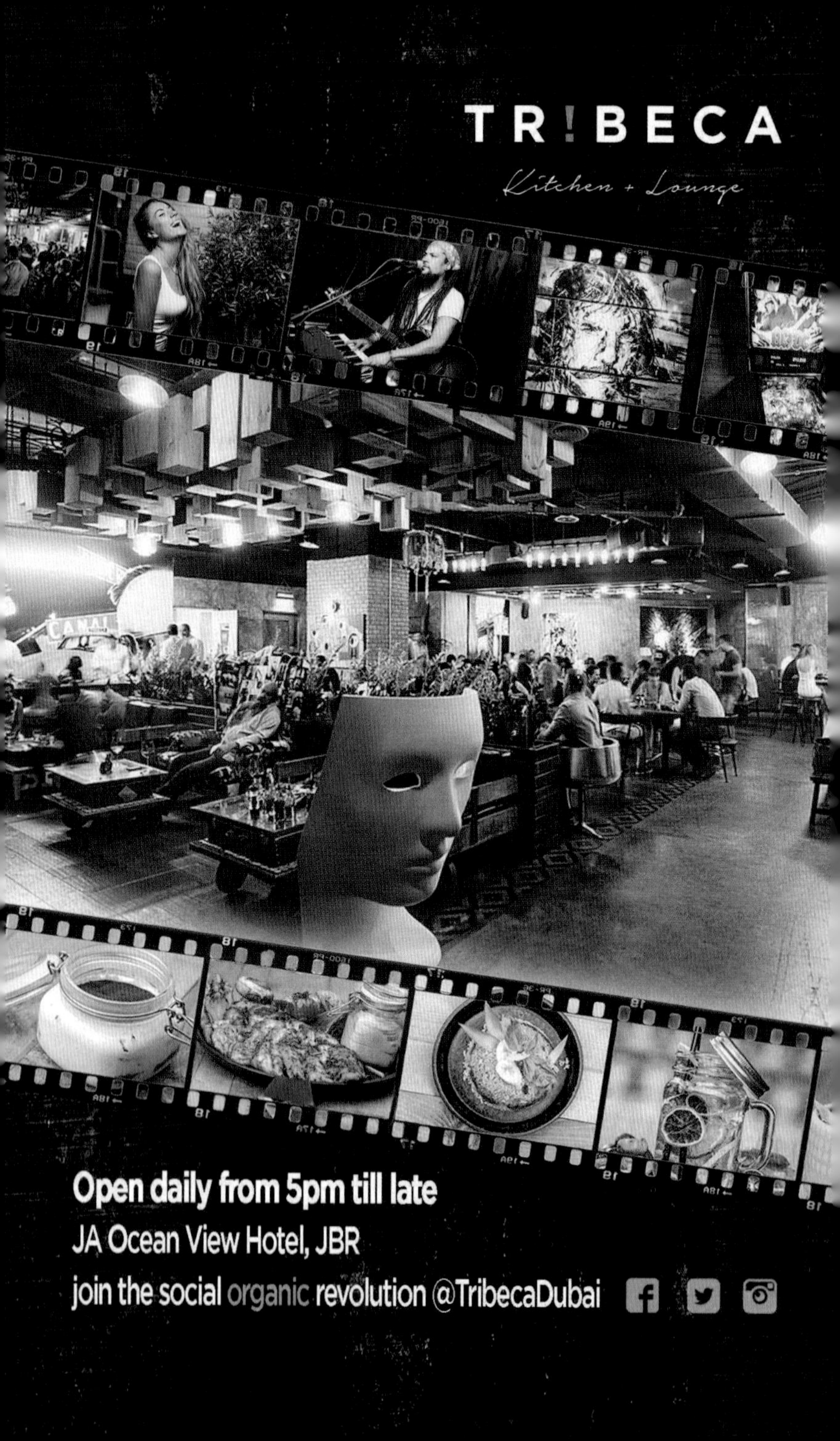
TR!BECA
Kitchen + Lounge
Open daily from 5pm till late
JA Ocean View Hotel, JBR
join the social organic revolution @TribecaDubai

★ Spice Souk

Between Baniyas Road & Al Khor Street. Metro Al Ras. **Open** times vary. **Map** p50 A2 ❼

Follow your nose from the gold souk to discover tiny alleyways lined with sacks full of fresh spices. Pick up cardamom and star anise, saffron and cinnamon, cumin, coriander and much more.

Restaurants

Abshar

Al Maktoum Road (04 223 0555, www.abshar.ae). Metro Al Rigga. **Open** noon-midnight daily. **Main courses** Dhs55-Dhs125. **Map** p50 C3 ❽ **Persian**

Housed in a converted villa with its own valet parking and massive outdoor bread oven, this Persian restaurant is a good spot for a casual dinner or lunch. Decor is a little on the kitsch side, with the ceiling painted to resemble the sky, complete with fluffy clouds. Lamb chops are cooked perfectly and the minced meat kebabs are flavoursome and tender.

Ashiana by Vineet

Sheraton Dubai Creek Hotel & Towers, Baniyas Road (04 207 1733, www.ashianadubai.com). Metro Union. **Open** noon-3pm, 7-11pm Mon-Thur, Sun; 7-11pm Fri, Sat. **Main courses** Dhs120-Dhs180. **Map** p50 C3 ❾ **Indian**

Backed by Michelin-starred Indian chef Vineet Bhatia – known for his other Dubai restaurant, Indego by Vineet – Ashiana is the place to come for superior Indian food in a grand setting. The attractive façade is like an Indian villa; once inside the theme is continued with traditional murals, dark wood, delicate chandeliers and intimate booths. Service is friendly and the food – including a tasting menu with wine pairings and a chef's choice menu – is very good, with some unexpected ingredients.

Bateaux Dubai

Baniyas Road, opposite ENBD Head Office (04 814 553, www.bateauxdubai.com). **Open** 8.30-11pm daily (boarding at 7.45pm). **Set menu** Dhs395 (with soft drinks); Dhs495 (with alcohol). **Map** p50 C3 ❿ **Modern European**

There are many vessels offering a night of food and entertainment on Dubai Creek: buffets, flashing lights and gaudy performances are de rigueur. Bateaux Dubai is an altogether classier affair. This is no old, wooden dhow but a modern cruiser with picture windows and viewing decks. The experience is enhanced by attentive service and an inventive menu.

★ China Sea

Al Maktoum Road, near Clock Tower Roundabout (04 295 9816). Metro Al Rigga. **Open** 10.30am-midnight daily. **Main courses** Dhs50-Dhs80. **Map** p50 D3 ⓫ **Chinese**

This oddball restaurant is popular with Chinese expats and for good reason: you won't get a more authentic Chinese dining experience in Dubai. A seafood tank, outlandish decor and plastic tablecloths all add to the quirky, low-key vibe. The menu offers delights such as fried sea cucumber.

Handi

Taj Palace, Al Rigga (04 223 2222). Metro Al Rigga. **Open** noon-3.30pm, 7pm-midnight

EXPLORE

Bateaux Dubai.

Legends.

daily. **Main courses** Dhs60-Dhs170. **Map** p50 C3 ⓬ **Indian**
Focusing on north Indian cuisine, Handi offers a variety of tandoori and other dishes in smart surroundings. The venue is not licensed but the cooking and ingredients are a cut above what you'd find in the city's more affordable canteen-style eateries.

JW's Steakhouse

JW Marriott Dubai, Abu Baker Al Siddique Road (04 607 7977, www.marriottdiningatjw.ae). Metro Abu Baker Al Siddique. **Open** 5pm-midnight Mon-Wed, Fri-Sun; noon-3pm, 5pm-midnight Thur. **Main courses** Dhs200-Dhs400. **Map** p50 C4 ⓭ **Steakhouse**
One of the most inviting restaurants in the city, the interior here is done out in gentlemen's club-style dark greens and wood tones, with faded newspaper clippings and black and white photographs on the wall. The atmosphere is warm, fixtures and fittings add to a sense of occasion. The venue prides itself on the quality of its meat but seafood also features prominently.

Legends

Dubai Creek Golf & Yacht Club, opposite Deira City Centre (04 295 6000, www.dubaigolf.com). **Open** noon-3pm, 7pm-midnight Mon-Thur, Sat, Sun; 7pm-midnight Fri. **Main courses** Dhs140-Dhs300. **Map** p51 F2 ⓮ **Steakhouse**
Legends scores highly from the moment you set foot on its terrace: the views of the Creek and the city skyline are the perfect backdrop for your steak and chips. Provenance is taken seriously here; the meat is sourced from Australia, Ireland, France and the US.

Minato

Radisson Blu Dubai Deira Creek, Baniyas Road (04 222 7171, www.radissonblu.com). Metro Union. **Open** 12.30-3pm, 7-11pm daily. **Set menus** Dhs220-Dhs340. **Sushi & sashimi platters** Dhs60-Dhs170. **Map** p50 B3 ⓯ **Japanese**
Minato certainly isn't the worst option after a day exploring the sights of Old Dubai. If you've spent an afternoon motoring up and down the Creek on an *abra*, there's nothing quite like a cold beer and a bowl of salty edamame to perk you up. The menu is varied: try the chicken gyoza or the Japanese omelette.

New Times

Al Maktoum Street, near Clock Tower Roundabout (04 250 1888). Metro Al Rigga. **Open** 11.30am-11.30pm daily. **Main courses** Dhs50-Dhs80. **Map** p50 C3 ⓰ **Chinese**
Fried chicken feet, sea cucumber with spinach sauce, duck's head chilli, preserved eggs and cold jellyfish. Not everyone will be a fan of New Times but it's the real deal and dozens of Chinese expats cram in here every night. Its utter refusal to become a standard Dubai eaterie adds to the charm.

BRIDGING THE GAP

What's the best way to cross the Creek?

Dubai's Creek is a psychological barrier for many who live in the city. Like Londoners who refuse to go south of the river, or New Yorkers who won't leave Manhattan, many Dubaians are put off heading to the 'Deira side'. It's perceived as being rather low-rent compared to the sparkly towers of Sheikh Zayed Road or the fancy yachts in the Marina.

Even for people who realise how worthwhile a trip can be, simply getting there can be off-putting. Traffic can build up towards the bridges, and the roads in Deira are often congested. The quickest way across is to avoid the roads altogether and take to the water. *Abras* chug back and forth for a dirham a time, and a trip on the ramshackle old wooden vessels is atmospheric and convenient. They go from each side of the Bur Dubai textile souk to Sabkha station (next to the spice souk) or Baniyas (a little further up the Creek).

Waterbuses provide an air-conditioned alternative on the same routes, and cost Dhs2 each way. To the uninitiated, they may appear like barges with a greenhouse on top, but they're cool, dry and as quick as *abras*; berths are next to the *abra* stations.

Another step up the ladder of nautical grandeur is the water taxi. These can be called, like road taxis, to come and collect you from the same stations as *abras* and waterbuses. To travel one stop costs Dhs50, or they can be booked for a half-day (Dhs200) or full day (Dhs400).

The cheapest option, though, is to go underwater. Down by Al Shindagha Tunnel, near the mouth of the Creek, there's a seldom-used pedestrian tunnel. It runs from just past the Diving Village on the Bur Dubai side to near the bus station on Baniyas Road on the Deira side. There are views out to the Gulf from each end, and it won't cost you a *fil*.

EXPLORE

Pyongyang Okryu-Gwan

Deira Business Village, near Clock Tower Roundabout (04 298 1589). Metro Deira City Centre. **Open** 10.30am-midnight daily. **Main courses** Dhs50-Dhs100. **Map** p50 D3 ⑰ **Korean**

Named after the North Korean capital, this venue offers a similar menu to its South Korean competitors in Dubai but it does offer a peek inside the soul of a secretive nation. Staff sometimes perform karaoke, pictures on the wall are for sale, and everything originates from North Korea. It may not be the best Korean restaurant in the city, but it's the most intriguing.

Sonamu

Asiana Hotel, Salahuddin Road (04 238 7777, www.asianahoteldubai.com). Metro Salah Al Din. **Open** 6.30-10am, noon-3pm, 6-11pm. **Main courses** Dhs80-Dhs150. **Map** p50 C4 ⑱ **Korean**

Dubai's Korean dining scene is dominated by budget eats but Sonamu, the flagship restaurant of the flashy Asiana Hotel, stands out. With its lofty ceilings and lacquered tables, it's a much more upmarket destination for a bowl of bibimbap. We love the pancake crammed full of prawns, squid and spring onion.

★ Traiteur

Park Hyatt Dubai, near Deira City Centre (04 317 2222, www.dubai.park.hyatt.com). **Open** 7pm-midnight Mon-Fri, Sun. **Main courses** Dhs150-Dhs250. **Map** p51 E2 ⑲ **French**

Given you have to stroll through the gorgeous lobby of the Park Hyatt Dubai to reach this restaurant, Traiteur needs to impress, and it succeeds. From the raised open-plan kitchen to its whalebone ceiling, it's both spectacular and intimate, with tables spaced far enough apart to whisper sweet nothings. The menu offers a mix of the classic and classically executed – the snails in garlic and parsley butter are an unctuous delight, the wagyu beef ribeye masterful.

Xiao Wei Yang Hotpot

Baniyas Road, near Radisson Blu, Dubai Deira Creek (04 221 5111). Metro Baniyas Square. **Open** 11.30am-1am daily. **Main courses** Dhs25-Dhs100. **Map** p50 B3 ⑳ **Chinese**

This is one of Dubai's hidden gems – the queue to get in speaks for itself – and while the decor may be basic the food is sublime. The broth hotpot sits on a hotplate at your table and you choose the ingredients to add; everything arrives fresh, vibrant and raw to be cooked in situ. Economical and fun.

Other locations International City (050 151 7228); Dubai Marina (04 421 4650).

Cafés & Bars

Chelsea Arms

Sheraton Dubai Creek Hotel & Towers, Baniyas Road (04 228 1111). Metro Union. **Open** noon-2am daily. **Map** p50 C3 ㉑

This is Dubai's oldest pub, dating to 1978, which – by local standards – is a lifetime. That's the only real reason to visit this spot in the ageing Sheraton Dubai Creek Hotel & Towers; you'll find regulars who look like they've been here every night since it opened.

Cielo Sky Lounge

Dubai Creek Golf & Yacht Club, near Deira City Centre (04 416 1800, www.cielodubai.com). **Open** 4pm-3am daily. **Map** p51 F2 22

This rooftop venue certainly looks the part: crisp white couches with a nautical touch of blue, sail-like canopies and uninterrupted views of the water and skyline. Drinks-wise there is an enormous range of cocktails and Spanish beers while a white, fruity sangria is another standout. For food, head downstairs to Casa de Tapas.

Hibiki

Hyatt Regency Dubai, Deira Corniche (04 317 2221). Metro Palm Deira. **Open** 7.30pm-3am Mon-Sat. **Map** p50 A3 23

Set in a Japanese-themed room with cherry blossom decorating the walls, Hibiki was one of the first karaoke lounges in the city and still attracts a good number of regular singers, and it's fun whether you take the mic or not. You can choose to sing in front of an audience, or in a private room with your friends. Busy at weekends, there is more room to exercise those vocal cords midweek.

Hofbräuhaus

JW Marriott Dubai, Abu Baker Al Siddique Road (04 607 7977, www.marriottdiningatjw.ae). Metro Abu Baker Al Siddique. **Open** 6pm-2am daily. **Map** p50 C4 24

If the atmosphere wasn't so warm and friendly, this German venue would be in danger of descending into kitsch. Authenticity comes from the choice of German beers, Bavarian bites on the menu and the regulars supping at the bar.

QD's

Dubai Creek Golf & Yacht Club, near Deira City Centre (04 295 6000, www.dubaigolf.com). **Open** 5pm-2am Mon-Wed, Sun; 5pm-3am Thur-Sat. **Map** p51 F2 25

QD's is an excellent alfresco, waterside spot, offering a late-night refuge for a mix of crowds and nationalities. With elements of a beer garden and a shisha bar, plus views over the Creek, it's unique.

★ Terrace

Park Hyatt Dubai, near Deira City Centre (04 317 2221, www.restaurants.dubai.hyatt.com). **Open** 5pm-2am daily. **Map** p51 E2 26

In an undisturbed Creekside spot, the Terrace offers rare tranquillity in the heart of Dubai. There are great sunset views, twinkling lights and live jazz later in the evening. Seafood snacks and serenity complement the drinks.

Shops & Services

Abu Hail Centre

Al Quds Street, opposite NMC Hospital (04 266 9600). Metro Abu Hail. **Open** 9am-1pm, 4-10pm Mon-Thur, Sat, Sun; 4-10pm Fri. **Map** p50 D6 27 **Mall**

With big names like BurJuman and Deira City Centre competing for shoppers' attention, it's a wonder that the Abu Hail Centre continues to attract any visitors. The vast majority of outlets sell traditional Arabic clothing for women but dotted around the mall's dark corridors are a few places of interest – perfume stores selling top-of-the-range scents at reasonable prices, for example.

Deira City Centre

Between Sheikh Rashid Road & Baniyas Road (04 295 1010, www.citycentredeira.com). Metro Deira City Centre. **Open** 10am-10pm Mon-Wed, Sun; 10am-midnight Thur-Sat. **Map** p51 E3 28 **Mall**

This major mall not far from the Creek has over 370 stores, 60 dining outlets, a VOX Cinema with 11 screens, and the Magic Planet indoor fun centre with arcade games and a bowling alley.

Al Ghurair Centre

Al Rigga Road, near Fish Roundabout (800 24227, www.alghuraircentre.com). Metro Union. **Open** 10am-10pm Mon-Wed, Sun; 10am-midnight Thur-Sat. **Map** p50 C3 29 **Mall**

Built in 1981, Al Ghurair Centre is Dubai's oldest mall, but in spite of its age its popularity hasn't waned. A bit of a maze spread over two floors, with corridors branching out at all angles, you can find anything here from Arabic jewellery and rugs to South African beauty products.

Toshkhana Trading

Al Khor Street, Gold Souk (04 225 4440). Metro Al Ras. **Open** 9.30am-10pm Mon-Thur, Sat, Sun; 4-10pm Fri. **Map** p50 A2 30 **Carpets**

Dubai's gold souk may not sound like an obvious location for solving your carpeting needs, but sitting on a main alleyway here is Toshkhana. Its range includes delicate, handmade silk and cotton rugs costing anything from Dhs1,500 to Dhs15,000, and sturdier woollen carpets priced between Dhs800 and Dhs1,500. For something a little more unusual, embroidered velvet-trimmed rugs with decorative jewel effects are on sale around the Dhs2,500 mark.

GARHOUD

If landing at Dubai International Airport, Garhoud will be the first part of Dubai you'll see. Initially it's not the most striking of areas but this unassuming district is home to a number of decent bars and restaurants. One of Garhoud's most popular destinations is the **Irish Village**, a bar that attracts expats from all over the city with its laid-back vibe and alfresco seating. You'd be

Dubai Tennis Stadium.

forgiven for thinking Garhoud was Dubai's Little Ireland as it's also home to the **Dubliner's** in the Le Méridien Dubai Hotel.

Every February Garhoud has its big moment in the spotlight when it hosts the Dubai Duty Free Tennis Championships (*see below*) at the **Dubai Tennis Stadium**. This competition is a key stop on the ATP World Tour 500 Series.

Sights & Attractions

Dubai Tennis Stadium

31A Street, near Jumeirah Creekside Hotel (04 282 4122). Metro GGICO. **Map** p51 F3 ㉛
This 5,000-seat stadium comes to life once a year for the Dubai Duty Free Tennis Championship, when the world's best descend on this corner of Garhoud. The complex occasionally hosts concerts as well. For tennis tickets, keep an eye on the official website, www.dubaidutyfreetennischampionships.com.

Restaurants

Blue Flame

Jumeirah Creekside Hotel, 31A Street (04 230 8459, www.jumeirah.com). Metro GGICO. **Open** 6-11pm Tue-Sun. **Main courses** Dhs165-Dhs365. **Map** p51 F3 ㉜ **Steakhouse**
There are seafood dishes as well as the expected meat at this hotel steakhouse, and they are often served in combination: scallops and duck breast, say, or beef short ribs and king prawn. The venue is a real looker, with a modern design, blue lighting and a futuristic pod in the centre of the dining area, used for cooking lessons.

Casa Mia

Le Méridien Dubai Hotel & Conference Centre, Airport Road (04 217 0000, www.casamia-dubai.com). **Open** 12.30-3.30pm, 7.30-11.30pm daily. **Main courses** Dhs140-Dhs300. **Map** p51 F4 ㉝ **Italian**
One of those amazing stuck-in-a-timewarp finds, Casa Mia shows its age but in all the right ways. A cute approximation of a rustic trattoria, complete with dark-wood furnishings and white-linen tablecloths, the walls proudly display awards from the 1990s – which makes it a positive dinosaur by local standards. The food is recognisably Italian and so is the pop soundtrack.

★ Kiku

Le Méridien Dubai Hotel & Conference Centre, Airport Road (04 217 0000, www.kiku-dubai.com). **Open** 12.30-2.30pm, 6.30-11pm daily. **Set menus** Dhs60-Dhs120. **Map** p51 F4 ㉞ **Japanese**

With its welcoming staff, cosy corners and an army of Japanese diners, first impressions here earn Kiku major kudos. Get a table near the busy kitchen and watch as chefs send out huge bowls of steaming ramen, crisp tempura, and basted meats bursting with umami. The venue sits across the road from Dubai's airport and lunchtime is noticeably hectic – worth it for the truly excellent ramen, though.

SoHo Grill

Century Village, 31A Street (04 286 8520, www.sohogrill.ae). Metro GGICO. **Open** noon-12.30am daily. **Main courses** Dhs90-Dhs200. **Map** p51 F3 35 **American**

If you're looking for a protein hit amid the myriad restaurants of Century Village, look no further than this New York-style bar and grill. With a louche canteen feel to the interior, this venue lends itself to a more casual dining experience; in the winter months you can eat alfresco. The menu is carnivore nirvana: steaks, burgers, dawgs, ribs and chicken.

Other locations Sheikh Zayed Road (04 343 4007); Wafi Mall, Oud Metha (04 396 6141).

Cafés & Bars

Cu-ba

Jumeirah Creekside Hotel, 31A Street (04 230 8459, www.jumeirah.com). Metro GGICO. **Open** noon-1am Mon-Wed, Sat, Sun; noon-2pm Thu, Fri. **Map** p51 F3 36

An eighth-floor, rooftop hangout, Cu-ba offers twinkly twilight views over the golf course and Creek. Fusing Cuban cool with a future-retro sheen, it's a decent spot for evening drinks under the stars. Tuesday is ladies' night, while the daily happy hour runs 6-8pm.

Dubliner's

Le Méridien Dubai Hotel & Conference Centre, Airport Road (04 217 0000, www.dubliners-dubai.com). **Open** noon-2am daily. **Map** p51 F4 37

A substantially smaller affair than the city's more well-known Irish stalwarts, there's a quaintness to the Dubliner's that's a tiny bit more authentic than its competitors. Serving as the home of Dubai's expat Celtic supporters, on match days it's transformed with a throng of football fanatics. But it remains homely enough to feel like a British or Irish neighbourhood local.

★ Irish Village

Century Village, 31A Street (04 239 5000, www.theirishvillage.com). Metro GGICO. **Open** 11am-1am Mon-Wed, Sat, Sun; 11am-2am Thur, Fri. **Map** p51 F3 38

The Irish Village is one of Dubai's larger Irish venues, with a spacious outdoor terrace. Inside is a little more traditional, with dark wooden furnishings and old-fashioned glass partitions; the space is adorned with antiques and quirky Irish memorabilia. Despite the venue's size, it gets so busy sometimes that you might have trouble finding a table. From September onwards, it comes into its own, particularly in the evenings when a cold drink on the terrace is irresistible.

IN THE KNOW GRIPPING STUFF

Make your way to Deira on a Friday afternoon to join the crowds watching the south Asian sport of *pehlwani*. These boisterous bouts of wrestling take place around 4pm near the old Deira Fish Market on Al Khaleej Road.

FESTIVAL CITY

Past Garhoud and further along the Creek, this entertainment complex tends to be quieter than other areas of Dubai due to its out-of-the-way location. There's plenty here, however, to keep the entire family happy.

At the heart of the complex is the **Festival Centre** shopping mall, with dozens of stores and some decent dining options including the **Hard Rock Café** and Emirati restaurant **Al Fanar**. Take a walk outside the Festival Centre and you'll discover another of the area's main draws, **Festival Marina**. From here you can look across the bobbing yachts to the Dubai skyline, which is particularly impressive at sunset. Golfers also find reason to visit Festival City thanks to **Al Badia Golf Club**. This course is just a stone's throw from the **Crowne Plaza Festival City** (*see p270*) and **InterContinental Festival City** (*see p269*) hotels. Both have plenty of bars and restaurants – the best are in the InterCon, not least the high-end French venue **Reflets par Pierre Gagnaire**.

Sights & Attractions

Al Badia Golf Club by InterContinental Festival City

Between Festival Boulevard & Al Badia Boulevard (04 601 0101, www.albadiagolfclub.ae). **Rates** vary depending on season. **Map** p51 H2 39

This 18-hole championship course feels a world away from the city, despite being just a 15-minute drive from Downtown. It's a challenging place to play, with water features, rivers and sand traps. Afterwards, unwind at the golf club's spa, where you can even experience a 'golf ball massage'.

Restaurants

Al Fanar

Canal Walk, Festival Centre (04 232 9966, www.alfanarrestaurant.com). **Open** 8.30am-11.30pm daily. **Main courses** Dhs25-Dhs60. **Map** p51 H2 40 **Arabic**

EXPLORE

This Emirati restaurant serves up local cuisine with a slice of history thrown in for good measure. Based in a converted pearl merchant's house, you can eat outside at the traditional *majlis* (meeting place) on floor cushions, or at the tables opposite. Inside, there are dozens of photographs of Old Dubai in the 1960s and Bedouin life. The restaurant's Souq Moshad sells traditional trinkets and is dedicated to the memory of the Indian spice merchant who imported the idea of street markets to the emirate.

★ Reflets par Pierre Gagnaire

InterContinental Festival City (04 701 1127, www.diningdfc.com). **Open** 7-11pm daily. **Main courses** Dhs220-Dhs340. **Map** p51 H2 41 **French**

If you're after destination haute-cuisine dining then Reflets should be on your shortlist. Pierre Gagnaire is a three-star Michelin chef and his style pervades everything here, from the sophisticated and highly developed combinations – your crab meat and dog cockles will be rubbed in farmhouse cider jelly – to the charming service. From the second you arrive in the luxurious dining room, with pink chandeliers, the decadence begins with an onslaught of amuse-bouches, and proceeds from there.

Terra Firma

InterContinental Festival City (04 701 1127, www.diningdfc.com). **Open** 7-11pm daily. **Main courses** Dhs140-Dhs350. **Map** p51 H2 42 **Steakhouse**

There's no view from this ground-floor, hotel restaurant, which is a shame as it sits alongside the Festival City Marina, but design features compensate: terrace tables illuminated by flaming lanterns, for example. As for the steaks, the American, Argentinian and Australian cuts impress, while there is also a good selection of seafood. Presentation stands out here: the cigar-themed dessert is served in an ashtray with icing sugar, ice-cream and prune cake.

Cafés & Bars

Belgian Beer Café

Crowne Plaza Festival City (04 701 1127). **Open** noon-2am daily. **Map** p51 H2 43

There's not much difference between the three Belgian cafés in Dubai, but if we had to choose, we feel the most affection for this one, the Festival City original. Make sure you visit early in the evening for great sunset views across the Creek accompanied by a pint of Belgian beer, chunky chips and mayonnaise. **Other locations** Grand Millennium, TECOM (04 429 9999); Madinat Jumeirah (04 447 0227).

Choix Patisserie & Restaurant par Pierre Gagnaire

InterContinental Festival City (04 701 1136, www.diningdfc.com). **Open** 7am-11pm daily. **Map** p51 H2 44

This is one of two venues in Dubai, in the same hotel, by three-star Michelin chef Pierre Gagnaire. It's also his first standalone pâtisserie anywhere in the world. There's an elegant dining room, or a terrace with shisha and views of the Burj Khalifa. The menus cover breakfast, afternoon tea, and à la carte lunch or dinner (featuring salads, pasta and *bento*

EXPLORE

Reflets par Pierre Gagnaire.

boxes). It's a refined café experience with some of the *je ne sais quoi* typical of his other venue, Reflets par Pierre Gagnaire (*see p60*), but at decidedly more accessible prices.

Hard Rock Café

Festival Centre (04 232 8900, www.hardrock.com/cafes/dubai). **Open** noon-2am daily. **Map** p51 H2 45

Famous around the world, Dubai's branch of the Hard Rock Café serves up what you expect: music memorabilia, super-sized portions of burgers and the like, and live rock entertainment. Its location, next to the Festival Centre, is perfect if you've had a long day shopping. When it comes to food, the Local Legendary is exclusive to the region: the burger is topped with date chutney, soft *kholas* dates and creamy cheese on a toasted bun with lettuce and tomato. After 10pm, under-21s aren't allowed as the place morphs into more of a bar.

Vista Lounge & Bar

InterContinental Festival City (04 701 1127, www.diningdfc.com). **Open** noon-2am Mon-Wed, Sat, Sun; noon-3am Thur, Fri. **Map** p51 H2 46

With incredible 26th-floor views across the Creek, it's surprising that Vista isn't better known. You might not have much company while enjoying a drink here, but it's undoubtedly a stunning venue. If you get peckish, there's a range of light bites including meze, samosas, spring rolls and mini pizzas. There's an intriguing, and expensive, range of champagne cocktails too.

IN THE KNOW
NEW FISH MARKET

At the time of writing, work was almost complete on Deira's new fish market at a cost of more than Dhs250 million. This major development will replace the popular original, depriving the city of what has been one of its most engaging visitor experiences. The old fish market opened in 1998 and is a popular attraction, with the daily hustle and bustle of traders selling fresh fish. The new market will feature stalls selling fresh and dried fish as well as fruit and vegetables; the building will also house a department store, hypermarket and restaurants.

Shops & Services

Festival City Mall

Festival City (04 232 5444, www.festivalcentre.com). **Open** 10am-10pm Mon-Wed, Sun; 10am-midnight Thur-Sat. **Map** p51 H2 47 **Mall**

At first glance, this huge shopping centre is just like the many others you'll find in Dubai. All the high-street brands are here, plus the UAE's only branch of IKEA. There's a good choice of restaurants as well, but the main draw – and what makes the mall stand out – is the outdoor area. Known as Canal Walk, the stretch alongside the marina is a pleasant place to stroll with *abras*, cafés and restaurants.

EXPLORE

Bur Dubai, Karama & Oud Metha

On the southern banks of the Creek and sprawling inland towards Jumeirah and Downtown Dubai is the fascinating and culturally rich district of Bur Dubai. Most of the city's heritage is condensed in a small area near the Creek here, and it's easy to walk around and hit a number of sites in one day. Karama, further south from the Creek, is a place for bargain hunters: you can buy everything from pashminas to phone covers for next to nothing; it's full of wallet-friendly Indian and Pakistani restaurants too. Oud Metha, which sits to the south of Bur Dubai and east of Karama, is far quieter, home to high-end restaurants and recreation facilities.

Creek Park.

Don't Miss

1 Dubai Museum Housed in the emirate's oldest building (p65).

2 Heritage & Diving Village Discover Dubai's past in this 'living museum' (p65).

3 Bayt Al Wakeel Arabic food and stunning Creek views (p68).

4 Karama Souk For bargains galore (p73).

5 Creek Park A relaxing green space beside the water (p75).

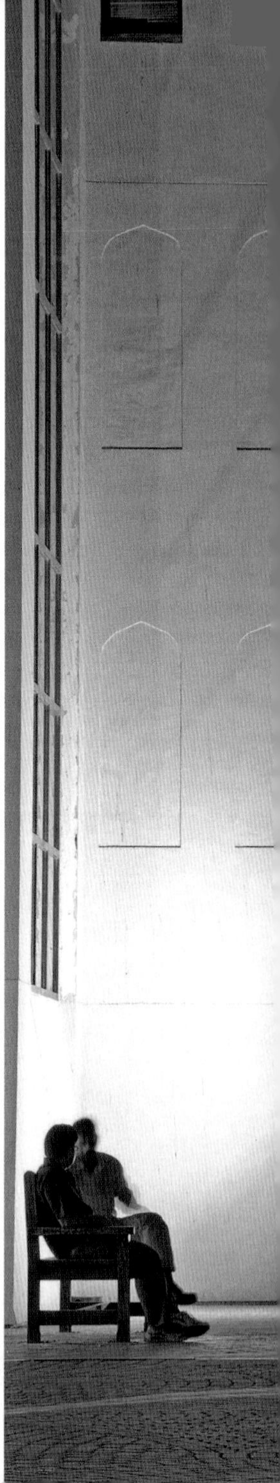

BUR DUBAI

As Dubai was settled in the 19th century, a residential area developed along the sandy southern banks of the Creek that became known as Bur Dubai. It was here that the emirate's rulers made their home, in sea-facing fortifications, and the district remains the seat of the Diwan (the Ruler's Office), Dubai's most senior administrative body. As the city grew, the area became home to embassies and consulates, creating an atmosphere of diplomatic calm, with commercial activity centred on the mouth of the Creek. Today the situation is changing fast and, although the banks of the Creek are still free from development, Bur Dubai has sprawled inland, with tower blocks springing up on practically every available inch of sand.

As the residential community has grown, so commerce has developed to support local residents. The once tiny souk has expanded dramatically, supermarkets and shopping malls have opened, and highways traverse the area. **Dubai Museum** makes a good starting point for exploration of Bur Dubai. From the museum, make your way northwards towards the Creek and enjoy the **textile souk**. Streets filled with fabric and tailoring shops lead you to the covered area of the **Bastakia souk**, which is filled with curios and souvenirs. Amid this cluster of market stalls is the entrance to one of Dubai's most scenic restaurants, **Bait Al Wakeel**, which offers unrivalled views across the Creek.

Outside Bayt Al Wakeel, you'll find the *abra* station, from where rickety boats can take you across the Creek to the Deira side for a bargain Dhs1 (*see p55* **Bridging the Gap**). After leaving Bait Al Wakeel, with the Creek ahead of you, walk to the left and you'll reach **Shindagha**, which features a collection of museums including the intriguing **Camel Museum** and the **Traditional Architecture Museum**. This area is one of the most traditional in the city, with many original buildings from the early 1900s still standing. Shindagha is also home to the **Heritage & Diving Village**, an outdoor museum that resembles a traditional village.

Heading away from the Creek and back towards Dubai Museum is **Al Fahidi Historical Neighbourhood** (*see p71* **Neighbourhood Watch**), one of Dubai's most picturesque heritage sites. Today, it houses some of the city's best cultural attractions, including the **Coffee Museum** and **XVA Gallery**.

Sights & Attractions

FREE Camel Museum

Al Shindagha, next to Heritage & Diving Village (04 392 0368, www.dubaiculture.gov.ae). Metro Al Ghubaiba. **Open** 8am-2pm Mon-Thur, Sun. **Admission** free. **Map** p66 A5 ❶

This museum celebrates the role of the camel in Arabian culture. The single-storey building surrounds a central courtyard and was originally used as a stable for the beasts. It has been restored and split into different sections with exhibits on the history of camels in the UAE, camel racing and the relationship between camels and the Arab people.

Abra station.

FREE Coffee Museum

Villa 44, Al Fahidi Historical Neighbourhood (04 380 6777, www.coffeemuseum.ae). Metro Al Fahidi. **Open** 9am-5pm Mon-Thur, Sat, Sun. **Admission** free. **Map** p66 B5 ❷

The history of coffee, as well as the different methods of preparing the beverage from around the world, are charted in this interesting and unusual museum. Exhibits include coffee-making paraphernalia and historical documents such as coffee adverts. After seeing all of the displays, you can – as you would expect – sample the goods at the custom-built brew bar.

FREE Coin Museum

Al Fahidi Historical Neighbourhood, near Al Farooq Mosque (04 353 9265, www.dubaiculture.gov.ae). Metro Al Fahidi. **Open** 8am-10pm Mon-Thur, Sun. **Admission** free. **Map** p66 B5 ❸

A collection of nearly 500 coins from across the Middle East. The museum has seven exhibition rooms with interactive displays on the different currencies. It may not sound fascinating, but the coins also tell the story of Dubai's trading history, which adds another dimension to the displays.

Dubai Museum.

★ Dubai Museum

Al Fahidi Street, near Arabian Court Hotel (04 353 1862, www.dubaiculture.gov.ae). Metro Al Fahidi. **Open** 8.30am-8.30pm Mon-Thur, Sat, Sun; 2-8.30pm Fri. **Admission** Dhs3; Dhs1 reductions. **Map** p66 B5 ❹

Al Fahidi Fort was built in 1787 as Dubai's primary sea defence, and also served as the ruler's residence. In 1970, it was renovated so the Dubai Museum could be housed within its walls. It's well worth a visit. The displays are creative and imaginative, allowing you to peek into an Islamic school, walk through a 1950s souk, watch traditional craftsmen at work and even experience the tranquil beauty of a night in the desert.

Grand Mosque

Next to Dubai Museum, Al Fahidi Street. Metro Al Fahidi. **Map** p66 B5 ❺

Although it may look like a historic building that has recently been restored, the Grand Mosque was actually built only a little over ten years ago – styled to resemble the original Grand Mosque that had stood on the site. Built in around 1900, the earlier mosque doubled as a religious school. Sadly, it was torn down in the 1960s and replaced with a smaller one.

★ FREE Heritage & Diving Village

Al Shindagha, off Al Mina Road (04 393 7151, www.dubaiculture.gov.ae). Metro Al Ghubaiba. **Open** 8am-8pm Mon-Thur, Sun; 3-10pm Fri. **Admission** free. **Map** p66 A5 ❻

This pleasant 'living museum' by the Creek, staffed by guides, potters, weavers and other craftspeople, focuses on Dubai's maritime past, and depicts the living conditions of the area's original seafarers, who harvested the waters of the Gulf for pearls and fish to trade. Static but entertaining displays chart the history of Dubai's pearling industry, and a tented village gives a glimpse into the Bedouin way of life that remained unchanged until well into the 20th century. During religious holidays, such as Eid Al Fitr and Eid Al Adha, traditional ceremonies are laid on, including sword dancing and 'wedding' celebrations. At such times old pearl divers are often on hand to recount tales of adventure and hardship.

Hindi Lane

Off Ali Bin Abi Taleb Street, between the Ruler's Court and Grand Mosque. Metro Al Fahidi. **Map** p66 B5 ❼

Along this tiny alleyway near the Dubai Museum, you'll find the city's only Hindu temple, plus dozens of little shops selling offerings and religious paraphernalia, from posters of Hindu deities to small figurines, keyrings to stickers. At the very end, you'll also find a small stall selling potted plants.

FREE Jumaa & Obaid Bin Thani House

Al Shindagha, next to Heritage & Diving Village (04 393 3240, www.dubaiculture.gov.ae). Metro Al Ghubaiba. **Open** 8am-9pm Mon-Thur, Sat, Sun; 4pm-10pm Fri. **Admission** free. **Map** p66 A5 ❽

Built in 1916, this is a fine example of a traditional local house. It was restored in 1998 and is home to an Arabic calligraphy exhibition on the first floor. The ground floor has been kept in the style of a traditional Emirati home – it's probably more interesting than the exhibits upstairs.

EXPLORE

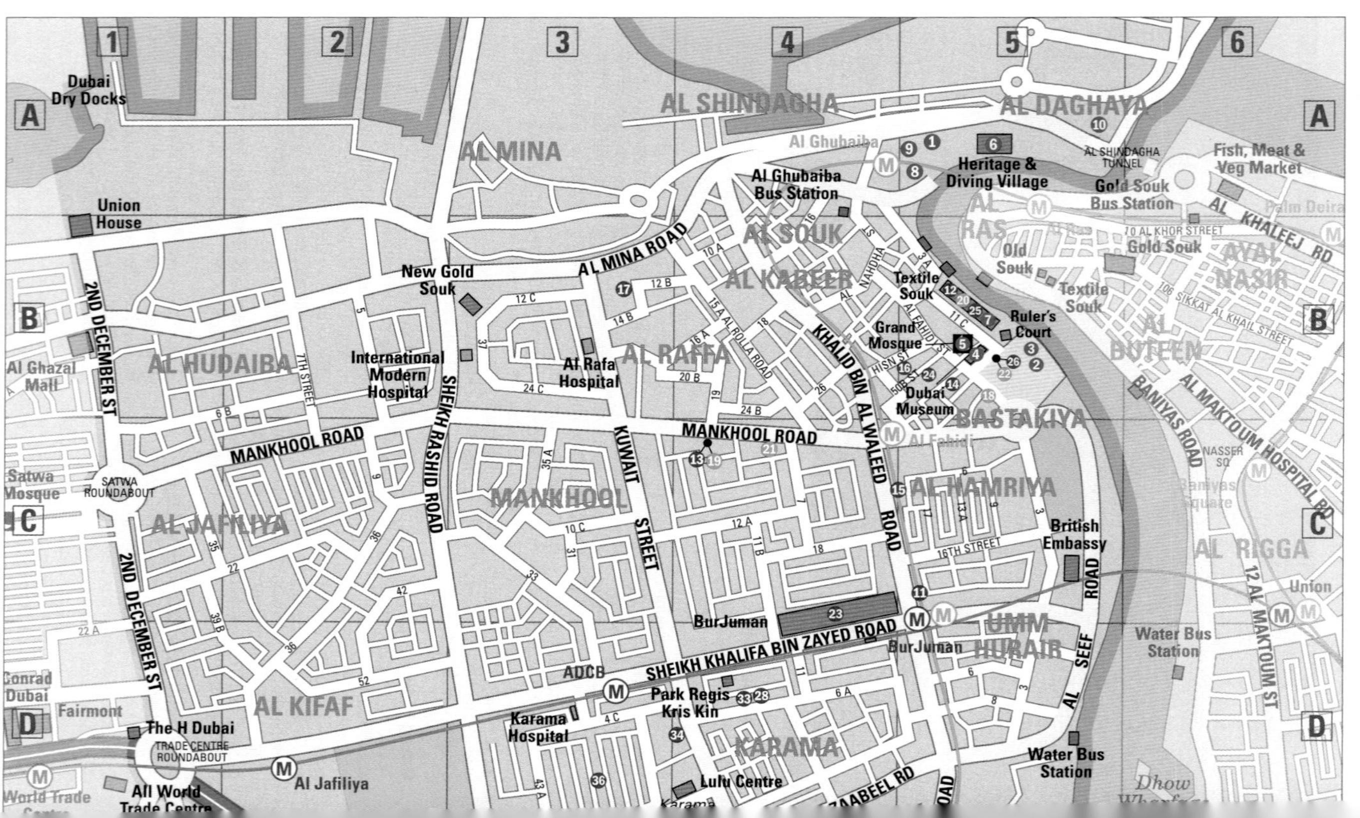

1
2
3
4
5
6
A
B
C
D
Dubai Dry Docks
AL SHINDAGHA
AL DAGHAYA
AL MINA
Al Ghubaiba
Heritage & Diving Village
AL SHINDAGHA TUNNEL
Fish, Meat & Veg Market
Union House
Al Ghubaiba Bus Station
Gold Souk Bus Station
AL RAS
Al Ras
Palm Deira
AL KHALEEJ RD
10 AL KHOR STREET
Gold Souk
AL SOUK
AYAL NASIR
AL MINA ROAD
AL KABEER
NAHDHA ST
Old Souk
Textile Souk
New Gold Souk
106 SIKKAT AL KHAIL STREET
2ND DECEMBER ST
12 C
12 B
14 B
15 A AL ROLLA ROAD
AL FAHIDI ST
Ruler's Court
Grand Mosque
AL BUTEEN
Al Ghazal Mall
AL HUDAIBA
7TH STREET
International Modern Hospital
SHEIKH RASHID ROAD
Al Rafa Hospital
AL RAFFA
KHALID BIN AL WALEED ROAD
HISN ST
Dubai Museum
BASTAKIYA
BANIYAS ROAD
AL MAKTOUM HOSPITAL RD
MANKHOOL ROAD
Al Fahidi
NASSER SQ
Baniyas Square
Satwa Mosque
SATWA ROUNDABOUT
AL JAFILIYA
MANKHOOL
KUWAIT STREET
AL HAMRIYA
British Embassy
AL RIGGA
16TH STREET
Union
BurJuman
UMM HURAIR
12 AL MAKTOUM ST
Water Bus Station
AL SEEF ROAD
SHEIKH KHALIFA BIN ZAYED ROAD
ADCB
Park Regis Kris Kin
Conrad Dubai
Fairmont
AL KIFAF
Karama Hospital
The H Dubai
TRADE CENTRE ROUNDABOUT
KARAMA
World Trade Centre
All World Trade Centre
Al Jafiliya
Lulu Centre
ZAABEEL RD
Dhow Wharfage

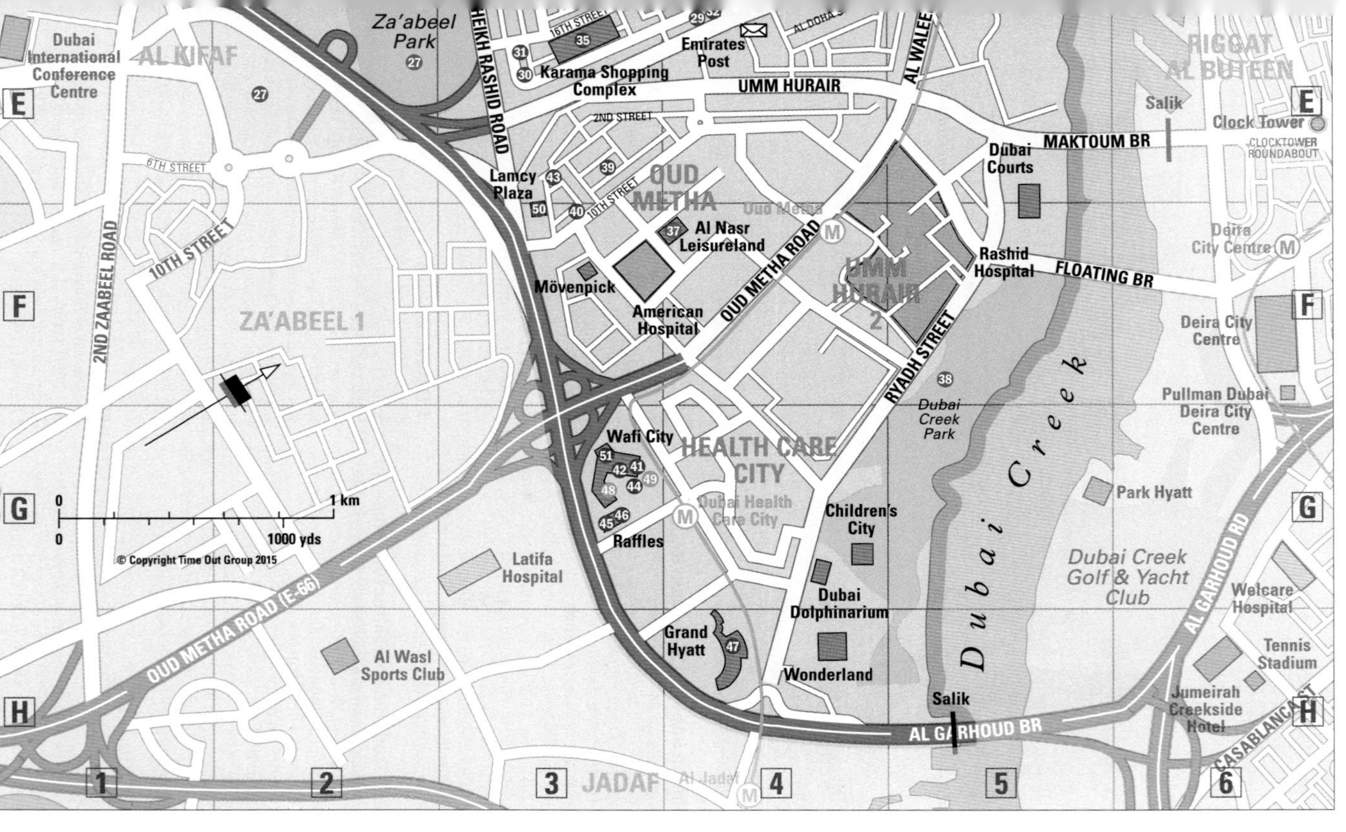
Dubai International Conference Centre
Al Kifaf
Za'abeel Park
Sheikh Rashid Road
16th Street
Emirates Post
Karama Shopping Complex
Umm Hurair
Al Waleed
Riggat Al Buteen
Salik
Clock Tower
Clocktower Roundabout
2nd Street
6th Street
Maktoum Br
Dubai Courts
Lamcy Plaza
Oud Metha
10th Street
Al Nasr Leisureland
Deira City Centre
2nd Zaabeel Road
10th Street
Rashid Hospital
Floating Br
Mövenpick
Umm Hurair 2
American Hospital
Oud Metha Road
Za'abeel 1
Ryadh Street
Deira City Centre
Pullman Dubai Deira City Centre
Dubai Creek Park
Dubai Creek
Wafi City
Health Care City
Park Hyatt
Dubai Health Care City
Children's City
1 km
1000 yds
Raffles
© Copyright Time Out Group 2015
Latifa Hospital
Dubai Creek Golf & Yacht Club
Al Garhoud Rd
Welcare Hospital
Dubai Dolphinarium
Oud Metha Road (E-66)
Grand Hyatt
Al Wasl Sports Club
Tennis Stadium
Wonderland
Jumeirah Creekside Hotel
Salik
Al Garhoud Br
Casablanca St
Jadaf
Al Jadaf
E
F
G
H
1
2
3
4
5
6

EXPLORE

View from Sheikh Saeed Al Maktoum House.

Sheikh Saeed Al Maktoum House

Al Shindagha, next to Heritage & Diving Village (04 393 7139, www.dubaiculture.gov.ae). Metro Al Ghubaiba. **Open** 8am-8.30pm Mon-Thur, Sat, Sun; 3-10pm Fri. **Admission** Dhs2; Dhs1 reductions; free under-7s. **Map** p66 A5 ❾

Built in 1896 out of coral covered in lime and sand plaster, this traditional house was the home of Dubai's former ruler until his death in 1958, hence its strategic position at the mouth of the Creek. Now restored and converted into a museum, it displays documents, stamps, currencies and a collection of old photographs of Dubai and its ruling family.

FREE Traditional Architecture Museum

Al Shindagha, next to Heritage & Diving Village (04 392 0093, www.dubaiculture.gov.ae). Metro Al Ghubaiba. **Open** 8am-2pm Mon-Thur, Sun. **Admission** free. **Map** p66 A5 ❿

A former residence of Sheikh Juma bin Maktoum, built in 1927, this house is now a museum showcasing the history of Dubai's traditional architecture and construction methods, with displays featuring tools used for building. It also has exhibits documenting the culture and history of the Emirati people.

Restaurants

Aryaas

Khalid Bin Waleed Road, near BurJuman metro station (04 357 7800, www.aryaasgourmet.com). Metro BurJuman. **Open** 7.30am-3.30pm, 5.30-11.30pm Mon-Thur, Sat, Sun; 7.30-11.30am, 1.30pm-midnight Fri. **Main courses** Dhs15-Dhs20. **No credit cards**. Map p66 C5 ⓫ **Indian**

With canteen-style dining downstairs, and a relaxed restaurant upstairs, Aryaas caters both for Bur Dubai's Indian community and westerners. It's worth overcoming any potential language barrier to order the southern Indian vegetarian thali: five different pots of curry, including a brilliant dahl and a surprising, but excellent, sweet tamarind concoction. In addition, you'll be served fluffy rice and a choice of breads.

★ Bayt Al Wakeel

Next to Textile Souk, off Ali Bin Abi Taleb Street, behind Dubai Museum (04 353 0530). Metro Al Ghubaiba. **Open** noon-11.30pm daily. **Main courses** Dhs35-Dhs125. **Map** p66 B5 ⓬ **Arabic**

As locations go, Bayt Al Wakeel takes some beating. Just around the corner from the textile souk, and jutting out into the Creek on stilts, Bayt Al Wakeel treats diners to picture-perfect views of Dubai as *abras* cross the water and larger ships cruise past. Dining alfresco is always popular, but the historic interior is impressive too, with large wooden doors. The menu is simple and fuss-free, with plenty of hot and cold meze, and grilled meat and fish.

Elia

Majestic Hotel Tower, Al Mankhool Road (04 501 2690, www.dubaimajestic.com). **Open** 7pm-midnight daily. **Main courses** Dhs50-Dhs100. **Map** p66 C4 ⓭ **Greek**

Elia is a rare gem: one of just a handful of Greek restaurants in Dubai. Given the quality of the food here, perhaps it's as simple as potential competitors not having the appetite for the fight. A sweet, romantic Mediterranean-style hideaway, set within the Majestic Hotel, Elia is an oasis of calm. Some may find a few of the meaty dishes bordering on heavy, but our recommendation would be to get yourself out on to the lovely terrace with a group of friends and while away a long and relaxed afternoon with shared meze plates – the likes of grilled calamari, cheese saganaki and feta cheese.

Mumtaz Mahal

Arabian Courtyard Hotel & Spa, Al Fahidi Street (04 351 9111, www.mumtazmahalrestaurant.com). Metro Al Fahidi. **Open** noon-3.30pm, 7pm-3am daily. **Main courses** Dhs40-Dhs135. **Map** p66 B5 ⓮ **Indian**

Stepping inside the Arabian Courtyard Hotel is like stepping into another world – and Mumtaz Mahal buys into the hotel's theme of extravagance. Booths are made from Indian carriages and musicians play traditional music while you eat. It's slightly strange, but charming none the less. Classic north Indian dishes are full of flavour, fragrant and spicy. Mumtaz Mahal is not a fine-dining restaurant but it's a good middle ground between Old Dubai's cafés and the high-end restaurants elsewhere in the city.

Picante

Four Points by Sheraton Bur Dubai (04 397 7444, www.picantedubai.com). Metro Al Fahidi. **Open** noon-3pm, 7pm-midnight daily. **Main courses** Dhs70-Dhs200. **Map** p66 C5 ⓯ **Portuguese**

With tiled floors, wooden beams and louvred shutters, Picante is an authentic, home-style setting for Portuguese cooking. It's a regular haunt of Mediterranean expats, so it's clearly doing something right. Seafood is particularly recommended, including the classic Portuguese *bacalhau a bras*, salted cod, with scrambled egg, parsley and crispy potatoes, served with cherry tomatoes and black olives. Prices are competitive, and the restaurant has food and drink deals, which makes it a hit with larger groups at weekends.

Rangoli

Cosmos Lane, Meena Bazaar (04 351 5873, www.rangolirestaurants.com). Metro Al Fahidi. **Open** 8.30am-11.30pm daily. **Thali** Dhs24-Dhs27. **No credit cards. Map** p66 B5 ⓰ **Indian**

By the time you get to Rangoli, having navigated the crowded, narrow streets of Meena Bazaar, dodging the shopkeepers trying to sell you watches, scarves and bags, you'll be grateful to take your seat. Head upstairs to try one of the vegetarian thalis, composed of the likes of yellow dahl, chickpea curry and potato curry, along with chapatis and popadoms – and they come with top-ups. If you dine à la carte downstairs, try the selection of puri (unleavened deep-fried bread). The original-style pani puri is some of the best you'll find in Dubai; sev puri is lighter, piled with salad and served with perfect sweet tamarind chutney.

Other location near Lamcy Plaza, Oud Metha (04 357 6710).

★ Signature by Sanjeev Kapoor

Meliá Hotel, Kuwait Street (04 386 8111, www.melia.com). **Open** noon-3pm, 7-11pm daily. **Main courses** Dhs70-Dhs200. **Map** p66 B3 ⓱ **Indian**

With sophisticated, restrained decor using dark-wood planks on the walls and low lighting, Signature by Sanjeev Kapoor is an upscale, romantic restaurant. The Indian cooking is rooted in the classics, with dishes such as a spicy rogan josh, but there are contemporary twists. Lemongrass butter chicken was creamy and fragrant, with the addition of *zaatar* spice lending some lemony local punch.

Cafés & Bars

Arabian Tea House

Al Fahidi Street, near the Ruler's Court (04 353 5071). Metro Al Fahidi. **Open** 8am-10pm daily. **Map** p66 B5 ⓲

Set in the historic Al Fahidi district, the Arabian Tea House is a large courtyard with plenty of seating, with net curtains overhead acting as shade from the sun. There are many different kinds of tea, as well as sizeable salads and sandwiches, all of which are good. But it's really about the experience and atmosphere.

Barrels Pub

Majestic Hotel Tower, Al Mankhool Road (04 359 8888). **Open** noon-3am daily. **Map** p66 C4 ⓳

An old favourite in the heart of Mankhool Road, Brit-pub Barrels has outlived much of the neighbourhood competition by sticking to what it does best: sports on the big screen, decent pub grub and friendly staff. And it's not as if you're spoiled for choice for places to have a drink in Bur Dubai.

★ Creekside

Al Suq Al Khabeer, next to Ruler's Court & Dubai Creek, Bur Dubai (04 359 9220, www.creekside dubai.me). Metro Al Fahidi. **Open** 8am-8pm daily. Map p66 B5 ⓴

Creekside describes itself as a 'cultural space and café'. True, there's art framed on the walls, but otherwise this place is all about the food. The café has a fantastic (you've guess it) Creekside location, in the heart of Old Dubai, accessible from the Al Fahidi Historical District. The food is said to be inspired by the location, although it actually seems pretty European. It's good though, starting with breakfast and moving on to great lunchtime salads (the Creekside summer salad is packed with grapefruit, burnt orange, grapes, cherry tomatoes, cucumber,

NEIGHBOURHOOD WATCH

Get a taste of old Dubai in Al Fahidi Historical District.

Located on the southern bank of the Creek, Al Fahidi Historical Neighbourhood has been carefully renovated to look as it did when it was first built in the early years of the 20th century. Narrow streets are bounded by sand-coloured houses with few features on the public side, affording privacy; inside, rooms are built surrounding a courtyard, providing a hidden haven. Wind towers, trapping the wind and funnelling it down into the house, were an ingenious solution to provide much-needed cooling in the time before electricity. The area is now pedestrianised, and stepping into the narrow alleyways is like taking a walk into Dubai's past.

This district was formerly known as Bastakia, from the first people to settle in the area, who were traders from Bastak in southern Iran. The ruler of Dubai encouraged such immigration in the early 1900s by granting favourable tax concessions. Many came and most stayed, which explains why so many Emiratis are of southern Iranian descent.

Many older UAE nationals tell of summers spent here, when entire families would sleep outside on raised platforms in order to escape the heat indoors. By the 1970s, however, Bastakia had fallen into disrepair, as families moved to modern air-conditioned flats.

Today, the regenerated area houses art galleries, cafés, restaurants and museums, including the **Coffee Museum** (*see p64*), **Coin Museum** (*see p64*) the **Arabian Tea House** (*see p69*) and **XVA Gallery** (*see p72*).

You can reach Al Fahidi by taking a short walk from Dubai Museum towards the Creek.

and smoked mackerel) and other standout dishes – a lamb burger is topped with Persian feta and aubergine chutney, and accompanied by rosemary fries.

Lucien Belgian Café

Ramada Dubai, Al Mankhool Road, (04 506 1158, www.ramadadubai.com). Metro Al Fahidi. **Open** noon-3am daily. **Map** p66 C4 ㉑

With exposed brickwork, retro European tourism posters and blackboard menus, Lucien is clearly reminiscent of other Belgium-themed venues in the city. However, in Bur Dubai, it stands out from the competition. It's a good spot for Belgian beer and hearty dishes.

XVA Café

Al Fahidi Historical Neighbourhood (04 353 5383, www.xvahotel.com). Metro Al Fahidi. **Open** 7am-10pm daily. **Map** p66 B5 ㉒

Amid the bustle of the Al Fahidi neighbourhood is this haven of a café, set in a quiet courtyard with a beautiful tree in the centre. Apple ice tea and fresh mint lemonade are wonderfully zingy and refreshing drinks. Well-presented food mainly consists of Lebanese-inspired vegetarian meze dishes.

Shops & Services

BurJuman

Corner of Khalid Bin Waleed Road & Sheikh Khalifa Bin Zayed Road (04 352 0222, www.burjuman.com). Metro BurJuman. **Open** 10am-10pm Mon-Wed, Sat, Sun; 10am-11pm Thur, Fri. **Map** p66 C4 ㉓ **Mall**

This high-end mall houses a range of designer stores for men and women, alongside a good mix of home furnishing and electronics stores. BurJuman tends to be a bit quieter than some of the city's other major malls, and it has some relaxing restaurants on the roof. It's also an easy mall to access, thanks to its dedicated metro station.

Meena Bazaar

Between Khalid Bin Waleed Street & Al Fahidi Street. Metro Al Fahidi. **Map** p66 B5 ㉔ **Market**

Referring to the area between Khalid Bin Waleed Street and Al Fahidi Street rather than a specific destination (though head for 50B Street and you're on the right track), Meena Bazaar is best visited at

EXPLORE

night, when the shops are lit up in twinkling lights and the district is at its busiest. Peruse ream after ream of fabric in one of the hundreds of textile shops, haggle over watches or admire the selection of extravagant traditional Indian outfits through the windows.

Textile Souk

Between Ali Bin Abi Taleb Street & Dubai Creek. Metro Al Ghubaiba. **Map** p66 B5 ㉕ **Market**

This bustling souk that runs alongside the Creek is the perfect place to pick up fabrics from the Indian subcontinent. You can find everything you need for suits, shirts and skirts, which a nearby tailor can whip up in no time. Haggling is encouraged, and you're sure to find a bargain.

★ XVA Gallery

Al Fahidi Historic Neighbourhood (04 353 5383, www.xvagallery.com). Metro Al Fahidi. **Open** 9am-6pm daily. **Admission** free. **Map** p66 B5 ㉖ **Gallery**

This gallery specialises in contemporary art from the Middle East, including Iran, and South Asia. Local and international artists display their works during the gallery's regular exhibitions. The gallery is part of a complex that also includes XVA Café (*see p71*) and XVA Art Hotel (*see p273*).

KARAMA

As synonymous with the trade in handbags, watches and the like as it is with excellent budget Indian and Pakistani restaurants, Karama is the ultimate place for shopping and scoffing on a shoestring. But it's not all about the main **Karama Souk** area, home to swathes of leather bag shops and dotted with cafés well worth visiting. Hit **Kuwait Road** too (between Za'abeel Road and Sheikh Khalifa Bin Zayed Road) for yet more great buys and eats.

Sights & Attractions

★ Za'abeel Park

Between Sheikh Zayed Road & Sheikh Rashid Road, near Lamcy Plaza (04 398 6888). Metro Al Jafiliya **Open** 8am-11pm Mon-Wed, Sun; 8am-11.30pm Thur-Sat. **Admission** Dhs5. **Map** p67 E2 ㉗

This huge, beautifully landscaped park is spread over two sections connected by pedestrian bridges. Popular with families and fitness fans, and quite busy at weekends, Zabeel also has a train that takes visitors on a park tour. There are some great shaded areas for parents with small children. Also available are barbecue/covered cooking areas, toilets, a bicycle track, jogging track, lake with boat hire, water fountains, children's edutainment centre and play zone, cricket pitch and plenty of refreshment kiosks. *See also p189.*

Restaurants

Betawi Café

Mabrooka 1 Building, 4B Street, near Park Regis Kris Kin Hotel (04 279 0302). Metro ADCB or BurJuman. **Open** noon-11pm Mon-Wed, Sat, Sun; 2-11pm Fri. **Main courses** Dhs15-Dhs30. **Map** p66 D4 ㉘ **Indonesian**

This budget Indonesian restaurant feels like it was born to be that hackneyed cliché, the 'hidden gem'. Based on a sleepy Karama backstreet, Betawi Café is that unique, authentic, ethnic, characterful-but-safe walk on the culinary wild side you've been dying to find. Serving affordable, wholesome and delicious food that bursts with flavours and spices, a few bites of classics like *gado gado, nasi padang* or *ketoprak* and you'll feel transported from said Karama side-street to a rainforest bamboo hut.

★ Calicut Paragon

Off Zabeel Road, behind Karama Park (04 335 8700, www.paragonrestaurant.net). Metro ADCB. **Open** 7am-12.30am daily. **Main courses** Dhs20-Dhs35. **Map** p67 E4 ㉙ **Indian**

Having to queue to get in a restaurant is surely a good sign, especially when it is in the heart of Dubai's 'curry corridor' of Satwa, Karama and Bur Dubai. Paragon is popular, and for good reason. The Keralan food is delicious and it is a brilliant choice for budget eats, with most main courses coming in at about Dh25. The menu is varied, but seafood is a speciality. Crab *thusar* is a thick, spicy sauce with a full crab broken up into it; it isn't dainty but it is delicious. This is food to delve into and enjoy, so leave any inhibitions at the door and take a trip to southern India.

Other location near NMC Hospital, Al Nahda (04 298 8858).

Manvaar

20B Street, near Karama Fish Market (04 336 8332). Metro Al Jafiliya. **Open** noon-3pm, 7pm-midnight. **Main courses** Dhs20-Dhs60. **Map** p67 E3 ㉚ **Indian**

This Rajasthani restaurant was renovated in 2014, removing some of its old charm but bringing in clean design. But one thing that hasn't changed is the superb food, particularly on the tandoori front. The *murg malai tikka* is a succulent carnival of flavour, while herbivores can safely deviate from the usual suspects (you know who you are, lentils…) and mix it up with an order of green peas masala.

Sallet Al Sayad

Off 16th Street, Sheikh Rashid Road (04 335 5722). **Open** noon-11pm daily. **Main courses** Fish charged by weight. **Map** p67 E3 ㉛ **Fish**

You could easily walk straight past this unassuming restaurant, but you'd be missing out if you did. Inside, Sallet Al Sayad feels traditional and cosy, with dark-wood furnishings and a fish bar near the entrance. The fish is served well seasoned with

Arabic spices, without being overpowering. This is a clean and simple restaurant that doesn't skimp on flavour, with friendly staff and even friendlier prices.

★ Venus

16th Street, between Lulu Centre and Karama Park (04 335 2113). Metro ADCB. **Open** 7am-midnight daily. **Main courses** Dhs15-Dhs20. **Map** p67 E4 ㉜ **Vegetarian Indian**

You'll get a warm welcome at Venus, a small, unpretentious caff serving vegetarian food. The menu is long, but the friendly staff will make suggestions. We say go for the thali – it's about as good here as anywhere in Dubai, and you'll get plenty of change from Dhs50. As well as the dahl and three vegetable curries, you'll get as much rice as you can manage and perhaps the best puri in the city.

★ Yalla Momos

4B Street, behind Park Regis Kris Kin Hotel (04 385 2233). Metro ADCB or BurJuman. **Open** noon-midnight daily. **Main courses** Dhs12-Dhs14. **Map** p66 D4 ㉝ **Nepalese**

Yalla Momos was Dubai's first eaterie dedicated to serving this little Himalayan dumpling. All you'll find here is a box-sized kiosk, with a little seating outside on the pavement, and a few tables and chairs inside. The menu is short but varied, with vegetarian and non-vegetarian dumpling recipes, available steamed or fried. Expect *momos* delivered to the table freshly cooked, still too hot to devour and perfectly twisted and formed in dough that is freshly prepared in-house. Excellent, cheap and moreish.

Shops & Services

Al Attar Centre

Next to Sunrise Supermarket, Kuwait Road (04 335 1020). Metro ADCB. **Open** 10am-11pm daily. **Map** p66 D4 ㉞ **Mall**

This small, shiny shopping mall sits slap-bang in the middle of Kuwait Road, and houses a range of tiny shops and kiosks selling everything from colourful smartphone covers to hair accessories, affordable clothing to tasty Filipino snacks. There are also a couple of casual eateries specialising in Asian cuisine.

Karama Fish Market

End of 18B Street, inside Karama Market. Metro ADCB. **Map** p67 E3 ㉟ **Market**

Pick up fresh and affordable produce at this market. Don't be put off by the sometimes jumbled seafood display – there's an enormous range of fresh fish, crabs and cephalopods available, and most stallholders will clean your purchases for you.

Karama Souk

18B Street, near Karama Park. **Map** p66 D3 ㊱ **Market**

If you came to Dubai for the bargain handbags, this is where you should be heading. You'll find leather goods in a huge range of colours and styles – but be sure to visit a few shops before parting with your cash, as prices for the same items can vary wildly. Also keep an eye out for the smaller shops selling pashminas in a variety of qualities (from Dhs10 to Dhs500 apiece) and small souvenirs.

EXPLORE

Za'abeel Park.

OUD METHA

Also known as Al Nasr (which means 'victory'), this small neighbourhood is home to a collection of restaurants and cafés, sports facilities, schools and landmarks including the American Hospital and **Mövenpick Hotel Bur Dubai** (*see p271*).

In the heart of Oud Metha, you'll find the retro charm of **Al Nasr Leisureland**. It may have seen better days, but it's an interesting glimpse of simpler times in Dubai. Not far from here is **Creek Park**, one of the city's most pleasant green spaces.

The area around Healthcare City is home to **Wafi Mall**, which is a notable landmark due to its pyramid shape. **Raffles Dubai** (*see p271*) is next door to Wafi, while another of Dubai's top hotels, the **Grand Hyatt** (*see p271*), is also in the district.

Sights & Attractions

Al Nasr Leisureland

12A Street, behind American Hospital (04 337 1234, www.alnasrll.com). **Open** Varies depending on activity. **Admission** Varies depending on activity. **Map** p67 F4 ㊲

Spread over 48 acres, this sports and leisure centre opened back in 1979 – and surprisingly little has changed since then. Here you can play retro arcade games or tennis, ice-skate, go bowling and much more. Just behind the complex, you'll find a couple of licensed restaurants, including Kiza Restaurant & Lounge and Khazana Restaurant.

Creek Park

Riyadh Road, opposite Rashid Hospital (04 336 7633). Metro Oud Metha. **Open** 8am-10pm Mon-Wed, Sun; 8am-11pm Thur-Sat. **Admission** Dhs5. **Map** p67 F5 ㊳

Stretching from the edge of Bur Dubai and down alongside the Creek towards Healthcare City is this attractive park, a lovely place to walk around, with plenty of greenery. There's a promenade alongside the water, with spectacular views of the city, as well as allocated barbecue spots, restaurants, kids' play areas, a go-kart track, bikes to rent and mini-golf. For a bird's eye view of the city, take a ride in the cable car, which carries you high over the park and Creek. You'll also find Children's City here (*see p188*), an education and adventure park for kids.

Restaurants

Adukkala

8th Street, near Lamcy Plaza (04 334 4043). **Open** 6am-3am daily. **Main courses** Dhs10-Dhs20. **Map** p67 E3 ㊴ **Indian**

It's not easy to find, but Adukkala is worth a visit. The decor is basic and the menu matches it, but the food is surprisingly good. The south Indian fare is clearly a hit with the local Indian expats; you'll usually find plenty of people tucking into thalis. There are also lots of fish choices as well as chicken curries and biryanis. Special set menus are great value at less than Dhs20.

Lan Kwai-Fong

10th Street, near Mövenpick Hotel & American Hospital (04 335 3680). **Open** noon-3.30pm, 6.30pm-midnight daily. **Main courses** Dhs30-Dhs40. **Map** p67 F3 ㊵ **Chinese**

A quirky, quality find in the backstreets of Oud Metha; don't let the uninspiring decor put you off. The restaurant itself is nothing like its Hong Kong namesake, and pretty much fulfills the Chinese restaurant stereotype: painted terracotta warriors are scattered to one side, and a rather depleted fish tank is plonked near the kitchen. The Cantonese cuisine is what makes a visit here worthwhile. The chefs have an impressively light touch, with the meat dishes, in particular, standing out. You won't regret dining here.

Medzo

Pyramids Wafi, Wafi Mall, Oud Metha Road (04 324 4100, www.pyramidsrestaurantsatwafi.com). Metro Dubai Healthcare City. **Open** 12.30-3pm, 7.30-11.30pm daily. **Main courses** Dhs100-Dhs200. **Map** p67 G3 ㊶ **Italian**

Understated, chic and feeling a little bit like someone's living room, Medzo is certainly one of the city's more elegant Italian eateries. In cooler months, the candlelit terrace is a good setting for a romantic date. Portions are generous, so skip the bread basket and save room for classic pastas and pizzas, or meat and fish mains, such as an enormous, melt-in-the mouth osso buco served atop saffron risotto rice, or seared wild sea bass, accompanied by a Provençal-style salsa.

Qbara

Pyramids Wafi, Wafi Mall, Oud Metha Road (04 709 2500, www.qbara.ae). Metro Dubai Healthcare City. **Open** 6pm-3am daily. **Main courses** Dhs150-Dhs250. **Map** p67 G3 ㊷ **Arabic**

This sophisticated restaurant presents modern Arabic food with flair in stunning surroundings. The colour scheme is all warm reds, black and gold, with lit cauldrons ablaze along the bar. A saxophonist provides a subtle backing track of cool jazz and the food is simply outstanding. Hot and cold meze come with some adventurous contemporary twists – lobster kibbeh with fresh herbs, say, or avocado labneh, plus crudités with truffle-scented labneh and houmous with honey-roasted parsnips. A must-try.

Sai Dham

Saleh Bin Lahej Building, 4th Street, near Lamcy Plaza (04 335 8788, www.sai-dham.com). **Open** noon-3.30pm, 7-11.30pm Mon-Wed, Sat, Sun; noon-3.30pm, 7-11.45pm Thur; 1-3.30pm, 7-11.45pm Fri. **Main courses** Dhs20-Dhs30. **Map** p67 E3 ㊸ **Indian**

Once you find your way inside (tip: there's a buzzer next to the door) you'll find a quaint little restaurant, minimally decorated but cosy. Sai Dham is a vegetarian restaurant specialising in Saatvik Bhojan, a pure form of cooking that does without onions, garlic, too many spices and oil (they bring negative energy, apparently). It may sound as if the food will be bland, but it's not. Order the thali and you'll get breads and rice as well as seven small pots of different curries; the dahl and paneer curry are the pick of the bunch.

Seville's

Pyramids Wafi, Wafi Mall, Oud Metha Road (04 324 4777, www.pyramidsrestaurantsatwafi.com). Metro Dubai Healthcare City. **Open** noon-1am Mon, Sat; Sun; noon-2am Tue-Fri. **Tapas** Dhs20-Dhs65. **Map** p67 G3 44 **Spanish**

There's a fine line between shabby-chic and shabby. Put it this way: Seville's by night looks considerably more charming than under the unforgiving gaze of the sun, which picks out its tatty edges. Fortunately, the food and service are far more uplifting, the former a classic line-up of tapas tropes delivered to a high standard, the latter a friendly bunch who know the menu inside out and are happy to chat through your choices to make sure you get what you need and don't order too much.

★ Solo Bistronomia & Vinobar

Raffles Dubai, 13th Street, Sheikh Rashid Road (04 370 8999, www.raffles.com/dubai). Metro Dubai Healthcare City. **Open** noon-3pm, 7-11pm daily. **Main courses** Dhs80-Dhs220. **Map** p67 G3 45 **Italian**

This Italian restaurant and wine bar is huge, a high-ceiling multi-functional space with exposed brickwork and a few quirky touches. The food is a two-tier affair: bar snacks and deli classics (antipasti, charcuterie and so on) in the bar area, and a wider selection on the restaurant menu. Plates here include authentic dishes like mushroom risotto and cacio e pepe (thick spaghetti tossed in cacio cheese and black pepper sauce), plus meat and fish mains. Although Dubai is awash with Italian dining, this place manages to stand out for its creative, yet unfussy and unpretentious menu.

★ Tomo

Raffles Dubai, 13th Street, Sheikh Rashid Road (04 357 7888, www.tomo.ae). Metro Dubai Healthcare City. **Open** 12.30-3.30pm, 6.30pm-1am daily. **Main courses** Dhs50-Dhs200. **Map** p67 G3 46 **Japanese**

Tomo is surprising in several ways. First, you might expect that a Japanese restaurant sitting at the top of one of Dubai's most recognisable hotels would be expensive. It is not. You might expect it to be exclusive. Nope, not that either. Is the food not that good then? Actually, it's pretty great. Grab a table on the terrace for views that stretch all the way from Dubai Festival City to the towers of Sheikh Zayed Road, and while you take them in, tuck into excellent value and delicious mains, many served *bento*-style.

Wox

Grand Hyatt Dubai, 9th Street, Sheikh Rashid Road (04 317 2221, www.restaurants.dubai.hyatt.com). Metro Dubai Healthcare City. **Open** noon-11.30pm daily. **Main courses** Dhs40-Dhs70. **Map** pH4 47 **Pan-Asian**

After a trek through the Grand Hyatt's huge indoor rainforest, you'll be rewarded with Wox, a casual

Tomo.

EXPLORE

noodle house that we'd love to call a well-kept secret – but the fact it's never empty means the secret clearly got out some time ago. It's refreshingly simple, and there aren't too many five-star hotels that can lay claim to such authentic, raw and competitively priced Asian dining. The theme is street food, with just a handful of tables set around the small central open kitchen, where two chefs thrash about with woks in unison. The menu is short and simple in scope, which means everything on it – noodles primarily – has been well road-tested, and can be knocked up in a storm.

Cafés & Bars

SPiN Dubai

Pyramids Wafi, Wafi Mall, Oud Metha Road (04 370 7707, www.dubai.wearespin.com). Metro Dubai Healthcare City. **Open** 6pm-1am daily. **Map** p67 G3 48

A bizarre combination of table-tennis hall and bar, founded by an older, respected Hollywood actress (Susan Sarandon), on paper SPiN sounds like the most eccentric of celebrity indulgences. But put your scepticism aside – SPiN is, quite simply, a blast. Although it's home to the headline-grabbing 'world's most expensive gold-plated table', SPiN is no exclusive playboys' paradise. With the right company, a game of table tennis can be a great giggle, and mixing in drinks, music and a nightclub atmosphere just multiplies the laughs.

Vintage

Pyramids Wafi, Wafi Mall, Oud Metha Road (04 324 4100, www.pyramidsrestaurantsatwafi.com). Metro Dubai Healthcare City. **Open** 5pm-1am Fri-Wed; 5pm-2am Thur. **Map** p67 G3 49

If you love cheese and wine, Vintage is the place for you. It's an intimate venue – ideal for couples and small groups. Bottles from its exquisite wine selection are paired with refined plates of cheese, freshly baked breads and cured meats. While its name may be Vintage, the decor is comfortable and elegant, with cosy plush sofas and chairs, plus cushions and soft carpeting.

Shops & Services

Lamcy Plaza

4th Street, Sheikh Rashid Road (04 335 9999, www.lamcyplaza.com). **Open** 10am-10.30pm Mon-Wed, Sun; 10am-midnight Thur, Fri; 10am-11pm Sat. **Map** p67 F3 50 **Mall**

This quirky mall, with its famously creepy robotic climbing clown, houses a range of affordable brands, such as Matalan, Bhs and Red Tag, a cinema, kids' play area and a '7XD' motion simulator to shake things up mid-shop.

Wafi

Oud Metha Road (04 324 4555, www.wafi.com). Metro Dubai Healthcare City. **Open** 10am-10pm Mon-Wed, Sat, Sun; 10am-midnight Thur, Fri. **Map** p67 G3 51 **Mall**

This pyramid-shaped building attracts fashion-conscious shoppers keen to keep up with the latest trends. It's a striking landmark due to its shape, but the best thing about this mall is the collection of excellent restaurants, many of which are licensed.

EXPLORE

IN THE KNOW FOOD TOURS

Arva Ahmed grew up in Dubai and has a passion for discovering the tiny hole-in-the-wall eateries along the backstreets of Old Dubai. Her company **Frying Pan Adventures** (www.fryingpanadventures.com) offers food tours with a difference that explore some of her favourite childhood spots in the city, as well as others that she has rooted out during years of trying and testing. For Palestinian falafels, Egyptian pastries and Syrian ice-cream, sign up for the Middle Eastern Food Pilgrimage (Dhs350 per person). For vibrant Indian food, the Little India on a Plate (Dhs380 per person) will take you through the streets of Meena Bazaar. Early risers will enjoy the Food Lover's Morning March (Dhs520 per person), which includes a trip to the spice souk, and there's a meat-focused tour for the most carnivorous foodies. Dates and times of tours vary, and bookings must be made online.

Downtown Dubai & Business Bay

Perhaps because it's home to the Burj Khalifa, the world's tallest building, Downtown Dubai is one of the most upmarket areas of the city. It's busy, but much more spacious than around JBR and the Marina, with excellent dining, drinking and shopping options. Burj Khalifa is really the only 'sight', though the Dubai Fountains are fun. And if malls are your thing, you'll be in your element at the Dubai Mall. Downtown is good for drinking and dining, but sadly lacking in budget accommodation. It's almost as central as you can get geographically – between Old Dubai and the beaches of Jumeirah. The upmarket vibe extends to Business Bay, full of smart office and apartment buildings, and the odd five-star hotel.

Burj Khalifa.

Don't Miss

1 Burj Khalifa The world's tallest building. Need we say more (p80)?

2 Dubai Fountain All-singing, all-dancing watery entertainment (p80).

3 Majlis Café Swap your latte for a Camelcino (p89).

4 Meydan Grandstand & Racecourse Take a tour of the stables at this famous course (p93).

5 Iris As close to cool as Dubai bars get (p97).

DOWNTOWN DUBAI

Downtown Dubai extends outwards from the landmark of the needle-like **Burj Khalifa** and the neighbouring **Dubai Mall**, and runs into Business Bay. At 830 metres (2,723 feet) at its tip, the Burj Khalifa holds the crown as the world's tallest building – and a ticket to At the Top, Burj Khalifa SKY takes you to the world's tallest observation deck.

Souk Al Bahar is your best bet for good restaurants with views of the **Dubai Fountain**, with its musical shows, while **At.mosphere** is a unique dining destination. The area is also rife with classy bars that sit in the Burj Khalifa's shadow, the best of which is **Calabar**, closely contested by **Above** in Sofitel Downtown Dubai. Your best bet for a casual pint or two, however, is friendly sports bar **Nezesaussi**.

Sights & Attractions

★ Burj Khalifa

800 2884 3867, www.burjkhalifa.ae. Metro Burj Khalifa/Dubai Mall. **Map** p81 B5 ❶

At the Top, Burj Khalifa Open 8.30am-midnight daily. **Admission** (8.30am-5pm, 7.30pm-midnight) Dhs125; Dhs95 reductions; fast track Dhs300. (5-7.30pm) Dhs200; Dhs160 reductions; fast track Dhs300.

At the Top, Burj Khalifa SKY Open noon-10pm daily. **Admission** *Mon-Thur, Sat, Sun* noon-7pm Dhs 500; 7-9.30pm Dhs300. *Fri* 9am-7pm Dhs500; 8-9.30pm Dhs300.

Little, if any, introduction is needed to the iconic needle-like structure that, at 830m (2,723ft) to its tip, is currently the tallest building in the world. Undeniably striking in appearance, it's quite something to see up close, even without buying a ticket to the top. To view the city from its observation deck several options are available and prices vary according to time booked (daytime and late evening slots are cheaper, 5.30-7pm coincides with sunset and is more expensive). A regular At the Top, Burj Khalifa ticket will take you to the 124th floor – 452m (1,480ft) up – but swindles you out of standing on the world's highest observation deck as it currently falls below both the platform of the Canton Tower in Guangzhou and the Skywalk of the Shanghai World Financial Centre. For roughly an additional Dhs300-Dhs500 you can purchase a 'SKY' ticket that allows access to a higher observation deck on the 148th floor, which at 555m (1,820ft) takes the title of the world's highest. Purchasing a ticket can be a gamble; in peak season slots get booked up in advance and are rarely available at the entrance, which means you can't make a decision based on the weather. Dusty, smoggy days are common in Dubai, which limits visibility. That said, it doesn't render the view disappointing, and useful little viewfinders are stationed around windows. It's also worth considering booking a visit for the evening, when the city lights make for a particularly spectacular sight.

If you're not fussed about climbing to the top of the tower, plenty of restaurants and cafés in Souk Al Bahar and the Dubai Mall offer great views if you can bag a table near the window or outside.

Dubai Aquarium

Dubai Mall (04 448 5200, www.thedubaiaquarium.com). Metro Burj Khalifa/Dubai Mall. **Open** 10am-midnight daily. *Last admission* 11.30pm. **Admission** Dhs70; Dhs55 reductions. **Map** p81 B5 ❷

See p88 **Dubai Mall.** *Photo p82.*

★ FREE Dubai Fountain

Burj Khalifa Lake, adjacent to Dubai Mall. Metro Burj Khalifa/Dubai Mall. **Shows** 1pm, 1.30pm & every 30mins 6-11pm Mon-Thur, Sat; 1.30pm, 2pm & every 30mins 6-11pm Fri. **Map** p81 B5 ❸

This Bellagio-esque music, water and light show is pretty impressive. Both these and the Vegas-located fountains were created by the same design agency, WET, based in California. They are – of course – another 'world's largest', cinching first place in the ranks of dancing fountains with ease. Jets of water shoot up to 50 storeys high and more than 6,600 superlights and 25 colour projectors are involved in each show. But, facts and figures aside, each show is quite cleverly 'choreographed'. This is particularly obvious if you're lucky enough to catch Michael Jackson's 'Thriller' on your visit, when the fountains appear to be performing the famous dance number. Other shows are co-ordinated to Andrea Bocelli's 'Con te partiro' and well-known Arabic dance track 'Shik Shak Shok'. The whole spectacle is made all the more impressive with the backdrop of the Burj Khalifa (the fountains are situated at its base). Mango Tree (*see p83*) has some of the best views from its terrace; other, cheaper options with excellent views of the show include Baker & Spice (*see p87*), Social House (*see p85*) and Madeleine Café & Boulangerie (04 438 4335, www.madeleinecafe.com).

Restaurants

Armani/Ristorante

Armani Hotel Dubai (04 888 3444, http://dubai.armanihotels.com). Metro Burj Khalifa/Dubai Mall. **Open** 7-11.30pm daily. **Main courses** Dhs130-Dhs290. Map p81 B5 ❹ **Italian**

Stepping into the Armani Hotel always engenders a sense of occasion, and that's true of its signature restaurant too. The interiors are what you'd expect from the Armani brand: clean, crisp and minimal. The real show-stopper, though, is the view – if you can grab a seat on the terrace. Could this be the best view of the Dubai Fountain from a restaurant? Quite possibly. As you would expect from a multiple award-winning

EXPLORE

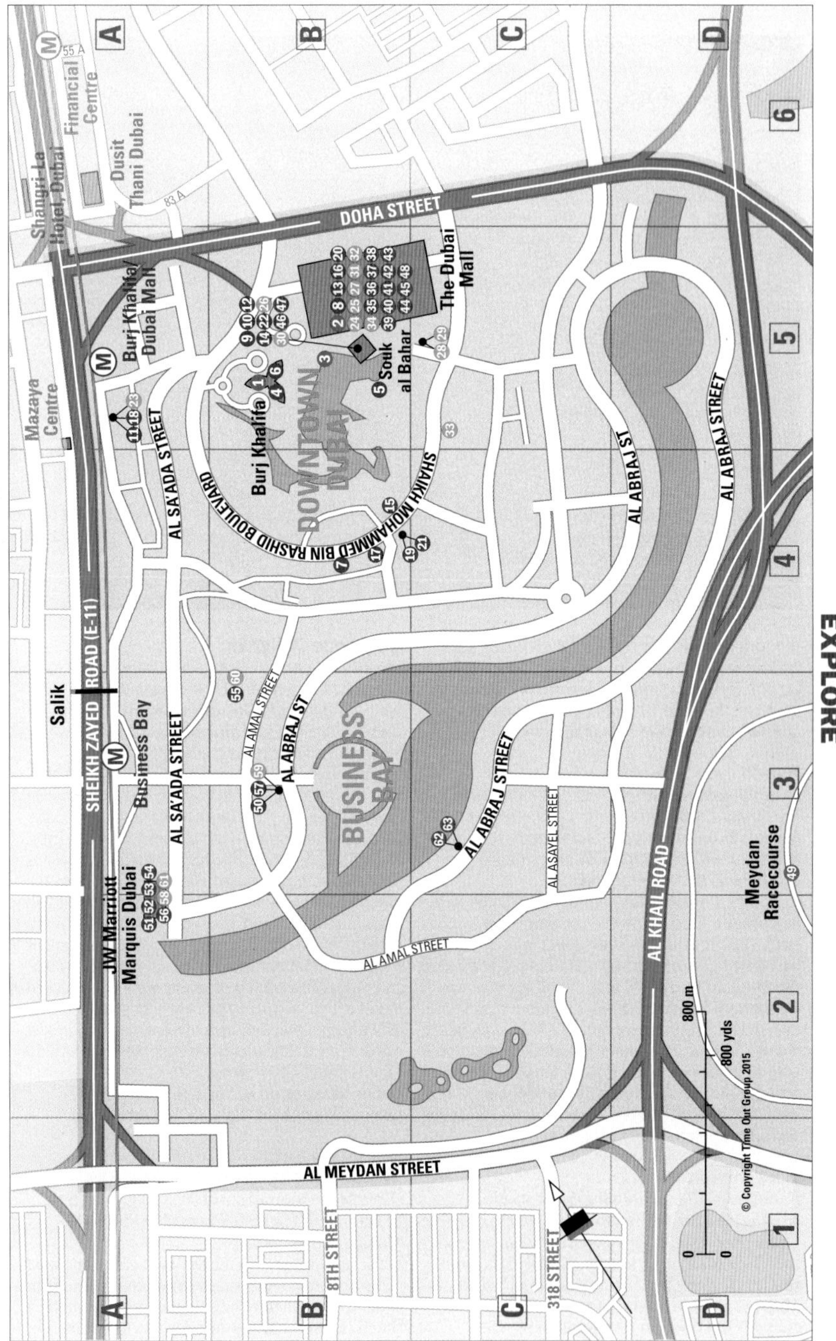
Financial Centre
Shangri-La Hotel, Dubai
Dusit Thani Dubai
DOHA STREET
Burj Khalifa/ Dubai Mall
Mazaya Centre
AL SA'ADA STREET
Burj Khalifa
DOWNTOWN DUBAI
Souk al Bahar
The Dubai Mall
SHAIKH MOHAMMED BIN RASHID BOULEVARD
AL ABRAJ ST
AL ABRAJ STREET
SHEIKH ZAYED ROAD (E-11)
Salik
Business Bay
AL AMAL STREET
BUSINESS BAY
JW Marriott Marquis Dubai
AL ASAYEL STREET
AL KHAIL ROAD
Meydan Racecourse
AL MEYDAN STREET
8TH STREET
318 STREET
800 m
800 yds
© Copyright Time Out Group 2015

EXPLORE

Dubai Aquarium. *See p80.*

restaurant, the food is excellent, each dish crafted to perfection with superb attention to detail. Yes, it's expensive, but this is one of Dubai's best Italian restaurants, the perfect location for a special occasion, and then there are those Fountain views.

Asado

Palace Downtown Dubai, Sheikh Mohammed Bin Rashid Boulevard (04 888 3444, www.theaddress.com/en/hotels). Metro Burj Khalifa, Dubai Mall. **Open** 7-11.30pm daily. **Map** p81 B5 ❺ **Argentinian**

This Argentinian restaurant serves up some of the best meat dishes in town – not only an enormous steak selection, but also intriguing options such as barbecued goat or venison stew. In fact, you'll find the level of creativity and execution you would expect from fine-dining restaurants, but with a buzzing atmosphere, impressive Burj Khalifa views and, above all, the space of more casual restaurants. This is more than just a fancy steakhouse, however, so ordering outside the grill will not disappoint. Where else in Dubai can you try braised pigeon, foie gras and purple potatoes with asparagus purée?

★ At.mosphere

Burj Khalifa (04 888 3444, www.atmosphereburjkhalifa.com). Metro Burj Khalifa/Dubai Mall. **Open** 12.30-3pm, 6.30-11.30pm daily. *Lounge* noon-2am daily. **Main courses** Dhs200-Dhs380. **High tea** *Window seat* Dhs580. *Regular seat* Dhs530. **Map** p81 B5 ❻ **Modern European**

See p86 **Oh What an At.mosphere!**

Barbecue Delights

Sheikh Mohammed Bin Rashid Boulevard (04 434 3443, www.barbecuedelights.com). Metro Burj Khalifa/Dubai Mall. **Open** 12.30-4pm, 7pm-12.30am daily. **Main courses** Dhs35-Dhs65. **Map** p81 B4 ❼ **Afghan/Indian/Pakistani**

Serving Afghan, Pakistani and north Indian cuisine, with a few token Middle Eastern dishes thrown in for good measure, this casual eaterie is surprisingly good, specialising in – you guessed it – barbecued and grilled delights. The high-ceilinged interior is pleasant, with tables and chairs spilling on to the pavement outside. We recommend the barbecue fish tikka and malai tikka, the former beautifully marinated with red chilli, ginger, garlic and coriander seeds and accompanied by a tangy tamarind sauce, and the latter made up of tender skewered chicken pieces with a mild herby marinade. If you steer clear of Western dishes and stick to what the chefs do best – grilled meats and south Asian staples such as dahl – you really can't go wrong.

Other locations The Walk, JBR (04 423 0632); Lamcy Square, Oud Metha (04 335 9868/9869).

Brandi Pizzeria

Dubai Mall (04 325 3336). Metro Burj Khalifa/Dubai Mall. **Open** 10am-12.30am Mon-Wed, Sun; 10am-1.30am Thur-Sat. **Pizzas** Dhs60-Dhs98. **Map** p81 B5 ❽ **Pizza**

While most eateries in the Dubai Mall can be found in the rambunctious food courts or lining the Lower Ground level near the Dubai Fountain, Italian import Brandi is tucked away in a far quieter corner. As such, it doesn't get as busy as it deserves, but the pleasant, relaxed atmosphere is all the better for it. Watch the dough being tossed and stretched before your eyes before being smothered in fresh, quality toppings and slid into the oven. Fans of hot and cold combos should opt for the Don Eduardo, a focaccia-dough base, baked with olive oil and herbs and then topped with creamy burrata, rocket, cherry tomatoes, shaved parmesan, olive oil and a sprinkling of salt. More classically minded? You can't go wrong with simple margherita – a heart-melting combination of sloppy tomato and mozzarella, crowning a thin, crisp base.

CLAW BBQ

Souk Al Bahar (04 432 2300, www.clawbbq.com). Metro Burj Khalifa/Dubai Mall. **Open** 5pm-2am daily. **Seafood** Dhs70-Dhs290. **Buckets** (for two people) Dhs230-Dhs330. **Map** p81 B5 ⑨ **Seafood**

The clue's in the name at CLAW BBQ, where you'll be served up huge buckets of crab legs. Inside, it's wall to wall Americana. Drinks are served in square jars and the bar staff are kitted out as lumberjacks to add to the theme. While crab is the speciality, there's also a variety of fish and barbecue dishes, and burgers. But it's those generous buckets of crab legs that steal the show. It's a messy affair trying to prise the meat out of legs with the tools provided, but it's worth the effort. And with large sides of fries and grilled corn on the cob, you're in for a substantial feast.

Fuego

Souk Al Bahar (04 449 0977, www.fuegodubai.com). Metro Burj Khalifa/Dubai Mall. **Open** noon-1am daily. **Main courses** Dhs50-Dhs200. **Map** p81 B5 ⑩ **Mexican**

This modern Mexican concept in Souk Al Bahar has the style and sophistication of a cool lounge bar and is as far removed from Tex-Mex style as it's possible to be, while still serving (very good) fajitas. An artfully presented, tangy ceviche selection comes in mini shot glasses of tuna, red snapper and shrimp flavours. More unusual Mexican dishes include lamb shank barbacoa (wrapped in a banana leaf and served with Mexican rice) or a stomach-busting Molcajete Special, a Mexican version of a mixed grill. You would be hard pressed to find a broader or better Mexican menu in the city.

Green Spices

Sofitel Downtown Dubai (04 503 6117). Metro Burj Khalifa/Dubai Mall. **Open** 6.30-11.30pm Mon-Sat. **Main courses** Dhs55-Dhs130. **Map** p81 A5 ⑪ **Pan-Asian**

Sofitel Downtown Dubai's pan-Asian restaurant has an evening buffet, teppanyaki tables and an à la carte menu. Although the buffet looks enticing, the food is average in comparison to the à la carte dishes, which are mainly composed of traditional Thai choices. There's an interesting selection of spring and summer rolls, with multiple combinations, including ingredients like spicy tuna wrapped in lettuce, and prawns, ginger, peanuts, lime and roasted coconut wrapped in a betel leaf. The dessert selection is similarly intriguing: the icy water chestnut soup makes for a refreshing end to the meal.

Karma Kafé

Souk Al Bahar (04 423 0909, www.karma-kafe.com). Metro Burj Khalifa/Dubai Mall. **Open** 3pm-2am Mon-Thur, Sun; noon-2am Fri, Sat. **Main courses** Dhs69-Dhs109. **Map** p81 B5 ⑫ **Pan-Asian**

On paper, it would be easy to write Karma Kafé off as a case of style over substance. Situated in Souk Al Bahar, with a terrace overlooking the Dubai Fountain, and a glam lounge-club setting inside, you'd expect it to be a tourist's dream serving up Asian bites to party people. But once the fountains cease and the phones are put aside, you can expect to sit down to some of the best Asian food in town. Every dish is a work of art on a plate, meticulously presented and prepared. And they taste as colourful as they look. Sushi is a particular highlight, paying lip service to tradition while offering daring new ingredients. The pitch here is more nightlife than candlelight and white tablecloths, but the pricing is good, and it's a surprisingly romantic venue for a date.

★ Katsuya by Starck

Dubai Mall (04 315 3633, www.katsuyarestaurant.com/dubai). Metro Burj Khalifa/Dubai Mall. **Open** 11am-midnight daily. **Main courses** Dhs45-Dhs180. **Map** p81 B5 ⑬ **Japanese**

Created by a dynamic duo in the form of master sushi chef Katsuya Uechi and renowned designer Philippe Starck, Katsuya is not at all what you might expect from a mall restaurant. It's stylish, carefully laid out and a million miles from boisterous echoe-y food courts. The menu is a thoughtful combination of classics and more unusual fusion dishes. Despite sounding impressive, the sushi rolls are actually among the more disappointing dishes; one of the stand-outs, on the other hand, is the edamame houmous – a delightful example of Far East meeting Middle East. It's a joy to not quite know what to expect, when much of Dubai's casual Japanese dining scene serves up identical fare.

Mango Tree

Souk Al Bahar (04 426 7313). Metro Burj Khalifa/Dubai Mall. **Open** 12.30-11.30pm daily. **Main courses** Dhs60-Dhs230. **Map** p81 B5 ⑭ **Thai**

Mango Tree's top-floor Souk Al Bahar balcony offers one of the best vantage points for catching the Dubai Fountain in full flow. With such a selling point, it would be easy for Mango Tree to get complacent in the kitchen, but thankfully there's no sign of that happening. The duck rice paper rolls and steamed sea bass are fresh and zesty, while old favourites like pad thai are most definitely up to scratch (and generously portioned). Service is warm and slick – staff are clearly well practised at politely explaining that the terrace is already booked. So that's our top tip – to avoid dining indoors and missing those views, make sure you book well in advance.

Mayrig

Sheikh Mohammed Bin Rashid Boulevard (04 453 9945, www.mayrigdubai.com). Metro Burj Khalifa/ Dubai Mall. **Open** noon-1am Mon-Thur, Sun; noon-1.30am Fri, Sat. **Main courses** Dhs55-Dhs80. **Map** p81 B4 ⓯ **Armenian**

A meal at this little Armenian restaurant can feel a little like dining in someone's living room, thanks to the homely decor. There is also an inviting outdoor terrace where you can take in views of the Burj Khalifa. Enticing dishes include houmous *basterma* – houmous topped with Armenian smoked beef – and the delicate *havgitov basterma* – an Armenian smoked beef canapé topped with quail's egg. Both are delicate, flavoursome and a delight to eat. Traditional *mante* – minced meat dumplings topped with a tomato sauce, yoghurt and sumac spice – is also pleasant enough, but perhaps too subtly spiced for some palates. The Armenian staff are friendly and happy to recommend dishes from their homeland.

Milas

Dubai Mall (04 388 2313, www.milas.cc). Metro Burj Khalifa/Dubai Mall. **Open** 9.30am-11.30pm Mon-Wed, Sun; 9.30am-12.30am Thur-Sat. **Main courses** Dhs5-Dhs100. **Map** p81 B5 ⓰ **Arabic**

Stylishly modern Milas is done out in black with flashes of purple neon, but serves traditional Emirati and Arabic favourites – and has a largely Emirati clientele. Bread is wonderfully hot and fluffy; salads and meze dishes include the likes of classic tabouleh, *moutabal* and falafel, joined by dishes less familiar to those used to the Lebanese canon, such as *aseda jazar*, carrot with cardomom and saffon, mashed to a paste. Snacky dishes include shawarmas, and mains are grills and stews such as chicken with marrow and tomato, served with rice.

Omnia by Silvena

Sheikh Mohammed Bin Rashid Boulevard (04 552 0129, www.omnia.co). Metro Burj Khalifa, Dubai Mall. **Open** 6-11pm Mon-Wed, Sun; 12.30-11pm Thur-Sat. **Main courses** Dhs120-Dhs300. **Map** p81 B4 ⓱ **Contemporary Arabic/international**

An Emirati brasserie by chef Silvena Rowe, and her first formal dining venture in the region. Its modern cooking is inspired by local and Middle Eastern cuisine, and raw and gluten-free recipes. Dishes tend to come stylishly dressed with generous amounts of foam and herbs. They don't all hit the mark but there are some stellar flavour combinations, such as the cauliflower mousse, which comes with colourful, crisp baby vegetables and circled in a vibrant green and aromatic basil oil. Raw tiramisu is a clever riff on this Italian classic, using very different flavours of walnut, date and coconut, alongside traditional coffee, to impressive effect. There's an emphasis on locally sourced ingredients, such as Gulf prawns

EXPLORE

and UAE-produced ricotta cheese, and since the venue is unlicensed, emphasis has been placed on creating some interesting mocktails and juices. The space itself is modern, bold and shiny.

Red Grill

Sofitel Downtown Dubai (04 503 6666). Metro Burj Khalifa/Dubai Mall. **Open** 6.30-11.30pm Mon-Sat. **Main courses** Dhs200-Dhs285. **Map** p81 A5 ⑱ **Steakhouse**

The Red Grill is a tiny dining space, hidden behind huge glass cabinets of wine. And it isn't actually red – more neon pink and purple. To one side is an open kitchen, and to the other a large terrace. The menu offers a fairly typical grill-house choice of largely European starters (carpaccios, tartares, burrata), classic European main courses, plus a lengthier steak selection and a few grilled seafood options (monkfish, sea bass and lobster). While grills are pricey (Dhs200 and upwards), they come with a choice of one side, one potato dish, one sauce and a selection of mustards and salts. The Red Grill does show some promise in terms of creativity from the kitchen. Oyster and sea bass tartare, for example, comes attractively presented in oyster shells, resting in a sandy-looking concoction made with breadcrumbs and squid ink, sharpened up with a touch of yuzu. The final result, however, can feel a little rough around the edges.

★ La Serre

Vida Downtown Hotel, Sheikh Mohammed Bin Rashid Boulevard (04 428 6969, www.laserre.ae). Metro Burj Khalifa/Dubai Mall. **Open** *Bistro* noon-3pm, 7-11pm daily. *Boulangerie* 6.30am-10.30pm daily. **Main courses** Dhs115-Dhs385. **Map** p81 B4 ⑲ **French bistro/bakery**

With a huge glass front overlooking Sheikh Mohammed Bin Rashid Boulevard, La Serre is set over two floors, the upper one being the posher bistro and the lower the slightly cheaper Boulangerie. From the bistro menu, the seafood bears particular mention, with a veritable jamboree of mussels, langoustines and prawns all cooked perfectly, whether seared langoustine with gnocchi and truffle butter, or grilled tiger prawns with aji amarillo peppers. Desserts are top quality, with playful twists on French classics. The downstairs boulangerie is the perfect spot for long lazy breakfasts thanks to its bright and airy atmosphere. Bag a seat by the huge window and settle in to watch the world go by, coffee and croissant in hand.

Social House

Dubai Mall (04 339 8640). Metro Burj Khalifa/Dubai Mall. **Open** 9am-10.30pm Mon-Wed; 9am-midnight Thur-Sat; 9am-10.30pm Sun. **Main courses** Dhs60-Dhs110. **Map** p81 B5 ⑳ **International**

Social House is a busy spot with a buzzing, bustling vibe, and with good reason. There's an enormous menu, offering everything from breakfast to pho soups, classic salads and sushi to Malay curries, pasta and fish and chips. The latter is particularly noteworthy especially if you're very hungry; two huge pieces of juicy fish encased in crispy, flaky batter and accompanied by zingy home-made tartare

EXPLORE

Mayrig.

OH WHAT AN AT.MOSPHERE!

Dining at the top of the world.

During peak hours, an At the Top experience at the Burj Khalifa will set you back a minimum of Dhs200 per person (more for a fast-track or SKY ticket). If you're budgeting for this anyway, your dirhams may be better spent on afternoon tea at **At.mosphere** (*see p82*), where – from Dhs530 per person – you can marvel at the view while sipping on unlimited teas, coffees and mocktails, and dining on a selection of treats. Set on floor 122, At.mosphere is only three below the observation deck. Service is impeccable, and the stylish lounge is a formal venue but not a stuffy one.

For the traditional tea, a tasty square of quiche is followed by sandwiches, including smoked salmon and cream cheese, and turkey breast with peppers on rye bread. There's also a main course, with vegetarian options available. Perfectly pretty cakes and dainty scones follow, and mocktails are also on the menu – the likes of Mandarin iced tea with spiced ginger and pear, or iced coffee with Caribbean coconut cream.

Alternatively, you can book a (pricier) table for dinner. You'll be asked to give your credit card details – the first indication that this is a special occasion experience. Getting to the restaurant is also far from simple, with access gained through the Armani Hotel, before heading up and down a number of escalators, stairs and lifts. But this just adds to the sense of occasion and anticipation. The view when you finally step out of the lift is nothing short of spectacular. A minimum spend is required to reserve a window seat, and we reckon it's worth it – after all, it's not every day that you dine in the world's highest restaurant. Stick to At.mosphere's special – a juicy steak cooked in the Josper grill – and you'll be mightily impressed. Follow it up with one of the top-notch desserts and you might just be able to tear your eyes away from the view – for a few seconds.

EXPLORE

sauce and roughly cut chips. Overall, it's a good spot to have a quick bite at a good price. Plus, you can catch a reasonable view of the Dubai Fountain from a few choice tables inside if the outdoor area is full.

★ Toko

Vida Downtown, Sheikh Mohammed Bin Rashid Boulevard (04 442 8383, www.toko-dubai.com). Metro Burj Khalifa/Dubai Mall. **Open** noon-3.30pm, 7pm-2am daily (last food orders midnight). **Sushi & sashimi** Dhs55-Dhs85. **Main courses** Dhs80-Dhs320. **Map** p81 B4 ㉑ **Japanese**

Toko ticks almost every box. The setting is fantastic, with a stylish, atmospheric garden area as well as a quiet indoor space in view of the open kitchen. The ambience suits the decor; there's a buzz about the place and it is clearly a hit with the beautiful people of Dubai. The food is superb: the flavours, imaginative ingredients and quality of produce are hugely impressive, as is the range of dishes, which run from sushi and sashimi to tempura (try the huge prawns with dashi broth), meat and fish dishes. The miso salmon is a house favourite, but try the Alaskan crab as well; the white meat is topped with a zesty citrus crumb. Toko is an exciting, stylish place to eat fabulous food.

Zahr El Laymoun

Souk Al Bahar (04 448 6060, www.zahrel-laymoun.com). Metro Burj Khalifa/Dubai Mall. **Open** 10am-midnight daily. **Meze** Dhs20-Dhs35. **Map** p81 B5 ㉒ **Arabic**

Filled with hanging greenery, plant pots, watering cans, flowery cushions and mini wooden benches, Zahr El Laymoun looks and feels something like a modish country cottage – quite a contrast to the surrounding Souk Al Bahar. Pull up a chair outdoors on the terrace that just about overlooks the Dubai Fountain, or grab one of around ten tables indoors, and then tuck into all manner of Lebanese dishes on a menu that leans towards healthy eating, with fresh, zingy salads like tabouleh and fattoush, hot meze dishes like fuul and falafel, plus tender main-course grills. While French fries tend to be the accompanying side of choice at many similar restaurants, here it's all about oil-free oven baked or grilled potatoes. The salads, in particular, are highly recommended.

Cafés & Bars

The Boulangerie at **La Serre** (*see p85*) is a great spot for a leisurely breakfast.

Above

Sofitel Downtown Dubai (04 503 6666, www.abovedxb.com). Metro Burj Khalifa/Dubai Mall. **Open** 6pm-3am daily. **Map** p81 A5 ㉓

This impressive new rooftop lounge can be enjoyed day or night, but evening is the best time to visit. There are both indoor and outdoor areas, and from the inside, the large windows perfectly frame the Burj Khalifa. Picture-perfect indeed. Sophisticated without being too pretentious, the bar and lounge area is done out in striking white, and the private terrace is adorned with palm trees, a reflection pool and private cabanas. The indoor space also has a retractable roof for when the weather permits, lending an airy indoor-outdoor feel. Signature cocktails are light and fruity.

Angelina

Dubai Mall (04 442 8814, www.thedubaimall.com). Metro Burj Khalifa/Dubai Mall. **Open** 9am-11pm Mon-Wed, Sun; 9am-midnight Thur-Sat. **Map** p81 B5 ㉔

The heritage of this Parisian import is about as far flung as it gets from the Dubai Mall. Having opened in 1903 in the French capital, the original Angelina boasted regulars like Coco Chanel, making this chic café a neat fit for the mall's Fashion Avenue. It's artfully designed to create that Parisian pavement café illusion. Inside, there's an imposing pâtisserie counter and a dining room decorated *grand café*-style. The menu offers breakfast dishes, bistro fare and desserts from the pâtisserie counter. Angelina is a pleasant spot for a Parisian-style coffee and cake stop-off, and the savouries are fine too, but this kind of over-the-top, high-end (and pricey) European-style establishment has become over-hyped in the UAE, and is no match for the French original.

Other location Mall of the Emirates (04 379 4560).

Armani/Dubai Caffè

Dubai Mall (04 339 8396). Metro Burj Khalifa/Dubai Mall. **Open** 10am-11pm Mon-Wed, Sat, Sun; 10am-midnight Thur, Fri. **Map** p81 B5 ㉕

Armani/Dubai Caffè offers something that most mall eateries are often unable to achieve: impressive food and super-fast service. It's quiet in the mornings and jam-packed in the evenings and afternoons, but the level of service and quality of food remain the same visit after visit. Whether you're after some fresh orange juice, toast and coffee, or exquisite seafood pasta and freshly made fruit mocktails, you'll find it here. Just keep in mind that while your belly might thank you for the delicious feed, your wallet most certainly won't.

Baker & Spice

Souk Al Bahar (04 427 9856, www.bakerandspiceme.com). Metro Burj Khalifa/Dubai Mall. **Open** 8am-11pm daily. **Map** p81 B5 ㉖

Baker & Spice reigns supreme in Souk Al Bahar thanks to its prime location beside the Dubai Fountain. A bright and airy venue with a beautiful terrace overlooking the water, it's a calm and relaxing escape from the bustling atmosphere of nearby Dubai Mall. Food begins with breakfast (eggs, pancakes, shakshouka) and goes on to pastries, light savouries and mains. We're impressed with the gnocchi and seemingly never-ending supply of freshly baked bread. The coffee is worth going back for, too,

DUBAI MALL

Everything from shopping to snorkelling.

The Dubai Mall is perhaps the only one we know where you could easily while away an entire day without running out of things to do. First, there's the surprisingly entertaining **Dubai Aquarium** (*see p80*), inhabited by penguins, stingrays, sharks and a five-metre (16-foot) crocodile. The huge ten-million-litre (22-million-gallon) tank is visible from the shopping areas of the mall and is two storeys high. It's mesmerising to watch, and the underwater zoo running through it can be accessed with an Aquarium ticket. Snorkelling and diving experiences are also available.

So, what about the shopping? Well, there are more than 1,000 outlets, although you'll need an impressive sense of direction to find anything specific – the sheer scale of this mall can be frustrating at the best of times and infuriating at the worst. Our advice: do everything you can to avoid weekend afternoons and evenings. If you have the time and the patience, however, you'll come across retail gems from all corners of the globe. This really is the mall that has it all. There's a souk area full of high-end Arab jewellery shops; Fashion Avenue is where you'll find the likes of Louis Vuitton, Chanel and the **Armani/Dubai Caffè** (*see p87*); another atrium is home to luxury jewellery stores such as Cartier or Van Cleef & Arpels and watch brands such as Tag Heuer and Rolex. Scattered across the mall are recognisable high-street brands from all over the world, and dotted in between you'll come across stores you've never heard of, nor are likely to hear of again.

If shopping isn't up your children's street, why not drop them off at **KidZania** (*see p189*), where they can experience a child's version of the grown-up world. There's also an **ice rink** (04 448 5111, www.dubaiicerink.com), a **cinema** (www.reelcinemas.ae) and access to **At the Top, Burj Khalifa** (*see p80*), as well as numerous cafés where you can sit back and enjoy the half-hourly shows at the **Dubai Fountain** (*see p80*). Cross the bridge from here to get to **Souk Al Bahar** (*see p93*), where more souk-style shopping awaits along with multiple restaurants and bars.

as is the friendly service. Make this your coffee pit stop if you're in the Dubai Mall or Souk Al Bahar.

Bestro

Galeries Lafayette, Dubai Mall (04 339 9933, www.galerieslafayette-dubai.com). Metro Burj Khalifa/Dubai Mall. **Open** 10am-10pm Mon-Wed, Sun; 10am-midnight Thur-Sat. **Map** p81 B5 27

Bestro is one of a handful of raw-food and vegan venues to have popped up in Dubai in the past 12 months. It is, however, the only one of these to currently offer food that strictly adheres to both philosophies. The space is relaxed, there are plenty of healthy juices and a short food menu that manages to encompass pizzas, spaghetti, curries and Asian noodles. Even the pizza bases and zucchini spaghetti strands are, like the rest of the menu, gluten- and sugar-free. The pizza arrives as a plate of little crackers, but is absolutely delicious, while the Asian-style noodles are a mixture of thick, udon-shaped zucchini, and flat, thin, fettucine-like slices of raw carrot.

Cabana

The Address Dubai Mall, Dubai Mall (04 8883444, www.theaddress.com). Metro Burj Khalifa, Dubai Mall. **Open** 9am-midnight Mon-Thur, Sun; 9am-12.30am Fri, Sat. **Map** p81 C5 28

Thanks to its location on the pool deck of the Address hotel – with views of the Burj Khalifa and a lush garden – this bar is usually full and buzzing. There aren't many places where you can relax poolside on a sun lounger, feeling as if you're at a beach resort, yet close to the tallest building in the world. But Cabana offers just that. Everything about the bar – down to the shady decking and the staff's lifeguard-inspired polo shirts – makes you feel as if you're at the beach. But remove your shades, glance upwards and glimpse the Burj Khalifa towering overhead, and you'll realise you're actually in the heart of one of the world's fastest-growing cities. The drinks menu isn't ambitious but you come here for the relaxed ambience over moden mixology.

Calabar

The Address Downtown Dubai, Mohammed Bin Rashid Boulevard (04 888 3444, www.theaddress.com). Metro Burj Khalifa, Dubai Mall. **Open** 6pm-2am daily. **Map** p81 C5 29

This hip bar has spectacular views of the Burj Khalifa and the Dubai Fountain. Diners can choose to sit inside the large venue, but the real attraction lies on its terrace. The bar tends to draw a young and hip crowd who flock to enjoy after-work drinks, and maybe some shisha, tapas and sharing platters. Sit on one of the venue's comfy beanbag chairs to soak in your surroundings, from the relaxing lounge music to the Downtown skyline. The setting is beautiful and can be intimate if you find a cosy corner.

Left Bank

Souk Al Bahar (04 368 4501). Metro Burj Khalifa/Dubai Mall. **Open** noon-2am daily. **Map** p81 B5 30

The Souk Al Bahar Left Bank is a dark and moody lounge bar, not half as stylish as it wants to be, but the length of the drinks menu alone makes it a pleasant place to idle away some hours. Although much quieter than its sister bar in the Medinat Jumeirah, which has more of a pre-clubby feel, it does get busy at weekends.

Other location Medinat Jumeirah, Jumeirah Beach Road, Umm Suqeim (04 368 6171).

Majlis Café

The Souk, Dubai Mall (056 287 1522, www.themajlisdubai.com). Metro Burj Khalifa, Dubai Mall. **Open** 10am-midnight Mon-Wed, Sun; 10am-1am Thur-Sat. **Map** p81 B5 31

Swap your usual coffee of choice for a Camelccino at Majlis Café – the first camel milk café in the city. You can also stop here for a cup of Arabic coffee, *qahwah*, served from a traditional coffee pot. If your preference is for tea, there are a number of regional options along with some local cold drinks, including a sparkling *karkadeh*, made with dried hibiscus flowers. As with the coffees, all baked goods here are made with camel milk including éclairs, fruit tarts and a selection of muffins.

Markette Restaurant & Crêperie

Dubai Mall (04 339 8173, www.thedubaimall.com). Metro Burj Khalifa/Dubai Mall. **Open** 9am-11.30pm daily. **Map** p81 B5 32

Next to the Cheesecake Factory and directly opposite the Dubai Mall's aquarium is this café specialising primarily in sweet crêpes and savoury galettes. Despite the mall location, Markette manages to achieve something of the feel of a Parisian café-meets-farmhouse kitchen. There's a long list of sweet and savoury pancake options, plus salads, soups, sandwiches, burgers and Asian- and Italian-inspired main courses.

Nezesaussi

Manzil Downtown Dubai (04 428 5888, www.vida-hotels.com/en/manzi). Metro Burj Khalifa/Dubai Mall. **Open** 5pm-2am Mon-Thur, Sun; noon-2am Fri, Sat. **Map** p81 C5 33

Short for New Zealand, South Africa and Australia, Nezesaussi has always been, first and foremost, a rugby-lover's pub. Inside, walls are covered with sports memorabilia and TV screens. A rugby-ball-shaped bar sits in the centre of the room, with more TV screens above it. Sports from Formula One to the Premier League, NBA play-off games to Wimbledon tennis are shown here. As one would imagine, there's a wide variety of beer available on tap and by the bottle. There's also an intriguing menu of beer cocktails. A twice-daily happy hour runs from 5pm to 7pm and 11pm to closing, with drinks at Dhs25 (a good discount on the regular prices) – a real score if it happens to coincide with your game. Kick back for kick-off and make this your sports bar of choice.

Shakespeare and Co.

Dubai Mall (04 434 0195, www.shakespeare-and-co.com). Metro Burj Khalifa/Dubai Mall. **Open** 7am-1am daily. **Map** p81 B5 34

Kitsch decor abounds at well-known Dubai mini-chain Shakespeare and Co., with its trademark distressed pastel furniture, fripperies, pink cushions and lace doilies as far as the eye can see. The menu's not all dainty cakes, however, with a good selection of sandwiches, salads and heartier pizza, pasta and meat mains. There are cakes too, of course, with French pastries, viennoiserie, macaroons, petits fours, marshmallows and ice-cream. Service is fast and efficient. This is good food at wallet-friendly prices.

Other locations Arabian Ranches Shopping Centre, Sheikh Mohammed Bin Zayed Road, Arabian Ranches (04 447 0444); Dubai Marina Mall, Dubai Marina (04 457 4199); Ibn Battuta Mall, Jebel Ali (04 553 0689); Safa Centre, Al Wasl Road, Jumeirah (04 394 1121); Souk Al Bahar, Downtown Dubai (04 425 7971); Village Mall, Jumeirah (04 344 6228).

Shops & Services

Bloomingdale's

Dubai Mall (04 350 5333, www.bloomingdales.com). Metro Burj Khalifa/Dubai Mall. **Open** 10am-10pm Mon, Wed, Sun; 11am-10pm Tue; 10am-midnight Thur-Sat. **Map** p81 B5 35 **Department store**

The first international location of the New York City department store giant. You can get Arabic-motif versions of the iconic 'little neon bag' featuring Turkish evil eyes and hands of Fatima, beautifully made home items and high-end fashion from designer labels as well as up-and-coming boutique brands like Finders Keepers and Mink Pink. There's also a little Magnolia Bakery counter for your red velvet cupcake fix and a Bloomie's Ice Cream.

IN THE KNOW RIDING THE DUBAI TROLLEY

A new addition to Dubai's transport system is Downtown's hop-on-hop-off trolley. The vintage-style cars are emission-free and hydro-powered, and once it's fully open the route will cover seven kilometres (4.5 miles). It's certainly not the quickest way to see the sights of Downtown, but in an area plagued by traffic you won't do much better in a car or on foot. For more information, *see p289*.

Candylicious

Dubai Mall (04 330 8700, www.candyliciousme.com). Metro Burj Khalifa/Dubai Mall. **Open** 10am-10pm Mon-Wed, Sun; 10am-midnight Thur-Sat. **Map** p81 B5 36 **Food & drink**

Yet another largest in the world, Candylicious is a humungous sweet shop: a 930sq m (10,000sq ft) space crammed with confectionery of all kinds, from a life-sized lollipop tree, jelly beans in floor-to-ceiling dispensers, oversized Hershey bars and 'I heart Dubai' rock candy. A variety of novelty items like Tootsie Roll neck pillows are also on sale.

Shakespeare and Co.

Rang Mahal. *See p94.*

Daiso

Dubai Mall (04 388 2902, www.daisome.com). Metro Burj Khalifa/Dubai Mall. **Open** 10am-midnight daily. **Map** p81 B5 37 **Fashion/accessories/homewares**

Japanese shop Daiso is a bigger, cheaper, kitschier version of sleek shops like Muji. It stocks just about everything – baking equipment, utensils, make-up, fancy dress, stationery, clothes, DIY products, food, gifts and more besides – for next to nothing. Most of the products have the same minimalist look that Japan is famous for.

KAS Australia

Dubai Mall (04 366 9386, www.kasaustralia.ae). Metro Burj Khalifa/Dubai Mall. **Open** 10am-10pm Mon-Wed, Sun; 10am-midnight Thur-Sat. **Map** p81 B5 38 **Fabrics/homewares**

Pick up bold cushion covers and bedding from this Australian brand. Bright colour-blocked prints and geometric patterns are the order of the day. There are also beach towels and a small number of home accessory items. If you want to easily spruce up your bedroom, this is the place to do it.

★ Kinokuniya

Dubai Mall (04 434 0111, www.kinokuniya.com). Metro Burj Khalifa/Dubai Mall. **Open** 10am-10pm Mon-Wed, Sun; 10am-midnight Thur-Sat. **Map** p81 B5 39 **Books**

Kinokuniya is a bibliophile's heaven. Enter with caution as it's easy to lose a good few hours wandering through the endless shelves of books, with sections for more genres than we can count. More than half a million books are housed here, and thousands of magazines, in English, Arabic, Japanese, French, German and Chinese. Beach reading: sorted.

Level Shoe District

Dubai Mall (04 388 2012, www.levelshoedistrict.com). Metro Burj Khalifa/Dubai Mall. **Open** 10am-1am Mon-Wed, Sun; 10am-2am Thur-Sat. **Map** p81 B5 40 **Shoes**

Level Shoe District's slogan, 'Let the shoe begin', fits this artful home of designer shoes perfectly. Heels are suspended in bird cages or placed on podiums in angelic spotlights. Corthay, Giuseppe Zanotti, Alaia, Ancient Greek Sandals, Christian Louboutin, Nicholas Kirkwood and Sophia Webster are among the 350 brands on display in the huge space, which also includes Vogue Café, a bespoke cobbler, a foot spa and VIP shopping, styling and concierge services.

Liu Jo

Dubai Mall (04 339 9001, www. liujo.com). Metro Burj Khalifa/Dubai Mall. **Open** 10am-midnight daily. **Map** p81 B5 41 **Fashion**

The main line of this Italian brand includes lots of polished pieces such as tailored shorts, jackets and dresses. The shop also stocks the Liu Jo Jeans collection, which is more dressed-down and edgy, and will make you want to rock denim every day.

Marina Exotic Home Interiors

Dubai Mall (04 388 2012, www.marinahomeinteriors.com). Metro Burj Khalifa/Dubai Mall. **Open** 10am-midnight Mon-Wed, Sat, Sun; 10am-1am Thur, Fri. **Map** p81 B5 42 **Furniture**

A Dubai-based home store, Marina is a prime example of the recent trend for vintage-looking items and contemporary Asian design. While much of the furniture will be too big to fit into your suitcase, if you've got the budget you will almost certainly be tempted to have it shipped home. This is the kind of place where you can pick up a travel trunk that opens into a home bar, intricately carved Indian cabinets and midcentury modern-style leather chairs. An intriguing combination of retro, rustic and avant-garde design.
Other locations Spinneys Centre, Al Safa, Jumeirah (04 394 2541); The Walk, Jumeirah Beach Residence (04 437 0239); Souk Madinat Jumeirah, Umm Suqeim (04 368 6050); Mall of the Emirates (04 341 0314).

Mauzan

Dubai Mall (04 339 9505, www.mauzan.com). Metro Burj Khalifa/Dubai Mall. **Open** 10am-midnight daily. **Map** p81 B5 ㊸ **Fashion**
When it comes to hijabs and abayas, consider Mauzan an authority on all things cool. Mauzan collections are a modern take on the traditional; Miss Mauzan is a diffusion line of more casual clothing.

O' de Rose

Galeries Lafayette, Dubai Mall (04 339 9933, www.o-derose.com). Metro Burj Khalifa, Dubai Mall. **Open** 10am-10pm Mon-Wed, Sun; 10am-midnight Thur-Sat. **Map** p81 B5 ㊹ **Fashion/homewares**
A Dubai-grown 'ethnic-chic' boutique selling cushions covered in embroidered Arabic motifs and arabesque coffee tables inlaid with mother of pearl. Almost everything is a brightly coloured statement piece of fashion or home decor, from the minimal shisha pipes and Moroccan tea sets to the Sarah's Bag *tawleh*-inspired DAMA clutches made popular by Amal Clooney (a hint of the price bracket you can expect).
Other location Al Wasl Road, Al Manara, Umm Suqeim (04 348 7990).

Scotch & Soda

Dubai Mall (04 325 3327, www.scotch-soda.com). Metro Burj Khalifa/Dubai Mall. **Open** 10am-10pm Mon-Wed, Sun; 10am-midnight Thur-Sat. **Map** p81 B5 ㊺ **Fashion**
Don't let the 'Amsterdam couture' tag scare you off; there are interesting pieces here with fantastically meticulous detailing at prices that won't leave you out on the streets. We particularly like the well-worn look of the clothes, giving a vintage vibe.

Souk Al Bahar

Downtown Dubai (www.soukalbahar.ae). Metro Burj Khalifa/Dubai Mall. **Open** 10am-10pm Mon-Sat, Thur; 2-10pm Fri. **Map** p81 B5 ㊻ **Mall**
Almost identical in concept to Souk Madinat Jumeirah, Souk Al Bahar is situated just over the small bridge from the Dubai Mall. It's actually better known for housing a number of popular restaurants in pole position in front of the Dubai Fountain and Burj Khalifa than for its stores and shops. Mostly you will be met with jewellery stalls – with typical prices varying wildly from around Dhs100 to Dhs1,000 – full of standard hand of Fatima and Turkish eye motifs. There are some nice pieces to be found, though, so if you fancy a leisurely mooch away from the crowds before or after dinner, head here.

The Camel Company

Souk Al Bahar (04 421 0087, www.camelcompany.ae). Metro Burj Khalifa/Dubai Mall. **Open** 10am-10pm Mon-Thur, Sat; 2-10pm Fri. **Map** p81 B5 ㊼ **Souvenirs**
A souvenir shopper's dream, with all the usual postcards, magnets, mugs and novelty gifts that you could want, but with less tack. Designs are by commissioned artists and inspired by local Arabic heritage, so there are camel-, palm tree- and minaret-adorned stationery sets aplenty, as well as cute glass camel-topped drink stirrers, adorable soft toys and Arab family-themed Matryoshka nesting dolls.

World of Pets

Lower Ground Parking, Dubai Mall (04 388 2455, www.worldofpetsme.com). Metro Burj Khalifa/Dubai Mall. **Open** 10am-10pm daily. **Map** p81 B5 ㊽ **Pet acessories**
There are few places in the world where you might find a designer pet boutique and spa, but Dubai is one of them. Pick up doggy deodorant, temporary coloured styling gels, and a whole range of shampoos that include, but are by no means limited to, tear-free shampoo, dry shampoo and products for detangling, dry and sensitive scalped pets, brightening coats and curly hair.

EXPLORE

BUSINESS BAY

There's not much to see in Business Bay, but it's a place to stop off on your way to or from the **Meydan Grandstand & Racecourse** for lunch, dinner or a drink. The soon-to-open **Dubai Design District** – planned as an artistic enclave (*see p95*) – will add an extra dimension to the area, although how successful the endeavour will be remains to be seen.

Sights & Attractions

FREE Meydan Grandstand & Racecourse

04 327 0077, www.dubaiworldcup.com/visit/meydan-grandstand. **Open** *Sept-Apr* times vary according to races; phone or see website. **Admission** *General admission* free. *Premium seating* phone or see website for latest ticket prices. *Stables tours* Dhs250; Dhs150 reductions. **Map** p81 D3 ㊾

You can spot Meydan Grandstand from a couple of miles away – it's an imposing space-age building that stretches for 1.5 kilometres (nearly a mile). The racecourse it overlooks is home to the world's richest race, the Dubai World Cup, and the day it takes place is one of the most anticipated social events of the year. The Grandstand is solar-panelled and has seating for 60,000 spectators, while the two courses – one dirt, one turf – have a combined length of more than 4km (2.5 miles).

During racing season, from September to April, you can book on to a Stable Tour (04 381 3405, www.stabletours.meydan.ae, 7.30am-noon Tue-Wed) to explore parts of the racecourse usually off-limits to the public. The price of a ticket includes breakfast at Farriers before meeting a trainer and taking the guided tour, which includes the equine swimming pools and gives you a chance to get up close to some of the world-class racehorses housed here. The tour then heads back to the Grandstand for a look at the parade ring, jockeys' room and the race-night dining facilities, plus some tea and coffee in Qube Sports Bar. The Grandstand remains closed to the public outside racing season, and during the season it only opens on race days, usually Thursdays from 5pm. However, if you don't fancy a tour, but are still keen to see the course, the Meydan hotel has several bars and restaurants that overlook it.

► *For more on the Dubai World Cup, see p96* **A Day at the Races**.

Restaurants

Ananta

Oberoi Dubai, Al A'amal Street (04 444 1407, www.oberoihotels.com). Metro Business Bay. **Open** 7-11.30pm Mon-Thur, Sat, Sun; 2.30-3.30pm, 7-11.30pm Fri. **Main courses** Dhs110-Dhs425. **Map** p81 B3 ⑩ **Indian**

Sleek and stylish, the decor of Ananta is a world away from most Indian restaurants. You'll find beautifully presented dishes, created using some serious chef skills. The five-course tasting menu, including amuse-bouches and palate cleansers, is a brilliant way to explore what's on offer, and good value. You'll get a combination of dumplings in yoghurt and mint, fois gras and tandoori chicken, wagyu beef with biryani, tandoori prawns, and chocolate dosa and deep fried kulfi to finish. It is all fantastic, with each dish expertly thought out and presented. For an upmarket, smart meal, you'll be hard pressed to find better.

Izakaya

JW Marriott Marquis Dubai, Sheikh Zayed Road (04 414 3000, www.jwmarriottmarquisdubailife.com). Metro Business Bay. **Sushi & sashimi** Dhs15-Dhs75. **Open** 6pm-midnight Mon-Sat. **Map** p81 A2 ⑪ **Japanese**

You might expect rather a lot from the restaurants within the city's tallest hotel – not least in the views department. While venues such as Prime 68 (*see below*) and Vault (*see p97*) deliver, Japanese restaurant Izakaya doesn't fare so well: it's an essentially windowless space. Take heart, then, from the food: seaweed salad is fresh, tangy and full of different textures. From the robata grill, the *kusi yaki* wagyu beef skewer (soft, juicy and beautifully seasoned) with spicy tomato salsa is excellent, while the lobster tempura is certainly a luxurious treat – though not the highlight of our meal. Staff are welcoming and Izakaya offers a perfectly decent night out – if not with all the pizzazz of its neighbours.

Prime 68

JW Marriott Marquis Dubai, Sheikh Zayed Road (04 414 3000). Metro Business Bay. **Open** 6pm-midnight daily. **Main courses** Dhs125-Dhs575. **Map** p81 A2 ⑫ **Steakhouse**

Perched up on the 68th floor of the JW Marriott Marquis, with huge windows, stunning views are almost guaranteed if dining at this boutique steakhouse. You'll need to book well in advance to secure a window seat, but even if you end up away from the view, the experience is still an impressive one. Light tones of cream and white help create a relaxed ambience, as do welcoming staff, and despite its high-end credentials, the place doesn't feel stuffy. Steaks are hefty, and include three 10oz filets. There's an array of sauces and butters to complement the steaks – featuring luxury ingredients such as truffle – plus add-ons including grilled lobster tail and meat rubs.

Prime Steakhouse

Meydan Hotel, Nad Al Sheba (04 381 3111, www.meydanhotels.com). **Open** 7-11.30pm daily. **Main courses** Dhs130-Dhs480. **Map** p81 A3 ⑬ **Steakhouse**

When it comes to location, Prime Steakhouse can safely claim to be unique. Up on the fifth floor of the Meydan, it overlooks the impressive racecourse, which is one of the greenest views in the city. If you're lucky – or just call in advance – you'll land one of the window seats, with two huge, high-backed

IN THE KNOW BAY SQUARE

The clue is in the name, and Business Bay consists mainly of businesses, along with a smattering of residential apartment buildings and hotels, plus a few restaurants and bars. But new addition Bay Square is set to change the vibe. It's home to branches of a number of the city's popular homegrown cafés, such as **Circle Café** (Building 7, 04 552 1403, www.circle-cafe.com), the **Pantry** (Building 6, 04 558 7161, www.pantrycafe.me) and **BookMunch** (www.bookmunchcafe.com; *see p120*).

DUBAI DESIGN DISTRICT

Creating an art quarter.

The image of Dubai as a city with no real emerging artistic identity is one that many local residents are keen to change, and in the past few years they've had some success at doing just that. Alserkal Avenue in Al Quoz (*see p130*) is one prime example of an upcoming artistic hub.

It's unfortunate, then, that many new developments that set out to emulate a cool east London or Williamsburg vibe tend to come off as a bit contrived. Dubai is a new city, so there are very few urban areas that have that same rough-around-the-edges feel so often found in other major global cities, which can organically emerge as artistic districts. Almost everything – perhaps unintentionally – ends up with a polished, brand-new feel.

Still to be completed, the **Dubai Design District**, or d3 (*pictured*), seems poised to join the ranks of the city's wannabe-hipster spots. It's described as being a 'creative hub' and a space for artists, designers and creatives, and will be home to shops, studios, galleries, pop-ups and eateries.

The d3 district has been carefully planned, and therein lies its main problem: it already lacks the spontaneity of places such as Berlin's Kreuzberg, Rome's Pigneto or Seoul's Gangnam-Gu, which grew into their identities over time. There are bound to be shops and cafés of note when d3 is completed, and it's still too early to predict whether it will surprise and emerge with its own unique character, but if it sticks to form it's unlikely to become the equivalent of art hubs in other cities.

chairs that look out over the course, offering an unrivalled sense of privacy and comfort. It can often be quiet here, maybe due to the out-of-the-way location. Steaks can be ordered by the 100g, so you won't need to worry about overindulging, although the delicious, tender, flavourful meat does encourage that. Staff are happy to offer information on different cuts. Mini desserts, at only Dhs20 a pop, end the meal on a sweet note, and the reasonable final bill will leave you with a smile on your face.

★ Rang Mahal

JW Marriott Marquis Dubai, Sheikh Zayed Road (04 414 3000, www.jwmarriottmarquisdubailife.com). Metro Business Bay. **Main courses** Dhs120-Dhs220. **Open** 6pm-midnight daily. **Map** p81 A3 54 **Indian**

Celebrity chef Atul Kochhar has nailed upmarket Indian dining at this stylish restaurant. The dark room, with low orange lighting, is very romantic. Huge carved wooden pillars break up the space, making it feel more intimate. The menu is an exciting mix of familiar dishes, created with flair and high-end ingredients. The starter of soft shell crab, which comes with a salad of crab meat, micro greens and passion fruit, is fantastic, as are the Scottish *lassooni* scallops with garlic and cauliflower. Spicing is subtle enough to add flavour without ovrewhelming the delicate seafood. Main courses are just as decadent, the butter-tossed lobster in malai curry, with a mustard and coconut sauce is a favourite. The rendering of a traditional lamb khada masala, meanwhile, takes the classic dish up another level. *Photos p92.*

The Pizza Guys

Executive Towers, Tower F, Mezzanine Level at Bay Avenue (800 843 4897, www.thepizzaguys.ae). Metro Business Bay. **Open** 11am-10.30pm Mon-Wed, Sat, Sun; 11am-11pm Thur, Fri. **Pizza** Dhs64-Dhs68. **Map** p81 B3 55 **Pizza**

The Pizza Guys commitment to quality is such that they won't deliver beyond Business Bay, Downtown Dubai and DIFC, lest your pizza arrive in anything less than perfectly gooey, piping-hot condition. It's a tiny venue, and while there are

A DAY AT THE RACES

Dress up to the nines for this very special occasion.

On the last Saturday in March every year, the racing season concludes with World Cup Day. This £19.5 million event features 18 races – including the world's richest horse race, the Dubai World Cup, with its £6.5 million purse – and an after-race concert with well-known stars (past performers include Kylie Minogue).

Prior to this, and running concurrently to the domestic racing at Meydan from January to March, is the World Cup Carnival, held over 11 race days, where international horse races are entered by some of the most high-profile owners, horses, jockeys and trainers in the world. As you would expect, it's a dressy affair, with 'Best Dressed Lady', 'Best Hat' and 'Most Elegant Lady' prizes to be won in the Jaguar Style Stakes. The lady judged Best Dressed wins the use of a Jaguar F-type convertible for one year. 'Most Elegant' gets a Longines watch.

Free admission is possible on regular race nights, but on Dubai World Cup Day general admission is charged at Dhs25. These tickets must be purchased in advance and allow access to a limited area for spectating. Otherwise, ticket prices start at around Dhs450 for apron views, where you can access the bars and a food court, and increase into the thousands depending on area and hospitality package. Children under the age of six are not permitted in these areas.

seats inside, they're not the most comfortable. They claim their pizzas are authentic, New York-style, artisanal, fresh pies – and they're not exaggerating. Try the Wall Street Special, covered in herb-roasted chicken, oven-roasted rosemary and olive oil potatoes, with creamy stracciatella cheese and fior di latte mozzarella. The five-cheese pizza with burrata and smoked scamorza is another home-run hit for flavour combinations.

Tong Thai

JW Marriott Marquis Dubai, Sheikh Zayed Road (04 414 3000, www.jwmarriottmarquisdubailife.com). Metro Business Bay. **Main courses** Dhs140-Dhs320. **Open** 6pm-midnight Tue-Sun. **Map** p81 A2 56 **Thai**

The sense of occasion at Tong Thai begins even before you reach your table. Arriving at the venue, diners are warmly welcomed and ushered down a long, ornate corridor, suddenly emerging into the dining space, where towering walls reach skywards and dramatic ceiling-high windows offer views of the Business Bay neighbourhood. After a start like this, it's a relief that the food doesn't disappoint. Classics such as tom yum have been perfected but don't bore, salads burst with fresh taste, while both the curries and stir-fries pack plenty of depth and flavour. Moreover for this standard, prices aren't extortionate, portions are ample and white rice is provided free of charge. As a package, Tong Thai is hard to beat.

Umai

Oberoi Dubai, Al A'amal Street (04 441 4444, www.oberoihotels.com). Metro Business Bay. **Open** 12.30-3.30pm, 7-11.30pm Mon-Thur, Sun; 7-11.30pm Fri. **Sharing plates** Dhs65-Dhs165. **Map** p81 B3 57 **Pan-Asian**

While some new openings become the talk of the town before anyone's taken the time to try a bite, other far more worthy ventures appear to slip under the city's radar. Umai is one of these. Meticulously decorated in a blend of sleek modernity and traditional Far Eastern touches, there's a Japanese focus to the decor, while the food wanders into pan-Asian territory. Alongside a large sushi selection, plus teppanyaki and yakitori grill dishes, there's Chinese dim sum and stir-fry and noodle dishes from across the Far East. In fact, it's the more daring dishes – the likes of grilled scallops with ruby grapefruit, plum liqueur and *umeboshi* and butter sauce – that put this place in the must-visit category. Well, that and the service – on our last visit the staff were warm, funny and incredibly well informed.

Cafés & Bars

In addition to the venues listed below, there are branches of **BookMunch**, **Circle Café** and the **Pantry Café** in Bay Square (*see p94* **In the Know**).

GQ Bar

JW Marriott Marquis Dubai, Sheikh Zayed Road (04 440 9300, www.gqbardubai.com). Metro Business Bay. **Open** noon-2am daily. **Map** p81 A2 58

Much like the publication of the same name, GQ Bar is aimed firmly at suave gentlemen. It's understated, but unquestionably upmarket, with faux-vintage sofas, hipster chairs and a clever use of funky lighting. For any other bar, a location in the world's tallest hotel might be a big part of the charm – but with an informed dining menu and some interesting-sounding drinks, this bar doesn't require a swanky address to justify itself. Prices are predictably on the high side but this is hardly a surprise – GQ is more George Clooney than Liam Gallagher.

★ Iris

Oberoi Dubai, Al A'amal Street (056 951 1442, www.irisdubai.com). Metro Business Bay. **Open** 6pm-2am daily. **Map** p81 B3 59

Take yourself up to the 27th floor of the Oberoi to find yourself in a buzzing bar with a music stage to the rear and a DJ supplying blissed-out house beats. Through a clever mixture of atmosphere (it's an outside venue, but the large windows create the sense you're still in a room) the vibe is effortlessly contemporary, with clean woods, glass and funky lights blending together seamlessly. As for the drinks, they are prepared with panache and although this isn't the most pocket-friendly place, it's undeniably good quality and, most importantly, ever so slightly cool.

Kcal

Executive Towers, Bay Avenue (600 595955, www.kcalhealthyfastfood.com). Metro Business Bay. **Open** 11am-11.30pm Mon-Thur, Sat, Sun; noon-11.30pm Fri. **Map** p81 B3 60

Kcal serves burgers, mains, desserts and shakes made from whey powder. Dishes are tasty enough, if not that filling, but Kcal's USP is that the menu includes calorie counts – with mains coming in at under 300 calories – along with other nutritional info. Chicken features heavily in Thai curries, southern grilled chicken, chicken seasoned Mexican style and chicken teriyaki, but there are also beef options and meatballs, served with aubergine noodles.

Vault

JW Marriott Marquis Dubai (04 414 3000, www.jwmarriottmarquisdubailife.com). Metro Business Bay. **Open** 5pm-3am daily. **Map** p81 A3 61

Sitting on the 71st and 72nd floors, this lounge is a record-breaker as the highest hotel bar in the world (avoid the faux pas of comparing it to the Burj Khalifa's At.mosphere, *see p82*, an independent venue not located in a hotel, which sits on the 122nd floor). Accessed from the hotel's lobby via two elevator rides, the bar gets its name from the heavy bank safe-style doors that mark its threshold. Inside is all black and gold, and there's an inventive drinks menu that majors on vodkas, with many different brands on offer. Pleasantly, and far too rarely for Dubai, the lower of the two floors is kept smoke-free. Despite the bar's elevated status, there are better Downtown views to be found in Dubai (see the aforementioned At.mosphere), but the full-length windows still offer dizzying panoramas of the skyline.

Shops & Services

Milena Fashion

Damac Tower, Al Abraj Street (04 438 7029, www.milenafashion.com). Metro Business Bay. **Open** 10am-7pm Mon-Thur, Sat, Sun. **Map** p81 C3 62

In a less-frequented area of Business Bay, hidden behind a stationery store, this large boutique is a rare find: it stocks beautiful Italian-designed beachwear (some on the rather skimpy side) and other garments. As well as bikinis and one-pieces we spied sequinned booty shorts, sandals, kaftans and flirty dresses from labels including Pin-Up Stars and Borsalino.

Tatiana Tailoring

Damac Tower, Al Abraj Street (04 452 9229, www.tatianatailoring.com). Metro Business Bay. **Open** 10am-7pm Mon-Thur, Sat, Sun. **Map** p81 C3 63

If you've bought something at Milena Fashion and it doesn't quite fit right, take it next door to this chic women's tailor, which offers bespoke garments of high quality as well as alterations. Staff can create everything from business suits to dresses and skirts and eveningwear.

IN THE KNOW JW MARRIOTT MARQUIS DUBAI

This 72-storey hotel (*see p273*) is currently the world's tallest, but even without this title it would have become one of the most talked-about spots in the city. Its award-winning restaurants include **Rang Mahal** (*see p95*), **Tong Thai** (*see p96*) and **Prime 68** (*see p94*). Several of its bars have become nightlife hotspots, among them **VIP Room** (*see p199*), **GQ Bar** (*see left*), **Vault** (*see left*) and sports bar **Velocity** (04 414 3000, www.jwmarriottmarquisdubailife.com). It's also the venue for **Deep Like Thursdayz**, one of the best house music nights in the city, where T-shirts, sandals and beards rule over chinos and high heels and, in the cooler months when it takes place on the terrace, fairy lights lend an 'alternative' vibe. Finally, the **Lemon Jam**, which takes place on Saturday afternoons and continues into the evening, is a delightfully chilled-out event around the pool, where you can sip on mason-jar cocktails while listening to anything from an acoustic set to some psychedelic dub-reggae.

EXPLORE

DIFC to Dubai World Trade Centre

Located between Downtown and Za'abeel Park, this area is defined by its glistening skyscrapers, high-end hotels and award-winning restaurants. It's also a centre of business and home to major international companies. This ensures that the area is buzzing, particularly on weekday evenings when local office workers pour into the bars and restaurants. You'll also find some intriguing art galleries clustered around DIFC, as well as major events taking place at the Dubai World Trade Centre – which hosts everything from comedy to sport. With three metro stations and pedestrian-friendly streets, this is one of the city's most accessible areas.

La Petite Maison.

Don't Miss

1 Best DIFC dining Book in for a treat at La Petite Maison (p102) or Zuma (p103).

2 40 Kong Drinks with stunning skyline views (p108).

3 Art galleries Explore the DIFC's art hub (p111).

4 Blue Bar Buzzing music-focused bar with bands and gig DVDs (p110).

5 Dubai World Trade Centre Catch an event at this vast venue (p110).

DIFC

Situated just off Sheikh Zayed Road, and a stone's throw from a whole host of other entertainment areas, the Dubai International Financial Centre, the free-trade zone referred to almost universally by its acronym DIFC, doesn't sound – or look – like a place you'd want to spend your holiday. But amid the sterile business environment are some of the city's finest restaurants. **La Petite Maison** and **Zuma** are multiple winners of *Time Out Dubai*'s best restaurant award, and are both located in this district. Some cool bars complement this high-end dining selection, while some of the city's best art can be seen in the cluster of galleries in Gate Village (*see p111* **Gallery-Hopping Guide**). Most of the galleries deal with contemporary work, with the **Opera Gallery** sometimes showcasing pieces from modern masters, including Salvador Dalí, Alexander Calder and Andy Warhol.

Restaurants

★ Café Belge

Ritz-Carlton DIFC, Gate Village (04 372 2222, www.cafebelge.com). Metro Financial Centre. **Open** noon-2am Mon-Thur, Sun; 6pm-2am Fri, Sat. **Main courses** Dhs100-Dhs300. **Map** p101 C3 ❶ **Belgian**

Café Belge's terrific seafood menu specialises in spot-on mussels, but also encompasses the likes of poached john dory, chilled razor clams and seared turbot, as well as a fantastic spread of oysters. It's a great spot for a lazy lunch, even if the chips are below par – they need to be crispier and less floury for optimum dunking in the mussels' sauces. Everything from the furniture to the music to the extensive beer menu makes you feel as if you're in Bruges. There's a terrace but it doesn't have views.

Center Cut

Ritz-Carlton DIFC, Gate Village (04 372 2323, www.ritzcarlton.com). Metro Financial Centre. **Open** 6-10.30am, noon-2.30pm, 6.30-11pm Mon-Thur, Sun; 6-11am, noon-2.30pm, 6.30-11pm Fri, Sat. **Main courses** Dhs180-Dhs500. **Map** p101 C3 ❷ **Steakhouse**

> **IN THE KNOW DIFC LAWS**
>
> As a free zone, the rules in DIFC differ from those in other parts of the city. One of the first things you'll notice is that standalone restaurants and bars can serve alcohol. In most parts of Dubai, only establishments in hotels have liquor licences. The usual rules still apply when it comes to being drunk outside and public displays of affection.

Dimly lit to such an extent that it's actually quite hard to see, Center Cut is an imposing fine-dining destination. But despite first impressions, it's not at all snooty: staff are warm and friendly, and the atmosphere relaxed. And when it comes to the food, Center Cut shines brightly. The menu is concise, but features everything you would want from a steakhouse, including some standout starters and salads. An organic beetroot dish is a wonderfully tangy combination of sweet and savoury flavours. Steaks are soft, tender and flavourful, and desserts maintain the high standards. There's no need to fear the final bill either: the cherry on the top of a satisfying dining experience.

Clé

Al Fattan Currency House (04 352 5150, www.cle-dubai.com). Metro Financial Centre. **Open** noon-2am daily. **Sharing plates** Dhs65-Dhs400. **Map** p101 C3 ❸ **Arabic**

The wave of modern Arabic dining in Dubai continues with the opening of Clé, with well-known Australian-Lebanese chef and cookbook author Greg Malouf at the helm. A sleek black interior is offset with pockets of shine; gilded Kalashnikovs are used as lamp stands and seats are padded, Chanel-style. Lebanese dishes are lovingly couched in tradition, then creatively shaken up with new twists. It's high end and high quality, and confident without being intimidating. There's a similar charm to the service.

★ Gaucho

Gate Village 5 (04 422 7898, www.gauchorestaurants.ae). Metro Emirates Towers. **Open** 11.30am-midnight Mon-Wed, Sat; 11.30am-2am Thur, 11.30am-1am Fri. **Main courses** Dhs120-Dhs180. **Map** p101 C3 ❹ **Argentinian**

Sophisticated, stylish, masculine, chic – it's not surprising that Gaucho is regularly packed with city slickers. The chrome fittings, monochrome palette and cow-print chairs add to the confident vibe. Steaks are the speciality, of course, and the knowledgeable staff will explain the numerous and well-procured cuts at length. Simply put, if you can afford premium prices, you can have a steak here that you will never forget. But before that, try the duck and beef empanadas, and round off your meal with a salted dulce de leche and hazelnut cheesecake. This is one of Dubai's top-tier restaurants.

Mint Leaf of London, Dubai

Emirates Financial Towers (04 706 0900, www.mintleaf.ae). Metro Financial Centre. **Open** noon-11.30pm daily. **Main courses** Dhs70-Dhs230. **Map** p101 C2 ❺ **Contemporary Indian**

Winging its way from the British capital to the Emirates, Mint Leaf of London, Dubai promises a contemporary take on authentic Indian cooking. The interior is upmarket – a mixture of textural effects, and stencil-like motifs over walls, ceilings

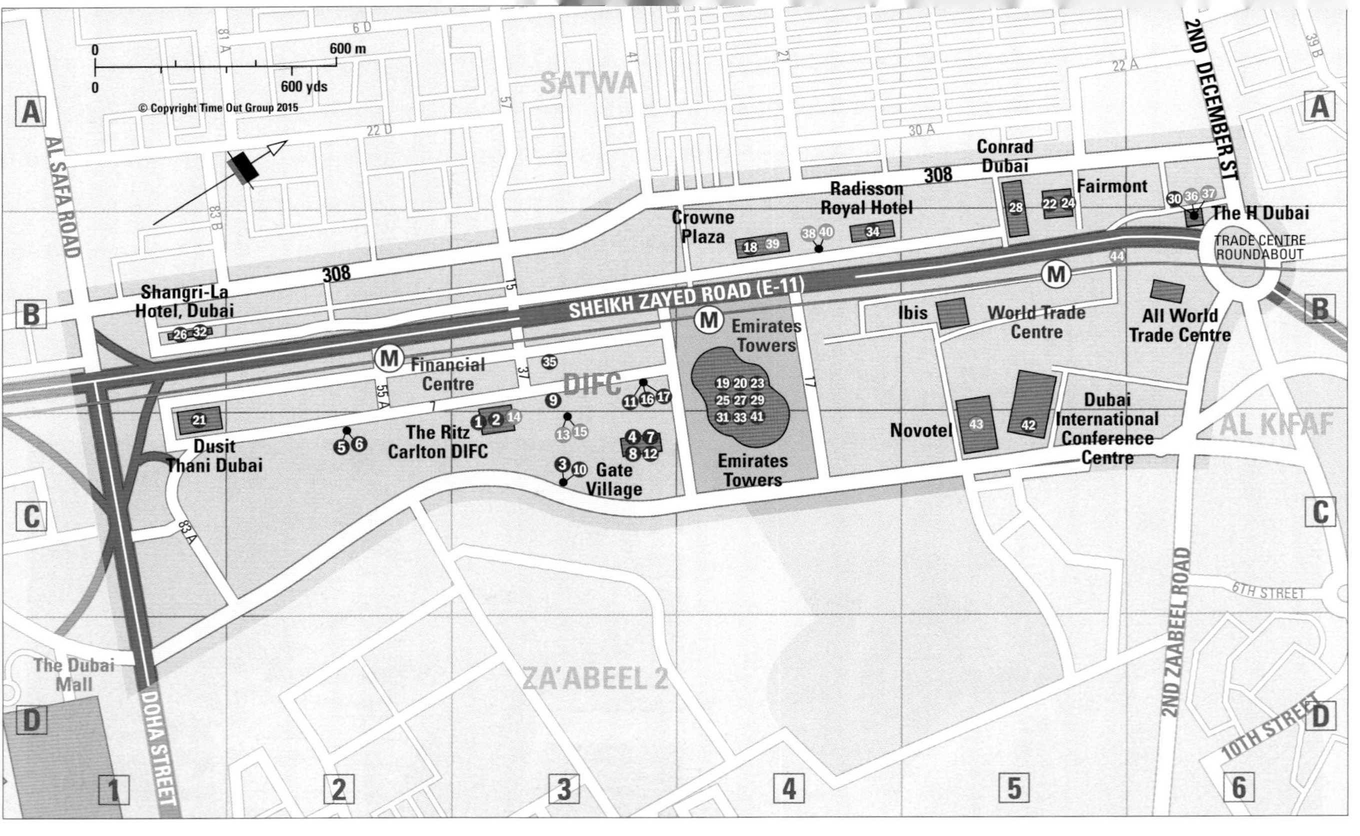
0
600 m
0
600 yds
© Copyright Time Out Group 2015
SATWA
AL SAFA ROAD
2ND DECEMBER ST
Conrad Dubai
Fairmont
Radisson Royal Hotel
Crowne Plaza
The H Dubai
TRADE CENTRE ROUNDABOUT
308
Shangri-La Hotel, Dubai
SHEIKH ZAYED ROAD (E-11)
Emirates Towers
Ibis
World Trade Centre
All World Trade Centre
Financial Centre
DIFC
Novotel
Dubai International Conference Centre
AL KIFAF
Dusit Thani Dubai
The Ritz Carlton DIFC
Gate Village
Emirates Towers
6TH STREET
2ND ZAABEEL ROAD
ZA'ABEEL 2
The Dubai Mall
DOHA STREET
10TH STREET

EXPLORE

Zuma.

and cushions, in black and white, with a few softening creams and beiges. Some dishes have classic Indian roots; others are unexpected or with a fusion element, such as soft-shell crab, wild mushroom and fennel soup with white truffle oil, or scallops with coconut moilee. Our verdict on this smart new joint: dishes are good, rather than exciting or inspiring, especially considering the prices.

Nay

Emirates Financial Towers (04 351 6660, www.nayrestaurant.com). Metro Emirates Towers. **Open** 12.30pm-1am Mon-Wed, Sat; 12.30pm-3am Thur, Fri. **Sharing plates** Dhs25-Dhs50. **Map** p101 C2 ❻ **Arabic**

This enormous restaurant is named after a type of Arabic flute. Apt, then, that its motto is: 'Where food and beverage meet to compose a splendid melody.' And Nay takes both food and entertainment seriously. It's a great place to share meze with a group of friends and enjoy the performance of the Brazilian dancers. There are some contemporary Mediterranean influences in the dishes. Houmous green *rihan*, for example, is a refreshing mix that contains pesto and basil; the home-made Lebanese white cheese comes mixed with dried mint and basil and topped with a light ratatouille sauce – a good mix of tart, tangy flavours. The outdoor terrace is vast and vibrant.

★ La Petite Maison

Gate Village 8 (04 439 0505, www.lpmdubai.ae). Metro Emirates Towers. **Open** noon-3.15pm, 7-11.15pm daily. **Main courses** Dhs100-Dhs250. **Map** p101 C3 ❼ **French**

La Petite Maison continues to live up to its reputation of being one of the finest French spots in town, equally good for lunch or dinner. From the extensive menu our suggestions would include the lamb cutlets, which are the finest we've had in this city, the spectacular burrata with tomatoes and basil, the octopus in lemon oil, the mushroom risotto and the lobster tagliatelle. Competition for La Petite Maison springs up regularly, but right now it seems to be coming out on top.

Roberto's

Gate Village 1 (04 386 0066, www.robertos.ae). Metro Emirates Towers. **Open** noon-3pm, 7pm-midnight daily. **Main courses** Dhs100-Dhs200. **Map** p101 C3 ❽ **Italian**

Roberto's is a romantic spot, designed with classical elegance, with white linen tablecloths and tiny tealight candles lit after dark. From a traditional Italian menu, we like simple starters such as burrata (mozzarella and cream) with sweet tomatoes and basil as well as sophisticated dishes such as aragosta – lobster carpaccio served with salad and black truffle caviar. Of the pasta dishes, the spaghetti carbonara with wagyu beef bacon is mouthwateringly good. There are great views of Dubai's skyline.

Royal China

Building 4 (04 354 5543, www.royalchina dubai.com). Metro Emirates Towers. **Open** 11.30am-11.30pm daily. **Main courses** Dhs100-Dhs120. **Map** p101 B3 ❾ **Chinese**

A grand, charcoal-hued Chinese-themed dining room with bright red accents awaits diners at this upmarket London import serving Hong Kong-style cuisine. Order jasmine flower tea to sip while you wait for your starters; it's an artful creation, which springs open into a bloom once in hot water. The steamed platter of dim sum is impeccably fresh. Deep-fried and wok-tossed salt and pepper squid is well seasoned and the batter crunchy. Crispy fried aromatic duck is carved nearby, put into pancakes and then whipped over to the table – it's wonderfully crunchy.

Sass Café

Al Fattan Currency House (04 352 7722, www. sasscafe-dubai.ae). Metro Emirates Towers. **Open** 7pm-midnight Mon-Wed, Sun; 7pm-1am Thur, Fri; 9pm-midnight Sat. **Main courses** Dhs150-Dhs250. **Map** p101 C3 ❿ **French/Italian**

The original Sass Café is apparently frequented by the rich and famous in Monaco. In its Dubai incarnation, a red carpet flanked by floodlit pools leads diners up to the distinctly nightclub-style entrance. Beyond the blacked-out front door, the sense of being in a club continues. The dark-walled dining room is so dimly lit that the visibility of the food is not the best and non-smokers may feel a little put off having to dine in smoky, bar-like surroundings. The menu is filled with French- and Italian-inspired dishes, many designed for sharing and reasonably priced, considering the glitzy nature of the venue. While we're not wowed by the interior and ambience, it's the fairly high standard of the food that would call us back.

SushiArt

The Marble Walk, Gate 5 (04 800 220, www. sushiart.ae). Metro Financial Centre. **Open** 11am-11pm daily. **Sushi & sashimi** Dhs7-Dhs20. **Map** p101 B3 ⓫ **Japanese**

A firm favourite with DIFC's number-crunching crowd, Dubai's first SushiArt outlet doesn't boast as attractive a beachside location as its younger sibling (now open at the Beach, opposite Jumeirah Beach Residence), but it certainly does a stronger trade on weekday lunchtimes. It's also done well to mask what is essentially a food court-style setting, with the French-Japanese chain's trademark minimalism and black decor. Be sure to try the dishes created by Joël Robuchon – because everything else is pretty much the same as what you'll find on every other sushi menu in town. Adventurous palates may take to Robuchon's (creative, but hard to love) crispy lobster roll, which features banana, yuzu mango sauce and soy leaf. His low-carb cut'n'roll invention featuring surimi, avocado and carrots wrapped in cucumber is light and refreshing. Quick, creative Japanese eats.

★ Zuma

Gate Village 6 (04 425 5660, www.zumarestaurant. com). Metro Emirates Towers. **Open** 12.30-3.30pm, 7pm-12.45am daily. **Mains** Dhs200-Dhs250. **Map** p101 C3 ⓬ **Japanese**

A multiple award-winner and an established force at the highest echelons of Dubai's Japanese fine-dining scene, Zuma is a classy, contemporary and enormously popular hangout for the UAE's most affluent residents and visitors. It pulls in a regular lunchtime crowd, but it's in the evenings when this place really comes into its own. Each and every dish on the menu is consistently impeccable, from starters such as beef tataki and prawn and black cod gyoza to mains including yuzu pepper jumbo tiger prawns and spicy tenderloin, right through to the green tea desserts.

Cafés & Bars

Caramel

Unit 1, Building 3 (04 256 677, www.caramel group.com). Metro Emirates Towers. **Open** 11am-2am Mon-Thur, Sun; 7pm-2am Fri, Sat. **Map** p101 C3 ⓭

The name is a Las Vegas export, but this chic lounge-bar-restaurant is surprisingly elegant, low-lit and understated. It serves some truly great food, too, mainly bar bites such as the Kobe barbecue beef sliders and mac and cheese, but with a few posher dishes such as apple endive salad, *scarpetta rigatoni malenzane* and Cajun blackened shrimp. There may be a lengthy wait for a table.

No.5 Lounge & Bar

Ritz-Carlton DIFC, Gate Village (04 372 2323, www.ritzcarlton.com). Metro Financial Centre. **Open** 6pm-2am daily. **Map** p101 C3 ⓮

The standalone terrace, a relatively new addition to the otherwise pleasant but unremarkable No.5 Lounge, really makes this place worth a trek across town. Sitting a couple of floors up in the midst of DIFC's gleaming, angular high-rises, it feels remarkably spacious, offering a novel perspective by being neither on the ground floor nor at the top. Crucially, it's accessible via a walkway from DIFC, removing the need to ever step inside the hotel.

★ Gramercy

Precinct Building 3 (04 377 511, www.thegramercy bar.com). Metro Financial Centre. **Open** noon-2am daily. **Map** p101 C3 ⓯

The Gramercy has had a makeover that has taken it from 1920s New York speakeasy to an art deco Parisian bar. Food is still rooted in the gastropub style, with a British feel. You'll find proper fish and chips with mushy peas here, as well as brilliant burgers. There's an extensive selection of cocktails and craft beers from around the world. There's a good after-work atmosphere during the week and regular live music nights.

Shops & Services

Bespoke

Shop 8, Level B1, The Gate (04 363 7237, www.bespoke.ae). Metro Emirates Towers. **Open** 10am-8pm Mon-Thur, Sun. **Map** p101 B3 ⑯ **Tailor**

This tailor is a little more expensive than those in Satwa or Bur Dubai, but you'll receive a well-cut suit that's fitted to a T. The service from the Parmar family is consistently excellent.

Cobbler

Marble Walk, Gate Building (04 386 3490, www.cobbler.ae). Metro Emirates Towers. **Open** 9am-7pm Mon-Thur, Sun; 9am-6pm Sat. **Map** p101 B3 ⑰ **Shoe repairs**

An old-school cobbler specialising in traditional repairs, shoe care and patina, as well as bespoke business shoes and gentlemen's accessories.

SHEIKH ZAYED ROAD

This stretch of skyscrapers from the World Trade Centre roundabout to the flyover for Dubai Mall features some of the city's biggest hotels and a plethora of restaurants and bars. Despite being situated either side of a mammoth motorway, it's actually one of the easiest parts of the city to walk around. While cars hurtle along the Sheikh Zayed Road towards Sharjah in one direction and Abu Dhabi in the other, pedestrians are kept a safe distance away on service roads lined with everything from coffee shops to spas.

You'll find some of the city's most extravagant establishments along this stretch, including the zebra print-clad monument to excess that is **Cavalli Club, Restaurant & Lounge**, plus the all-singing, all-dancing cabaret restaurant the **Act** and the weird and wonderful world of **Cirque Le Soir** (for both, *see p200*).

See even more of the glitzy side of Dubai while browsing the high-end stores of **Jumeirah Emirates Towers Boulevard**, or let your hair down with a night at two expat favourites: **Fibber Magee's**, or **Rodeo Drive** for an altogether different vibe.

Restaurants

Al Fresco

Crowne Plaza Dubai, Sheikh Zayed Road (04 331 1111, www.crowneplaza.com/dubai). Metro Emirates Towers. **Open** noon-11pm daily. **Main courses** Dhs50-Dhs130. **Map** p101 B4 ⑱ **Italian**

Although the dated decor of this small eaterie is in need of a revamp, the food is certainly up to scratch. There's a comforting, home-cooked quality to simple Italian dishes such as a sharing plate of assorted cold cuts served with crisp, buttery rosemary fried bread, pickles and aged balsamic vinegar. Sadly, there's not much buzz about the place and diners are mostly made up of single hotel guests, but its quiet, friendly atmosphere does create the perfect setting for a peaceful catch-up with friends.

Alfie's

Jumeirah Emirates Towers, Sheikh Zayed Road (04 319 8088). Metro Emirates Towers. **Open** noon-3pm, 7pm-midnight daily. **Main courses** Dhs70-Dhs190. **Map** p101 B4 ⑲ **British/international**

A proper British den of fish and chips plus all the trimmings, with art deco styling, a retro feel and a separate cigar room. The menu allows some influences from elsewhere – a little Mexican here, some Thai there – but the establishment prides itself on British classics and lots of manly things cooked in a manly manner on the grill. Prices are good, too, with frequent deals. Just make sure you save room for pudding. The apple crumble is a knockout.

★ Alta Badia

Jumeirah Emirates Towers, Sheikh Zayed Road (04 366 5866, www.jumeirah.com). Metro Emirates Towers. **Open** noon-3pm, 6pm-midnight Mon-Thur, Sat, Sun; 6pm-midnight Fri. **Main courses** Dhs150-Dhs220. **Map** p101 B4 ⑳ **Italian**

This restaurant's USP is its view. Perched on the 50th floor of Jumeirah Emirates Towers and looking out towards the Gulf coast, the view is breathtaking day or night. Food served in the classy, white-table-clothed dining room is northern Italian and inspired by traditional recipes. You'll find burrata, gnocchi and pasta dishes, as well as meat and fish mains. Scallops are perfectly cooked and come with creamy butternut squash and wild mushrooms. Another standout is the rich oxtail ravioli, which comes with a creamy parmesan sauce and fragrant black truffle. For a romantic Italian meal, you won't find much better in Dubai.

Benjarong

Dusit Thani Dubai, Sheikh Zayed Road (04 343 3333, www.dusit.com). Metro Financial Centre. **Open** noon-3pm, 7-11.30pm daily. **Main courses** Dhs70-Dhs250. **Map** p101 C1 ㉑ **Thai**

As perhaps the best-known Thai hotel chain, there's a fair amount of expectation that accompanies a visit to the Dusit Thani's signature restaurant, Benjarong. But in Dubai, they get just about everything right. The venue looks, and more importantly feels, great – the ornate but restrained colonial-tinged decor has an understated charm, elegant without being glitzy, creating the vibe of a family-run joint rather than a global hotel chain. And the somewhat safe menu is lifted by the fact that the kitchen faultlessly delivers the goods. Kick off with the *khong wang ruammit* appetiser platter, then dive into one of the classic curries, and you won't go wrong. Extra touches such as magnificent views of the cityscape from the venue's 24th-floor location, an impressive mixed drinks selection and an authentic live music duo playing traditional Thai music seal the deal.

Alta Badia.

Cavalli Club, Restaurant & Lounge

Fairmont Hotel, Sheikh Zayed Road (04 332 9260, http://dubai.cavalliclub.com). Metro World Trade Centre. **Open** 9.30pm-3am Mon-Sat; 9pm-3am Sun. *Food served* 9.30-11.30pm Mon-Sat; 9-11pm Sun. **Main courses** Dhs200-Dhs350. **Map** p101 A5 ㉒ **Italian**

From the zebra-print elevator to the sparkling chandeliers, everything about this venue is set out to dazzle. Inspired by the Italian designer with a penchant for flashy designs, there's more zebra print on the chairs and crockery with monochromatic motifs. The venue is also a club and so a reasonable choice if you're going on to a night on the dancefloor. Unfortunately, the menu doesn't excite half as much as the decor or the DJs. It is a simple, modern Italian menu with a selection of risottos and pastas alongside some meat or fish main courses. Portions are small, though very neatly presented. *Photo p106.*

ET Sushi

The Boulevard, Jumeirah Emirates Towers (04 366 5866, www.jumeirah.com)). Metro Emirates Towers. **Open** noon-11.30pm Mon-Thur, Sun; noon-3pm, 7-11.30pm Fri, Sat. **Sushi & sashimi** Dhs25-Dhs125. **Map** p101 B4 ㉓ **Japanese**

Like many of Emirates Towers Boulevard's eateries, ET Sushi is a swish and handy spot for a business lunch or midweek meal, rather than a destination restaurant. There's a conveyor belt with a good variety of sushi and sashimi – we like the crisp and light soft-shell crab tempura and the gloriously soft yellowtail sashimi – as well as a menu featuring some more high-end Japanese dishes. A refreshing fruit mochi is a good way to round off a meal.

Exchange Grill

Fairmont Dubai, Sheikh Zayed Road (04 311 8316, www.fairmont.com/dubai). Metro World Trade Centre. **Open** 7pm-midnight daily. **Main courses** Dhs200-Dhs500. **Map** p101 A5 ㉔ **Steakhouse**

In the sleek setting of this New York-themed restaurant, with black leather seats and moody lighting, you'll find chunky steaks alongside daintier starters and sides. Presentation is impressive: the crab cake starter is a light way to kick off the meal, and is served with a small parcel of cream cheese topped with caviar. Steaks, too, look the part, with clean presentation, from the petite fillet mignon options up to larger cuts for hungry carnivores. The odd dish misses the mark but many are close to perfection. The second-floor restaurant doesn't have views.

Hakkasan

Jumeirah Emirates Towers, Sheikh Zayed Road (04 384 8484, www.hakkasan.com). Metro Emirates Towers. **Open** noon-4pm, 7pm-1am daily. **Main courses** Dhs140-Dhs300. **Map** p101 B4 ㉕ **Contemporary Chinese**

Cavalli Club, Restaurant & Lounge. *See p105.*

It's the dimly lit, sexy ambience and private booth seating that draw diners to this London import, as much as the excellent contemporary Chinese food. Despite being expensive, tables are booked in two-hour slots, but the dining experience here means it's still a popular choice for special occasions. The menu lists extravagant delicacies such as peking duck with royal beluga caviar and braised Japanese abalone. Slightly less pricey, the Hakka dim sum platter features pristinely fresh dumplings of scallop, prawn and chive and sea bass. Crispy duck salad with pomelo, pine nut and shallots is crunchy and more-ish, the citrus offsetting the fattiness of the duck. There are novel takes on standard Chinese dishes, too, including sesame prawn toast with foie gras.

Hoi An

Shangri-La Dubai, Sheikh Zayed Road (04 405 2703, www.shangri-la.com). Metro Emirates Towers, Financial Centre. **Open** 7pm-midnight daily. **Main courses** Dhs130-Dhs150. **Map** p101 B1 ㉖ **Vietnamese**

Hoi An is named after the coastal trading city in central Vietnam. The name apparently translates as 'peaceful meeting place', which is a pretty fair description of this warm, cosy space on the first floor of the Shrangri-La. The service can be a little scatter-shot but is always cheery, and waitresses are likely to recommend one of the set menus, a great way for a single diner to sample a selection of appetisers and mains, as well as soup and dessert. Nice touches such as amuse-bouches and palate-cleansing sorbets help put Hoi An a step above the competition.

Ivy

The Boulevard, Jumeirah Emirates Towers, Sheikh Zayed Road (04 319 8767, www.theivydubai.ae). Metro Emirates Towers. **Open** 8am-11pm Mon-Wed, Sun; 9am-11.30pm Fri; 9am-11pm Sat. **Mains** Dhs140-Dhs260. **Map** p101 B4 ㉗ **British**

Shipped in wholesale from Covent Garden, the Ivy Dubai does suffer by comparison when it comes to the walk up – whereas in London it's hidden away on a backstreet, here in Dubai it is to be found amid the retail glitz of Jumeirah Emirates Towers. That it makes up for this discrepancy is down to some excellent staff (with all of the Ivy brand's cheeky politeness), identikit decor of stained glass, wood panelling and discreet booths, as well as the same comfort food favourites that have made its sister gaff such a go-to spot for famished famous folk. The Ivy is all about long afternoons filled with shepherd's pie, calf's liver, and a proper taste of England. And boy, does it deliver on its promise.

Marco Pierre White Grill

Conrad Dubai, Sheikh Zayed Road (04 444 7444, http://conradhotels3.hilton.com).

Metro World Trade Centre. **Open** 5.30pm-midnight daily. **Mains** Dhs120-Dhs300. **Map** p101 B5 ㉘ **Modern European**
Often packed to the rafters, Marco Pierre White's second launch (opened in 2013) is still going great guns, despite high prices. Situated on the mezzanine of the Conrad Dubai's glamorous golden lobby, it's an atmospherically lit den of decadence, the flames of the open grill occasionally illuminating darkened corners. The food – mainly from the grill – varies wildly in terms of quality. Try, for instance, the terrific roast bone marrow to start. Lobster, on the other hand, is less successful. Save room for the brilliant puddings.

Al Nafoorah

Jumeirah Emirates Towers, Sheikh Zayed Road (04 319 8088, www.jumeirah.com). Metro Emirates Towers. **Open** noon-4pm, 7pm-midnight daily. **Main courses** Dhs60-Dhs300. **Map** p101 B4 ㉙ **Arabic**
At the Emirates Towers branch of this restaurant, the ambience is set by musicians playing on the terrace that overlooks the space-age towers. Meze dishes are fresh and zingy: the Al Nafoorah salad is a crisp and refreshing mix of cucumbers, tomatoes, lettuce, green chilli, mint, parsley and lemon vinaigrette. For Lebanese dining in an impressive setting that won't break the bank, Al Nafoorah is a good choice.
Other location Jumeirah Zabeel Saray, Palm Jumeirah (04 453 0444).

Okku

The H Dubai, Sheikh Zayed Road (04 501 8777, www.okku.com). Metro World Trade Centre. **Open** noon-3pm, 7pm-12.30am Mon-Thur, Sun; 7pm-12.30am Fri, Sat. **Main courses** Dhs120-Dhs450. **Map** p101 B6 ㉚ **Japanese**
Long one of Dubai's coolest nocturnal haunts, Okku is a swish, stylish nightspot knocking out excellent food. While the crowds may pour in on Thursday and Friday nights for fancy drinks and moody surroundings, there's no need to reserve your sampling of this Japanese fusion fare only for the weekends. Throughout the week, the restaurant-lounge is open for lunch as well as dinner, with an excellent-value tezukuri lunch. Try the ebi gyoza to start, and stick with the seafood theme for mains – the black cod donburi is delicate yet filling, not to mention fantastically tasty. If you're just around for nibbles, order the organic salmon carpaccio, tender slivers of the Scottish fish layered with daikon cress, cherry tomatoes and an intriguing shiso-yuzu pesto. Warm-hearted service is the icing on the cake. Okku may be stylish, but it's not too cool to show you a good time.

Rib Room

Jumeirah Emirates Towers, Sheikh Zayed Road (04 366 5866, www.jumeirah.com). Metro Emirates Towers. **Open** noon-3pm, 6pm-midnight Mon-Thur, Sun; 6pm-midnight Fri, Sat. **Main courses** Dhs150-Dhs550. **Map** p101 C4 ㉛ **Steakhouse**
Despite being located off the lobby in Jumeirah Emirates Towers, the Rib Room feels secluded and exclusive. The dark interior is stylish and spacious, with cushioned seating lining the walls and tables filling the centre of the space. When it gets busy – and it often does – the atmosphere is buzzing and it feels like the place to be. Its popularity comes down to its hearty steaks. There are grain-fed American, Australian and Canadian cuts as well as grass-fed Argentinian steaks, while ribeye, striploin and tenderloin are the choicest cuts. Seafood-lovers are catered for, to a degree, especially when it comes to starters; there's also a concise choice of seafood mains. It's worth saving space for dessert, especially the creamy banana parfait with dulce de leche.
Other location Jumeirah Zabeel Saray, Palm Jumeirah (453 0444).

Shang Palace

Shangri-La Hotel, Sheikh Zayed Road (04 279 0302). Metro Financial Centre. **Open** 12.30-3pm, 7pm-midnight Mon-Fri, Sun; 11am-3pm, 7pm-midnight Sat. **Sharing plates** Dhs50-Dhs200. **Map** p101 B1 ㉜ **Chinese**
If you're looking for a decent Chinese meal between Deira and New Dubai, where most of the city's Far Eastern restaurants are located, Shang Palace should be high on your list. It may not have the hip vibe of its DIFC competitor, Royal China (*see p103*), but with its traditional decor, round-table dining room and quality food, the experience feels

authentic. The mixed appetiser platter is ideal for sharing and a nice prelude for what's to come: the likes of small servings of barbecued chicken, marinated jellyfish with spicy sauce, chilled cucumber and beef short ribs. The peking duck is carved and rolled into pancakes for you at the table, courtesy of a chatty server. There is also a variety of claypot dishes on the menu, including king scallop with asparagus and black truffle, and aubergine with shrimp in spicy sauce.

Tokyo@thetowers

The Boulevard, Jumeirah Emirates Towers, Sheikh Zayed Road (04 366 5866, www.jumeirah.com). Metro Emirates Towers. **Open** noon-3pm, 7-11.30pm daily. **Main courses** Dhs50-Dhs125. **Map** p101 C4 ㉝ **Japanese**

Tucked away upstairs in the Emirates Towers Boulevard shopping mall, Tokyo@thetowers serves up enjoyable teppanyaki with a little light acrobatics from the chefs. Want to be right where all the action is? Pull up a chair at the teppanyaki tables to watch food and utensils fly into the air before making it on to your plate, or sit cross-legged at one of the tatami tables for a more secluded vibe.

Tresind

Radisson Royal Hotel Dubai, Sheikh Zayed Road (04 308 0440, www.tresind.com). Metro World Trade Centre. **Open** noon-3pm, 7pm-midnight daily. **Main courses** Dhs100-Dhs160. **Map** p101 B4 ㉞ **Contemporary Indian**

Tresind promises not just modern, but 'modernist' Indian cooking. It's in a space to match (one that has already seen at least two other concepts come and go within the past few years). Tresind has kept the same clean white interiors as the last Arabic venture, but still feels fresh and new, with hardly any extra detailing compromising its minimalist look. Food is ambitious and intriguing, without being pretentious and – for the most part – exceptionally elegant in both appearance and taste. Bearing that in mind, it's not unduly expensive.

Zaroob

Jumeirah Tower, Sheikh Zayed Road (04 327 6060, www.zaroob.com). Metro Financial Centre. **Open** 24 hours daily. **Main courses** Dhs10-Dhs30. **Map** p101 B3 ㉟ **Arabic**

Something different for Dubai: graffiti covers corrugated iron lining the walls and manga-style cartoon characters decorate the ceiling. Thanks to the delectable dishes on offer for astoundingly low prices, this cool comic book-style Lebanese street food restaurant is perennially packed with all kinds of patrons, from businesspeople in suits to expats and students from around the world. Zaroob serves outstanding, fresh and juicy shawarmas for a nominal Dhs10, as well as other light bites and sandwiches. It's well worth a visit – even if you have to wait a while for a table.

Cafés & Bars

For bar-restaurant-nightclub hybrid **Amika**, *see p196*. Dinner-cabaret venue the **Act** and circus-style bar and club **Cirque du Soir** (for both, *see p200*) both offer entertainment alongside food and drinks.

★ 40 Kong

The H Dubai, Sheikh Zayed Road (04 355 8896, www.40kong.com). Metro World Trade Centre. **Open** 6pm-3am daily. **Map** p101 B6 ㊱

Asian-themed rooftop lounge 40 Kong is the last word in style and chic. It's also among the tallest outdoor terraces in the city, hovering amid Sheikh Zayed Road's towering skyscrapers. While you're likely to need a table reservation to bag the best views, it's the meticulous service, mixed drinks and good vibes that will keep this on the cool list for years to come. There's good food, too, with an international menu offering dishes such as beef tartare, lobster crostini, veal rack and sea bass alongside classic wagyu mini burgers.

Bapas

The H Dubai, Sheikh Zayed Rood (04 385 8881, www.bapas-online.com). Metro World Trade Centre. **Open** noon-1am Mon-Thur, Sun; 11.30am-3am Fri, Sat. **Map** p101 B6 ㊲

Claiming to offer a Belgian take on tapas – geddit? – Bapas is a classy Downtown bar that is as focused

Fibber Magee's.

on the dining as it is on the drinking. So expect top-notch bar bites, classic mussels and the like. Not that the drinks disappoint, with a great range of beer, Belgian and otherwise, and a notable wine cellar. Dark and intimate on week nights but healthily buzzing at the weekend, Bapas snugly fills the gaping gap between pub and upmarket lounge, and is a great place to catch up with friends.

Fibber Magee's

Behind Saeed Tower One, Sheikh Zayed Road (04 332 3100, www.fibbersdubai.com). Metro World Trade Centre. **Open** 8am-2am daily. **Map** p101 B4 38

A longstanding institution of the emirate, there are legions of Dubai expats who won't let you utter a bad word about good ole Fibber's. The city isn't short of Irish-themed drinking holes, and everyone has a favourite, but the small scale, hearty grub, timeless feel and rich history of this place mean it's probably the most authentic of the bunch. And if you're hungry, you're in luck, as portions are huge, especially the steak and mushroom pie, which features chunky lumps of meat in a rich gravy under a puff pastry topping.

Oscar's Vine Society

Crowne Plaza Hotel Dubai, Sheikh Zayed Road (04 331 1111, www.ihg.com). Metro World Trade Centre. **Open** 6pm-midnight daily. **Map** p101 B4 39

One of the oldest wine bars in the city, Oscar's Vine Society ignores the current trend for chic chrome modernism in favour of the other cliché – the rustic French watering hole. Of course, the chances of recreating provincial France on the fourth floor of a Sheikh Zayed Road hotel are minimal. Which is why the floral tablecloths, vintage bike, chalkboards, stone floor and ceiling-tall wall painting of a French boulangerie are ridiculous enough to feel kitsch rather than contrived. Oozing soul, with friendly staff, good food and a decent cellar, Oscar's is a breath of fresh air.

Rodeo Drive

Next to Radisson Royal Hotel, Sheikh Zayed Road (04 386 9617). Metro World Trade Centre. **Open** 6pm-3am daily. **Map** p101 B4 40

Swap your diamonds for denims and prepare for a riotous ride at this haunt behind Sheikh Zayed Road. The American bar has gained plenty of fans for its emphasis on fun and entertainment – specifically of the raucous frat-party variety. Sitting centre stage, slap bang in the middle of the room, is a bucking bronco (free to every punter, all you need to do is sign a waiver), while there are separate areas dedicated to every college kid's favourite sport – think ping-pong balls and plastic cups of beer (there's even an open beer pong tournament). The drinks menu features an impressive range of shorts and great deals almost every night of the week. But while the bargains may

EXPLORE

IN THE KNOW
CATCH A SHOW AT DWTC

With its huge conference halls and performance spaces, Dubai World Trade Centre is one of the biggest venues in the city. Major artists who have performed here include British comedians Jack Dee and John Bishop; *Disney on Ice* and *The Illusionists* have been staged here; and it has hosted sports events from kickboxing to five-a-side football championships. During major international sporting events, such as the FIFA World Cup, one of the centre's exhibition halls is turned into a dedicated venue with big screens, comfy seating, shisha and a restaurant service. Exhibitions and conventions play a major role in the life of DWTC. Among the most popular are the Middle East Film and Comic Con, which usually takes place in April and celebrates cult entertainment and popular culture. During Ramadan, part of the centre is turned into the Majlis, which serves *iftar* and *suhour* in an Arabesque setting. There's a Ramadan night market too.

be available daily, this place only really gets going towards the tail end of the week.

Shops & Services

Jumeirah Emirates Towers Boulevard

Jumeirah Emirates Towers, Sheikh Zayed Road (04 319 8732, www.jumeirah.com). Metro Emirates Towers. **Open** 10am-10pm Mon-Thur, Sat, Sun; 4-10pm Fri (most shops). **Map** p101 C4 41 **Mall**

Quiet and exclusive, with a string of expensive designer boutiques, this mall is good for window shopping even if you can't afford to buy. You'll find the likes of Bvlgari, Cartier and Rivoli here, among other big names.

► *If you start to get hungry, Hakkasan (see p105), the Ivy (see p106) and Tokyo@thetowers (see p108) are all located here.*

DUBAI WORLD TRADE CENTRE

Heading away from Downtown and north towards the older part of town is Dubai World Trade Centre, a major exhibition and conference space next to Sheikh Zayed Road. Big events take place here all year round, from trade shows to music gigs (*see above* **In the Know**). There are a couple of restaurants and bars in the vicinity, but it's also just a stone's throw from venues in bustling Sheikh Zayed Road and the DIFC.

Restaurants

Options by Sanjeev Kapoor

Convention Tower, Dubai World Trade Centre (04 444 6488, www.sanjeevkapoor.com). Metro World Trade Centre. **Open** noon-2.30pm, 7-11pm daily. **Main courses** Dhs100-Dhs200. **Map** p101 C5 42 **Indian**

If you like your venues filled with shiny things, hanging things and lots of paraphernalia, you'll appreciate the opulent Options. What you order – or, if our experience is anything to go by, what your waiter chooses for you – is likely to be good: we particularly like the seafood platter starter, which can be shared by two; it comes with two kinds of prawn, tandoori salmon, lobster and fried white fish, all perfectly marinated in a variety of flavours. From the mains, the smoky goat curry and creamy chicken tikka curry also hit the spot, both rich and packed with flavour. Options is a full-on experience – from the service and ambience to the food.

Other location Mövenpick Hotel Deira, Deira (04 444 6488).

Cafés & Bars

Blue Bar

Novotel World Trade Centre Dubai, Sheikh Zayed Road (04 332 0000, www.novotel.com). Metro World Trade Centre. **Open** noon-2am daily. **Map** p101 C5 43

A cosy, dimly lit venue modelled on a European jazz bar, with guitars and saxophones on the wall, the Blue Bar is one of the few places in town where music truly takes priority. There are bands every Thursday, Friday and Saturday – these days leaning towards rock, pop and funk over jazz, but still among the best in the city – and if you stop by on weeknights expect to be entertained by the bar's library of cool and credible gig DVDs, with favourites including Dizzy Gillespie and David Gilmour. It's well priced, too, with good drinks promotions and decent food, while staff are warm and friendly.

McGettigan's DWTC

Dubai World Trade Centre, Sheikh Zayed Road (04 378 0800, www.mcgettigans.com). Metro World Trade Centre. **Open** noon-2am Mon-Thur, Sat, Sun; 2pm-2am Fri. **Map** p101 B5 44

With its relaxed pub vibe and warm welcome, this spot is busy all week – even at weekends when the surrounding offices are empty. It's a top spot to hear quality acoustic covers from some of the city's best singers and musicians, and on match days it's a great place to watch live sport. With a real community feel and quirky promotions – check social media for one-offs, such as football-themed freebies depending on who scores – this is hands down one of the best pubs in the city.

Other location Bonnington Hotel, Jumeirah Lakes Towers (04 356 0000).

GALLERY-HOPPING GUIDE

The DIFC is home to some of the city's finest contemporary art galleries.

Ayyam Gallery *Podium Level, Gate Village 3 (04 323 6242, www.ayyamgallery.com).* **Open** 10am-6pm Mon-Thur, Sat, Sun.
This Syrian gallery features contemporary art collections with a focus on Damascus. There are regular exhibitions and permanent installations. Check the website for the latest information.
Other location Ayyam Art Centre, Alserkal Avenue, Al Quoz (04 323 6242).

Cuadro *Gate Village 10 (04 425 0400, www.cuadroart.com).* **Open** 10am-8pm Mon-Thur, Sun; noon-6pm Sat.
A gallery with a focus on international art, Cuadro hosts curated exhibitions and residencies, as well as offering education and consultation services. The exhibitions are wide-ranging and the artists-in-residence are a mixture of local and international, which makes for an intriguing collection of work.

Opera Gallery *Gate Village 3 (04 323 0909, www.operagallery.com).* **Open** 10am-10pm Mon-Thur, Sun; 4.30-11pm Fri, noon-11pm Sat.
Shows works by world-famous artists, such as Salvador Dalí and Andy Warhol, plus contemporary greats from China and elsewhere. The regular exhibitions are carefully curated.

RIRA Gallery *Gate Village 3 (04 369 9339, www.riragallery.com).* **Open** 10am-8pm Mon-Thur, Sun; noon-6pm Sat.
The RIRA Gallery maintains a focus on Iranian contemporary artists, with a roster of monthly exhibitions.

Empty Quarter *Gate Village 2 (04 323 1210, www.theemptyquarter.com).* **Open** 10am-10pm Mon-Thur, Sun; 2-8pm Sat.
Dedicated to photography, with a flexible space and decent library. The Empty Quarter promotes young and emerging photographers through various mediums, including fine art and street photography. Its range of essays, documentaries and books is a great resource.

Jumeirah & Satwa

Just half a century ago, Jumeirah was a fishing village several kilometres outside Dubai. It developed southwards from Satwa's borders, and the oldest part, known as Jumeirah 1, remains one of the most desirable addresses in Dubai. The city's first chic malls and coffee shops were here, and it's still popular with those with plenty of leisure time and in search of a latte or a manicure (often known as Jumeirah Janes). Some Western residents refer to it, with tongue firmly in cheek, as the Beverly Hills of Dubai. Along the Jumeirah Beach Road, Jumeirah Mosque is one of the city's most striking, and the only one in the emirate to allow non-Muslims to have a peek inside, as part of a guided tour. Also here are various malls, the shameful Dubai Zoo and several public beaches. Neighbouring Satwa is bustling with street life, restaurants and a mishmash of nationalities that make up this lively community.

BoxPark.

Don't Miss

1 Kite Beach Prime stretch of sand with a focus on watersports (p114).

2 Ravi Restaurant Excellent, affordable Pakistani food (p125).

3 Jumeirah Mosque Fine modern Islamic architecture and guided tours (p117).

4 BoxPark Cutting-edge fashion (p122).

5 Jumeirah Fishing Harbour Eclectic dining at the water's edge (p116).

ينظر المرء ما قدمت يداه ويقول الكافر يا ليتني كنت ترابا

JUMEIRAH & AROUND

Jumeirah is tricky to access by public transport. There are four metro stops – Noor Bank, Business Bay, Financial Centre and Burj Khalifa Dubai Mall – from where it's easiest to catch a taxi to your destination. For Jumeirah 3 alight at Noor Bank; for Jumeirah 2 and areas surrounding Safa Park alight at Business Bay; for Jumeirah 1 head to Financial Centre or Burj Khalifa Dubai Mall. From there, a taxi should cost around Dhs15-Dhs20.

In many ways, Jumeirah epitomises the stereotype of the Dubai lifestyle. The neighbourhood is associated with affluent expat families and life tends to consist of mums' coffee mornings, lazy lunches, shopping and afternoon visits to the many parks, beaches and salons that populate the area. It's no surprise that Four Seasons Hotels (*see p279*) chose it as the location for its Dubai property.

Jumeirah is serviced by two main roads: Jumeirah Beach Road, which runs along the coast, and Al Wasl Road, which runs parallel a few blocks inland. A haphazard network of streets lined with luxury villas links the two. Development grew outwards from around here, and left from those early days, lining the beaches, are a number of small, quaint bungalows in picturesque little clusters. These are predominantly Emirati homes and are virtually impossible to get hold of, for either rent or purchase. The area is also the locale of **Jumeirah Mosque**, the only one in Dubai to allow non-Muslims inside for guided tours. **Majlis Ghorfat Umm Al Sheif**, also open to visitors, began life as a 20th-century royal retreat and a place where the royal family heard petitions from their subjects.

The Jumeirah lifestyle can seem very LA. Head to somewhere like **Comptoir 102**, which is minutes from the beach, and you'll find hordes of health-conscious, early-morning-beach-yoga types loading up on buckwheat pancakes, avocado scrambled eggs and activated charcoal lemon juices (yes, this is a genuine health craze), while browsing through the high-end jewellery and furniture on display in this concept store-cum-café.

Jumeirah is home to some prime beach stretches, and the **Corniche** project (*see p117* **In the Know**) allows the public to stroll along much of the shoreline. **Kite Beach** (www.thekitebeach.com) is one of the city's biggest. Beach games and watersports rule at weekends, when the water is dotted with stand-up

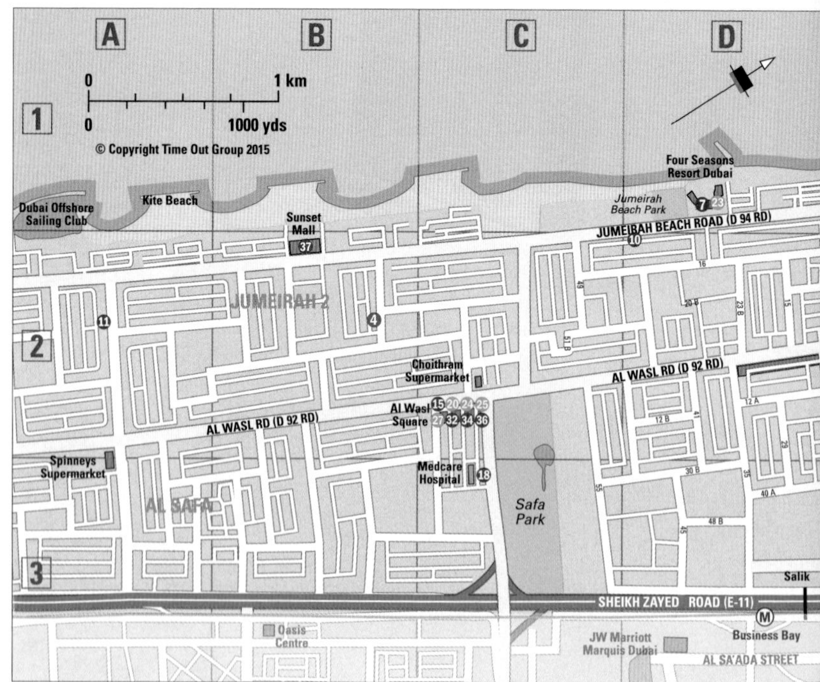

paddleboarders, kitesurfers and the occasional surfer on the rare occasion that there is enough swell. There are multiple stalls, vendors and beachfront eateries here too. Paddleboards are available for rent for Dhs35 per hour, and beach tennis – a fusion of beach volleyball and tennis – is also popular. **Beach Tennis ME** (055 268 6090, www.btmesports.com) has a great set-up. You can take a lesson in the sport or grab your mates and hire a sandy court to play a few matches. Kitesurfing is exhilarating once you get the hang of it and **DuKite** (050 758 6992, www.dukite.com) offers lessons and courses, and hires equipment. Food outlets that have set up shop on the beach include food truck SALT, which serves chicken or wagyu beef sliders from a retro silver van, and Egyptian seafood restaurant Barracuda's (04 394 0408, www.barracudarestaurant.net) for fresh and simply cooked fish.

If you head to the stretch of coast behind **Sunset Mall** there are a few little coves defined by small rocky breakwaters that are ripe for underwater exploration – just make sure you stay on the inside to avoid encounters with vessels.

In this chapter, we have also included some venues in the neighbouring inland residential districts of Al Wasl and Al Safa.

World Islands

The waters off Jumeirah are home to the famed World Islands. Much ado was made about this development way back when it was announced. For the time being, however, it's still a case of much ado about nothing. The islands (that roughly resemble a map of the world, if you squint from space) are still for the most part uninhabited, and only two are actually available to visit: Lebanon and Germany. If you really feel the need to check them out, the **Island** (050 617 6507, www.theisland.ae, Dhs300 adults, Dhs150 children, free under-5s, including boat transfer) on **Lebanon Island** has its own beach club with a pool, volleyball court, bar, restaurant and two beaches, where you can spend the day. It hosts a Friday brunch, but your money would be better spent elsewhere at one of the city's award-winning Friday events (*see p145* **Party Brunches**).

Dubai Tourism & Travel Services runs a boat tour to **Germany Island**, which takes you along the coast past the Burj Al Arab and Jumeirah Beach Hotel. Once on the island, a sign reads 'Willkommen in Deutschland', and that's about it. After a few pictures, it's time to head back. At Dhs475 per person – including light refreshments – you'd be better off booking a yacht charter

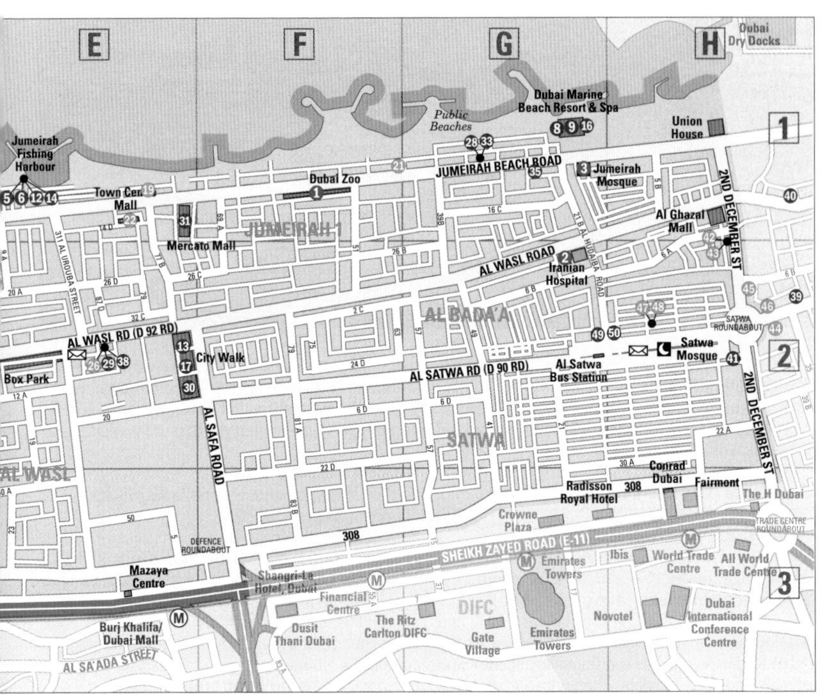

EXPLORE

JUMEIRAH FISHING HARBOUR

Take your pick from this eclectic bunch of waterfront restaurants.

This little dining district may only house a handful of venues, but there's a lot of variety here, from Thai or Indian to vegan desserts.

Mint Leaf (*see p119*), not to be confused with DIFC-based Indian Mint Leaf of London, serves classic Indian food amid pale walls, white furnishings, colourful glass chandeliers and hammered brass lanterns. **Charm** (*see p117*) is a Thai restaurant with 360-degree views of the surrounding coast and relatively affordable classic Thai food. Brazilian café **Boteko Brasil** (*see p117*), meanwhile, has a few intriguing, unusual items on the menu, such as a gnocchi made with chickpeas rather than potato and served with Brazilian favourite *carne seca* (sundried beef).

But the restaurant that has attracted the most attention is **Omnia Gourmet** (04 343 7181, www.omniagourmet.co). This is largely down to the fact that well-known chef Silvena Rowe is at the helm. At her café-deli, the concept is farm-fresh, healthy food. Most ingredients are sourced from within the region, including UAE-produced burrata, which is served with locally grown heirloom tomatoes. Most dishes are gluten-free, while desserts are all sugar-free, and some are vegan or for those on a raw-food diet.

(*see p167* **All Aboard**). Alternatively, book the World Journey flight tour with Seawings (www.seawings.ae, Dhs1,895 per person) and see the islands from the air, along with fabulous views of the city coastline.

Sights & Attractions

Dubai Zoo

Jumeirah Beach Road, Jumeirah 1 (04 349 6444). **Open** 10am-5pm Mon, Wed-Sun. **Admission** Dhs3. **No credit cards. Map** p115 F1 ❶

The animals at Dubai Zoo are the survivors, and progeny, of a private collection now owned by the Dubai Municipality. The conditions are shabby and animals enjoy little freedom. There are allegedly plans to relocate but, despite many promises over the years, there has been little action. There are lions, tigers, giraffes, bears, reptiles and birds, but it's up to your conscience whether or not you'd actually enjoy a visit.

Iranian Mosque

Al Wasl Road, Jumeirah 1, next to the Iranian Hospital. **Map** p115 G2 ❷

Sitated within the complex of the impressive Iranian Hospital – but visible from the road – Dubai's Iranian Mosque is covered in intricate blue mosaics with floral Persian motifs and Qur'anic calligraphy. The adjacent hospital is similarly decorated. Al Wasl Road runs right through the middle of the hospital complex, so you can get a good view of the mosque's exterior (entry is forbidden to non-Muslims).

★ Jumeirah Mosque

Jumeirah Beach Road, Jumeirah 1. **Tours** 10am Tue, Thur, Sat, Sun. **Admission** Dhs10. **No credit cards. Map** p115 G1 ❸

A fine example of modern Islamic architecture, and one of Dubai's most photographed sights, Jumeirah Mosque stands at the northern end of Jumeirah Beach Road. The Sheikh Mohammed Centre for Cultural Understanding (04 353 6666, smccu@emirates.net.ae) organises visits (no children under five). You'll walk through the mosque with a small group before putting questions to your guide about the building and the Islamic faith. You must wear modest clothing (no bare legs or arms, and women must cover their heads).

Majlis Ghorfat Umm Al Sheif

Jumeirah Beach Road, Jumeirah 3; look for brown heritage signposts when nearby (04 394 6343). **Open** 8.30am-1.30pm, 3.30-8.30pm Mon-Thur, Sat, Sun; 3.30-8.30pm Fri. **Admission** Dhs1. **No credit cards. Map** p114 B2 ❹

Built in 1955 in traditional style from coral and stone, this building was used by the late Sheikh Rashid bin Saeed Al Maktoum, the founder of modern Dubai, as a summer retreat and *majlis* – a place where he could hear the petitions of his subjects. The fact that many of the plans for modern Dubai were probably hatched in such a simple structure, by a man who had known nothing of 20th-century luxury for most of his life, is remarkable.

Restaurants

Boteko Brasil

Jumeirah Fishing Harbour, Jumeirah 2 (600 562227, www.botekobrasil.com). **Open** 9am-10pm daily. **Main courses** Dhs20-Dhs50. **Map** p115 E1 ❺ **Brazilian**

See p116 **Jumeirah Fishing Harbour**.

Charm

Jumeirah Fishing Harbour, Jumeirah 2 (04 344 8895). **Open** noon-midnight daily. **Main courses** Dhs40-Dhs60. **Map** p115 E1 ❻ **Thai**

See p116 **Jumeirah Fishing Harbour**.

Coya

Four Seasons Resort Dubai at Jumeirah Beach, Jumeirah 2 (04 316 9600, www.coyarestaurant.com). **Open** noon-3pm, 7-10.30pm daily. **Main courses** Dhs80-Dhs500. **Map** p114 D1 ❼ **Peruvian**

The launch of Coya inside the Four Seasons Resort was highly anticipated in the wake of the success of the London opening. The place certainly looks the part: the main dining room has wow-factor dimensions and is sumptuously decorated in wood, leather, stone and metal (walls have a distressed metallic sheen). The Peruvian cuisine is of a high standard: red snapper ceviche is a lovely balance of heady truffle and sharp, fresh yuzu; and the prettily plated scallop tiradito is as delicate and elegant in appearance as taste. Shame the service wasn't up to scratch on a recent visit: the two-hour time slot, not mentioned at time of booking, was particularly annoying.

Flooka

Dubai Marine Beach Resort & Spa, Jumeirah 1 (04 346 1111, www.flooka.com). **Open** 12.30-3.30pm, 7-11.45pm Mon-Thur, Sun; noon-11.45pm Fri, Sat. **Main courses** prices vary. **Map** p115 G1 ❽ **Seafood**

With views of the beach and light-wood decor, Flooka has a relaxed coastal feel. Aside from the Arabic and Mediterranean à la carte options, there's a selection of fresh fish, lobster and prawns displayed on ice at the front of the restaurant. Staff are quick to take orders here, but they're sometimes lacking when asked for more information about the menu. If you choose to go à la carte, portion sizes are generous; it's a bit of a mixed bag when it comes to quality, though.

★ Loca

Dubai Marine Beach Resort & Spa, Jumeirah 1 (04 346 1111, www.locauae.com). **Open** noon-midnight daily. **Main courses** Dhs60-Dhs160. **Map** p115 G1 ❾ **Mexican**

Loca is probably better known as a watering hole and nightspot rather than a restaurant, but bag a table on the periphery of the noisy hubbub and you'll be able to enjoy some good Mexican food. As is the trend in Dubai, guacamole is prepared tableside, and the creamy texture and mildly spicy flavour is a good indication of what is to come: nothing too adventurous or imaginative, but a 'better-than-pub-grub' meal. Fajitas sizzle at your table in six different flavours. It's the tacos, though, that stand out: served in a soft or hard shell, and generously accompanied with beans and rice, they're great for sharing. Loca

IN THE KNOW STROLLING THE CORNICHE

The Corniche is a Dhs100m project designed to revamp a 14-kilometre (8.5-mile) stretch of coastline, from Sunset Beach in Umm Suqeim, in the shadow of the Burj Al Arab, right down to the Dubai Marine Beach Resort & Spa in Jumeirah 1. Featuring a boardwalk and jogging track, the Corniche allows beachgoers to stroll almost uninterrupted – save for a small section between Jumeirah 1 and 2 where the strip is briefly broken between the new Four Seasons hotel down to Jumeirah Beach Park. Dotted along the route are showers, changing facilities, toilets, benches, shaded seating areas and small kiosks selling refreshments.

goes the extra mile with Mexican desserts such as fried ice-cream and banana empanada.

Manga Sushi

Beach Park Plaza, opposite Jumeirah Beach Park, Jumeirah Beach Road, Jumeirah 2 (04 342 8300). **Open** 11am-11.30pm Mon-Wed, Sat, Sun; 11am-1am Thur, Fri. **Sushi & sashimi** Dhs25-Dhs50. **Main courses** Dhs45-Dhs70. **Map** p114 D2 ⑩ **Japanese**

Head to this Japanese eaterie in Beach Park Plaza for some decidedly quirky manga-themed dining. From kitsch cartoon decor to the anime and wacky talent shows screened on the walls, the Japanese theming is all around you. And, really, it's what this place is all about. It's best to stick to the extensive array of sushi and sashimi to avoid disappointment when it comes to the food, as hot dishes tend not to be up to scratch, and service is slow too. A place to focus on the fun, rather than the food.

Maria Bonita's

Umm Al Sheif Street, Jumeirah 2 (04 395 5576, www.mariabonitadubai.com). **Open** noon-midnight daily. **Main courses** Dhs55-Dhs75. **Map** p114 A2 ⑪ **Mexican**

With its bright bunting, makeshift outdoor terrace and quirky vibe, this casual restaurant has the feel of a Mexican roadside diner. If you want your meal fried, covered in cheese and slopped with salsa and guacamole, then this is the place for you. It lacks the fast-food veneer of international Tex-Mex outlets around the city, and it's this originality and charm that has made it an enduring stalwart. The guacamole is freshly prepared at your table and whichever variety of wrap you opt for – steak, chicken or prawn – it'll come well stuffed and greasy. *Photo p120.*

Other location Green Community (04 885 3188).

Mint Leaf

Jumeirah Fishing Harbour, Jumeirah 2 (04 343 1651). **Open** 1-11pm daily. **Main courses** Dhs25-Dhs65. **Map** p115 E1 ⑫ **Indian**

See p116 **Jumeirah Fishing Harbour**.

Mo's

City Walk, Jumeirah 1 (04 344 3305, www.caramel group.com). **Open** 8am-midnight daily. **Main courses** Dhs55-Dhs85. **Map** p115 E2 ⑬ **Diner**

American diner-restaurant Mo's, like most of the venues in this area, offers plenty of outdoor seating, and inside looks like a fancy yet accessible American steakhouse. As one would expect, the menu runs to burgers, classic deli sandwiches and appetisers such as gravy-coated Tater Tots and 'crock of chilli'. Servers are helpful and friendly, and seem genuinely pleased to see diners enjoying their food.

★ Omnia Blue

Jumeirah Fishing Harbour, Jumeirah 2 (04 343 7339). **Open** noon-11pm daily. **Sliders** Dhs20-Dhs70. **Map** p115 E1 ⑭ **American**

Omnia Blue is the second venue to have opened under the Omnia umbrella, headed up by chef Silvena Rowe. An American menu of burgers and sliders are joined by US comfort-food favourites like mac 'n' cheese. The nautically themed room is decked out in blue and white stripes complete with driftwood on the ceiling and a ship's wheel hanging from the wall. The outdoor dining area faces directly on to the harbour. Burgers and sliders include a few Middle Eastern twists, plus locally caught lobster; there are also a few healthy eating elements, such as organic quinoa sliders. The Emirati lobster mac 'n' cheese was decadently rich and cheesy, its topping of almond and pistachio lending an Arabic – if rather oversweet – edge. It's fun, outdoors and different, but we couldn't say these are the best burgers in Dubai. Its prolific use of local lobster makes it stand out, though. *Photo p120.*

Smiling BKK

Al Wasl Square, Al Wasl Road, Al Wasl (04 349 6677, www.smilingbkk.com). **Main courses** Dhs35-Dhs95. **Open** 11am-midnight daily. **Map** p114 C2 ⑮ **Thai**

As any old Dubai hand will tell you, Smiling BKK is a bona fide piece of the emirate's dining history. But times have changed. Known for kooky pictures, ripped magazine pages and Thai tourist T-shirts lining every inch of wall, this is no longer the only independent eaterie exhibiting Western-tinged irony with reckless abandon. In fact, some of the venue's natural charm and relaxed vibe has been curbed. Still, the food remains decent: the classic red curry and tom yum are both hard to fault.

Other location 2nd Street, Garhoud (04 286 8060).

Sho Cho

Dubai Marine Beach Resort & Spa, Jumeirah 1 (04 346 1111, www.sho-cho.com). **Open** 7pm-3am Mon-Fri, Sun. *Last food orders* 11.45pm. **Map** p115 G1 ⑯ **Japanese**

Sho Cho's location, overlooking the sea at Dubai Marine Beach Resort, is stunning. The outdoor area is bathed in low, blue lighting and the place can be very romantic (though the tables may be a little too close together for a total romantic experience). Food isn't at all bad either: soft-shell crab spring rolls are a must-try starter; also good are the vegetable gyoza, the dumplings filled with shiitake mushrooms and fried until crispy; there's a wide selection of sushi and sashimi, and mainly fish-based mains – all with deliciously fresh fish. But really it's about location, location, location.

Y by Yabani

City Walk, Jumeirah 1 (04 344 3371, www.yabanirestaurants.com). **Open** noon-1am daily. **Sushi** Dhs30-85. **Map** p115 E2 ⑰ **Japanese**

Situated in the pedestrian-friendly alleyway of City Walk mall, you'll find this attractive-looking Japanese eaterie, born in Beirut, now with a branch in Dubai. Y by Yabani looks the epitome of Japanese style, with clean lines, bright interior and wooden tables. The menu focuses on sushi and sashimi, and includes some fusion, especially Peruvian, influences. Scallop *tiradito*, for example, is an elegant plate of pretty little scallop slices, simply topped with a red splotch of rocotto chilli and a single coriander leaf. From the wide selection of maki rolls, the crazy maki, with crabstick, mixed vegetables, tobiko and tempura crunch, is a tasty alternative to traditional sushi. The food may not represent the height of Japanese cuisine, but there's something very pleasant about the dining experience here.

Zurna

Wasl Square, Al Wasl Road, opposite Safa Park, Al Wasl (04 328 5043). **Open** noon-midnight Mon-Thur, Sun; 9am-1am Fri, Sat. **Map** p114 C3
18 **Turkish**

Zurna's simple menu of traditional Turkish fare includes wraps, kebabs, soup, meze dishes and salads. Also on the menu are dishes such as *ali nazik* – minced, grilled chicken served with spiced, chargrilled aubergine and a garlic yoghurt sauce. Zurna is a homely and friendly spot, but if you don't want to stop for long you can also pick up a selection of Turkish baked goods to take away, including sesame crusted Turkish bagels and tahina rolls.

Cafés & Bars

Biker's Café

Jumeirah Beach Road, near Mercato Mall, Jumeirah 1 (04 349 3585, www.bikerscafe.com). **Open** 7am-1am daily. **Map** p115 E1 19

This motorcycle-themed café in the bustling heart of Jumeirah offers an expansive menu to satisfy the appetites of road-weary bikers and the general public. The indoor and outdoor seating areas are pleasant and comfortable, and while the staff-recommended Biker Burger is not so good, the beef medallions are – that is if you're happy to wait quite some time for your order. There's a good range of desserts, though, like traditional Emirati *luqaimat* (sweet dumplings), with honey date syrup, and *khabees* (made with Emirati semolina, caramelised sugar and saffron).

BookMunch

Wasl Square, Al Wasl Road, Al Wasl (04 388 4006, www.bookmunchcafe.com). **Open** 7.30am-10pm Mon-Wed, Sun; 8am-10.30pm Thur-Sat. **Map** p114 C2 20

A great little place serving a café menu of cakes, sandwiches, salads and all-day breakfasts in a vibrant book-lined space. There are brightly patterned chairs, and equally brightly coloured whoopie pies on display at the small pâtisserie counter at the back. There's a particularly large selection of children's books and a cute, tent-like reading corner at the back, so BookMunch is a family-friendly spot.

Comptoir 102

Jumeirah Beach Road, opposite Beach Centre, Jumeirah 1 (04 385 4555, www.comptoir102.com). **Open** 8am-10pm daily. **Map** p115 F1 21

A relatively new French concept store and café, Comptoir 102 is housed inside a beautiful bungalow on Beach Road, complete with a dreamy outdoor terrace and beautiful furniture. This may not be a café

Omnia Blue. *See p119.*

EXPLORE

DUBAI MARINE BEACH RESORT & SPA

The place to party, whatever your vibe.

One of the only nightlife spots in the area, other than the expensive Four Seasons Resort, Dubai Marine Beach Resort & Spa is a huge space with 15 bars, restaurants and clubs, so you can easily spend a whole night here flitting from one to the other.

Barefoot Lounge is a good option for sundowners. Relax on a beanbag, drink in hand, with your toes in the sand. **Lounge Bar** is a dressier venue serving cocktails and spirits, with a 1920s jazz vibe. For a livelier atmosphere, head to **Serai**. It's a once-hip club that's starting to feel a bit dated, but it has plenty of promotions; music leans towards international-Arabic fusion. **Boudoir** is a swanky faux-Parisian venue that gets very lively – which is the upside. The downside is that the club is a bit too preoccupied with upholding an aura of exclusivity, so front-of-house staff can be very rude. **A Club** follows a similar track of attempted glamour, which it doesn't really pull off, but it does host some fun nights: Best of Hip Hop on Tuesdays, Thursdays and Sundays; Russian night on Wednesdays; House meets Pop on Fridays, and pop with live entertainment on Saturdays.

Dubai Marine Beach Resort & Spa
Jumeirah Beach Road, Jumeirah 1 (04 346 1111, www.dxbmarine.com).

EXPLORE

for everyone, though, as it focuses on mostly vegan, raw and dairy-free food. The daily-changing menu lists two or three dishes for each course, and we've been consistently impressed by the fresh juices. Be warned that Comptoir doesn't come cheap: expect to spend around Dhs300 for a light lunch and drinks for two.

Mama Tani

Town Centre, Jumeirah 1 (04 385 4437, www.mamatani.com). **Open** 8.30am-10pm daily. **Map** p115 E1 22

Friendly service, a laid-back atmosphere and fresh breads are the three things Mama Tani has going for it – not to mention good coffee and fresh decor. And although it's in a mall, the Town Centre on Jumeirah Beach Road is more peaceful than many. The menu mainly consists of sandwiches, made with the fresh *khameer* (Emirati flatbread) that Mama Tani does so well. Ingredients are always fresh and there's a good variety to choose from.

Mercury Lounge

Four Seasons Jumeirah Beach, Jumeirah 2 (04 270 7777, www.mercurydubai.com). **Open** 5pm-2am Mon, Wed-Sun. **Map** p114 D1 23

The rooftop lounge of the Four Seasons is chic, design-centric and has 360-degree views. The elegant outdoor spot is home to various bars. The upmarket Mercury Lounge has a creative cocktail list, and makes much use of dry ice and smoke for that modern cocktail-magic experience. It's pricey, though – the Cinema Set signature cocktail (Maker's Mark whiskey infused with caramel popcorn, cola syrup, Angostura bitters and lime juice) will set you back Dhs85. More classic options sit around the Dhs65 mark. As a treat, though, the mouth-watering cocktails and beautiful setting do make for a special combination.

Pantry Café

Wasl Square, Al Wasl Road, Al Wasl (04 388 3868, www.pantrycafe.me). **Open** 7.30am-10pm Mon-Thur, Sun; 8.30am-10pm Fri, Sat. **Map** p114 C2 24

A large warehouse-style café with big windows, cement flooring and exposed ceilings. The decor may verge on cool, but the temperature can verge on freezing. Chilliness notwithstanding, the menu is a pleasant assortment of appetising breakfast dishes, soups, salads, rice, noodles and gourmet burgers. Toasted muesli is a standout: a gorgeous layered concoction of gooey honey, tangy yoghurt, crispy muesli and a sweet mixed-berry compote. Coffee is excellent.

Spontiphoria

Wasl Square, Al Wasl Road, Al Wasl (04 338 8827, www.spontiphoria.com). **Open** 7am-1am Mon-Thur, Sun; 10am-midnight Fri, Sat. **Map** p114 C2 25

PARK LIFE

BoxPark is breathing new energy into Al Wasl Road.

Smack-bang between Safa Park and trendy shopping-and-dining district City Walk on Al Safa Street, **BoxPark** has brought a new buzz to Al Wasl Road. The colourful new strip takes its inspiration from London's own cutting-edge shopping district of the same name in Shoreditch, and has capacity for 30 cafés and restaurants, and 14 shops.

Stock up on funky stationery and home accessories at **Typo** (www.typo.com), a cool South African shop. For a major interior design statement, head to **Urbanist** (04 348 8002). It's a vintage-inspired shop with a small selection of one-off clothing pieces and quirky armchairs. For some truly unusual fashion finds, your best bet is **Rundholz** (www.studiorundholz.de). The German womenswear brand features bold pieces with a gender-neutral feel (so no clingy, second-skin dresses here) and lots of monochrome that works on any age. If you want something casual, though, there's always dedicated onesie shop **OnePiece** (04 343 63691, www.onepiece-me.com), featuring high-quality, zipped, sweater-material jumpsuits from three Norwegian twentysomethings who established the brand in 2009.

Shopping sustenance comes in a few wonderful forms: **Logma** (800 56462) serves a contemporary take on Emirati and Khaleeji (Gulf) cuisine, warranting visits from Dubai's ruling family, while **Shish Fish** is inspired by Istanbul's fish restaurants. Turkish chefs create some of the nation's best-known dishes including fish served skewered on a bed of charcoal. Sample Azerbaijani cuisine at the **Jag Restaurant** (www. jagrestaurant.com) or bite into fresh mozzarella (made fresh on site daily using local dairy and traditional Italian techniques) at **Bianca Mozzarella** (04 345 5300, www. bianca.ae). You can order the creamy cheese with a variety of sides, or opt for Italian mains, sandwiches or pasta. Truffle burrata and ricotta are among other cheeses available.

When it comes to ice-cream, two establishments are taking the city by storm. **GROM** (www.grom.it/en) serves more than 20 flavours of *gelato* – including stracciatella, coffee and caramel, pistachio and sorbets – with organic fresh fruit. **Dri Dri** (04 553 0647) has more adventurous flavours, including liquorice and custard cream, plus delicious sorbets such as kiwi fruit and grapefruit.

BoxPark's shops are open 10am-10pm Mon-Wed, Sat, Sun, 10am-midnight Thur, Fri. The restaurants and cafés are open 10am-midnight daily.

This little boutique and bake shop is often overlooked for the popular Pantry Café opposite. But, if you're looking for somewhere quieter to stop, or enjoy browsing little gift-shop type items while you sip on coffee, take a seat here instead. Decor is firmly feminine – white with lots of pinks, pastels and flowers. But the cakes are good (try the Friday special lychee rose cake), as are unusual desserts such as spiced cinnamon chocolate soup, a chocolate burger and a cookie pizza. A breakfast happy hour from 8am to 9am on weekdays gives customers a free coffee with their breakfast, and you can get 25% off coffee after the first order.

Tasha's

Galleria Mall, Al Wasl Road, Jumeirah 1 (050 640 8816, www.tashascafe.com). **Open** 7.30am-11pm daily. **Main courses** Dhs65-Dhs170. **Map** p115 E2 ㉖

Marble-look floor tiles, pillars and palm trees lend a colonial look to Tasha's. If you visit in the evening, you'll find two menus to choose from: a classic café list of salads and sandwiches, and a more elaborate selection of bistro-stye plates. We advise sticking to salads and the café selection, though, as the mains can be inconsistent. Tasha's shines at cakes: carrot cake, at Dhs40 a slice, seems expensive, but it's likely to be one of the finest you've tasted.

Yamanote Atelier

Wasl Square, Al Wasl Road, Al Wasl (04 388 1811, www.yamanoteatelier.com). **Open** 8am-10pm daily. **Map** p114 C2 ㉗

An unusual addition to Jumeirah, Yamanote Atelier is a modern Japanese pâtisserie, simply and elegantly designed. In the centre is a display of freshly baked buns, pastries and breads in wicker baskets. Buns range from deep-fried doughnuts filled with beef curry and coated in panko crumb to chocolate custard-filled sweet dough buns decorated to look like cartoon characters Hello Kitty and Totoro. Other specialities include melon buns (so named due to their appearance, rather than flavour) and buns filled with red bean paste. Everything is made from scratch in-store.

Shops & Services

Ayesha Depala

The Village Mall, Jumeirah Road, Jumeirah 1 (04 344 5378, www.ayesha-depala.com). **Open** times vary. **Map** p115 G1 ㉘ **Fashion**

This talented young Indian designer's Dubai boutique is awash with silk, chiffon, tulle and lace, all in soft, serene colours. Her collections are the epitome of femininity – as is the store itself, with lilac walls, sparkling chandeliers and a chic chaise longue. From long evening gowns, to baby-doll dresses and delicate cardigans, each garment is beautifully cut and timelessly stylish. The boutique is due to relocate in 2015; check the website for details.

Cities

Galleria Mall, Al Wasl Road, next to Emirates Post, Jumeirah 1 (04 343 4301, www.citiesstore.com). **Open** 10am-10pm Mon-Wed, Sat, Sun; 10am-midnight Fri. **Map** p115 E2 ㉙ **Homewares**
See p127 **One of a Kind**.

City Walk

Corner of Al Wasl Road & Al Safa Street, Jumeirah 1 (800 637227, www. citywalk.ae). **Open** times vary; phone or check the website for information on individual stores. **Map** p115 E2 ㉚ **Mall**

This outdoor shopping strip has a few high-end boutiques and designer shops, but nothing that warrants making a special trip here. There are a few convenient places to stop for a quick bite on the move – burger joints, takeaway chains and a few other outlets dedicated to the likes of frozen yoghurt and rice pudding – and a supermarket. Edo Sweets (04 344 0833) is worth a look for its range of *mochi* flavours.

Mercato Mall

Jumeirah Beach Road, Jumeirah 1 (04 344 4161, www.mercatoshoppingmall.com). **Open** *Mall* 10am-10pm Mon-Thur, Sat, Sun (some stores open at 1.30pm Fri). *Spinney's supermarket* 10am-midnight daily. *Cinema* 10am-late daily. **Map** p115 E1 ㉛ **Mall**

A fairly standard small mall with a bunch of high street shops along the lines of Mango, Nike, Reiss, Diesel and Mac. There's also a supermarket, cinema and children's play area, plus various coffee shops and a food court.

EXPLORE

Odd Piece

Wasl Square, Al Wasl Road, Al Wasl (04 388 3733, www.the-oddpiece.com). **Open** 10am-9.30pm Mon-Thur, Sat, Sun; 3-9pm Fri. **Map** p114 C2 ㉜ **Furnishings**

Stocks vintage, midcentury and contemporary furniture from across the globe, hand-picked by owner Arwa from souks, markets and trade shows in Italy, France, Morocco, South Africa and more.

S*uce

Village Mall, Jumeirah Beach Road, Jumeirah 1 (04 344 7270, www.shopatsauce.com). **Open** 10am-10pm daily. **Map** p115 G1 ㉝ **Fashion**
See p127 **One of a Kind**. *Photo p124*.

S*uce Gifts

Wasl Square, Al Wasl Road, Al Wasl (04 388 3488, www.shopatsauce.com). **Open** 10am-10pm daily. **Map** p114 C2 ㉞ **Fashion**

Quirky bits and bobs at the gift-shop version of popular (and expensive) boutique S*uce (*see above*).

S*uce Lite

Jumeirah Centre Mall, Jumeirah Beach Road, Jumeirah 1 (04 344 7270, www.shopatsauce.com). **Open** 10am-10pm daily. **Map** p115 G1 ㉟ **Fashion**
See p127 **One of a Kind**.

Verona Chocolatier

Wasl Square, Al Wasl Road, Al Wasl (04 388 3484). **Open** 10am-11pm daily. **Map** p114 C2 ㊱ **Food & drink**

Verona stocks all manner of locally produced confectionery, including so-called 'healthy chocolate' and elaborately decorated and brightly coloured creations. You'll also find intricate chocolate towers and the gift sets that are characteristic of most high-end chocolate shops in the city.

West LA Boutique

Sunset Mall, Jumeirah Road, Jumeirah 3 (04 394 4248, www.westlaboutique.com). **Open** 10am-10pm daily. **Map** p114 B2 ㊲ **Fashion**

See p127 **One of a Kind**.

Zayan the Label

Galleria Mall, Al Wasl Road, Jumeirah 1 (04 344 0104, www.zayan.com). **Open** 10am-10pm Mon-Wed, Sat, Sun; 10am-midnight Thur, Fri. **Map** p115 E2 ㊳ **Fashion**

See p127 **One of a Kind**.

SATWA

Satwa is a kooky neighbourhood that mixes Arabic, Indian, Pakistani and Filipino culture in the heart of Dubai. Its ramshackle buildings and streets make a delightful contrast to the relentless towers and highways across the rest of the city.

Any night of the week, the cafés on 2nd December Street are worth a stop for a freshly squeezed juice and to people-watch the area's residents as they promenade – everyone from young Filipino men done up like surfer dudes to extended Emirati families in search of ice-cream. At the top of this strip, and near Pars Iranian restaurant, are municipal basketball courts that remain busy even through July and August. You'll find dozens of Filipino, Asian and Arabic men playing here, in the kind of local community scene not often found in Dubai.

Around the corner from Al Diyafah Street (to give it its former name; *see below* **In the Know**) is Al Satwa Road, which, with its flashes of neon colour, is the heart of the area – part Manila, part Islamabad and part 'old' Dubai. Take a stroll down this noisy, chaotic street and peruse a huge range of fabrics, shop after tiny shop of Indian and Pakistani sweets, bargain homewares and clothes. Check out **Raoof Sweet Restaurant** (04 344 3184) for delicious halwa, *gulab jamun* and *jalebi* and **Pan de Manila** (*see p126*) for traditional Filipino baked goods.

S*uce. *See p123.*

IN THE KNOW NAMING THE DAY

Until December 2011, 2nd December Street – Satwa's arterial main road – was called Al Diyafah Street. The name was changed by Sheikh Mohammed bin Rashid Al Maktoum, vice president and prime minister of the UAE and ruler of Dubai, to mark UAE National Day, which falls on 2 December.

Restaurants

Lola's Best Restaurant

Opposite Al Hana Centre (04 398 9193). Metro Al Jafiliya. **Open** 8am-2am Mon-Wed, Sat, Sun; 8am-3am Thur, Fri. **Main courses** Dhs15-Dhs30. **Map** p115 H2 ㊴ **Filipino**

Lola's is worth a look for those curious about Filipino cuisine. The room is basic, but clean, and a TV was blaring as solo diners enjoyed their lunch break on a recent visit. The menu comes with colourful pictures, and staff are handy at explaining dishes and making recommendations. But Lola's lets itself down with scattershot inconsistency from the kitchen. The mixed noodle dish, *pancit fiesta*, is a decent stomach-filler, if on the greasy side. But the house special of stuffed grilled fish, *pinaputok na bangus*, is often too dry. On the other hand, everything is very cheap – many dishes are less than Dhs20 – and Lola's is not a bad place to fill up and try something different.

Mannaland Korean Restaurant

Al Mina Road (04 345 1300). Metro Al Jafiliya. **Open** 11am-3pm, 6-11pm daily. **Main courses** Dhs55-Dhs150. **Map** p115 H1 ㊵ **Korean**

Mannaland is one of the city's more affordable real Korean restaurants – though it will still set you back more than a cheap Chinese or Filipino meal in an equivalent venue. That said, there's value in the free kimchi served up once you've taken your seat in the small but clean space. Food is fantastically authentic: we love the *yachae bulgogi* (marinated beef with mixed vegetables), with thin beef strips and bags of flavour, bulked up with a side of steamed rice.

★ Ravi Restaurant

Satwa Road (04 331 5353). Metro Al Jafiliya. **Open** 5am-2am daily. **Main courses** Dhs10-Dhs25. **Map** p115 H2 ㊶ **Pakistani**

There's nothing grand about Ravi, just excellent, extremely affordable Pakistani food. It's very basic (plastic tablecloths, polystyrene cups) but the focus is on the cooking. There's a menu, but staff will tell you what is available and recommend what to have. The dahl fry is amazing – gently spiced lentils in a silky yellow sauce – as is the mutton peshwari (spicy and a little sweet, with tender meat, full of flavour). Naans, crispy on the outside and soft in the middle, are the perfect way to make sure you get every drop of the delicious sauce. It's hard not to love Ravi, a restaurant that's well worth seeking out.

Other location Sheikh Khalifa Bin Zayed Street, Al Karama (04 352 8090).

Cafés & Bars

Boston Bar

Jumeira Rotana (04 345 5888, www.rotana.com). Metro Al Jafiliya. **Open** noon-12.30am daily. **Map** p115 H1 ㊷

An old expat favourite, Boston Bar is said to be modelled on the bar from US sitcom *Cheers*, and it attracts all manner of characters and eccentric old Dubai hands. On our last visit one such old-timer – a regular we can only presume, clad in a Stetson and cowboy boots – had brought along his own tambourine.

Brauhaus

Jumeira Rotana (04 345 5888, www.rotana.com). Metro Al Jafiliya. **Open** 6pm-2.30am daily. **Map** p115 H1 ㊸

It may not have the largest selection of German hop beverages on offer, but what Brauhaus does have in buckets is cosy pub appeal, and the great advantage of being one of Satwa's lesser-stomped drinking grounds. Perfect for a low-key, generously proportioned plate of bratwurst with friends.

IN THE KNOW TAILOR MADE

Aside from its wonderful little street-side eateries, Satwa is also known for its tailors. Many have been in business for 30 years or more and the tailors can skilfully copy and recreate almost any garment for – generally – between Dhs250 and Dhs400, depending on the design. **Coventry Tailoring** (17B Street, off Al Satwa Road, opposite Emirates Post Office, 04 344 7563) is hidden (like most) down an alley off Al Satwa Road and has a loyal customer base. For best results, bring in the item you want copied or detailed photographs so you can discuss your needs with the tailors. You'll need to bring your own fabric, but there are plenty of shops nearby selling a vast variety of fabrics. **Dream Girls** (Al Satwa Road, near Emirates NBD, 04 349 5445) is another renowned spot with fantastic tailors who will continue to modify your garment until it's perfect. And if you've got a few favourite dresses you want copied or made in different fabrics, **Deepa's** (opposite Emirates Post Office, 04 349 9733) can do the job brilliantly, and the finishes are beautiful. They're also experienced enough to let you know if something simply won't work: if you brought in a cotton dress you wanted remade in silk, they'd tell you if it wouldn't hang right.

Legends Sports Bar

Chelsea Plaza Hotel, Satwa Roundabout (055 738 8527, www.legends-sportsbar.com). Metro Al Jafiliya. **Open** noon-3am daily. **Map** p115 H2 44

Legends may not be able to deliver on its promise of offering 'good times, good food and good sport' all the time, but this American-style saloon bar is a solid venue. A ramshackle array of framed memorabilia lines the bits of the walls not taken up by TV screens (for sport), while a large portion of the floor is given up to pool tables and arcade games, although there's something of a dancefloor for the live music on Thursday and Friday nights. Snackwise, the nachos – a gargantuan mound – are perfect for hungry spectators to munch on while taking in a match. The burgers come heaped with toppings and drinks are reasonably priced.

Al Mallah

2nd December Street (04 398 4723). Metro Al Jafiliya. **Open** 6.30am-3am daily. **Map** p115 H2 45

An old stalwart on the bustling 2nd December Street scene, Al Mallah is the place to go for simple Arabic fast food. Skip the meze, which are much better elsewhere (try Sidra across the road), and munch on the winning shawarmas and falafel sandwiches.

Pan de Manila

Al Mankhool Road, across from Al Hana Centre (056 799 5722). Metro Al Jafiliya. **Open** 9am-midnight daily. **Map** p115 H2 46

This bakery serves freshly baked sweets from the Philippines, such as chocolate crinkles, *pandesal*, *ensaymada*, *hopia*, pineapple pie and the swiss-roll-like Brazo de Mercedes.

Saleh Mohd Bakery

11th Street, opposite Satwa Mosque, off Al Satwa Road (no phone). Metro World Trade Centre. **Open** 7am-11pm daily. **Map** p115 H2 47

Some real treats can be found poking out of Satwa's hole-in-the-wall kitchens. One such is this Iranian side-street gem, just opposite Satwa Mosque. Watch as a speedy duo of bakers roll out dough and sweep it into the oven, before whipping it back out moments later and throwing it on to the fresh pile in the window. The result is a stretchier, doughier roti, roughly the size of a hub cap.

Satwa Palace

Opposite Satwa Mosque, Al Satwa Road (04 342 2070). Metro World Trade Centre. **Open** 10am-10pm daily. **Map** p115 H2 48

Despite being home to some great Pakistani and Indian restaurants, finding a good pre-noon savoury snack to munch on while you trawl through Satwa's textile stores is not that easy. Take our advice and head to Satwa Palace. While the delightfully surly cashier won't waste any niceties on you, he'll oblige enough to scoop you a few vegetable samosas out of the window. Crunchy on the outside, full of flavour within and just Dhs1 each, it can't hurt to grab a bagful.

Shops & Services

Wadi Zabeel

Al Satwa Road (no phone). Metro World Trade Centre. **Open** 9am-midnight daily. **Map** p115 G2 49 **Food & drink**

Peruse chocolates with quirky fillings – from kiwi creams to mango – plus rows and rows of roasted nuts. Stacked to the ceiling, prices start from a reasonable Dhs20 per kilo of colourful confectionery, and while they may not be the most fantastic quality, they're perfect party-bag fillers for kids' birthdays.

Yousif Abdul Aziz Thyme & Herbs

Opposite Al Satwa Bus Station (04 331 3964). Metro World Trade Centre. **Open** 10am-10pm daily. **Map** p115 H2 50 **Food & drink/spices**

Wafts of cardamom and incense float out on to the street to tempt passersby inside this small store. Peruse Omani frankincense and pottery holders for burning the incense in, plus saffron, dried thyme and rosewater, while the shopkeeper cheerfully points out and explains different products. You can also pick up a bag of disc-shaped Pakistani figs for Dhs10 and a large bag of roasted, salted cashews for Dhs5.

ONE OF A KIND

Indie shops are making their mark in Jumeirah.

Dubai's malls are generally pretty predictable, with the same big brands predominating. For something different, head to the stretch of calm consumerism between the Jumeirah Mosque and the tumbledown Dubai Zoo. Some of the city's best independent retailers are based in malls on this stretch of Jumeirah Beach Road, and discerning shoppers flock here to find them.

First stop is the **Village Mall**, home to **S*uce** (*see p123*), one of the most cutting-edge fashion retailers in the city – it also has a branch at the Dubai Mall. If you love the original S*uce but your purse can't deal with the prices, cross the road to **Jumeirah Centre Mall**, where you'll find **S*uce Lite** (*see p123*), which sells last season's leftovers. You're likely to spot super-cool labels such as Sass & Bide, Antoni & Alison, Citizens of Humanity, See (the Chloé concession) and Johnny Loves Rosie. You can save yourself anything from 40 to 80 per cent by rummaging around.

Sunset Mall is a newer addition to the Dubai shopping scene and houses a good few boutiques, most of which are very expensive. **West LA Boutique** (*see p124; pictured*), however, is a great little place full of urban and LA-inspired clothes and accessories. You'll need to catch a sale if you're looking for bargains, though.

The **Galleria** is on Al Wasl Road and is home to a few boutiques that are definitely worth a browse, including **Zayan the Label** (*see p124*), a high-end space with a mixed bag of edgy and whimsical modern pieces. **Cities** (*see p123*) is a design and concept store located in the same mall with some eclectic home furnishings such as cool coffee tables, über-modern lamps and geometric candelabras, as well as a selection of large sculptures.

EXPLORE

Al Barsha & Umm Suqeim

Umm Suqeim is where Old Dubai and New Dubai meet. Like its neighbour Jumeirah, it was one of the first areas to profit from the boom years. Today, it's filled with expensive villas, many now converted into medical clinics, spas, boutiques or jewellery shops. The jewel in its crown is the emirate's most familiar sight – the sail-shaped Burj Al Arab hotel. Almost as familiar to Dubai residents is the nearby Jumeirah Beach Hotel, which has its own – more accessible but still very fancy – places to eat. There's also a waterpark, and two of Dubai's biggest hotels in the sprawling Madinat Jumeirah – with restaurants, bars and shops.

You'll not find much glitz and glamour in Al Barsha outside of the Mall of the Emirates shopping complex (complete with its own indoor ski slope). What you will find are dozens of cafés, restaurants and a few sports bars, mostly catering for non-Western expats.

Madinat Jumeirah.

Don't Miss

1 Skiing in a shopping mall Try out the indoor slopes at Ski Dubai (p130).

2 Pierchic Twice the winner of Time Out Dubai's Most Romantic Restaurant award (p141).

3 Shimmers Beach restaurant and bar with views of Burj Al Arab (p144).

4 Bu Qtair Fish shack on the beach (p138).

5 Madinat Jumeirah Old-style souk with new-style bars and restaurants (p137).

AL BARSHA

This somewhat down-at-heel, rough-and-ready area may not seem to offer much in the way of tourist destinations at first glance, but right in the middle of Al Barsha is **Mall of the Emirates**. It may not match the record-breaking Dubai Mall in terms of size or variety, but it does offer some high-end fashion outlets, a plethora of restaurants and Dubai's indoor ski slope **Ski Dubai**. Bar and restaurant **Après** overlooks it. The mall is also home to **Ductac** (*see p216*), a theatre and community arts centre. The glittering **Kempinski Hotel** (*see p281*) houses quirky Spanish restaurant **Salero**, and hidden away in Harvey Nichols is the fantastic Moroccan restaurant **Almaz by Momo**.

Outside of the mall you can head to **Barsha Pond Park**, where you can hire bikes and go-karts, stroll around the pond and soak up the atmosphere.

Heading out of the area along the Sheikh Zayed Road towards Downtown you'll find a few smaller malls and the Al Manara and Al Quoz areas. **Al Manara** is mostly residential, but there is a stretch of the road with half a dozen likeable cafés. Nearby is the industrial estate-cum-arty area of **Al Quoz**, which is home to the **Courtyard Playhouse** (*see p216*), award-winning café **Tom & Serge**, gallery hub **Alserkal Avenue**, and some street food and music festivals.

EXPLORE

Sights & Attractions

Alserkal Avenue

Street 8, Al Quoz, take the Al Manara Road exit off Sheikh Zayed Road (050 556 9797). Metro Noor Bank or FGB. **Open** Mon-Thur, Sun; opening times of galleries vary. **Map** p131 C5 ❶

For a city that prides itself on extravagance, it's somewhat ironic that one of Dubai's least glamorous enclaves is effectively home to its artistic lifeblood. Set within the industrial streets of Al Quoz is the thriving art hub Alserkal Avenue. Street art lines the walls of the former industrial units that are now occupied by galleries, edgy art spaces and a few small businesses. Regular open nights and street-food festivals see the area filled with fashionistas and Dubai's dozen or so hipsters. It's not the prettiest place to visit, but there's nowhere else like it in Dubai.

FREE Al Barsha Pond Park

Off Al Barsha Road, near Emirates NBD bank. Metro Mall of the Emirates. **Open** 8am-11pm Mon-Thur, Sun; 8am-11.30pm Fri, Sat. **Admission** free. **Map** p131 D2 ❷

An oasis of green in predominantly sand-infiltrated Al Barsha, this park is built around the perimeter of a man-made lake and is popular with joggers, families, fitness fiends, kids' birthday parties and picnickers. It also plays host to the Ripe Night Market, an organic food market and street food gathering every Saturday (except in summer). There's a jogging track, bicycle hire, basketball and tennis courts, playgrounds and fitness equipment, and kiosks selling popcorn and soft drinks.

Bounce

Building 32, 4B Street, off Shiekh Zayed Road, Al Quoz (04 3211 400). Metro Noor Bank or FGB. **Open** 10am-10pm Mon-Wed, Sat, Sun; 10am-midnight Thur; 9am-midnight Fri. **Admission** from Dhs80 per hour. **Map** p131 C5 ❸

In a warehouse in Al Quoz, nestled in between a row of industrial compounds, lies Bounce – basically a trampoline park for grown-ups. Over 2,320sq m (25,000sq ft) there are 80 trampolines in divided into five activity areas: the free-jumping zone, the dodgeball pit, the big-bag area (three long trampolines with a huge stunt airbag at the end to jump on to), the slam dunk (which has two basketball hoops at one end) and the performance zone, where those with serious skills can try wall-running tricks.

Hint Hunt

Times Square Centre, off Shiekh Zayed Road (04 321 2242). Metro Noor Bank or FGB. **Open** 10am-9pm daily. **Admission** Dhs110. **Map** p131 C5 ❹

A site-specific team game that sees groups of three to five people locked in a room to try to find clues that will help them solve a mystery and therefore escape. You have 60 minutes to find out why you're there, following clues that eventually lead to the answer. Probably not one for the claustrophobic, but certainly good fun for everyone else.

★ Ski Dubai

Mall of the Emirates (04 409 4090). Metro Mall of the Emirates. **Open** 9am-midnight daily. **Admission** free; skiing from Dhs150. **Map** p131 C3 ❺

While the skiing draws up to 1,500 daily visitors to Ski Dubai, the Middle East's only indoor snow resort, it actually has much more to offer. The centre, which is covered with real snow all year round, covers 22,500sq m (242,260sq ft) – the size of three football fields – and is 25 storeys high. With its alpine-style restaurants and temperatures hovering around -1°C, you could almost kid yourself you're in the Alps. Snow Park is a 3,000sq m (32,260sq ft) snow-covered cavern within the centre, with a tobogganing hill: you can shoot down its twin track on a lightweight sledge. Alternatively, roll down the hill in a giant zorb ball, even jumping a 3m (10ft) ramp.

There are five ski runs that vary in height, gradient, length and difficulty. Beginners can take lessons, while experienced skiers and snowboarders can practise moves on the centre's longest run, which stretches 400m (1,300ft) and drops more than 60m (197ft). Or you can show off on the jumps and rails in the free-style zone, or attempt the world's first indoor black run. If that sounds too tame, ride the snow bullet, the world's first indoor sub-zero zip line. *Photo p132.*

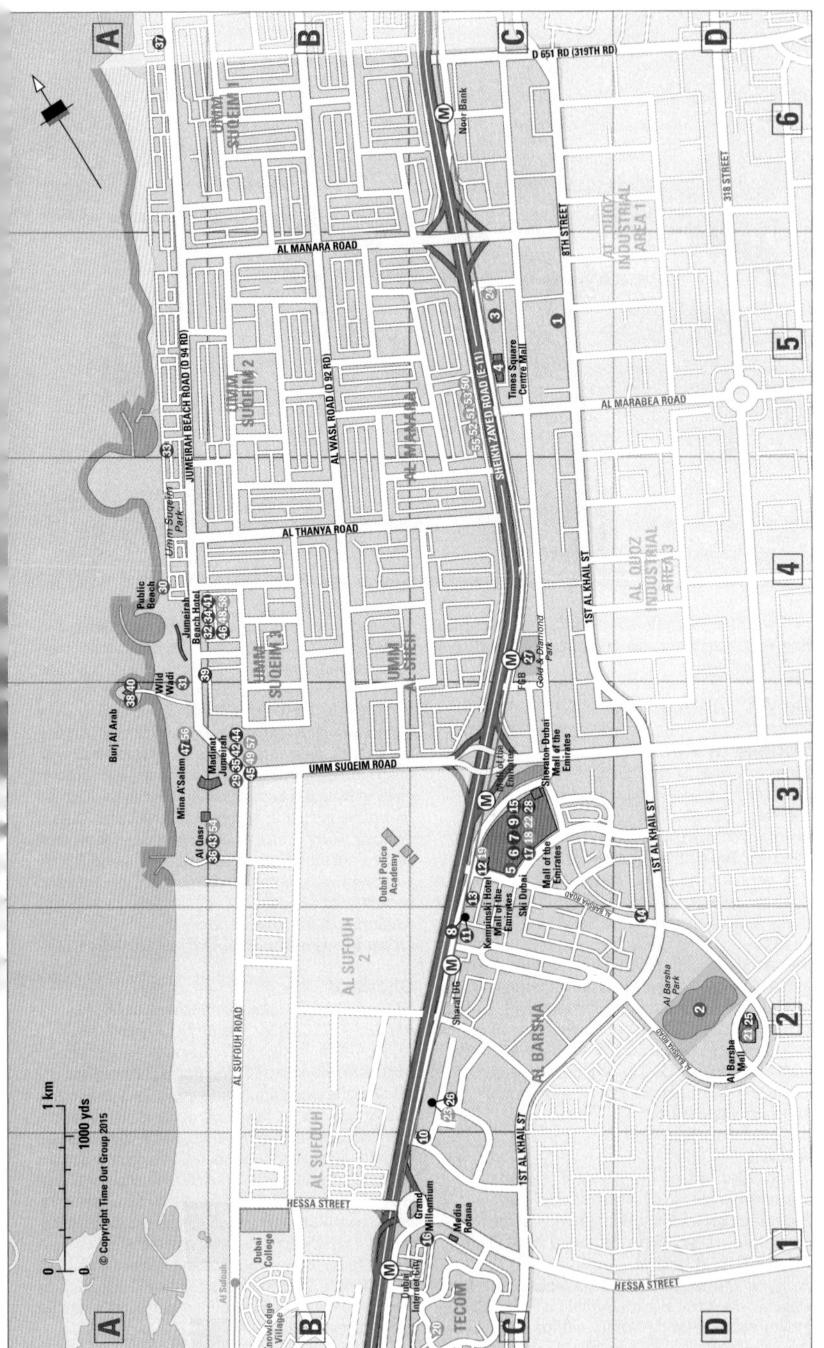

UMM SUQEIM 1
UMM SUQEIM 2
UMM SUQEIM 3
AL MANARA
UMM AL SHEIF
AL QUOZ INDUSTRIAL AREA 1
AL QUOZ INDUSTRIAL AREA 3
AL SUFOUH 2
AL SUFOUH
AL BARSHA
TECOM
D 651 RD (319TH RD)
AL MANARA ROAD
8TH STREET
318 STREET
JUMEIRAH BEACH ROAD (D 94 RD)
AL WASL ROAD (D 92 RD)
SHEIKH ZAYED ROAD (E-11)
AL MARABEA ROAD
AL THANYA ROAD
1ST AL KHAIL ST
UMM SUQEIM ROAD
AL SUFOUH ROAD
HESSA STREET
AL BARSHA ROAD
Noor Bank
Times Square Centre Mall
Umm Suqeim Park
Public Beach
Jumeirah Beach Hotel
Wild Wadi
Burj Al Arab
Mina A'Salam
Madinat Jumeirah
Al Qasr
FGB
Gold & Diamond Park
Sheraton Dubai Mall of the Emirates
Mall of the Emirates
Dubai Police Academy
Kempinski Hotel Mall of the Emirates
Ski Dubai
Sharaf DG
Al Barsha Park
Al Barsha Mall
Grand Millennium
Media Rotana
Dubai Internet City
Dubai College
Knowledge Village
Al Sufouh
0 1 km
0 1000 yds
© Copyright Time Out Group 2015
EXPLORE

Ski Dubai. See p130.

If you don't fancy the sports, you can always meet Ski Dubai's very own penguin family – they'll melt the hardest heart.

Restaurants

★ Almaz by Momo

Harvey Nichols, Mall of the Emirates (04 409 8877, http://momoresto.com). Metro Mall of the Emirates. **Open** noon-11.30pm Mon-Thur, Sun; noon-12.30am Fri, Sat. **Main courses** Dhs40-Dhs190. **Map** p131 C3 ❻ **Moroccan**

The people behind this restaurant's design have done an excellent job of making you forget you're in the Mall of the Emirates. Ornate lanterns throw shadows across exquisitely tiled walls and light up the sparkly domed ceiling. There's a glitzy bar area and a separate shisha room towards the rear. The Moroccan food is authentic and excellent, both the classic tagines and couscous dishes, and some of the Levantine-style starters. Drinks include cocktails and some creative mocktails. The place really comes into its own at night, when a DJ spins Arabic tunes and there's a lively buzz.

Asha's

Mall of the Emirates (04 324 4100, www.ashasrestaurants.com). Metro Mall of the Emirates. **Open** 10am-midnight Mon-Thur, Sun; 10am-1am Fri, Sat. **Main courses** Dhs40-Dhs70. **Map** p131 C3 ❼ **Indian**

Asha, in this instance, is Asha Bhosle, the Hindi singer and actress. Her restaurant serves north-west Indian cuisine and the menu is filled with classics alongside some more modern dishes and family recipes. Her influence is all over the menu, with anecdotes and explanations about the food. It's a warming touch that complements the decor, which makes you feel you're in a restaurant rather than a mall, and the service, which is knowledgeable and helpful. Among the starters, *papdi chat* is beautifully presented, with crispy discs layered with yoghurt, mint and chutney; chicken soup is fragrant and light. From the long list of mains, including kebabs and vegetarian dishes, *dhaniya murg* (chicken cooked in a yoghurt and cashew nut sauce) is spicy and fresh, while *mirch baingan ka salan* comes in a thicker sauce, with chunks of baby aubergine and coconut. Like Asha herself, this restaurant is dependable and classy.

Other location Wafi Mall, Oud Metha (04 324 4100).

Gharana

Holiday Inn Al Barsha, off Shiekh Zayed Road (04 323 4333). Metro Sharaf DG. **Open** 7.30-11.30pm Mon-Thur, Sun; 7.30pm-12-30am Fri, Sat. **Mains** Dhs40-Dhs100. **Map** p131 C2 ❽ **Indian**

'Gharana' means family, and you're certainly made to feel welcome at this lively restaurant. From the rich, vibrant saffron-and-gold walls to the music from the five-piece house band, Gharana embraces its guests in its warm-hearted ambience; and diners embrace the place back and sing along with the house band. The menu includes an extensive selection of classic curry, rice and vegetable dishes from across India, but really, Gharana is more about fun than the food. One thing to bear in mind is that it's on the ground floor of the Holiday Inn, so there are no views to speak of.

Al Hallab Restaurant & Sweets

Mall of the Emirates (04 341 1880, www.alhallabrestaurant.com). Metro Mall of the Emirates. **Open** noon-11.30pm Mon-Thur, Sun; noon-12.30am Fri, Sat. **Main courses** Dhs40-Dhs190. **Map** p131 C3 ❾ **Arabic**

Al Hallab is a smart restaurant with Arabesque furnishings, white linen tablecloths, well-presented staff and first-rate classic Lebanese cuisine. The long meze list includes the usual pastries, kibbeh and halloumi alongside salads like tabouleh and fattoush. Dishes like boiled brain salad tossed with garlic and olive oil are a sure sign that this place means business. Main-course grills are served with rice, a side salad and fries. Some of the desserts can be a bit of a let-down, so probably best to concentrate on meze and mains. **Other location** Dubai Mall, Downtown Dubai (04 330 8828).

Koreana

Next to Ibis Al Barsha, off Sheikh Zayed Road (04 392 9918). Metro Sharaf DG. **Open** 11.30am-3.30pm, 6pm-11am daily. **Main courses** Dhs40-Dhs 100. **Map** p131 C1 ❿ **Korean**

'No-frills' can sound like a slight on a restaurant – but when it comes to Koreana, that's certainly not the intention. We love how firmly the focus is put on the food here. In a city of swanky restaurants, pulling up a perch in this casual Korean eaterie is a welcome treat. Among our favourite dishes are the slivers of beef and fresh vegetables cooked on a hotplate at the table, the meaty dumplings and sticky potato noodles. In fact, flavours across the board are simple but compelling. If you thought you didn't like Korean food, think again.

Royal Buddha

Holiday Inn Al Barsha, off Sheikh Zayed Road (04 323 4333). Metro Sharaf DG. **Open** 7-11pm daily. **Main courses** Dhs60-Dhs160. **Map** p131 C2 ⓫ **Thai**

You'll find all the classic Thai tastes at Royal Buddha, from sticky rice to peanut sauce, soups to noodles and curries. With slightly jarring music and a big Buddha in the centre of the room, this Holiday Inn restaurant has the feel of an exotic outpost in a remote rural town, but friendly staff make the place inviting. Dubai's Thai dining scene is particularly strong, so the Royal Buddha may struggle to stand out among its competitors. But in this part of town, it's worth a visit.

★ Salero Tapas & Bodega

Kempinski Hotel, Mall of the Emirates (04 409 5888, www.kempinski.com). Metro Mall of the Emirates. **Open** noon-1am Mon-Thur, Sun; noon-3am Fri, Sat. **Tapas** Dhs40-Dhs70. **Map** p131 C3 ⓬ **Spanish**

Tucked away in the Kempinski you'll find Salero – one of the few Spanish or tapas restaurants in the city. Its entrance, lined with shelves of Spanish cookbooks and produce, sets the scene for this fun, informal and lively venue. Dishes are authentic – we're particularly keen on the seafood, such as razor clams with garlic and parsley and Galician octopus with potatoes. There's frequent entertainment with flamenco dancers or a Spanish guitarist. Happy hours, tapas deals and paella of the day offers seal the deal.

The Sky

Golden Tulip Al Barsha Hotel (04 341 7750, www.goldentulipalbarsha.com). Metro Sharaf DG. **Open** noon-2.30pm, 6-10.30pm daily. **Main courses** Dhs40-Dhs160. **Map** p131 C3 ⓭ **Korean**

Looking a little like someone's living room (perhaps down to the huge TV screen and speakers set up for karaoke in the corner), the Sky serves up the kind of homely Korean food that suits the surroundings, and the large groups of Koreans who dine here. From the lengthy menu, try a hearty bowl of *bibimbap* (meat served on squidgy rice, then mixed up with sweet and spicy sauces), or the greasy but guiltily satisfying seafood pancake.

Spice

Ramada Chelsea Hotel, Mafraq Road (04 501 9000). Metro Mall of the Emirates. **Open** 1-3pm, 7pm-1am daily. **Main courses** Dhs40-Dhs100. **Map** p131 D2 ⓮ **Indian**

This hotel is not known for its catering, but this restaurant is an exception, serving elegant Indian classics wth refined flavours: poppadoms are served with a lovely papaya chutney; a vegetarian okra dish is tangy and gingery; aloo gobi potatoes with cauliflower or creamy yellow dahl with cumin and garlic are a great accompaniment to a selection of breads. Juicy lamb chops are sent through the tandoor oven on massive skewers, and there's also a good selection of seafood dishes, including fish tikka. The dining room has a stage for entertainment, though there isn't something on every night.

St Tropez Bistro

Mall of the Emirates (04 341 3415, www.sttropez.ae). Metro Mall of the Emirates. **Open** 11am-11.30pm daily. **Main courses** Dhs70-Dhs275. **Map** p131 C3 ⓯ **French**

It may be accessed through Mall of the Emirates, but St Tropez is nothing like a typical shopping mall restaurant. With exposed-brick and white-painted walls and pale banquette seating, this is most definitely an upmarket break from scouring the shops. A classic French bistro menu (*escargots, moules* and the like) is joined by a selection of steaks – they're very good, accompanied by frites and a selection of sauces. Being one of the few places in the mall where you can have wine or beer with your meal is another plus.

Toshi

Grand Millennium Dubai, TECOM (04 429 9999). Metro Internet City. **Open** 5.30-11.30pm daily. **Main courses** Dhs80-Dhs195. **Map** p131 C1 ⓰ **Asian fusion**

In our experience, the first thing staff are likely to do when you arrive at Toshi is introduce you to their generous all-in theme nights. Our advice: ignore them. While those buffet packages are remarkable value, it's the à la carte dishes that really shine: classics like green curry are packed with zest, while more complicated dishes such as the steamed whole sea bass are also successful. The venue isn't exciting, despite pleasant 18th-floor views, but you will eat well.

Tribes

Mall of the Emirates (04 395 0660, www.tribesrestaurant.com). Metro Mall of the Emirates. **Open** 9am-midnight Mon-Wed, Sun; 9am-1am Fri, Sat. **Main courses** Dhs50-Dhs230. **Map** p131 C3 ⓱ **Meat/global**

This lively African-themed restaurant serves up an extensive, mainly meaty menu of burgers, ribs and steaks, with inspiration from around the African continent and beyond – from Moroccan spicy lamb chops to Kalahari roast lamb. There are steaks to suit every appetite and preference, from small 105g rump and sirloin cuts, all the way up to T-bone slabs, plus wagyu. Service is famously warm, thanks to the African staff. If you want to escape from the crowds, ask to be seated inside, under the domed ceiling.

Cafés & Bars

★ Après

Mall of the Emirates (04 341 2575). Metro Mall of the Emirates. **Open** 11.30am-1am Mon-Sat, Wed; 11.30am-2am Thur, Fri. **Map** p131 C3 ⓲

If you're looking for a few drinks and a quick bite to eat with an unusual view, then look no further than Après at Mall of the Emirates, which overlooks Ski Dubai. Inspired by European ski resorts, the casual lounge, bar and restaurant aims to create an *après ski*-style experience. It offers a little more than the average bar food menu with an array of fresh, contemporary European dishes, including a warming French onion soup with caramelised onions in a rich beef broth topped with gruyère cheese. Pizzas from the wood-fired oven are ideal for sharing. The choices of beers and wines aren't mindblowing, but typical of Dubai. The cocktail selection is a little better.

Aspen Café

Kempinski Hotel, Mall of the Emirates (04 409 5999). Metro Mall of the Emirates. **Open** 24hrs daily. **Map** p131 C3 ⓳

Defying all stereotypes afforded to hotel lobby restaurants, this classy French-style café serves surprisingly good food. Menus are displayed on iPads and the service is swift. The bread basket (baked in-house) has the best bread we've tasted in the city, and there is also a good selection of sandwiches. Lobster bisque (the soup is theatrically poured over the medallions of lobster at the table) is a must-try and heftier main courses include a grand café-style weiner schnitzel. Aspen also serves English-style afternoon tea and breakfast.

Crown & Lion

Byblos Hotel Dubai, TECOM (04 448 8000). Metro Internet City. **Open** 11am-3am daily. **Map** p131 C1 ⓴

Reliably busy whenever there's a Premier League football match on, this British-themed pub attracts a predominantly male crowd. The food isn't the cheapest, but it's hard to argue with the gargantuan portions, and there are also regular food deals and a happy hour to take advantage of if you're around at the right time. Pub classics include home-made pies with mashed potato and gravy, fish and chips, and burgers.

Klayya Bakery & Sweets

Al Barsha Mall, 23rd Street (04 325 5335). Metro Mall of the Emirates. **Open** 8.30am-10pm daily. **Map** p131 D2 ㉑

Set in Al Barsha Mall, one of Dubai's quieter shopping centres, is this gem of a café. The small but perfectly formed space, brightened up by colourful patterned cushions and seating, is one of the city's best places to try Emirati food. Breakfast is a highlight, with dishes coming with *karak* tea – a sweet, creamy and spiced hot drink – and traditional bread. We like the *chebab* (a warm saffron-infused pancake) and *ryood yerena*, baked eggs in a tin pot, on a bed of sticky, sweet dates. Another good choice is the *ryoog* Bur Dubai, a shakshuka-type dish with eggs baked in a sweet tomato sauce with a hint of chilli.

Rich Café

Mall of the Emirates (04 341 0945). Metro Mall of the Emirates. **Open** 8am-midnight Mon-Wed, Sun; 8am-2pm Thur-Sat. **Map** p131 C3 ㉒

Bright and airy, with comfortable seats and high-chairs for little nippers, the Rich Café has a distinctly relaxed and friendly vibe. On the menu are soups and sandwiches, mains, freshly baked pastries, sweet treats and breakfast dishes. English breakfast with mini chicken sausages, grilled mushrooms, baked beans, eggs and toast. If you fancy something altogether more decadent, the French breakfast is a good choice: two thick slices of bread flavoured with vanilla, dressed with mixed berries and drizzled with maple syrup. With a bill coming in at under Dhs100 for two dishes and coffee, this place is good value.

Taste Initiative

The Change Initiative, off Shiekh Zayed Road (04 376 9213, www.thechangeinitiative.com). Metro Sharaf DG. **Open** 8am-6pm daily. **Map** p131 C2 ㉓
Serving organic, gluten-free and vegan dishes, with a genuine effort to use responsibly sourced and unprocessed ingredients, this eco store is a welcome addition to Dubai's bloated food scene. High ceilings, generous space and a light colour palette create a pleasant environment. The decent breakfast range (served until noon on weekdays and 1pm on weekends) encompasses everything from granola and porridge to pancakes, eggs and more. At lunch there are interesting salads, hearty sandwiches made with bread that's been baked on the premises, plus quiche, pies, pizza, pasta and grills. Even the ice-cream is from the Taste Initiative's own *gelateria*. If only more places adopted the same approach.

★ Tom & Serg

Al Joud Centre, near Ace Hardware, Al Quoz (056 474 6812, www.tomandserg.com). Metro Noor Bank or FGB. **Open** 8am-4pm Mon-Thur, Sun; 8am-6pm Fri, Sat. **Map** p131 C5 ㉔
If you know good food and really good coffee, you know Tom & Serg. In arty Al Quoz, it's a spacious open-plan café and eaterie spread over two floors. The cool, distressed-industrial design and even cooler staff are unusual for Dubai. The short menu throws up some interesting dishes, including a superfood salad – a veritable explosion of everything that's green and good for you, topped with grilled chicken, nuts and seeds. The flourless chocolate cake is another Tom & Serg signature dish, perfect when washed down with one of their famous coffees. It's not very quiet, due to the concrete-look ceiling and constant stream of customers, but it's well worth a trip here.

Shops & Services

Al Barsha Mall

Al Barsha, (04 409 9000). Metro Mall of the Emirates. **Open** 10am-10pm Mon-Wed, Sat, Sun; 10am-midnight Sun. **Map** p131 D2 ㉕ **Mall**
A short hop away from Mall of the Emirates is Al Barsha Mall, which is tiny in comparison to its neighbour. Here you'll find independent clothes

Après.

shops for kids and adults, jewellery, a supermarket and a food court. You'll most likely find locals in here, as it's close to lots of Al Barsha's big villas.

The Change Initiative

Off Sheikh Zayed Road (800 824, www.thechange initiative.com). Metro Sharaf DG. **Open** 8am-9pm daily. **Map** p131 C2 ㉖ **Ethical products**

This store dedicates its trade entirely to upcycled and sustainable products, from Frank Gehry cardboard chairs to an eco-fuel VW, clothes and bags made from jute, energy-saving appliances, and even homewares made from old tyres. It's all the work of Indian founder and CEO Gundeep Singh, who has lived and worked in the UAE for more than 13 years. He hopes the store will trigger new practices here and help consumers make more responsible choices. Ambitious, yes, but he has some big names behind him: Robert Kennedy Jr, nephew of the former US president, is one of the board members.

Gold & Diamond Park

Off Sheikh Zayed Road, Al Quoz (04 362 7777). Metro FGB. **Open** 10am-10pm Mon-Thur, Sat, Sun; 4-10pm Fri. **Map** p131 C4 ㉗ **Jewellery mall**

Dubai is a major gold trading hub, but if you'd rather not venture to the gold souk down by the Creek, the shops here are a good alternative. The Park is essentially a mall hosting more than 90 jewellers, with shops where you can pick up ready-made pieces and, in some cases, un-set precious stones such as emeralds and sapphires, as well as diamonds. If you can't find what you want, the knowledgeable and skilled staff at the eternally busy Cara (04 323 2776, www.carajewellers.com) will custom-make, or modify, jewellery to your specifications. It will also exchange old jewellery. Unlike most malls in New Dubai, you can haggle here.

★ Mall of the Emirates

Al Barsha (04 409 9000). Metro Mall of the Emirates. **Open** 10am-1am daily (shops close at 10pm Mon-Thur, Sun, midnight Fri, Sat). **Map** p131 C3 ㉘ **Mall**

Just about anything you could want you can find in this huge mall. There are a dozen banks, two hotels, a cinema, a kids' play area, a supermarket, department stores, a theatre, restaurants and cafés, pharmacies, opticians, tailors, florists, car rentals, and more. And that's before you've even thought about the shops available, which include UK high street favourites Marks & Spencer, H&M, Topshop and Next. There's also a smattering of high-end designer stores including Versace, Roberto Cavalli, Giorgio Armani, Ralph Lauren and Gucci.

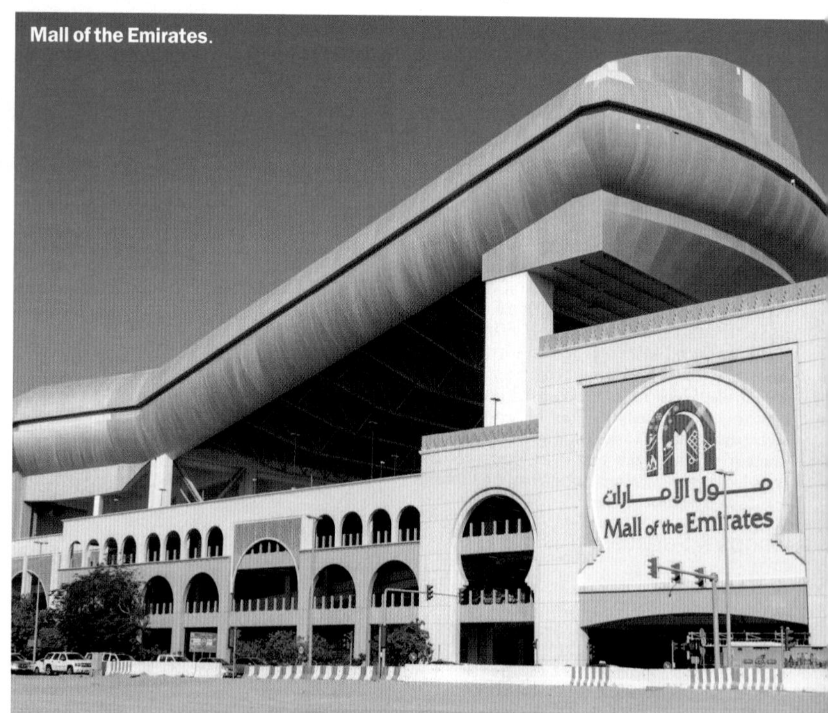

Mall of the Emirates.

UMM SUQEIM

For destinations in this area, you'll need to take a taxi from either First Gulf Bank (FGB) or Mall of the Emirates station – we've indicated which is closest in the reviews below – which should cost roughly Dhs12-Dhs25.

Umm Suqeim is a predominantly residential area that is more or less an extension of Jumeirah. **Sunset Beach** is public and stretches away from **Jumeirah Beach Hotel** (*see p279*) and the Burj Al Arab, giving it particularly lovely views at sunset. The **Burj Al Arab** (*see p279*) itself, the sail-shaped tower on an artificial island that has been described as the world's first seven-star hotel, is perhaps Dubai's most iconic sight. On shore beside it are maze-like streets of villas interrupted by **Jumeirah Road** – or Beach Road as many call it – and the **Al Manara** area, which has a few good cafés.

The **Madinat Jumeirah**, a souk-style shopping destination built in the style of traditional Emirati buildings with faux wind towers, is one of Dubai's biggest tourist attractions (and traps). It's pretty and pleasant, particularly between October and March when you can sit outside and enjoy the canals and greenery. The Madinat, its two hotels (Al Qasr and Mina A' Salaam), the Jumeirah Beach Hotel and Burj Al Arab are all neighbours and occupy the same stretch of exclusive coastline. Adjacent is the **Wild Wadi Waterpark**, which has a relatively limited selection of rides, but is nonetheless a fun day out that children, in particular, will love.

Sights & Attractions

★ Souk Madinat Jumeirah

Junction Umm Suqeim Road & Jumeirah Road. Metro Mall of the Emirates. **Open** times vary for individual shops & restaurants. **Map** p131 B3 ㉙

The building is dotted with stalls selling things like painted Turkish bowls and ethnic sequined slippers for ten times the price of an authentic souk, in addition to a few caricature stands and artists who will write your name in sand in a bottle. Its coffee shops are mostly Costa Coffees and Cinnabons. If you can look past all this, however, you will find that Souk Madinat Jumeirah is not totally without charm. The waterside setting is appealing. The outdoor areas are pretty and pleasant for whiling away a few hours; Frioul Bistro de Luxe (*see p139*) has a great canal-side terrace with views of the Burj Al

Dhow & Anchor.

Arab. There are also a few good bars and the Dubai version of famed Ibiza club Pacha (*see p198*). Sadly most of the shops are chains.

FREE Sunset Beach

Next to Jumeirah Beach Hotel, off Jumeirah Road. Metro First Gulf Bank (FGB) station. Metro Mall of the Emirates. **Admission** free. **Map** p131 A4 ㉚

This public beach is quite small by comparison to others like Kite Beach (*see p114*), and gets extremely busy at weekends. There are no facilities here either. Most hotels in the area have access to either their own private beach, or are closer to the beach at JBR.

★ Wild Wadi

Where Umm Suqeim Road meets Jumeirah Road. Metro Mall of the Emirates. **Open** *Nov-Feb* 10am-6pm daily. *Mar-May* 10am-7pm daily. *June-Aug* 10am-8pm daily. *Sept, Oct* 10am-7pm daily. **Admission** over 1.1m in height Dhs275; under 1.1m in height Dhs230; free under-2s. **Map** p131 A3 ㉛

Wild Wadi is a fairly sizeable waterpark and its nine rides and attractions are more than enough to keep you occupied for the better part of a day. The family-style rides – Tantrum Alley and the Burj Surj – rather tame affairs at most waterparks, are surprisingly exciting. The Jumeirah Sceirah lives up to its name; it has two tandem slides and begins with standing on a trap door that falls away from under you. More relaxed rides include a wave pool and lazy river. There's also a surf experience ride and a kids' adventure play structure.

Restaurants

Beachcombers

Jumeirah Beach Hotel (04 406 8999). Metro Mall of the Emirates. **Open** 7.30-11.30am, 12.30-4pm, 6.30-11.30pm Mon-Thur, Sun; 7.30-11.30am, 1-4pm (weekend brunch), 6.30-11.30pm Fri, Sat. **Evening buffet** Dhs235. **Seafood buffet** (Thur) Dhs315. **Map** p131 A2 ㉜ **Pan-Asian**

If you can land a seat on the large outdoor terrace, with its uninterrupted view of the Burj Al Arab, you will have an undisputed 'Dubai moment'. This pan-Asian restaurant serves a wide variety of cuisine, with regular nights offering a different nation's food, or food themes, in the form of a buffet. Whichever night of the week you decide to visit (you might find Barbecue Night, Street Food Festival or Taste of Malaysia, for example), you can be assured of a generous spread including everything from soups and salads, through satisfying mains and on to indulgent desserts such as chocolate fountains. The set-up includes a number of cooking stations for dishes made while you wait. With so many cuisines churned out by the kitchen, the food can be slightly hit and miss, but it's a romantic spot, and there's generally something that you'll enjoy. It's a hit with families by day, when an à la carte menu is served, and there's brunch too.

★ Bu Qtair

Road 4D, near Burj Al Arab (055 705 2130). Metro FGB. **Open** 10.30am-3pm, 6.30-11.30pm daily. **Fish/prawns** sold by weight; average Dhs60. **No credit cards. Map** p131 A5 ㉝ **Seafood**

This casual seafood café is a popular entry in many Dubai residents' little black book. Located in a residential area along Jumeirah Beach Road, you'll find queues most evenings at the unassuming spot, with punters happily waiting for a plastic table and chair to become available. There are no reservations and the food served is catch of the day. Whatever you order, it'll be marinated in a mildly spicy seasoning before being fried and served with rice or paratha and curry sauce. Simple but delicious. Staff are swift and efficient, and they have to be to ensure that tables are turned over quickly for the waiting hordes. No James Bond-style aquariums here, then; just the freshest fish, simply served.

Dhow & Anchor

Jumeirah Beach Hotel, Umm Suqeim (04 366 5866). Metro Mall of the Emirates. **Open** noon-1am daily (food served noon-11.30pm). **Main courses** Dhs120-Dhs135. **Map** p131 A4 ㉞ **Gastropub**

Head here for some superior pub-style food, albeit in slightly more dressed-up surroundings than your average local. The restaurant is on one side and a bar with screens on the other. Dishes include dainty salads like peas and goat's cheese, as well as more sturdy fare like juicy wagyu beef burgers and old-fashioned fish and chips. It's nothing fancy, and it quite likes it that way. So do we. There are views of the Burj Al Arab from the terrace.

Frioul Bistro de Luxe

Madinat Jumeirah (04 567 0011, www.frioulbistrodeluxe.com). Metro Mall of the Emirates. **Open** noon-1am Mon-Wed, Sat, Sun; noon-3am Thur, Fri. **Main courses** Dhs60-Dhs180. **Map** p131 B3 ㉟ **French**

Named after the Frioul islands off the southern coast of France, this Madinat Jumeirah eaterie has a style of French-Mediterranean chic that has become increasingly popular in Dubai. There's white, summery seating outside, and the all-white theme continues inside as well. On the menu, a one-page list that doubles up as a place setting, expect frogs' legs, merguez sausages, bouillabaisse and bone marrow – classic dishes produced with verve and a modern gloss. The cocktail menu also shines. It goes the whole French hog by including absinthe in the Starlight (other ingredients are vodka, basil, pineapple and lemon), but it remains light and refreshing.

Al Hambra

Al Qasr Hotel, Madinat Jumeirah (04 366 6730). Metro Mall of the Emirates. **Open** 6-11.30pm Mon-Thur, Sat, Sun; 12.30-4pm, 7-11.30pm Fri. **Tapas** Dhs30-Dhs100. **Main courses** Dhs170-Dhs400. **Map** p131 B3 ㊱ **Spanish**

One of the many restaurants in Madinat Jumeirah's sprawling complex, Al Hambra wins instant points for its romantic *abra* (a traditional boat) access route down the hotel's seafront waterway and its terrace, which has great views of the Burj Al Arab. Meals begin with some tasty tomato potato bread, served with a punchy aioli and olives on the side. There are some genuine highlights on the menu, such as outrageously good Spanish anchovies, patatas bravas with a perfectly crisp exterior, beef cheeks and light stewed octopus.

The Hamptons

Jumeirah Beach Road, next to KFC (04 331 5118, www.hamptonsdubai.com). Metro FGB. **Open** 8am-11pm daily. **Map** p131 A6 ㊲ **Global**

Taking its name from the exclusive getaway in New York State, the Hamptons Café – in a very residential-looking white villa – looks something like its New York namesake. Inside, the space feels exceptionally, pleasantly domestic, more like a stylish home than a café; there is also a roof terrace. It's on the small side and so can feel busy, but service is slick. Menus are presented on iPads, and the selection is a posh, internationally inspired brasserie-style list

EXPLORE

Bu Qtair.

AL MANARA'S CAFÉ STRIP

A little oasis of café culture.

There's not much that would lure a visitor to Al Manara. Adjacent to Umm Suqeim, it's an area that's almost exclusively made up of villas with the odd supermarket. However, there is one strip of road running parallel to and facing Sheikh Zayed Road where you'll find a little row of cafés, some of which are definitely worth stopping off at.

With Australian roots, **Jones the Grocer** (*see p144*) made waves when it arrived as a cool and contemporary gourmet café and food store. Breakfast is a standout, with perfect eggs florentine, fresh orange juice, doughy but crispy bread straight out of the oven and freshly brewed coffee. Next door, **Bystro** (*see p144*) has steadily gained a following for its cool wood interior, fantastic food and sensational coffee. There's a kids' corner and a wonderful pâtisserie display case in the centre of the room. **Crumbs Elysee** (*see p144*) has a tacky and twee exterior but serves excellent Middle Eastern breakfasts, fresh juices and delightful European pastries, including almond bostock, filled with a decadent almond paste and big enough for two. Its sister restaurant and neighbour is a branch of **Reem Al Bawadi** (*see p144*), a Lebanese restaurant and shisha lounge popular with local and expat youth. It's an excellent spot for tasting good Lebanese fare for reasonable prices and in a relaxed setting. The latest addition, **Bertin Bistro & Restaurant** (*see p144*), is one concept split in two. The two-level building looks like a 1920s art deco villa. On the ground floor is a bakery-meets-bistro, with food from the Alsace region of France – the homeland, we are led to believe, of the fictional M Bertin. Upstairs is a restaurant with an outdoor terrace, which serves Spanish and Moroccan cooking, the destination of Bertin's travels.

that ranges from buttermilk fried chicken and East Hampton fish pie through to Moroccan lamb tagine and Thai beef noodle salad. It's a pleasant, attractive and popular spot that's worth a try even if the food is sometimes a bit hit and miss.

Junsui

Burj Al Arab (04 301 7600, www.jumeirah.com). Metro Mall of the Emirates. **Open** 7-10.30am, 12.30-3.30pm, 6-11.30pm daily. **Lunch buffet** Dhs505. **Dinner buffet** Dhs560. **Map** p131 A3 ㊳ **Pan-Asian**

The last thing you expect from the Burj Al Arab is to bag a bargain, and the first thing you expect is quality. Junsui meets expectations in both those criteria. Ordered according to cuisine, on offer are specialities from China, Japan, Korea, Thailand and Indonesia, with a range of live cooking stations. An extensive sushi counter serves wonderful, freshly cut sashimi that's among the best we've tasted. The dim sum station is equally successful, but the live teppanyaki and Korean grill are less remarkable. Buffet prices don't include drinks, and it's clear that by dining at Junsui you're paying a premium for the address. However, if you want to sample a variety of Asian tastes at a single meal and cost isn't an issue, dive in.

Kaftan

Jumeirah Beach Road, opposite Wild Wadi (04 338 9688, www.kaftan-restaurant.com). Metro FGB. **Open** 9am-1am Mon-Wed, Sat, Sun; 9am-2am Thur, Fri. **Main courses** Dhs75-Dhs145. **Map** p131 A4 ㊴ **Turkish**

'Turkish cuisine and fine art' is this restaurant's tagline, and it's a more elegant-looking spot than many of the emirate's Turkish eateries; it also sets itself apart by serving Ottoman dishes in addition to Turkish classics. There's a large outdoor area, while inside are artworks depicting the kaftan of the restaurant's name. The menu features Turkish meze dishes – stuffed vine leaves, *boreki* rolls, and so on – along with grilled mains and casseroles, such as *hunkar begendi* (lamb stew with aubergine). Food doesn't always match the upmarket setting.

Al Mahara

Burj Al Arab (04 301 7600). Metro Mall of the Emirates. **Open** 12.30-3pm, 7pm-midnight daily. **Main courses** Dhs350-Dhs665. **Map** p131 A3 ㊵ **Seafood**

Located on the lower level of the iconic Burj Al Arab, Al Mahara is an intimate and romantic restaurant with a stunning central aquarium. The seating circles the tank, giving everyone a view of the marine life within – it's a Dubai classic. The aquarium may be the restaurant's USP, but the food is never a letdown. Every dish, even the bread, is like a work of art, executed with attention to detail. Dover sole is delicately wrapped into roulades and the sauces are applied to the plate with flair. Combinations are creative and exciting: for example, seared scallops with herb 'Viennoise' come with braised fennel and endive with roasted pear, onion confit in ginger and turmeric jus. Salted caramel mousse is a dessert worth holding out for. Needless to say, it's a pricey evening out – even if you skip the caviar list – but for a one-off special experience it's worth it. The venue has a strict dress code, so gents without jackets may have to borrow one. *Photos pp142-143.*

La Parilla

Jumeirah Beach Hotel (04 366 5866). Metro Mall of the Emirates. **Open** 6.30pm-midnight daily. **Main courses** Dhs190-Dhs490. **Map** p131 A4 ㊶ **Argentinian**

Chilean sea bass and a Caribbean prawn dish are both tempting, but it's the massive selection of steaks that keeps the crowds coming here; they're some of the best in the city. This Jumeirah Beach Hotel restaurant, with remarkable 25th-floor views of the Burj Al Arab, has been one of the most consistently excellent in the city over the last few years. Excellent service and Latin music dancing complement the excellent food. Try the Australian wagyu with roasted root vegetables and fries, with mushroom truffle sauce.

Perry & Blackwelder's

Souk Madinat Jumeirah (04 366 5866). Metro Mall of the Emirates. **Open** noon-2am daily. **Main courses** Dhs60-Dhs145. **Map** p131 B3 ㊷ **American barbecue**

It may have the appearance of a bar, but Perry & Blackwelder's is an American smokehouse, with a full menu of dirty food, from smoked mesquite beef short ribs to sloppy joe sandwiches with barbecue sauce. On the ground floor terrace you can sit at dining tables or dine sitting on beanbags (if you can work out the logistics of enjoying finger-licking food while sat on one). Here, you'll also spot and smell the restaurant's famed meat smoker at work. Among the other Deep South soul food classics are fried chicken wings, cornbread and biscuits; and smoked turkey with candied yams, collard greens and mac'n'cheese. The two-tone fries, a mix of potato and sweet potato, are top-notch. Food arrives with a simple canteen-style presentation. Overall, this is a laid-back, accessible and relatively affordable spot for drinks and comfort food… with plenty of napkins.

★ Pierchic

Al Qasr Hotel, Madinat Jumeirah (04 366 6705). Metro Mall of the Emirates. **Open** 12.30-3pm, 6-11.30pm daily. **Main courses** Dhs110-Dhs375. **Map** p131 B3 ㊸ **Seafood**

Pierchic has long had the reputation for being one of the most romantic restaurants in Dubai. It's a stylish space over the water at the end of a long wooden pier on stilts, with light-wood tables and a stunning Swarovski crystal light installation. Arrive early and you can enjoy a pre-dinner drink at the pod-like bar and take in the unrivalled view of the Burj Al

Al Mahara. See p141.

Arab. The seafood-heavy menu incorporates caviar and oysters, plus soups and salads. Main courses include some lovely combinations – baked organic salmon with cannellini bean, snow pea and tomato salad and red pepper sauce, for example. Lobster thermidor is a crustacean delight, beautifully presented with roasted cauliflower and a mustard sauce. The unique location, however, remains the defining factor and you'll be hard pressed to find a more impressive, or romantic, venue.

Times of Arabia

Souk Madinat Jumeirah (04 368 6044). Metro Mall of the Emirates. **Open** 10am-2am daily. **Main courses** Dhs115-Dhs200. **Map** p131 B3 ⓮ **Arabic**
On a Friday night, this spot in the Madinat Jumeirah is bursting at the seams – booking ahead is recommended, particularly at weekends. Decked out to resemble a traditional *majlis*, with reds, blacks and mosaic patterns, Times of Arabia has a classic Middle Eastern vibe. The hot and cold mezes include good versions of typical Lebanese favourites: baba ganoush, houmous with and without meat, halloumi and spinach fatayer score better than the grilled meats, which can sometimes be a little dry. This is a good place to soak up the views of the Madinat's waterways and, considering its location, prices are good too. We suggest making a meal out of meze.

Toscana

Souk Madinat Jumeirah (04 366 6730). Metro Mall of the Emirates. **Open** noon-11.30pm daily. **Main courses** Dhs80-Dhs145. **Map** p131 B3 ⓯ **Italian**
With wooden tables, chunky ceiling beams and hanging brass saucepans, Toscana is something like an Italian country kitchen. Reservations aren't accepted, so if you're fussy about getting an al fresco spot overlooking the water you may face a bit of a wait, but once seated, expect service to be friendly and efficient. You won't need too long perusing the concise but well-rounded menu, which only has a few options when it comes to mains but plenty of pizzas and pastas – both very good. Definitely one of the best-value options in the Madinat complex and perfect for those with kids in tow.

La Veranda

Jumeirah Beach Hotel (04 406 8520). Metro Mall of the Emirates. **Open** 11.30am-10.30pm Mon-Wed, Sat, Sun; 11.30am-11.30pm Thur, Fri. **Pizza** Dhs80-Dhs99. **Map** p131 B4 ⓰ **Pizza**
Simple food and a waterside alfresco setting give this Italian a laid-back, rustic charm. It's right on the sand and the wooden decking is decorated in warm, cheerful yellows; Mediterranean stoneware jugs filled with oil and balsamic sit on each table. The menu is unpretentious, if a little limited, but

fans of classics like bruschetta (served on slices of perfectly crisp bread) won't be disappointed. The pasta dishes are fine – generous in portion size, slightly lacking in flavour – but the pizzas, baked in a traditional stone oven, have light, fluffy crusts piled with liberal amounts of topping and creamy, indulgent mozzarella.

Zheng He's

Mina A'Salam Hotel, Madinat Jumeirah (04 366 6730). Metro Mall of the Emirates. **Open** noon-2.30pm, 7-11.30pm daily. **Main courses** Dhs95-Dhs178. **Map** p131 A3 47 **Chinese**

Its romantic setting on the waterways of Mina A'Salam help make Zheng He's one of the city's most popular Chinese restaurants. The food is good, but the relaxed atmosphere and regal Far Eastern decor will win you over if your meal doesn't. Some dim sum dishes take a modern, fusion approach, like foie gras, diced chicken-filled yam or spinach, crab roe and caviar dumpling. The crispy fried soft-shell crab starter is a winner, accompanied by green mango, coriander, sour plum and lime dressing. There are fusion elements to some mains too, such as braised foie gras abalone, joining more classic dishes like roast duck with pancakes and cucumber. Save room for inspired desserts such as the tantalising chilled lemongrass jelly with dragon fruits and lemon sorbet.

Cafés & Bars

360°

Jumeirah Beach Hotel (04 406 8741). Metro Mall of the Emirates. **Open** 5pm-2am Mon-Wed, Sun; 5pm-3am Thur-Sat. **Map** p131 A4 48

If you had guests in town for one night only, where would you take them? Matters of season, taste, budget and age aside, there's a high chance that 360° would spring to mind for most expats faced with that question. It's just… well, 360°. Watching the sun set behind the Burj Al Arab, before a night partying on that distinctive circular dancefloor, on a promontory a kilometre out to sea, is a quintessential Dubai experience. The consistency of the soundtrack – particularly from Friday night mainstays Audio Tonic – keeps clued-up clubbers coming back for more.

The Agency

Souk Madinat Jumeirah (04 366 5866). Metro Mall of the Emirates. **Open** 1pm-1am Mon-Wed, Sun; 1pm-2am Thur; 4pm-2am Fri; 5pm-1am Sat. **Map** p131 B3 49

A simple but sleek wine bar with a waterside terrace that manages to combine smart and casual with aplomb. It's without pretension and is a good spot for pre- or post- dinner drinks, particularly if you're in the mood for a quiet evening.

Bertin Bistro & Restaurant

Sheikh Zayed Road, across from Times Square Centre, Al Manara (04 321 9239). Metro Noor Bank. **Open** *Downstairs* 8am-10.30pm daily. *Upstairs* 9.30am-1am daily. **Map** p131 C5 50
See p140 **Al Manara's Café Strip**.

★ Bystro

Sheikh Zayed Road, across from Times Square Centre, Al Manara (04 336 8056, www.bystrodubai.com). Metro Noor Bank. **Open** 8am-10.30pm Mon-Thur; 8.30am-10.30pm Fri, Sat; 8am-5pm Sun. **Map** p131 C5 51
See p140 **Al Manara's Café Strip**.

Crumbs Elysee

Sheikh Zayed Road, Al Manara (04 346 8899, www.crumbselysee.com). Metro Noor Bank. **Open** 6am-9pm daily. **Map** p131 C5 52
See p140 **Al Manara's Café Strip**.

Jones the Grocer

Sheikh Zayed Road, across from Times Square Centre, Al Manara (04 346 6886, www.jonesthegrocer.com). Metro Noor Bank. **Open** 8am-10.30pm Mon-Thur, Sun; 9am-10.30pm Fri, Sat. **Map** p131 C5 53
See p140 **Al Manara's Café Strip**.
Other location Etihad Travel Mall, Sheikh Zayed Road (04 388 1038).

Koubba

Al Qasr Hotel, Madinat Jumeirah (04 366 6730). Metro Mall of the Emirates. **Open** 5pm-2am Mon-Wed, Sat, Sun; 5pm-3am Thur; 4pm-3am Fri. **Map** p131 B3 54
Koubba is a rung above its neighbours – and most lounge bars in the city – a sublime piece of escapism, combining the exotics of *The Arabian Nights* with the class and service of a top-notch lounge bar. Its greatest triumph is taking the Arabian theme and making it feel not in the least tacky. The exotic rugs, traditional curios, patterned cushions and twinkly lanterns call to mind everything from Moroccan souks to starlit desert skies. Outside, the terrace is similarly lovely and has views of the Burj Al Arab and the sea. If it's just the one round you stay for, we'll be surprised.

> **IN THE KNOW REEL TIME**
>
> The **Dubai Moving Image Museum** (MCN Hive Building, Tecom, Al Barsha, 04 421 6679, www.dubaimovingimagemuseum.com) is a new archive tracing the history of photography and film from the 1700s up to modern movie-making. A collection of more than 300 items includes a Kaiser-Panorama that dates back to 19th-century Germany.

Reem Al Bawadi

Sheikh Zayed Road, across from the Times Square Centre, Al Manara (04 330 6663, www.reemalbawadi.com). Metro Noor Bank. **Open** 6am-3am daily. **Map** p131 C5 55
See p140 **Al Manara's Café Strip**.
Other locations Sheikh Mohammed Bin Rashid Boulevard, Downtown (04 443 9690); Dubai Marina Walk (04 452 2525); Jumeirah Beach Road, Jumeirah 3 (04 394 7444); Ramada Deira, Salahuddin Road, Deira (04 259 6111).

★ Shimmers

Mina A'Salam Hotel (04 366 5866). Metro Mall of the Emirates. **Open** noon-1.30am daily. **Map** p131 A3 56
In many respects, Shimmers is like a deluxe beach shack, with wooden floor, heavy furniture, a slatted roof and no walls. It's a great spot for sundowners, offering Burj views without Burj prices, and does a mean line in shisha in the evenings. And with the Arabian Gulf on one side, the Mina A'Salam on another and a perfect view of the Burj on another, it's a charming spot.

Trader Vic's

Madinat Jumeirah (04 366 5646). Metro Mall of the Emirates. **Open** noon-3pm, 6pm-1.30am daily. **Map** p131 B3 57
Trader Vic's has been serving its signature formula of mixed drinks and Polynesian-themed revelry worldwide since the 1930s. Essentially, it's a take on a 1950s American tiki bar, best known for kitsch and sugary drinks served in tacky vessels like totem poles, skulls and barrels – most famously mai tais and the lethally strong and sweet Tikki Pukka Pukka (order with caution). The food is adequate if you fancy a few nibbles at the bar and a lively Cuban band plays most nights. Selected drinks are half price at happy hour. (7-9pm daily).
Other locations Al Fattan Tower, Jumeirah Beach Residence (04 399 8993); Crowne Plaza, Sheikh Zayed Road (04 305 6399); Festival City Mall, Festival City (04 255 9000).

Uptown Bar

Jumeirah Beach Hotel (04 366 5866). Metro Mall of the Emirates. **Open** 6pm-2am daily. **Map** p131 A4 58
Step out of the 24th-floor interior of this bar – which is perfectly nice, but not particularly memorable – and on to the balcony, and you'll find yourself gazing down at an extraordinary view of Jumeirah, with roads receding to a vanishing point and the Burj Al Arab glowing on the horizon. Come back at night and it's even more extraordinary, as the city becomes an abstract drawing in fluorescent light. Bar snacks are expensive for what you get, and it's hard to escape the feeling that Uptown Bar isn't made for food anyway – it's there for alfresco drinking and chatting, and soaking up the view.

EXPLORE

PARTY BRUNCHES

Celebrating Friday afternoon.

If there's one thing Dubai has no shortage of, it's brunches. A Dubai brunch is quite different to a brunch elsewhere in the world. These aren't lazy late breakfasts accompanied by coffee and tea. These brunches are (mostly) all-you-can eat and drink parties. On a Friday (or, occasionally, Saturday) afternoon, Dubai lets its hair down.

Almost all restaurants and lots of bars have a Friday brunch. They run the gamut from posh, multi-course tasting menus with matching wines to buffet and booze events. But some have a little (or a lot) more wow factor than others, and those at the Madinat Jumeirah's luxury hotels Al Qasr and Mina A'Salam are right at the top of the pile.

In **Al Qasr** (*see p279*; 04 366 8888, 12.30-4pm Fri, with soft drinks Dhs475, with sparkling wine Dhs575, with champagne Dhs795), the hotel's three restaurants come together to put on an extravagant, special-occasion brunch. It takes over a lot of the hotel, so it's an immense affair, with live cooking stations and bars lining the walkways and a huge range of global dishes available.

Mina A'Salam (*see p281*; 04 366 8888, 12.30-4pm Fri, with soft drinks Dhs450, with sparkling wine Dhs535) also serves its brunch from its three restaurants. Among the many culinary highlights is a cheese room: that's right, a whole room devoted to *fromage*. You can enjoy your brunch outside, on tables along the waterways of the Madinat Jumeirah – a lovely spot in the cooler months.

Another brunch in the same vein is **Bubbalicious** (04 399 4141, www.westinminaseyahi.com, 1-4pm Fri, with soft drinks Dhs450, with sparkling wine and alcoholic drinks Dhs550, with champagne and alcohol Dhs650) at the **Westin Dubai Mina Seyahi Beach Resort & Marina**. Once again spread over three restaurants, the mind-blowingly extensive spread includes a hideaway *Alice in Wonderland* dessert station, and other themed stations with cuisines from all over the world, paired with drinks, including spirits drunk out of a hollowed watermelon.

Saffron's brunch in **Atlantis The Palm** (*see p282*; 04 426 2000, 12.30-4pm Fri, with alcohol Dhs550) can only be described as unrestrained opulence (and inebriation – this is for over-21s only). The normally rather bland restaurant explodes with boisterous activity every Friday when the clock strikes (half-past) noon. This brunch tends to attract diners of the ostentatious kind who are out for nothing short of a raucous party. There are more than 220 dishes to choose from, many with a loose Asian theme. Huge sections are devoted to sushi, Chinese, Thai and Indian, as well as European staples, salads and desserts. Far more popular than any of these, however, are the omnipresent drinks stations.

EDEN Beach Club (*see p156*; 04 277 1477, 1-5pm Sat, with house alcohol Dhs495, with champagne Dhs595) also attracts party-goers and sun-worshippers keen to parade by the pool at its Saturday brunch. Food here tends towards the fresh and light and dishes are served in courses at your table as you sip on sangria or spirits. It's a young and fashionable crowd so dress to impress, and maybe buy a new swimsuit for this brunch-turned-bikini-pageant.

Al Sufouh & Palm Jumeirah

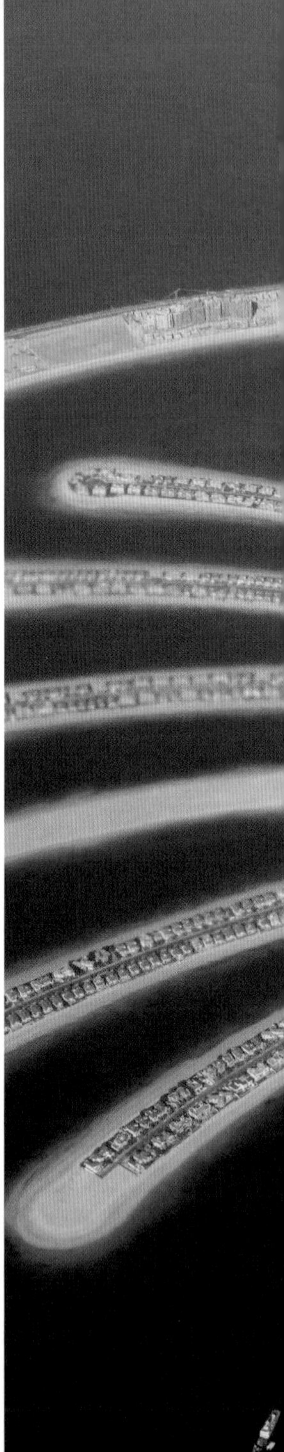

Al Sufouh stretches, roughly, from the Burj Al Arab down to Dubai Marina, between Sheikh Zayed Road and the coast. Drive down Al Soufouh Road and you'll pass a series of royal palaces on either side. Al Sufouh Beach is a pleasant sunbathing spot away from the masses. On the other side of the road, and a world away from the beach paradise vibe, are the workaday free zones of Knowledge Village, Internet City and Media City.

Stretching away from the coast are the famed Palm Jumeirah islands, arranged to resemble a palm tree – and if you view them from the air they do look like just that. The huge Atlantis The Palm offers an impressive vista as you approach.

China Grill.

Don't Miss

1 Atlantis The Palm Showy but fun ocean-themed resort (p155).

2 Beach bars The best location for a sandy sundowner (p154, p159).

3 China Grill Seriously stylish New York import (p152).

4 101 Dining Lounge & Bar Take a romantic boat ride to dinner at one of Dubai's best restaurants (p156).

5 Bubbalicious For a blow-out Friday brunch (p148).

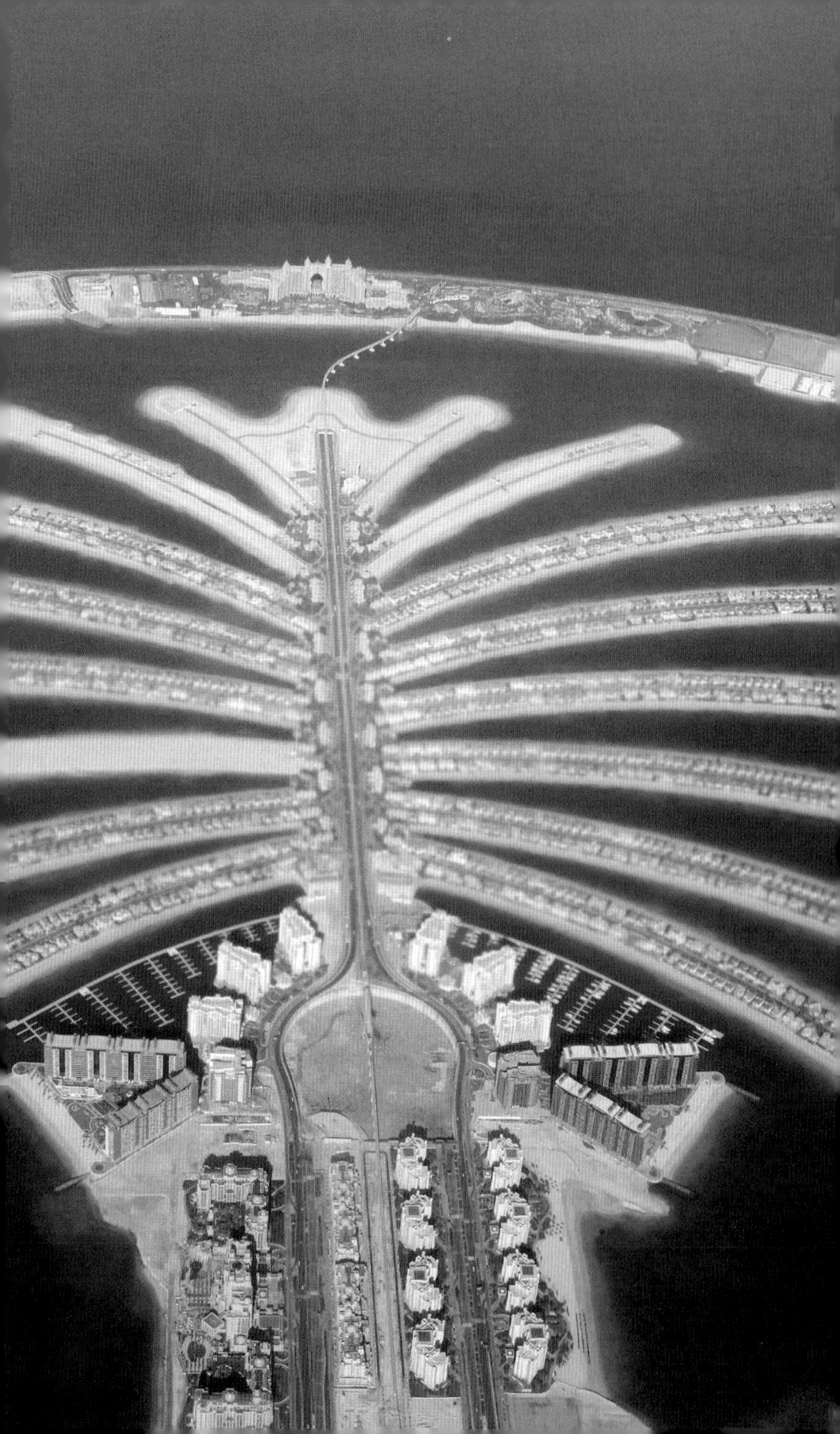

AL SUFOUH

Drive down Al Sufouh Road from Burj Al Arab, heading towards Dubai Marina with the coast on your right, and you'll pass a series of palaces and mansions. The grassy lawns outside the white palace walls used to be inhabited by palace peacocks, which would lazily wander up and down the road, but these have recently been replaced by a mysterious herd of bunny rabbits. **Al Sufouh Beach** – nicknamed Black Palace Beach – remains public and, although tricky to access (there's a rough track across sand dunes), is a pleasant sunbathing spot away from the masses. Over the road, a striking all-black palace constructed from black marble can be glimpsed amid some dense greenery. Just off the coastline you can see Sheikh Mohammed Bin Rashid Al Maktoum's private island, where his yacht – one of the largest in the world at more than 150 metres (500 feet) – is often moored.

Juxtaposing the beach paradise vibe, on the other side of Al Sufouh Road, are the **free zones** (*see p152* **In the Know**) just over the road. They are neither an eyesore nor particularly picturesque and have – as is common in Dubai – laughably literal names. **Knowledge Village** is mostly home to Middle Eastern branches of international universities as well as language schools and the like. Next door, **Media City**, predictably, is the base for the majority of the city's (and region's) news, broadcasting and publishing companies, including CNN and Thompson Reuters. **Internet City** is a regional technological hub where Fortune 500 companies such as Facebook, HP, Cisco Systems and Google have set up offices.

Although the Palm Jumeirah packs a punch when it comes to beachy bars, the nearby mainland has two of the best in the city: lively **Barasti** and the elegant **Jetty Lounge** are two variations of a beach-bum bar, while the **Observatory** is the place to go for aerial coastal views. Restaurants in this area are mostly high-end, save for a couple of casual cafés in Media and Internet Cities, like **1762**, which are frequented by suited businesspeople during the lunchtime rush. The **Westin Dubai Mina Seyahi Beach Resort & Marina** (*see p284*) has a couple of good options: popular New York fusion restaurant **China Grill** and laidback Italian **Bussola**. It's also the setting for one of the city's most famous blow-out brunches, **Bubbalicious** (*see p145* **Party Brunches**). Friday brunch is an institution in Dubai and this famous spread takes over three restaurants, with acrobats, globally themed food stations and, of course, bubbly.

Aside from the public Al Sufouh Beach, the coastline is occupied by beach clubs (*see p149* **Beach Bliss**) attached to five-star hotels located here, most of which have day passes available that include access to pools as well as beaches.

Sights & Attractions

Al Sufouh Beach

Off Al Sufouh Road. Tram Al Sufouh.
Map p151 E5 ❶

This is a small public beach sandwiched between two palaces on Al Sufouh Road. It's difficult to spot as the road veers off to it at a big sandy patch between two palaces. There are no mod cons like toilets or changing rooms but it's less popular than other beaches – a good choice if you're after a peaceful spot.

Emirates Golf Club

Emirates Golf Club, Sheikh Zayed Road (04 380 1234, www.dubaigolf.com). Metro Nakheel.
Map p150 C6 ❷
Majlis course *Oct-Apr* 18-hole Dhs995 Mon-Thur, Sun; Dhs1,100 Fri, Sat. *May* 18-hole Dhs795.
Faldo course *Night golf* Oct-Apr 18-hole Dhs425; 9-hole Dhs255.
Both Open from 6am daily. **Last tee-off time** *9 holes* 9.35pm Mon-Thur, Sun; 7.55pm Fri, Sat. *Driving range* last bucket 9.30pm daily.

One of the most beautifully landscaped courses in the city, the Majlis course is home to the European PGA Tour Omega Dubai Desert Classic and has won multiple awards, while the Faldo course is the only fully floodlit 18-hole course in the UAE. Playing here is unique – the atmosphere is that of a lush and peaceful course, while the towering apartment blocks of Jumeirah Lakes Towers rise above the palm trees and remind you that you are playing bang in the centre of a huge city. All fees include cart hire and range balls before play.

One&Only Royal Mirage Beach

Al Sufouh Road (04 315 2105, http://royalmirage.oneandonlyresorts.com). Tram Media City.
Open 10am-sunset daily. **Admission** *Day pass with reservation* Dhs300; Dhs225 reductions. *Day pass without reservation* Dhs400; Dhs350 reductions. **Map** p150 C5 ❸
See p149 **Beach Bliss**.
► *For a review of the hotel, see p282.*

Restaurants

Bussola

Westin Dubai Mina Seyahi Beach Resort & Marina, Al Sufouh Road (04 511 7136, www.bussoladubai.com). Tram Media City. **Open** noon-2.45pm, 7-10.45pm daily. **Main courses** Dhs140-Dhs220. **Pizzas** Dhs60-Dhs105. **Map** p150 C5 ❹ **Italian**

Diners can sit upstairs on the terrace and dine on wood-fired pizzas, or downstairs in the main restaurant or patio, where there's a regular Italian menu. The majority of families opt for the upstairs section, leaving downstairs pretty much child-free. The problem, however, is that if one member of your party wants pizza and the others don't, you have a bit of a dilemma. Seafood dishes are second to none, and

EXPLORE

BEACH BLISS

Join the club and soak up the sun in style.

Public beaches are all well and good, but to have a day at the beach Dubai-style – if you're not staying in a coastal hotel with its own beach – treat yourself to a beach club and bask in cocktails, bar snacks, sun loungers and swimming pools, as well as the sun.

Sofitel The Palm's **Moana** (*see p157*) offers a brunch-and-beach package on Fridays (with soft drinks Dhs300, with house alcohol Dhs450). In addition to four courses of sublime seafood, you'll get complimentary beach access and slices of apple to snack on while you relax. There's eco-golf (hitting balls of fish food into the sea), paddleboarding, water volleyball and a daily beach and pool happy hour from 4pm, plus little buzzers for food and drinks service at your sun lounger.

For an adult-friendly day on the beach, **EDEN Beach Club** (*see p156*), perched at the very tip of Palm Jumeirah's crescent, is your best bet. There's no entertainment for kids; it's all grown-up and sophisticated, done out in pale blue and white. Behind the row of stylish cabanas is a long pool designed more for taking a cooling dip rather than doing laps, but you can swim up to the well-stocked bar. There's a lounge area, a beach bar and a restaurant; some tables even have their own private plunge pools. Latin beats play throughout the club at just the right volume by day, adding to the stylish but blissed-out feel, but when the sun goes down on weekend evenings, this far-flung corner of the Palm ramps up the volume and is transformed into an Ibiza-style beach party with high-tech lighting, top international DJs, dancers and acrobats.

Families, on the other hand, will enjoy **Riva Ristorante, Bar & Beach** (*see p156*) which has a lively laid-back vibe and a shallow faux-beach pool that's ideal for small kids to play in. A small bar sits poolside, but well out of reach of children. As the club is tucked on the east side of the Palm Jumeirah's trunk, the beach has a lagoon feel. Pack snorkels – there are lots of fish to be spotted – and kayaks and paddleboards are available for hire. The sun loungers on the beach face away from the water, which is a shame given the lovely view of the Burj Al Arab. The restaurant serves superb Mediterranean food from a more varied menu than you would expect of a beach club, and impresses enough to warrant a visit on its own.

Similarly, **Fairmont The Palm** (*see p156*) is perfect for just about everyone – families can lounge by the winding pool (with lots of lifeguards) while their kids frolic. And if they don't fancy a dip there's also a play area with water cannons. Just off the pool, Seagrill on 25° Restaurant & Lounge has a pleasant setting. If you don't have kids, you'll still enjoy Fairmont The Palm. The pool is big enough to give them a wide berth, or you can head down to the beach itself, where the loungers and cabanas are set away from the action.

The beach club of the **One&Only Royal Mirage** (*see p148*) is partly by the pool and partly on the sand. It's popular with older couples and families, and with no music playing, it's the ideal place to relax and read. There's only one pool, but it's large, and in the summer months you'll be grateful for the heavily shaded areas around it. Don't expect to be waited on hand and foot, though: you'll have to walk to other restaurants around the property if, for example, you'd like fries with your toasted sandwich from the pool bar.

One&Only Royal Mirage.

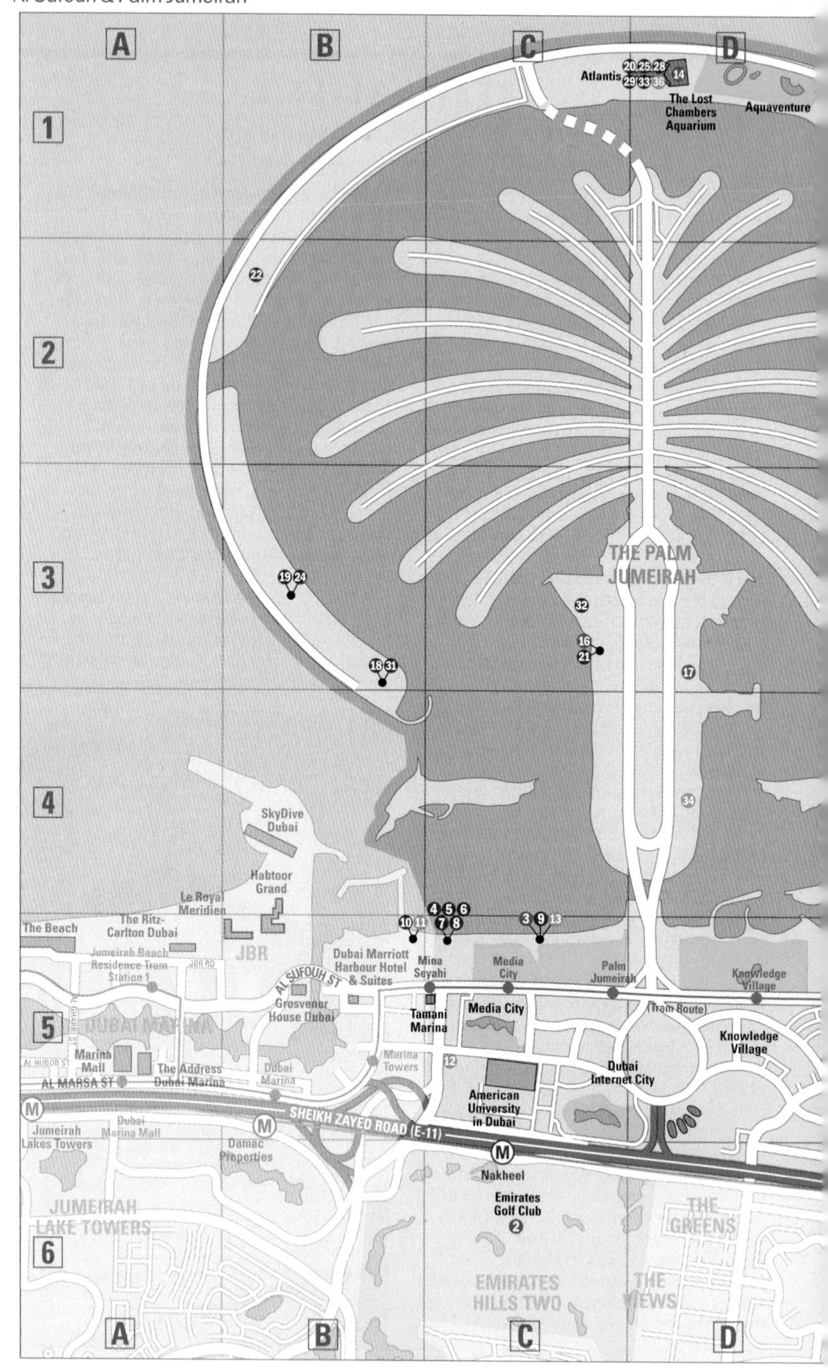
Atlantis
The Lost Chambers Aquarium
Aquaventure
THE PALM JUMEIRAH
SkyDive Dubai
Habtoor Grand
Le Royal Meridien
The Ritz-Carlton Dubai
The Beach
Jumeirah Beach Residence Tram Station 1
JBR
JBR RD
Dubai Marriott Harbour Hotel & Suites
Mina Seyahi
Media City
Palm Jumeirah
Knowledge Village
AL SUFOUH ST
Grosvenor House Dubai
Tamani Marina
Media City
(Tram Route)
Knowledge Village
DUBAI MARINA
AL GHARBI ST
AL HUBOB ST
Marina Mall
The Address Dubai Marina
AL MARSA ST
Dubai Marina
Marina Towers
Dubai Internet City
American University in Dubai
SHEIKH ZAYED ROAD (E-11)
Jumeirah Lakes Towers
Dubai Marina Mall
Damac Properties
Nakheel
Emirates Golf Club
JUMEIRAH LAKE TOWERS
THE GREENS
EMIRATES HILLS TWO
THE VIEWS

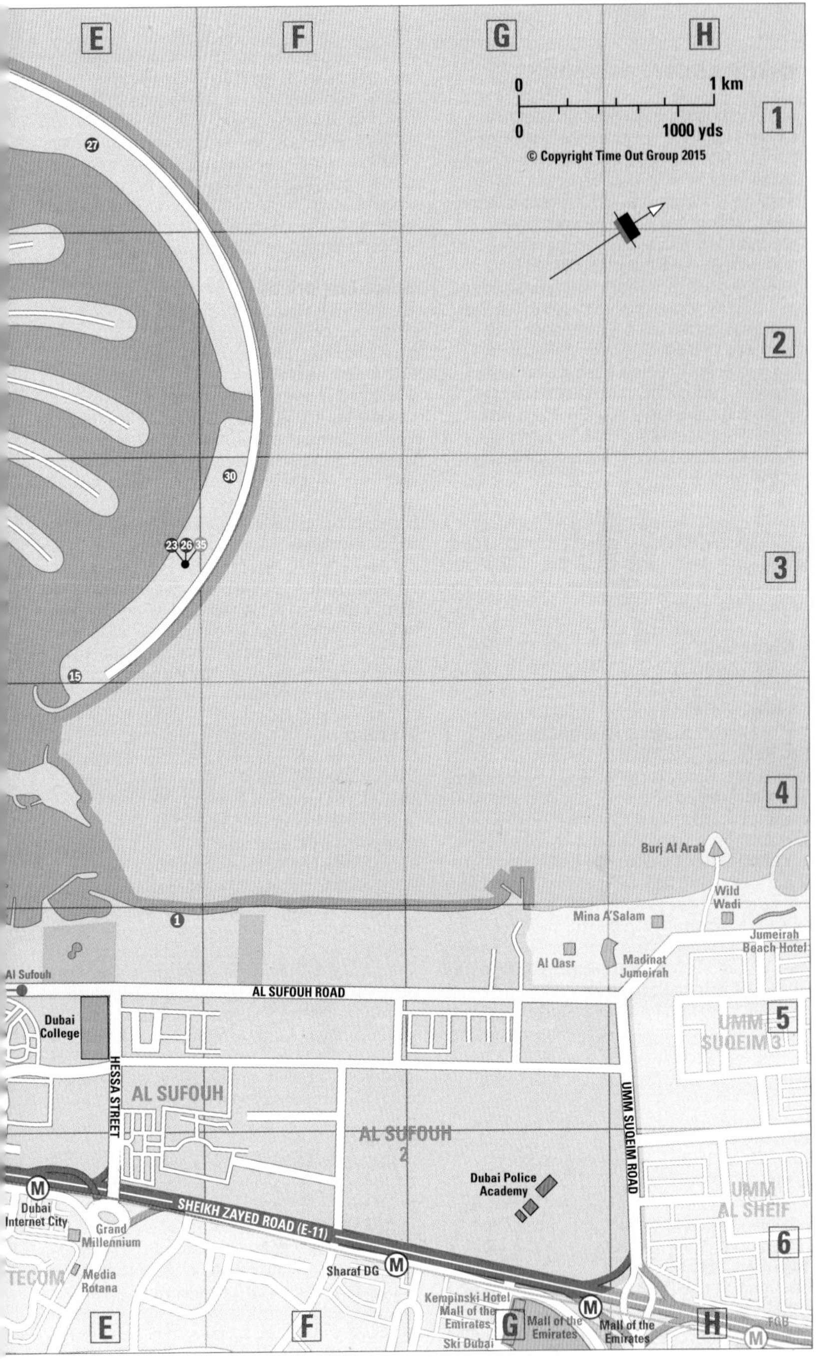
E
F
G
H
0
1 km
0
1000 yds
© Copyright Time Out Group 2015
1
2
3
4
5
6
27
30
23
26
35
15
1
Burj Al Arab
Wild Wadi
Mina A'Salam
Jumeirah Beach Hotel
Al Qasr
Madinat Jumeirah
Al Sufouh
AL SUFOUH ROAD
Dubai College
UMM SUQEIM 3
HESSA STREET
AL SUFOUH
AL SUFOUH 2
UMM SUQEIM ROAD
Dubai Police Academy
UMM AL SHEIF
M
Dubai Internet City
SHEIKH ZAYED ROAD (E-11)
Grand Millennium
TECOM
Media Rotana
Sharaf DG
Kempinski Hotel Mall of the Emirates
Ski Dubai
Mall of the Emirates
Mall of the Emirates
FGB

IN THE KNOW FREE ZONES

Areas in Dubai that have been created as tax- and duty-free zones are known as free zones. The government set up a number of these, specialising in different industries, as a way to incentivise foreign investment and to encourage overseas companies to base their Middle Eastern branches in Dubai. The UAE has complicated laws regarding setting up and owning businesses in the country, one of which used to require new businesses to have at least one local partner with a 50/50 stake. Although this law has been modified, basing a company in a free zone means that it doesn't apply at all. There are more than 20 free zones in the city and the concept has been hugely successful in attracting business investors to the emirate.

pasta is freshly made and served perfectly al dente, though it can lack a little bit of punch. The place looks great, though, and the vibe is friendly: a good choice for impressing a date.

★ China Grill

Westin Dubai Mina Seyahi Beach Resort & Marina. Tram Media City. **Open** 6-11pm Mon-Wed, Sat, Sun; 6pm-midnight Thur, Fri. **Main courses** Dhs105-Dhs385. **Sushi & sashimi** Dhs60-Dhs115. **Map** p150 C5 ❺ **Pan-Asian**

China Grill is an outpost of a 27-year-old brand from New York – an early adopter of the Asian fusion concept. Tucked around the back of the Westin on Al Sufouh Road, you'll find a spacious and dimly lit mezzanine level lounge bar. Just below it is the dining space, with high ceilings elegantly adorned with large shell-like lanterns and Chinese vases on the walls. Sharing plates come with plenty of twists, with a list ranging across dim sum, sushi and salads. There are also dishes available as small or large plates, such as barbecued pulled lamb with steamed buns, and lobster and scallion pancake with truffle butter. While an original idea that is nearly 30 years old may not be mind-blowing in today's fusion-familiar market, China Grill still offers plenty of character and quality.

Hunters Room & Grill

Westin Dubai Mina Seyahi Beach Resort & Marina, Al Sufouh Road (04 511 7136, www.huntersdubai.com). Tram Media City. **Open** 6-10.45pm Mon-Wed, Sat, Sun; 6-11.45pm Thur; 7-11.45pm Fri. **Main courses** Dhs145-Dhs320. **Map** p150 C5 ❻ **Steakhouse**

This dimly lit restaurant deep within the Westin is a striking spot, with oversized design features and open kitchen slap bang in the middle of the dining area. There are large tables for big groups and couples find space at the back. When it comes to the steaks, there is plenty of information to help you make an informed choice, with the different cuts of meat on display and the staff forthcoming with detailed descriptions. But while the meat is of good quality, it is slightly let down by uninspired side dishes. Dessert, though, is an interesting experience, with some unusual ingredients, including a pumpkin dish featuring basmati rice ice-cream.

Spice Emporium

Westin Dubai Mina Seyahi Beach Resort & Marina, Al Sufouh Road (04 511 7136, www.spiceemporiumdubai.com). Tram Media City. **Open** 7-10.45pm Mon-Wed, Sat, Sun; 7-11.45pm Thur, Fri. **Main courses** Dhs60-Dhs150. **Map** p150 C5 ❼ **Thai**

With chic, minimal furnishings, dark wooden tables and low lounge-style seats, the Westin's signature spot feels of-the-moment, despite being a Dubai dining fixture since 2008. Seasoned Thai chef Khamphun is at the helm, offering a traditional take on his homeland's flavours. The set menus and sharing deals offer the best overview of the restaurant's signature dishes, and make for good value too. The Thai Feast package may feature well-trodden classics such as chicken green curry, pad Thai, tom yam and beef satay, but you'll rarely find them tasting as fresh or flavoursome as they are here. A top Thai option that refuses to tire.

★ El Sur

Westin Dubai Mina Seyahi Beach Resort & Marina, Al Sufouh Road (04 399 7700). Tram Media City. **Open** 7pm-1am daily. **Tapas** Dhs35-Dhs165. **Main courses** Dhs110-Dhs210. **Map** p150 C5 ❽ **Spanish**

The city's best Spanish restaurant by a nose, El Sur has a good atmosphere, great food and excellent service. Dishes arrive in appealing fits and starts – a sharing platter of incredible meats here, a perfect octopus carpaccio there, and the best garlic prawns we've had this side of San Sebastian. The steak, meanwhile, is sublime. The only slight downside is the setting. It's not a big space, and has been decorated smartly and airily to compensate. But its proximity to a rowdy bar, and a terrace that has ambience but not a great view, takes away a little when it comes to the romantic factor.

Tagine

One&Only Royal Mirage, Al Sufouh Road (04 399 9999, http://royalmirage.oneandonlyresorts.com). **Open** 7-11.30pm Tue-Sun. **Main courses** Dhs105-Dhs270. **Map** p150 C5 ❾ **Moroccan**

The courtyard setting and musical entertainment lend an inviting ambience to this Moroccan restaurant. Dishes such as *d'jaj kammama* (braised chicken with onion, black pepper, saffron and cinnamon, garnished with honey, apricots, fried almonds and

KINGDOM OF ATLANTIS

Tackle the thrill rides or tuck into superb seafood at Atlantis The Palm.

Atlantis The Palm (*see p155*) is a sprawling ocean-themed resort that sits more or less at the head of the Palm Jumeirah's outer crescent. Encompassing a waterpark, dolphin bay and aquarium, it's an impressive sight. Rooms are luxurious and lavish, but everything has the feel of a Disneyland resort, rather than a five-star hotel. Thankfully, this doesn't extend to all the restaurants, some of which are fantastic. **Nobu** (*see p157*) offers Japanese food from the world-famous brand and a welcome respite in its cool interior; **Ossiano** (*see p157*) serves superb seafood.

Aquariums are everywhere, though the fish are just as impressive in the tank at the Dubai Mall. Things are jazzed up here, though, with a scattering of lost city-style objects. The **Lost Chambers Aquarium** (*see p155*) will delight young children, and the behind-the-scenes tour is a rare opportunity to see how aquariums operate. One aquarium tank is viewable as you descend a staircase down a corridor from the lobby en route to the hotel restaurants, or you can have your own private viewing while taking a bath by booking one of the two underwater suites.

Aquaventure waterpark (*see p155*) has a number of rides that pass through shark-filled tanks, as well as rides for thrill-seekers such as the 27-metre (88-foot) Leap of Faith or Poseidon's Revenge, which involves a trap door and speeds of up to 60kmh (37mph). And children aren't forgotten, of course, with family-friendly rides and adventure play areas.

If you want to get even closer to the marine life, for an extra fee on top of your Aquaventure ticket you can also feed stingrays (Dhs175) or go on a Shark Safari in the Shark Lagoon (Dhs295). You can swim or dive with dolphins at **Dolphin Bay** (*see p155*) and make friends with sea lions at **Sea Lion Point** (*see p155*). There are a variety of experiences available for both of these that are priced based on your level of interaction with the marine life. Diving and snorkel experiences are also available in the Ambassador Lagoon.

For a review of the hotel accommodation at Atlantis, *see p282*.

IN THE KNOW GETTING TO PALM JUMEIRAH

To access Palm Jumeirah via public transport, you'll need to take the tram to Palm Jumeirah station and then either catch a taxi to your destination (around Dhs20) or ride the (notoriously expensive) monorail across to Atlantis The Palm. For superb views of the islands and Atlantis on approach, though, the monorail is worth the extra cost.

grilled sesame seeds) – should be bursting with bold flavours, but in reality can be underspiced. On the other hand, portions are huge, so they're good value for money, provided you have a big appetite. Not a place for superb cuisine, then, but it's not a bad choice for a taste of Morocco in pleasant surroundings.

Watatsumi

Le Méridien Mina Seyahi Beach Resort & Marina, Al Sufouh Road (04 399 3373, http://watatsumi.ae). Tram Mina Seyahi. **Open** noon-3pm, 7-11.30pm Mon-Thur, Sun; 7-11.30pm Fri, Sat. **Main courses** Dhs80-Dhs185. **Map** p150 B5 ⑩ **Japanese**

Watatsumi's setting is a little lacking in warmth, despite plenty of potential in the rounded space and modish furniture, and though beach-facing windows run a portion of the perimeter, don't expect a sea view. Service, however, is charming, helpful and spilling over with recommendations, and the cooking is very good: dishes run from sushi and maki to robatayaki, tempura, noodles, mains and more; we particularly like the crispy soft shell crab and the salmon teriyaki. However, given the muted atmosphere and lack of pizzazz, the prices may make your eyes water slightly.

Bars & Cafés

★ Barasti

Le Méridien Mina Seyahi Beach Resort & Marina, Al Sufouh Road (04 318 1313, www.barastibeach.com). Tram Mina Seyahi. **Open** 11am-1.30am Mon-Wed, Sat, Sun; 11am-3am Thur, Fri. **Map** p150 B5 ⑪

If you utter the word 'Barasti', chances are that the person you're talking to will know it and have been at least once. Since opening its doors in 1995, the beachside venue has become a Dubai institution, a rite of passage for newbies arriving in the emirate and a landmark for tourists. The upstairs outdoor area is home to a huge bar and fairy lights lead down a boardwalk to the sand where there are more tables and another bar. The lower level also accommodates a large stage for live acts and DJs, which give the venue a club-like atmosphere come the early hours.

Jetty Lounge.

EXPLORE

However, if you opt for a table close to the water on the far left corner of the beach, it's still quiet enough for a conversation. It is busy throughout the day, whether you pop in early to lounge on the beach or swing by at night to watch sport, grab a drink or dance on the sand. The beauty of the venue is its ability to appeal to everyone, and the crowd is usually a mix of young and old. It does have a tendency to get a bit rowdy in the evenings – particularly with the post-brunch Friday crowd – but it's a failsafe for liveliness and a one-size-fits-all boozy spot.

Garden on 8

Media One Hotel, Media City (04 427 1000, www.mediaonehotel.com). Tram Media City.
Open 5-11.30pm daily. **Map** p150 C5 ⑫
Designed to look like a homely pub garden, the new Dubai Media City bar sits adjacent to the Media One Hotel's more established poolside outlet Dek on 8. Casual, but not devoid of a few interesting quirks, the spacious venue boasts fake grass and potted plants, while lawn gnomes lurk behind rows of large picnic tables. It's a simple but creative space, with a wall garden of fresh vegetables and herbs cultivated by the chefs, plus furniture made from recycled and reused materials. Other notable objects include a wishing well, and for the sentimentalists, a fence full of padlocks, designed to look like they've been left by people to remember their significant others. Perhaps unlike its eighth-floor neighbour, there are plenty of places to sit here – you can choose to park your rear on one of the aforementioned benches, take a seat at the bar counter, loiter at the tall barrel-style tables or kick back in the small, cosy sofa area.

★ Jetty Lounge

One&Only Royal Mirage, Al Sufouh Road, Al Sufouh (04 399 9999, http://royalmirage.oneandonlyresorts.com). Tram Media City.
Open 2pm-2am daily. **Map** p150 C5 ⑬
The secret of Jetty Lounge is in its tone: background chill-out tunes, comfy cushions and candles make this place scream style – quietly. It's as though someone ordered a chic European lounge that was accidentally delivered to the beach. But it works and, miraculously, it tends not to attract pretentious idiots to soak up the twilight and enjoy the drinks – even the cheapest grape on the menu is delicious. It's how we'd imagine an Ibiza for grown-ups would look and sound, with those chill-out zones staying at just the right decibel.

PALM JUMEIRAH

For information on how to access venues on Palm Jumeirah, *see p154* **In the Know**.

Nothing says 'Dubai' more than manmade islands. The Palm Jumeirah islands, stretching out off the coast at Al Sufouh, were arranged somewhat more successfully than the World Islands to resemble a palm tree – though the full shape can only be discerned from the air. On the ground, however, there's not much to distinguish driving along its roads to any other road in the city. Since you can't make out the overall shape of the islands from the ground, the main draw of visiting them – aside from the novelty of standing on a man-made, palm tree-shaped island – is **Atlantis The Palm**, impressive on approach because of its sheer size (though the monorail above the road slightly detracts from the sight). Once you reach it, you can occupy yourself with dolphin encounters, waterparks, beach bars and some of the priciest restaurants in the city. The Palm Jumeirah is also home to some other – fantastic – restaurants. Then there are beach clubs: at **Fairmont The Palm** and **Riva Ristorante, Bar & Beach**. And last, but certainly not least, there are the beautiful views as you round the East Crescent. As you look back across the water towards the coast there's a view encompassing the Burj Al Arab, Jumeirah Beach Hotel, the Madinat hotels and the Burj Khalifa. A photo opportunity if ever there was one.

Sights & Attractions

Atlantis The Palm

All *04 426 2000, www.atlantisthepalm.com.*
Map p150 D1 ⑭
★ **Aquaventure Open** 10am-sunset daily. **Admission** Dhs250 over 1.2m tall; Dhs205 under 1.2m tall. Free for hotel guests.
Dive & snorkel experiences Open Varies; phone or check website. **Admission** *Ultimate Dive* (for certified divers) Dhs950. *Atlantis Diver Discovery* (for non-certified divers) Dhs1,150. *Ultimate snorkel* Dhs250 per person.
Dolphin Bay Open 9.30am-4.30pm daily. **Admission** *Dolphin Photo Fun* Dhs425. *Dolphin Encounter* (shallow water) Dhs795. *Dolphin Adventure* Dhs960. *Royal Swim* Dhs1,100. *Dolphin scuba dive* Dhs1,450. *Observer pass* Dhs300; Dhs100 (hotel guests). *Encounter photographs* from Dhs75. Prices are inclusive of access to the Aquaventure waterpark, the Lost Chambers aquarium and a meal deal at one of the waterpark restaurants. Visitors should note that an expensive Observer Pass is charged to view the interaction of friends and family with the dolphins from the lagoon shore.
★ **Lost Chambers Aquarium Open** 10am-11pm daily. **Admission** Dhs110; Dhs80 children. *See p153* **Kingdom of Atlantis**.
Sea Lion Point Open 9.30am-4.30pm daily. **Admission** *Sea Lion Photo Fun* Dhs425. *Sea Lion Discovery* Dhs645 per person. *Encounter photographs* from Dhs75. Prices are inclusive of access to Aquaventure waterpark, the Lost Chambers aquarium and a meal deal at one of the waterpark restaurants.
▶ *For a review of the hotel, see p282.*

EXPLORE

★ EDEN Beach Club
Rixos The Palm, East Crescent (04 277 1477, www.edenbeachclub.com). **Open** Varies; call or check website for details. **Day pass** Dhs100 Mon-Thur, Sun; Dhs200 Fri, Sat. Welcome drink included. **Map** p151 E3 ⑮
See p149 **Beach Bliss.** *Photos pp158-159.*

Fairmont the Palm Health & Beach Club
Fairmont The Palm (04 457 3388, www.fairmont.com/palm-dubai). **Open** sunrise-8pm daily. **Day pass** Dhs200, Dhs150 reductions Mon-Thur, Sun; Dhs250, Dhs150 reductions Fri, Sat. **Map** p150 C3 ⑯
See p149 **Beach Bliss.**
► *For a review of the hotel, see p282.*

Riva Ristorante, Bar & Beach
Shoreline Apartments Building 8 (04 430 9466, www.riva-beach.com). **Open** *Beach* 7am-7pm daily. *RIVA Bar* noon-midnight daily. *Pool* 7am-9pm daily (adults only 7-9pm). *Gym* 7-10pm daily. **Day pass** Dhs100, Dhs50 reductions Mon-Thur, Sun. Dhs175, Dhs85 reductions Fri, Sat. *Gym access* additional Dhs50. **Map** p150 D3 ⑰
See p149 **Beach Bliss.**

EXPLORE

Restaurants

In addition to the venues below, there's superb Mediterranean food and a varied menu at beach club **Riva** (*see above*).

★ 101 Dining Lounge & Bar
One&Only The Palm Dubai (04 440 1030, http://thepalm.oneandonlyresorts.com). **Open** 12.30-3.30pm, 7-11pm daily. **Main courses** Dhs85-Dhs280. **Map** p150 B3 ⑱ **Mediterranean**
Set in the idyllic surroundings of One&Only The Palm, reachable by boat from Jetty Lounge (*see p155*) and jutting out into the tip of the Palm's furthest reaches, 101 Dining Lounge & Bar starts winning awards pretty much as soon as you're strolling down the jetty that takes you to it. Once there, the stunning decor – it's like a sort of high-end floating shack with sail ceilings blowing in the wind out in front of you as you gaze into the deep blue distance – keeps up the romantic vibe. And then comes the food. A mix of top-drawer Mediterranean and European dishes, weighted towards Spanish, with a great collection of tapas and a selection of paellas. We heartily recommend the octopus cooked on the Josper charcoal barbeque. It is, frankly, a delight.

Amala
Jumeirah Zabeel Saray (04 453 0444, www.jumeirah.com). **Open** 6pm-1am Mon-Thur, Sun; 1-4pm, 6pm-1am Fri, Sat. **Main courses** Dhs85-Dhs110. **Map** p150 B3 ⑲ **Indian**
Amala is a rather regal restaurant in the luxurious Jumeirah Zabeel Saray, serving refined and authentic curries, biryanis and meats from the tandoor oven. Food is beautifully presented: no big bowls of curry here; portions are delicate. Try the mixed chaat starter, a delightful combination of pastries, with potato, tomato, lentil and savoury vermicelli, which all have a kick to them. *Pahhadi murgh tikka* – chicken marinated with nuts and cheese, with egg white – has lovely subtle spicing. There are many creative main courses, but we like a traditional *tandoor murgh kali mirch* (black pepper chicken), or lamb biryani. As is fitting for the opulent surroundings, you get well looked after in Amala.

Asia Republic
Atlantis The Palm (04 398 9193, www.atlantisthepalm.com). **Open** noon-10pm Mon-Wed, Sat, Sun; noon-11pm Thur, Fri. **Main courses** Dhs30-Dhs70. **Map** p150 D1 ⑳ **Pan-Asian**
Asia Republic might be based in Atlantis, but don't expect the resort's typical five-star glitz. This cosy pan-Asian eaterie specialises in noodles, and with around a dozen tables, simple wooden furnishings and a tick-a-box menu system, is definitely a place geared towards a quick bite rather than destination dining – hence its popularity with families fresh from the neighbouring Aquaventure attraction. As a casual eaterie it shines, both in the noodle dishes upon which it builds its livelihood, and more exotic appetisers and dim sum plates.

Ba
Fairmont The Palm (04 457 3338, www.dineatba.com). **Open** 7-11.30pm Mon-Wed, Sat, Sun; 7pm-midnight Thur, Fri. **Main courses** Dhs88-Dhs168. **Map** p150 C3 ㉑ **Chinese**
One of the city's fancier Chinese restaurants, this two-level venue features dramatic decor and dimmed lighting. There's a selection of somewhat uninspired dim sum, including the usual spring rolls and steamed buns. Soups are good, though, and the shrimp wonton comes with a well-seasoned broth and parcels of wonton with Chinese vegetables. The mains are marginally more adventurous, with both sea cucumber and abalone on the menu, as well as wok-fried chilli crab and steamed lobster.

Brunello
Kempinski Residences Palm Jumeirah, Crescent West (04 444 2501, www.kempinski.com). **Open** 7-11am, 12.30-3.30pm, 7-11pm daily. **Main courses** Dhs90-Dhs360. **Map** p150 B2 ㉒ **Italian**
Given its out-of-the-way location, it would be easy to overlook Brunello, but its modern Mediterranean fare is something to take notice of. A simple buffet is on offer, but it's worth eating à la carte. While many Italian restaurants err on the side of caution, sticking to traditional menu form and content, Brunello sticks its neck out with some intriguing inclusions – such as seared scallops with orange blossom, basil and bitter dark chocolate, an unexpectedly winning combination. It also produces skilled renderings of

traditional dishes. Sadly, the restaurant is rather let down by its harsh decor. Ask to be seated outside, surrounded by the hotel's landscaped grounds, where the atmosphere is livelier.

Bushman's Restaurant & Bar

Anantara Dubai The Palm Resort & Spa (04 567 8304, http://dubai-palm.anantara.com). **Open** 6.30-11.30pm daily. **Main courses** Dhs75-Dhs355. **Map** p151 E3 ㉓ **Australian**

Australian food is rare in Dubai, let alone Australian cooking with a fine-dining edge. As such, Bushman's Restaurant & Bar occupies a small niche in an otherwise diverse dining scene. Inside, the space is fun and full of character, with little design touches reflecting Australian culture. Service tends to be excellent and, in the case of senior staff, also Australian, which sets the tone for the experience of eating here. The menu spans a selection of gourmet Australiana, including emu, kangaroo, barramundi, 'bugs' (like little flat-tailed lobster) and 'yabby' (crayfish), prepared with plenty of international fusion touches from around the globe – from Italy to Asia.

Lalezar

Jumeirah Zabeel Saray (04 453 0444). **Open** 3pm-midnight daily. **Main courses** Dhs140-Dhs190. **Map** p150 B3 ㉔ **Turkish**

Decked out in shades of brown, cream, white and – of course – gold, Lalezar fits in well with the opulence of Jumeirah Zabeel Saray. The outdoor terrace is a particularly fine spot to dine when the weather permits. But it's not all about looks. The menu is authentic Turkish and staff are happy to help pick out their favourites among the classics and house specialities. Grilled meats are juicy and tender, and a seafood platter features very fresh fish and crustaceans, perfectly grilled. Prices are on the steep side, but it's worth it for this fine taste of Turkey in opulent surroundings.

Levantine

Atlantis The Palm (04 426 2626, www.atlantis thepalm.com). **Open** 7pm-2am daily. **Set menu** Dhs285. **Map** p150 D1 ㉕ **Arabic**

This sprawling restaurant has low tables and seats reminiscent of an Arabian *majlis* (meeting place where guests are entertained). The decor is bright and unfussy with red, cream and orange dominating the colour scheme and a relaxed, homely atmosphere, and the vibe is relaxed. Set menus offer an abundance of food and great value for money: the Adonis presents a good spread of Lebanese meze dishes and mains, of which the sea bream is a standout. The nightly entertainment, with musicians and belly dancers, sees the laid-back vibe dissipate as the volume is cranked up to full blast – you'll have to shout at the top of your voice to be heard. Levantine is a great place to dine with the family or with a big group of friends. Just don't expect an evening of quiet conversation.

Mekong

Anantara Dubai The Palm Resort & Spa (04 567 8304, http://dubai-palm.anantara.com/mekong). **Open** 6.30-11.30pm daily. **Main courses** Dhs85-Dhs180. **Map** p151 E3 ㉖ **Pan-Asian**

Warm and ornate, with eclectic Asian theming including outside seating in rickshaws, pillars in the shape of Chinese vases and colourful wooden shutters decorating the ceiling, Mekong has a similarly eclectic menu. It runs the gamut from Chinese to Thai and Vietnamese dishes (with helpful flags next to each dish), produced in a large open kitchen at the back. The dishes it turns out – from beijing duck to scallops on a fresh, sour salad of mint and shredded green papaya – are competent, but it's the space itself that's the real draw.

★ Moana

Sofitel The Palm (04 455 6677, www.sofitel-dubai-thepalm.com). **Open** 7-11.30pm daily. **Main courses** Dhs145-Dhs350. **Map** p151 E1 ㉗ **Seafood**

Seafood restaurant Moana is situated just in front of the hotel's main pool, with the private beach beyond. If the weather permits, it's a wonderful spot to sit outside and enjoy lunch. The food is impeccable, too. The ceviche and tartare platter, for example, is served with a coconut lemongrass sauce; Italian-style lobster is made all the more appealing by the addition of wild mushrooms, lemon cream sauce, parmesan and pea risotto, while Singaporean-style red snapper is served in a mouthwatering laksa sauce with caramelised onions, baby spinach, red tobiko and coconut foam.

► *On Fridays, Moana offers a brunch-and-beach package. See p149* **Beach Bliss**.

Nobu

The Avenues, Atlantis The Palm (04 426 2626, www.atlantisthepalm.com). **Open** 7-11pm Mon-Wed, Sat; 7pm-12.30am Thur, Fri. *High brunch* noon-4pm Fri. **Dishes** Dhs70-Dhs280. **High brunch** with soft drinks Dhs395; with house alcohol Dhs595. **Map** p150 D1 ㉘ **Japanese**

Packed to the rafters with a moneyed crowd drawn to this celeb-friendly brand, Nobu ditches austere Japanese minimalism in favour of cosy sofa-style seating and large, almost rustic wood tables. The kitchen fires out chef Nobu's best-known and best-loved dishes, from miso black cod to yellowtail sashimi and jalapenos, through to soft-shell crab tempura, served atop squares of sweet watermelon and dressed with a tangy amazu ponzu sauce. If you're a fan of Japanese and fusion cuisine, a meal at Nobu's is a worthwhile experience – even if it does mean saving up for a couple of months.

Ossiano

Atlantis The Palm (04 426 2626, www.atlantisthepalm.com). **Open** 7-11.30pm daily. **Main courses** Dhs270-Dhs470. **Map** p150 D1 ㉙ **Seafood**

EDEN Beach Club. See p156.

Ossiano certainly has the wow factor. Diners descend a spiral staircase and are greeted by a huge aquarium teeming with sea life. Similar to the Burj Al Arab's Al Mahara (*see p141*), the aquarium is the restaurant's centrepiece; seats face it so you can't help but be transfixed by the brightly coloured tropical fish, rays and other marine life. Combined with an undulating ceiling, metallic sheen on the walls and low lighting, it's pretty amazing, and the same can be said of the cooking, which takes a sophisticated, contemporary approach to seafood, and majors on beautiful presentation. A great special occasion venue.

Social by Heinz Beck

Waldorf Astoria Dubai Palm Jumeirah (04 818 2222). **Open** 7pm-midnight daily. **Main courses** Dhs145-Dhs240. **Map** p151 F3 ㉚ **Italian**

With his restaurant La Pergola in Rome awarded three Michelin stars, Heinz Beck is among the most renowned chefs in the world. Launched in the Waldorf Astoria on the Palm, Social by Heinz Beck brings to Dubai what the chef terms a 'deformalised' yet still fine taste of his cooking style – a light, contemporary approach to Italian cuisine. Marinated salmon with ricotta, herbs, and lime, or scallops on a pea purée with artichoke vinaigrette, might be followed by the likes of rack of lamb with a green olive crust and Mediterranean vegetables. His Dubai venue is decorated in sophisticated tones, with a slightly masculine, New York edge, featuring dark wood, glass and cosy cushioned seating in soft greys.

STAY by Yannick Alleno

One&Only The Palm Dubai (04 440 1010, http:// thepalm.oneandonlyresorts.com). **Open** 7-11pm daily. **Main courses** Dhs100-Dhs440. **Map** p150 B3 ㉛ **Modern European**

French masterchef Yannick Alleno's STAY (the abbreviation standing for Simple Table Alleno Yannick, apparently) is about as must-try a dining experience as you can find in the city. Decor is stylish and service superior. Waiters assemble some dishes on your plate in front of you, placing items so delicately they might be made of explosives – that they do so and avoid pretension is testament to their charm and skill. From delicate seafood raviolis to melting wagyu beef, the menu is consistently excellent, executed perfectly and delivered with flair. And that's before you get to the 'dessert library', a temple to puds where the pastry chefs prepare dishes in front of guests, and encourage them to try before choosing. A magic end to an unforgettable experience.

West 14th

Oceana Beach Club (04 447 7601, www.west 14th.ae). **Open** 9.30am-midnight Mon-Thur, Sun; 9am-midnight Fri, Sat. **Main courses** Dhs170-Dhs499. **Map** p150 C3 ㉜ **Steakhouse**

West 14th comes into its own during the cooler months, with seating spilling out on to a large terrace, and views across the water to the Dubai Marina skyline. By night this view is particularly impressive, and chill-out tunes from a band add to the ambience. With such a pleasant setting, you'll be unsurprised to hear that it often gets busy here, which can take its toll on service at times. But there are some nice touches when it comes to ordering steaks, from a choice of knives to a trolley stocked full of mustards and other condiments. The steaks are good quality cuts, well cooked, with a complimentary sauce and a varied choice of sides. West 14th's American-inspired theme becomes clear by the time you reach dessert, with a decadent selection of chocolate-heavy sweets to enjoy.

★ Yuan

Atlantis The Palm (04 426 2626, www.atlantis thepalm.com). **Open** 12.30-4pm, 6-11pm Mon-Wed, Sat, Sun; 12.30-4pm, 6-11.30pm Thur; 6-11.30pm Fri. **Main courses** Dhs95-Dhs195. **Map** p150 D1 ㉝ **Chinese**

Setting itself apart from the rest of Atlantis The Palm, with its own standalone entrance, this lounge-style fine-dining Chinese eaterie is where you'll find the cool kids. Massive tables are inlaid with mother of pearl, while some are slightly raised on an illuminated platform, flanked with high-back chairs hung with beautiful silver and blue brocade. The food is excellent, but be prepared to pay top dirham. A wasabi prawn starter consists of massive crustaceans, smothered in a wasabi mayonnaise, while the steamed shrimp dumpling with yellow mustard is another highlight. Other favourites include crispy chicken salad with pomelo in mango plum dressing and a selection of clay pots. Desserts are a big deal here, particularly the raspberry sphere and foamy cheesecake.

Bars & Cafés

Of the beach clubs listed in this chapter, **EDEN Beach Club** (*see p156*), hidden away at one end of the Palm's crescent, offers the most adult-friendly experience, with a laid-back vibe, well-stocked bar and Latin beats.

Bidi Bondi

Shoreline apartments 1-5 (04 427 0515). **Open** 10am-mdnight Mon-Wed, Sat, Sun; 10am-1am Thur, Fri. **Map** p150 D4 ㉞

Bidi Bondi seems to be the antithesis of what the Palm's all about. A man-made paradise of golden beaches, luxury villas, castles and five-star resorts, it's the last place you'd expect to find an Aussie pub/bar so chilled you feel overdressed in a collar. Much of the charm is down to the location, because the bar isn't based inside a hotel – no walking across a crystal-lined lobby to reach the faux-dive pub – but at the bottom of an apartment block. Bidi's possesses that rare thing, a community feel; coming here is something akin to stumbling into a student union bar without being a member of the university.

Lotus Lounge

Anantara Dubai The Palm Resort & Spa (04 567 8304, http://dubai-palm.anantara.com). **Open** 11am-midnight daily. **Map** p151 E3 ㉟

If there's one thing Dubai could never have too many of (unlike malls), it's outdoor spots from which to enjoy the city's many stunning views. Lotus Lounge's terrace is just one of these (the Thai-inspired interior is not at all unpleasant, but by no means a knockout). There are few more serene spots from which to enjoy an elegant cold drink and some nibbles.

Nasimi Beach

Atlantis The Palm (04 426 2626, www.atlantis thepalm.com). **Open** 11am-midnight Mon-Thur, Sun; 9am-1am Fri, Sat. **Map** p150 D1 ㊱

Part bar, part restaurant, part club, Nasimi manages to do most things it attempts pretty well. Its beach parties are hugely popular and during beach renovations it managed to pull off several extremely well-attended and thoroughly enjoyable pool parties. And what better way is there to unwind than sprawled out on a beanbag on the beach with an ice-cold (if rather pricey) drink? Indoors, the atmosphere and aesthetics are just as pleasing, with heaps of space to accommodate the crowds and a drinks menu as interesting and varied as it is vast.

JBR & Dubai Marina

The Marina and JBR are at the heart of what is referred to, in somewhat tongue-in-cheek fashion, as 'new Dubai' (Old Dubai being the bits around the Creek that sprang up in the 1970s and '80s), and distinct from the Downtown development around the Burj Khalifa. There's a thriving hub of restaurants and cafés dotted along the promenade near the wharf, where gleaming motor yachts are berthed and scenic dhow trips can be arranged. An evening stroll around the waterfront pathway surrounding the Marina is particularly lovely.

The Marina and nearby JBR (actually Jumeirah Beach Residence, but no one calls it that) have become one of the busiest and most developed areas in Dubai, and as it has grown in scale, its food reputation has also grown. Stunning restaurants continue to open here, all within easy reach of one of Dubai's best public beaches.

The Observatory.

Don't Miss

1 Skydive Dubai For extreme airborne thrills (p167).

2 The Observatory Drink or dine with some of the city's best views (p171).

3 Pier 7 Seven diverse dining experiences under one roof (p170).

4 The Beach A swish new development that's a hit with food-lovers (p164).

5 Boat tour For a different angle on Dubai's dramatic skyline (p167).

JUMEIRAH BEACH RESIDENCE (JBR)

What began as a purely residential development, with a few shops and bars and a scattering of hotels, has grown into one of the busiest areas of the city. Over the past few years, modern, upscale developments like the Beach (*see p164* **The Beach**) have opened and now offer a number of design-centric, beachside eateries like **House of Curry** and **Eat Greek**. The Ritz-Carlton (*see p285*) adds to the upmarket atmosphere with its award-winning restaurants including sophisticated Italian **Splendido**, while bars like **Tribeca Kitchen + Bar**, with its kitsch decor of upcycled furniture and retro artwork, are adding a new, quirky element.

Thanks to the bustling beach, JBR has retained something of a laid-back vibe and become a prime location for a family day out thanks to the **Beach Waterpark** and cinema at **La Playa Lounge**. However, beware of the excessive traffic that plagues the area, particularly bad during rush hour, and eternally gridlocked at weekends. You'd be better off heading to Kite Beach (*see p114*) to sunbathe at peak times and to take a taxi rather than drive here in the evening to avoid the nightmare of trying to find a parking spot.

EXPLORE

Sights & Attractions

Beach Waterpark

The Beach (04 388 3223, www. arabianwaterparks. com). Tram Jumeirah Beach Residence Station 1. **Open** 8am-noon, 3-7pm daily. **Admission** Dhs60; Dhs50 children; day pass Dhs125. **Map** p163 B2 ❶

Head to the sand at JBR and you'll be greeted by a giant inflatable monolith of fun. This is the Arabian Water Park, an inflatable playground that's made up of trampolines, slides and climbing walls. Located a little way out from the beach, you have to swim out to reach it, but once there you can jump into the sea from a variety of trampolines, scale a climbing wall, launch your friends into the water with giant flippers and swing from one obstacle to another: this kind of fun shouldn't just be restricted to children. Book as a group for a complimentary hour.

Muscle Beach

The Beach, JBR (04 323 2323, www.whym.com). Tram Jumeirah Beach Residence Station 2. **Open** 6am-10pm Mon-Thur, Sun. **Admission** Dhs60 per hr. **Map** p163 B2 ❷

Dubai's bright, neon- and graffiti-covered Warehouse gym has followed the lead of California's Venice Beach, where fitness fans can work on their tans and triceps simultaneously. Muscle Beach is a gym that's entirely outdoors. But unlike in California, this Muscle Beach isn't an intimidating sprawl with rows of weights and bench presses. The 235sq m (2,525sq ft) gym sits on a raised platform with six spinning bikes, a rowing machine, multi-fitness rig and a selection of free weights. There are also qualified staff on hand to lead you through a class or assist with your workout – at the time of writing offerings include spinning (with bikes facing out to sea for inspiring views) and boot-camp. No membership is necessary, though, just sign up at the reception and pay as you go. Operation hours will change during the summer to beat the stifling heat with early morning and late evening sessions and plenty of water and towels on hand.

La Playa Lounge

The Beach (055 260 9650, www. laplayalounge. com). Tram Jumeirah Beach Residence Station 1. **Open** 4pm-2am daily. **Headsets** Dhs50 per person. **Map** p163 B3 ❸

This is the largest outdoor cinema screen in the UAE and screens films and sport that can be viewed from white sofas, while you tuck into a Black Angus cheeseburger or a plate of nachos, or enjoy a shisha. Headsets are handed out for the films – the venue is essentially a lounge first and a cinema experience second, so music still plays on the speakers during screenings. Films are generally popular Hollywood productions that are a year or two old; Premier League, Serie A and international football matches are also shown. The seating area is comfortable and if the temperature dips, staff will happily provide you with a blanket. Though this isn't a venue for diehard movie fans, it's certainly a fun place to chill out and enjoy an alfresco flick.

Restaurants

BiCE Ristorante

Hilton Dubai Jumeirah Resort, the Walk (04 318 2520). Tram Jumeirah Beach Residence Station 1. **Open** 12.30-11.30pm Mon-Thur, Sat, Sun; 1-11.30pm Fri. **Main courses** Dhs100-Dhs250. **Map** p163 B3 ❹ **Italian**

BiCE is a sophisticated spot. Tables are neat and clean, with white linen, and clinking glasses and diners' chatter provide the soundtrack in the large, smart space. The Italian cuisine encompasses both the simple and traditional, and the modish: starters run the gamut from top-quality buffalo mozzarella with tomatoes and peppery olive oil, say, to the likes of lobster carpaccio or crab cakes with avocado tartare and bell pepper sauce. Pasta dishes are excellent, from a simple penne arrabbiata to a rich ricotta and spinach tortelli with creamy white truffle sauce. Some mains feature luxury ingredients, like veal tenderloin with foie gras sauce, mashed potatoes and asparagus; others have a modern twist, such as prawns and scallops with vegetable timbale and citrus sauce.

Blue Jade

The Ritz-Carlton (04 318 6150, www.ritz-carlton. com). Tram Jumeirah Beach Residence Station 1. **Open** 5pm-midnight daily. **Map** p163 B4 ❺ **Pan-Asian**

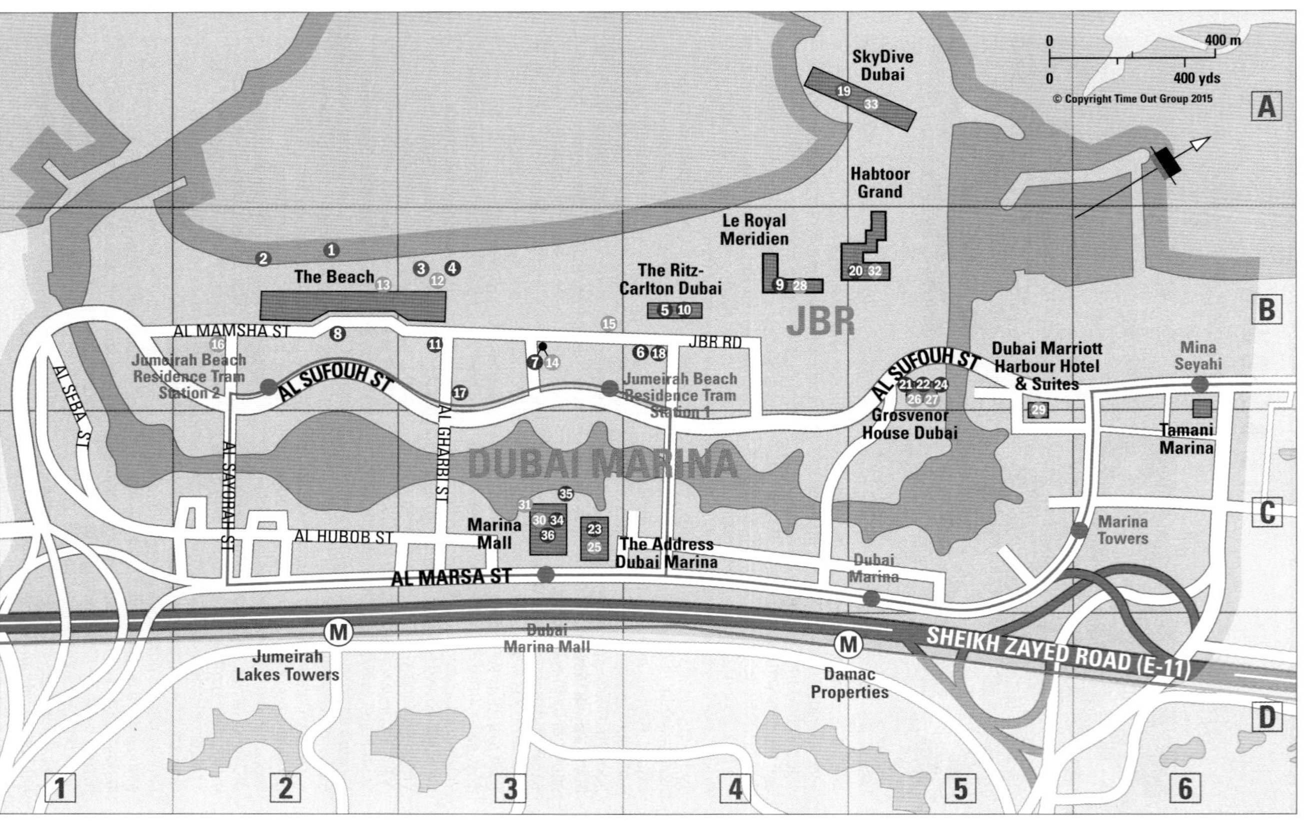
0
400 m
0
400 yds
© Copyright Time Out Group 2015
SkyDive Dubai
Habtoor Grand
Le Royal Meridien
The Ritz-Carlton Dubai
JBR
The Beach
AL MAMSHA ST
JBR RD
Jumeirah Beach Residence Tram Station 2
Jumeirah Beach Residence Tram Station 1
AL SUFOUH ST
AL SEBA ST
AL SAYORAH ST
AL GHARBI ST
DUBAI MARINA
Dubai Marriott Harbour Hotel & Suites
Grosvenor House Dubai
Mina Seyahi
Tamani Marina
Marina Towers
Marina Mall
The Address Dubai Marina
AL HUBOB ST
AL MARSA ST
Dubai Marina
Dubai Marina Mall
SHEIKH ZAYED ROAD (E-11)
Jumeirah Lakes Towers
Damac Properties
M
A
B
C
D
1
2
3
4
5
6

THE BEACH

A beachside development that's become a magnet for food fans.

At night, dreamy fountains set around fairy-light-spangled trees make for a romantic sight, while during the day the area is bright and bustling with beachgoers and families. This is the Beach, a development alongside the beach, opposite Jumeirah Beach Residence. The beach itself is public, but sadly lots of the space is taken up by sun loungers that, at Dhs110 per day, are costly to rent. Kayaks, paddleboards and other watersport equipment is available to rent from Dhs60. You can spend time frolicking at the **Beach Waterpark**, enjoy a film on sports at **La Playa Lounge** (for both, *see p162*) and there's a **Reel Cinemas** cinema (04 449 1903, www.reelcinemas.com) if you want to soothe your skin in a darkened room post-swim. In terms of shopping, there's not much to shout about – just a few outlets from well-known brands like Sephora and Victoria's Secret – but the development is turning into something of a foodie destination, with a fantastic collection of cafés and restaurants, all just a spade's throw from the beach.

Casual Californian burger bar the **Counter** (www.thecounterburger.com,), beloved of the likes of Robert Downey Jr and Leonardo DiCaprio, allows diners to create their own meals. Top your hormone- and antibiotic-free beef (or chicken or veggie patty) with more than 15 different types of cheese, one of 23 sauces and 44 different toppings. You can also opt for a burger served in a bowl with various salads. And if nothing there appeals, there's a choice of the restaurant's own 'expert builds'. **Eat Greek** (04 430 5249, www.eatgreekkouzina.com) has an open kitchen, a modern and slightly edgy east London look of exposed brick, combined with beachy, whitewashed accents and twinkly-lit bird cages hanging from the ceiling. It's cute, yet somehow still urban. We like the mixed grill, fava and classic Greek salad.

While the outdoor tables overlooking the beach at **House of Curry** (04 346 9740, www.houseofcurry.me) are popular in cooler months, it's the interior that really warrants investigating. Huge faux trees stand in the centre of the room, which has the look and feel of an atrium in an imagined Indian home. As well as Indian classics, the menu includes dishes such as tandoori crab, clam sukka and mussel curry. It isn't the finest Indian cooking in Dubai, but it does represent decent value and the setting is a bonus.

Order a bucket of seafood and say goodbye to table manners at **Aprons & Hammers** (04 456 7888, www.apronsandhammers.com) or go for a plate piled high with Lebanese falafel, manakeesh, shawarma and meze at the more affordable **Operation: Falafel** (04 338 3644). There's more good-value Arabic food at Levantine venue **Awani** (04 424 8082, 9am-midnight daily), plus shisha. It's open 24 hours daily.

Pappa Roti (04 420 0690, www.papparoti.ae) serves a caramelised coffee-coated bun with a buttery centre with its hot drinks, which is brilliant for a mid-morning snack, while **Morelli's** (www.morellisgelato.com) has a great selection of indulgent *gelato* flavours and desserts (for heaven in a bowl go for the banana caramel sundae). Grab-and-go juice counter **Fruteiro do Brasil** (04 423 3656) is great for beachy refreshments with its enless variety of fruity combos and exotic smoothies.

EXPLORE

The decor is a striking combination of super-stylish midcentury modern with oriental touches; food is contemporary Asian. The place looks stunning, but in Dubai one gets used to beautiful venues that trip up at the final hurdle, namely the kitchen. Not so here, with a menu that skirts through Thai, Japanese, Chinese and more, with dishes rooted in these traditions but not afraid of fusion. Among our favourites are black pepper beef – the twist here a Singaporean rather than Guangdong-inspired sauce – and a Szechuan-style hot pot that bursts with flavours. It's not cheap, but this classy contender is well suited to a special occasion.

Chinwaggery + Soul

Mövenpick Hotel Jumeirah Beach, the Walk (04 449 8888, www.moevenpick-hotels.com/). Tram Jumeirah Beach Residence Station 1. **Open** 5pm-1am daily. **Sandwiches** Dhs25-Dhs30. **Map** p163 B4 ❻ **American**

Dubai is no stranger to an American import, but put down the pancakes and hold the hamburger, because there is now a more sophisticated way to get a slice of the Big Apple. Over at the Mövenpick Jumeirah Beach, Chinwaggery + Soul is serving up refined fare in Manhattan-inspired surrounds. Chinwaggery is the second-floor bar, while Soul is the New York-style brasserie that now forms the bulk of the venue. Steaks lead the mains on the menu, with a range of Irish, Australian, American and French cuts available, but there are plenty of seafood dishes and a couple of vegetarian choices. Standards are high.

Frankie's Italian Bar & Grill

Al Fattan Tower (04 399 4311, www.rmal hospitality.ae). Tram Jumeirah Beach Residence Station 1. **Open** 12.30-3.30pm, 5.30pm-11.30pm daily. **Mains** Dhs80-Dhs250. **Map** p163 B3 ❼ **Italian**

Given it's the brainchild of shouty celebrity jockey Frankie Dettori and Marco Pierre White, who could hardly be described as a shrinking violet, it's not surprising that a meal at Frankie's is a lively and loud affair. This is not a criticism. Free of the pretension that can creep into some of the city's restaurants, here is an upmarket but down-to-earth venue that serves decent food accompanied by some funky piano playing and caters to everyone from families to first daters without making either feel awkward. True, five years in it is starting to show a little wear around the edges, and the waiting staff sometimes get the ratio of efficiency to rushing a little off kilter, but the menu is extensive and the dishes – in particular the ravioli choices – are tasty and presented with a flair that makes its price point reasonable, if not a steal.

Massaad BBQ Farm to Table

The Walk (04 362 9002, www.massaadfarmtotable.com). Tram Jumeirah Beach Residence Station 2. **Open** 11am-2am daily. **Main courses** Dhs40-Dhs150. **Map** p163 B2 ❽ **Arabic**

We're encouraged by the ethos of this restaurant, which claims to be the world's first farm to table restaurant and whose slogan is 'Eat well, eat local'. Food is light and healthily cooked and there's a good selection of Arabic salads, including a crisp and refreshing fattoush. Meat is sourced from local farms and grilled before your eyes in the open kitchen as classic Lebanese kebabs. There's not much space inside, and it's probably not somewhere to hang out all evening, but for a quick pit stop if you're on the Walk, or for takeaway, Massaad will serve you well.

★ Rhodes Twenty10

Le Royal Méridien Beach Resort & Spa (04 316 5550, www.rhodestwenty10.com). Tram Jumeirah Beach Residence Station 1. **Open** 7pm-midnight daily. **Main courses** Dhs95-Dhs190. **Steaks** Dhs100-Dhs460. **Map** p163 B4 ❾ **British**

This is the kind of restaurant you take your time to enjoy. On arrival, diners can enjoy a pre-dinner drink in the comfortable lounge; food orders are also taken here. The accomplished British cuisine includes such classics as Welsh rarebit and fish and chips – elevated from the everyday to the immaculate. Starters are served as sharing plates; the beetroot and cream cheese salad, served as towers, is a wonderfully light and fresh way to start the meal. Steaks and seafood dominate the mains. The food isn't complicated, but the high-quality ingredients and chefly skill shine through. Service is exemplary, and taking staff advice pays dividends, especially with their recommendation of the signature sticky toffee pudding.

Splendido

Ritz-Carlton Dubai (04 399 4000, www.ritz carlton.com). Tram Jumeirah Beach Residence Station 1. **Open** 6.30-11pm daily. **Main courses** Dhs70-Dhs250. **Map** p163 B4 ❿ **Italian**

You expect a certain degree of sophistication from the Italian restaurant in the Ritz-Carlton, and Splendido doesn't disappoint. The chic New York-style decor, smooth soundtrack and understated elegance are all present and correct. But it is when the place lets its guard down and acts a little less stuffy that the real charm appears: let the staff guide you out to the terrace to enjoy the alfresco setting with palm trees and sea views. Food is modern Italian, with an emphasis on quality ingredients and presentation. Creative combinations might include roasted duck breast with chickpea croquette and truffle honey. By night this is a romantic restaurant but visit in the day for a lazy afternoon in the sun.

Sukh Sagar

Rimal, the Walk (04 437 0188, www.sukhsagar.com). Tram Jumeirah Beach Residence Station 2. **Open** 11am-1am Mon-Thur, Sun; 11am-1.30am Fri, Sat. **Main courses** Dhs25-Dhs50. **Map** p163 B3 ⓫ **Vegetarian/Indian**

Located right on the Walk, this vegetarian restaurant is a great spot for alfresco dining. The menu is a bit confusing, with an international selection of Chinese wok dishes, pizza, pasta and quesadillas. But what this place does best is authentic Indian dishes. Dosas, in particular, stand out. Portions are very generous. Service can be hit and miss, but this is tasty, good-value vegetarian food in a great location.

Cafés & Bars

Chinwaggery + Soul (*see p165*) has a bar on its second floor.

Eggspectation

The Beach (04 430 7252, www.eggspectation.com). Tram Jumeirah Beach Residence Station 1. **Open** 7am-2am daily. **Map** p163 B3 12

Originally opened in Montreal back in 1993, and now with branches across the globe, Eggspectation is one of the many new additions to the Beach. As the name suggests, egg-fuelled breakfast dishes – available all day – dominate the menu, including riffs on eggs benedict, omelettes, full English breakfasts and more. There are plenty of other options if you don't feel like eggs, including flatbreads, burgers, salads and pasta, with a notable variety of mac 'n' cheeses. Like many venues in this beachside area, it has an ambient outdoor dining area.

Leopolds of London

The Beach (04 430 6841, www.leopoldsof london.com). Tram Jumeirah Beach Residence Station 1. **Open** 8am-11.30pm Mon-Wed, Sat, Sun; 8am-1.30am Thur, Fri. **Map** p163 B2 13

Gourmet café Leopold's of London has an attractive setting with outdoor seating overlooking the shore. Inside, it's decorated in a bistro style with marble tabletops, leather upholstery and dark wood. The menu varies with time of day, with a large range of breakfast dishes, a deli-style selection of sandwiches and bagels available in the afternoon, plus brasserie-style dishes. Whatever time you call in, you'll find a very appetising selection of modern café food, teas, coffees and cocktails.

MAKE Business Hub

Al Fattan Tower, the Walk (04 392 9216, www. makebusinesshub.com). Tram Jumeirah Beach Residence Station 1. **Open** 8am-8pm Mon-Thur, Sat, Sun; 10am-8pm Fri. **Map** p163 B3 14

Customers can choose from different packages that include hot drinks, food and internet access to make a visit here easier on the pocket. Food includes the delectable and seriously meaty MAKE burger, crispy chicken tenders and a distinctly moreish chocolate cake. This friendly café is a good choice for a quick bite, leisurely lunch or even a long working day.

Saladicious Deli

Sadaf, the Walk (04 423 0855, www.saladicious. com). Tram Jumeirah Beach Residence Station 1. **Open** 8.30am-midnight daily. **Map** p163 B3 15

As the name suggests, salad plays a big part in this deli's menu, and the Walk is all the better for it. In an unlicensed stretch of restaurants like this, a healthy eating venue stands out from the numerous burger joints and casual dining venues. The Temptation Salad here is one of our favourite dishes on the Walk, with its combination of creamy brie, strawberry, mandarin, caramelised walnuts and crostini potato. Dozens more can be sampled. Don't be fooled into thinking this is a one-trick pony, however, as further perusal of the menu throws up good sandwich options as well: Angus beef with Venezuelan flavours and cheddar cheese, anyone? There are mains too, but we prefer to stick to the salads and enjoy the outdoor vibe.

★ Tribeca Kitchen + Bar

JA Ocean View Hotel (050 345 6067, www.tribeca. ae). Tram Jumeirah Beach Residence Station 2. **Open** 6pm-1am Mon-Wed, Sat, Sun; 6pm-3am Thur, Fri. **Map** p163 B2 16

Tribeca Kitchen & Bar has been designed with the same industrial and urban feel that the bars and buildings in its New York namesake are known for. Its look is colourful, eclectic, and full of pop-art and pop-culture references: you'll find neon graffiti of the Statue of Liberty, comically huge, high-backed chairs, a 'reclaimed' loft in a combination of wood, brick and concrete, and oddities such as a suitcase crammed full of dollars chained to the ceiling. It serves a selection of organic wines and beers. There is a no-nonsense attitude about the venue – don't expect private VIP tables. It's this easygoing and friendly attitude that makes Tribeca work so well.

Shops & Services

Boutique 1

The Walk (04 425 7888, www.boutique1.com). Tram Jumeirah Beach Residence Station 1. **Open** 10am-11pm daily. **Map** p163 B3 17 **Mall**

Art-lovers should call in here, even if the idea of looking at art and design in a fashion store seems a bit odd. This store is a high-end multi-designer concept where you can pick up a Diane von Furstenberg dress or a Phillip Lim bag as well as funky home accessories, books and beauty products. A bit like a high-end version of Urban Outfitters.

Mood and Singways

Opposite the Ritz-Carlton, the Walk (04 437 6488, www.mood.ae). Tram Jumeirah Beach Residence Station 1. **Open** 10am-10pm daily. **Map** p163 B4 18 **Homewares**

Mood and Singways stocks an eclectic collection of modern home furnishings and accessories from European and Chinese brands. You'll find everything from art deco-style chairs, minimalist beds and retro coffee tables to Ingo Maurer lighting and Alessi kitchenware.

EXPLORE

ALL ABOARD

Boat tours and floating restaurants.

Hundreds of yachts are moored here and while the average visitor won't have their own, it's possible to book boat trips or hire a boat for you and your friends. It's always worth shopping around a bit for the best deal for your group size and budget. **Mala Yachts** (056 115 7422, www.malayachts.ae) and **Arabian Yachting** (055 217 3209, www.arabianyachting.com) both have reasonable prices and a fleet of small boats to accommodate smaller parties. There are often deals and discounts with many charter companies for advance booking too.

The **Captain Jack** (04 430 9941, Dhs60 per person) tour is great as a no-fuss open-air trip around the coastline in front of JBR and the Palm Jumeirah. It only takes an hour and soft drinks are provided. **Venus Floating Restaurant** (04 357 2200, www.venuscruises.com), on the other hand, is one of the few vessels to have a fully licensed bar on board and has wonderful views after dark of the lit-up Marina. There's a buffet dinner with unlimited soft drinks for Dhs180 per person and a *tanoura* dance show; alcoholic drinks are extra.

You can relax on board an enormous catamaran as you sail around the Palm Jumeirah, Atlantis and Burj Al Arab on a **Catamaran Cruise** (04 239 4760, www.partycruisedubai.com). Included in the price of Dhs550 per person is a four-hour trip, with a barbecue buffet, soft drinks, a DJ and on-board music, plus towels and snorkelling gear. A favourite part of the cruise is anchoring at the Burj Al Arab, where revellers can enjoy a swim in the shadow of one of the city's most iconic landmarks. There's no age limit, so it's good for families.

Long-standing nautical firm **Xclusive Yachts** (04 432 7233, www.xclusiveyachts.com) offers trips on a range of yachts, with prices starting from as little as Dhs1,000 per hour for a 12-person capacity boat up to Dhs4,000 for a vessel that can take 40 guests. For a bigger bash, a houseboat, with space for 80 revellers, costs Dhs6,000 per hour, while a party boat with space for 200 costs Dhs10,000 per hour. All boats come with a sound system and full crew, so soak up the sounds and leave the sailing to the pros. If you really want to go all out, hire a yacht from **Deep Sea Dubai** (050 450 1340, 055 902 0111, www.deepseadubai.com). Its bigger boats come with dancefloors, jacuzzis, barbecue areas and extra luxurious bathrooms.

DUBAI MARINA

Bars, restaurants and hotels are lined up along Dubai Marina, a relatively new part of the city. The Marina is a good example of Dubai's rapid development, with every inch taken up by apartments or other developments – some still under construction. **Pier 7** (*see p170* **Seven Up**) is an impressive development with seven restaurants over seven floors, **Grosvenor House** (*see p285*) and **Le Royal Méridien** are two of the area's oldest – but still impressive – hotels, with some great restaurants. Most of the shopping in this area is centred on **Dubai Marina Mall**, also home to a cinema, if you feel in need of respite from the heat.

In the evening it's possible to walk around the Marina, and the high-rise towers look most impressive once they're lit up and the sun goes down. There are 11 kilometres (seven miles) of track around the Marina, popular with runners.

Sights & Attractions

★ Skydive Dubai

Dubai Marina, Al Sufou Road (04 377 8888, www.skydivedubai.ae). Tram Jumeirah Beach Residence Station 1. **Open** 8am-4pm Mon-Sat. **Map** p163 A4 ⓳

Skydive from 3,960m (13,000ft) at Skydive Dubai's Palm Drop Zone. Arguably one of the best spots in the world for a jump, you can dive tandem for Dhs1,999, a price that includes a DVD of the jump and photographs. Licensed skydivers can jump for just Dhs120 (gear rental costs an additional Dhs110), with the option of a camera flyer and DVD video for an additional fee. Slots with your preferred time sometimes need to be booked a month or more in advance, but early morning slots from 5am can sometimes be booked with little notice. Book the last slot of the day to catch a spectacular view of the sunset as you jump. Jumpers must be over 18, no alcohol or drugs can be consumed beforehand, and you

IN THE KNOW BOOT CAMP

For fitness fanatics in need of a fix, **Elite Aesthetics** (055 536 7718, www.eadxb.com) runs a bootcamp with a difference. The trainers will have you pushing cars and running with parachutes strapped to you on the lawn and outdoor gym area next to Skydive Dubai. One-hour sessions (Dhs115) take place at 6am and 7.30pm, but days that the sessions run vary so phone to check.

must not scuba dive for 24 hours before your jump. A Dhs999 deposit is required at the time of booking, and reservations are for the check-in time, after which you should allow a minimum of three hours to complete the jump.

Restaurants

For dinner cabaret venue **Russian Cabaret at Tchaikovsky**, *see p201*.

Grand Grill

Habtoor Grand Beach Resort & Spa (04 408 4823, www.thegrandgrillsteakhouse.com). Tram Jumeirah Beach Residence Station 1. **Open** 1pm-midnight daily. **Main courses** Dhs95-Dhs140. **Map** p163 B5 ⑳ **African**

Dimly lit and decked out in eclectic African-themed knick-knacks, the Grand Grill stands out from other steakhouses in the city. The atmosphere is relaxed, and dining here provides a great chance to sample some traditional African dishes, from spare ribs to lamb cutlets and a whole host of other marinated meats. But don't miss out on the steaks, particularly the Kobe cuts, which are succulent, tender and great value for money. Side dishes also impress here, with generous portions of hearty, home-cooked goodness such as roasted root vegetables and creamy mashed potato.

★ Indego by Vineet

Grosvenor House (04 317 6000). Tram Jumeirah Beach Residence Station 1. **Open** 12.30-3pm, 7pm-midnight daily. **Main courses** Dhs150-Dhs250. **Map** p163 B5 ㉑ **Indian**

With exquisite food, service and ambience, Indego by Vineet lives up to expectations – and with the name of the first Indian chef to hold a Michelin star attached to it, the standard needs to be high. The setting is smart, in classic rather than contemporary style. The food is stunning. Malabari magic is just that: chilli paneer wrapped in a banana leaf, with broccoli, edamame beans and *idiyappam* noodles with a creamy malai sauce. Another starter, herb chop, is a perfectly pink piece of lamb, with sweet baby carrots, a carrot foam and goat's cheese samosa. Both are a perfect balance of restraint and inventiveness. Mains also blend tradition and creativity. Coastal *jigha* is a generous mound of prawns in a kaffir lime leaf, with coconut sauce, served on a bed of polenta; Punjabi chicken is a spiced breast on pea and aubergine mash with potato croquettes and a wonderful madkhani sauce. Outstanding.

Rhodes W1

Grosvenor House (04 317 6000, www.rw1-dubai.com). Tram Jumeirah Beach Residence Station 1. **Open** 7-11pm Mon-Sat. **Main courses** Dhs115-Dhs180. **Map** p163 B5 ㉒ **British**

Gary Rhodes's latest restaurant was a highly anticipated 2014 opening. From the entrance, where a Kew Garden-esque mixture of fake grass and white butterflies covers the walls, through to the bucolic murals inside, Rhodes W1 creates a pretty and airy modern-orangery-style space. The splashes of limey green and sunshine yellow create a distinctly contemporary cheery vibe. The restaurant describes itself as serving a modern take on British food. You will find some straight classics here, such as shepherd's pie with house-made brown sauce; other dishes have entirely unexpected twists, or are modern riffs on retro favourites, such as ginger beer battered monkfish scampi with sea salt straw potatoes, fennel slaw, ginger and sesame dressing. While the menu describes ingredients in modern, pared-down style, the flavours can be complex – but we've never found them confusing. A great dining experience.

EXPLORE

Ruth's Chris Steakhouse

The Address Dubai Marina (04 501 8779, www.ruthschris.ae). Tram Dubai Marina Mall. **Open** noon-4pm, 6pm-2.30am Mon-Thur, Sat, Sun; 12.30-3.30pm, 6pm-2.30am Fri. **Map** p163 C3 ㉓ **Steakhouse**

This dimly lit steakhouse in the suitably sleek setting of the Address Dubai Marina certainly looks the part, with its crisp white tablecloths and smartly attired staff. From the tables that line the window, there's a pleasant view of the Marina waterways, but the red, black and white colour scheme of the interior is inviting and welcoming enough to keep the attention of diners. The choice of steaks here is refreshingly concise, but with enough cuts to keep everyone happy – from juicy ribeyes to tender filets. Sides are indulgent, especially the gratin dishes, which are smothered in rich cheese. It's easy to lose track of time at Ruth's Chris, and if you want to extend your evening, there's a chilled-out lounge that's perfect for a few drinks.

Toro Toro

Grosvenor House Dubai (04 317 6000, www.torotoro-dubai.com). Tram Jumeirah Beach Residence Station 1. **Open** 8pm-2am daily. **Map** p163 B5 ㉔ **Latin American**

One of the most atmospheric venues in Dubai Marina, Toro Toro is a popular nightspot in its own right. But this pan-Latin lounge should not be overlooked when it comes to food, as you'll struggle to find a more imaginative and stylish place to eat this cuisine. The concept of celebrity chef Richard Sandoval's restaurant is all about sharing dishes, with the menu dominated by small plates of steak tartare, grilled octopus, ceviche and the like. The ceviche has become something of a signature dish, made with salmon, snapper, tuna or prawns. There's a tasting platter if you'd like to try a variety of dishes, and don't miss out some of the hot dishes either, including grills of wagyu steak or Chilean sea bass. This modern take on Latin cuisine is quite unlike anything else you'll find in the city.

Cafés & Bars

And Lounge

The Address Dubai Marina (04 551 9698). Tram Dubai Marina Mall station. **Open** 6pm-3am Tue-Fri. **Map** p163 C3 ㉕

Another NYC urban loft design, with a cosy, homely feel. The walls were transformed by painter Laurent Godard into murals of past-century icons like Audrey Hepburn, Jackie Kennedy and Martin Luther King Jr. Sofa seating areas are divided by wooden bannisters, making them more private than the high wooden tables around the bar. But the drinks list is the real highlight. Creative and original cocktails include Through the Looking Glass (Nikka whiskey, orange juice, mint, rosewater, sugar syrup and sparkling date juice) and Don't Be A… (tequila,

EXPLORE

Buddha Bar. *See p170.*

SEVEN UP

Pier 7 has seven fine restaurants on seven floors.

Cylindrical tower Pier 7 has fast become one of the city's best dining and drinking destinations. Each of the building's Marina-side floors houses a different and distinctive restaurant, and each has stunning Marina views, with balconies looking over the water.

Fumé (04 421 5669, www.fume-eatery.com), for example, is serious about its southern US-style smokehouse concept, so much so that it closes from 4pm to 7pm every day for a little in-house smoking. Refreshingly, Fumé dispenses with the frills so often associated with Dubai dining. You'll find its policy written down on a little card at the table, explaining why you shouldn't expect valet parking, or staff to pour your water, and so on.

Asian-fusion restaurant **Asia Asia** (04 276 5900, www. asia-asia.com) has a seductive setting, bathed in dark, sultry red-tinged lighting, furnished in jewel colours and golds. At the impressive entrance stands a triangle of terracotta Chinese warrior-esque figures, and more statues guide the way in to the main dining are through a tunnel of arches. The food is generally very good indeed, living up to the statement venue, and the bar is buzzing on a Tuesday for ladies' night, with three free drinks for ladies – including some great cocktails. Second pan-Asian eaterie **Cargo** (04 3618 129, www.cargo-dubai.com), equally popular as a restaurant and bar, is very different, a funky, laid-back space with high ceilings and industrial styling – exposed pipes and a bar made from wooden crates.

British venue the **Scene** (04 422 2328, www.thescenedubai.com) was launched by TV chef Simon Rimmer and is livening up British dining in Dubai. It's quite unlike anything else in the city: it's as if the owners raided every vintage shop in Hoxton and cleared out all the midcentury modern furniture. Food is traditional British at root, with fusion twists. Dishes can be brilliant, and the warm yet edgy appearance makes it an inviting prospect.

For Arabic cuisine, head to **Abd El Wahab** (04 432 5782). Lebanese meze classics such as houmous, fatteh and kibbeh come in generous portions, mains are the usual grilled meats and fish, all served by friendly and helpful staff.

Atelier M (04 450 7766, www.ateliermae) is more about nightlife than cuisine. Food is modern French and Asian fusion, with a focus on sharing plates, but overall it's pretty average. However, it occupies the top two floors of the building, so its chic rooftop bar, with panoramic views of the Marina, is hard to beat at night. Head here for post-dinner drinks, or to **O Cacti** (04 452 6699, www.ocactiuae.com), Pier 7's Latin American restaurant, which serves some tasty food, but is best enjoyed with a large group of friends, taking advantage of the generous drinks deals.

EXPLORE

lime juice, agave syrup and green tabasco). One – the As You Are – comes served in a plastic zip-lock bag on a wooden board. There's even a photo booth.

Buddha Bar

Grosvenor House (04 317 6000, www.buddhabar-dubai.com). Tram Jumeirah Beach Residence Station 1. **Open** 7.30pm-2am Mon-Wed, Sat, Sun; 7.30pm-3am Thur, Fri. *Last orders for food* 1am Mon-Wed, Sat, Sun; 2am Thur, Fri. **Map** p163 B5 26

One of the largest outposts of the glamorous chain, Buddha Bar has an impressively spacious dining room with striking red and gold chandeliers. The main bar and dining area is dominated by the brand's famous gilded statue and an entire wall of glass, with large windows looking on to the Marina; the lounge area has a sumptuous oriental vibe. Food is pan-Asian, and chilled-out loungey beats morph into livelier house music as the night progresses. *Photo pp168-169.*

Embassy

Grosvenor House (04 317 6000). Tram Jumeirah Beach Residence Station 1. **Open** 8pm-2am Tue, Wed, Sat; 8pm-3am Thur, Fri. *Last orders for food* 11.30pm. **Map** p163 B5 27

Spread across three floors of tower two at the swanky Grosvenor House, Embassy is a sleek bar, restaurant and club with views over Dubai Marina. There's a full Italian dinner menu, and a bar menu with popular items including a trio of mini burgers with fries, presented on a wooden slab and perfect for sharing, alongside seafood dishes and pizzettas. It's all super-swanky, with lush furnishings and mirrored walls, plus a dancefloor with LED lighting.

Maya Modern Mexican Kitchen & Lounge

Le Royal Méridien Beach Resort & Spa (04 399 5555, www.maya-dubai.com). Tram Jumeirah Beach Residence Station 1. **Open** *Restaurant* Sat-Wed 7pm-midnight, Thu-Fri 7pm-1am; *Lounge & bar* Sat-Wed 5pm-2am, Thu-Fri 5pm-3am. **Map** p163 B4 ㉘

This upscale and modern Mexican restaurant has a wonderful setting and a varied menu, and turns into a buzzing bar in the evenings, with seats outside on the lawn with beach views or inside in the impressive modish interior. Bar snacks are of a Mexican bent too, with several varieties of guacamole and cheesy nachos among them. The pitchers of sangria are robust and fruity.

★ Observatory

Dubai Marriott Harbour Hotel & Suites, Al Sufou Road (04 318 4795, www.observatory.dubai marriottharbourhotel.com). Tram Marina Towers station. **Open** 12.30pm-1am daily. **Map** p163 C5 ㉙

Best known for its popular drinks deals, particularly on a Thursday, the Observatory has one of the best views in Dubai. It sits on the 52nd floor of Dubai Marriott Harbour Hotel & Suites and looks out over the Marina and the Palm Jumeirah. Its interior is classic, chic and dark and looks particularly seductive at night; book a table and head here to watch Dubai's spectacular sunsets and have a romantic meal, or begin a night out here with a few drinks.

Le Pain Quoitidien

Dubai Marina Mall (04 441 2827, www. lepainquotidien.ae). Tram Jumeirah Beach Residence Station 1. **Open** 7.30am-11pm daily. **Map** p163 C3 ㉚

On the ground floor of Marina Mall, Le Pain Quotidien is perfectly placed for those in need of a snack while shopping, and the outdoor terrace has great views. There's an emphasis on organic, with chalkboards announcing: 'Don't panic, we're organic.' Wooden floors and furniture add a rustic feel. The smell of freshly baked bread greets you as you walk through the door and you'll find soups, salads, tartines, crêpes and quiches on the menu, alongside heartier mains.

Pier 7

Dubai Marina, next to Dubai Marina Mall (04 436 1020, www.pier7.ae). Tram Dubai Marina Mall Station. **Map** p163 C3 ㉛

See p170 **Seven Up**.

Underground Pub

Habtoor Grand Beach Resort & Spa (04 408 4221, http://grandjumeirah.habtoorhotels.com). Tram Jumeirah Beach Residence Station 1. **Open** 12.30pm-3am daily. **Map** p163 B5 ㉜

A fun London underground-themed British pub, built into a faux tube train, with tube memorabilia lining the walls. There are TV screens for sport, and it does a roaring trade in pints on Premier League game nights. Bands play regularly too. You can count on this place for a lively, friendly atmosphere.

★ Zero Gravity

Skydive Dubai drop zone, Al Sufou Road (04 399 0009, www.0-gravity.ae). Tram Jumeirah Beach Residence Station 1. **Open** 10am-2am Mon-Thur, Sun; 8am-2pm Fri, Sat. **Map** p163 A5 ㉝

Located directly in the 'drop zone' of SkyDive Dubai, this beach club-meets-lounge bar has grown in popularity as a hotspot for alfresco drinking. Although it's in the heart of Dubai Marina, the long, winding path down to Zero Gravity gives it a slightly exclusive air. It looks shiny and futuristic, done out in white and chrome, yet manages to feel laid-back and casual. By day, there are the views to enjoy. By night there's an impressive monthly lineup of international DJs; there's an international food menu too.

Shops & Services

Dubai Marina Mall

Emaar Drive (04 436 1020, www.dubaimarina mall.com). Tram Dubai Marina Mall Station. **Open** 10am-10pm Mon-Wed, Sat, Sun; 10am-midnight Fri, Sat. **Map** p163 C3 ㉞ **Mall**

A relatively small mall by Dubai's standards but with a number of international brands and designers as well as popular eateries like Carluccio's and YO! Sushi. There's also a Reel Cinemas and a handy selection of practical shops including a branch of Waitrose, an optician and a pharmacy.

Marina Market

Dubai Marina Mall Promenade, behind Dubai Marina Mall (www.marinamarket.ae). Tram Jumeirah Beach Residence Station 1. **Open** 10am-10pm Wed; 10am-11pm Thur-Sat. **Map** p163 C3 ㉟ **Market**

Independent artists and retailers peddle their wares along the edge of the Marina. It's a pleasant way to spend an hour or so – but not necessarily worth going out of your way for. There are no flea market-style piles to rummage through, possibly concealing hidden gems, but you will be able to pick up items like abstract oil paintings, handpainted silk scarves, jewellery made from cutlery and Turkish *peshtemals* (towels), albeit at much higher prices than at a Turkish souk.

Smitten

1st Floor, Dubai Marina Mall (04 451 9779, www. smitten-boutique.com). Tram Dubai Marina Mall station. **Open** 10am-10pm Mon-Wed, Sat, Sun; 10am-midnight Thur, Fri. **Map** p163 C3 ㊱ **Children**

A children's boutique, with clothes and accessories from international brands like Frangipani, Poupette La Plage and BW Chic Kids (plus some of the most adorable tutus you will ever see from Tutu Du Monde). Also in stock are maternity clothes and collections for mothers, but the focus is on beautifully made, unique items that kids – and their parents – will love.

Further Afield

Drive away from the coastline, towards the desert, and you'll find a hive of building activity. The stretch of major highway Sheikh Mohammed Bin Zayed Road between Arabian Ranches and Silicon Oasis is changing as elements of the Dubailand district – such as the City of Arabia and IMG Worlds of Adventure – are finally beginning to take shape. Nearby Motor City is home to the Dubai Autodrome, while the development of Dubai Sports City is well under way. Studio City sits between Arabian Ranches and Motor City, and is home to radio stations, film studios and production companies. Vast housing projects such as Arabian Ranches and Silicon Oasis have been built and plans are in place for more, including the larger-than-life Falconcity of Wonders. You'll need a car to explore, as the metro doesn't stretch this far yet, but make the effort as there's lots to see in these miniature 'cities'.

Camel racing.

Don't Miss

1. **Camel racing** Experience a traditional Emirati sport (p181).
2. **The Farm** Begin the day with breakfast at a lush oasis (p178).
3. **Dragon Mart** Rummage for bargains at this Chinese market (p180).
4. **Global Village** Quirky knick-knacks from across the globe (p178).
5. **Desert Palm** Catch a polo match and unwind in the desert (p180).

MOTOR CITY

Initially planned as part of the extensive plans – drawn up before the recession – for Dubailand, Motor City is now a mostly residential area built around huge entertainment centre the **Autodrome**.

Sights & Attractions

Al Qudra Road Cycle Path

Sheikh Mohammed Bin Zayed Road, then Al Qudra Road through Arabian Ranches and Studio City. Continue until you reach the signposted cycle track.

This unique track through the desert landscape and sand dunes is an absolute must for any cycling enthusiast. There's a small café and bike rental shop at the track entrance, but otherwise there are minimal facilities – arrive prepared with plenty of sun cream, water and a fully charged phone. The paths cover around 85km (53 miles) in total – including a 50km (31-mile) loop. The track passes desert hotel Bab Al Shams (*see p280* **Out and About**), which is a popular spot for snacks and refreshments en route.

Dubai Autodrome

Junction of Sheikh Mohammed Bin Zayed Road & Umm Suqeim Road (04 367 8745, www.dubaiautodrome.com). **Open** *Kartdrome* 9am-11pm daily. *Autodrome* see website for schedule. **Admission** free. *Kartdrome* Dhs120/15mins. *Experiences* from Dhs875.

Featuring a 5.4km (3.3-mile) circuit with six different configurations, plus a Kartdrome and Laserdrome, the Dubai Autodrome offers a number of entertainment options for petrolheads young and old. There are a number of 'Experiences', including an Easy Drift course and the chance to test-drive Clio Cup cars and Audis. The 1.2km outdoor Kartdrome track has 17 corners.

Restaurants

Cycle Bistro

Dubai Motor City Grandstand, Shop B6 (04 425 6555, www.facebook.com/thecyclebistro). **Open** 8am-8pm Mon-Thur, Sun; 8am-6pm Fri, Sat. **Main courses** Dhs60-Dhs80. **Health food**

This organic health food restaurant is located in the Cycle Hub, a popular cycle shop and club. It serves dairy-, sugar- and gluten-free foods, as well as paleo-friendly dishes, using locally sourced ingredients where possible. The wide-ranging menu covers breakfast, salads, burgers, wraps, soups, mains and desserts, plus kids' meals and a good choice of smoothies.

Oregano

Apex Building (04 447 0740, www.oregano restaurants.com). **Open** noon-11.45pm daily. **Main courses** Dhs35-Dhs50. **Italian**

Inspired by the cuisine of Liguria, this small Italian restaurant/pizzeria serves tasty, well-made dishes. Its simple, rustic interior makes the perfect pit-stop after an afternoon at the Kartdrome.

Sushi Counter

Ground Floor, Control Tower (04 375 1687, www.sushicounter.com). **Open** 11am-11.30pm daily. **Sushi** Dhs24-Dhs70. **Sushi**

A large part of the menu at this top-notch sushi chain consists of traditional rolls, sashimi and soups, but a selection of seasonal creations keeps things interesting: Arabic and Indian cuisine such as dahl and chutneys or sushi 'burgers' made with wafers, sashimi, vegetables and sauce.

Zaatar w Zeit

Kojak Buiilding, opposite the Autodrome (600 5222 31, www.zaartarwzeit.net). **Open** 8am-11.45pm daily. **Main courses** Dhs25-Dhs45. **Arabic**

If you're looking for fast food on the move, this well-loved Lebanese takeaway chain has a decent menu of authentic and modern *manakeesh*, salads and wraps. This branch has a pleasant interior – designed in a minimalist urban style – and there's outdoor seating too.

Cafés & Bars

Caffè Nero

Motor City Retail Strip, opposite the Autodrome (04 447 5419, www.caffenero.co.uk/uae). **Open** 6am-10.45pm daily.

This London-based chain specialises in Italian coffee. The paninis are decent, as is the cake and pastry selection, and they serve generous porridge portions during the breakfast rush to eat in or take away.

IN THE KNOW FALCONCITY OF WONDERS

This huge development still has no confirmed completion date, but lives up to Dubai's reputation for building ever bigger and wackier developments. Ever wanted to see a faux Eiffel Tower that's taller than the original? Or a set of pretend pyramids bigger than those that sit at Giza? This is your chance. Other structures will include a Taj Mahal (bigger than the original, of course), Leaning Tower of Pisa, Great Wall of China and Lighthouse of Alexandria. And why stop there? The **Falconcity of Wonders** (www.falconcity.com), laid out in the shape of a falcon, will also have a theme park, schools, shops, sports facilities and more than 5,000 residential units.

Caribou Coffee

Motor City Retail Strip, opposite the Autodrome (04 447 7963, www.cariboucoffee.com). **Open** 6.30am-11pm daily.

An outpost of the Boston-born chain that's pretty similar in look and feel to the other giants of the coffee industry, such as Costa or Starbucks. The menu is pretty much what you'd expect, with sandwiches and pastries, the coffee is pretty decent and there are sofas if you need to take the weight off your feet for a little while.

EXPLORE

Dubai Autodrome.

Shops & Services

Motor City Retail Strip
Motor City, opposite the Autodrome. **Open** varies. **Various**
This cluster of shops runs the length of the road that passes the Autodrome. There's a large supermarket and various other outlets, plus restaurants, cafés and takeaways.

Trek Bicycle Store Seih Al Salam
Exit Sheikh Mohammed Bin Zayed Road & pass Arabian Ranches & Studio City. Continue straight along Al Qudra Road until you reach the signposted cycle track. **Open** 6am-10pm Mon-Thur, Sun; 5am-9pm Fri, Sat. **Bike rental** Dhs40 per hr; Dhs105 per day. **Carbon road bike rental** Dhs80 per hr; Dhs175 per day. **Cycling**
Rents bikes and equipment for the Al Qudra Road Cycle Path (*see p174*). You'll need your passport to hire a bike.

DUBAI SPORTS CITY

Still in various stages of development, Dubai Sports City will be an expansive complex of leisure, sport, retail and housing when it's finally completed. It's an ideal base for visiting sports fanatics thanks to its Sports Village, which includes a number of Olympic or full-sized sports facilities, impressive state-of-the-art gyms such as Fit Republik, and the **Els Club** – an 18-hole championship course designed by legendary South African golfer Ernie Els. Two huge shopping and leisure areas – North Point and South Point – are planned for the area.

Sights & Attractions

Dubai International Cricket Stadium
Dubai Sports City (04 425 1111, www. dsc.ae). **Open** varies.
Cricket fans should time their trip to coincide with one of the major series held at the stadium each year, including some of the Pepsi Indian Premier League (IPL) in 2014. In just five years, the stadium has held more Twenty20 internationals than anywhere else in the world and the 25,000-seater has become a popular venue for concerts and other events.

Els Club
Dubai Sports City (04 425 1000, www.elsclub dubai.com). **Open** varies. **Golf** 18 holes/Dhs895. *Driving range* Dhs100.
This is one of the newest courses in the city, designed by former US Open champion Ernie Els. The course design draws on some of Els's favourite courses from around the world, such as Royal Melbourne

Els Club.

and Pinehurst No.2, and includes interesting elevation changes and wide fairways. There's also a reasonably priced driving range.

Restaurants

261 Restaurant

Els Club (04 425 1000, www.elsclubdubai.com). **Open** 6am-midnight daily. **Main courses** Dhs55-Dhs210. **Breakfast** Dhs35-Dhs85. **Global**

This is one of the few places in the city where you can pick up a proper bacon and egg sandwich or a full English with bacon, sausages and black pudding, and breakfast is served until 3pm. The rest of the menu is pretty varied: alongside classic pub grub such as steak and Guinness pie or sausage and mash, you'll find Thai salad, crabcakes, curries and hearty sandwiches.

Big Easy

Els Club (04 425 1000, www.elsclubdubai.com). **Open** 5-11pm daily. **Main courses** Dhs85-Dhs385 **Grill**

The meat-heavy menu at this South African grill includes classic options such as steak and *boerewors* (sausages), but there's also a wide selection of global dishes from Malay chicken curry to bouillabaisse. The simple decor won't win any awards, but the food is certainly worth a look if you're in the area.

Wooden Cellar

Canal Provence, Mediterranean Building (04 553 0467, www.woodencellar.com). **Open** 7am-8pm Mon-Thur, Sun; 10am-10pm Fri, Sat. **Greek**

A new restaurant and deli serving Greek cuisine inspired by traditional family recipes. Shop for artisanal Greek produce or take a seat and enjoy breakfast, lunch or an early dinner.

Cafés & Bars

Champs Café

Dome (04 448 1591, www.champscafe.ae). **Open** 10am-10pm daily. **Sandwiches & salads** Dhs15-Dhs30.

This child-friendly football-themed café is popular with local families after matches at the huge indoor football pitch. You can pick up simple salads and sandwiches, as well as fresh juices, teas and coffees. Health-conscious parents will be pleased to see that no pizzas or burgers feature on the menu, and prices won't break the bank.

Kickers Sports Bar

Near Dubai International Cricket Stadium (04 425 1111, www.dsc.ae). **Open** noon-11.30pm daily.

Walls are hung with signed sports paraphernalia and printed illustrations of players, and there are neon lights aplenty at this sports bar. Bar options are still limited in this area, so Kickers can get pretty busy at weekends or on game days. It's a huge space with big screens for international matches, pool tables and a large outdoor area.

Shops & Services

The **Motor City Retail Strip** (*see p176*) is just a five-minute drive away.

SHEIKH MOHAMMED BIN ZAYED ROAD AND ARABIAN RANCHES

Sights & Attractions

Arabian Ranches Golf Club

Arabian Ranches, Sheikh Mohammed Bin Zayed Road (04 366 3000, www.arabianranchesgolfdubai.com).

This par-72 course spans 100 hectares (247 acres) of grassy turf. The design mimics the natural desert landscape, similar to courses found in Arizona and California. Rates are seasonal so check the website for the latest prices. The club is home to several restaurants and bars, including Maison Mathis (*see p179*), Ranches Restaurant & Bar (6.30am-10pm daily), and Birdies Sports Lounge (7am-10.30pm daily) – as well as a nail salon (600 544 001, www.thenailspa.com).

Dubai Polo & Equestrian Club

Al Qudra Road, off Sheikh Mohammed bin Zayed Road, opposite Arabian Ranches and next to Dubai Studio City (04 361 8111, www.poloclubdubai.com). **Open** 6am-10pm (times of polo matches vary; phone or check the website).

Head here to catch a game of polo, or better yet, camel polo (the season runs from roughly October to April), while enjoying a drink on the terrace at Ippos Lounge (*see p180*). The on-site Dubai Polo Academy (050 887 9847, www.dubaipoloacademy.com) offers polo lessons, courses and stables tours.

Global Village

Exit 37, Sheikh Mohammed Bin Zayed Road (04 362 4114, www.globalvillage.ae). **Open** 4pm-midnight Mon-Wed, Sat, Sun; 4pm-1am Thur, Fri. Closed Apr-Nov. **Admission** Dhs15. *Economy pack* Dhs99 (4 tickets, 1 valet parking, Dhs75 to spend at Fantasy Island, 2 mini train tickets). *Family pack* Dhs199 (10 tickets, 2 valet parking, Dhs100 to spend at fantasy island, 4 mini train tickets).

This mega complex of shops and stalls has a kind of flea market vibe, with a difference. Split into sections themed by country, you can browse honey in the Yemen, carpets and upholstery in India and Pakistan, or Arabic lanterns in Syria. There are a grand total of 31 countries represented, in addition to a funfair (albeit a slightly lacklustre one), nightly fireworks display and numerous street-food stalls. Don't underestimate the scale – it's easy to spend a few hours here getting lost among endless stalls of knick-knacks at pretty cheap prices. The entrance to each country section is done up with a gimmicky façade mimicking the national architecture, but surprisingly it all comes together quite well and errs more on the side of eclectic than tacky. The quirky attractions don't end there: there's a Prehistoric Oceanarium that uses 3D to reconstruct prehistoric water creatures, an Illumination World using lantern art and LED lights to recreate famous buildings, an area full of sand sculptures, and another packed with moving animal sculptures.

IN THE KNOW A BRIEF HISTORY OF CAMEL RACING

One of the oldest sports in the Middle East, camel racing has a long and proud tradition, and until 2002 saw child jockeys ride the region's finest dromedaries (that's single-humped to the uninitiated) to possible victory. For the past decade, an ever-evolving procession of robots (yes, you read that right) have taken the place of humans, helping the sport break all previous speed records. In the past, children were commonly chosen to work as camel jockeys to save weight, but this has been outlawed in the UAE since 2002. The ban was designed to end the exploitation of foreign-born minors, who were often injured in races and badly treated. Following the ban, the UAE government has contributed millions of dirhams towards the repatriation of former child jockeys.

Restaurants

Al Arrab

Arabian Ranches Shopping Centre, Arabian Ranches, Sheikh Mohammed Bin Zayed Road (04 361 7070, www.alarrab.net). **Open** 11am-1am daily. **Shawarmas** Dhs29. **Arabic**

Al Arrab turns out tasty no-fuss Lebanese fare. Prices are reasonable, and outdoor seating and shisha are available. Order from the grill along with some saj bread, tabouleh and fattoush, or pick up a shawarma to go.

★ Farm

Al Barari Villas, Sheikh Mohammed Bin Zayed Road (04 392 5660, www.thefarmdubai.com). **Open** 7am-11pm daily. **Main courses** Dhs60-Dhs160. **Global**

Tucked away in the Al Barari compound, the Farm feels like a true escape from Dubai. A long, winding road with towering greenery on either side leads you gently to the entrance, an architecturally impressive space with outdoor terraces, pools and chirping

SEVENS HEAVEN

Rugby rules Dubai in December.

Situated approximately 40km (25 miles) outside the city, the **Sevens Stadium** (*see p181*) is home to the annual Dubai Rugby Sevens tournament (*www.dubairugby7s.com*). Fans flock here on the first weekend of December to see more than 3,000 players in action during three days of matches.

But you don't have to be a rugby fanatic to enjoy the event, which has become as much a Dubai institution as a sporting contest. Get on your dancing shoes and whatever fancy dress you can find, and head down for the party atmosphere and electrifying crowds at one of the biggest parties of the year.

There's beer and sunshine aplenty, plus a melting pot of nationalities – you'd be hard pressed to find a more lively crowd at any of the other Sevens tournaments around the world. Day three culminates with live music until midnight, after which a fleet of buses ferries revellers to Barasti to continue the party.

Despite the party vibe, the event is child-friendly, with dedicated family areas in the stands and a huge number of games and activities – such as bouncy castles and face painting – to keep little ones entertained.

Advanced single-day tickets are Dhs300; season tickets are Dhs500; under-12s go free.

wildlife. The all-smiling staff are attentive, although service can be a little slow. The well-judged menu is presented on an iPad – a concept that jars slightly with the natural vibe of the venue. The food, though, is excellent, with breakfast a particular highlight: mouthwatering sourdough bread, hot waffles with gooey syrup and perfectly cooked eggs benedict are all available. This is a great spot with good food that offers a brief respite from Dubai's hectic pace.

Maison Mathis

Arabian Ranches Golf Club, Arabian Ranches, Sheikh Mohammed Bin Zayed Road (04 450 1313, www.mm-argc.com). **Open** 7am-2am daily. **Main courses** Dhs95-Dhs165. **Belgian**

This Belgian bar-restaurant with views across the golf course is particularly pleasant during the cooler months, when all the floor-to-ceiling French windows are opened up. The vibe is chic and modern, but distinctly family-friendly with a climbing frame tucked into a corner of the terrace. Sadly, though, the menu isn't as authentic as you might expect. A small number of familiar Belgian dishes – foie gras terrine, steaming pots of mussels, perfectly cooked chips – line up alongside a wide variety of global fare: ribs, burgers, steaks, ratatouille and the like.

Dragon Mart.

Cafés & Bars

There's also a branch of popular local chain **Shakespeare & Co** (*see p91*) in the Arabian Ranches Shopping Centre.

Circle Café

Shop No.5, Ground Floor, EIT Building No.2 (04 276 6283, www.circle-cafe.com). **Open** 8am-10pm daily. **Main courses** Dhs40-Dhs75. **Salads & sandwiches** Dhs35-Dhs55.

This home-grown café has quickly become a favourite lunch spot with locals. The menu is fresh and (mostly) healthy, with wonderful salads such as wild rice with cherry tomatoes, shallots, mint, feta, black olives and yellow raisins, and mains such as Jamaican jerk chicken with coconut rice or grilled teriyaki glazed salmon. There are also more indulgent options, a selection of bagels, and some fantastic crowd-pleasing desserts (try the Oreo mousse covered in Nutella, salted caramel, banana, strawberries and toasted hazelnuts).

Ippos Lounge

Dubai Polo & Equestrian Club, Al Qudra Road, off Sheikh Mohammed bin Zayed Road, opposite Arabian Ranches and next to Dubai Studio City (04 361 8111, www.poloclubdubai.com). **Open** 4-11.30pm daily.

This laid-back bar has a terrace overlooking the polo fields, TVs screening sports, and a good selection of drinks and cigars. The decor is a combination of dark hardwood furniture, brown leather sofas and wooden beams – very much like a typical ranch.

Shops & Services

Arabian Ranches Shopping Centre

Arabian Ranches, Sheikh Mohammed Bin Zayed Road. **Open** varies.

This shopping centre houses a range of services, including a supermarket, optician, travel agent and pharmacy, plus a selection of fast food chains.

AL AWIR ROAD

Sights & Attractions

★ Desert Palm Hotel & Polo Club

Al Awir Road (04 323 8888, www.desertpalm.peraquum.com). **Admission** free. **Pool** Dhs195 per day. **Gym** Dhs195 per day. **Afternoon tea** Dhs110.

Situated on the very outskirts of the city, Desert Palm is a lush oasis of green polo fields, ringed by fantastic restaurants. Visit between October and May (Mon, Wed, Fri, Sat) and relax on the terrace while watching one of Dubai's best-loved sports. Afternoon tea is served to coincide with the matches. Afterwards, check into the LIME Spa or head to the gym or infinity pool (with polo field views). There are also tennis courts and outdoor running and mountain biking circuits. Desert Palm is tranquil and sophisticated, and although a day spent here won't come cheap, there's more than enough to keep you occupied.

Dragon Mart

Al Awir Road (www.dragonmart.ae). **Open** 10am-10pm Mon-Wed, Sat, Sun; 10am-11pm Thur-Sat.

This vast Chinese emporium on the way to Desert Palm is more than just a novelty. There are 3,950 shops in the market, which covers 150,000sq m and is more than a kilometre long. You'll find anything and everything – wholesale and retail – from home appliances, building materials, machinery and furniture to toys, textiles, clothing, plus other household and general items. It's divided into seven zones, and you could easily spend a whole afternoon lost in the overwhelming number of shops selling the oddest assortment of goods you could ever imagine. It's a bit out of the way, but definitely fun enough to warrant a visit if you enjoy a good rummage.

Restaurants

Rare

Desert Palm Dubai, Al Awir Road, next to International City (04 323 8888, www.desertpalm.peraquum.com). **Open** 7-11pm Mon-Thur, Sat, Sun; 7.30-11pm Fri. **Steak**

Desert Palm's steakhouse is a relaxed place to dine, with a spacious terrace during the winter, and the food is exquisite. Opt for the indulgent Australian wagyu and you won't be disappointed, but it's not all about steak. The miso black cod with soba noodles, enoki mushrooms and smoked tuna broth is sublime.

Cafés & Bars

Epicure

Desert Palm Dubai, Al Awir Road, next to International City (04 323 8888, www.desertpalm.peraquum.com). **Open** 7-11.30am, noon-10.30pm daily.

Epicure is a laid-back contemporary brasserie with a cool European vibe. It's open for breakfast, lunch and dinner, serving pastries, juices and a rustic selection of sandwiches and mains, plus a deli counter for takeaways. Plush sofas overlook the infinity pool – ideal for a leisurely coffee.

Polo Bar

Desert Palm Dubai, Al Awir Road, next to International City (04 323 8888, www.desertpalm.peraquum.com). **Open** 5pm-2am Mon-Sat.

As the name suggests, alfresco drinking is the order of the day here, with a terrace overlooking the green polo fields of the Desert Palm.

Red Bar

Desert Palm Dubai, Al Awir Road, next to International City (04 323 8888, www.desertpalm.peraquum.com). **Open** 5pm-2am Mon-Thur, Sun; midday-2am Fri, Sat.

A chic, modern lounge and cigar bar that serves inventive martinis. The espresso version is made by using captured smoke as an infusion, while the Ron Zacapa Sour features smoking curry leaves. Other fun options include coconut martini, coriander martini, and honey and marmalade martini.

DUBAI TO AL AIN ROAD

Sights & Attractions

Dubai Camel Racing Club

Al Marmoum Camel Racing Track, Dubai to Al Ain Road (E66) (04 832 6526, www.dcrc.ae). **Admission** free. **Open** varies.

The camel racing season runs from around October to February or March, culminating in a series of finals. Head over to the track, approximately 45 minutes from central Dubai, to witness for yourself these curious boxes bouncing around atop some of the UAE's finest desert-dwelling speedsters. The UAE's best, fastest camels compete on the desert track, reaching impressive speeds of up to 40km per hour (20 miles per hour). *See p178* **In the Know**.

Dubai Outlet Mall

Dubai to Al Ain Road (E66) (04 423 4666, www.dubaioutletmall.com). **Open** 10am-10pm Mon-Wed, Sat, Sun; 10am-midnight Thur, Fri.

The Dubai Outlet Mall is home to a huge selection of international brands – including Diesel, Kas Australia, Coach, Mango, ALDO and DKNY – selling off last season's stock at heavily discounted prices. Lesser-known outlets include S*uce – a Dubai-based brand selling fashion and accessories from local and international contemporary designers – where you can pick up one-of-a-kind pieces at much cheaper prices than branches in the central malls.

Sevens Stadium

Dubai to Al Ain Road (E66), at intersectin with Jebel Ali-Lahbab Road (04 809 6605, www.thesevens.ae). **Open** varies.

One of the biggest sporting venues in the country, with room for six cricket ovals, four tennis and netball courts, and a basketball court, plus pitches for rugby, football, Gaelic football, Aussie rules and more. *See p179* **Sevens Heaven**.

Restaurants

The **Dubai Outlet Mall** (*see above*) has a food court with fast-food options such as Burger King, KFC, New York Fries and other big-brand takeaways, as well as a Starbucks and one or two mediocre coffee shops. If you're looking for something a little more *haute*, **Rare** (*see left*) at Desert Palm or the **Farm** (*see p178*) at Al Barari are both within a 20-minute drive of the outlet mall and around half an hour from the Camel Racing Club.

Shops & Services

If you're in need of an ATM, money exchange services or left luggage facilities, **Dubai Outlet Mall** (*see above*) can accommodate.

Arts & Entertainment

Children

With year-round sun and endless sandy beaches, entertaining children can be as simple as packing a bucket and spade. But there's more to Dubai than this for little ones. Despite being a desert city, there are pleasant oases of green amid the skyscrapers, which offer affordable, down-to-earth fun. Then there's the other side of Dubai, with its mega developments such as the world's largest indoor ski slope, aquariums stocked full of marine life and waterparks with exhilarating rides. Needless to say, your children won't be bored. To keep up to date with all the latest family events, make sure you buy *Time Out Dubai Kids*, on the shelves every month.

WILDLIFE

Animal Sanctuary & Petting Farm

Khawaneej, off Al Warqaa Road (050 273 0973, www.poshpawsdubai.com). **Open** 9am-5pm daily. **Admission** free (donations welcome).

This animal sanctuary looks after lots of donated, unwanted or rescued animals. Children can pet and feed an array of creatures including sloths, porcupines, ponies, llamas and ducks. Entry is free, but as the sanctuary is a non-profit organisation, all donations are welcomed.

★ Dolphin Bay & the Lost Chambers

Atlantis The Palm, Palm Jumeirah (04 426 1030, www.atlantisthepalm.com/marine-water-park). Tram Palm Jumeirah (then monorail to Atlantis). **Open** 10am-10pm daily. **Admission** *Dolphin Bay* prices on enquiry. *Lost Chambers* Dhs100; Dhs70 under-13s. **Map** p308 A1.

Swim with dolphins at Dolphin Bay, before checking out the Lost Chambers aquarium, which is home to more than 65,000 marine animals. Prices include entry to Aquaventure Waterpark (*see p190*), making this a good option for an action-packed day.

Dubai Aquarium & Underwater Zoo

Dubai Mall, Downtown (04 448 5200, www.thedubaiaquarium.com). Metro Burj Khalifa or Dubai Mall. **Open** 10am-10pm Mon-Wed, Sun; 10am-midnight Thur-Sat. **Admission** Dhs100-Dhs250. **Map** p310 H5.

If your children get tired of traipsing around the shopping avenues of Dubai Mall, then a trip to Dubai Aquarium & Underwater Zoo offers respite. Mind you, it features its own never-ending avenue: a 48m (157ft) aquarium tunnel, surrounded by sharks and stingrays. There are more than 33,000 marine creatures in the aquarium, a 750kg (2,205lb) Australian saltwater crocodile, and various opportunities for diving with the fish.

Dubai Dolphinarium

Gate 1, Creek Park (see p188 for listings; 04 336 9773, www.dubaidolphinarium.ae). Metro Dubai Healthcare City. **Open** varies; check website for latest times. **Tickets** Dhs70-Dhs120. **Map** p311 K3.

Take your seat for an action-packed aquatic show, where graceful bottlenose dolphins and playful seals dance, sing, juggle, play ball, jump through hoops and even paint.

Falcon Heritage & Sports Centre

Muscat Street, Nad Al Sheba (04 327 2854). **Open** 7am-6pm (8am-2pm for tours) Mon-Thur, Sun. **Admission** free. **Map** p309 D4.

Learn more about falcons and their important place in Emirati culture at this cracking sanctuary. The multi-purpose centre has a falcon souk and a shop for all the necessary falconry equipment, but the main highlight is the onsite museum. Within the museum are exhibitions answering every conceivable question you might have about falcons and, of course, there are real-life falcons too.

★ Snow Penguins

Mall of the Emirates, Al Barsha (04 409 4242, www.skidubaipenguins.com). Metro Mall of the Emirates. **Open** 10am-11pm Mon-Wed, Sun; 10am-midnight Thur; 9am-midnight Fri; 9am-11pm Sat. **Admission** Dhs150-Dhs850. **Map** p318 D3.
Ski Dubai, inside Mall of the Emirates, isn't just for those looking to hurtle down the indoor snowpark's enormous slope. There are penguins to gawk at too. It's possible to see the animals from the viewing windows inside the mall, but you can also pay for more up-close experiences with gentoo and king penguins.

ARTS & CRAFTS

Clay Sculpture for Kids

Ductac, Mall of the Emirates, Al Barsha (04 341 4777, www.ductac.org). Metro Mall of the Emirates. **Open** 11.30am-12.30pm (beginners), 1-3pm (advanced) Sat. **Map** p318 D3.
Unlock your kids' artistic potential, improve concentration, observation and hand-eye co-ordination.

Dubai International Art Centre

Villa 27, Street 75B, Jumeirah (04 344 4398, www.artdubai.com). **Open** 8.30am-5.30pm Mon-Wed, Sat, Sun; 9am-4pm Thur. **Map** p316 C12.
This non-profit centre holds classes in all artistic media, from mosaics to calligraphy.

Mirath Art Center

Amwaj 3, The Walk, Jumeirah Beach Residence (04 434 0128, www.mirathcenter.com). Tram Jumeirah Beach Residence 2. **Open** 9am-6.30pm Mon-Wed, Sat, Sun. **Map** p318 B1.
Creative art courses and workshops for all ages, starting from four years.

Thejamjar

17A Street, Al Quoz (04 341 7303, www.thejamjardubai.com). Metro FGB. **Open** 10am-8pm Mon-Thur, Sat; 2-8pm Fri. **Map** p318 E2.
Thejamjar is a fun, hands-on art studio, offering three-hour creative sessions, including supplies, for artists of all ages.

Picasso Project

Al Areesh Club, Al Badia (050 352 0844). http://picassoprobernadett.wix.com. **Sessions** 3.30pm Wed (subject to change; phone or check the website). **Admission** Dhs80. **Map** p311 L4.
Arts and crafts workshops for children aged 18 months to nine years. Kids get creative with all kinds of materials and techniques.

BEACH CLUBS

Club Joumana

Jebel Ali Beach Hotel, Jebel Ali (04 814 5555). **Open** 9am-6pm daily. **Rates** Dhs180 Mon-Thur, Sun; Dhs250 Fri, Sat; half-price 5-12s.
Make sure you get to Joumana early at weekends – they sometimes have to turn people away by 10am. This is a great place to take the children, with plenty of activities. Watersports are also offered, including windsurfing (from Dhs150 for rental per hour), waterskiing (Dhs250 including rental and 20mins instruction), sailing (from Dhs170 per hour) and kayaking (Dhs100 per hour).

Club Mina

Le Méridien Mina Seyahi Beach Resort & Marina, Umm Suqeim (04 399 3333). Tram Mina Seyahi. **Open** 9am-7pm daily. **Rates** Dhs225 Mon-Thur, Sun; Dhs350 Fri, Sat. **Map** p318 B2.
Club Mina has five pools, a 500m beach, gym, steam room, sauna, tennis courts and volleyball courts. It also provides facilities for a generous number of watersports, with banana boating, boat trips, windsurfing, waterskiing and sailing, as well as beach volleyball, table tennis, golf and aerobics classes. There's also a jogging circuit and a dedicated lap pool for swimmers.

Dubai Marine Beach Resort & Spa

Jumeirah Beach Road, Jumeirah 1 (04 346 1111). **Open** 8am-8pm daily. **Rates** Dhs100 Mon-Thur, Sun; Dhs225 Fri; Dhs150 Sat. **Map** p314 D8/D9.

Thejamjar.

RIVA Beach Club.

This Jumeirah beach club is like a little village, with shops, varied alfresco restaurants, bars and a spa. The two pools and beach are a little smaller than those in the actual Marina area, but that only makes it feel more exclusive. It also has a kids' pool, a tennis court and gym.

Habtoor Grand Beach Resort & Spa

Dubai Marina (04 399 5000). Tram Mina Seyahi. **Open** 8.30am-7.30pm daily. **Rates** Dhs150 Mon-Wed, Sun; Dhs250 Thur-Sat. **Map** p318 B2.
This busy beach club features a pool, slide and beach bar, and guests also have full access to a host of watersports provided by the Habtoor Grand's privately managed marina and boat charter company, Nautica 1992. Activities include windsurfing, water-skiing, wakeboarding, banana boating and para-sailing. Fishing charters are available. Other outdoor sports include beach football and beach volleyball.

Ritz-Carlton Dubai Beach Club

The Walk, Jumeirah Beach Residence (04 399 4000). Tram Jumeirah Beach Residence 1. **Open** 7am-6pm daily. **Rates** Dhs500 adults; Dhs750 couples; Dhs300 children. **Map** p318 B2.
Beach Club guests have access to all the hotel's facilities including the spa and fitness equipment, pools, beach and tennis courts. Children can join in with the kids' club and pool. Watersports are available for an additional cost.

RIVA Beach Club

Shoreline Apartments, Building 8, Palm Jumeirah (04 458 1811, www.riva-beach.com). **Open** 7am-7pm daily. **Rates** Dhs100 Mon-Thur, Sun; Dhs175 Fri, Sat. **Map** p318 C1.
RIVA has its own stretch of private beach with more than 200 sunloungers laid out (all available for day hire), a climate-controlled pool, a gym, fully licensed gazebo bar, steam rooms and an alfresco restaurant. Kayaks and paddleboards are available for hire. The RIVA complex is also home to outlets offering everything from beauty by Kalm and pampering by Dreamworks to the Palm's favourite florist, Bliss.

BOWLING

Al Nasr Leisureland

Oud Metha Road, behind American Hospital, Oud Metha (04 337 1234, www.alnasrll.com). Metro Oud Metha. **Open** 9am-11pm daily. **Rates** Dhs 5 admission; Dhs15/game. **Map** p311 J3.
The ageing Al Nasr Leisureland may not look like much from the outside, but there's plenty to do here. The entertainment complex features an eight-lane bowling alley, plus an ice rink, tennis courts, go-karts and a rollercoaster.

Dubai Bowling Centre

Al Meydan Street, Al Quoz (04 339 1010, www.bowlingdubai.com). Metro FGB. **Open** 10am-midnight Mon-Wed, Sat; 10am-2am Thur; 10am-1.30am Fri. **Rates** Dhs17-Dhs25/game. **Map** p309 D3.
This large bowling alley has 16 lanes plus plenty of other facilities including an arcade, café and gym with a sauna and jacuzzi.

Switch

Ibn Battuta Mall, The Gardens (04 440 5961). Metro Ibn Battuta. **Open** 11am-midnight Mon-Wed, Sun; 10.30am-midnight Thur-Sat. **Rates** vary.
Always busy due to its prime location within Ibn Battuta Mall, this alley has 12 lanes plus karaoke booths and a café.

Yalla! Bowling Lanes & Lounge

Mirdif City Centre, Mirdif (04 800 386, www.theplaymania.com). **Open** 10am-10pm Mon-Wed, Sun; 10am-midnight Thur-Sat. **Rates** Dhs20/game Mon-Wed, Sun; Dhs25/game Thur-Sat.

Inside Mirdif City Centre, this high-tech bowling alley provides an escape from the shops. There are 12 lanes plus a video games area and pool tables.

ICE-SKATING & SNOWSPORTS

Dubai Ice Rink

Dubai Mall, Downtown (04 448 5111, www.dubaiicerink.com). Metro Burj Kahlifa/Dubai Mall. **Open** 10am-10pm Mon-Wed, Sun; 11.15am-midnight Thur-Sat. **Rates** Dhs60 public session; Dhs80 disco session. **Map** p310 H5.

This Olympic-sized ice rink is a good place to skate – as long as you're not put off by the hordes of rink-side spectators. There are open sessions to just slide around or disco sessions with music and lights.

Galleria Ice Rink

Hyatt Regency Dubai, Corniche Road, Deira (04 209 1234). Metro Palm Deira. **Open** 10am-12.30pm, 1-3.30pm, 4-6.30pm, 7-10pm Mon-Sat; 10am-12.30pm, 1-4.30pm, 5-9.30pm Sun. **Rates** Dhs40 Mon-Wed, Sun; Dhs45 Thur-Sat. Dhs60 disco nights Thur, Fri. **Map** p313 J1.

This old-school ice rink has been around since 1980 and is a bit quieter than the one in the Dubai Mall. Thursdays and Fridays are Disco Nights, with music and lights to accompany sliding around on the ice.

★ Ski Dubai

Mall of the Emirates, Al Barsha (04 409 4000, www.theplaymania.com). Metro Mall of the Emirates. **Open** 10am-11pm Mon-Wed, Sun; 10am-midnight Thur; 9am-midnight Fri; 9am-11pm Sat. **Rates** Dhs225-Dhs500. **Map** p318 D2.

The world's biggest indoor ski slope. You can also try tubing and tobogganing in the snowpark area, or see the penguins (*see p185*). If you'd like to hurtle down the ski slope in a giant ball, that's possible too. *Photo p189.*

HORSE RIDING

Al Ahli Riding School

Amman Street, Al Qusais (04 298 8408, www.alahliclub.info). Metro Stadium. **Open** 9am-9pm daily. **Rates** on request. **Map** p311 L1.

A pony club for children four and above. The school organises beach and desert rides, and runs lessons.

Dubai Polo & Equestrian Club

Emirates Road, Arabian Ranches (04 361 8111, www.poloclubdubai.com). **Open** 6am-11pm daily. **Rates** Dhs35 pony rides for ages 3-7. **Map** p308 A5.

It's not all about polo at this club, which also offers pony rides for little ones. All levels are welcome.

Jebel Ali Golf Resort & Spa

JA Jebel Ali Golf Resort, Jebel Ali (04 814 5555, www.jaresortshotels.com). **Open** 7am-11.30am, 3.30-7.30pm Tue-Sun. **Rates** available on request.

Children aged four and above can enjoy a 25-minute pony ride around the pleasant grounds of the resort. Opening times can change in summer.

Meydan Racecourse

Al Meydan Road, Nad Al Sheeba (04 327 0000, www.dubairacingclub.com). **Racing** *Sept-Mar* 7.30am-noon Tue-Wed. **Rates** Dhs250; Dhs150 4-12s. **Map** p309 D4.

Go behind the scenes at the impressive Meydan Racecourse, which hosts the richest day in horse racing – the Dubai World Cup. The day starts with breakfast before a stable tour where guests can meet the trainer and horses.

MUSEUMS

Al Ahmadiya Museum

School & Heritage House, Al Khor Street, near Gold House building, Al Ras, Deira (04 226 0286, www.dubaiculture.gov.ae). Metro Ras. **Open** 7.30am-7.30pm Mon-Thur, Sat, Sun; 2.30-7.30pm Fri. **Admission** free. **Map** p312 H3.

Visiting a school while on holiday may not be many children's idea of fun, but Al Ahmadiya should pique their interest. Established in 1912, it was the first school in Dubai.

Dubai Heritage Village

Al Shindagha, Bur Dubai (04 393 7139, www.dubaiculture.gov.ae). Metro Al Ghubaiba. **Open** 7.30am-10pm Mon-Thur, Sat, Sun; 3-11pm Fri. **Admission** free. **Map** p312 G3.

A stone's throw from the Creek is this recreation of a Bedouin village. You can also see local people demonstrating traditional crafts such as pottery and basket-weaving.

Dubai Museum

Al Fahidi Fort, Bur Dubai (04 353 1862, www.dubaiculture.gov.ae). Metro Al Fahidi. **Open** 8.30am-8.30pm Mon-Thur, Sat, Sun; 2.30-8.30pm Fri. **Admission** Dhs3; Dhs1 children. **Map** p312 H4.

Situated inside the renovated Al Fahidi Fort in the heart of the city's historic district, Dubai Museum has plenty to keep children amused. A large cannon at the entrance attracts interest from the start, while inside the museum there are various displays and hands-on exhibits telling Dubai's history.

GREAT OUTDOORS

Al Barsha Pond Park

Al Barsha 2, off First Al Khail Street. Metro Mall of the Emirates. **Open** 8am-11pm Mon-Thur, Sat; 8am-11.30pm Fri, Sat. **Admission** free. **Map** p318 D3.

This lesser-known park in Al Barsha, not far from Mall of the Emirates, has real charm. With a large lake in the centre and plenty of shady spots to lay down a picnic blanket, it makes a peaceful retreat from city life. The perimeter of the lake is a smooth, 2.5km (1.5-mile) padded jogging track, which is ideal for pushing a stroller in the sunshine, letting kids work off some energy on a bicycle, or getting some exercise on rollerblades. There are three separate children's play areas, with sand flooring and a variety of activities to keep all ages entertained, and sun canopies above the equipment to keep them cool. There's beach volleyball, too, on a dedicated court.

Beach chalets

Al Mamzar Park, Al Mamzar, about 5km north of Al Hamriya Port (04 296 7454). **Open** 9am-9pm Mon-Wed, Sun; 9am-10pm Thur-Sat. **Admission** Dhs30 per car; Dhs5 per person. **Chalets** Dhs200 per day for 6-person chalet; Dhs150 per day for 4-person chalet.

Al Mamzar Park has a number of air-conditioned chalets, complete with outside barbecue facilities, shower rooms, seating areas, and space to prepare your picnic. Perfect for families with little ones that need to shelter from the sun or have a nap.

Boating lake

Safa Park (see right for listings). **Rates** Dhs40/20 mins. **Map** p310 F5/G5.

Safa Park is the place to head for if the children fancy climbing aboard a rowing boat and having a paddle around a pretty lake. Boats take two to four people.

Cable car

Creek Park (see below for listings), near the park's main restaurant. **Open** 8am-11pm daily (5-9pm in summer). **Tickets** Dhs25; Dhs10 children.

Creek Park has a cable car. And why not? Suspended 30m (98ft) in the air, the cable car runs the entire 2.3km (1.5-mile) length of the park and provides a bird's-eye view of the city. You'll be able to see as far as the Dubai Marina in one direction and Sharjah in the other.

Children's City

Gate 1, Creek Park (see below for listings; 334 0808, www.childrencity.ae). **Open** 9am-8pm Mon-Thur, Sat; 3-9pm Fri. **Tickets** Dhs15; Dhs10 under-16s.

Designed for kids from two to 15 years old, Children's City has a planetarium, the Al-Ajyal Theatre and galleries teaching youngsters about nature, the human body, culture, and computers and communication.

★ Creek Park

Al Riyad Street, Oud Metha (04 336 7633). Metro Oud Metha or Dubai Healthcare City. **Open** 8am-10pm Mon-Wed, Sun; 8am-11pm Thur-Sat. **Admission** Dhs5. **Map** 311 K3

When it comes to entertaining children, few green spaces in Dubai can beat Creek Park. Located in a picturesque position alongside Dubai Creek, the park benefits from a sea breeze which helps to keep everyone cool on warm days. The park is home to a cable car and Children's City (for both, *see left*).

Al Mamzar Park

Near Al Hamriya Port, Al Waheda (04 296 6201). **Open** 8am-10pm Mon-Wed, Sun; 8am-11pm Thur-Sat. **Admission** Dhs30 per car; Dhs5 per person.

This large park has four pristine beaches with calm waters, a large section of manicured lawn, palm trees, barbecue facilities, play areas for children, swimming pools and winding paths to take a stroll or ride a bicycle. The real highlight is being able to choose between green space, with lots of shade, and the stretch of sandy beach. Lifeguards are on duty on the beach and sun loungers are available.

Mushrif Park & International Village

Near Mirdif City Centre, Mirdif (04 288 3624). **Open** 8am-10pm Mon-Wed, Sun; 8am-11pm Thur-Sat. **Admission** Dhs10 per car; Dhs3 per person.

This vast park is full of little surprises. In fact, it's so big that it's the only park in Dubai you can drive through to fully explore. Visitors can spread out a picnic blanket, get some exercise in one of the two 25m pools, visit a bird aviary, or let the children climb and swing in the play areas dotted around the park. Children also love exploring the International Village, with 13 models of traditional houses from around the world, including a replica of a traditional German *hausbarn*, a Thai house, and even a blue toadstool house. In the Bedouin area, there's a traditional village mocked up with tents, goats and a water well. To explore further, you can take camel and horse rides or even board a train that takes you round the park.

RIPE Market

Gate 1, Za'abeel Park (see p189 for listings). **Open** 9am-3pm Fri.

As well as a vast range of farm-fresh food and craft items to browse and buy, there's a petting zoo, pony rides, sand art activities and live music to keep the little ones entertained.

Safa Park

Between Al Wasl & Sheikh Zayed Road Interchange 2, Al Safa (04 349 2111). **Open** 8am-11pm daily. **Admission** Dhs3. **Map** p310 F5/G5.

With a vast expanse of manicured lawns, over 16,000 trees and plants, and a striking cityscape in the distance, Safa Park is one of the prettiest places to spend time with the family. Look around and you will see families on picnic rugs, sporty types jogging the perimeter of the park and yoga enthusiasts contorting bodies on mats. Head into the park at the main Al Wasl Road entrance (Gate 3) to discover a Ferris wheel, bumper cars, large bouncy castle and carousel. There's also a boating lake (*see left*).

Ski Dubai. *See p187.*

Safa 2 Park

Off Al Wasl Road, Al Safa 2 (050 420 2892). **Open** 8am-11pm Mon-Thur, Sun; 8am-11.30pm Fri, Sat (women and children only Mon-Thur, Sun). **Admission** free.

This miniature version of Safa Park is the place to go when you want peace and quiet. It's open only to women and children during the week, making it the ideal meeting point for groups of mums and kids. Bring a ball, as Safa 2 has a small-scale football pitch, which is perfect for letting little kickers release some energy with friends. There are also play areas dotted around, built on sand to prevent injuries. Safa 2 is one of the better parks in Dubai for picnic benches, so you can bring along lunch and feed the children in reasonable comfort.

Stargate Theme Park

Gate 4, Za'abeel Park (see below for listings). **Open** 10am-10pm Mon-Wed, Sat, Sun; 10am-midnight Thur, Fri. **Admission** free.

Head to this educational theme park to enjoy high-tech mazes, an ice rink, a rollercoaster, an art gallery, an e-library and a karting track. BMX enthusiasts should bring their bikes to explore the trail. Buy a charge card for Dhs2 and top it up with credit to get the most out of the facilities.

★ Za'abeel Park

Between Sheikh Zayed Road & Sheikh Rashid Road, near Lamcy Plaza, Bur Dubai (04 398 6888). Metro Al Jafiliya. **Open** 8am-11pm Mon-Wed, Sun; 8am-11.30pm Thur-Sat. **Admission** Dhs5. **Map** p315 H9.

Za'abeel Park straddles Sheikh Zayed Road and is linked by a pedestrian footbridge. The large park has a lake, plenty of shaded seating, barbecue facilities, play areas for children, and refreshment kiosks. It's also home to the Stargate Theme Park (*see left*).

PLAY CENTRES

Aquaplay

Mirdif City Centre (800 534 7873, www.aquaplayme.com). **Open** 10am-10pm Mon-Wed, Sun; 10am-midnight Thur-Sat. **Admission** Dhs5-Dhs20 per attraction.

This play centre features fountains, dodgems on water and a giant soft play and climbing area. Rechargeable cards are available for Dhs2; top up Dhs5-Dhs20 for each attraction.

★ KidZania

Dubai Mall, Downtown (04 448 5222, www.kidzania.ae). Metro Burj Khalifa/Dubai Mall. **Open** 9am-9pm Mon-Wed, Sun; 9am-11pm Thur; 10am-11pm Fri, Sat. **Admission** Dhs140 4-16s; Dhs95 2-3s. **Map** p310 H5.

'Let's pretend' as you've never seen before – fighting fires, performing on stage and piloting a plane is all in a day's work for KidZania residents.

Little Explorers

Playnation, Mirdif City Centre, Mirdif (800 534 7873, www.theplaymania.com/little-explorers). **Open** 10am-midnight daily. **Admission** Dhs130; Dhs90 for workshops.

Aimed at children aged two to ten, this fantastic interactive learning centre houses 97 exhibits across five learning zones – perfect for curious little monsters. There are also daily workshops with constantly changing topics.

Magic Planet

Deira City Centre and Mall of the Emirates (04 295 4333, www.magicplanet.ae). Metro Deira City Centre or Mall of the Emirates. **Open** 10am-midnight daily. **Admission** free; pay per ride.

Whizzing, buzzing and whirring, Magic Planet is possibly the noisiest of play areas. With its arcade games, fairground rides and bowling, you'll find it hard to tear children away.

Mini Monsters

off Sheikh Zayed Road, near Dubai Garden Centre, Al Quoz (04 341 4459, www.minimonsters.ae). Metro FGB. **Open** 9am-7pm Mon-Wed, Sun; 9am-8pm Thur-Sat. **Admission** Dhs50. **Map** p318 E3.

Mini Monsters is dubbed the largest indoor soft play area in the UAE, and this multi-storey jungle gym is a great place to set active, energetic kids loose. There are party rooms and entertainment for rent, as well as a reasonable café.

Playnation

Mirdif City Centre, Mirdif (800 534 7873, www.playnationme.com). **Open** 10am-11pm Mon-Wed, Sun; 10am-midnight Thur; 9am-midnight Fri; 9am-11pm Sat. **Admission** varies.

From indoor skydiving to the Sky Trail obstacle course, bowling lanes to climbing walls, plus branches of Magic Planet and Johnny Rockets, Playnation caters to most children's wishes.

Sega Republic

Dubai Mall, Downtown (04 448 8484, www.segarepublic.com). Metro Burj Khalifa/Dubai Mall. **Open** 10am-11pm Mon-Wed, Sun; 10am-1am Thur-Sat. **Admission** Dhs15-Dhs30; Dhs175 day pass for all rides. **Map** p310 H5.

Mega-modern indoor theme park offering hyperactive horrors a dose of extreme stimulation.

WATERPARKS

★ Aquaventure

Atlantis The Palm, Palm Jumeirah (04 426 1000, www.atlantisthepalm.com). Tram Palm Jumeirah. **Open** 10am-sunset daily. **Admission** Dhs250; Dhs205 below 1.2m. **Map** p308 A1.

Brave the Leap of Faith, a vertical drop, or take it easy on the River Ride. Find a blow-up ring and get pulled by the waters to the rides and waves.

★ Wild Wadi

For listings, see p138.

A plethora of water slides, including the Jumeirah Sceirah and the Flowrider, and a 'fake wave' to surf.

Wonderland Water Park

Al Riyadh Street, next to Creek Park, Oud Metha (04 324 3222, www.wonderlanduae.com). Metro

Wild Wadi.

ARTS & ENTERTAINMENT

Dubai Healthcare City. **Open** 10am-8pm daily. **Admission** Dhs125; Dhs60 under-5s. **Map** p311 K3.
This retro amusement park has a number of classic water rides including a log flume, rapids and slides. There's also a theme park on the site for combined fun.

RESTAURANTS & CAFÉS

★ BookMunch Café & Bookshop

For listings, see p120.
BookMunch combines food with a love of books at this small but perfectly formed café in Al Wasl Square. There's a great selection of books lining the walls so children can browse while you eat or sip coffee. The laidback atmosphere encourages lingering, and there's a tent-like reading corner at the back.

Café Ceramique

Town Centre Jumeirah, Jumeirah 2 (04 344 7331, www.cafeceramique.ae). **Open** 9am-11pm daily. **Main courses** Dhs50-Dhs100. **Map** p316 C12.
If you fancy a bit of painting with your lunch or dinner, this is a good spot, especially for smaller, more active family members, who can decorate ceramics while they eat. A wide variety of dishes includes hearty breakfasts, soups, sandwiches, salads, burgers and gourmet crêpes.

Crumbs Elysee

Sheikh Zayed Road, Al Manara (04 346 8899, www.crumbselysee.com). Metro FGB. **Open** 6am-9pm daily. **Main courses** Dhs50-Dhs100. **Map** p308 C3.
Busy, but not frantic, with children running around and the aroma of fresh bread and coffee hitting you as you walk in the door, Crumbs Elysee is a great place to bring the family on a weekend morning. Friendly staff are adept at dealing with smaller family members – high chairs, colouring papers and crayons are produced before you've even had time to sit down.

Frankie's Italian Bar & Grill

For listings, see p165.
Conceived by Marco Pierre White and celeb-jockey Frankie Dettori, this upscale diner welcomes and caters especially to families before 9.30pm. The menu is extensive, and the dishes are tasty and presented with a flair that makes the prices reasonable, if not a steal. Busy, and rightly so.

Kiddies Café

Lake Shore Tower, Cluster Y, Jumeirah Lakes Towers (04 360 8571, www.kiddiescafe.com). Metro Jumeirah Lakes Towers. **Open** 10am-7pm daily. **Main courses** Dhs30-50. **Map** p318 B2.
Enjoy an afternoon with your children at the Kiddies Café. The youngsters can run wild in the colourful and well-equipped play area, while you relax in the on site café. There is a variety of art and crafts activities, plus puppet shows, storytelling, movie nights and birthday party packages.

IN THE KNOW
SUMMER SURPRISES

When the temperature starts to rise to melting levels, it's time to head indoors. But that doesn't have to mean the arrival of boredom. Dubai Summer Surprises runs from July to September and features a number of programmes and events for children. One of the biggest is **Modhesh World** (www.modheshworld.com/en), a huge entertainment zone inside Dubai World Trade Centre, with live shows, games and theme-park rides.

Maria Bonita's Taco Shop

For listings, see p119.
With its bright bunting, mixed-colour cushions, makeshift outdoor terrace and quirky vibe, this casual Al Wasl restaurant has the feel of a Mexican roadside diner. Nachos, burritos, fajitas, tacos, quesadillas – if you want your meal fried, covered in cheese and slopped with salsa and guacamole, then this is the place for you. There's a good children's menu, too.

Reform Social & Grill

The Lakes, Emirates Hills (04 454 2638, www.reformsocialgrill.ae). **Open** 8am-midnight Mon-Wed, Sat, Sun; 8am-1am Thur, Fri. **Main courses** Dhs200-Dhs250. **Map** p318 B3.
Excellent British pub grub. Reform is a welcoming place for lunch with the children. There's a children's menu with the likes of fish and chips, sausage rolls and spaghetti bolognese, and an ice-cream parlour for dessert.

Shakespeare & Co

Dubai Marina Mall (04 457 4199, www.shakespeare-and-co.com). Tram Dubai Marina Mall. **Open** 7am-1am daily. **Main courses** Dhs50-Dhs100. **Map** p318 A2.
Kitsch decor abounds, with distressed pastel furniture, pink cushions and lace doilies as far as the eye can see. The quirkiness abates when it comes to the menu, however, with a good selection of sandwiches, salads and heartier pizza, pasta and meat main dishes to choose from. It's perennially popular with the 'buggy brigade' on account of its great kids' meals. **Other locations** around the city.

Urbano

Souk Al Bahar, Downtown (04 435 5666). Metro Burj Khalifa/Dubai Mall. **Open** noon-11pm Mon-Wed, Sat, Sun; noon-midnight Thur, Fri. **Main courses** Dhs100-Dhs150. **Map** p310 H5
Vast Italian-style restaurant that offers quick snacks and slap-up dinners; there's a children's menu too. The little ones will be entertained by the view of the Dubai Fountain and the Burj Khalifa towering above.

Film

Dubai's arthouse cinema scene is still young, but projects such as the Scene Club and the annual Dubai International Film Festival in December are giving locals the chance to see a wider range of films from all corners of the globe. In addition, this young country is beginning to produce more work of its own. Big multiplexes still dominate the landscape, though. Dubai-style decadence even extends to filmgoing, with special 'experiences' available, where moviegoers can stretch out on a luxury recliner and enjoy table service while watching the latest big-screen blockbuster. Dubai's weather is an asset when it comes to outdoor screenings: a number of alfresco cinemas spring up in the winter months, where you can relax on a beanbag, drink in hand, while enjoying anything from old classics to new releases.

CINEMAS

Dubai has more big branded cinemas than you can shake a stick at – just head for any mall. For a truly indulgent experience, get a Gold Class ticket at **Vox Cinemas, Mall of the Emirates** (Dhs120, 600 599905, www.voxcinemas.com) or try the **Platinum Movie Suites at the Dubai Mall** (Dhs130, 04 449 1903, www.reelcinemas.ae).

But film fans should also try and seek out the smaller venues listed below or plan their trip to coincide with the Dubai International Film Festival to catch some interesting independent productions.

Arthouse

Scene Club

Main Auditorium, Dubai Knowledge Village Conference Centre, Al Sufouh Road (04 391 0051, www.thesceneclub.com). Metro Dubai Marina, or tram Knowledge Village. **Tickets** free. **Map** p318 C2.

The Scene Club entertains hundreds of Dubai film fans every month with its free (for now) monthly screenings of independent movies, either fresh from the international festival circuit or carefully curated classics. The Scene Club has previously shown *No Man's Land*, directed by Danis Tanovic; *Wadjda* by Saudi director Haifaa Al Mansour; and Feo Aladag's *When We Leave*. It also manages to bring filmmakers and producers from around the world to host Q&A sessions after screenings. The venue at Dubai Knowledge Village has a capacity of 400 and tickets are allocated on a first-come, first-served basis. You need to register for membership beforehand on the website, but that doesn't guarantee admission, so arrive early to avoid missing out.

Other institutions

Cinematheque of Bastakiya

XVA Gallery, Al Fahidi Historical Neighbourhood, Bur Dubai (04 353 5383, www.xvagallery.com). Metro Al Fahidi. **Tickets** free. **Map** p312 H3.

IN THE KNOW CHILL ZONE

Remember to take a light jumper to the cinema with you. Over-enthusiastic air-conditioning can make the auditorium resemble a wind tunnel and two hours can feel like a very long time indeed.

XVA Gallery screens a variety of films and documentaries every night in its courtyard café in Al Fahidi Historical Neighbourhood, also a quiet and quaint venue for a relaxed dinner. Films here are a real mixed bag and could be anything from a recent award-winning feature or cult classic to smaller independent productions. Phone the gallery beforehand for updated information on screenings: a different film is chosen each day, there is no set schedule and currently no information is published online.

Outdoor screenings

The largest outdoor cinema screen in the UAE is **La Playa Lounge** *(see p162)* at the Beach, JBR. It screens sports and classic films, viewed from the comfort of white sofas. The places listed here are generally closed during the hottest months, from June until the end of August.

JLT Park

Amphitheatre in front of Armada Towers, Cluster P, JLT (www.greateventsdubai.com). Metro Damac. **Screenings** 7.30pm Fri, Sat. **Tickets** free. **Map** p318 A2.

A free outdoor cinema that screens kids' films on a Friday and films for adults on a Saturday night. All screenings start at 7.30pm, though there is entertainment before they start and a good array of food stalls – selling sushi, pizza and crêpes – and independent traders selling arts and crafts. And there's no need to worry too much about chatter from the crowd: for the most part people are respectful when the film is on. Previous films have included Che Guevara biopic *The Motorcycle Diaries* and East Germany-set movie *Goodbye Lenin!*

IN THE KNOW
NOISY NEIGHBOURS

Don't expect to enjoy your film in silence at Dubai's big multiplex cinemas. For many locals, especially teenagers, films serve merely as a backdrop to frenzied texting and mobile phone conversations, garrulous socialising, noisy consumption of snacks and, in some cases, bouts of prolonged snoring. A few well-aimed tuts are usually as far as anyone goes to combat the problem. Families with infants frequent even age-inappropriate films and it's not unusual for outbreaks of clapping, whooping and cheering to take place in response to on-screen events. Smaller venues and independent festivals seem to attract a slightly more respectful crowd.

Reform Social & Grill

Reform Social & Grill, the Lakes (04 454 2638, www.reformsocialgrill.ae). Metro Damac. **Screenings** 8pm Tue. **Tickets** free. **Map** p318 B2.

Fairy lights, picnic tables, comfy outdoor sofas and beanbags are the set-up at this British-themed venue. Book a table if you feel like tucking into hotdogs and burgers but we suggest arriving early to bag a comfy seat in front of the screen. Order a pitcher of Pimm's or a glass of wine, grab some popcorn and pick 'n' mix (served out of big old-fashioned jars) and settle in. Although there's an adjoining play area, it's not ideal for children – the crowd is mainly adult due to the bar. Showings are arranged in themed months.

Scene Club.

Movies Under the Stars.

Most of the films are light-hearted and nostalgic with lots of old faves such as *Four Weddings and a Funeral*, *Back to the Future* and *Legally Blonde*.

Movies Under the Stars

Wafi Pyramids Rooftop Gardens, Oud Metha (04 324 4100, www.pyramidsrestaurantswafi.com). Metro Al Jadaf. **Screenings** 8pm Sun. **Tickets** free. **Map** p311 J3.
Seating is on giant beanbags in front of a decent-sized screen. Tasty snacks are available, such as popcorn, burgers, shawarmas and cheesy nachos, and there's also a full bar. Be patient for your snacks, though, and order once the film starts to avoid the mad rush at the beginning. Staff take orders from the ground – if you head over to the bar area, you'll end up waiting an age to place your order. Also take a fleecy blanket to wrap yourself in for a cosy night.

IN THE KNOW CENSORSHIP

Censorship is an issue for film-lovers in Dubai, who often have a hard time following a story after cuts made to meet cultural sensibilities leave the movie in tatters. A stir was caused when a whole 45 minutes was cut from *The Wolf of Wall Street*, leaving the film completely incomprehensible. Broadly speaking, the Dubai Department of Censorship will cut any nudity and overt sexual references, as well as any homosexual scenes. Political comments relating to Arab governments or anything deemed defamatory towards Islam are out, as is anything that comes even close to recognising Israel. Films shown at festivals are technically considered to be private screenings – rather than general release – and are screened without cuts.

Foreign-language

Alliance Française Dubai (Street 18, Oud Metha, Bur Dubai & Oud Metha, 04 335 8712, www.afdubai.org) regularly holds arts and cultural events, including film screenings, at various locations around Dubai – phone or check the website for updated information. To catch Bollywood flicks, head to **Golden Cinemas** (corner of Al Ghubaiba Road & Al Nahda Street, near Al Ghubaiba metro station, Bur Dubai, 04 393 3393) in Al Ghubaiba.

Festivals

Since its launch in 2004, the **Dubai International Film Festival** (www.dubaifilmfest.com) has continued to grow in scale; now one of the premier platforms for emerging Arab filmmakers in the region, it has become a major annual event, attracting a truly international host of guests and screening films from all corners of the globe every December. Independent films from the UAE, France, Georgia, Iraq, Japan, Yemen, Lebanon and more are screened alongside well-known US titles such as *American Hustle* and *Birdman*. There's also a wide range of talks, workshops and panel discussions.

ESSENTIAL DUBAI FILMS

Six movies that capture the essence of this vibrant desert metropolis.

CHAMP OF THE CAMP
MAHMOOD KAABOUR (2013)
A documentary about life in Dubai's labour camps that follows participants in a huge Bollywood singing and trivia competition across more than 70 camps. It's an emotional film – narrated entirely by the participants – interweaving the suspense of the competition with intimate scenes offering an unprecedented look at daily life for Dubai's labourers.

CITY OF LIFE
ALI MOSTAFA (2009)
Tracking the lives of three of Dubai's residents, *City of Life* (starring Natalie Dormer) reflects on the everyday existence of three very different people: a Romanian flight attendant, a young Emirati and an Indian taxi driver. The people, social issues and locations will resonate strongly with anyone familiar with Dubai, and it's absolutely on point in its portrayal of the city.

DJINN
TOBE HOOPER (2010)
The first horror film to come out of the UAE was directed by Tobe Hooper, the man behind *The Texas Chainsaw Massacre*. It's set in a haunted apartment building in Ras Al Khaimah and was filmed in both the northern Emirate and Dubai. The film weaves together traditional Emirati culture, Qur'anic cosmology and folklore, and modern-day horror thrills.

DUBAI
RORY B QUINTOS (2005)
A Fillipino romantic drama shot in the UAE about two brothers who fall in love with the same woman. It's a bit dated, and a little bit cheesy, but it follows the characters to some of the most scenic spots in the city.

FAST & FURIOUS 7
JAMES WAN (2015)
Vin Diesel, Tyrese Gibson, Michelle Rodriguez and Ludacris spent time filming at some of Abu Dhabi's most iconic locations, including Emirates Palace and the Corniche. A car chase was also spotted being filmed in the city centre.

HAPPY NEW YEAR
FARAH KHAN (2014)
This is an entertaining *Oceans 11*-style Bollywood production in which a street fighter assembles a team to steal some famous diamonds from Atlantis The Palm. It was one of the highest-grossing Bollywood films of all time, and includes an array of extravagant dance numbers and action stunts. There are plenty of aerial shots of the city – including some impressive New Year's Eve firework displays on the Palm Jumeirah.

Fast & Furious 7.

Nightlife

Long regarded as the 'party emirate', Dubai is home to countless nightclubs and bars of varying quality and salubriousness, and regularly attracts top DJs. The club scene has begun to diversify dramatically: where once house and R&B ruled the day, it's now not unusual to hear high-profile venues playing indie, electro, soul and even metal. Dubai's crowds come out to play late, so clubs may seem dead until midnight or even 1am, which only leaves a couple of hours of partying before home time.

The music scene is on the up with more and more international acts dropping by, while venues such as MusicHall, the Music Room and the Fridge are turning up the nightlife notch on a smaller scale.

Dubai's strict laws are tempered with signs of increasing alt activity as cabaret begins to muscle in on the action, and nightlife offerings are increasing at the same rate as skyscrapers.

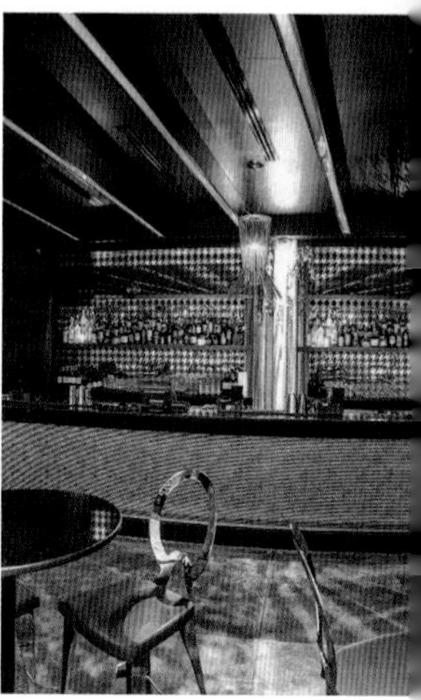

CLUBS

360°

Jumeirah Beach Hotel, Umm Suqeim (04 406 8741, www.jumeirah.com). Metro Mall of the Emirates. **Open** 5pm-2am Mon-Wed, Sun; 5pm-3am Thur-Sat. **Map** p318 E2.

For review, *see p143*.

Amika

H Dubai, Sheikh Zayed Road (04 358 0044, www.h-hotel.com). Metro World Trade Centre. **Open** 6pm-3am daily. **Map** p315 G9.

Amika multitasks brilliantly as a bar, restaurant and club. This old-school party fave has decent resident DJs and a buzzing dancefloor. Check out nights such as deep house concept City of Lights on Thursdays, Urban Fever on Fridays and Arabica on Saturdays. See the venue's Facebook page for the latest listings.

Cavalli Club

Fairmont Hotel, Sheikh Zayed Road (04 332 9260, www.cavalliclub.com). Metro World Trade Centre. **Open** 9.30pm-3am Mon-Sat; 9pm-3am Sun. **Map** p315 G9.

Cavalli is opulence personified. Done out in the most elaborate concoction of shapes, colours and eras (think zebra-skin chairs, chandeliers and furry lifts), the whole venue seems to have been constructed to be as outlandish, flamboyant and expensive as possible. Which, of course, makes it an absolute must-do Dubai experience. Fortunately, the endless stream of high-end DJs and guest stars – if not the prohibitively high prices – will keep you coming back for more.

Embassy

Grosvenor House, Dubai Marina (04 317 6000, www.embassy-dubai.com). Metro DAMAC. **Open** 8pm-2am Mon-Wed, Sat, Sun; 8pm-3am Thur, Fri. **Map** p318 B2.

Embassy spreads across three floors, and each tier has a different theme and USP. The 43rd floor is all about retro dance (think Pulp's 'Disco 2000' video), the 44th floor is a big spender's lounge paradise, and the top deck houses a signature restaurant with stunning views. Sadly, the tiny dancefloor lacks anything resembling an atmosphere, partly thanks to a policy forbidding simultaneous drinking and dancing. This isn't a club dancefloor, but more a neon-lit corner for guests to stumble around for a few minutes before returning to their cordoned-off table. Embassy's redeeming quality is its ladies' night, with generous canapés included with the three free drinks deal.

Kasbar
One & Only Royal Mirage, Jumeirah Beach Road, Al Sufouh (04 399 9999, www.oneandonlyresorts.com). Tram Dubai Media City. **Open** 9.30pm-3am Mon-Sat. **Map** p318 B2.

This Royal Mirage club has an upmarket vibe thanks to its over-25s entry policy. Rather than trying to appeal to the stumbling, party-hungry masses, it's aiming at an older, more sophisticated crowd who want to party in peace. That's not to say that Kasbar is stuffy – it still has a pretty laid-back vibe, and while there's a slight air of aloofness, it's not the same ego-boosting VIP trip that comes with some of the big-brand clubs in Dubai.

★ Mahiki
Jumeirah Beach Hotel, Jumeirah Beach Road, Umm Suqeim (04 380 7731, www.mahiki.ae). Metro Mall of the Emirates. **Open** 7pm-3am Mon-Fri; 10pm-3am Sat. **Map** p318 E2.

Mahiki's USP is its Polynesian theme: a totem-style wooden figure holds a vigil over the (decent) dancefloor, straw lines the ceiling, and a window-shaped hole has been painted on one wall with the view of a tropical sunset. It's not immediately clear if the decor is misjudged or an impressive stab at irony. The music policy, though, gives it away. Lurching from '80s soft rock to trance, Mahiki can't be taking itself too seriously – a quality we admire given Dubai's often pompous nightlife. There's no denying the impact Mahiki has had on the local scene, proving that glitz and glamour are not always the answer, and that late in the evening many clubbers would rather leave their inhibitions at the door and dance like a loon than pose indoors wearing sunglasses. An undeniably fun spot.

Movida
Radisson Royal Hotel, Sheikh Zayed Road (055 174 4449, www.movida-dubai.com). Metro World Trade Centre. **Open** 11pm-3am Wed-Sat. **Map** p315 G10.

Arriving straight from London – where Kate Moss, Jay-Z and Beyoncé all partied – Movida set out to join Dubai's most exclusive club venues. Three years on and it no longer has novelty on its side, but it has retained a sense of class. Movida is smaller than much of the competition, and intimacy and attention to detail are evident in the sleek purple furnishings, large velvet booths and neon glow. Instead of a collective dancefloor, each booth has its own floor-lit platform. It's yet another example of an attempt to emulate the moneyed elements of nightlife in cities such as London and LA, but somehow Movida manages to pull it off better than most.

★ Nasimi Beach
Atlantis The Palm, Palm Jumeirah (04 426 2626, www.atlantisthepalm.com). Tram Palm Jumeirah. **Open** 11am-midnight Mon-Thur, Sun; 9am-1am Fri, Sat. **Map** p308 A1.

For review, *see p159*.

ARTS & ENTERTAINMENT

Provocateur.

★ Pacha

Souk Madinat Jumeirah, Umm Suqeim (04 567 0000, www.pacha.ae). Metro Mall of the Emirates. **Open** 8pm-3am Tue-Sat (times vary Thur, Fri); 10pm-3am Sun. **Map** p318 E2.

Set across three floors, Pacha comprises the Main Room, Red Room and Rooftop. The Main Room, on the ground floor, serves dinner accompanied by live shows involving aerial acts and acrobatics before the venue transforms into a 'nightlife experience' with house music from the world's best DJs and local artists. Independent venue the Fridge (*see p205*) heads up the entertainment and aims to offer plenty of musical variety, so expect deep and soulful house in the rooftop lounge space, nu disco in the Red Room, and more mainstream house beats in the Main Room.

People by Crystal

Raffles Dubai, 13th Street, Sheikh Rashid Road (050 292 2912, 052 922 0222). Metro Dubai Healthcare City. **Open** 11pm-3am Thur-Sat. **Map** p311 J3.

People by Crystal is an explosion of glamour and extravagance located at the tip of the five-star Raffles Dubai pyramid. The huge windows with magnificent panoramic city views are as nothing compared to the gold decor, white leather seating and illuminated dancefloors that make up the club's interior. And that's not to mention the flashing light shows, big-name acts, confetti that regularly pours from the ceiling or the huge metal gorillas at the door. Expect a packed house and a lively atmosphere in what is one of the city's most popular dance clubs.

Provocateur

Four Seasons Resort Dubai at Jumeirah Beach, Jumeirah 2 (055 211 8222, www.provocateurdubai.com). **Open** 10pm-3am Thur, Fri. **Map** p316 B13.

This is the first US nightlife brand to open up in the UAE, modelled on the New York flagship and playing host to a roster of Grammy award-winning international DJs and niche electronic dance music producers. The design exudes glamour and sophistication – most of the space is dedicated to VIP tables and bottle service, with booths and tables stretching out along both sides of the room. For those not sitting at one of the VIP tables, there's ample room to stand at the back of the club next to the bar, and revellers are able to jump on the central stage to dance at any point. The club also injects an element of fun with a large bathtub and gigantic teddy bear positioned on stage that guests can pose with throughout the night, making for endless Instagram fodder – it's a clever marketing ploy on the club's part and a quirky addition to any night out. Book a table in advance, as there's no guestlist and entry without a reservation is limited.

Q43

Media One Hotel, Dubai Media City, Al Sufouh (04 443 5403, www.q43dubai.com). Metro Nakheel. **Open** 11am-3am Mon-Thur, Sun; 2pm-3am Fri; 2pm-2am Sat. **Map** p318 B2.

We're not really sure what Q43 is yet. Part pub, part club, it's pushing its trendy urban identity with zeal, throwing everything into its crusade to create a modern, stylish environment: distressed furniture, dingy club-like lighting and murals that

IN THE KNOW VISUAL SENSATION

The first Dubai edition of global dance festival **Sensation** (www.sensation.com, tickets from Dhs450) took place in 2014, with a line-up including Roger Sanchez and Martin Garrix playing to a sold-out crowd of 15,000. What began in Amsterdam has spread across the world to the US, Thailand, Turkey, South Africa and Italy, and the theme changes from event to event – 2014 was titled 'Source of Light', while other global editions had themes of 'Innerspace', 'Dreamcatcher', 'Mythology' and 'Into the Wild'. There's a stricter-than-strict dress code so the crowd matches the seriously psychedelic visuals that have made the event so famous (don't take the dress code lightly; you have zero chance of getting in if you don't adhere to it). There are performers and pyrotechnics aplenty, and while you won't find the kind of drug-fuelled hedonism that you would in Sensation's country of origin, it's one of the best events in the city.

are so tasteless they manage to add a slice of hipster chic. There's also a DJ and, above the sleek black pool tables, what looks like unravelled chainmail dangling from the lights.The main thing that sells this venue, though, isn't the decor or the panoramic views from the 43rd floor, or even the attempt at New York loft-inspired edginess – it's the size, location and variety of the place.

★ Societe

Marina Byblos Hotel, Dubai Marina (04 443 5403, www.societe.ae). Metro Dubai Marina. **Open** 10pm-3am Tue-Fri. **Map** p318 B2.

Societe will suit if you yearn for a time when Madonna was in her pomp and *Dirty Dancing* was the movie soundtrack of the moment. Groups of middle-aged women get down to the Backstreet Boys and Belinda Carlisle, alongside glamorous twentysomethings, in a cheesy party atmosphere. The club's been decked out à la 1950s, with faux bookcase wallpaper and oversized lampshades that wouldn't look out of place in your granny's sitting room. Remarkably, the look provides just enough class to prevent the venue slipping into the 'dive' category, but it's rough enough around the edges to avoid the clinical sense of elitism that plagues the majority of Dubai's swanky clubs. If you're the sort of clubber who likes to station yourself on an exclusive table to set yourself up for an evening of posing, and you see yourself as above tapping your toe and reminiscing over bygone soundtracks, Societe isn't for you. However, if you like your clubs unpretentious, busy and unfailingly fun, then you'll find these qualities in abundance.

VIP Room

JW Marriott Marquis, Sheikh Zayed Road, Business Bay (052 881 8888, www.viproom-dubai.com). Metro Business Bay. **Open** 11pm-3am Tue, Thur, Fri. **Map** p310 G5.

This large, circular venue is lit with moody hues and LCD screens. After midnight, the club explodes with a frenzied energy – although much of the space is given over to tables and you'll need a reservation to make the most of a night here. But for a glitzy evening out of no-expense-spared indulgence, VIP Room is hard to beat.

Warehouse

Le Méridien Dubai Hotel & Conference Centre, Garhoud (04 217 0000, www.warehouse-dubai.com). Metro Airport Terminal 1. **Open** noon-1.30am daily. **Map** p311 J1.

This place is best known as a rowdy, budget brunch option, and Friday evenings invariably produce a party atmosphere on the dancefloor. Warehouse multitasks as a chic wine bar, sushi restaurant, swanky drinking spot and nightclub, and DJs spin classic dancefloor fillers to get the crowds moving, to good effect. A decent weekend spot.

White Dubai

Grandstand Rooftop, Meydan Racecourse, Business Bay (050 443 0933, www.whitedubai.com). Metro Business Bay. **Open** 10pm-3am Thur-Sat. **Map** p309 D4.

This decadent, exclusive Beirut clubbing import has quickly become the hottest spot to party under the stars, taking up a huge rooftop terrace. It has a tiered, amphitheatre-style set-up around a central bar, and everything is, predictably, white. Thanks to its Meydan location, some distance away from the centre of Dubai, the venue feels wonderfully airy and spacious. It's certainly refreshing to party away from the claustrophobic, smoky dancefloors and skyscraper-surrounded outdoor terraces of the rest of the city.

Zinc

Crowne Plaza Dubai Hotel, Sheikh Zayed Road (04 331 1111, www.ichotelsgroup.com). Metro Emirates Towers. **Open** 10pm-3am daily. **Map** p315 G10.

Now more than a decade old, Zinc has seen more packed dancefloors than most of the competition combined. What keeps the punters coming back? An unabashed reputation for crowd-pleasing clubbing. Zinc's resident DJs supply a soundtrack of mainstream chart hits with the occasional dance track thrown in. Long-running club nights include Manic Mondays' cabin crew deals, ladies' nights on Tuesdays and Wednesdays, and DJ Greg Stainer's reliably banging Club Anthems every Thursday. In the face of newer, hipper and glitzier competition, Zinc continues to thrive.

CABARET

★ Act

Shangri-La Hotel, Sheikh Zayed Road (04 355 1116, www.theactdubai.com). Metro Financial Centre. **Open** 8.30-11.30pm Mon, Wed; 8.30pm-3am Thur, Sun. **Map** p317 E12/F12.

The closest Dubai comes to the full-blown drama of legendary cabarets such as Paris's Moulin Rouge, this Shangri-La restaurant (set menus Dhs320-Dhs495) is as dramatic, atmospheric and downright entertaining as anything you're ever likely to experience in the city. Where else could you dine while a woman dances with half a dozen hula hoops and a man dressed as a hipster bear lurches between tables? The Act is styled like a theatre, with tables in and among the performances (of which there are many, including magic, music and, memorably, dance). Thankfully, the cast of talents includes a chef turning out exciting Peruvian dishes, timed to arrive between the various acts that take to the stage. The concept is tapas and sharing platters with three set menus available, ranging from Applause at Dhs320 to Encore at Dhs495. This isn't a place to be shy – go all out and indulge in plates such as quinoa-coated prawns with passionfruit, five-spice lamb shank, and wagyu ribeye with mango and truffle chimichurri.

★ Cirque Le Soir

Fairmont Dubai, Sheikh Zayed Road (04 995 5400, www.cirquelesoir.com/dubai). Metro World Trade Centre. **Open** 10.30pm-3am Mon, Tue, Thur, Fri. **Map** p315 G9.

London's original Cirque Le Soir (née: du Soir) was once the place to see and be seen; within months of its 2009 launch the likes of Leonardo DiCaprio, Usher, Scarlett Johansson and Lady Gaga had all stopped by. Naturally Dubai – home of the opulent, extreme and extravagant – followed suit with its own venue. While it has attracted a fair few famous faces, the UAE venue was never going to outshine its older brother – but it does do a good job of recreating the vibe of dynamism and decadence. Decorated in dim hues, visitors are greeted by an eccentric cast of circus stereotypes: burlesque dancers take to the

IN THE KNOW LADIES' NIGHT

Ladies' night in Dubai is huge. In a city where the gender ratio of residents is so off balance that there are roughly three times more men than women, clubs and bars have embraced ladies' night deals with a passion – give free drinks to the ladies and the men will follow (and spend the money). Deals usually consist of around three free drinks, such as a spirit and mixer or cocktails from a specially created menu. Some venues might offer free-flowing sparkling wine or canapés instead, while others have à la carte menu discounts, but you can almost guarantee that whichever bar or nightclub you head to, it will run a ladies' night. Tuesdays are a popular choice, making it your best bet for a party vibe on a week night, but be sure to check beforehand as offers and days vary from venue to venue.

podiums and fairies spin on ropes suspended from the ceiling, while jugglers and clowns tend the tables. Each evening the whole motley crew takes to the stage for a tub-thumbing, fire-breathing stage show, which is utterly captivating the first time you see it.

Tchaikovsky Restaurant

Marina Byblos Hotel, Dubai Marina (04 448 8222, www.marinabybloshotel.com). Metro Jumeirah Lakes Towers, or Tram Jumeirah Lakes Towers 2. **Open** 8pm-3am Tue-Sun. **Map** p318 B2.

This all-singing, all-dancing venue in Dubai Marina is a must-visit for its doo-wop dancing, disco lighting and traditional Russian dishes (mains Dhs80-Dhs110). The opulent decor falls short of sophisticated, but is endearing when paired with some of the weird and wonderful acts that take to the stage (expect two-man bands accompanied by disco lights and Russian cabaret). The bilingual English-Russian menu features page after page of dishes, from *selyodka pod shuboy* (a traditional herring dish) to caviar.

ALTERNATIVE NIGHTS

If you're on the hunt for quirk rather than twerk, seek out the city's alternative nightlife events instead of heading to its better known VIP venues. Locations for most of the nights vary from weekend to weekend, so check the website before setting off.

Analog Room

Q Underground, Holiday Inn Al Barsha, Sheikh Zayed Road (www.analogroom.com). Metro Mall of the Emirates. **Open** 10pm-3am Thur. **Map** p318 D3.

While its tagline 'the one and only truly alternative night in Dubai' might be a little over the top, there's no denying the impact Analog Room has had on the city's underground electro scene since its launch in early 2013 at the Q Underground. Keeping up regular Thursday nights ever since, and programming an intelligent stream of leftfield international guests, Analog Room's playlist might not fill floors at commercially minded superclubs, but attracts legions of the faithful week in, week out. The guys have also recently gone out into the light with sets at Story Rooftop Lounge.

Bad House Party

Casa Latina, Ibis Al Barsha, Sheikh Zayed Road (www.facebook.com/thebadhouseparty). Metro Dubai Internet City. **Open** varies. **Map** p318 D2.

One of the youngsters on the alternative scene, Bad House Party offers up a much-needed guitar night, filling the void that was left when Loaded imploded and Step On went fancy by shifting to Media One. Expect to hear a buzzing mix of punk stormers, indie tracks that didn't chart and other eclectic tunes when the party starts at Casa Latina on the first Thursday of every month.

Boombox

Various locations (www.ohmevents.com).

After a lengthy tenure at the Music Room that saw Boombox host some huge names from hip hop's pantheon – we're talking De La Soul's Maseo, NWA's DJ Yella, Public Enemy's DJ Lord and Wu-Tang 'associate' DJ Sueside – local MC Eslam Jawaad's alternatively minded hip hop night recently moved to Casa Latina. Keep a close eye on the website for what's up next.

Act.

Sunny Vibe-Up.

Deep Crates Cartel

Q Underground, Holiday Inn Al Barsha, Sheikh Zayed Road (www.deepcratescartel.com). Metro Mall of the Emirates. **Open** varies. **Map** p318 D3.

It was with a sniffle and a whimper that we heard the news that Deep Crates was folding its regular Casa Latina Thursday evenings at the end of 2013. Well, now it's back – with a new regular Friday night at Q Underground. Expect a mix of hip hop, soul, and reggae from the Cartel's reggae wing Drop Dread, plus an international guest every month or so.

Dust

Various locations (www.facebook.com/dustdxb).

Dust are purveyors of woozy club nights, danceable disco and cool electronic sounds. Fresh from hosting NYC edit king John Morales, the DJ collective is now launching a new Turntables of the Gulf concept, in conjunction with affiliate podcast brand RBMA Radio Quarter Tone Frequency. Expect ten hours of top tunes from the likes of New Yorkers Nickodemus, DRM and former Jungle Brother Bam, plus a roster of local mic men including Hamdan Al-Abri and rappers Jibberish and Toofless.

Electric Days

Various locations.

We've heard some grumbles that the music policy – mixing up credible house and electro flavours – isn't all that alternative and that the guest list-only door policy is far from the come-all-serve-all mentality you usually associate with underground nightlife. But Electric Days, which takes place every Friday, attracts a refreshingly cliquey clientele and has a welcome non-mainstream ethos. True, it's not a place for grubby jeans, but this recent winner of our Best Alternative Night of 2014 is the rooftop party of the moment. Recent guest appearances have included German duo Smash TV and US producer Tone of Arc.

GlobalFunk

Various locations (www.facebook.com/GlobalFunkDXB).

After more than a decade in Dubai, GlobalFunk is the big daddy of the city's bass scene – and has a CV to go with it. Having hosted the likes of Roni Size, Goldie, LTJ Bukem, DJ Marky, DJ Hype and more big-hitters than we can list over the years, the semi-regular drum'n'bass event is keeping things ticking over nicely with appearances by the likes of the legendary Andy C and MC LowQui.

Something Big

Various locations (www.facebook.com/somethingbigdubai).

Since launching in October 2012, Something Big has consistently brought an engaging roster of international bass names to Barsha's Catwalk. And it recently went out into the open air and teamed up with Croatia's renowned bass haven Outlook Festival for a Super Yacht Party with headliners Icicle (of Shogun Audio) and Ant TC 1 (of Dispatch Recordings).

Step On

DEK on 8, Media One Hotel (050 464 9390, www.facebook.com/StepOnDubai). **Open** varies. **Map** p318 B2.

Dubai's longest-running indie night has been spitting out guitar anthems at stacks of venues across town over the years, and is currently keeping things classy with regular happenings at the Dek on 8. Expect to hear the likes of Miami Horror, Klaxons, Babyshambles, Placebo, Panic! at the Disco, the Chemical Brothers, Johnny Cash and the Strokes.

Sunny Vibe-Up

Various locations (www.facebook.com/sunnyvibeupdubai).

With a firm focus on reggae, hip hop, soul and anything with a groove, Deep Crates' monthly-ish rooftop party is going from strength to strength. Despite moving its signature night to a Friday, we're told that Sunny will continue to run monthly during the cooler months, acting as a daytime pool party and offering a free shuttle bus to the new happening at the Q Underground later on.

COMEDY

Dubai has a well-established comedy scene, which continues to expand. As well as the regular shows listed below, there are many more one-off events that take place throughout the year. Check out the latest magazine copy of *Time Out Dubai* or visit www.timeoutdubai.com for the most up-to-date listings.

Chuckle Club

Various locations (www.facebook.com/thechuckleclub).

This comedy club is based in Bahrain, but tours Dubai once a month. Previous comedians on the tour have included Yianni Agisilaou, who improvises skilfully with whatever a room throws at him; Los Angeles native Chris Garcia, who has worked with comedians Reggie Watts and Robin Williams; and the undeniably funny Geordie comic Carl Hutchinson, who has supported American wrestler Mick Foley and English funyman Chris Ramsey on their sell-out tours. The venue changes for each tour, so check the Facebook page or *Time Out Dubai* for the latest information.

Dubai Laughing Comedy Club

1UP Bar, Boutique 7 Hotel & Suites, TECOM (050 843 2877, 050 796 4344, www.dubailaughing.com). Metro Dubai Internet City.
Open varies. **Map** p318 C2.

This is one of the most active comedy clubs in Dubai, with a packed schedule throughout the year and plenty of local talent on the mic. Two of the club's regular shows are Beat the Gong, in which 15 comics perform for five minutes each; and Get Set... Laugh, the UAE's only improv comedy game show.

★ Laughter Factory

Various locations (04 355 1862, www.thelaughterfactory.com).

Having started back in May 1997 at the Hyatt Regency, this is now billed as the longest-running regular comedy show in the UAE. It's renowned for serving up a reliable roster of decent comedians every month, with past shows featuring the likes of Frankie Boyle, Russell Peters and Michael McIntyre. It's also a great place to spot up-and-coming comics.

MUSIC

Rock & pop

The winter months in Dubai are prime time for outdoor concerts and festivals. **Zero Gravity** (www.0-gravity.ae) has a huge outdoor space and a monthly roster of international DJs. It's also the venue for the recently launched DXBeach festival – the inaugural edition saw performances from the likes of Jess Glynne, Mark Ronson and Sneaky Sound System. **Dubai Media City Amphitheatre** (Dubai Media City, Al Sufouh) plays host to a number of concerts, festivals and events in its grassy park beside a lake, including the Dubai Jazz Festival (www.dubaijazzfest.com). Globe-trotting bands such as One Direction have graced the stage of the **Dubai Sevens Stadium** (*see p179*), and the **International Stadium** (*see p176*) in Sports City is one of the city's newest outdoor concert venues.

Each November, the Yasalam after-race concerts (www.yasalam.ae, www.thinkflash.ae) take place at du Arena on **Yas Island** (www.yasisland.ae) in Abu Dhabi as part of the Formula One Abu Dhabi Grand Prix. Past performers have included Jay Z, Eminem, Pharrell Williams and

IN THE KNOW FRESHLY GROUND SOUNDS

Indie musicians gather to play on a stage strewn with fairy lights in the surprisingly charming surroundings of the Dubai Garden Centre, while the audience lounges on AstroTurf and munches on popcorn and hotdogs. **Freshly Ground Sounds** (www.freshlygroundsounds.com) is about as chilled out as things get and anyone can sign up to perform, so the (mainly acoustic) acts can vary widely in style and ability. But you can't beat the community vibe, especially during the cooler months. Independent artists, designers and others also set up stalls at the twice-monthly events, which get pretty packed so show up early with a blanket to claim your spot. Check the website beforehand as the venue can vary.

Armin Van Buuren. As part of a push to revitalise tourism in the UAE's capital city, an increasing number of live music events are moving emirate to Abu Dhabi and taking place at du Arena.

Classic Rock Coffee

Dubai Healthcare City, Oud Metha (www.classicrockcoffeedxb.com). Metro Dubai Healthcare City. **Open** 7am-10pm daily. **Map** p311 J3.

Coffee and rock music may seem an unlikely marriage, but they blend together well at this café, where you can sit on drums and sip your latte surrounded by icons of the genre. There's a library of music magazines, private listening stations and monthly gigs. Musicians can also bring in their instruments and arrange a jam session on the stage.

Club Seven

Park Regis Kris Kin, Bur Dubai (04 377 1213, www.dubsevendubai.com). Metro Burjuman. **Open** 7.30pm-3am daily. *Concerts* 9.30pm. **Map** p315 J6.

The booming nightclub at the top of the Park Regis Kris Kin is a great place for live music. With a bassy sound system and luminous dancefloor, the venue creates a party atmosphere every night of the week. The club has two house bands – Apple of 7 and Pure Mix. Both play a mix of pop, R&B, rock and Filipino classics, with special performances at the weekend.

Irish Village

Century Village, 31A Street, Garhoud (04 239 5000, www.theirishvillage.com). Metro GGICO. **Open** 11am-1am Mon-Wed, Sat, Sun; 11am-2am Thur, Fri. **Map** p311 K2.

A home for live music from Ireland and beyond, the Irish Village has a reputation for fun rock, Celtic folk and acoustic music. The venue accommodates up to 3,500 people for gigs by global stars such as Bob Geldof, Sinéad O'Connor and Macy Gray.

Marines Club

Seaview Hotel, Mina Road, Bur Dubai (04 355 8080). Metro Al Fahidi. **Open** 10pm-3am daily. **Map** p312 F5.

This Filipino bar in Old Dubai is home to fun rock band the Golden Stars, who play everything from AC/DC to Led Zeppelin, with a knock-out lead singer. They also take requests from the crowd.

Maxx Music Bar & Grill

Citymax Hotels, Al Barsha (04 409 8000). Metro Mall of the Emirates. **Open** 6pm-3am daily. *Concerts* 10pm. **Map** p318 D3.

This buzzing bar has become a beacon of live music in Al Barsha, with bands playing six nights a week. The spacious venue is decorated with cool pop-art images of legends such as John Lennon and Jim Morrison, which sets the tone for a night of quality music. Brand-new resident band Blast Beats have just signed up – expect everything from rock to funk.

Music Room.

McGettigan's

Bonnington, Cluster J, Jumeirah Lakes Towers (04 356 0560, www.mcgettigans.com). Metro Jumeirah Lakes Towers. **Open** 7.30pm-2am daily. **Map** p318 A2.

An Irish pub simply has to have live music – and McGettigan's doesn't disappoint. This pub in Jumeirah Lakes Towers has another branch in the Dubai World Trade Centre, and both have a resident band, with Irish bands such as the Coronas and Paddy Casey flown in frequently to perform. Between the two venues, punters can enjoy six nights of live music a week. The DWTC resident band, Boz Boz, have been rocking the joint for three years and play Thursday nights. The Friday brunch crowd at JLT can enjoy a set from the Maplejacks, a quartet with rich harmonies, with Scitzophonic taking to the stage in the evening.

MusicHall

Jumeirah Zabeel Saray, Palm Jumeirah (056 270 8670, www.themusichall.com). Tram Palm Jumeirah. **Open** 9pm-3am Thur, Fri. **Map** p318 B1.

MusicHall is famed for its eclectic roster of musicians. Each act typically plays three songs followed by a 15-minute interval, when chart-friendly fare tends to be spun. The bill might include funked-up Otis Redding and Stevie Wonder tracks; an eastern European folk duo playing the spoons; traditional Greek opera and guitar music (and dancing); or Bob Marley tunes performed by a talented solo drummer. Line-ups are shuffled every couple of months and

each act is carefully selected by famed Beirut-born Greek-Lebanese founder Michael Elefferlades (we know his heritage because it's engraved above the entrance, alongside an image of his face).

Music Room

Majestic Hotel Tower, Bur Dubai (04 359 8888, www.themusicroomdubai.com). Metro BurJuman. **Open** 6pm-3am daily. **Map** p312 H5.

This venue doesn't care for genres – it's hosted acts including Apache Indian and Guns N' Roses' Bumblefoot – and welcomes allcomers. It's the kind of place where you'll hear salsa and samba one night, heavy metal and rock the next. The crowd is as diverse as the music, and the vibe is always laid-back and fun with dancing guaranteed.

★ Rock Bottom Café

Regent Palace Hotel, Bur Dubai (04 396 3888, www.rockbottomcafe.com). Metro BurJuman. **Open** 10pm-3am daily. **Map** p313 J5.

It's not the classiest establishment in town, but the Rock Bottom Café attracts a lively throng of expats and tourists all week long. And it's one of the few venues that offers live music every night of the week. The Rock Bottom is something of an institution in Dubai, and both the TECOM and Bur Dubai branches provide a showcase for new talent as well as established bands. Regardless of what you might make of the music on the stage, the venue has great acoustics, professional lighting and an energetic, feel-good vibe.

Other location Ramee Rose Hotel, TECOM, Al Barsha (04 450 0111).

Seville's

Wafi Pyramids, Oud Metha (04 324 4100, www.pyramidsrestaurantsatwafi.com). Metro Dubai Healthcare City. **Concerts** 9.30-11.30pm Mon, Thur, Fri. **Map** p311 J3.

If you like your food spicy and your music with a Latin flavour, check out Seville's for classic Spanish guitar music. The restaurant hosts themed nights every Monday, Thursday and Friday. Lively salsa classes are also held on Tuesdays.

IN THE KNOW COOL CUTS

The **Fridge** (Alserkal Avenue, Al Quoz, Al Barsha, 04 347 7793, www.thefridgedubai.com) may be housed in an unassuming warehouse in Al Quoz, but inside performers use the space for all manner of showcases, mini gigs and recitals (check the Facebook page to see what's on). One recent success at the venue was the Dubai Street Jam, a hip hop showcase for the UAE's up-and-coming urban music talent, which may become a regular event. The space has great lighting and stage facilities, and its cool location within the trendy Alserkal Avenue art district makes it a hub for the city's creatives.

LOUDER ENTERTAINMENT

The lowdown on Dubai's live music scene with Amy Wilkinson-Lough.

Louder Entertainment (www.louderentertainment.com), a newcomer to Dubai's live music scene, has made a name for itself by bringing Drake (pictured) and Michael Bublé to the region for the first time. We chatted to the company's founder, Amy Wilkinson-Lough, to find out what it takes to work with some of the world's biggest artists.

How did Louder Entertainment begin and how did it come to Dubai?
I've been in the music industry since the age of 17. I started out with Gatecrasher and then I moved out here to run two really successful events – Deep Nights at Trilogy, which is now Pacha, and Peppermint, which was at the World Trade Centre. Both were electronic dance music nights and were led by big-name DJs who could easily pull in 10,000 people. I then went over to Sydney and worked with Future Music Festival, but every ounce of me knew that at some point I'd come back and set up Louder Entertainment.

We're not here to do anything different, there's no gap in the market for us, but our motto is 'for the people, by the people' because we want to give a little bit back. With Gary Barlow, for example, we brought in a school choir, and for Drake and Bublé we used university kids as photographers, bloggers and artist liaison. We're also very keen to encourage people who want to get involved in the industry to come and have a chat. I know when I started out, finding people to talk to who would answer questions was never easy, so we stand by that motto and want to be an approachable business.

Dubai's live music scene has snowballed over the past couple of years. Was it quite tough as a new company to break on to a scene with so many big players?
It's very easy to come into a market like this and be nothing more than a flash in the pan, so my main aim was to make sure we came with a very clear two-year strategy. I think people often don't understand the risk, the hard work, the tears, you name it, that goes into putting these shows together. It's much more than building a stage and the artist showing up. A lot of people have no idea how many people it takes, how long you have to work for and, most importantly, the financial implications of getting it right – it's definitely not for the faint-hearted. And in order to compete with the guys who were already here, and who've got a big reputation, we needed to come out fighting with some big guns. We knew that we had the Bublé and Drake deals, so we knew that we could pull those out of the hat – which hopefully has made people realise that we're here to stay and that they should be confident in us as a brand.

Which direction do you hope to see Dubai's live music industry going in the coming years?
When you're all in competition, it becomes a bit of a bidding war and the artists become so expensive that commercially you just can't make shows happen, so it would be great to see everybody working together more cohesively, so that we can plan as a group when these guys are going to be coming. We have to keep offering such a diverse range of artists so hopefully everybody gets to go to something. But I think Dubai is heading in the right direction. Within the next two years it will be on a par with the rest of the world as a place at the forefront of artists' minds when they start their global touring plans.

What would you say is the best thing about being in Dubai right now as a live music entertainment agency?
For me, it's the energy. The city is still new and therefore it's very easy to go and talk to the right people and get them to get behind what you're doing. The Destination Dubai campaign is top of the list for everybody in terms of tourism right now, and I think when you put on big live events it adds value for everybody; the restaurants do well, the hotels do well, the airlines do well, and everybody benefits.

Any hints for what's next for Louder?
I'd like to see a few more festivals out here. I think losing Sandance was a big shame, so we'll be looking at festival opportunities as well as the live shows. I obviously can't reveal artists, but we've got some exciting things coming up and I can tell you that we do have projects confirmed right into 2016.

Jazz

★ Blue Bar

Novotel Dubai World Trade Centre, Downtown Dubai (04 332 0000). Metro Dubai World Trade Centre. **Open** 8pm-2am Mon-Wed, Sun; 8pm-3am Thur; noon-3am Fri; noon-2am Sat. *Concerts* 9.30pm-midnight Mon, Tue; 11pm-2am Thur; 10.30pm-1am Fri. **Map** p315 H10.

The intimate Blue Bar is an authentic jazz and blues venue. Book a table up close to the stage for the best experience. Thursday nights see resident band Fox Five Force playing blues, pop and classic rock, while Friday nights are set to swing with Abri.

Frioul Bistro de Luxe

Souk Madinat Jumeirah, Umm Suqeim (04 567 0011, www.frioulbistrodeluxe.com). Metro Mall of the Emirates. **Open** 8am-1am Mon-Wed, Sat, Sun; 8am-3am Thur, Fri. *Concerts* 9pm-midnight Thur, Fri. **Map** p318 E2.

This elegant French restaurant also hosts a quality jazz band with some excellent singers on Thursday and Friday nights. Whether you choose to eat here or not, you're welcome to enjoy the show from the bar. On Fridays, Kerrie-Anne presents a classic jazz playlist.

Ivy Jazz Lounge

Boulevard, Jumeirah Emirates Towers, Sheikh Zayed Road (04 319 8767, www.theivydubai.ae). Metro Emirates Towers. **Open** noon-midnight Mon-Wed, Sat, Sun; noon-1am Thur, Fri. *Concerts* 7.30-11pm. **Map** p310 H4.

Start the weekend with some swing and enter a world of 1920s glamour at the Ivy's Jazz Lounge. Enjoy a vibrant night of finger-clicking tunes as Ciaran Fox performs a swing set with a pianist, mixing Frank Sinatra with a touch of Michael Bublé. There's no minimum spend and no need to book a table, but it does get busy, so calling to reserve a spot in advance will save you standing all night.

Jazz@PizzaExpress

Cluster A, Jumeirah Lakes Towers (04 441 6342, www.pizzaexpressuae.com). Metro Jumeirah Lakes Towers. **Open** varies. **Map** p318 A2.

On Mondays, duo Matt and Chad perform rock and pop covers; Tuesdays and Thursdays are for jam sessions hosted by Abri & Funk Radius. Wednesday nights see the restaurant transported to the swinging '30s with jaunty jazz and lindy hop dancing. Weekend crowds are serenaded by an eclectic blend of soul and pop, with seasoned musicians and up-and-coming artists taking to the open mic on Sundays.

TR!BECA Kitchen + Bar

Ocean View Hotel, The Walk, Jumeirah Beach Residence (050 345 6067, www.tribeca.ae). Tram Jumeirah Beach Residence 2. **Open** 5pm-3am daily. *Concerts* 10pm-3am Fri. **Map** p318 A2.

This New York-inspired bar and kitchen opened its doors in 2015, serving organic food and drinks with a dose of soulful entertainment. Every Friday, home-grown resident musician Adam Baluch delights diners with his individual style of guitar mixed with beatboxing, singing and rapping.

Jazz@PizzaExpress.

Outdoors

Living in Dubai can sometimes make you forget about the rugged natural scenery lurking just beyond the city limits. If you have a couple of days spare, or even just a day, it's possible to explore terrain that's a world away from skyscrapers and motorways. Hidden in the wilderness are hiking trails of varying difficulty, stunning camping spots, lush oases and even glimpses of a lifestyle that has largely disappeared from the region. The less adventurous can still experience the beautiful rolling scenery of the UAE's sandy deserts by booking a desert safari. Back in the city, head to the beach for a kitesurfing lesson or to rent a paddleboard. Sporty types can take advantage of the outdoor running tracks and gyms, or sign up for a spot of beach yoga.

Avoid strenuous activities in the summer when temperatures can easily rise above 50°C (122°F). Always make sure you're properly prepared, with a GPS, maps, compass, guidance notes and plenty of water, plus protective gear: headwear, sunglasses and sun cream should be worn by all.

ACTIVITIES

Boat trips

See p167 **All Aboard**.

Bungee jumping

Gravity Zone
Power Play Football, opposite Dubai Bowling Centre, Al Quoz 1 (056 364 8778, www.gravityzone.co).
Rates Single jump Dhs360; tandem jump Dhs550.
Put your nerves through the shredder as you leap from a platform 92m (300ft) in the air. There's also the option to jump backwards from a 50m (160ft) platform – if you think you're hard enough.

Camel trekking

Al Sahra Equestrian Centre
Jebel Ali Lehbab Road (04 427 4055, www.jaresortshotels.com). **Rates** 90mins Dhs200; Dhs400 with champagne.
Head to this equestrian centre out in Dubai's sandier pastures to embark on a camel excursion, where, if you're lucky, you'll spot wildlife such as desert foxes and owls. A champagne option is available, too. So if you're looking to pop the big question this year, this is one special way to do it.

Deep-water soloing

Absolute Adventure
Dibba, Musandam (www.adventure.ae).
Rates Dhs495-Dhs695.
Not for the faint-hearted or clammy-handed, this dangerous sport involves climbing along rock faces overhanging water, without ropes. Your exit is directly into the deep water below. Don't try this alone – expert companies such as Absolute Adventure offer trips to Dibba.

Desert drumming

Dubai Drums
Gulf Ventures Camp, Al Awir (04 347 2129, www.dubaidrums.com). **Rates** (including barbecue and drum rental) Dhs300; Dhs100 6-13s; free under-5s.
Musically inclined, or just like to make a racket every now and then? This family-friendly pursuit sees participants sit together for an evening of guided drumming under the stars, plus a barbecue dinner. Visit the website for the monthly schedule.

Dune-bashing

Big Red

Accessible from Dubai-Hatta Road (E44).
One of the oldest attractions in the region, this well-known sand dune is something of a local landmark situated just off the Dubai–Hatta Road (E44), where the colour of the landscape changes from yellow to red. Just don't expect to have the place to yourself – tour companies run two trips a day to the dune. The area is also popular with residents keen to practise their dune-bashing skills (which basically involves driving over the sand in a 4x4). There's also a stretch of road at the foot of Big Red with numerous outfits renting quad bikes and dune buggies, which you can take for a spin in a designated area. Try Golden Desert (052 948 4616, 056 263 6956, www.golden desert-dubai.com).

Horse-riding

Mushrif Equestrian Club

Mushrif Park, Al Khawaneej Road (050 103 0243, www.mushrifequestrianclub.wordpress. com). **Rates** Dhs300.
Open to seasoned riders as well as newcomers to equestrian pursuits, Mushrif Equestrian Club's desert rides take in the varying terrain of the park over 90 minutes. Every month, the club also offers rides under the auspicious full moon.

Motorcycling

Dubai Motorcycle Tours

Prestige Motorcycle Tours & Rentals, Dubai Investment Park (055 953 2064, www.dubai motorcycletours.com). **Rates** from Dhs1,590.
Fancy yourself as a bit of a petrolhead? Don some leathers and hit the open road with one of Prestige Motorcycle's tours of the UAE, which range from day trips up to eight-day excursions across the country. You'll meet like-minded bike-lovers and learn heaps about the local landscape, plus see the Emirates as never before.

Skydiving

★ Skydive Dubai

Al Sufou Road, Dubai Marina (04 377 8888, www.skydivedubai.ae). Tram Jumeirah Beach Residence Station 1. **Open** 8am-4pm Mon-Sat. **Map** p318 B1.
Skydive over Palm Jumeirah from a height of 3,960m (13,000ft) with Skydive Dubai.

Survival skills

Bear Grylls Survival Academy

Dibba, Musandam (0044 1483 424438, www.beargryllssurvivalacademy.com). **Rates** Dhs2,023.

Skydive Dubai.

Bear Grylls Survival Academy. See p209.

The intrepid ex-Special Forces British adventurer has launched a survival academy in Dibba, on the Musandam peninsula – just a two-hour drive from Dubai. There are two courses available, one for adults and one for families, each lasting 24 hours. Groups are taught how to survive the desert sun, build and light a fire, find and purify water, deal with snakes and scorpions, use a survival knife and cross difficult terrain, as well as how to scale hills, abseil, crawl and run back to civilisation.

Yoga on the beach

Talise Spa

Madinat Jumeirah, Umm Suqeim (04 366 6821, www.jumeirah.com). Metro Mall of the Emirates. **Rates** Dhs80. **Map** p318 E2.

Salute the setting sun over the ocean. In winter, Talise Spa hosts these unique outdoor group yoga experiences every evening on the beach, with views of the Arabian Gulf and Burj Al Arab.

BOOTCAMPS

Beach Bootcamp

The Beach, JBR (04 311 6571, www.originalfitnessco.com). Tram Jumeirah Beach Residence Station 1. **Schedule** 6am Tue, Thur, Sun; 7am Fri. **Rates** Dhs75. **Map** p318 A2.

This bootcamp (on the lawn next to the open-air cinema) is ideal for those who want to train outdoors. The class uses a combination of high-intensity interval training circuits, as well as traditional exercises such as push-ups, crunches and burpees. Classes are quite small and tend to include a variety of fitness levels. Running on the sand is challenging, but spurred on by an enthusiastic instructor, you'll leave feeling great.

TribeFit

Silverene Tower, Dubai Marina (800 87423, www.tribefit.com). Metro Dubai Marina. **Rates** Dhs100. **Map** p318 A2.

While this bootcamp is by no means a walk in the park – think sprints, squats, push-ups, crunches and a whole lot of sweating – it's one of the more enjoyable ones out there. Catering to all fitness levels, it takes place along the waterfront of Dubai Marina, just below TribeFit's gym – the sea breeze is a welcoming factor at times, and you can expect some friendly camaraderie among the attendees. The one-hour session combines tabata-style training (20 seconds of hard training followed by ten seconds of rest, repeated eight times) with high-intensity exercises.

CAMPING TRIPS

Al Dhafra Beach, Abu Dhabi

Drive straight down Sheikh Zayed Road (E11) through Abu Dhabi. Follow the signs towards Danat Jebel Dhanna Resort or Al Dhafra Golf Links. The

MOUNTAIN HIGH

Take a hike on Jebel Shams.

Jebel Shams is the highest mountain in Oman, standing at 2,999 metres (9,840 feet). The good news is that you can drive to 2,000 metres (6,560 feet), where there's an excellent base camp known as Jebel Shams Heights (23° 13.616'N, 57° 12.131'E). You can either bring your own camping gear or rent basic huts with bathroom facilities at very reasonable rates. Remember to take your passport, GPS, charged mobile phone and sturdy walking boots.

From base camp, the hike to the summit is long and strenuous. It takes at least 12 hours, so is probably best left to very fit and experienced hikers. But don't be too disappointed – there are other well-marked trails that offer spectacular scenery. A short drive from base camp is Al Khataym, the start of a hike along an ancient donkey trail leading to the abandoned village of As Sab. It's relatively flat, on good paths and takes about four hours there and back.

For a longer mountain hike, drive back down to the old village of Al Ghul and follow a path up through the village and on to the canyon rim (known as the 'Grand Canyon' of the Middle East): from Al Ghul, it will take a fit hiker about six hours to reach the base camp. If this sounds too strenuous, drive to Al Hamra and then to Misfat al Abriyin, an old village with an incredible maze of traditional *falaj* water channels and ancient buildings. Enjoy a stroll around and don't forget to bring your camera with you.

STEP TO IT

Make the most of Dubai's outdoor running tracks and gyms.

Exercise in Dubai doesn't have to happen indoors in a private club: there are some free outdoor options. **Al Barsha Pond Park** is an oasis of green in sandy Al Barsha. Built around the perimeter of a man-made lake, it has a pleasant running track and fitness equipment. **Al Quoz Pond Park**, meanwhile, seems to be in an odd location, wedged in a corner where two roads meet, with a sign at the entrance reading 'Families and residents only'. It has basic exercise equipment, a running track and a water fountain.

Ittihad Park on Palm Jumeirah is a palm tree-lined promenade-style affair surrounded by a 3.2-kilometre (two-mile) jogging track. Squarely aimed at keen runners, this place is perfect for an early morning or evening jaunt. Landscaped rockeries and the odd water feature improve the scenery on the straight running route, and there's even a variety of gym equipment along the way. Sadly, greenery is lacking, except for the palm trees.

Jumeirah Beach Residence's the **Beach** (*see p164*) has a coastal running track, as well as **Muscle Beach** outdoor gym (*see p162*) – but the track may be difficult to navigate through weekend crowds as it runs down the centre of the main promenade. The running track at spacious **Kite Beach** (*see p114*) may be quieter and its small cafés are pleasant for some after-workout refuelling, and more casual than the venues in the Beach. **Skydive Dubai** (*see p167*) also has a small outdoor gym next to the Marina, with various equipment including climbing ropes and monkey bars.

Al Barsha Pond Park

Near Emirates NBD Bank, Al Barsha. **Open** 8am-11pm Mon-Thur, Sun; 8am-11.30pm Fri, Sat. **Admission** free. **Map** p318 D3.

Al Quoz Pond Park

Al Khail Road & Al Meydan Street, Al Quoz. **Open** 8am-11pm Mon-Thur, Sun; 8am-11.30pm Fri, Sat. **Admission** free. **Map** p309 D3.

Ittihad Park

Between Golden Mile buildings 2 & 3, Palm Jumeirah. Tram Palm Jumeirah. **Open** 24hrs daily. **Admission** free. **Map** p318 C1.

Al Barsha Pond Park.

ARTS & ENTERTAINMENT

beach can be accessed through the golf club by driving into the clubhouse entrance before the hotel roundabout and driveway. The drive can take up to three hours – it's a long, straight road, but there's some great scenery, especially after passing the outskirts of Abu Dhabi city. There have been sightings of sea turtles and flamingos in this area. It's a great place for diving, snorkelling and stand-up paddleboarding, so take swimming gear. If fishing is your game, you can try to catch some snapper, queen and trevally.

Khasab and Al Sayah Plateau, Musandam

If you're prepared for a longer drive (four hours from Dubai) and perhaps planning two nights out of the city, why not try the northern approach to Musandam from Al Rams? This can be reached by following the road through Ras Al Khaimah straight up to the border. Pass through the border at Al Rams (border fees apply: a ten-day tourist visa costs OMR5, about Dhs50) and drive along the spectacular coast road to Khasab. On the first night, camp on the beach at Khasab. From there, head up into the mountains, find the track to the Al Sayah Plateau and camp in fields a few kilometres further on (25° 57.862'N, 56° 12.334'E). Enjoy hiking, mountain biking or just chilling out in the camp and admiring the views. An option for your third day could be an early-morning drive back to Khasab and a dhow cruise (Dhs250 per person, Arabian Tours, 050 628 9667, book in advance), during which you can see dolphins and snorkel around Telegraph Island. You'll need to take bikes, snorkels and Oman car insurance – the latter can be arranged in advance or at the border. Check the up-to-date border information (www.rop.gov.om); you may need to apply in advance for a road permit to enter Musandam. And don't forget your passport.

IN THE KNOW PADDLE POWER

Most beach clubs have paddleboards or kayaks available for hire on an hourly basis, but **Kite Beach** (*see p114*) is one of the best public areas in which to paddleboard due to its ample space. **DuKite** (*see p215*) rents paddleboards as well as kitesurfing equipment. Dubai sunsets are nothing short of spectacular. So, for a novel way to watch the sun go down, rent a board, paddle out and watch the sun sink into the horizon.

Ras Al Khaimah

Follow Emirates Road heading north towards Ras Al Khaimah, then take the J119. Head south-east along the truck road for 2.5km (1.5 miles) and turn left on to a hard gravel track leading to the small farms at 25° 37.398'N, 55° 51.091'E. The drive takes about 1.5 hours. Camp near the farms (but not too close – you don't want to disturb the locals), or, if you have a 4x4, explore the sand dunes. There are many good sand

Kitesurfing. *See p215.*

IN THE KNOW
TEST YOUR LIMITS

The **Urban-Ultra Hajar 100** off-road run takes place in March and covers a 100km (62-mile) trail through some beautiful scenery, taking in mountain passes, Jeep tracks and stunning sand dunes. Physically fit, determined and well-prepared runners should get to the finish. When it comes to a challenge, however, the **Musandam Adventure Race** (Khor Najd, Khasab, Oman), held in February, is arguably the toughest in the region. A gruelling 35km (22-mile) sea kayak is followed by a 20km (12-mile) trail run, and you finish with a whopping 65km (40-mile) mountain bike ride. It can be completed as a team, or, if you dare, solo – although, to our knowledge, there's no record of a solo competitor reaching the finish line. To sign up for either event, visit www.premieronline.com.

tracks in the area, linking camel pens and small oasis farms. Banyan trees, palms, wild birds and Arabian oryx can be seen on an early-morning walk or drive around the camp. There are no facilities, so take everything with you, including plenty of food and drink. The hard track can be reached with care in a two-wheel-drive car. Camp in an open space, and be aware of other off-roaders coming over sand dunes.

Umm Al Quwain

Take Emirates Road north towards Ajman, turning off when you see signs for Dreamland Waterpark. Head for Al Rafaah. The drive takes about an hour. You can camp on the beach to the north and south of Al Rafaah. Visit the old fishing villages along the peninsula at Al Raas: take fishing gear and binoculars to spot wild birds. If you have a kayak, you can explore the mangroves along the coast. Choose your spot with care – some areas, especially those close to the river outlet, are dry at low tide but flooded at high tide. Also, take care not to camp on private property. Those who prefer to camp away from the coast road can find a secluded spot just off the main road. Try the area close to 25° 37.021'N, 55° 44.855'E.

Wake Evolution.

SAILING

Dubai Offshore Sailing Club

Off Jumeirah Road, Jumeirah (04 394 1669, www.dosc.ae). **Map** p308 C2.

If you're an avid sailer, or just interested in learning the ropes, DOSC is the best place to go. There are two-day courses for adults and children, as well as taster courses for youngsters (aged six to seven), which give a general introduction to sailing. Non-members can hire boats in advance from Sunday to Thursday. Proof of competency must be provided by either a RYA Level 2 certificate, or an assessment with one of the club instructors (to arrange an assessment and check the latest rates, contact sailingadmin@doscuae.com).

WATERSPORTS

DuWePlay

Marina Walk, Dubai Marina (056 693 0663, www.duweplay.com). **Open** 6am-6pm daily. **Rates** *30mins* Dhs300. *1hr* Dhs580. *Half-day* Dhs1,750. *Full-day* Dhs3,000. **Map** p318 B2.

This Marina outfit offers a full range of watersports, including wakeboarding, waterskiing, wakesurfing and wakeskating, as well as doughnut and banana boat rides.

★ Dukite

Kite Beach, Jumeirah (050 758 6992, www.dukite.com). **Open** 7am-5pm daily. **Rates** *Full equipment* Dhs250/hr. *Kite only* Dhs200/hr. *Board only* Dhs100/hr. *Harness only* Dhs50/hr. **Map** p308 C2.

Head down to the aptly named Kite Beach to try your hand at the popular sport of kitesurfing. If you need a lesson, advance booking is essential.

Wake Evolution

Jumeirah Fishing Harbour, Jumeirah (056 397 9538, www.wake-evolution.com). Metro FGB. **Rates** *20mins* Dhs200. *1hr* Dhs500. *Half-day* Dhs1,800. **Map** p316 B12.

Wake Evolution offers wakeboarding sessions, but if you're already a dab hand at that, have a go at trickier wakesurfing. Drinks are provided on board.

Xtreme Wake

Dubai Marina (056 342 3012, www.xtremewakeuae.com). Metro Dubai Marina. **Open** sunrise-sunset daily. **Rates** 1hr Dhs550. 2hrs Dhs1,100. 3hrs Dhs1,600. Half day Dhs2,000. **Map** p318 B2.

If you've never stepped on to a wakeboard or water-skis before, Xtreme Wake has some great instructors to guide you through the basics (included in the price). For more seasoned wakers, they provide tips to improve technique. Try to book the sunrise session, before there are too many boats out on the water to make things choppy. The boats can accommodate up to seven people, and drinks are provided.

DESERT SAFARIS

Numerous companies offer desert trips from Dubai.

Most outfits will pick you up from your accommodation before heading out towards the desert. What's included in the safari package varies; some offer trips to camel farms, others stop off to let you rent quad bikes and buggies for a 30-minute session. All should include dune-bashing in a 4x4 and a sunset photo-op stop, where you can also try out things such as sandboarding. On the whole, they all offer enjoyable, though inevitably touristy, experiences.

Arabian Adventures (04 303 4888, www.arabian-adventures.com) is one of the best-known – and more expensive – companies. It runs several different trips, including one to the Dubai Desert Conservation Reserve (DDCR). Expect to pay around Dhs300-Dhs400 for a standard day trip, depending on the season. All safaris end at one of a few desert camps for a buffet and an Arabian belly dancing and *tanoura* show. Shisha, henna and camel rides are also available.

For something a little more special, check out the Heritage Dinner Safari from **Platinum Heritage** (04 388 4044, www.platinum-heritage.com), which promises to show guests Dubai as it was 50 years ago. The experience includes transport in a vintage Land Rover, a meal among the dunes, camel rides, shisha and more. Prices start at Dhs545 (Dhs445 for children).

Performing Arts

Dubai's performing arts scene is still very much in its infancy and there are only a handful of dedicated venues, which double up to host both theatre and dance performances. But the situation looks set to improve dramatically in 2016, with the new Dubai Opera scheduled to open as part of the Opera District in Downtown Dubai, which will provide a huge boost to the city's cultural landscape. In the meantime, arts-lovers will have to make do with the sporadic shows taking place at the city's limited venues. For the most up-to-date information about arts events in the city, visit www.timeoutdubai.com.

VENUES

The venues below are usually only open to the public when there's a performance on, so it's best to call or check the website for listings. **Ductac** and the **Madinat Theatre** are also the most popular venues for dance events in the city. In 2015, the Madinat presented the Opéra National de Paris and a performance of *Romeo and Juliet* by Les Ballets de Monte-Carlo. Ductac, meanwhile, staged contemporary shows including *Orthello – The Remix* by the Chicago Shakespeare Company and the Sharmila Dance Extravaganza, performed by its in-house dance school.

Courtyard Playhouse

4B Street, Al Quoz 1, near Alserkal Avenue (056 986 1761, www.courtyardplayhouse.com). **Map** p308 C3.

Dubai's only improv theatre, an intimate venue with just 70 seats, offers something completely different on Dubai's performing arts scene. On the improv side, there are three regular shows that often involve audience participation. Maestro features ten performers selected at random to improvise scenes, with the audience asked to vote them off until only one remains. Two teams of improvisers compete against each other in Theatresports, with a panel of judges scoring the contest. Speechless involves performers being given a random topic from which they have to improvise a PowerPoint presentation. The Courtyard also hosts a night for up-and-coming comedians, as well as its King Gong show, when the audience can vote off under-performing acts.

Ductac

Mall of the Emirates, Al Barsha (04 341 4777, www.ductac.org). Metro Mall of the Emirates. **Map** p318 D3.

The Dubai Community Theatre & Arts Centre, known almost universally as Ductac, is a non-profit venue that hosts a wide range of shows. Theatre performances regularly appear on the schedule, but the centre also hosts dance, music and comedy events. Its main Centrepoint Theatre can seat 543 for Ductac's biggest shows, while there are also smaller studios for more intimate performances and art exhibitions. For longer-term visitors, Ductac holds workshops on subjects such as sculpture, photography and dance. The in-house Arts Materials Shop is the place to go for supplies, while the Old Library is one of the city's biggest libraries with more than 20,000 books in stock.

Madinat Theatre

Souk Madinat Jumeirah, Al Sufouh Road, Umm Suqeim (04 366 6546, www.madinattheatre.com). Metro Mall of the Emirates. **Map** p318 E2.

Nestled in the middle of Souk Madinat Jumeirah, this plush-looking venue has hosted everything from Chinese circus performances to Christmas pantomimes, comedy shows to Russian ballet. The theatre is on two levels and can seat 442 across the stalls and balcony. This is one of the most impressive venues in Dubai, with a foyer of grand columns and marble floors, and a main auditorium featuring tiered seating and a huge stage. Its location in Souk Madinat Jumeirah means that you're spoilt for choice when it comes to pre-show drinks and post-show meals.

Dance classes

Arthur Murray Dance School
Reef Tower, Jumeirah Lakes Towers (04 448 6458, www.arthurmurraydubai.com). Metro Jumeirah Lakes Towers. **Open** 1-10.30pm Mon-Thur, Sun; 11am-3.30pm Sat. **Classes** vary. **Map** p318 A2.
This Dubai branch of the US dance franchise offers private dance lessons. There are also regular group lessons teaching various styles, including Latin, waltz and ballroom. Call for latest prices and times.
Other location Souk Al Bahar, Downtown Dubai (04 450 8648).

Dubai Dance Academy
Yassat Gloria Hotel Apartments, TECOM (055 362 6435, www.dubaidanceacademy.com). Metro Dubai Internet City. **Open** times vary. **Classes** from Dhs70 per hr. **Map** p318 C2.
This school aims to bring skilled French ballet training to Dubai. It's run by Reiko M-Cheong, a professional ballet dancer with more than 20 years' experience. Lessons are available for kids and adults.

James & Alex Dance Studios
Concord Tower, Dubai Media City (04 447 0773, www.jamesandalex.com). Tram Palm Jumeirah. **Open** 2-10pm Mon-Wed, Sun. **Classes** from Dhs55. **Map** p318 B2.
You can try out salsa, tango, ballet, zumba, hip hop, contemporary, musical theatre, pole fitness and more at this modern 370sq m (4,000sq ft) venue, which is equipped with three studios. Kids' musical theatre company Hayley's Comet (www.hayleyscomet.com) is also based here.

Sharmila Dance
Ductac, Mall of the Emirates, Al Barsha (04 341 4777, www.sharmiladance.com). Metro Mall of the Emirates. **Open** times vary. **Classes** Dhs60. **Map** p318 D3.
Sharmila's classes are a mix of hip hop, street jazz, funk, jazz and lyrical contemporary, and the schedule changes every two weeks. Ballet classes are also available. There are two annual shows organised by the studio, the Sharmila Dance Extravaganza and the Sharmila Dance Gala. A summer workshop is also organised every year.

TUNING UP

The new Opera District will revolutionise Dubai's arts scene.

When it opens in 2016, the Opera District should provide a massive boost to Dubai's performing arts scene. At the centre of the development will be **Dubai Opera** (www.dubaiopera.com), a multi-format venue that will be able to stage concerts, opera, musicals, ballet and contemporary dance. Depending on the configuration, the venue will be able to seat up to 2,000 people.

This being Dubai, the opera house won't be the only part of the development. Developer Emaar has announced plans for a museum of modern art, two art hotels, design studios and galleries. Serviced apartments, a shopping mall and a waterfront promenade will also make up part of the district, which will be located off Sheikh Mohammed Bin Rashid Boulevard in Downtown Dubai.

But it's the impending arrival of the opera house that will really make a big difference in the city. This flagship project is long overdue and should result in more international touring companies stopping off in Dubai, as well as encouraging the fledgling local scene.

Spas

Ritual pampering is big business in the emirate; it's an area in which the visitor is utterly and bewilderingly spoilt for choice. Dubai's spa scene ranges from the sublime, such as Talise Ottoman Spa's lavish Royal Hammam, to the downright cynical: spoilt toddlers scoffing cupcakes during their bubblegum pink manicures at the Hello Kitty Beauty Spa. Every new hotel worth its body wrap and facials has ten pages of treatments to offer, but what could be more Dubai than slathering your face in 24-carat gold? If a trip to the spa here is going to demonstrate anything, it's that everything you've ever heard about the city is right on the money. Just be prepared to spend some.

FIVE-STAR SPAS

Ahasees Spa

Grand Hyatt, Oud Metha (04 317 2336, www.hyatt.com/ahasees-spa-dubai). Metro Dubai Healthcare City. **Open** 9am-9pm daily. **Full-body massage** from Dhs500/hr. **Map** p311 J3.

Situated inside the Grand Hyatt hotel, Ahasees is surprisingly understated and serene, with a menu of treatments that pays homage to Dubai's maritime and desert-dwelling heritage. Wooden floors lend an oddly Swedish sauna feel, but nevertheless deliver an earthiness to the minimalist decor. Head here to try scrubs using Dubai sand and crushed pearls, plus seaweed wraps and frankincense essential oils.

IN THE KNOW MEDISPAS

Dubai is rapidly becoming a hotspot in the Middle East for plastic surgery and other cosmetic procedures. Thanks to a region-wide obesity epidemic, liposuction is one of the most sought-after procedures in the city. Medispas and clinics (many of them lining Jumeirah Beach Road and Al Wasl Road) offering surgical treatments as well as non-surgical, Harley Street-style 'lunchtime lipo' sessions, using such techniques as ultrasound biocavitation, which claim to use radio frequency to break down fat cells. Botox and fillers remain popular, as does rhinoplasty, with breast augmentation and hair implants also selling well.

Amara Spa

Park Hyatt, Deira (04 602 1235, www.dubai.park.hyatt.com/hyatt/pure/spas). Metro GGICO. **Open** 9am-10pm daily. **Full-body massage** from Dhs495/hr. **Map** p311 K2.

Amara is well known for its couples' packages and treatment rooms, which include a private outdoor rain shower. All treatments (which range from anti-cellulite wraps to golf massages to cryotherapy facials) are themed around four different precious stones and their supposed healing qualities: sapphire to de-stress, relax and calm; emerald to detoxify, cleanse and heal; ruby to revitalise, 'defy' age and protect; and diamond to energise, clarify and revive.

Armani/Spa

Armani Hotel, Burj Khalifa, Downtown Dubai (04 888 3888, www.dubai.armanihotels.com/spa-en). Metro Burj Khalifa/Dubai Mall. **Open** 9am-9pm daily. **Full-body massage** from Dhs520/50mins. **Map** p317 F14.

This deeply design-driven space abandons conventional spa cosiness in favour of seriously expensive, yet austere, monotone decor and hazy overhead lighting that wouldn't feel out of place in a horror film. Cold and slightly creepy though it may be, it's still worth visiting for a massage if only to say you've been rubbed up and down in the world's tallest hotel, and to make use of the outdoor pool, which boasts views of Dubai's most exclusive neighbourhood.

B/Attitude Spa

Grosvenor House Tower 2, Dubai Marina (04 402 2200, www.battitudespa-dubai.com). Metro Damac. **Open** 8am-10.30pm daily. **Full-body massage** from Dhs525/hr. **Map** p318 B2.

If the Buddha Bar franchise launched a spa, this is what it would look like (and coincidentally, the funky Asian nightspot is just next door in Tower 1). Spagoers should prepare to be surrounded by dragon motifs and deities, classical Far Eastern illustrations, and vibrant colours and patterns while they enjoy some of the 40-odd East-meets-West treatments on offer. The spa also has a hammam, complete with mini marble slab, and traditional Thai massages conducted on a mattress on the floor.

Cleopatra's Spa

Wafi Pyramids, Oud Metha (04 324 7700, www.cleopatrasspaandwellness.com). Metro Dubai Healthcare City. **Open** *Women* 9am-9pm daily. *Men* 10am-9.30pm Mon-Thur, Sat, Sun. **Full-body massage** from Dhs335/hr. **Map** p311 J3.

Part of Dubai's ancient Egypt-inspired Wafi complex, which also houses a shopping mall, several restaurants and bars, Cleopatra's is heavily themed. While some of the decor looks a little dated, the spa's unpretentious, relaxed vibe has helped secure its popularity in the face of dozens of swankier options opening up nearby. Besides, how many other places indulge your inner child by claiming chocolate syrup baths as a legitimate spa therapy?

Conrad Spa

Conrad Dubai, Sheikh Zayed Road (04 444 7440, www.conraddubai.com/en/leisure/conrad-spa). Metro World Trade Centre. **Open** 6am-10pm daily. **Full-body massage** from Dhs420/hr. **Map** p315 G9.

This spa offers facials and full-body treatments for men and women. Facilities include a relaxation zone, plunge pool and outdoor swimming pool.

LIME Spa

Per Aquum Desert Palm, Al Awir (04 323 8888, www.desertpalm.peraquum.com/lime-spa). **Open** 9am-9pm daily. **Full-body massage** from Dhs380/hr.

Sure, looking out on to a polo field while someone works the tension out of your glutes might not be everyone's bag, but spa-going equestrian fiends would be hard pushed to find anything that matches

B/Attitude Spa.

up to this suburban spot. LIME offers a (relatively) short menu of treatments, but one that includes a caviar and pearl facial – while you may be on the outskirts of the city, you're still very much in Dubai.

Mandara Spa

The H Dubai, Sheikh Zayed Road (04 501 8270, www.mandaraspa.com). Metro World Trade Centre. **Open** 9am-10pm daily. **Full-body massage** Dhs365/50 mins. **Map** p315 G9.

There are ten treatment rooms, saunas, steam rooms and relaxation lounges at the Mandara Spa in the H Dubai. Treatments using techniques from around the world are available.

One&Only Private Spa

One&Only The Palm, Palm Jumeirah (04 440 1040, http://thepalm.oneandonlyresorts.com). **Open** 10am-9pm daily. **Full-body massage** from Dhs535/hr. **Map** p318 B1.

Palm Jumeirah's most secluded retreat, and arguably its classiest, is no stranger to the odd visiting VIP or celebrity guest. Staff are big on luxury and privacy – an ethos reflected in the spa, which offers big-bucks packages for the ultimate day retreat. The Palm Indulgence for two features access through a secluded VIP entrance, a private rhassoul with water jets in the double scrub room, two hours of treatments and a two course lunch, for £480 (Dhs2,720).

Raffles Spa

Raffles Dubai, Oud Metha (04 314 9870, www.raffles.com). Metro Dubai Healthcare City. **Open** 9am-9pm daily. **Full-body massage** from Dhs479/hr. **Map** p311 J3.

While the spa is inside the pyramid-shaped Raffles hotel, and part of the ancient Egypt-inspired Wafi complex, the pharaonic theme isn't too heavily present. The menu of treatments, however, does list a few options that even pharaohs might have approved – the Egyptian gold facial in particular features the real thing. There's also a ladies' hair salon and men's grooming lounge.

ShuiQi Spa

Atlantis The Palm, Palm Jumeirah (04 426 1020, www.atlantisthepalm.com/shuiqi-spa-fitness). Tram Palm Jumeirah (then monorail). **Open** 10am-10pm daily. **Full-body massage** from Dhs510/hr. **Map** p308 A1.

Like much of the gaudy pink hotel that contains it, ShuiQi is immersed in an underwater theme. Unlike the rest of the property, however, the spa actually feels pretty magical and – dare we say – even classy. Small streams line the ornate corridor off which treatment rooms lie, and it's a nice change to know you're listening to the sound of actual fountains rather than a CD of panpipes and running water. Head here to try treatments such as the Dubai Glamour Ritual (featuring scrub, massage and facial). There's also a Medi Spa offering Botox and teeth whitening, plus salons for men and women.

IN THE KNOW AYURVEDIC THERAPIES

With an enormous number of Asian expats contributing to Dubai's population of more than two million, demand for traditional ayurvedic treatments is high. While you'll often find an *abhyanga* (warm oil) massage or two on the menus of generic spas all over town, there are dozens of small, dedicated ayurveda centres in the city too. While most of them stick to the more enjoyable side of the 5,000-year-old natural healing philosophy (try **Breath & Health** on Al Wasl Road, 04 348 9940, www.breathandhealth.net), administering massages and drizzling warm oil over various body parts to heal imbalances in the three humours (*vata*, *pitta* and *kapha*) and ailments, some take things a step further into purging and draining territory. Not for the faint-hearted, or the unacquainted. Should you wish to indulge your curiosity, try **Panchakarma Ayurveda & Yoga Centre** on Bur Dubai's Bank Street (04 397 0790, www.panchakarmadubai.com).

Softouch Spa

Kempinski Mall of the Emirates, Al Barsha (04 409 5909, www.kempinski.com/en/dubai/mall-of-the-emirates). Metro Mall of the Emirates. **Open** 24hrs daily. **Full-body massage** from Dhs480/hr. **Map** p318 D3.

Attached to the bustling Mall of the Emirates (home to Dubai's infamous snow-smothered indoor ski slope), the Kempinski hotel's spa focuses on treatments that follow the ancient principles of Ayurveda. Handier for shoppers needing a quick boost between extravagant purchases are the spa's express treatments, which include scalp massages, leg and feet treatments, and puffy eye therapies.

Spa at the Ritz-Carlton

Ritz-Carlton Dubai, JBR (04 399 4000, www.ritzcarlton.com). Tram Jumeirah Beach Residence 1. **Open** 10am-10pm daily. **Full-body massage** from Dhs480/hr. **Map** p318 A2.

This tranquil retreat is what we imagine one of the more (read, few) tasteful palaces of Dubai's sheikhs might look like on the inside. Ornate doorways, floating pools of tea lights and tonnes of cream marble set the tone, while the spa menu includes all the usual suspects – de-stressing massages, slimming wraps and deep-cleansing scrubs, as well as a couple of standouts such as the jet-lag body massage and a hammam.

Talise Spa Burj Al Arab Jumeirah.

Spa InterContinental

InterContinental Dubai Festival City, Festival City (04 701 1257, www.ihg.com). **Open** 10am-11pm daily. **Full-body massage** from Dhs415/hr. **Map** p311 K3.

Entering this spa on the northern side of the Creek, you're met with an entrance that resembles a night sky. Sadly, the entrance is just about the only thing that impresses about this pampering haven as none of the rest of the decor stands out, and the treatments are not especially unusual or interesting. However, it's worth noting that there's a whole page on the menu dedicated to men's facials and massages.

Talise Ottoman Spa

Jumeirah Zabeel Saray, Palm Jumeirah (04 453 0456, www.jumeirah.com). **Open** 9am-9.30pm daily. **Full-body massage** from Dhs479/hr. **Map** p318 B1.

One of the largest Turkish-style hammams in the Middle East, Talise Ottoman is held in high esteem by Dubai's spa devotees for its mega-luxurious spin on Istanbul's baths. As well as a traditional scrubbing down with olive-oil soap and flannel mitts, you can also unwind with a session in the shiver-inducing snow room, or go for the signature 'sultan's massage'.

Talise Spa Al Qasr

Al Qasr, Madinat Jumeirah (04 366 6818, www.jumeirah.com). **Open** 9am-10pm daily. **Full-body massage** from Dhs525/hr. **Map** p318 E2.

Said to be a personal favourite of Dubai's ruler and UAE vice president and prime minister, Sheikh Mohammed bin Rashid Al Maktoum, this branch of Jumeirah Group's Talise chain is pretty much exactly what you'd picture if asked to imagine an Arabian take on a spa. The comfy central relaxation area resembles a luxurious *majlis*, while the scent of frangipani flowers pervades the private garden and pool. If you can only pick one treatment, go for a massage (try the Talise sea shell experience) in a private outdoor cabana, next to the garden's small waterfall.

Talise Spa Burj Al Arab Jumeirah

Burj Al Arab, Umm Suqeim (04 301 7365, www.jumeirah.com). **Open** 9.15am-9pm daily. **Full-body massage** from Dhs895/55mins. **Map** p318 E2.

One of the most instantly recognisable buildings in the world, the Burj Al Arab is so swanky you can't even set foot on the small island that houses it without a reservation of some sort. This is the place to go for a facial if you really want to give your friends back at home something to turn green for. If you do book in, however, be prepared for the fact you're paying through the nose for the address rather than the best treatment in town. Everything you'd expect is on the menu, including caviar and gold facial options, and a romantic moonlight swim package for two, which features a couples massage, private swim in the infinity pool, champagne, roses and monogrammed Burj Al Arab bathrobes to take away with you.

BOUTIQUE SPAS

De La Mer Day Spa

Jumeirah Beach Road, Umm Suqeim (04 328 2775, www.delamerspa.com). **Open** 9am-9pm Mon-Thur, Sat, Sun; noon-9pm Fri. **Full-body massage** from Dhs300/hr. **Map** p318 E2.

One of many ladies-only villa spas and salons that line Jumeirah Beach Road and Al Wasl Road, De La Mer offers everything from massages to manicures to deep stretching classes. Located inside what is, to all intents and purposes, a large house, the all-round grooming haven has a private pool, state-of-the-art gym and beauty salon in addition to its numerous treatment rooms. There are typically weekly promotions and offers, so it's worth checking the website for the latest announcements to see where you can save before making a reservation.

Purple Sanctuary

Al Wasl Road, Jumeirah (04 348 9679, www.thepurplesanctuary.com). **Open** 9am-8pm daily. **Full-body massage** from Dhs350/hr. **Map** p318 E2.

Formerly home to the Thai Privilege Spa, the Sanctuary is another villa-dwelling business, this time offering treatments that feature a range of natural ingredients, from pumpkin to aloe vera to papaya, alongside classic Thai therapies. Even lairy children are catered for, with a special kid-calming massage designed to tame even the most boisterous of expat brats.

SensAsia Urban Spas

Emirates Golf Club, Sheikh Zayed Road (04 417 9820, www.sensasiaspas.com). Metro Nakheel. **Open** 10am-10pm daily. **Full-body massage** from Dhs399/hr. **Map** p318 B2.

This cool, down-with-the-kids spa chain, the brainchild of an expat massage-addict, has now grown from one outlet to four across the city. SensAsia's therapists hail from massage meccas such as Bali and Thailand, and as a result they really know their stuff. Treatments have funky names – book in for a Sole to Seoul massage, perhaps, or a Pamper Me Silly half-day package. If you like a great massage with quality products and expert staff, but without all the excessive faff of a five-star hotel spa, this place was made for you.

Other locations Souk Al Manzil, Downtown (04 456 0866); Village Mall, Jumeirah Beach Road (04 349 8850); Al Natura Beach Club, Palm Jumeirah (04 422 7115).

Spa Cordon

Sky Gardens, DIFC (04 421 3424, www.spacordon.com). Metro Financial Centre. **Open** 10am-10pm daily. **Full-body massage** from Dhs375/hr. **Map** p310 H4.

A popular escape for stressed-out city workers from the nearby Financial Centre, Cordon offers vegan mani-pedis alongside a short menu of massages, mud scrubs and facials. It may be located in a small spot in a residential building, but the spa makes up for a lack of space with soothing, earthy decor. Prices are also fairly competitive for the often pricey neighbourhood. Fancy something a bit bespoke? Customised combinations of massages and facials, scrubs and facials or scrubs and massages start from Dhs480 for 90 mins. Not bad.

IN THE KNOW MALE GROOMING

Far from being disparaged or mocked, a well-groomed man is a thing to be celebrated in Dubai, and indeed across the UAE. You only have to look at the immaculate facial hair of the country's rulers to see how much a full beard is valued, and many men spend painful hours in the clinic under a laser to make that sharp, defined hairline on their face and neck official. A good beard is culturally associated with maturity and wisdom, and you'll find a growing number of male grooming lounges catering to this symbol of manhood – the newest of which is **Jazz Lounge Spa** on Umm Suqeim Road in Al Barsha (04 395 7338, www.jazzloungespa.com). Well-kept extremities are also the norm – most barbers offer a manicure and pedicure service to keep your tips and toes in good nick.

Escapes & Excursions

Escapes & Excursions

Formerly known as the Trucial States when they were under British rule, the seven emirates – Abu Dhabi, Ajman, Dubai, Fujairah, Ras Al Khaimah, Sharjah and Umm Al Quwain – each have strong individual identities. They all came together in 1971 as the United Arab Emirates and since then each one has grown in status.

Set on the eastern edge of the Arabian peninsula, the UAE has Qatar to its north-west, Saudi Arabia to the west and south, and Oman to the south-east and north-east. For most tourists, Dubai is the first – and often only – port of call in the UAE. But beyond its bright lights and shopping centres is a world of sun-drenched beaches, remote mountain escapes, endless expanses of desert and culturally diverse towns and cities.

THE LIE OF THE LAND

Less than two hours down the road from Dubai is the capital of the UAE, **Abu Dhabi** (*see below*). If you head in the other direction, you'll find an array of attractions, beginning with Dubai's slightly chaotic northern neighbour, **Sharjah** (*see p233*), and then **Ajman** (*see p232*). But from there on, you'll begin to see the wild side of the UAE, especially amid the mountains and dunes of **Ras Al Khaimah** (*see p236*). The east coast, too, offers plenty of natural wonders, especially at **Fujairah** (*see p235*), where excellent snorkelling and diving await.

Public transport has been improving over the years, but it still remains sporadic the further you travel from the cities. Our advice, if you're heading out of Dubai, is to rent a 4x4 and explore what the UAE has to offer at your own pace.

ABU DHABI

Few places in the world have undergone such rapid change as Abu Dhabi. Only 50 years ago, the few small villages in the emirate were mainly connected by centuries-old camel trails. The discovery of oil, and the explosion of money in its wake, triggered a building boom that is still pushing skyscrapers up from the sand.

But this is not the first boom to hit the emirate. In the 1800s, Abu Dhabi grew rich from pearls. However, a global recession and competition from Japanese cultured pearls broke the local industry; Abu Dhabi returned to poverty, becoming the poorest of the emirates. And so it remained until the discovery that would shape both the emirate's and much of the world's history for the next half century and more.

In 1958, huge offshore oil reserves were found. Abu Dhabi became the first of the Gulf states to export oil in 1962, earning an estimated US$70 million per year throughout the 1960s. Today, roughly two million barrels of oil are exported from the United Arab Emirates every 24 hours. Current estimates suggest this will continue for the foreseeable future.

Under the rule of Sheikh Khalifa bin Zayed Al Nahyan, president of the UAE, Abu Dhabi shows no signs of letting up on its rapid development.

Tourism is at the forefront of the emirate's plans, with some hugely ambitious projects on the horizon. Of these, the project receiving the most attention is **Saadiyat Island**. The island is on course to be reimagined as a cultural hub, with five world-class museums set to land on its shores: the Guggenheim Abu Dhabi, Louvre Abu Dhabi, Maritime Museum, Performing Arts Centre and Zayed National Museum.

At its heart, though, Abu Dhabi remains a traditional Middle Eastern city, which means it's advisable to watch your behaviour, even when just passing through. Overt drunkenness and lasciviousness should be confined to private places, and revealing outfits are best avoided, especially during Ramadan.

Sightseeing & shopping

Getting your bearings can be tricky in Abu Dhabi, as it's a city made up of multiple islands. At the heart of the capital is **Abu Dhabi Island**, which features many attractions of note, both cultural and gaudy. Among these is the immense **Sheikh Zayed Grand Mosque** (*see p230* **In the Know**), which is open for non-Muslim visitors.

To realise just how far the city has come in such a short space of time, visit the **Heritage Village** (Breakwater, near Marina Mall, 02 681 4455), a faithful representation of a small nomadic camp. The village features a goat's-hair tent and a campfire with coffee pots, and there are also plenty of old-fashioned craft shops to browse.

From Heritage Village, you can easily nip across to the jaw-dropping **Emirates Palace** (West Corniche Road, 02 690 9000, www.kempinski.com). As with Dubai's Burj Al Arab, the Emirates Palace calls itself a seven-star hotel: even if you don't stay to confirm or dispute the self-aggrandisement, a visit to high-end Emirati restaurant **Mezlai** (02 690 7999), stylish club **Etoiles** (02 690 8960) or the luxurious Emirates Palace Spa is worth the splurge.

When it comes to shopping, Abu Dhabi has its fair share of the gigantic malls that the UAE is famous for. On Abu Dhabi Island there are four major malls, of which the most pleasant is **Marina Mall** (02 681 2310, www.marinamall.ae), which sits on a causeway jutting out beside the gates of the Emirates Palace. The newest and shiniest shopping centre is **Yas Mall** (02 414 6401, www.yasmall.ae), which features all the major high-street brands plus a huge cinema and the ultimate in unlikely desert experiences: an indoor snowpark called Snow City.

Sun, sea & sand

There's a lot of sand in Abu Dhabi, and a fair amount of it forms beaches. **Saadiyat Public Beach** (sun lounger Dhs50 Mon-Thur, Sun, Dhs75 Fri, Sat), on Saadiyat Island, provides views of even more sand in the wave-like sweep of dunes, an endless horizon and plenty of marine life lurking beneath the water's surface. If you want to be closer to the city centre, then the

Sheikh Zayed Grand Mosque.

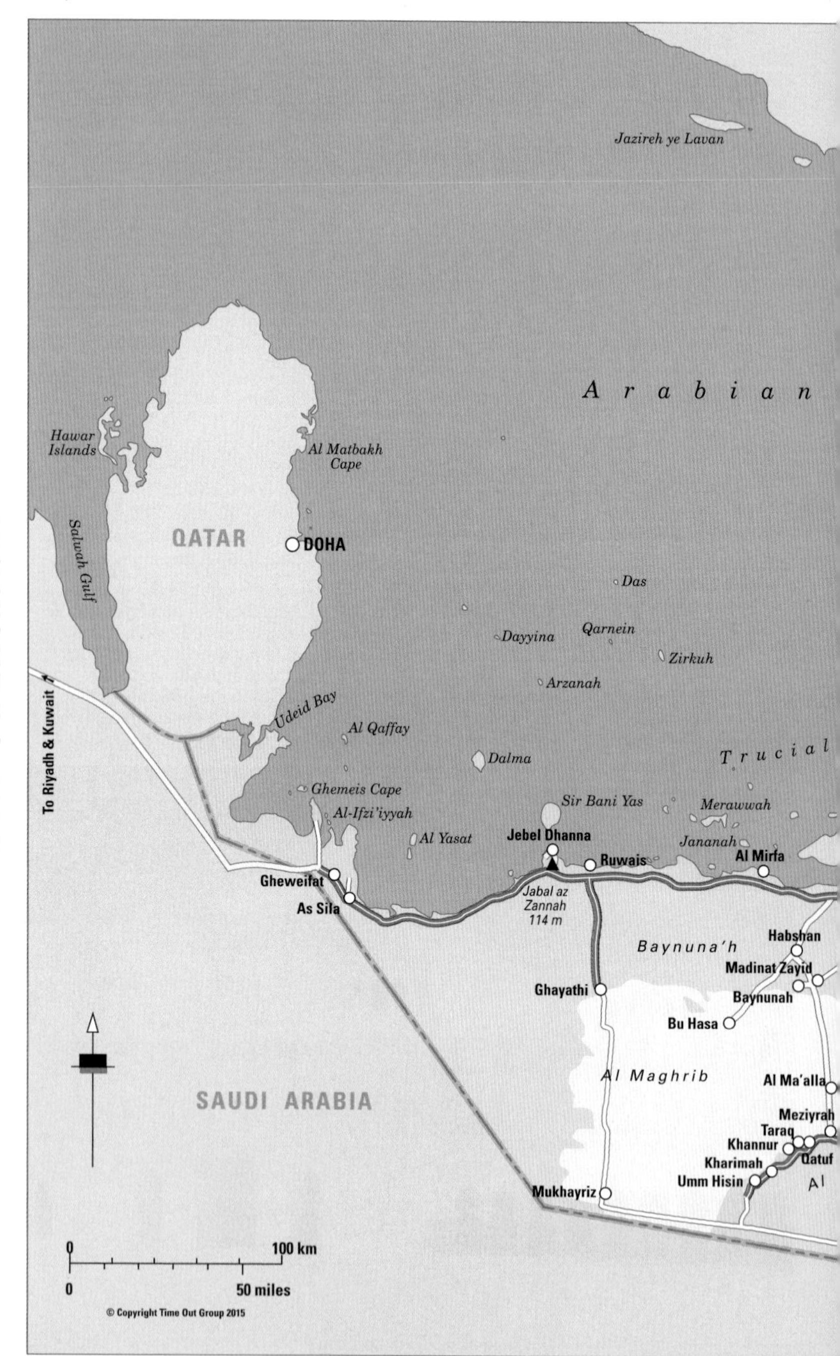

Jazireh ye Lavan
Arabian
Hawar Islands
Al Matbakh Cape
Salwah Gulf
QATAR
DOHA
Das
Dayyina
Qarnein
Zirkuh
Arzanah
Udeid Bay
Al Qaffay
Dalma
Trucial
To Riyadh & Kuwait
Ghemeis Cape
Al-Ifzi'iyyah
Sir Bani Yas
Merawwah
Al Yasat
Jebel Dhanna
Jananah
Ruwais
Al Mirfa
Gheweifat
As Sila
Jabal az Zannah 114 m
Habshan
Baynuna'h
Madinat Zayid
Ghayathi
Baynunah
Bu Hasa
Al Maghrib
Al Ma'alla
SAUDI ARABIA
Meziyrah
Taraq
Khannur
Qatuf
Kharimah
Umm Hisin
Al
Mukhayriz
0
100 km
0
50 miles

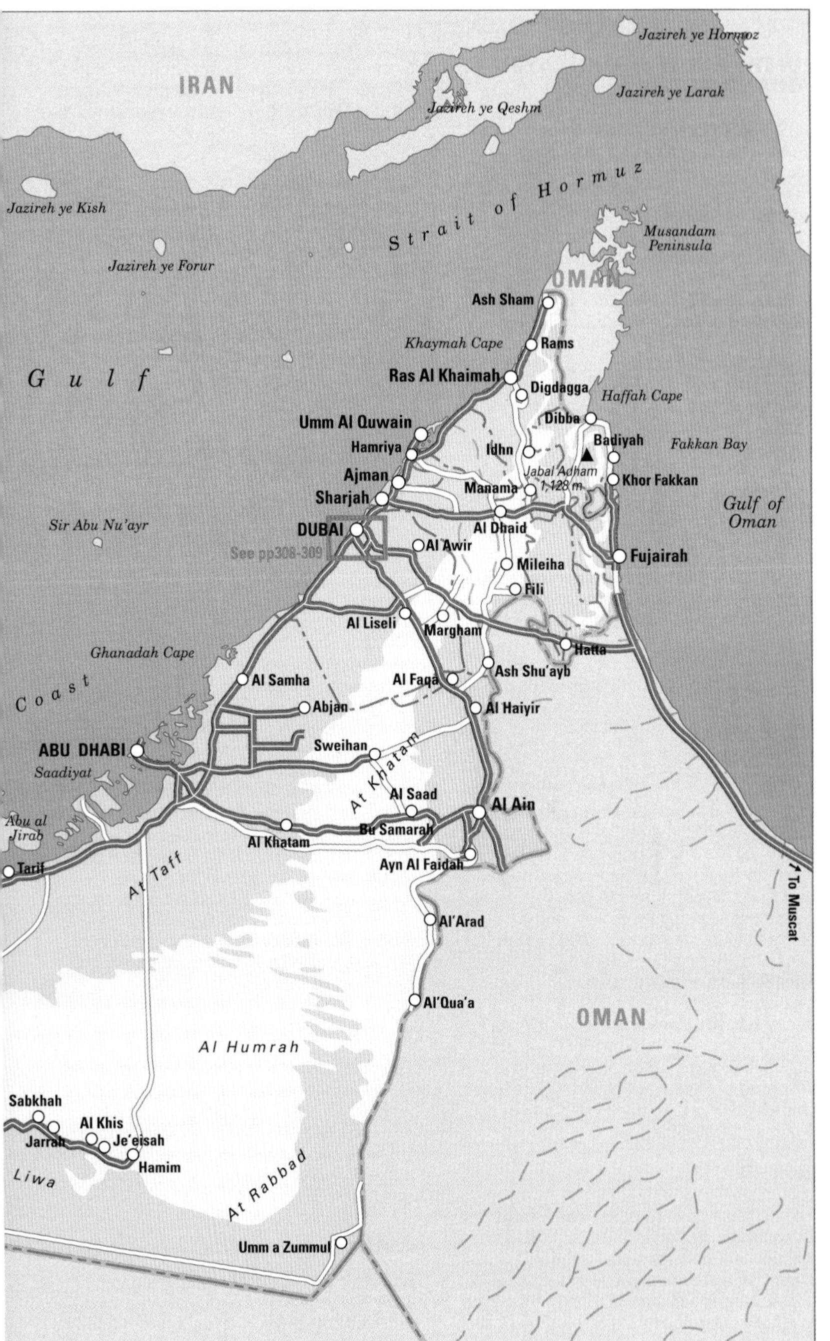

ESCAPES & EXCURSIONS

IN THE KNOW SHEIKH ZAYED GRAND MOSQUE

The **Sheikh Zayed Grand Mosque** (02 441 6444, www.szgmc.ae/en) was designed to 'unite the world', at least in its materials and architecture. More than 3,000 workers employed themes from Italy, Germany, Morocco, India, Turkey and Iran when building the mosque, which is capable of holding almost 41,000 people. The Grand Mosque contains 1,000 columns and 20,000 marble panels inlaid with intricate semi-precious stones. Continuing its superlative theme, the mosque also boasts one of the largest chandeliers ever built and the world's biggest hand-knotted carpet, by Iranian designer Ali Khaliqi, in its main prayer hall. Tours are free of charge, last around an hour and offer some interesting insights into the mosque's history, design and role in the community. Make sure you take ID with you – it's used as a deposit when you 'hire' the compulsory local dress.The mosque is open 9am-10pm Mon-Thur, Sat, Sun; it opens on Fridays in the afternoon after prayers.

Corniche beach (sun lounger Dhs25) is well placed. With six kilometres (four miles) of beautiful sand and views to the other islands, it's also safe for bathing, with plenty of lifeguards on duty. It's worth noting that Corniche beach is split into three sections: two for families and one for singles and groups. **Al Bateen** (sun lounger Dhs50) is another good option, popular among families thanks to its picnic spots and play parks.

Despite the often scorching temperatures, the capital isn't devoid of greenery, with plenty of parks to enjoy during the cooler months. One of the city's most serene spaces is **Baynunah Park** (Bainunah Street, opposite the InterContinental Hotel). This expanse of green has a wilder feel to it than the other more manicured parks around the city. **Khalifa Park** (Eastern Ring Road, near Al Bateen Airport) is one of the biggest in Abu Dhabi, with canals and fountains as well as swimming for women and children. For children, **Khalidiyah Park** (opposite Areej Tower) is always a popular choice.

Yas Island life

In 2006, there was water where **Yas Island** now lies, connecting the mainland to Al Juabail Island. But billions of dollars and thousands of tonnes of sand later, it has been transformed into a shopping and entertainment island and, as such, makes a popular stop for visitors to Abu Dhabi.

Given the amount of money sunk into the Persian Gulf to raise Yas Island from the seabed, it's appropriate that one of its main attractions is **Ferrari World** (02 496 8000, www.ferrariworldabudhabi.com), a Maranello-red theme park with go-karts real and virtual, a miniature Ferrari that whizzes around a suitably shrunken Italy and a high-speed (naturally) rollercoaster. After all that, some water should come as a welcome relief, and there's plenty of it at **Yas Waterworld** (02 414 2000, www.yaswaterworld.com), the country's first sustainable waterpark, where you can take your pick from more than 43 rides and slides.

For something more sedate, take in a round of golf at **Yas Links** (02 810 7710, www.yaslinks.com). The course runs plenty of deals, including rounds paired with meals at the club's restaurants, so check the website for the latest offers.

As an island created for entertainment, it's no surprise that there are plenty of eating and drinking options. **Stills Bar & Brasserie** (Crowne Plaza Yas Island, 02 656 3061) is a good spot for some gourmet pub grub. **Rush** (Yas Viceroy, 055 780 0086) and **O1NE** (Leisure Drive, near Yas Tunnel, 052 788 8111) are popular nightclubs. Or you could take a stroll along Yas Marina: as well as stunning superyachts, you'll find bars and restaurants including **Iris** (055 160 5636), a swish venue filled with beautiful people, and **Stars & Bars** (02 565 0101), a popular sports bar based on the original in Monte Carlo.

For shopping fans, **Yas Mall** (02 414 6401) is a haven of designer outlets, boutique shops and department stores. There are also scores of places to eat and drink, a 20-screen cinema, a family entertainment zone and a hypermarket.

Yas Island also hosts the **Abu Dhabi Grand Prix**, which is arguably the biggest event on the city's calendar. And it's not just motor racing. In fact, the on-track action tends to take a backseat to the off-track festivities. F1 weekend in the capital has become synonymous with some of the biggest names in music rocking the Yas Marina Circuit. The likes of the Who, Kylie Minogue, Jay Z and Muse have performed over the years.

Getting there

The journey from Dubai Marina to Yas Island can take less than an hour by car, making Abu Dhabi the perfect short trip. Dubai and the capital are also well connected by public transport, with the E101 bus departing from Ibn Battuta Metro Station for Abu Dhabi Central Bus Station every 30mins. A single ticket costs Dhs25.

AL AIN

Technically part of the Abu Dhabi emirate but big enough to warrant its own write-up, the Garden City of Al Ain is an oasis – both literally

WILD ABU DHABI

Island life is just a short hop from the city.

Abu Dhabi isn't all shopping and high-end restaurants; there's natural beauty just a short distance from the sprawling city. Much of the emirate's wilderness is on its islands, with each one offering a different experience. **Sir Bani Yas Island** was originally the private retreat and royal nature reserve of Sheikh Zayed bin Sultan Al Nahyan, the former ruler of Abu Dhabi and president of the UAE, and today it's one of the country's most pristine wildlife reserves. It's home to over 10,000 free-roaming animals, including Arabian oryx, gazelles, giraffes, hyenas and cheetahs. And, this being the UAE, the island is also home to a five-star retreat – Desert Islands Resort & Spa by Anantara (02 656 1399, www.desertislands.anantara.com). The island can be accessed from Jebel Dhanna pier, about 210 kilometres (130 miles) west of Abu Dhabi.

Closer to the city is **Al Sammaliah Island**, home to ostriches, emus, lizards, gazelles and wildfowl. It's overseen by the Emirates Heritage Club (02 558 4474); contact them before heading over as the island is private property. Al Sammaliah is just five minutes by powerboat from Al Raha Beach Hotel.

Also near the capital is **Al Futaisi**. This island remains largely undeveloped. Well worth checking out is the tranquil mangrove lagoon, an Arabian fort and a miniature zoo. You can catch the ferry here from Al Bateen Marina.

Sir Bani Yas Island.

and metaphorically – from the sky-piercing buildings and clamour of Dubai. Set in the middle of the peninsula, Al Ain escapes the humidity of the coastal cities, making it a popular weekend escape in the summer.

Steeped in culture and history, Al Ain was also the hometown of the late Sheikh Zayed bin Sultan Al Nahyan, who was the founder of the UAE. His former childhood home is now **Al Ain Palace Museum** (Al Ain Street, 03 751 7755).

It's also worth checking out the many forts and towers in the area. One of the highlights is **Al Qattara Fort**, where recent construction uncovered a large haul of historic artefacts. Visitors can view many of these finds, including pottery, stone and daggers, in the underground exhibition within the **Al Qattara Arts Center** (Al Ain Street, 03 761 8080, www.adach.ae), which is adjacent to the tower.

The emirate's highest peak, Jebel Hafeet, is another big draw and people flock here on the weekends to enjoy the views and the natural hot springs that flow beneath the mountain. Water also bubbles up elsewhere in Al Ain, sustaining the six oases in the city, each of which are listed as a UNESCO World Heritage Site. **Al Ain Oasis** (Al Mutawaa, 03 711 8208) is the largest of the six, with more than 147,000 palm trees, watered by the underground *falaj* irrigation system, where vertical boreholes are connected by gently sloping tunnels, allowing water to flow by gravity to where it's needed most. This ancient system of irrigation was first developed in Persia.

Water also plays its part in making **Wadi Adventure** (Jebel Hafeet, 03 781 8422, www.wadiadventure.ae) an unlikely destination for white-water adventures: this is the first rafting, kayaking and surfing facility in the Middle East and – naturally – it's man-made and about as far from the sea as it's possible to get in the UAE.

For something more serene, visit **Al Ain Zoo**, the country's biggest (Nahyan The First Street, 03 782 8188, www.awpr.ae).

As with the rest of the UAE, the best time to visit Al Ain is during the winter, but the elevation of Jebel Hafeet means that it can be considerably cooler than Dubai during the height of summer.

Eating & drinking

Al Ain isn't known for its nightlife, but if you're looking for a lively atmosphere try **Trader Vic's** (Al Ain Rotana, 03 754 5111, www.rotana.com) for cocktails and decent food. For alfresco Lebanese and Arabic bites, that can be enjoyed with shisha, **Makani** (Hilton Al Ain, 03 768 6666, www.hilton.com) is a good bet.

Where to stay

Perfect for a short getaway, the **Al Ain Rotana** (Al Mutawaa, 03 754 5111, www.rotana.com/alainrotana) has large rooms and chalets, and plenty of facilities such as a gym, squash courts and separate pools for adults and children.

If you're looking to combine your trip with a round of golf, check out the **Hilton Al Ain** (Al Sarooj, 03 768 6666, www.hilton.com), which has a nine-hole course plus plenty of family activities.

Getting there

By car From Dubai, simply take the E66, which will take you straight to the heart of Al Ain.
By taxi A taxi from Dubai is going to set you back between Dhs200 and Dhs250, so it's cheaper and more convenient to rent a car.

AJMAN

Ajman is the smallest emirate in the United Arab Emirates. Although it lies just north of Sharjah, with urban sprawl joining the two cities, it remains a long way from its flashier cousin further south. Old beige low-rise buildings, forts that wear the look of history, and people in no particular rush to get anywhere are commonplace in tiny Ajman.

The perfect introduction to Ajman is a walk along the Corniche, taking in the view of an unbroken stretch of white sand and emerald waters. You can spend hours here, relaxing on the beach or in one of the many shorefront cafés. If you happen to be staying overnight at one of the coastal hotels, you'll have unlimited access to some of the best private beaches in the country.

Sharjah.

For a slice of culture, head to **Ajman Museum** (Al Hosn roundabout, Aziz Street, 06 711 6666). This 18th-century fort was initially the ruler's residence and then used as a police station before finally opening to the public as a museum. It's got a good collection of old weapons and tools, old photographs and reconstructions of Bedouin days gone past.

For anyone interested in snapping up a bargain, a trip to **Ajman Souk** is an absolute must. Found between Al Masafi and Al Dhaid on the E88 road, it features trinkets, handicrafts, carpets, *abayas* and other traditional items and souvenirs. Aside from the goods on offer, the impressive architecture of the market makes the trip worthwhile.

Eating & drinking

For an initiation into the mixed flavours of Zanzibari cuisine, try **Zanzi Bar** (Kempinski Hotel Ajman, 06 714 5555). Further down on the Corniche, there are plenty of charming outdoor cafés that are perfect for watching the sun go down.

Hotels

The five-star **Kempinski Ajman Hotel** (Sheikh Humaid bin Rashid Al Nuaimi Street, 06 714 5555, www.kempinski.com) is a world in itself. There are loads of bars and restaurants, plus a licensed bowling alley. For something a little more affordable, check out the **Ramada Hotel & Suites Ajman** (Sheikh Khalifa bin Zayed Street, 06 740 4666, www.ramadaajman.com). It features an indoor pool, two restaurants and a spa.

Getting there

By bus The E400 goes from Union Square Metro Station in Dubai to Ajman, departing every 30mins and costing Dhs10 for a single ticket.
By car From Dubai, take Sheikh Zayed Road, then Sheikh Rashid Road. Turn on to Al Daid Road at Sharjah Cultural Square and take a left on to Al Wasl Road. Follow this to Ajman.
By taxi It will cost Dhs130-Dhs150 to travel from Dubai to Ajman.

SHARJAH

Only 60 kilometres (40 miles) from the hedonism of Dubai is an altogether different city. Sharjah is a much more conservative place, so much so that alcohol is unavailable. There are also decency laws that prohibit the mixing of unmarried or unrelated men and women, and a fairly restrictive dress code. It has gone down an alternative route to the other emirates and focused on culture, complemented by strong Islamic traditions. And the city has been recognised for its efforts. In 1998, it was crowned Cultural Capital of the Arab World by UNESCO, before being named Islamic Culture Capital of 2014. So it's no surprise there are more museums and galleries here than elsewhere in the UAE.

Sharjah Art Museum is the largest of its kind in the Gulf (Arts Area, Al Shuwaihiyeen, 06 568 8222, www.sharjahmuseums.ae), with a collection focusing on modern and contemporary Arab artists, and also includes some 19th-century orientalist works. The history of settlement in the region is long, and **Sharjah Archaeology Museum** (Helwan, Sheikh Rashid bin Saqr Al Qasimi Road, 06 566 5466, www.sharjahmuseums.ae) has some fascinating displays. Excavations have revealed evidence of human settlements in Sharjah stretching back 125,000 years, and one of the oldest artefacts in the museum is an ivory comb that was found inside an alabaster bowl, which dates to 2200-2000 BC.

Bringing cultural activities rolling up to date, the **Sharjah Classic Cars Museum** (Airport Road, 06 558 0222, www.sharjahmuseums.ae) displays more than 100 of the machines whose

thirst has fuelled development in the UAE and whose roads have transformed the region. Cars on show include a 1915 Dodge Brothers Model 30-35 and a 1969 Mercedes-Benz 600 Pullman.

There's interesting work being done by contemporary Arab artists, and **Maraya Art Centre** (Al Qasba, 06 556 6555, www.maraya.ae) has much of it on display, in curated temporary exhibitions. The centre also runs art workshops for children and adults, and language classes.

To get out of the car and stroll, head to **Sharjah Cultural Square**, lined with rich Islamic architecture, and dominated by a huge sculpture of the Qur'an. The square is the site of Ahmed Bin Hanbal Mosque, the Cultural Centre, the Diwan Al Amiri (Ruler's Court) and Sharjah City Hall.

No visit to Sharjah is complete without being taken to the casbah, or Al Qasba as it is more properly known, with its musical fountain, *abra* rides on the canal, and an array of restaurants. But the most striking attraction is the huge **Eye of the Emirates Wheel** (www.alqasba.ae). This 60-metre (200-foot) Ferris wheel offers views stretching over Sharjah and all the way to Dubai from its air-conditioned cabins.

A short walk from Al Qasba is the Al Majaz Waterfront development, where you can watch the **Sharjah Fountain** (www.almajaz.ae), which shoots water up 100m (300 feet) in the air in time to music. It's also possible to take *abra* tours across the water for scenic views of the city's art venues (www.almajaz.ae).

Eating & drinking

There's plenty of good Arabic food in Sharjah. **Falafil Al Comodor** (opposite Al Majaz Park, 06 553 5280) serves arguably the best falafel in the UAE. If you want something more substantial, **Zahr El-Laymoun** (Al Majaz Waterfront, 06 552 1144, www.zahrel-laymoun.com) deals in succulent kebabs and other grilled Lebanese treats. Seafood fans should check out **Fish Corner** (Al Qasba, 06 556 8884, www.alqasba.ae). Traditional Egyptian cuisine can be found at **Grand Abu Shakra** (Al Qasba, 06 536 5656, www.alqasba.ae).

If you want a drink of something stronger than a mocktail, then you'll have to travel back to Dubai or further north to Ajman. The **Kempinski Hotel Ajman** (Sheikh Humaid bin Rashid Al Nuaimi Street, 06 714 5555, www.kempinski.com) is a 20-minute taxi ride from the centre of Sharjah and has bars enough to satisfy the thirstiest of visitors.

Where to stay

Due to its proximity to Dubai, there really isn't much need to stay in Sharjah overnight. But if you do fancy an overnight break, try the **Radisson Blu Resort** (Corniche Road, 06 565 7777, www.radissonblu.com). This five-star property has a private beach, a range of watersports, and many restaurants, including a Canton Chinese one.

Fujairah.

Getting there

By bus There are a number of buses operating between Dubai and Sharjah. Buses depart from Union Metro Station, Al Sabkha, Satwa, Al Ghubaiba Bus Station, Deira City Station and Abu Hail, heading towards Al Jubail Bus Station in Sharjah. A one-way ticket costs Dhs10.
By car It couldn't be simpler to drive to Sharjah from Dubai. Just get on the Sheikh Zayed Road and follow the very clear signs to Sharjah.
By taxi A taxi from Dubai Marina to Sharjah Corniche costs around Dhs120.

FUJAIRAH

Situated along the east coast of the UAE, facing into the Gulf of Oman, is Fujairah. Unlike its six fellow emirates, this part of the country is almost entirely mountainous, with spectacular scenery.

Geographically, Fujairah is slightly confusing, with the region of Dibba, in particular, having less than clear borders. Due to its slightly troubled history, Dibba is split into three parts under three different jurisdictions: Fujairah, Sharjah and Musandam, Oman. In this chapter, mentions of Dibba will refer to the part ruled by Fujairah, known as Dibba Al Fujairah, which is in the north of the emirate.

In a region where the sound of construction is all but omnipresent, Fujairah presents a welcome relief, with many of its attractions rooted in the history of the area. There are many archaeological sites, castles, forts, watch towers and mosques. In fact, Fujairah is home to the UAE's oldest mosque – **Al Bidyah Mosque** (Fujairah-Dibba Road), which was built over 500 years ago.

Another important site is **Fujairah Fort** (Fujairah city, opposite Ruler's Court). Believed to have been built in 1640, the fort is a mud-brick landmark that sits on the hill above the city, 20 metres (65 feet) above sea level and surrounded by date orchards and the remains of old buildings. For many years, this was the only stone building on the entire Fujairah coast. Although the British caused considerable damage when their gunboats opened fire on it in the early 1900s, the fort has since been restored and is definitely worth a visit. If you're still craving history after your visit, the **Fujairah Museum** (Dhs2 adults, Dhs1 children) is located just south of the fort.

But the past has a way of throwing strange customs into the present, and few can be stranger than seeing bullfights on the Arabian peninsula. The Fujairah version, bull butting, doesn't involve swords or matadors. Instead, two bulls face off against each other, locking horns and shoving until the loser is pushed to the edge of the arena. The Portuguese, whose own version of bullfighting is less bloody than the Spanish, are thought to have introduced the custom to the region in the 16th century but it was embraced by the locals, who made it their own over the centuries. The contest attracts large and vocal crowds, with few Western faces on view. Bull butting takes place at 5pm on Fridays, with a break for Ramadan, next to Café Maria on Corniche Road in Fujairah city.

Diving and watersports are another big attraction, as the sea life in the Gulf of Oman is more diverse than that of the Arabian Gulf. **Snoopy Island** (named after the cartoon dog, because it resembles him, if you're far away, and squinting) is a huge favourite for snorkellers and divers. Located just off Al Aqah Beach, it's an easy swim from the mainland, during which you'll be accompanied by a colourful array of marine life. On a good day you can also expect to see sharks, eels, angelfish and even turtles. For those who don't fancy the swim, kayaks are available for rent.

Eating & drinking

While the dining scene in Fujairah is fairly casual, you'll still find plenty of pleasant places to try. Overlooking the dive site of the same name, **Dibba Rock Restaurant** (Royal Beach Alfaqeet Hotel & Resort, 09 244 9444, www.royalbeach.ae) is hard to beat when it comes to location, and serves up international cuisine. For something a bit more romantic, head to **Waves** (Fujairah

Rotana Resort & Spa, 09 244 9888, www.rotana.com) for a candlelit dinner on the beach. For those wanting to up the romance quotient, a butler and roses are potential extras. Staying in the Fujairah Rotana, there's **Sharkey's** beach bar, which is good for a laid-back evening of alfresco cocktails. But Fujairah isn't simply about chilling out on the sand. **Bliss** (Iberotel Miramar Al Aqah Beach Resort, 09 244 9994, www.miramaralaqah.com) is one of the emirate's fanciest clubs.

Where to stay

Although it's more than 30 years old, the **Hilton Fujairah Resort** (Al Faseel Street, 09 222 2411, www.hilton.com) is a reliable favourite, located just outside Fujairah city. A relaxed Spanish vibe permeates the place. There are 104 rooms, suites and villas, all with balconies.

On the way to Dibba, you'll come across the **Le Méridien Al Aqah Beach Resort** (Dibba Road, 09 244 9000, www.lemeridien-alaqah.com). This family-centred complex offers snorkelling, diving, kayaking and parasailing.

In Dibba itself is **Royal Beach Hotel** (Suwayfah, 09 244 9444, www.royalbeach.ae). It provides comfortable rooms or three-bedroom chalets, and has its own private beach, swimming pool and kitchen, while not costing too much.

Getting there

By bus The E700 runs from Union Square Metro Station to Fujairah city. It departs once every hour and a single ticket costs Dhs20.

IN THE KNOW
SPOOKY STORIES

Speak to locals, and you may hear stories of the *djinn* that haunt the buildings of the abandoned fishing village of Jazirat Al Hamra. But this isn't the only spooky spot in the emirate. Al Qasimi Palace (Sheikh Rashed bin Said Road, Al Dhait North) was built in the late 1980s and is said to have been abandoned after many strange occurrences: furniture being thrown around, the sound of a woman screaming and sightings of little 'children' staring at passers-by. These strange goings-on were the inspiration behind 2013 Tobe Hooper-directed horror movie *Djinn*, which was filmed entirely in the UAE, including at Jazirat Al Hamra. In the film, an Emirati couple move into an apartment building in Ras Al Khaimah, built on the site of the former fishing village. The move proves to be a terrible mistake.

By car To reach Fujairah from Dubai, take the E11 through Sharjah and follow it to Dhaid. Continue through Dhaid until Masafi, where you turn right onto the E89, which will take you to the centre of Fujairah city. For Dibba, follow the same route and then signs for Dibba. Dibba is about 2hrs 30mins by car from Dubai.

RAS AL KHAIMAH

As the northernmost emirate in the UAE, Ras Al Khaimah aptly translates as 'top of the tent'. It was the last of the emirates to join the UAE, eventually becoming part of the region on 11 February 1972.

The emirate has long been famous for its rolling sand dunes and desert experiences, but is currently undergoing vast development in order to compete with its more tourism-savvy southern sisters. One of the most talked-about schemes is Al Marjan, a collection of four islands that officials hope to turn into an entertainment hub based on Ibiza and Miami.

But that's still in the future, and for now Ras Al Khaimah offers a rare glimpse into the past, with easily accessible sites of historical importance. One of the most striking is **Jazirat Al Hamra** (off the E11, next to Al Jazeera Port), an abandoned village of crumbling 19th-century buildings. But for one day a year, Jazirat Al Hamra returns to life: on the National Day (2 December), the village's former residents return for a reunion party.

For a look even further back in time, take a trip to **Shimal Archaeological Site** (near the modern village of Shimal, eight kilometres (five miles) north-west of Ras Al Khaimah city), which is the largest site of pre-Islamic archaeology in the emirate. Visit the cemetery and a medieval fortress known as the 'Palace of the Queen of Sheba'. At the cemetery, there are approximately 250 tombs of monumental size. Since 1976, British and German archaeologists have uncovered a variety of impressive artefacts at the site that are now on display in the **National Museum of Ras Al Khaimah** (Al Hisn Road, 07 233 3411).

Overlooking Shimal is **Dhayah Fort** (off Al Rams Road, 15 kilometres (9.5 miles) north-west of Ras Al Khaimah city), a scenic location with wonderful views of the mountains and sea. The fort was a strategic military fortification that played a major role in the history of the UAE.

The heat renders outdoor sport difficult in the emirates, but there is one breed of competitor that revels in the heat: camels. Camel racing is the traditional sport of the UAE and the place to see it is **Al Sawan Camel Track** (off the E18, Digdaga), with races usually held on Friday and Saturday from 6.30am to 8.30am between September and April. To make the experience more immersive, jump into your 4X4 and race around the track alongside the animals.

Golf has become increasingly popular in Ras Al Khaimah over the past few years. **Al Hamra Golf Club** (07 244 7474, www.alhamragolf.com) has an 18-hole championship course and a more manageable par-3 academy course, as well as a Belgian Beer Café for afterwards.

Eating & drinking

The arrival of the five-star behemoths has transformed Ras Al Khaimah's dining scene. For steak, the New York-inspired **Lexington Grill** in the Waldorf Astoria (Vienna Street, 07 203 5555) is hard to beat; afterwards head to the sophisticated **Cigar Bar** or intimate lounge **17 Squared**.

For excellent Lebanese dishes and live Arabic music, try **Al Jazeera** (Hilton Al Hamra Beach & Golf Resort, 07 244 6666) or, if you're craving Indian, **Passage to Asia** (Hilton Ras Al Khaimah Resort & Spa, 07 228 8844).

Where to stay

There are some undeniably striking hotels in Ras Al Khaimah. The **Waldorf Astoria** (Vienna Street, 07 203 5555, www.waldorfastoria3.hilton.com) opened in 2013 and quickly established itself as one of the country's leading properties, with 346 luxurious rooms and a fantastic spa. The **Cove Rotana Resort & Spa** (E11 motorway, Al Dhait South, 07 206 6000, www.rotana.com) is set in a beautiful location, with cobbled paths and Nubian-styled villas interspersed with lagoons, looking out to the Arabian Gulf. If you're looking to get away from everything, **Banyan Tree Al Wadi** (Al Mazraa, 07 206 7777, www.banyantree.com) is the perfect retreat – a desert resort, hidden among the dunes.

Getting there

By car From Dubai, take the E11 towards Sharjah; Ras Al Khaimah is well signposted. Stay on the E11, which will take you straight into the city. It takes around an hour to reach Ras Al Khaimah from Dubai International Airport.

UMM AL QUWAIN

A trip to Umm Al Quwain is full of contrasts. You'll see historic forts dotted around the landscape, an old harbour overlooking the dhow building yard, and coral stone houses depicting ancient architecture. But there's more to Umm Al Quwain than this. It is also home to a slightly bizarre waterpark, a holiday resort that freely sells alcohol and a motor-racing circuit where you can get behind the wheel.

But let's start with the traditional side of the emirate. Formerly the emirate's police headquarters, **Umm Al Quwain Fort and Museum** (Old Town Area) has an attractive *majlis* room with wooden balconies and high ceilings. There is also a great collection of antiques, jewellery and weapons.

Umm Al Quwain also has some natural attractions worth seeking out. To the east of the peninsula are eight sandy islands – Al Sinniyah,

Old Muscat.

Jazirat Al Ghallah, Al Keabe, Al Sow, Al Qaram, Al Humaidi, Al Chewria and Al Harmala – surrounded by a dense forest of mangrove trees. The islands can be spotted from the old town, and you can see fishermen navigating along Madaar Creek (which runs between the islands) looking for a catch. Afterwards, visit the Old Harbour, where craftsmen still make dhows in the traditional manner, and the surrounding coral stone houses are a great example of the original architecture in the emirate.

Now for the gaudy side of Umm Al Quwain. Contrasting with the quaint, quiet history of the emirate is **Dreamland Aqua Park** (06 768 1888, www.dreamlanduae.com). Opened in 1997, it has more than 30 wet and dry rides and slides, a spot for camping, and a huge pool bar. A short drive from Dreamland Aqua Park is **Emirates Motorplex** (06 768 1166, www.motorplex.ae), a place dedicated to burning off large amounts of the petrol drilled from the UAE in the pursuit of car and motorcycle racing.

Eating & drinking

You'll struggle to find fine dining in Umm Al Quwain, with the offerings far more casual than those in Dubai. **Beach Bar** at Flamingo Beach Resort (06 765 0000, www.flamingoresort.ae) is a bit rough around the edges, but is in a prime location next to the sand, while **Aquarius** at Barracuda Beach Resort (06 768 1555, www.barracuda.ae) serves up international fare.

Where to stay

Again, five-star luxury is hard to find in this emirate, but there are some pleasant places to stay. **Umm Al Quwain Beach Hotel** (Al Muroor Road, Exit 90, 06 766 6647, www.uaqbeachotel.com) is worth a stopover if only for its expansive sea views and spacious swimming pool. The **Barracuda Beach Resort** (06 768 1555, www.barracuda.ae) may be best known for its large off-licence, but it also has a variety of interesting accommodation options, plus a pristine beach, swimming pools and a jacuzzi.

Getting there

By car To avoid the chaos of Sharjah's road system, it's probably best to get on the Sheikh Mohammed Bin Zayed Road out of Dubai and keep heading north towards Ras Al Khaimah. Umm Al Quwain will be well signposted. Alternatively, Emirates Road will also take you in the same direction.

By taxi It'll be expensive. Expect to pay Dhs220 or more for a one-way journey. Hiring a car is a better option.

Oman

Although the Sultanate of Oman is the UAE's neighbour, it has a distinctive culture and vast areas of wilderness, making the crossing of the border more than worthwhile.

While Dubai and Abu Dhabi have their record-breaking skyscrapers and mega projects, Oman has taken a different approach to development. Without the oil wealth of the UAE, the sultanate has had to pursue different strategies. When Sultan Qaboos bin Said deposed his father in a bloodless coup in 1970, the country had only ten kilometres (six miles) of paved roads and two hospitals. Today, it's a modern nation, where you'll find an intriguing mix of traditional culture and forward-thinking developments.

Located south of the UAE, Oman is a huge country that stretches down the south-eastern coast of the Arabian Peninsula, with the exclave of Musandam (*see p240*) to the north of the UAE also ruled by the sultanate. It's more than 1,000 kilometres (600 miles) from the capital, Muscat, to the city of Salalah in the south close to the Yemen border, with the landscape marked by the jagged Hajar mountain range and the eastern encroachment of the Empty Quarter desert. But you don't have to venture far to get a taste of a fascinating country.

MUSCAT

The Omani capital runs at its own pace, which is much slower than Dubai and Abu Dhabi. Another striking difference from the cities of the UAE is the lack of skyscrapers – the tallest building in Muscat is the ten-storey Sheraton Hotel building. Instead, low whitewashed buildings are backed by the toffee-coloured Hajar mountain range on one side and the glistening Gulf of Oman on the other.

One significant splash of grandeur in the city is the **Sultan Qaboos Grand Mosque** (Ghubra). Constructed from Indian sandstone, the mosque is ornately decorated with white and grey marble panelling; it has the world's second largest hand-woven carpet, and the giant dome is made of stained glass triangles. Make sure you dress conservatively, and women should remember to bring a scarf to cover their hair.

The heart of the city is **Muttrah** and the area commonly referred to as **Old Muscat**, which was the original walled city of the capital. On cooler days, it's possible to walk between these two areas, starting on the sweeping Muttrah Corniche, with its views of dhows bobbing on the bay and the 16th-century Muttrah Fort perched up on the jagged rocks overlooking the harbour. The Corniche is also home to **Muttrah Souk**, which, in its architecture, ambience and alleys, gives a sense of a traditional Arabian

KEEPING OMAN BEAUTIFUL

Preserving the Sultanate's natural environment.

The Sultanate of Oman is home to vast areas of beautiful wilderness and, in order to help preserve its natural good looks, the country's travel industry is developing a keen interest in environmental matters and community responsibility.

High up in the rugged mountains near the historic town of Nizwa is **Alila Jabal Akhdar** (+968 2534 4200, www.alilahotels.com/jabalakhdar), a resort that has been designed to blend into the environment and take as little as possible from it. Alila Jabal Akhdar was constructed to Leadership in Energy & Environmental Design (www.usgbc.org/leed) principles, using traditional Omani building techniques and materials.

Six Senses Zighy Bay (*see p241*), meanwhile, runs a number of programmes at its resort in Musandam, such as funding for modern irrigation networks in the arid region and a project to protect the stunning reefs around the peninsula.

On the Ash Sharqiyah coast of Oman, about three hours south of Muscat, the **Ras Al Jinz Turtle Reserve** (+968 9655 0606, www.rasaljinz-turtlereserve.com) is helping to protect the habitat of the sea turtles that nest on the beaches. The reserve conducts guided excursions every night to view the turtles and witness the nesting process. There's simple accommodation available in rooms and eco-tents.

marketplace. While the old traders have been largely displaced by vendors of tourist tat, the surroundings and ambience still convey something of a lost world and there are still a few bargains to be found. Most shops are open 9.30am-1pm, 4.30-10.30pm Mon-Thur, Sat, Sun; 4.30-10.30pm Fri.

A pleasant stroll along the Corniche will take you to Riyam Park, famous for its giant incense burner. From the park, there's a great view of Muttrah Fort, the Corniche and the sea.

Keep going past Riyam Park and you'll get to Old Muscat. Time your visit here for a cooler part of the day, for the best way to explore this area is on foot, when you can wander amid the winding streets. There are a couple of museums in the area, the pick of which is the **Bait Al Zubair** (Al Sidyah Street, +968 2473 6688, www.baitalzubairmuseum.com), which displays Omani handicrafts, model boats, ornaments, jewellery and antique weapons. Next door to Bait Al Zubair is **Gallery Sarah** (+968 2208 4747, www.gallerysarah.com), which hosts bi-monthly exhibitions for up-and-coming local and established international artists. It also sells a range of paintings and photographs.

Also keep an eye out for the blue, white and gold Al Alam Palace in Old Muscat, which Sultan Qaboos uses for greeting dignitaries. It isn't open to the public, but the approach to its multi-coloured façade is a masterclass in the architecture of state aggrandisement.

Eating & drinking

Muscat doesn't have many high-end dining destinations, but you can still find a good meal. **Mumtaz Mahal** (near Qurum Park, +968 2460 5907) serves excellent Indian food and is convenient for drinks with a view at **Left Bank** (+968 2469 3699) – just nip across the car park. Some way out of town, but with a wide variety of restaurants, is **Shangri-La Barr Al Jissah Resort & Spa**. We recommend **Al Tanoor** (+968 2477 6565) for its beachside terrace.

Where to stay

Oman is positioning itself at the higher end of the tourism market, and the standard (and price) of hotels reflects this. You'll have no trouble finding a five-star property, such as the spectacular **Chedi** (Al Khuwair, +968 2452 4400, www.ghmhotels.com) with its infinity pools and beachside setting. A little less grand, but perfectly comfortable, is the **Crowne Plaza Muscat** (Qurum, +968 2466 0660), on a hill overlooking Qurum Beach, and the **InterContinental Muscat** (Shatti Al Qurum, +968 2468 0000), a short walk from Shatti Beach.

Getting there

By car The drive from Dubai to Muscat takes around four hours. Follow the E44 towards Hatta on the border. From there, it's a fairly straightforward road to Muscat.

By air Flydubai, Emirates and Oman Air operate direct flights between Dubai and Muscat, which take less than an hour.

MUSANDAM

Situated at the northern tip of the Arabian Peninsula, above and surrounded by the UAE but ruled by Oman, Musandam is perhaps the most scenically spectacular region in the entire Gulf. Life on the Musandam Peninsula moves at an even slower pace than it does in the rest of the country, and there are plenty of deserted beaches on which to spread a towel before taking a leisurely swim in the azure waters lapping at the shore. And located only three hours or so from Dubai (depending on the border crossing), it's the perfect spot for an overnighter or a day excursion.

Musandam is sometimes called the 'Norway of the Middle East'. While that might sound like typical tourist-PR language, a trip by 4x4 to **Khor Al'Najd**, a beautiful waterway surrounded by rocky hills, suggests that the claims are not entirely misplaced – although there's not quite so much greenery on view. A dhow cruise through these waterways and channels is the best way to appreciate the wild, bleak scenery; Khasab Travel & Tours, based in the Atana Khasab hotel, can arrange cruises and tours (+968 2673 0464, www.khasabtours.com).

While the hills tumbling down to the sea are largely bare of life, the opposite is true underwater. Reefs fringe Musandam, providing

Musandam.

excellent dive sites, and whale sharks are often spotted between May and October. Visibility is variable, but usually between ten and 15 metres (30-50 feet). **Extra Divers Musandam** (www.musandam-diving.com, +968 2673 0501) runs courses and daily trips. The Strait of Hormuz is thick with plankton, which means it's rich in fish life. And where there are lots of fish, there will be dolphins, too, year round. **Dolphin Travel & Tourism** (+968 2673 0659, www.dolphintour.net) offers dhow cruises in search of cetaceans.

The capital of Musandam is **Khasab**, situated at the northern end of the peninsula. It was a purely maritime city until the construction of the coastal highway, and the port is still the main area of interest. While the hills around Khasab might be barren, the sea teems with life, as seen when fishermen cast their nets, while Iranian smugglers continue to unload goats from camouflaged boats as they have done for over 200 years. **Khasab Castle** (+968 2458 8820), overlooking the harbour, was once the eastern coast's main line of defence against invaders. It was built in the 16th century, with the central tower believed to be even older. There's a mini museum within its walls.

Eating & drinking

A good, cheap and cheerful option in Khasab, serving grills and juices as well as Indian fare, is **Al Shamaliah Grill Restaurant** (+968 2673 1147). It's mostly local men dining at this establishment, which can be found on the left from the main mosque by the souk. For drinks, there really are very few options. **Darts Bar** (+968 2673 0777), an English-themed pub in the Atana Khasab hotel, is a small and quiet watering hole, and by far the best option in town.

Where to stay

In Khasab town, there are two good options from an Omani hotel chain: Atana Khasab and Atana Musandam. **Atana Khasab** (+968 2673 0777, www.atanahotels.com) is situated slightly to the north of the town, while the unlicensed **Atana Musandam** (+968 2673 0888, www.atanahotels.com) is close to the port. Further south in Musandam is **Six Senses Zighy Bay** (+968 2673 5555, www.sixsenses.com) near Zighy village. You can arrive at this hideaway by 4x4 along a mountain road, speedboat or by paragliding in, before enjoying the resort's elegant sophistication and stunning panoramas.

Getting there

By car Driving from Dubai, follow the Sheikh Mohammed Bin Zayed Road north, past Sharjah and through Ras Al Khaimah. The border crossing is about half an hour's drive out of Ras Al Khaimah. You'll need to pay Dhs35 for an exit stamp, and OMR5 for the Omani visa. Make sure you have the required car insurance for Oman as well. From the border, it's 38 kilometres (24 miles) to Khasab.

In Context

History

From sleepy backwater to soaring metropolis in record-breaking time.

With its gleaming skyscrapers, love of modernity and apparent lack of anything more than ten years' old, you'd be forgiven for thinking that Dubai is a mere child of a city, albeit one undergoing an incredible growth spurt. Although it's true that the city that headline writers know and love only really took shape during the last decade, settlements dating from the early fifth and sixth centuries have been found in what is now the modern suburb of Jumeirah. These relics indicate that with the advent of Islam, and the rule of the Umayyad and the Abbasid dynasties, Dubai was already established as a stop-off point for the caravans serving Iraq.

Sheikh Rashid Al Maktoum, Sheikh Mohammed Al Maktoum & Sheikh Maktoum Al Maktoum with legal advisor Adi Bitar, 1968.

TAMING THE GULF

Until recently, the emirate hasn't been very good at preserving its historic sites. The almost hysterical construction boom that began in the 1990s, and which went into overdrive in 2003, has morphed Dubai into a bustling metropolis, welding together Arab and Western cultures, sometimes successfully, other times awkwardly, but almost always at the cost of its traditional architecture and old buildings. Consequently, there are precious few mementoes of Dubai's more distant past.

It was the lure of pearl trading that really put Dubai on the global map; Venetian jeweller Gasparo Balbi made the first written reference to 'Dibei' in 1580, during a search of the East to uncover a lucrative source of the precious jewels.

Strategically located on a ten-kilometre (six-mile) creek, Dubai started its remarkable evolution from small, sleepy fishing village to dynamic city some time during the 18th century. The town was wedged between the two powerful clans that held sway over the lower Gulf – the Bani Yas of Liwa Oasis, who went on to settle in Abu Dhabi, the modern capital of the UAE; and the Qawasim, based in the northern emirates and parts of what would become Oman.

The Qawasim's powerful navy had already triggered the ire of the British Empire's ruling classes, which led to the area becoming known as the 'Pirate Coast' owing to the agile, armed Arab dhows that plundered ships from the East India Trading Company. The disruption to British commercial interests prompted a show of superior naval power that brought the ruling families of this part of the Arabian coastline to their knees. Britain, fearing attempts from Russia and France to challenge its dominance of the region, then signed exclusivity treaties with the leaders of the Trucial States, offering protection and non-interference in local politics on the condition that leaders didn't even correspond with other global powers. Dubai and the rest of the Trucial Coast were now firmly within the sphere of British influence.

MAKTOUM RULE

In 1833, the era of Maktoum family rule began, probably as a result of an internal quarrel among the Bani Yas of Abu Dhabi, when violent conduct on the part of its leader, Sheikh Khalifa, prompted the emigration of around 800 members of the Al Bu Falasah branch of the tribe. There was little resistance in Dubai to Obaid bin Said and Maktoum bin Butti, who took over the then village-sized settlement along the Creek. Following Obaid's death a few years later, Maktoum took the reins of power, ushering in the bloodline that continues to rule Dubai today. The Maktoums based themselves in Shindagha, which provided easy access to the sources of Dubai's wealth: the Gulf for pearling and fishing, and the Creek for trade. In 1820, Mohammed bin Hazza, then ruler of Dubai, signed the trading village's first preliminary truce with London, all too aware of the superior manpower of neighbouring Abu Dhabi and the Qawasim, who controlled much of the northern emirates and what is now Oman.

Under the protection of the British navy, which helped to stamp out the constant disruptions to trade caused by raids among the various tribes along the Trucial Coast, Dubai concentrated on making money. Like the other city ports that later formed the United Arab Emirates, Dubai evolved around its creek, an inlet from the sea. And like the other creeks along the northern coast, Dubai's creek suffered from sandbars formed at its entrance by strong tides but at least it was much longer than those of its neighbours, paving the way for the cargo ships that would make Dubai its fortune. Because the waves were pacified by sandbars, the pearling industry thrived, and its wares were exported to India and Europe. Trade with India and Persia encouraged more foreign traders to open up shop in the city port; the town was already developing its reputation as being not only open for business, but a place that warmly welcomed non-Arabs to take their share.

In the mid-19th century, Shindagha may have been the preserve of around 250 Arab homes, but the neighbouring Bur Dubai community was the base for almost 100 houses belonging to Indian traders. Across the Creek, Deira boasted 1,600 compounds, housing Arabs, Persians and Baluchis from what is now Pakistan. Deira souk was also thriving, with around 350 shops.

BUDDING DUBAI

It was the liberal, open-minded Maktoum bin Hashar, whose rule began in 1894, who capitalised on Dubai's emergence as a business and commercial centre. In the late 19th century, Dubai exempted almost half the men working in the pearling industry from taxes. Although more divers worked the pearl banks in Dubai than in any other Trucial State, the ruler ended up receiving only half the revenue of neighbouring Abu Dhabi.

No matter: Dubai's population exploded. As the pearl industry brought more and more wealth to the town, Sheikh Maktoum implemented business-oriented policies that attracted traders from Lingah, the Persian port on the other side of the Gulf. Run by the Qawasim family, Lingah had, through the 1800s, acted as the main entry point for goods coming into the Gulf. The Persians, desperate for tax revenue, wrested control of the port from the Arabs at the turn of the century, replacing Arab officials with Persians and then Belgians, whose rigid bureaucracy and high tariffs persuaded merchants to head off in search of cheaper trade environments on the Arab side of the Gulf.

At the beginning of the 20th century, Sheikh Maktoum made Dubai a free zone by abolishing commercial taxes. He also courted the big players in the Persian warehousing trade, offering cheap land to important Indian and Persian traders. As he attracted these trade giants, others followed. In the first two decades of the 20th century, Dubai's population doubled to around 20,000, rapidly catching up with Sharjah, its larger neighbour and sometime trade rival.

Traders who had reckoned on a temporary sojourn in Dubai settled in the city once it became clear that taxes and regulations in Persia were there to stay. The pearling industry was now booming. Many people emigrated from the Persian district of Bastak, part of the Arab-dominated province of Lars, naming their newfound home on the Creek after their homeland; Bastakia soon became another thriving commercial area.

Sheikh Maktoum's power rose with the fortunes of his city state. He began the process of building bridges between the rival sheikhdoms of the coast, calling a meeting of the Trucial leaders in 1905 that foreshadowed the creation of the federation that was to be agreed nearly 70 years later.

THE BUBBLE BURSTS

After years of growing prosperity, Dubai and the rest of the Gulf fell prey to the worldwide recession of the 1930s, a warning to leaders that the trade-based city's fortunes would ebb and flow with the tide of global economic prosperity. The pearling industry first became a victim of the weak international demand for luxury goods, and then the Japanese discovery of cultured pearls finished it off, throwing thousands of pearl fishermen out of work. In the final years of the trade, financiers were taking up to 36 per cent annual interest on the loans that captains needed to fit out boats and hire staff. As the pearling industry declined, traders redoubled their efforts in black market deals with Persia, where tariffs continued to soar far higher than in those ports on the Arabian Peninsula.

The pearling industry continued to decline. Dubaians with Persian connections built up their illicit cargo trade, making up for the city's lost revenue, but the increasing financial inequities between the traders and the recently unemployed Arab pearl divers amplified societal pressures. Further north in Kuwait, yearnings for political reform influenced the setting up of a parliament, giving the country the most developed political system in the Gulf.

Mirroring growing unease within Dubai society, splits within the royal family also emerged. The ruler's cousin, Mani bin Rashid, led the reform movement that challenged the ruling family's autocratic rule. Domestic slaves came closer to freedom, not because the British decided to enforce their ban on trading slaves, but because owners could no longer afford them. It wasn't until after World War II that the UK government started to enforce general manumission after having called a halt to the trading of slaves within the Gulf states a century earlier.

Against this background of social flux, events turned violent in October 1938. Sheikh Saeed and his followers set up their base in Bur Dubai, while his cousins lined up against the ruler across the Creek in Deira. After mediation from neighbouring sheikhs and the British political agent, or colonial ambassador, in Bahrain, Sheikh Saeed agreed to the setting up of a consultative council or *majlis* ('place of sitting'), heading up a cohort of 15 members, all of whom were proposed by leading members of the community who theoretically had the power to veto his decisions.

Sheikh Saeed was a reluctant leader, and only attended the first few sessions, smarting at a system in which his office was allocated an eighth of the national budget, the remainder earmarked for the *majlis*'s projects. He still controlled the treasury, and was hesitant to open up the state coffers for the council's projects, such as building state-run schools for the general populace, regulating the customs service and its payroll, adjusting tariffs, and setting up a council of merchants to oversee the city-state's expanding commerce.

Six months after the council's foundation, Sheikh Saeed ordered loyal Bedouin to storm and dissolve it. A strong believer in benign autocratic rule, he suspected that some of his royal rivals were exploiting the *majlis* for their own benefit. Although short-lived, Dubai's six-month flirtation with democracy nonetheless had lasting implications at the highest levels. It sounded the political death knell for Sheikh Saeed; he devolved most of his authority to his son, Sheikh Rashid, who in time initiated many of the ideas of civic development proposed by the council's members.

POST-WAR DEVELOPMENT

Although spared the horrors that Europe and Asia endured during World War II, Dubai still struggled during those six tough years. Trade was brought to a near standstill, and short supplies of rice and sugar caused hunger to grip parts of the city. The British government, which was landing seaplanes in the Creek throughout the conflict, imported food supplies that were to be rationed among the population. Never ones to miss a money-spinning trick, Dubai's traders began buying up some of these supplies and smuggling them to Iran's black market, where shortages were even more pressing.

Malnutrition was an even greater issue in the countryside, which was still ruled by autonomous nomadic tribes and where contacts with the coastal regions could be difficult. There was almost constant warfare as the tribes fought for rations, and the leaders of Abu Dhabi and Dubai argued over the boundary between their territories. Open warfare between the two distant relatives, as well as among their allied and rival tribes of the hinterland, continued after World War II until the high level of casualties from Bedouin raids and counter-raids prompted townsfolk and tribesmen to demand peace in 1948. The British authorities took it upon themselves to research the boundary dispute and draw the new frontier – London's first direct intervention in the internal politics of the Trucial States.

DUBAI STRIKES OIL

Although trade remained at the core of Dubai's development, a revolutionary new prospect came the Trucial States' way in the early 1950s: oil. For a couple of decades, most petroleum engineers had concluded that large deposits would be found somewhere along the Trucial Coast. After all, massive reserves had been found across the Middle East, and particularly in the Arabian Peninsula and the Gulf. Oil had first been discovered in Iran in 1908; Bahrain had started significant exports in 1936; and on the eve of World War II, neighbouring Saudi Arabia had found the first of its huge reservoirs. Companies began to explore across the region, frantically searching for more deposits of black gold. Petroleum Development (Trucial Coast), a British-owned company, won the concession to search for oil across the Trucial States and Oman.

But the war put a stop to the exploration, condemning the emirates to more years of poverty, and encouraging thousands of locals to emigrate to neighbouring Kuwait and Saudi Arabia to work on the massive post-war oil development projects there. Although a consortium formed by British Petroleum and France's Total found commercially viable oil deposits off the coast of Abu Dhabi in 1958, progress was limited in Dubai's onshore and offshore exploration blocks.

COMMERCIAL WHEELS TURN

Nevertheless, Dubai sought to capitalise on the massive trade opportunities brought by oil companies. Mortgaging Dubai with a huge loan from oil-rich Saudi Arabia and Kuwait of around Dhs3.1 million, an amount that far outstripped the city's yearly income, Sheikh Rashid had the Creek dredged by an Australian firm. The ambitious project, which allowed vessels of up to 500 tonnes to anchor there, greatly increased shipping capacity. The emirate's trade levels jumped by 20 per cent, outpacing the growth in neighbouring Sharjah, which had been snapping at Dubai's heels. Gold smuggling, which peaked in 1970, contributed to the new surge in business. The 3.5 per cent import levies imposed on dhows and steamers docking along its wharfage became the emirate's biggest revenue earner after the war.

After seeing off Sharjah's maritime trade competition, Sheikh Rashid also took on his neighbour's airport. Sheikh Sultan of Sharjah had started levying taxes on gold arriving at Sharjah airport, which grew commercially on the back of the Royal Air Force base there.

Offshore oil installation.

In 1960, Sheikh Rashid opened an airport, little more than an airstrip made from the hard sand found in Dubai's salt flats, which he expanded a few years later as demand for weekly flights to the UK grew. An open skies policy allowed any airline to use the airport at a cheaper cost than any other in the region, triggering its eventual rise as an international passenger and freight hub.

Before then, though, Dubai struck black gold. In 1966, oil was discovered in an offshore field; exports began three years later. The prospect of imminent oil exports, along with severe overcrowding of the Creek and the commercial centres around it, persuaded the government in 1967 to start building a Dhs367 million seaport, known as Port Rashid, which eventually opened in 1972 and was expanded again in 1978.

Trade and oil combined to give economic growth a massive injection. The petrodollar boom had finally arrived in Dubai, even though its oil reserves and revenues were minnow-like compared with its oil-rich neighbour Abu Dhabi. The population sky rocketed as migrant labour poured into the city to extract the oil and to build and maintain the public services that Sheikh Rashid, remembering the demands of the reform movement when he was being groomed for power, made a high priority for his government. In 1967, as the government planned Port Rashid, the population stood at 59,000. Five years later, in 1973, the city had doubled in size. By the end of the booming 1970s, 250,000 people lived in Dubai.

INDEPENDENCE

In 1967, Britain decided that its moment in the Middle East was over. London announced its intention to withdraw from its colonial outposts east of Suez, giving the Trucial States a departure date of 1971. Unlike in Aden, in southern Yemen, where years of insurgency showed a stark desire to see off the imperialists, the leaders of Dubai and the other Trucial States felt almost abandoned by the hasty nature of the British retreat. The Conservative opposition of the day also criticised the Labour government's decision to withdraw, arguing that British business exposure across the Gulf amounted to much more than the Dhs117.5 million annual cost of maintaining the presence of British forces in the area, and that withdrawal would merely encourage new imperialists, such as the

UAE President Sheikh Zayed bin Sultan Al Nahyan with Margaret Thatcher.

Soviet Union, to extend their influence over a region of vital strategic importance owing to its oil deposits.

Some of the Trucial leaders hoped the Conservative government, once it gained power, would reverse the decision to withdraw, but it wasn't to be. Sheikh Zayed of Abu Dhabi and Sheikh Rashid of Dubai met at the frontier between their two emirates, and agreed to form a federation that would jointly decide foreign, defence and social policy. At the encouragement of the British, the rulers of the Trucial States Abu Dhabi, Dubai, Sharjah, Ajman, Umm Al Quwain, Ras Al Khaimah and Fujairah met in Dubai with the leaders of Bahrain and Qatar in February 1968 to discuss a federation.

The nine leaders of these islands, city states and desert regions met on several occasions in the run-up to independence in 1971, discussing models of federation. Differences plagued the meetings, with Bahrain's larger, better-educated population suspicious of a federation in which political power would be spread evenly across the nine emirates, rather than being based on the population of each emirate. Bahrain, having ended border disputes with Iran, told the other prospective federation members that it would retain its independence. Qatar chose the same path. In July 1971, with the British withdrawal approaching, the seven Trucial leaders met and hammered out a federal document. Six of them, excluding Ras Al Khaimah, signed the provisional constitution, which was then used to proclaim a federation in November 1971.

Ras Al Khaimah had felt undervalued in the negotiations, and wanted to focus on three Gulf islands that Iran had occupied once the British forces left the area. But once the other emirates agreed to take on the issue of Abu Musa and the Greater and Lesser Tunb islands, it too acceded to the federation in February 1972.

The federation was born, led by Abu Dhabi, owing to its disproportionate financial contribution to the federal budget, but with significant autonomy for all emirates in local affairs. Sheikh Zayed Al Nahyan became the country's first president; Sheikh Rashid, who through the 1970s pressed for more autonomy for his free-wheeling emirate, acted as Zayed's vice president and prime minister.

PETRODOLLAR BOOM

The 1970s were a decade of excess across the Gulf. Petrodollars flowed into the area as the world's seemingly unquenchable appetite for oil lapped up the region's exports. Oil revenues spiralled ever higher during the price shock of 1973 and 1974, triggered by the Arab producing states' boycott of nations supporting Israel in the third Arab-Israeli conflict. Dubai has never had the oil revenues that its rich neighbour Abu Dhabi enjoys (by 1980, Dubai's annual oil income stood at US$3 billion compared with Abu Dhabi's US$15 billion), but these revenues went a long way towards helping Dubai to develop the infrastructure it needed to realise fully the potential of its core economic activity, trade and commerce.

FAMILY FEUD

Questioning the unity of purpose between the country's seven emirates is something of a taboo in the United Arab Emirates (UAE). However, historians privately recount stories of arguments between the leaders of all the emirates, especially the two powerhouses, oil-rich Abu Dhabi and commerce-friendly Dubai. Go back 50 years, and the two emirates were locked in all-out war, with the two leaders' Bedouin allies carrying out raids on the other's territory over three bloody years. Rivalries have cooled since the leaders of the seven Trucial States came together under one flag in the early 1970s. But even in those early days of unity, Dubai's Sheikh Rashid, although committed to the union, fought to give his emirate as much autonomy as possible.

Abu Dhabi's superior size and population have translated into greater political power. The discovery of huge oil reserves in Abu Dhabi gave Sheikh Zayed's emirate even more financial clout, as well as military muscle. When the UAE was formed, Abu Dhabi earned ten times more money from its oil revenues than Dubai and those earnings still vastly outstrip its neighbour's. Factor in its huge investments in Western markets (one of the most high-profile being Manchester City football club) and the capital controls maybe 90 per cent of the UAE's national wealth.

The federal government developed around Abu Dhabi's financial largesse. This helped the union's development, but sparked fears in Dubai and other poorer emirates, which were concerned that Abu Dhabi's bureaucrats, keen to control the disbursement of their funds, would whittle away at the emirates' close-knit tribal roots. In 1979, the UAE was in crisis, as Abu Dhabi pushed for more centralised authority than the other emirates would accept. The crisis abated as Sheikh Rashid accepted the post of UAE prime minister, while securing the rights of individual rulers to continue developing their emirates along their own lines.

The threat of international turmoil in the 1980s, as the Iran-Iraq War loomed large over the region, glued the emirates together. With the Islamic Revolution boiling in Iran and civil shipping under attack in their own backyard, the seven emirates' petty squabbles paled into insignificance. Abu Dhabi continued to fund generous welfare systems for the entire country, especially the resource-starved northern emirates.

Today, Abu Dhabi and Dubai still have different characters. Abu Dhabians are more restrained and conservative than go-getting Dubaians, and this was most evident when Dubai unilaterally allowed foreigners to own freehold property – which triggered a massive building boom after 2003. Abu Dhabi sat silently on the sidelines for a while, but evidently took notes, as it has since embarked on an ambitious programme of its own, developing natural islands, building a Formula One race track and overhauling the city's infrastructure – although there are no plans for mile-high towers or flashy theme parks.

There will no doubt have been a sense of schadenfreude at the level of pain the seemingly invincible Dubai suffered after the credit crunch. But nobody is denying that the city's dynamic economy has also brought international recognition and offers many lessons in how to move away from reliance on oil – along with a few hard-learned examples of what not to do.

DUBAI'S INDUSTRIAL REVOLUTION

Dubai, founded as a trade hub, quickly used growing oil revenues to diversify its economic base to include heavy industry. With abundant oil and gas resources, the emirates had a competitive advantage in large-scale industrial projects that require vast amounts of energy. Dubai's first great industrial project took the form of Dubai Dry Dock, constructed in 1973 as a ship repair yard, which Sheikh Rashid passed on to his third son and current ruler, Sheikh Mohammed. This venture also benefited from the outbreak of maritime war between Iran and Iraq, serving the steady stream of tanker war victims. Two years later, the Dubai Aluminium Co, or Dubal, was set up with an initial investment of Dhs5.1 billion, which took advantage of cheap oil to create one of the world's most profitable smelters.

As well as industrial projects, the oil wealth of the 1970s brought modern infrastructure. By the end of the decade, another bridge and a tunnel complemented the original Maktoum Bridge linking Bur Dubai with Deira. Dubai's population rose to 207,000 in 1977, compared with 20,000 in the 1940s.

As Dubai grew, so did the number of roads, hospitals and schools. The police force, set up in 1956 under the command of British officers, came under local control in 1975. Immigrants started their own schools, complementing the state-run schools that catered for locals and expatriate Arabs.

Whereas the 1970s spelt industrial development, the 1980s saw the arrival of big-time commerce. While strong global demand for oil underpinned the soaring revenues enjoyed by oil-producing countries, Dubai continued to diversify. The World Trade Centre, opened in 1979, attracted some of the world's biggest companies to set up local or regional headquarters in Dubai. Once again, cynics whispered that the centre, today dwarfed by the high-rises of Sheikh Zayed Road, was too far from the central commercial district in Deira. But little did it matter, as foreign companies set up shop in a land free of bureaucracy, boasting political stability and liberal social mores. The city kept booming through the 1980s.

THE AGE OF TOURISM

In the 1970s, business people travelling to Dubai were hard pushed to find a single decent hotel. Sheikh Rashid even built a guesthouse to accommodate these early visitors. By 1975, the InterContinental had opened on the Deira side of the Creek, but never satisfied the growing hordes of travellers touching down at the new airport.

How times change. By the 1990s, after the death of Sheikh Rashid, Dubai was busy reinventing itself as a tourist destination.

There were 42 hotels in 1985, 272 in 2002 and 493 by 2008. The establishment in 1985 of Emirates, the Dubai-based international airline, helped the tourism sector flourish as the airline encouraged its passengers to stop over in the emirate en route to Asia, Africa or Europe. With start-up capital of Dhs36.7 million, the airline rapidly expanded, even managing to stay profitable through the global travel slump after the terror attacks of 11 September 2001.

With its oil reserves running out, Dubai has turned increasingly to tourism. International events such as the Dubai World Cup horse race, desert rally and golf, tennis and rugby tournaments helped fuel the boom. But it's Dubai's love affair with shopping that has sustained the emirate's industry. The Dubai Shopping Festival, launched in 1996, attracts around 3.5 million people to the city every year. A second shopping festival, Dubai Summer Surprises, was introduced in 1998, attracting Gulf visitors who are used to the soaring summer temperatures that put off many Western tourists. Combined with sea, sun and liberal attitudes to entertainment, annual tourist numbers have now reached around 7.5 million, six times the city's resident population.

A NEW ERA

In January 2006, following the death of Sheikh Maktoum bin Rashid Al Maktoum, his younger brother, Sheikh Mohammed, assumed power in Dubai. There was little doubt that he would be named leader. Accordingly, the transition between leaders was smooth and any changes in government policy were barely noticeable.

BLACK GOLD TO WHITE COLLAR

Dubai's plan was, and continues to be, to attract professionals from across the globe. One of the emirate's most successful ventures to date is the formation of corporate free zones, where businesses in roughly the same industries are gathered in a corporate park, encouraging networking and new businesses. Dubai Internet City (DIC), announced in 1999, was the first such attempt to attract more professionals to the emirate. The venture was tailor-made to lure high-tech firms, offering tax-free 100 per cent ownership (outside free zones businesses need a local partner).

PROPERTY BOOM

Dubai's property boom, which exploded in 2003 with the introduction of freehold properties, is yet another reason why the emirate continues to make headlines across the globe. The repatriation of money from Western markets to the Middle East, especially the UAE, after 11 September 2001 gave Dubai's budding property industry a significant boost. Close to Dhs3.67 trillion poured into various sectors of the Middle Eastern market, a fair chunk of which went into Dubai's construction projects. Wealthy investors purchased dozens of apartments and villas, and small-time investors purchased an apartment or two at rock-bottom prices.

Developments such as Emaar's the Greens (the first rent-to-own scheme) and the Marina sparked buying crazes among expatriates and investors interested in making Dubai either their home or a destination for holidays. Nakheel's record-breaking Palm islands and the World attracted a number of heavyweight investors and celebrities as keen on owning a property in Dubai as they are about letting the world's media know about it. Local and international interest in Dubai's properties was substantial, with no one quite prepared for the unprecedented influx of cash into the market.

Interestingly, for the first couple of years, there wasn't a single law to safeguard foreign homeowners and their properties. Instead, investors nervously relied on the clauses in their contracts with developers, and hoped that the imminent law they heard so much about would give them the comfort of government-sanctioned freehold status they desperately needed. In March 2006, after months of speculation, the law was implemented. Foreigners now have the legal right to buy properties in designated areas across the emirate, and they can register the properties in their own names with another new agency, the Real Estate Regulatory Authority (RERA).

Even before the law was announced, Dubai's property market was one of the fastest-growing in the world. In the first five years of freehold sales, the market broke through one financial ceiling after another in a dizzying rise into the financial stratosphere. People who bought properties off-plan in 2002 and 2003 saw their investments more than triple and sometimes quadruple in value.

If it all seemed too good to last, that's because it was. As the world entered a new era of restricted credit in 2008, speculation on property in Dubai reached ludicrous proportions: by that summer, anyone with enough money for a ten per cent deposit could make an initial payment on an off-plan property, then 'flip' it for a handsome profit. When the bubble burst at the end of that summer, those same investors were left high and dry. House prices fell by more than 40 per cent, many smaller developers went bust and thousands were stuck with properties that they couldn't afford. The bigger government-backed developers were not immune from the sudden exodus of cash from the market.

It was a worrying time for residents of a city that had only seen property world record after world record broken, as well as almost weekly announcements of some of the most ambitious construction projects in the world – including a planned underwater hotel, and another city next to Dubai, reported to be twice its size. Many multi-billion dollar projects were put on indefinite hold with little chance of them being finished – or even started – in the near future. People lost jobs and left the country. Prices came down. Roads, in a city famous for its traffic jams, got quieter. But, yet again, the city adapted in a way that it has many times in its history.

BOUNCING BACK

Meanwhile, Dubai seemed fully committed to keeping up appearances. Media crews from around the world decamped on to Palm Jumeirah in September 2008, ready to report on the grand opening of Atlantis The Palm. And they weren't disappointed. Two thousand guests from around the world were invited to the opening party, reported to have cost US$5 million. They included A-list Hollywood actors such as Robert De Niro, Wesley Snipes and Charlize Theron, plus Mischa Barton and Lindsay Lohan, as well as some of the biggest names in the world of entertainment. Kylie Minogue is said to have been paid US$2 million to play for the assembled guests, as four Michelin-starred chefs – Nobu Matsuhisa, Giorgio Locatelli, Michel Rostang and Santi Santamaria – cooked. Fireworks, reported to be seven times the amount set off for the opening of the Beijing Olympic Games, lit up the night sky.

The following month, Terminal 3 at Dubai International Airport opened, dedicated to Emirates Airlines and planned as a place to house the A380, the world's largest airplane. Then, in January 2013, Concourse A opened, upping the capacity of Dubai International Airport from 60 million passengers per year to 75 million. Later, in March, Emirates – the national airline founded by Sheikh Mohammed Bin Rashid Al Maktoum – finalised a non-equity codeshare merger with Qantas. The strategic move significantly boosted passenger traffic through Dubai thanks to Qantas moving its stopover location from Singapore on its flights from Europe to Australia. By the end of the year it was estimated that the aviation sector alone – including Dubai Airports, the Emirates Group, and other businesses such as Duty Free – accounted for 16.5 per cent of Dubai's GDP.

And that's not all – Concourse D, an extension of Dubai International Airport Terminal 1, is scheduled for completion in 2015, and it's estimated that annual passenger traffic will increase to 100 million, annually, by the end of the decade. The new Maktoum International Airport in Jebel Ali is currently estimated to surpass Dubai International Airport in size and scale once completed, with projections of an annual capacity of 200 million passengers.

THE WORLD EXPO AND BEYOND

In 2013, the city won its bid to host the World Expo 2020, an event expected to attract more than 20 million visitors to the emirate and create thousands of jobs.

The opportunity was well timed. Dubai diversified its economy long ago to avoid relying on the country's finite supply of oil, and tourism had already proved to be one of the city's biggest assets. But 2014 brought more setbacks, as Dubai began to feel the effects of falling oil prices. The cost of living went up, but no plans were made by the government to curb spending or investment domestically; instead it remained committed to plans for the Expo and sure in its ability to boost the economy.

In a city that has already experienced so much change during its relatively short lifetime, it's difficult to predict whether plans will stay on track up to 2020. But what can be said with certainty is that the period leading up to Expo – and the period after it – will be anything but boring.

KEY EVENTS

Dubai in brief.

1580 First written reference to 'Dibei'
1820 Dubai signs the General Maritime Peace Treaty with Britain
1833 Dubai becomes an independent settlement of Abu Dhabi; rule of the Maktoum family begins
1841 Smallpox epidemic breaks out in Bur Dubai
1892 Trucial States are founded
1894 Fire devastates much of Deira
1947 Border dispute between Dubai and Abu Dhabi escalates. Britain intervenes to draw new frontier.
1954 Dubai Municipality established to help with city planning
1956 The Dubai police force is established; first concrete house is built
1958 Sheikh Saeed dies; succeeded by Sheikh Rashid
1963 Maktoum Bridge opens, the first crossing over the Dubai Creek
1966 Oil is discovered in Dubai
1967 Building of Port Rashid begins; Britain announces its intention to withdraw from the region
1971 Seven Trucial States meet; all but Ras Al Khaimah sign a federal document, forming the United Arab Emirates (UAE), with Sheikh Zayed Al Nahyan as its first president
1972 Ras Al Khaimah joins the federation
1973 Port Rashid in downtown Dubai completed; the dirham adopted as the single UAE currency
1975 The Dubai police force comes under local control for the first time; Al Shindagha Tunnel opens, running beneath the Creek
1976 Building of Jebel Ali port begins; Garhoud Bridge opens across the Creek
1979 Dubai World Trade Centre opens; the Jebel Ali Free Zone is established; the border between Abu Dhabi and Dubai is agreed
1980 Dubai's annual oil income stands at US$3 billion, while Abu Dhabi's reaches US$15 billion
1983 Jebel Ali port completed
1985 The Dubai-based international airline Emirates is established
1986 Sheikh Saaed's house is restored and opens for tourists
1990 Sheikh Rashid dies; he is succeeeded as ruler by Sheikh Maktoum
1996 First Dubai World Cup, the world's richest horse race, takes place
1999 Burj Al Arab, the world's first 'seven-star hotel', opens in December. Dubai Internet City (DIC) opens
2001 Work begins on the first of the Palm group of islands, Palm Jumeirah
2003 Expatriates are granted permission to purchase freehold properties; Dubailand, the world's biggest collection of theme parks, announced
2004 Sheikh Zayed bin Sultan Al Nahyan dies; his son, Sheikh Khalifa bin Zayed Al Nahyan becomes UAE president
2005 Ski Dubai, an indoor ski slope with real snow, opens at the Mall of the Emirates; Dubai International Finance Centre (DIFC) opens
2006 Sheikh Maktoum bin Rashid Al Maktoum dies; his brother, Sheikh Mohammed bin Rashid Al Maktoum, becomes ruler of Dubai; the official weekend changes from Thursday and Friday to Friday and Saturday
2007 Salik road toll system comes into effect; the Floating Bridge and Business Bay Bridge across Dubai Creek open
2008 New Garhoud Bridge opens; Atlantis Hotel opens on the Palm, with opening party attended by a host of Hollywood stars
2009 Dubai Metro opens; construction is finished on Burj Dubai, the world's tallest building
2013 Expansion of Dubai International Airport and merger of Qantas with Emirates significantly increases airport traffic; Dubai wins bid to host World Expo 2020

Architecture

From wind towers to the world's tallest tower.

With a hunger for innovative landmarks, and a peerless aptitude for publicising them, Dubai has produced multiple architectural feats to showcase its ambition and wealth around the world. When a *Vanity Fair* article hailed the city's 'skyline on crack', it wasn't far off the mark; Dubai, it can safely be said, is not the sleepy fishing town it was half a century ago.

But if you look behind the buzzwords and the bombast, you'll discover that something quite extraordinary has taken place. And although it's easy to scoff at the more outlandish projects, it's impossible not to be impressed by the outside-the-box thinking that has transformed this city.

Textile Souk, Old Dubai.

THE GROWTH SPURT

Unlike major cities such as London or New York, Dubai's architectural history is astonishingly compressed: wind tower houses replaced palm-frond shelters in the early 20th century; following the oil boom, these were torn down to make way for concrete apartment blocks; and those in turn were replaced by skyscrapers. However, the city's design trend is turning full circle, with a penchant for Arabian chic seeing architects incorporating wind towers – which originally worked as an early form of air-conditioning – into their designs for five-star hotels.

With the first exports of oil from the area taking place in the early 1960s, Dubai set about dragging itself into the 20th century with an almost religious zeal. The mantra 'out with the old, in with the new' and the urgent need for mass housing resulted in the razing of most of its old town and the rapid rise of towers and cheap apartment blocks. It wasn't until the 1990s that the government turned its attention to preserving and restoring what was left of the old town.

Critics maintain that only the UAE's neighbour, Oman, offers true examples of traditional Gulf architecture, but there are still pockets of authenticity left in early 21st-century Dubai, mainly in the Al Fahidi Historical District.

In terms of contemporary architecture, the audacious Burj Al Arab hotel became an instant icon upon completion, and started Dubai's passion for breaking height records. Meanwhile, international architects got busy creating cities-within-cities, the world's tallest tower, Burj Khalifa and the Palm Jumeirah. But the debate still rages among architects over ways to develop a local architectural language that looks to Dubai's past as well as its gleaming future.

BACK IN THE DAY

It was the Bani Yas tribe – ancestors of the Bedouin – who first set up camp in the deserts and mountains of Abu Dhabi and Dubai in the 18th century. They split their time between animal-hide tents, ideal for winter wanderings, and *arish* or *barasti* (palm-frond shelters) for summer months spent on date plantations. *Barasti* were also popular among fishermen, pearlers and traders.

Coastal areas had blocky homes built from bricks of fossilised coral bonded with *sarooj* (a

Dubai Museum.

blend of Iranian red clay and manure, dried and baked in a kiln) or a lime mixture derived from seashells and plastered with chalk and water paste. Large courtyard houses built of *farush* (beach rock) and covered with lime plaster have been excavated in Jumeirah and dated to the second century of the Islamic era (ninth century AD). When a branch of the Bani Yas – the Maktoums – settled by the Creek in the early 19th century, more permanent homes were built using *guss* (mud blocks) and roofed with palm fronds, materials that kept the temperature down. Rooms usually opened on to an airy central courtyard restricted to family use, and male guests were entertained in a separate *majlis* (meeting room). In many newer villas, the *majlis* is in the main house, a layout that is still familiar to Dubaians living in villas built in the 1970s and 1980s.

Public buildings in the 18th and 19th centuries were mostly stone forts, which doubled up as seats of government, and mosques. Al Fahidi fort, believed to be Dubai's oldest building, now home to **Dubai Museum** (*see p65*), was built around 1799 to guard landward approaches to the town. Parts of the old Dubai wall, built in the early 1800s, can be seen in the **Al Fahidi Historical District** (*see p71*).

As Dubai's pearling industry boomed in the late 1800s, Bedouin and mountain communities began to gravitate towards the coastal trading villages. The simple, outwardly minimalist homes they built were decorated inside with intricate rugs and outside by wooden latticework on windows and elaborately carved doors. This tradition has continued in the brightly painted metal doors and gates on old villas by the beach, and there are some great examples of antique wooden doors in Al Fahidi.

Historians disagree about whether these decorations were traditionally Arab, based on Islamic designs, or inspired by Indian decorative principles. Homes were built close to one another, with shady *sikkas* (narrow alleys) running down towards the water.

By the late 19th century, spurred in part by a devastating fire in 1894, Deira's wealthy began to build their homes from coral stone and gypsum, although the poor still lived in *barasti* buildings. Today, *barasti* huts are constructed to shade farm workers in the desert, picnickers in villa gardens and cocktail drinkers at busy beach bars.

Majlis Gallery.

Sheikh Saeed Al Maktoum House (*see p68*) was built in 1896 on the southern bank of the Creek in Shindagha as a residence for the ruling family; it remained their home until Sheikh Saeed's death in 1958. Probably one of the first houses in the area to sport Iranian-inspired wind towers, it is a traditional coral-block structure built around a large central courtyard. The Emirati historian and architect Rashad Bukhash, formerly head of the Historical Buildings Section of Dubai Municipality, has described the Sheikh Saeed Al Maktoum House as 'the best example of traditional architecture, with all the wooden decorative elements – such as carved latticework and teak doors – that were typical of the times'. The restored house now acts as a museum, displaying old photographs and historical documents.

By the mid 20th century, a village of around 50 compounds, each with a wind tower or two, had built up along the Bur Dubai side of the Creek in an area called Bastakia, now renamed the Al Fahidi Historical District. It remained more or less intact until the 1980s. A collection of wind-tower shops still exists by the *abra* (boat) station; other fine examples open to the public are the **Majlis Gallery** and **XVA** (*see p72*), a restored café, gallery and guesthouse. Former residents of Bastakia today look back with fondness to less hurried times, when families were self-sufficient – with livestock kept and slaughtered at home – and a shopping trip involved taking a rowed *abra* to the souks of Deira.

A CITY IS BORN

Dubai's pace of urbanisation – like every other facet of life in what was then the Trucial States – was dramatically accelerated by the discovery of oil in the early 1960s, first in Abu Dhabi and then in Dubai. The city's skyline was transformed following the formation of the UAE in 1971, largely due to the explosion in Dubai's population.

The first house built from concrete blocks was constructed in Dubai in 1956, but much of the population continued to live in *barastis* until well into the 1960s. Typically, extended families grouped together into compounds separated by thin alleyways; transport was by donkey, camel or *abra* until the 1960s, when the first roads opened.

Even before the oil days, Dubai's ambition was evident. Sheikh Rashid, who succeeded his father in 1958, spent his first few years in power setting up a Municipal Council, building and widening roads, constructing the first airport and bridging the Creek. The advent of the car had created the need for the establishment of a system of land management and ownership – as people losing half their compound to a widened road required compensation – and the concept of town planning was introduced. Working out who owned what in the tribal quarters of the city proved tricky, but became essential as land values rose. Territory outside built-up areas and any reclaimed land belonged to the ruler – a decree that continues to this day.

International commentators were sceptical about Sheikh Rashid's grand plans, but there was no shortage of believers; Dubai's population doubled to 120,000 between the late 1960s and early '70s, and by 1981 had reached well over a quarter of a million. The few apartment blocks that sprung out of the desert around Deira's **Clock Tower Roundabout** (1963) in the 1960s weren't lonely for long, and by the mid '70s the Creek was lined with low- and high-rise structures. Already soaring fortunes, built on increased trade, went stratospheric during the oil crisis of 1973, and the government began construction in earnest. Developing infrastructure took precedence – the Shindagha tunnel and Al Maktoum Bridge, the dry docks at Port Rashid, mosques, hospitals, schools and power stations all date from around the late 1960s and early '70s. Sadly, however, the need for urgent residential and office accommodation led to some entirely uncharismatic blocks being erected.

One exception is **Dubai Municipality** (1979), on the Deira side of the Creek, a building that's still widely admired for its abstract sensitivity – although the inner glass courtyard and water pools, which create a cool microclimate, weren't added until the 1980s. The **Dubai World Trade Centre** (**DWTC**, *see p110*), also built in 1979 and at the time the signature Dubai landmark, and its highest building at 39 storeys, hasn't enjoyed the same favour. Unmistakeably of its time, the DWTC is now dwarfed in size and renown by Jumeirah Emirates Towers, and in function by the nearby hotels, built to accommodate delegates to 2003's World Bank and IMF meetings.

Dubai's ritual building up and tearing down saw many of the smaller structures of the 1960s and '70s cleared to make way for a rising wave of brand-new skyscrapers. But tradition sat cheek by jowl with the shiny and the modern: timber for interiors and furniture was still imported to the Creek on wooden dhows and, even in the early 1980s, Bur Dubai was still a wind-tower village compared to Deira's burgeoning metropolis across the water.

By the end of the decade, Dubai's passion for novelty began to soften slightly, perhaps owing in part to the emergence of the first wave of local architecture graduates. Rumour has it that Prince Charles, the UK's ambassador for architectural conservatism, expressed great enthusiasm for wind towers on a tour of Bastakia, encouraging Dubaians to start conservation projects. Meanwhile, the launch of Emirates airline in 1985 brought increasing numbers of tourists hungry for a taste of Arabia. The first restoration project, Sheikh Saeed's House, was completed in 1986, and through the 1990s another 70 buildings were saved. Architects began incorporating traditional or Islamic elements into their designs. The thoroughly 1980s **Deira Tower** (1980) in

Dubai World Trade Centre.

Jumeirah Emirates Towers.

National Bank of Dubai.

Baniyas Square, for example, has a distinctive circular white 'cap' like that worn by Emirati men under their *ghutra* (headdress).

INTO THE MILLENNIUM

Upon Sheikh Rashid's death in 1990, his sons set about furthering their father's plans to create the Hong Kong of the Middle East, with new buildings dedicated to commerce and tourism. Dubai's macho love affair with the tower became ever more fervent, and foreign architects' efforts to relate their buildings to the local environment ranged from the ultra-literal to the ultra-kitsch. Some managed to be both: visitors heading into the city from the airport can't miss the mock aircraft hull of **Emirates Aviation College**. **Jumeirah Beach Hotel** (1997, *see p279*) represents a surfer's dream wave, and the unusually low-rise **Dubai Creek Golf & Yacht Club** (1993), the billowing sails of a dhow. Other architects' favourites include Ott's **National Bank of Dubai** building (1998) on the Creek at Deira, known locally as the 'pregnant lady'. Supported by two giant columns, the gold, glass and granite sculptural tower nods to the curved hulls and taut sails of *abras* and dhows, but in a subtly contextual manner.

Ott is also responsible for the nearby **Hilton Dubai Creek** (2001, *see p269*), a minimalist's dream. **Jumeirah Emirates Towers** (*see p276*) is equally sleek. The hotel tower rises 355 metres (1,165 feet) – take a ride in the exhilarating glass lifts to experience it. **Children's City** (*see p188*) in Creekside Park has a Duplo-style series of exhibition rooms, and is equally unashamedly modern and unusual in that it provides a spatial as well as a formal experience – as does the **One&Only Royal Mirage** (*see p149*), which uses elements of traditional Islamic architecture. The impressive **Madinat Jumeirah** (*see p137*), a massive hotel and souk complex that opened in 2004, also harks back to the days of wind towers and coral-block hues.

Of course, it was with the opening of the Madinat's neighbour, the **Burj Al Arab** hotel (*see p283*), in late 1999 that Dubai really earned its reputation as an architect's playground. Tom Wright of Atkins aimed to build a 'state-of-the-art, almost futuristic building' that was 'Arabic, extravagant and super-luxurious'.

The Burj became an instant icon and the most recognised landmark in the city. Built

ON THE DRAWING BOARD

Some of the mega projects planned for Dubai.

Dubai residents are used to announcements of grand projects and to living within view (and earshot) of building sites. Not all the fantastic ideas come to fruition and some take longer than others to materialise, but here are ten projects planned to be completed in time for Expo 2020.

ALADDIN CITY

A 16-square-kilometre (six-square-mile) complex of towers striding out into the Dubai Creek inspired by, what else, mythical characters including Sinbad and Aladdin. It's said to include offices, at least one hotel and some of the buildings will look like Aladdin's lamp. The project is expected to be finished in 2016, though, at the time of writing, work hadn't begun.

AL HABTOOR CITY

Another one that was almost complete at the time of writing – indeed, you can see part of this huge hotel tower lit up and fountains flowing in the garden, while other sections of the building are barely started. There are three hotels and residential blocks planned for this area of Business Bay, with landscaped gardens and tennis courts.

BLUEWATERS ISLAND

If there's one thing that spoils the Beach at JBR at the moment, it's the construction work that's happening just off the coast. That work is to create Bluewaters Island, which will include housing and commercial properties as well as the Dubai Eye – the world's largest Ferris wheel. Estimated completion date is 2018.

DEIRA ISLAND

This project, based off Deira, will add more than 40 kilometres (25 miles) to Dubai's coastline. Planned for the site are shops, a night souk, hotels, beaches, an amphitheatre and marinas.

DUBAI CREEK HARBOUR

The world's tallest twin towers are billed to be part of this vast development on Dubai Creek. The complex will include offices, retail space, residential units and hotels.

DUBAI FRAME

On the edge of Zabeel Park, a huge picture frame-like structure is rising steadily upwards. It was supposed to be finished in late 2015, but that seems unlikely. Once completed, it will give people the chance to view the city from a clear glass walkway 150 metres (490 feet) up in the air.

DUBAI OPERA HOUSE

At the time of writing, this project to inject some culture into Downtown Dubai was almost finished. The design is based on an Arabian dhow (traditional sailing boat) and it will hold 2,000 people and stage opera, theatre, concerts and other productions.

DUBAI THEME PARKS

Due to open in autumn 2016, this massive entertainment site alongside the main road to Abu Dhabi will include Bollywood Parks, Legoland Dubai and Motiongate Dubai.

DUBAI WATER CANAL

This monumental project has already altered a sizeable chunk of Dubai's landscape. The canal will connect Business Bay with the Arabian Gulf and cuts through Sheikh Zayed Road, Safa Park, Al Wasl and Jumeirah before reaching the coast. It will create a space for waterside restaurants, hotels and other tourism opportunities – and lower the temperature in the area.

MUSEUM OF THE FUTURE

With a planned completion date of 2017, this elliptical, egg-shaped structure is due to appear near Jumeirah Emirates Towers, on Sheikh Zayed Road. It will provide interactive demonstrations of new technologies, and host conferences and workshops.

some 300 metres (985 feet) offshore, it was the world's tallest hotel at 321 metres (1,053 feet) when it opened, and is supported by 250 columns descending 40 metres (130 feet) into the seabed. Rumour has it that sand from around the base has to be hoovered out every night to prevent subsidence, and that the tower sways by up to 30 centimetres (12 inches) at the top. Even if you can't afford a night's stay in the hotel, you can check out its 28 double-height floors of pure opulence by booking into one of the restaurants or bars.

By the late 1990s, however, local architects were beginning to mutter about an identity crisis among Dubai's buildings. For some, the attempts by the likes of the Royal Mirage and intimate eco-retreat **Al Maha Desert Resort & Spa** (*see p280*) to allude to local or regional history were key to creating a contextual and distinctive Dubai 'look'. For people who question the notion of 'Islamic architecture', these attempts amounted to mere pastiche: they say that Dubai's age-old position on the trading crossroads and its new identity as a global city necessitate the sort of universal buildings that you'll see if you take a drive down Sheikh Zayed Road or walk by the Marina.

Dubaians often wryly joke that they go to sleep alone at night only to wake up next to a skyscraper the following day. But while European, American and Asian capitals have patronised the new breed of superstar architects, Dubai has taken that course less often. Reflecting the transient and impatient nature of the new Dubai, many of the structures look impressive, but few of them are truly innovative, especially when it comes to satisfying environmental concerns. Critics ask why today's architects have yet to master the use of cool air, shade and natural light perfected in wind-tower houses.

BOOM, BUST AND BOUNCING BACK

By the mid 2000s there was a fevered property boom that seemed unstoppable. New mega-projects were announced on what seemed like a daily basis, and each one was more audacious than the last.

Then the global credit crunch hit Dubai in late 2008. With investors fleeing the market and credit all but impossible to find, many developments ground to a halt. Some, like the sprawling Dubailand area, are officially

Dubai Marina.

postponed rather than cancelled, but it is highly unlikely that they will see the light of day any time soon.

However, Dubai has bounced back from the crash, and once again people are moving to and investing in the city. The biggest and most striking structure to open since 2008 is the **Burj Khalifa** (*see p80*). Standing at almost 830 metres (2,723 feet) high, work on the tallest building in the world started in 2004 and was completed in 2009; it officially opened a year later.

The Burj Khalifa's design, by Skidmore, Owings and Merrill (SOM) of Chicago, was inspired by Arabian minarets and desert flowers, as well as Frank Lloyd Wright's 1956 plans for the Illinois Sky-City in Chicago. Wright's building was impossible to create then, but by the 2000s the technology existed to construct a similar structure.

The tower helped the surrounding area – now called Downtown Dubai – to grow too. Other recent structures in the area include the record-breaking **Dubai Fountain** (*see p80*) and **Dubai Mall** (*see p88*), as well as the historic-looking **Souk Al Bahar** (*see p93*), the restaurant-lined Sheikh Mohammed Bin Rashid Boulevard and the **Address Downtown Hotel** (*see p273*).

However, some huge projects never recovered, among them the **World Islands** (*see p115*) and **Palm Jebel Ali**, which dwarfs its Palm Jumeirah sister but stands empty.

The city has spread further towards Abu Dhabi with the creation of **Dubai Marina** (*see p171*), with Jumeirah Beach Residence on one side of the Sheikh Zayed Road and the Jumeirah Lakes Towers development – with residential towers surrounding man-made lakes – on the other.

A driverless metro was opened in 2009 and connects Jebel Ali to Dubai International Airport. A tram also opened in the Marina in 2014, changing the infrastructure of the area further.

Dubai's ever-changing landscape doesn't look like being finished any time soon, with billions of dollars being pumped into it ahead of 2020, when Dubai will host Expo 2020, the first time the international event has been held in the Middle East and North Africa region. As ever, Dubai's rulers will be using the occasion to show how far the city has come since its days as a fishing village.

Essential Information

Hotels

If you've got money to burn, you'll have no trouble finding a hotel in Dubai. The city that gave birth to the world's only 'seven-star hotel' (even if the Burj Al Arab did give itself that title) is the place to experience the uppermost in luxury. Dubai is also home to the huge, iconic and nautically themed Atlantis The Palm, the equally popular Jumeirah Beach Hotel, and the Armani brand's first foray into the hotel business – the sleek, chic Armani Hotel Dubai – at the foot of the Burj Khalifa. In fact, one striking thing about the Dubai hotel scene is the sheer quantity of properties: it seems as if every chain on the planet has at least one hotel here.

If you don't have money to burn, package deals can offer a cost-effective way to stay in a hotel that would otherwise be out of reach, while the low season during the searing summer months, as well as Ramadan, also mean lower-than-usual prices.

STAYING IN DUBAI

When it comes to accommodation in Dubai, you'll soon realise that some areas are far more expensive than others. Hotels in the older parts, including Deira and Bur Dubai, tend to be cheaper due to the age of the properties, the lack of space and the slightly chaotic nature of the locations. Of course, this isn't a strict rule, as the **Park Hyatt Dubai** in Deira and **Raffles Dubai** in Oud Metha demonstrate. But, in general, if you're looking for an absolute bargain, head to Old Dubai.

Downtown Dubai is, understandably, high-end and expensive – especially if you decide to stay in the **Armani Hotel Dubai** at the foot of the world's tallest building.

The stretch of beach from Jumeirah to Dubai Marina is home to some of the city's most iconic and luxurious properties, including the **Jumeirah Beach Hotel**, the **Burj Al Arab** and the Madinat Jumeirah resort, which contains **Al Qas**, **Dar Al Masyaf** and **Mina A'Salam**. Dubai Marina is one of the liveliest areas and there's no shortage of hotels here, particularly along the Walk at Jumeirah Beach Residence. Fierce competition on this stretch means you have a better chance of getting a good deal, with everything from the **Ritz-Carlton Dubai** to more affordable places such as **JA Ocean View Hotel** and **Amwaj Rotana**.

And don't forget about Palm Jumeirah, site of one of the world's most famous hotels, **Atlantis The Palm**. Expect a wallet-busting visit if you book into a property on the man-made Palm.

Hotels in Dubai have star ratings, but these aren't the most reliable measure as there's no universal standard or governing body overseeing the ratings. We've listed hotels according to price. For Deluxe hotels, expect to pay Dhs1,500 and above for a standard double; Expensive Dhs1,000-Dhs1,499; Moderate Dhs500-Dhs999; and Budget under Dhs500. But note that this is just a guide: prices vary wildly depending on the season, with significant discounts during the summer.

DEIRA, GARHOUD & FESTIVAL CITY

Deluxe

Park Hyatt Dubai

Dubai Creek Golf & Yacht Club, Deira (04 602 1234, www.dubai.park.hyatt.com). Metro Deira City Centre. **Map** p311 K2.

Nestled amid the greenery of the golf course, alongside a scenic stretch of the Creek, the Park Hyatt Dubai oozes calm and luxury. Its Moroccan architecture and low, whitewashed buildings are the perfect backdrop for days spent lounging by the pool, while the interiors are tasteful and modern. The bedrooms are minimal but inviting, and all have designer bathrooms. There's a collection of great restaurants and bars, and after dinner you can take a leisurely stroll along the Creek, watching boats bobbing up and down on the water. Bliss.

Expensive

Al Bustan Rotana

Casablanca Street, Garhoud (04 282 0000, www.rotana.com). Metro GGICO. **Map** p311 K2.

A stone's throw from Dubai International Airport, the Al Bustan Rotana has a reputation as a conveniently located business hotel. But there's more to the place than meetings and conferences, with an array of restaurants, a swimming pool and a well-equipped gym. Standard bedrooms are a reasonable size with large beds, but wardrobe space is lacking and the bathrooms are dated. A handful of rooms come with their own private terraces facing the pool deck. Executive club levels are an improvement, with larger rooms, a dedicated check-in area, TV lounge and breakfast area.

Hilton Dubai Creek

Baniyas Road, Deira (04 227 1111, www3.hilton.com). Metro Union. **Map** p313 L4.

One of Deira's classiest hotels, the Hilton is home to award-winning restaurants and some buzzy bars. The rooms are statements in contemporary luxury, and the comfortable beds and ultra-cool black and white bathrooms prove there is substance beyond the style. This hotel is an excellent choice if you need to stay in Deira.

Hyatt Regency Dubai

Deira Corniche, Deira (04 209 1234, www.dubai.regency.hyatt.com). Metro Palm Deira. **Map** p313 J1.

Built in 1980, this vast 400-room stalwart sits close to the Creek amid the hustle and bustle of downtown Deira. Due to its out-of-the-way location – around 7km (4 miles) from Downtown Dubai and even further from the Marina and Jumeirah's beaches – the Hyatt Regency has created something of a siege mentality and is almost completely self-sufficient. You'll find plenty of eateries (including a revolving restaurant), bars, an ice rink, tennis courts, swimming pools and a nine-hole pitch-and-putt golf course.

InterContinental Dubai – Festival City

Dubai Festival City (04 701 1111, www.ihg.com). **Map** p311 K3.

This enormous hotel can accommodate up to 500 guests and boasts some great restaurants, including French fine dining at Reflets par Pierre Gagnaire. The hotel has an informal feel, and rooms are modern and smartly designed. The shops and restaurants of Festival City are next door, there are two golf courses nearby and the airport is only a couple of minutes away. With its Creek and Festival City Marina views, this is a scenic as well as convenient option.

Jumeirah Creekside Hotel

2nd Street, Garhoud (04 230 8555, www.jumeirah.com). Metro GGICO. **Map** p311 K2.

This sleek, glass-covered building is well located for the airport, but has more style than some of the hotels nearby. There are decent restaurants and bars inside, and it's a short walk to Century Village, where you'll find the ever-popular Irish Village pub.

JW Marriott Hotel Dubai

Abu Baker Al Siddique Road, Deira (04 262 4444, www.marriott.com). Metro Abu Baker Al Siddique. **Map** p311 J1.

This is an elegant hotel that stands out from its surroundings in the older part of town. The comfortable rooms offer an old-world charm that's rare in Dubai hotels. The pool and leisure facilities are nothing to write home about – aside from the massive gym and training area – but are perfectly acceptable. There are a couple of excellent restaurants, including the award-winning JW's Steakhouse.

Le Méridien Dubai Hotel & Conference Centre

Airport Road, Garhoud (04 217 0000, www.lemeridien-dubai.com). **Map** p311 K2.

This sprawling hotel complex is popular for stopovers due to its proximity to the airport, but don't worry about noise – it's not directly under the flight path. Rooms are dated, but some offer pleasant views of the gardens and pool area. There's a health club and gym on site, plus the popular Le Méridien Village, which bursts into activity at night thanks to the many alfresco restaurants and bars.

Sheraton Dubai Creek Hotel & Towers

Baniyas Road, Deira (04 228 1111, www.sheratondubaicreek.com). Metro Union. **Map** p313 J2.

This striking tower rising from the Deira side of the Creek doesn't quite achieve the same effect inside, where the decor is business-like. A long escalator leads up to a dimly lit foyer, where various restaurants include Indian venue Ashiana by Vineet and Creekside Japanese Restaurant. Rooms are comfortable and affordable, though somewhat lacking in character. If you want to discover the older side of town, this hotel is ideal; it's a stone's throw from the *abra* boat station, and the gold and spice souks.

Taj Palace Hotel

36A Street, Al Rigga Road, Deira (04 223 2222, www.tajhotels.com). Metro Al Rigga. **Map** p313 L3.

This five-star slice of extravagance in downtown Deira is immediately noticeable thanks to its glass and steel façade. In keeping with Muslim practice, no women work in the hotel after 11pm and no alcohol is served. These Islamic values have made Taj Palace popular with guests from other Gulf countries. The rooms are large, combining wooden floors and stylish furnishings. There's a rooftop pool and tranquil spa. If you don't mind foregoing a glass of wine with dinner, one of the best restaurants in the hotel is Indian eaterie Handi.

Moderate

Asiana Hotel

Salahuddin Road, Deira (04 238 7777, www.asianahoteldubai.com). Metro Salah Al Din. **Map** p311 J1.

As the name suggests, this hotel has an Asian influence, from the decor to the restaurants. You'll find Korean, Japanese and Filipino cuisine, with signature Korean restaurant Sonamu particularly impressive. Rooms are fairly standard, but perfectly comfortable. It's in the heart of Deira, so it's popular as a business destination.

Coral Deira

Al Muraqqabat Street, Deira (04 224 8587, www.hmhhotelgroup.com/coraldubaideira). Metro Al Rigga. **Map** p311 J1.

This large five-star hotel on Al Muraqqabat Street draws tourists from the Gulf due to the fact that it doesn't serve alcohol. It's relatively stylish, especially once you get past the slightly gaudy lobby. The standard rooms are spacious enough and tastefully decorated, and modern-day comforts include Villeroy & Boch bathrooms with elegant tubs.

Crowne Plaza Festival City

Dubai Festival City (04 701 2222, www.ihg.com). **Map** p311 K3.

A slightly cheaper option to the neighbouring InterContinental, but still a more than comfortable place to stay. It's primarily a business hotel, but is near Al Badia Golf Club and adjacent to the Festival City shopping centre. Rooms are warm and welcoming, and it contains a branch of the popular Belgian Beer Café.

Marco Polo Hotel

Al Muteena Street, Deira (04 272 0000, www.marcopolohotel.net). Metro Salah Al Din. **Map** p313 K2/L2.

With an eclectic smattering of decent dining options, including British, Chinese and Filipino, plus a pleasant swimming pool and gym, the Marco Polo fares well in this price bracket and location. Although at first glance there's nothing to distinguish it from its competitors, it's a relaxed place with no pretensions.

Metropolitan Deira Hotel

Clock Tower Roundabout, Al Maktoum Road, Deira (04 295 9171, www.habtoorhotels.com). Metro Al Rigga. **Map** p311 J1.

This hotel is an old timer by Dubai standards, having been around since 1998. These days, it's looking a bit tired, but still offers welcome respite from the crowds around downtown Deira. You'll find comfortable and clean rooms here, though the hotel's main draw is its location near the famous Deira Clock Tower, the Creek and the Deira City Centre shopping centre.

Millennium Airport Hotel

Casablanca Road, Garhoud (04 702 8888, www.millenniumhotels.ae/millenniumdubai). Metro GGICO. **Map** p311 K2.

This hotel, as you'd guess from the name, is aimed squarely at visitors stopping over in Dubai from the nearby airport. Nonetheless, it's an impressive place, with an elegant and inviting marble-heavy lobby, large swimming pool and green spaces that make it a low-key family favourite. Rooms are large (a twin could easily sleep four adults), airy and have pleasant garden views. Beds and wardrobes are both ample, with a subtle Arabic touch running through the decor and furnishings.

Radisson Blu Hotel, Dubai Deira Creek

Baniyas Road, Dubai Creek, Deira (04 222 7171, www.radissonblu.com/hotel-dubaideiracreek). Metro Union. **Map** p313 J3.

This was Dubai's first five-star hotel, occupying a prime location on the Creek since the 1970s. It still boasts a host of excellent restaurants and some interesting decor, but is starting to look a little ragged around the edges. One thing that never gets old are the stunning views of the Creek. If you're looking for a hotel in the heart of the old town action, this is the place to stay.

Budget

Dubai Youth Hostel

Al Nahda Road, Al Qusais (04 298 8151, www.uaeyha.com). Metro Stadium. **Map** p311 L1.

Dubai isn't known as a backpacking destination, but cash-strapped travellers can get a comfortable night's sleep at this popular youth hostel. There are single rooms, doubles and dorms to choose from, breakfast is included in the price, and there's even a swimming pool. And it's only a couple of minutes' walk from Stadium metro station. It's wise to book in advance; members of the Youth Hostel Association can get a discount.

Nihal Hotel

Al Maktoum Road, Deira (04 295 7666, www.nihalhoteldubai.ae). Metro Al Rigga. **Map** p311 J2.

This 70-room three-star hotel is located slap-bang in the middle of Deira, close to the Clock Tower Roundabout. It's not the most impressive hotel, aesthetically speaking, but at these sorts of prices you can't complain. Rooms are basic, with nothing lavish about the bathrooms, but clean and comfortable.

BUR DUBAI & OUD METHA

Deluxe

★ Grand Hyatt Dubai
Sheikh Rashid Road, Oud Metha (04 317 1234, www.dubai.grand.hyatt.com). Metro Dubai Healthcare City. **Map** p311 J3.
This 674-room behemoth is packed full of amenities, such as tennis courts, a fitness centre, spa, swimming pools and an indoor rainforest. There are also 13 bars and restaurants, including Singaporean Peppercrab and Indian iZ. Rooms are decorated with contemporary Arabic touches and the bathrooms feature massaging showers and colossal tubs.

★ Raffles Dubai
13th Street, Sheikh Rashid Road, Oud Metha (04 324 8888, www.raffles.com/dubai). Metro Dubai Healthcare City. **Map** p311 J3.
The Raffles name is synonymous with luxury, and its Dubai outpost is no exception. In a city full of grand lobbies, Raffles' high-ceilinged version still manages to impress, while the opulent decor continues through to the rooms and suites. There's the indulgent Raffles Spa, seven restaurants and bars, including the impressive Japanese eaterie TOMO, award-winning Italian Solo Bistronomia & Vino Bar, and exclusive nightclub People by Crystal.

Expensive

Mövenpick Hotel & Apartment Bur Dubai
19th Street, Oud Metha (04 336 6000, www.moevenpick-hotels.com). **Map** p311 J3.
The location is nondescript, amid the sprawl of Oud Metha, just off the Sheikh Rashid Road. But you'll find pleasant, good-sized rooms here, with comfy beds and adequate furnishings. If you have a bit more cash to splash, the suites and executive rooms are a significant step up from the standard ones, with jacuzzis in the bathrooms. The business and fitness facilities (including a rooftop pool) are impressive. The pick of the restaurants is Chutney's, which serves authentic north Indian cuisine.

Moderate

Arabian Courtyard Hotel & Spa
Al Fahidi Street, Bur Dubai (04 351 9111, www.arabiancourtyard.com). Metro Al Fahidi. **Map** p312 H4.
This huge hotel towers over the historic Al Fahidi district in Bur Dubai; despite the traditional façade, it's fairly new. It's only a short distance from Dubai Museum, Meena Bazaar and the Creek, making it a good choice if you're interested in exploring the city's heritage side. Many of the spacious bedrooms have Creek views.

Ascot Hotel & Royal Ascot Hotel
Khalid Bin Waleed Road, Bur Dubai (04 352 0900, www.ascothoteldubai.com). Metro Al Fahidi. **Map** p312 H4.
Located on the bustling Khalid Bin Waleed Road, the Ascot is the perfect base if you want to explore the historic areas of Bur Dubai. The rooms have modern decor and are of a good size. For an extra couple of hundred dirhams, you can stay in the Ascot's adjacent five-star sibling – the Royal Ascot Hotel.

Raffles Dubai.

Majestic Hotel Tower Dubai
Al Mankhool Road, Bur Dubai (04 359 8888, www.dubaimajestic.com). **Map** p312 H5.
If you want to be within striking distance of the Al Fahidi district, Jumeirah and the Sheikh Zayed Road, this 28-storey hotel is a good option. Rooms are spacious, with an Arabesque theme and opulent furniture. There's also an outdoor swimming pool. The Majestic also has a decent reputation for dining and nightlife: Greek restaurant Elia was highly commended in the European section of the 2015 *Time Out Dubai* Restaurant Awards, while Barrels is a good spot for a relaxed pint, and the Music Room the place to go for live music.

Ramada Dubai
Al Mankhool Road, Bur Dubai (04 351 9999, www.ramadadubai.com). Metro Al Fahidi. **Map** p312 H5.
A little way outside the most hectic areas of Bur Dubai, the Ramada is primarily a business hotel, but is fine for tourists. The rooms are large, although most overlook air-conditioning units of neighbouring buildings, building sites or the busy streets below. There's a small pool, gym, sauna and spa.

★ XVA Art Hotel
Al Fahidi Street, Bur Dubai (04 353 5383, www.xvahotel.com). **Map** p312 H4.
For something that stands out from the crowd, look no further than XVA. This three-in-one boutique hotel, café and art gallery occupies a coral and clay building that was constructed nearly 80 years ago. It's been restored and now offers a unique accommodation option in the city. There are only a handful of rooms, so you'll need to book early.

Budget

Citymax Hotels Bur Dubai
Kuwait Street, Bur Dubai (04 407 8000, www.citymaxhotels.com). **Map** p315 G6/H6.
This clean, minimal hotel offers a more peaceful environment than many of its neighbourhood rivals. It has a pleasant pool deck and decent restaurants, including north-western Indian cuisine at Claypot. The rooms are basic, but a good size for the money.

Golden Sands Hotel Apartments
Al Mankhool Street, near BurJuman, Bur Dubai (04 355 5553, www.goldensandsdubai.com). Metro Al Fahidi. **Map** p313 J5.
Offering sizeable fully serviced self-catering apartments, this is a good choice for those who are planning a slightly longer stay. Options range from studios to four-bedroom apartments, with extras such as a gym, sauna and squash courts. Monthly rates are also available.

President Hotel
Trade Centre Road, Karama (04 334 6565, www.presidenthoteldubai.com). **Map** p315 H7.
Fittingly for its location in bargain-heavy Karama, this 50-room hotel seems as happy to offer knock-down prices as the traders working behind it. Dimly lit hallways lead to equally gloomy rooms that boast views of other buildings and the busy roads around Karama. The beds are quite small, and the tiny bathrooms just about adequate, but for the price and the location, it's hard to complain.

DOWNTOWN DUBAI & BUSINESS BAY

Deluxe

Address Dubai Mall
Financial Centre Road, Downtown Dubai (04 438 8888, www.theaddress.com). **Map** p310 H5.
Of five Address hotels in Dubai, three are in Downtown, including this one. As the name suggests, it's next to the Dubai Mall, the world's largest shopping centre, with a walkway connecting the two. The hotel has 244 rooms and suites, from the cosy Deluxe Room all the way up to the utterly vast Presidential Suite. The Address Dubai Mall has some great alfresco dining options with views of the Dubai Fountain and Burj Khalifa.

Armani Hotel Dubai
Burj Khalifa, Downtown Dubai (04 888 3888, http://dubai.armanihotels.com). Metro Burj Khalifa. **Map** p317 F14.
Giorgio Armani's first foray into the hotel world is in the world's tallest tower: the Burj Khalifa. It's dark, sleek and exudes a very masculine feel, with smooth stone and mahogany dominating the decor. While there's no beachside access, you'll find a decent enough pool by the spa, which offers 'designer healing'. There are 160 guest rooms and suites to choose from, but most people are partial to the ones offering views of the Dubai Fountain and across Downtown. The restaurants are some of the best in the city, including the award-winning Italian Armani/Ristorante. *Photos p274.*

★ JW Marriott Marquis Dubai
Sheikh Zayed Road, Business Bay (04 414 0000, www.marriott.com). Metro Business Bay. **Map** p310 G5.
Get into Dubai's record-breaking spirit by spending a few nights in the high-flying surroundings of the world's tallest hotel. This 72-floor, twin-tower skyscraper reaches 355m (1,165ft) and contains more than 1,600 guest rooms. Needless to say, the views are incredible, especially from the Sea View rooms. All rooms have floor-to-ceiling windows to maximise the outlook, while the decor is a tasteful blend of wood and neutral colours. The restaurants are all worth checking out, and the Saray Spa is one of the city's most tranquil.
► *For more on the Marriott hotel's facilities, see p97* **In the Know**.

Oberoi, Dubai

Sheikh Zayed Road, Business Bay (04 444 1444, www.oberoihotels.com/hotels-in-dubai). Metro Business Bay. **Map** p310 G5.

This Indian hotel chain's Dubai outpost may seem a little out of the way, but it's a luxurious destination in a part of the city that is set for major development. Once finished, the Business Bay Canal is set to flow past the hotel, but until then it will remain slightly stuck out on its own. There are 252 bright and airy rooms and suites to choose from, all with large windows, and one of the city's finest Indian restaurants, Ananta.

★ Palace Downtown Dubai

Sheikh Mohammed Bin Rashid Boulevard, Downtown Dubai (04 428 7888, www.theaddress.com). **Map** p317 F14.

Built in an old Arabian style, the Palace (part of the Address chain) looks very different from most of the other hotel developments around Downtown. Its palm-fringed swimming pool has views of the Burj Khalifa, and the Arabesque design makes the area particularly atmospheric at sunset. Many of its restaurants have front row seats of the Dubai Fountain, and its spa continues the palatial theme.

Sofitel Dubai Downtown

Sheikh Zayed Road, Downtown Dubai (04 503 6666, www.sofitel.com). Metro Burj Khalifa. **Map** p317 E14.

One of Downtown's newest hotels, offering a luxurious sanctuary near the Burj Khalifa and the Dubai Mall. Design has a distinct French flair, and some of the rooms have stunning views of the Burj Khalifa. The So Spa offers plenty of treatments, and there's a handful of high-end restaurants as well.

Expensive

Manzil Downtown Dubai

Sheikh Mohammed Bin Rashid Boulevard, Downtown Dubai (04 428 5888, www.vida-hotels.com). **Map** p310 H5.

The Manzil reopened in 2015 following a significant revamp. From the outside, its Arabesque façade is distinctive, while inside the design is more contemporary. The hotel keeps it simple throughout: rooms are stylish with minimal clutter, and there's a pleasant pool surrounded by sun loungers. It's not flash, but a homely destination in the middle of Downtown.

★ Vida Downtown Dubai

Sheikh Mohammed Bin Rashid Boulevard, Downtown Dubai (04 428 6888, www.vida-hotels.com). **Map** p317 F15.

This stylish hotel opened in 2013 and, along with the nearby Manzil (*see above*), is one of the stand-out properties on the popular Downtown boulevard. Owned and operated by the same company, it is similar to the Manzil in look and feel, but a little less

Armani Hotel Dubai. *See p273.*

Arabesque. Dining options in the hotel are fantastic, with La Serre and Toko both firm favourites with the city's foodies. Rooms have free internet access, flat-screen TVs, and are refreshingly minimal for Dubai.

Moderate

Radisson Blu Hotel, Dubai Downtown
Al Asayel Street, Business Bay (04 450 2000, www.radissonblu.com/hotel-dubaidowntown). **Map** p310 H5.
Its position is not as convenient as hotels on Sheikh Mohammed Bin Rashid Boulevard or the Sheikh Zayed Road, but that keeps prices down, and it's still only a short taxi ride from the action. The standard rooms are on the simple side, but there are some slightly more extravagant suites. The dining options are nothing special, but the pleasant rooftop pool has skyline views.

Ramada Downtown Dubai
Sheikh Mohammed Bin Rashid Boulevard, Downtown Dubai (04 330 7330, www.ramadadowntowndubai.com). **Map** p317 F15.
You'll find the Ramada set back from the Boulevard on the edge of Burj Khalifa Lake. It has 181 suites, ranging from studios to a four-bedroom penthouse with views of the Burj Khalifa. Numerous facilities include badminton and squash courts, a gym and a relaxing outdoor swimming pool.

DIFC, SHEIKH ZAYED ROAD & DWTC

Deluxe

Al Murooj Rotana
Al Safa Street, DIFC (04 321 1111, www.rotana.com). **Map** p317 F13.
Opposite the Dubai Mall though separated from it by a major road, the Al Murooj Rotana is a self-contained property surrounded by a man-made lake. Its setting is awkward for pedestrians – as are most places in Dubai – but it's only a ten-minute taxi ride from Jumeirah Beach. Rooms are comfortable and contemporary, and there's a pleasant pool area and well-equipped gym and spa. Business travellers will applaud the excellent meeting facilities. The hotel is also home to raucous British pub Double Decker.

Conrad Dubai
Sheikh Zayed Road (04 444 7444, www.conraddubai.com). Metro World Trade Centre. **Map** p315 G9.
This impressive hotel has a business-like feel, but also plenty of luxurious touches to make it an indulgent leisure destination. The rooms and suites are stylish and spacious, offering views of either the Arabian Gulf or Sheikh Zayed Road. Marble bathrooms and rain showers add another level of luxury. There's also an incredibly relaxing spa and signature restaurants including Marco Pierre White Grill.

Fairmont Dubai

Sheikh Zayed Road (04 332 5555, www.fairmont.com/dubai). Metro World Trade Centre. **Map** p315 G9.

A monolithic testament to all things stylish, this business hotel is the definition of 21st-century Arabian chic. Often compared to a castle, the design is actually based on a traditional Arabic wind tower. It contains 394 rooms and suites, 3,700sq m (40,000sq ft) of spa facilities and myriad dining and nightlife venues. Two of Dubai's most extravagant nightspots – Cavalli Club (*see p196*) and Cirque Le Soir (*see p200*) – are also attached to the hotel. The guest rooms and suites are huge, with sweeping views of the Sheikh Zayed Road.

H Dubai

Sheikh Zayed Road (04 501 8888, www.h-hotel.com). Metro World Trade Centre. **Map** p315 G9.

Sitting next to a busy roundabout, the H Dubai is better suited to business visitors who need to be close to the action rather than leisure travellers. But it's still a pleasant place to stay, with its inviting Arabesque decor and tranquil spa. Rooms are modern and masculine, with wooden floors and neutral furnishings. Floor-to-ceiling windows offer an excellent view of the city, especially if you're near the top (33rd) floor. Visitors with huge wads of cash can reserve the Sky suite, situated on the 29th and 30th floors.

Jumeirah Emirates Towers

Sheikh Zayed Road (04 330 0000, www.jumeirah.com). Metro Emirates Towers. **Map** p310 H4.

These visually striking towers are a symbol of Dubai, and the business hotel inside them is one of the city's finest. A sophisticated lobby lounge and atrium dominate the ground floor, while glass lifts shoot up and down the 52 floors. Rooms are big, with stylish furnishings, attractive dark wood tables and panoramas that never fail to impress. The hotel has its own pool and spa, plus plenty of shops and restaurants on the ground-floor Jumeirah Emirates Towers Boulevard.

★ Ritz-Carlton DIFC

Gate Village, DIFC (04 372 2222, www.ritzcarlton.com). Metro Financial Centre. **Map** p310 H4.

Bold without being brash, this five-star hotel has retained plenty of European-style charm and, despite being at the heart of the busy Dubai International Financial Centre (DIFC), retains a sense of sanctuary once you step inside. It also fields some impressive restaurants in the shape of Center Cut steakhouse and Café Belge. There are 341 tastefully decorated rooms, 80 suites and two royal suites for a seriously grand stay. None of this comes cheap, of course.

Shangri-La Hotel, Dubai

Sheikh Zayed Road (04 343 8888, www.shangri-la.com). Metro Financial Centre. **Map** p317 E12/F12.

The smart, serene foyer of this immaculate hotel has welcomed many celebrities, and the views it provides over the dramatic Sheikh Zayed Road skyline are second to none. The spacious standard rooms impress with their minimalist chic, while the suites dazzle with their luxurious fittings. The business facilities are state of the art, and there are several top restaurants including Vietnamese establishment Hoi An.

Expensive

Crowne Plaza Dubai

Sheikh Zayed Road (04 331 1111, www.ihg.com). Metro Emirates Towers. **Map** p315 F10.

Guests staying at this stalwart hotel are spoilt for choice when it comes to eating and drinking, with 13 restaurants and bars to try. The location is great too – at the Creek end of Sheikh Zayed Road, and a short taxi ride from major sights such as the Dubai Mall and Jumeirah's beaches. The interiors are starting to look a bit dated and the standard rooms are smallish, but the views of the Sheikh Zayed Road are as good as from any of its rivals, while its business and leisure facilities are impressive for the price bracket.

Dusit Thani Dubai

Sheikh Zayed Road (04 343 3333, www.dusit.com). Metro Financial Centre. **Map** p317 F12.

The Dusit Thani manages to stand out amid the eccentric architecture of the Sheikh Zayed Road with its unusual design – intended to represent two hands in prayer. This Thai-style aesthetic is evident throughout, from the Asian-chic rooms to the smart sarong-wearing staff. Rooms are modern, with floor-to-ceiling windows boasting city views. Guests can work out in the well-stocked gym or laze in the open-air pool on the 36th floor. Business travellers like the location, but its proximity to the Dubai Mall appeals to holidaymakers too.

Radisson Royal Hotel, Dubai

Sheikh Zayed Road (04 308 0000, www.radissonblu.com). Metro World Trade Centre. **Map** p315 G10.

Situated just across the Sheikh Zayed Road from the World Trade Centre, this hotel is perfect for corporate travellers. It has extensive business and meeting facilities, including the funky and colourful Origami meeting rooms. For leisure travellers, there are plenty of restaurants and a spa, plus a shuttle bus service to the beach.

Towers Rotana

Sheikh Zayed Road (04 343 8000, www.rotana.com). Metro Financial Centre. **Map** p317 F12.

Surrounded by grander and considerably more expensive five-star properties, the Towers Rotana attracts a younger clientele than its neighbours. Rooms range from average to cosy in size, but they're very comfortable, and the views over Jumeirah and Satwa are hard to beat. Decor is light and airy

Four Seasons Resort Dubai. *See p279.*

in both the bathrooms and bedrooms, and there's a large pool space and gym in a separate wing. While pitched predominantly at business travellers, the Rotana is seconds from the bars and restaurants on the Sheikh Zayed strip.

Warwick Hotel Dubai

Sheikh Zayed Road (04 506 9600, www.warwickhotels.com/dubai). Metro Financial Centre. **Map** p317 F12.

The four-star Warwick is one of the newest hotels on the Sheikh Zayed Road and offers good access to DIFC. It has all the amenities that you'd expect, from the rooftop swimming pool to a spa and business services. Accommodation options range from deluxe rooms to penthouse suites that occupy the 37th to 42nd floors.

Moderate

Hotel Novotel World Trade Centre Dubai

Dubai World Trade Centre, Sheikh Zayed Road (04 332 0000, www.novotel.com). Metro World Trade Centre. **Map** p315 H10.

This no-nonsense Novotel proves that lower prices doesn't mean boring or basic. The lobby – all dark wood, open space and ordered sophistication – is suitably stylish, while the guest rooms, although small, aren't cramped. The hotel holds little appeal to sun-seekers, offering only a small pool and gym, but it will score highly with business people and those operating along Sheikh Zayed Road. The central location will probably save you a bundle on taxi fares to boot, plus it's next to the World Trade Centre metro station.

Budget

Hotel Ibis World Trade Centre Dubai

Dubai World Trade Centre, Sheikh Zayed Road (04 332 4444, www.accorhotels.com). Metro World Trade Centre. **Map** p315 G10.

This fuss-free hotel has excellent access to Dubai's financial district and the exhibition halls of the World Trade Centre. As you'd expect from the price bracket, facilities are basic and there's no swimming pool. Rooms are on the small side too. But it has a sophisticated feel for a three star and is a sound choice for the shoestring traveller who has no desire for fancy extras. And it's fantastic value for money, which is difficult to find in Dubai.

JUMEIRAH & SATWA

Deluxe

Dubai Marine Beach Resort & Spa

Jumeirah Beach Road, Jumeirah 1 (04 346 1111, www.dxbmarine.com). **Map** p314 D9.

Situated right at the start of Jumeirah Beach Road, this slightly older establishment is a beachfront

hotel that's closer to the city's business districts than most. It's made up of 33 low-rise, villa-style buildings and 15 themed restaurants and bars, which means at night you can gaze at the stars without a skyscraper in sight. Two swimming pools, a kids' pool and a (smallish) private beach make up the rest of the resort, which has a family feel despite the lively nightfront options.

★ Four Seasons Resort Dubai

Jumeirah Beach Road, Jumeirah 2 (04 270 7777, www.fourseasons.com/dubaijb). **Map** p316 A14/B14.
After years of hotel inactivity along Jumeirah Beach Road, this resort arrived in October 2014 to offer a new luxury option in the area. Set on a serene stretch of beach, it has 237 spacious rooms and 49 suites, with views of the Arabian Gulf from one side and Downtown Dubai on the other. The numerous facilities include ten restaurants and lounges, three pools, tennis courts, a gym and a spa. *Photos p277.*

Moderate

Capitol Hotel

Al Mina Road, Satwa (04 346 0111, www.capitol-hotel.com). **Map** p312 G5.
This Capitol is a basic affair with reasonably sized standard rooms boasting huge beds and views of the area's busy roads. The suites are large and welcoming with a well-decorated living space, and can be extended through the use of an adjoining twin room. Sadly, it's let down by its facilities; the rooftop is home to an underwhelming swimming pool, the gym is pokey and the restaurants nothing special. It's situated close to both Satwa's bustling streets and the beach, and nothing is more than a short taxi ride away.

Jumeira Rotana

2nd December Street, Satwa (04 345 5888, www.rotana.com). **Map** p314 F8.
Despite the name, this hotel is actually in shore-free Satwa rather than sandy Jumeirah. That said, it's a pleasant place to stay, with a casual atmosphere and a mix of business and leisure guests. The spacious and light bedrooms come with generously sized beds, plenty of wardrobe space and entertaining views over the backstreets. Rates are reasonable too.

Budget

Chelsea Plaza Hotel

2nd December Street, Satwa (04 398 2222, www.crimsonhotels.com/chelseaplaza). **Map** p315 F8.
Next to Satwa roundabout, this old-fashioned nine-storey hotel delivers far more in terms of comfort, style and facilities than its mundane exterior promises. Most rooms have a clear view of the bustling streets below, and there are complimentary beach and airport transfers to boot.

Holiday Inn Express Dubai – Safa Park

Next to Safa Park, Al Wasl Road (800 4642, www.ihg.com). Metro Business Bay. **Map** p310 G5.
A good budget option in a convenient location, close to both Downtown and Jumeirah. Rooms are basic but clean, and facilities minimal but acceptable for the price. It has an all-day restaurant and a simple bar (imaginatively named 'The Bar'), but Downtown and Sheikh Zayed Road are a short taxi ride away with many more dining options.

AL BARSHA & UMM SUQEIM

Deluxe

The Madinat Jumeirah resort, a faux 'traditional souk' with its own private beach, has various accommodation choices, including hotels Al Qasr and Mina A'Salam and the private villas of Dar Al Masayaf. The resort also has some good (if pricey) souvenir stores, a health club and spa, and plenty of award-winning restaurants and bars.

Burj Al Arab Jumeirah

Jumeirah Road, Umm Suqeim 3 (04 301 7777, www.jumeirah.com). **Map** p318 E2.
See p283 **Luxury Lounging**.

★ Jumeirah Al Qasr

Al Sufouh Road, Umm Suqeim (04 366 8888, www.jumeirah.com). **Map** p318 D2.
Al Qasr (meaning 'The Palace') is designed to reflect a sheikh's summer residence. Grand yet elegant, it has palm trees, beautiful rugs and furniture, elaborate flower arrangements, and each of the spacious rooms comes with a private balcony – it's well worth paying extra for a view of the sea. It's also home to one of the city's most romantic restaurants, Pierchic, which is set on its own pier. With views of the Burj Al Arab and the sea, you can easily sunbathe away the hours, but it's linked by private canals to the other restaurants and attractions in the Madinat Jumeirah resort, so you'll never run out of things to do.

Jumeirah Beach Hotel

Jumeirah Road, Umm Suqeim 3 (04 348 0000, www.jumeirah.com). **Map** p318 E2.
One of the best-known hotels in Dubai, designed to look like a cresting wave, this regal establishment sits at the top of Jumeriah Road with unparalleled views of the Burj Al Arab and what is known locally as Sunset Beach. It's a five-star beach resort, with all the facilities you'd expect, including beach clubs, dive centre and kids' club. It's also next door to Wild Wadi, one of the best waterparks in Dubai. There's a range of rooms and suites, as well as private villas with their own pools and gardens.

Jumeirah Dar Al Masyaf

Al Sufouh Road, Umm Suqeim (04 366 8888, www.jumeirah.com). **Map** p318 E2.

OUT AND ABOUT

Some interesting and exotic lodgings lie further afield.

Jebel Ali is best known for its huge port and sprawling industrial area, but it also has a few options for tourists. The **Mövenpick Ibn Battuta Gate Hotel** (The Gardens, Jebel Ali; 04 444 0000, www.moevenpick-hotels.com) is famous for the huge archway separating the two wings of the building. It's an opulent property, with vast Arabian-style chandeliers adorning the expansive lobby, off which you'll find an array of restaurants. It's a bit far out of town, but right next to the Ibn Battuta metro station and the mall of the same name.

Further along the Sheikh Zayed Road is **JA Jebel Ali Golf Resort** (Exit 13, Sheikh Zayed Road, Jebel Ali; 04 814 5555, www.jaresortshotels.com). There's a nine-hole course, but it's not all about golf here. The resort has two hotels: JA Jebel Ali Beach Hotel, with 231 rooms and suites, and JA Palm Tree Court, offering 208 family-friendly one- and two-bedroom suites.

For a more serious golfing holiday, check into **Address Montgomerie Dubai** (Emirates Hills, off Al Khamila Street; 04 390 5600, www.theaddress.com), where the 18-hole championship course was designed by Colin Montgomerie. The hotel is quite small, with just 21 rooms and suites.

Per Aquum Desert Palm Dubai (Al Awir Road; 04 323 8888), about 20 minutes from Downtown Dubai, offers chic luxury in the midst of manicured polo fields. The 28 suites are complemented by private pool villas.

For those looking to experience the desert while still within touching distance of the city, there are two great options. **Bab Al Shams Desert Resort & Spa** (Al Qudra Road, opposite Endurance City; 04 809 6100, www.meydanhotels.com/babalshams) is built in an Arab fort setting around an oasis; its walls, courtyards, walkways and water features make for an atmospheric experience. **Al Maha Desert Resort & Spa** (Dubai Desert Conservation Reserve, Al Ain Road; 04 832 9900, www.al-maha.com) is 50 minutes from Downtown Dubai, but feels a lot further away. Arabian oryx and gazelles can be seen from the infinity pool or the decks of every suite.

Mövenpick Ibn Battuta Gate Hotel.

Even by Dubai's high standards of service and luxury, the Dar Al Masyaf summer houses are something special. These 29 palatial villas are some of the most sought-after beachfront properties in the city, offering the privacy of secluded surroundings combined with access to the rest of the Madinat's extensive facilities. The two-storey buildings are wonderfully elegant, with one pool to every three villas, intricately landscaped gardens and 24-hour butler service: enough to excite even the most blasé of travellers.

Jumeirah Mina A'Salam

Al Sufouh Road, Umm Suqeim (04 366 8888, www.jumeirah.com). **Map** p318 E2.

Entering here is like walking into a history book. The lobby features fountains, polished stone and scented flowers, and reception staff are decked out in elegant robes. Not that you'll be in a hurry to get away from the hotel because it has some wonderful dining options too. Rooms are large, comfortable and Arabic in style with Persian carpets and ornate designs. Mina A'Salam translates as 'harbour of peace', so you can be sure of a good night's sleep.

Kempinski Mall of the Emirates

Mall of the Emirates, Al Barsha (04 341 0000, www.kempinski.com). Metro Mall of the Emirates. **Map** p318 D3.

Located at one of Dubai's most famous shopping centres, the Kempinski is also known for being next to Ski Dubai – the Middle East's only indoor ski slope. This is a Kempinski hotel through and through, so you can expect five-star luxury the moment you check in. If a room or suite isn't enough, book a 'chalet', which comes with snow-side views and even a fake roaring fire. Assorted restaurants and bars include decadent pool bar Mosaic and Spanish eaterie Salero Tapas & Bodega.

Expensive

Sheraton Dubai Mall of the Emirates

Mall of the Emirates, Al Barsha (04 377 2000, www.sheratondubaimalloftheemirates.com). Metro Mall of the Emirates. **Map** p318 D3.

For shopaholics seeking a little bit of luxury, this hotel is the perfect choice. Connected to Mall of the Emirates via a walkway, it also links to the mall's metro station and is convenient for trips to the beach. Decent nightlife options include alfresco bar Vantage, and there are top-notch fitness and spa facilities.

Moderate

Gloria Hotel

TECOM, Sheikh Zayed Road (04 399 6666, www.gloriahoteldubai.com). Metro Dubai Internet City. **Map** p318 C2.

Set just off the Sheikh Zayed Road and right next to an entrance for Dubai Internet City metro station, Gloria Hotel is in a great location. It doesn't serve alcohol so is popular with guests from the Gulf, but there are hotels nearby that have decent bars. You can choose from spacious suites with either city or sea views, both of which are pretty spectacular.

Grand Millennium Hotel Dubai

TECOM, Sheikh Zayed Road (04 429 9999, www.millenniumhotels.ae). Metro Dubai Internet City. **Map** p318 C2.

TECOM isn't the most glamorous area of Dubai, which could explain why this solid five-star hotel is so affordable. While rooms aren't enormous, the suites are generous and the city views impressive. There's also an outdoor heated pool, jacuzzi, fitness centre and a spa that offers Moroccan hammam treatments.

Media Rotana

TECOM, Sheikh Zayed Road (04 435 0000, www.rotana.com). Metro Dubai Internet City. **Map** p318 C2.

This large hotel has a business feel, but is comfortable enough for leisure travellers. The 536 rooms range from the modest 33sq m (350sq ft) club room to a premium suite complete with free evening cocktails. It has some fairly standard dining options, but the business facilities are excellent.

Budget

Grand Excelsior Hotel

Al Barsha Road, Al Barsha 1 (04 444 9999, www.grandexcelsior.ae). **Map** p318 D3.

At first glance, the Grand Excelsior resembles a cruise ship beached amid the Barsha apartment buildings. It's slightly dated, but the rooms are a good size for the price. There are some dubious entertainment venues inside, including Copacabana, which, despite its name, looks like it's been modelled on an English pub.

Ramada Chelsea Hotel Al Barsha

23rd Street, Al Barsha 1 (04 01 9000, www.ramada.com). **Map** p318 D3.

With fairly basic but large rooms, this is a good option for the cost-conscious. It also has an outdoor pool and some average spa facilities, though not enough amenities to warrant a long time spent indoors. But Mall of the Emirates is a shortish walk away, where you'll find plenty of entertainment and a metro station.

Ramee Rose Hotel

TECOM, Sheikh Zayed Road (04 450 0111, www.rameehotels.com). Metro Dubai Internet City. **Map** p318 C2.

There are 126 basic rooms in this unassuming hotel in TECOM. It's a good place to base yourself if you don't plan to spend too much time inside. There's a small outdoor pool and a basic gym, plus a lively night out waiting at Rock Bottom Café.

AL SUFOUH & PALM JUMEIRAH

Deluxe

Anantara Dubai The Palm Resort & Spa

East Crescent, Palm Jumeirah (04 567 8888, www.dubai-palm.anantara.com). **Map** p318 D1.
Out on the far eastern side of the Palm, this resort has 293 rooms and villas, offering unspoilt sea views in a location that feels a world away from the city. The decor is beautifully simple, and if you can get a sea-view room or villa, you'll never want to leave. The Thai-inspired spa also shouldn't be missed.

★ Atlantis The Palm

Palm Jumeirah (04 426 2000, www.atlantisthepalm.com). **Map** p308 A1.
One of the most famous landmarks in Dubai, this iconic hotel was the first to open on the Palm and is still one of the city's biggest draws. The decor has a nautical theme and, fittingly, there are plenty of watery activities to enjoy, including the Lost Chambers Aquarium, Dolphin Bay (for swimming with dolphins) and Aquaventure Waterpark. It offers 1,000-plus rooms and over 100 suites; if you can, book one of the Imperial Club rooms. These include access to the Club Lounge, which has a great selection of free food and drinks. Otherwise, 17 fine restaurants, bars and lounges offer an array of cuisines.

Fairmont The Palm

Golden Mile, Palm Jumeirah (04 457 3388, www.fairmont.com/palm-dubai). **Map** p318 B1.
Located on the main drag of the Palm is the suitably luxurious Fairmont. There are plenty of activities to keep guests entertained, such as a beach club, spa and a popular kids' club. The interesting mix of restaurants includes Mashrabiya Lounge for one of the city's best afternoon tea experiences. The hotel has 381 rooms and suites, some with views of the Arabian Gulf and Dubai Marina skyline.

★ Jumeirah Zabeel Saray

West Crescent, Palm Jumeirah (04 453 0000, www.jumeirah.com). **Map** p318 B1.
The architects behind Zabeel Saray have been inspired by the Ottoman Empire. Opulence pours from every wall and it feels grand, but slightly overwhelming too – you wouldn't want to walk into this place in scruffy shorts and flip flops. Rooms and suites are as luxurious as it gets, but with a more classical feel, so the vibe is elegant rather than tacky. The on-site Talise Ottoman Spa, one of Dubai's grandest, offers traditional Turkish hammam treatments.

Kempinski Hotel & Residences Palm Jumeirah

West Crescent, Palm Jumeirah (04 444 2000, www.kempinski.com). **Map** p308 A1.
This luxury beach hotel on the Palm has European decor, manicured lawns and its own private beach. There are 244 suites, penthouses and villas; the last are lavish five-bedroom properties with their own pools, jacuzzis and private beach access. The hotel is a bit out of the way on the West Crescent, but the restaurants and bars keep guests entertained.

Le Méridien Mina Seyahi Beach Resort & Marina

Al Sufouh Road (04 399 3333, www.lemeridien-minaseyahi.com). Tram Mina Seyahi. **Map** p318 B2.
The guest rooms are pleasant enough, if a bit dated, but try to book a sea-facing Club Room – as well as a better view, you'll get complimentary airport transfers and DVD rentals thrown in, along with a free buffet breakfast, afternoon tea and cocktail hours in the Le Méridien Club Lounge. The hotel has a prime location on a decent stretch of beach and the kids' club is excellent, with a full range of activities. Weekends at the ever-popular beach bar Barasti can be particularly raucous, so if you're travelling with a family, request a room as far from the noise as possible or you'll be awake listening to revellers until the early hours of the morning.

One&Only Royal Mirage

Al Sufouh Road (04 399 9999, http://royalmirage.oneandonlyresorts.com). Tram Media City. **Map** p318 B2.
It can be hard sometimes to escape the modern metropolis that is Dubai, but once through the gates of the One&Only Royal Mirage, you'll have no problems forgetting the skyscrapers and traffic. One of the city's most secluded and hidden-away hotels, situated amid 65 acres of manicured lawns and beach frontage, it's for visitors who want to seriously relax. It's home to one of the city's hottest beach bars, Jetty Lounge, where you can sit and watch the Palm's many luxury boats and Dubai's beautiful people.

One&Only The Palm Dubai

West Crescent, Palm Jumeirah (04 440 1010, http://thepalm.oneandonlyresorts.com). **Map** p318 B1.
The One&Only The Palm has an exclusive island getaway feel, complete with honeymoon atmosphere. There are fantastic views of the mainland to enjoy and it's also one of the quietest five-star resorts in town. Rooms will blow you away: even the most basic option is a secluded, three-level 'Manor House' – but be sure to insist on a beach view or you might be left looking out at a less glamorous pathway. Of the three restaurants, don't miss STAY by Yannick Alléno, a high-end French venue. *Photos p284.*

Rixos The Palm Dubai

East Crescent, Palm Jumeirah (04 457 5555, http://thepalmdubai.rixos.com). **Map** p318 C1.
Each of the 230 rooms and suites here has at least one balcony with a sea view. It's secluded due to its location out on the East Crescent, but there's plenty to do, from beach clubs to a spa, while the hotel also runs a complimentary water taxi to Dubai Marina.

LUXURY LOUNGING

Book a date with decadence at the 'seven-star' Burj Al Arab.

Dubai's most famous hotel is every bit as extravagant and outrageous as you've heard. The tallest hotel in the world when it was built in 1999, the **Burj Al Arab** (*see p279*) appointed itself two stars more than official ratings allow, and watched as press inches, bookings and room rates rocketed. The landmark building, whose sail-like structure recalls dhow trading vessels and is a tribute to the region's seafaring tradition, stands on its own man-made island some 280 metres (920 feet) offshore, linked to the mainland by a slender, gently curving causeway. Taller than the Eiffel Tower, it has its own helipad on the 28th floor for guests who prefer to fly from Dubai's airport rather than ride in one of a fleet of 14 white Rolls-Royces across a bridge that shoots jets of flame to acknowledge the arrival of a VIP.

After the sleek and stylish exterior, the garishly overwrought interior can come as something of a shock; it's definitely not a place for people with egalitarian sensibilities or an aversion to gilding. A triumphant waterfall cascades into the lobby and is flanked by floor-to-ceiling aquariums so vast the staff have to don scuba gear to clean them. Bedrooms are 8,000 square metres of 22-carat gold leaf that covers columns, ceilings, panels and every tap. Huge golden pillars reach up into the atrium: greens, reds and blues all vie for prominence in a reminder that style in Dubai is as much a case of volume as it is of taste.

However, if you have the cash to splash, a night here will earn you unlimited holiday bragging rights – after all, how many people do you know who have stayed in a (admittedly self-appointed) seven-star hotel? Each room at the Burj is a duplex suite and there are 202 in total, including two royal suites on the 25th floor. All are equipped with the latest technology: internet access, a 42-inch plasma screen TV, and, in keeping with the sheer decadence, a remote control allowing you to see who's at the door and let your guests in without having to leave the comfort of your armchair. The management at the Burj Al Arab prides itself on the hotel's personalised service. Each suite has its own butler and each floor its own guest service desk. An unbeatable view of Dubai's coastline can be enjoyed from the Al Muntaha restaurant, which is suspended 200 metres (656 feet) above the Gulf and reached by an express panoramic lift travelling at six metres per second.

If you can't afford a bed at the hotel (a standard room will set you back at least Dhs5,000 a night), but still want to see the obscene affluence of its interiors for yourself, book in for afternoon tea or cocktails. There's a minimum spend of Dhs350 per person at Sky View Bar, while afternoon tea costs Dhs620 per person. But it's just about worth the expense to say you've been inside one of the world's most famous buildings.

★ Sofitel Dubai The Palm Resort & Spa

East Crescent, Palm Jumeirah (04 455 6677, www.sofitel-dubai-thepalm.com). **Map** p308 B1.
The Sofitel stretches along a private beach, but it's also one of the greenest resorts on the Palm, with palm trees dotted around the low-rise complex. There are rooms, apartments, suites and villas to choose from, 12 restaurants and bars, and a luxurious spa.

Waldorf Astoria Dubai Palm Jumeirah

West Crescent, Palm Jumeirah (04 818 2222, www.waldorfastoria3.hilton.com). **Map** p308 B2.
With a private beach, this is a relaxing getaway on the West Crescent. The luxurious rooms and suites are light and airy, and all have sea views. For those looking for a more active holiday than just sunbathing, there's a dedicated watersports centre.

Westin Dubai Mina Seyahi Beach Resort & Marina

Al Sufouh Road (04 399 4141, www.westinminaseyahi.com). Tram Mina Seyahi. **Map** p318 B2.
The Westin is a stately complex, full of people looking to enjoy the good life. The rooms stand out because of the hotel's 'Heavenly' beds and sweeping sea views. The Westin's beach is a place to see and be seen, and the watersports centre is one of the best in the city.

Moderate

Media One Hotel

Al Falak Street, Dubai Media City (04 427 1000, www.mediaonehotel.com). Tram Mina Seyahi. **Map** p318 B2.
This affordable business hotel has a modern vibe, chic design and regular promotions and offers that are worth keeping an eye out for. Rooms are split into four categories – hip, cool, calm and chill-out – depending on what kind of holiday you want to have. Media One is also home to some popular bars, including Q43 on the 43rd floor and outdoor bars DEK on 8 and Garden on 8.

Radisson Blu Hotel, Dubai Media City

Dubai Media City, next to Media City Amphitheatre (04 366 9111, www.radissonblu.com). Metro Nakheel, or Tram Dubai Media City. **Map** p318 B2.
This place is geared towards business travellers, as it's surrounded by the offices of international companies, but it's an ideal place to mix business with pleasure. The rooms and facilities are nice enough, with the slightly larger Business Class rooms your best bet, as they come with access to the Business Lounge for free food and drink, and DVDs. Business rooms are also in the East Tower – a lot quieter than the West Tower where the noise of bar revelry can keep you up until 2am. Rates are reasonable and, depending on when you book, can be a bargain.

Budget

Holiday Inn Express Dubai Internet City

Behind Zayed University, Knowledge Village (800 4642, www.holidayinnexpress.com/internetcity). Tram Knowledge Village. **Map** p318 C2.
The location isn't amazing, but this budget hotel has some great amenities for leisure travellers, despite its business credentials. It's surrounded by the learning

One&Only The Palm Dubai. *See p282.*

institutes of Knowledge Village, so there's not much to see in the vicinity – but you can catch the tram to Dubai Marina. There's also a complimentary shuttle service to Mall of the Emirates. Rooms are basic.

DUBAI MARINA & JBR

Deluxe

Address Dubai Marina

Next to Dubai Marina Mall, Dubai Marina (04 436 7777, www.theaddress.com). Tram Dubai Marina Mall. **Map** p318 A2.

This hotel occupies a prime position on the water's edge, next to the yachts moored in the Marina. The luxurious rooms are tastefully decorated and most offer views over the Marina and surrounding skyscrapers. There are a couple of bars and restaurants, including all-day dining venue Mazina and laid-back pool bar Shades. The hotel is right next door to Dubai Marina Mall if you're looking for a shopping fix.

Ritz-Carlton, Dubai

The Walk, Jumeirah Beach Residence (04 399 4000, www.ritzcarlton.com). Tram Jumeirah Beach Residence 1. **Map** p318 A2.

It's all about the Ritz style here, and standards are as high as you'd expect. Try to get a room at the Club Level, where you can enjoy breakfast, hors d'oeuvres, afternoon tea and loads of goodies through the day at the Club Lounge as part of the room rate. There's a 350m (1,150ft) private beach and huge landscaped gardens, plus the various attractions of the Walk at JBR on the doorstep.

Expensive

DoubleTree by Hilton Hotel Dubai

The Walk, Jumeirah Beach Residence (04 453 3333, http://doubletree3.hilton.com). Tram Jumeirah Beach Residence 2. **Map** p318 A2.

This is one of the newest hotels along the Walk at JBR, with plenty of fresh facilities for leisure travellers. There's a private beach, infinity pool, spa, gym and some decent dining options, including the Kitchen Table, which spills out on to the terrace by the pool. The hotel has 110 suites, containing one to three bedrooms, all with balconies.

Dubai Marriott Harbour Hotel & Suites

Al Sufouh Road, Dubai Marina (04 319 4000, www.marriott.com). Tram Marina Towers. **Map** p318 B2.

Located in Dubai Marina, this Marriott hotel is right next to the action – and a fair bit of construction. The good news is that it hardly affects your stay as you won't hear any noise from your suite. Only one-, two- and three-bedroom suites are available. With kitchens and living rooms, they're more like fully furnished apartments – ideal for families travelling with children. But do insist on a suite on a higher floor as the international AZ.U.R restaurant and bar on the fifth floor can get busy. There are other restaurants, both in the hotel and around the neighbourhood, as well as a nearby convenience store.

Grosvenor House Dubai

Al Sufouh Road, Dubai Marina (04 399 8888, www.grosvenorhouse-dubai.com). **Map** p318 B2.

KEEPING IT LOCAL

Dubai's home-grown hotel chains offer something different.

The multicultural make-up of Dubai is reflected in its range of hotels. And while the international chains occupy some of the prime locations in the city, Dubai's home-grown hotel groups own arguably the most iconic properties in the emirate.

Jumeirah Group, which was founded in Dubai in 1997, operates the ultra-luxurious **Burj Al Arab** (*see p279*), one of the world's most famous hotels. **Al Qasr** (*see p279*), **Dar Al Masyaf** (*see p279*) and **Mina A'Salam** (*see p281*) within the Madinat Jumeirah complex, plus the **Jumeirah Beach Hotel** (*see p279*), are other well-known properties run by the company. If you stay at a Jumeirah property, you'll probably be able to enjoy discounts or free use of the facilities at the chain's other hotels.

The Address is owned by Dubai's Emaar Properties and has five high-end hotels. The Address Downtown Dubai, **Address Dubai Mall** (*see p273*) and Palace Downtown Dubai occupy enviable positions around the Burj Khalifa, while **Address Dubai Marina** (*see p285*) is the company's property in 'New Dubai'. **Address Montgomerie Dubai** (*see p280* **Out and About**), meanwhile, is perfect for serious golfers.

At the other end of the scale, **XVA Art Hotel** (*see p273; pictured*) is a more down-to-earth option, and unique in the city. Housed in a building that was constructed nearly 80 years ago, this hotel, café and art gallery is a rare chance to experience staying in a traditional setting – a slice of Dubai before the mega projects arrived.

One of the first hotels to be built in Dubai Marina, this consists of two towers that feature a range of accommodation options. The standard Deluxe Rooms are perfectly comfortable, but it's worth upgrading to a Premier Room, which gives access to the Grosvenor Club Lounge on the 44th floor with its stunning views and complimentary food and drink. Grosvenor also has a prime location, but none of the crawling traffic neighbouring Jumeirah Beach Residence is known for. You're a short walk from popular nightspots, but far enough away to be able to sleep peacefully.

Habtoor Grand Beach Resort & Spa

Off Al Sufouh Road, Jumeirah Beach Residence (04 704 8888, www.habtoorhotels.com). **Map** p318 B2.

This rather ornate (and occasionally over-the-top) Marina hotel is perched on the edge of Jumeirah Beach Residence, with good access to the area's attractions. Families have their pick of outdoor pools, kids' clubs, a private beachfront and plenty of restaurants. If you want to sit back and unwind with a cocktail in hand, check out XL Beach Club, which promises international DJs and artists. Rooms are extensive and have a contemporary feel that's meant to bring Arabic hospitality to life. For the best sea vistas, book one of the higher Tower rooms.

★ Hilton Dubai Jumeirah Resort

The Walk, Jumeirah Beach Residence (04 399 1111, www3.hilton.com). Tram Jumeirah Beach Residence 1. **Map** p318 A2.

The JBR Hilton was one of the first to arrive in the area, back in 2000. While the years since have seen JBR transformed beyond recognition, the Hilton retains a sense of calm. But step out of the hotel and you'll be on the Walk, home to hundreds of cafés and shops. Although there's a free beach on the doorstep, we'd strongly recommend staying within the Hilton Beach Club and making the most of the VIP facilities and watersports area. The rooms lack some of the opulence that has come to be expected from a Dubai hotel and the building's exterior is starting to show signs of ageing. Having said that, rooms are clean, well presented and more than three-quarters of them have a small balcony and sea view. Add in the beachfront location and Hilton service, and you've got one of the most in-demand holiday locations in the city.

InterContinental Dubai Marina

Jumeirah Beach Road, Dubai Marina (04 446 6777, www.ihg.com). Tram Jumeirah Beach Residence 1. **Map** p318 A2.

This hotel opened in June 2015 in a prime Dubai Marina location. With a tram station and the myriad attractions of Jumeirah Beach Residence nearby, it is ideally placed for a lively Dubai stay. There are 328 rooms, suites and residences, which look out on to the Marina's yachts. Restaurants include Ynot Bar & Kitchen, serving wine, cheese and tapas-style dishes, and Marina Social, the first restaurant in the Middle East from acclaimed British chef Jason Atherton.

Mövenpick Hotel Jumeirah Beach

The Walk, Jumeirah Beach Residence (04 449 8888, www.moevenpick-hotels.com). Tram Jumeirah Beach Residence 1. **Map** p318 A2.

Centrally located on the Walk, the Mövenpick is a great choice if you want to combine dining out with daily trips to the beach. The 294 rooms and suites are spacious enough, and some offer sea views. You can relax by the infinity pool, lounging in cabanas while taking in views of the Arabian Gulf. There are a couple of bars and restaurants on site, or you can venture out to the Walk for a whole world of choice.

Sheraton Jumeirah Beach Resort

The Walk, Jumeirah Beach Residence (04 399 5533, www.sheratonjumeirahbeach.com). Tram Jumeirah Beach Residence 2. **Map** p318 A2.

A stylish resort property with a good stretch of sand, decent beach club, spacious gardens and a fine pool. Popular with European package tourists, the hotel blurs the five-star lines with the overall vibe being comfortable rather than lavish. Rooms are large and overlook either the sea and resort area or JBR.

Sofitel Dubai Jumeirah Beach

The Walk, Jumeirah Beach Residence (04 448 4848, www.sofitel-dubai-jumeirahbeach.com). **Map** p318 A2.

This is a tastefully decorated hotel, which is welcome in often gaudy Dubai. Rooms definitely have a luxurious feel, but head to the higher floors for the best view. The outdoor pool is adequate, especially when it goes into the shade for about an hour during the sweltering summer months. Guests receive a complimentary beach kit, including a beach mat, towel and water bottle.

Moderate

Amwaj Rotana

The Walk, Jumeirah Beach Residence (04 428 2000, www.rotana.com). Tram Jumeirah Beach Residence 2. **Map** p318 A2.

The Amwaj Rotana, while lacking its own private beach, manages to compete with JBR rivals through its laid-back approach and impressive facilities. The rooms offer some of the best sea views in Dubai, stretching from the Marina entrance to Burj Al Arab, and the casual restaurants are worth a visit, whether or not you're a guest. Italian Rosso is invariably busy, while Japanese Benihana offers regular specials.

JA Ocean View Hotel

The Walk, Jumeirah Beach Residence (04 814 5599, www.jaresortshotels.com). Tram Jumeirah Beach Residence 2. **Map** p318 A2.

This hotel has 342 rooms and suites, all with a sea view. The outdoor pool overlooks the Arabian Gulf and there's a health club, jacuzzi and sauna. The hotel is also home to Gaelic-inspired bar Girders and Girders Garden, both of which can get quite rowdy.

Getting Around

ARRIVING AND LEAVING

By air

There are two international airports in Dubai, with most travellers likely to fly into **Dubai International Airport (DIA)** in Garhoud. The other airport is **Al Maktoum International**, which is on the other side of the city in Jebel Ali. The airports share a website (www.dubaiairports.ae) and phone numbers (call centre 04 224 5555, immigration 04 800 5111).

DIA has three terminals, with Terminal 3 catering primarily to Emirates, but with Qantas also flying out of there. Almost all other major airlines arrive at Terminal 1. The smaller Terminal 2 caters largely for low-cost flights, including budget airline Flydubai, which flies to other Middle Eastern destinations, Eastern Europe and South Asia.

The major airlines using Al Maktoum International are Gulf Air and Qatar Airways. Operations are expected to increase at this airport, but for the time being DIA is the hub.

Before you leave the terminal, you'll see Dubai Duty Free (04 800 4443), which is the last chance to purchase alcohol before entering Dubai's 'hotel-only' licensing restrictions (*see p292* **Customs**).

Airport facilities at DIA include internet and banking services, shops, restaurants, business services, bars, pubs and a hotel. Al Maktoum International has slightly fewer facilities, but you'll still find plenty of shops and restaurants.

To and from the airport

DIA is in Garhoud, about 5km (3 miles) from Downtown.

If you're staying at one of the big hotels, you'll get a complimentary shuttle bus or limousine transfer to and from the airport. Otherwise, taxis are the most convenient and practical form of transport. There's a Dhs20 surcharge on pick-up from the terminal (instead of the usual Dhs5). This means that the journey from the airport to Bur Dubai costs around Dhs40, and the return journey is Dhs20 or so. It takes about ten minutes to get to Bur Dubai; Jumeirah, Dubai Marina and the hotel beach resorts are half an hour away.

Another option is the RTA-operated **Sky Bus**, or **Terhab**, service, which runs from all three terminals at DIA to various hotels around the city. One way tickets cost Dhs15, to be paid by Nol card (*see p289*), which can be purchased at airport information kiosks.

The **Dubai Metro** red line stops at DIA Terminals 1 and 3. Single journeys range from Dhs3 to Dhs7.5 depending on how many zones you travel through. A one-day pass costs Dhs20 and offers unlimited travel.

Al Maktoum International Airport is situated in Jebel Ali, about 55km (35 miles) from Downtown. There's no Metro service, so taking a taxi is the best option. The starting fare is Dhs20, with a journey to Dubai Marina taking about 30 minutes.

The F55 **bus** connects the airport to its nearest Metro station at Ibn Battuta Mall, while the F55A travels to Satwa Bus Station when the Metro is in operation. But note that bulky luggage is not allowed on buses.

Call 04 284 4444 or 04 800 9090 for more details, or visit www.rta.ae.

Airport parking

There are short- and long-term parking facilities available at DIA. Tariffs vary depending on the terminal. For Terminals 1 and 2, expect to pay from Dhs20 per hour up in short stay, and Dhs100 per day in long stay. For Terminal 3, the daily rate is Dhs240. At Al Maktoum International, all car parking is free.

Airlines

All airlines operating into DIA are listed on the airport website.

By road

The UAE is bordered to the north and east by Oman, and to the south and west by Saudi Arabia. Road access to Dubai is via the Abu Dhabi emirate to the south, Sharjah to the north, and Oman to the east. There is no charge for driving between emirates, but travel to or from Oman or Saudi Arabia requires you to show your passport, driving licence, insurance and visa. The visa for Oman costs RO5 (Dhs47) for UAE residents or RO20 (Dhs190) for tourists.

At the border, your car is likely to be searched; carrying alcohol is prohibited. All the highways linking Dubai to the other emirates and Oman are in good condition. Ensure your vehicle and the air-conditioning are in good working order, as it's inevitably hot at most times of the year, and the drive through the Hajar Mountains to Muscat, the capital of Oman, takes approximately five hours. Check with the Royal Oman Police (+968 2456 9392, www.rop.gov.om) before you leave for any important changes in travel policy. For traffic enquiries, contact RTA (04 800 9090, www.rta.ae, www.dubaipolice.gov.ae). *See also below* **Navigation**.

NAVIGATION

Thanks to its modern road system, it's fairly easy to get around most of Dubai. However, in some places the infrastructure has struggled to cope with the growth of the city, most notably the Garhoud and Maktoum bridges spanning the Creek and the Shindagha tunnel underneath it, as well as Dubai Marina in the new part of town. During rush hours (7-9am, 5-8pm Mon-Thur, Sun), serious tailbacks can develop.

Despite the relatively good road system, Dubai can be a dangerous place to drive. There are high numbers of road accidents and deaths, caused largely by speeding and poor lane discipline. Many drivers tailgate, chat away on their mobiles and don't use their indicators or mirrors.

The easiest way to get around by road is in a taxi (*see p289*). Water taxis or *abras* (*see p290*) are also available on the Creek, but won't help you get around the whole city.

The Dubai Metro (*see p289*) has two lines – Red and Green – that cover some major areas of the city, but not all. Dubai's public buses are not tourist friendly, and are primarily used by people unable to afford cars or taxis. The biggest problem with getting around Dubai, though, is the lack of an accurate system of street names. Some of the larger roads and streets are known by their name, but most are just numbered. This means your destination is usually identified by a nearby landmark, typically a hotel or building. However, this may change with the introduction of the Makani geo-addressing system. *See also p291* **Addresses**.

PUBLIC TRANSPORT

Nol card

Using public transport in Dubai becomes simpler if you have a Nol card. These smart cards can be pre-loaded with credit, which is deducted when you check-in and check-out at Metro or tram stations, as well as when using buses and water transport. There are also plans to fit taxis with Nol card readers.

As a visitor, there are two Nol card options: Silver or Gold. The Silver card provides access to the standard carriages on the Metro, tram and Dubai ferry, while the Gold card can be used in the premium carriages, which are more spacious and have leather seats.

Both the Silver and Gold Nol cards cost Dhs25, and include Dhs19 of useable credit. To find out more, visit www.nol.ae.

Buses

The public bus system is rarely used by tourists, due to the convenience of taxis and Dubai Metro. The service is cheap but routes can be convoluted and at times erratic.

For timetables, prices and route maps, it's best to check online (www.rta.ae), or to use the RTA's Wojhati journey planning website (http://wojhati.rta.ae). You can also call the main information line (24 hours, seven days a week; 04 800 9090).

To use a bus in Dubai, you will need a Nol card, which has to be scanned on the card reader when entering and exiting the bus. All buses are fitted with information screens that display the upcoming stops, although these are often not working. Eating, drinking and smoking are not allowed on the bus, and the front three rows of seats are reserved for women. Be sure to always have a valid Nol card with you while travelling on the bus, as inspectors carry out random checks and fine offenders Dhs200.

Metro

The driverless, fully automated Dubai Metro runs on two lines: the 52km (32-mile) Red line between Rashidiya and Jebel Ali, and the 22.5km (14-mile) Green line between Etisalat and Creek stations. The Red line is likely to be the most useful while visiting the city, with it passing through major stops such as Mall of the Emirates, Dubai Mall/Burj Khalifa and BurJuman in the heart of Bur Dubai. It also services Terminals 1 and 2 at Dubai International Airport. The Green line links to the Red Line at BurJuman and Union stations.

All the Metro trains are air-conditioned, as are the stations and walkways. Over the last few years, the Metro has become increasingly busy, especially during rush hours (7-9am, 5-8pm Mon-Thur, Sun). During these times, it's unlikely that you'll get a seat, and even getting on the train may be difficult. However, this being Dubai, there is a premium option in the form of the Gold Class, which comes complete with leather seats and is usually slightly less crowded during rush hour, but more expensive than the regular class. There are also designated sections for women, which are increased during rush hour.

A single journey on the Metro starts from Dhs3 for travel between one zone, rising to Dhs7.5 for more than two zones. Single Gold Class journeys start from Dhs6 and rise to Dhs15.

To plan a journey, visit http://wojhati.rta.ae or call 04 800 9090.

Monorail (Palm Jumeirah)

Opened in April 2009, with plans for numerous stations between Dubai Internet City and Atlantis the Palm, the monorail currently stops at only two stations. Passengers can get on at Gateway Towers and travel to Atlantis the Palm. However, the arrival of the Dubai Tram (*see right*) has justified the existence of the monorail somewhat with a link between Palm Jumeirah tram station and Gateway Towers.

The trains are automatic and driverless, running approximately every 15 minutes between 10am and 10pm every day. Tickets cost Dhs15 one way, and Dhs25 return.

Taxis

Official taxis are well maintained, air-conditioned and metered. Fares are 1.71 per kilometre, with the price for flagged-down taxis starting at Dhs5 between 6am and 10pm, and Dhs5.5 between 10pm and 6am. Pre-booked taxis start at Dhs8 during the day, and Dhs12 at night. The minimum fare is Dhs12.

Taxi drivers usually have a reasonable grasp of English, so you shouldn't find it too difficult to explain where you want to go. They also have a reputation for being honest, so if you leave something in a taxi, your driver might find a way to return it to you. Failing this, call the company you used and give the time, destinations (to and from) and taxi number, and they will do their best to help. If you get a receipt the driver's details will be on there.

One problem you are likely to encounter in a taxi is drivers complaining about a lack of change. It's always worth carrying smaller denominations, otherwise you may end up getting into an argument. Driving standards also tend to vary wildly, with some drivers extremely erratic behind the wheel. To book an official RTA taxi, call 04 208 0808.

Unofficial taxis are best avoided, as they tend to be older cars with poor air-con and they may rip you off. If it's the only option available, be sure to agree on a price first.

Tram

The Dubai Tram was officially launched on 11 November 2014, and runs for 10.6km (6.5 miles) from Dubai Marina to Al Sufouh. There are 11 stations with stops at Jumeirah Beach Residence, Dubai Marina Mall and Palm Jumeirah, where it links to the Palm monorail. It links to the Dubai Metro at Jumeirah Lakes Towers and Damac Properties (Dubai Marina) stations. Trams arrive every six minutes at peak times, and every 12 minutes during regular hours, with it in operation from 6.30am to 1.30am Mon-Thur, Sat, Sun and 9am to 1.30am Fri. There is a flat rate of Dhs3 for travelling on the tram with a Nol card, or Dhs4 if purchasing a single ticket. A journey in the Gold Class will cost Dhs6. There is also a women-only carriage.

Ask Dubai residents about the tram, and you may hear complaints about it being slow (it travels at 12mph and takes 42 minutes to complete a round trip) and the fact that it has caused traffic chaos in the Marina. But come the searing heat of summer, the Dubai Tram makes a lot more sense.

To find out the timetable and other information, visit http://dubaitram.rta.ae or call 800 90 90.

Trolley

At the time of writing, the hydrogen- and electric-powered Dubai Trolley was set to begin operation along on a 1km (half-mile) stretch of Downtown Dubai. Running along Sheikh Mohammed Bin Rashid Boulevard, it will eventually link up major attractions such as Dubai Mall and Souk Al Bahar. Each trolley will be able to carry 74 passengers, with seating available inside or on the open deck.

Water taxis

Abras are water taxis that ferry Dubai workers and tourists across the Creek for Dhs1. The boats run between 5am and midnight, carry about 20 people and take just a few minutes to make the crossing from Bur Dubai on the south bank of the Creek to Deira on the north, or vice versa.

Other options for travelling by water in Dubai include the Water Bus, which operates on the Creek between Al Seef and Al Ghubaiba, as well as around Dubai Marina. Fares range from Dhs2 to Dhs5.

For longer trips – which are more like mini cruises, but can still be used to travel around the city – there's the Dubai Ferry. The most practical option is the route between Dubai Marina and Al Ghubaiba on the Creek. It costs Dhs50 for a regular single ticket, or Dhs75 in Gold Class.

DRIVING

People drive on the right in Dubai. Seatbelts are compulsory in the front seats and recommended in the back. In residential areas, the speed limit is normally between 40kph (25mph) and 80kph (50mph). On the highways within the city, it's 100kph (60mph); outside the city, it's 120kph (75mph).

Although there are, in theory, fines and bans for a whole series of offences, in practice enforcement of these is pretty erratic. While you may have to pay up to Dhs1,500 if you're caught going through an amber or red light, don't expect much in the way of road rules or driving etiquette if you venture out by car.

Traffic fines & offences

A comprehensive official traffic police website (www.dubaipolice.gov.ae) lists the details of licence requirements, contact numbers and fines for offences.

There is zero tolerance on drinking and driving. If you're caught driving or parking illegally by the police, you'll be issued with a fine. If caught by a speed camera, you'll normally be fined Dhs500, although if you're speeding at excessive levels this may be higher. When hiring a car, it's routine to agree to pay for any fines you incur. You can check whether you've racked up any offences on www.dubaipolice.gov.ae or call 04 800 7777. Fines can be paid online, or at the Muroor (Traffic Police Headquarters), near Galadari Roundabout on the Dubai–Sharjah road.

Traffic accidents

If you're involved in a serious traffic accident, call 999; if it's a minor collision, call the police on 04 398 1111. If you do not report scratches or bumps to the traffic police, insurers will almost certainly reject your claim. Third-party vehicle insurance is compulsory.

If the accident was a minor one and no one was hurt, move the car to the side of the road and wait for the police to arrive. If there is any doubt as to who is at fault, or if there is any injury (however slight), do not move the car, even if you are blocking traffic. If you help or move anyone injured in an accident, the police may hold you responsible if anything happens to that person.

Breakdown services

There are two 24-hour breakdown services, the **AAA (Arabian Automobile Association)** (04 266 9989, www.aaauae.com) and **IATC Recovery (International Automobile Touring Club)** (04 800 4282, www.iatcuae.com).

If you are driving when the car breaks down, try to pull over on to the hard shoulder. The police are likely to stop and will give assistance. If you're in the middle of high-speed traffic, it will be unsafe to get out of the car. Instead, use a mobile to call the police from the relative safety of your vehicle.

Vehicle hire

Most major car-hire companies have offices at Dubai's airports and five-star hotels. Before renting a car, check the small print, and especially clauses relating to insurance cover in the event of an accident, as this can vary from company to company.

Drivers must be over 21 to hire a small car, or 25 for a medium (two-litre) or larger 4x4 vehicle. You'll need your national driving licence (an International Driving Permit is best, although it isn't legally required). You'll also need your passport and one of the major credit cards. Prices range from about Dhs80 per day for a small manual car, to Dhs1,000 for something like a Lexus LS430.

Avis
04 425 0306, www.avis.com.
Budget
04 295 6667, www.budgetuae.com.
Hertz
04 206 0206, www.hertzuae.com.
National Car Rental
04 251 6211, www.national-me.com.
Thrifty
04 295 4878, www.thriftyuae.com.

Fuel stations

There are 24-hour petrol stations on all major highways. Most petrol stations also have convenience stores selling snacks and drinks.

Parking

Many areas in the city centre have paid parking in a bid to reduce congestion. Prices are reasonable (Dhs2 for a one-hour stay, depending on location), but it isn't easy to secure a parking space. Paid parking areas operate at peak times (generally from 8am to 6pm), and it's usually free outside of these hours, as well as on Fridays and public holidays.

If you park illegally or go over your time limit, the penalty charge is Dhs200. Generally your car hire company will pay the fines for you and charge them to you at the end of your lease.

Particular black spots include the warren of streets in 'old' Bur Dubai, the stretch of Sheikh Zayed Road between the Crowne Plaza and Shangri-La hotels and most of Deira. Parking in shopping malls is free in most places, although BurJuman and Mall of the Emirates are exceptions. At BurJuman, parking is free on Fridays and public holidays, and free for the first two hours on weekdays; thereafter it is Dhs20 per hour. At Mall of the Emirates, it is free to park on Friday and Saturday, and for the first four hours on weekdays; after this, it is Dhs20 per hour.

There tend to be huge queues at all the malls on Thursday and Friday evenings. Most hotels have extensive parking facilities and a valet service for visitors.

Road signs

Road signs are given in English and Arabic, but the sheer scale of the highway system means that you have to stay alert.

WALKING

The city was not designed for pedestrians. Certain areas lack pavements and the sheer size of some highways can mean waiting up to 20 minutes just to cross. It's not uncommon for pedestrians to take a taxi to get to the other side of the road. Due to the intense heat and humidity, an outdoor stroll is out of the question between June and September.

Resources A-Z

TRAVEL ADVICE

For up-to-date information on travel to a specific country – including the latest on safety and security, health issues, local laws and customs – contact your home country government's department of foreign affairs. Most have websites with useful advice for would-be travellers.

AUSTRALIA
www.smartraveller.gov.au

CANADA
www.voyage.gc.ca

NEW ZEALAND
www.safetravel.govt.nz

REPUBLIC OF IRELAND
foreignaffairs.gov.ie

UK
www.fco.gov.uk/travel

USA
www.state.gov/travel

ADDRESSES

Dubai can be difficult to navigate. Although street addresses are slowly being introduced to the city, at the present time all official locations are simply given by post box numbers. The majority of roads are numbered, but not identifiable by anything other than nearby landmarks. Any resident will happily point you towards Mall of the Emirates or the Jumeirah Beach Hotel, but few will know an actual address. Taxi drivers know most of the significant landmarks, but it's always worth carrying a map with you. The most common reference points are hotels, shopping malls, restaurants and some of the bigger supermarkets such as Spinneys and Choithrams.

But all of this could be about to change with the introduction of Makani, a geo-addressing system for the city. The ten-digit Makani number gives the location of a building's entrance, with large buildings, such as the Dubai Mall, having different numbers for each entrance. At the time of writing, the system was yet to be fully utilised, but it appears to have the potential to eliminate confusion regarding locations. Visit www.makani.ae for more information.

We've also included a number of useful city maps at the end of this guide; *see pp308-318*.

AGE RESTRICTIONS

You must be 18 to drive in Dubai (21 to rent a car) and to buy cigarettes, although the latter rule does not appear to be vigorously enforced.

In restaurants and bars, you must be 21 to drink. It's illegal to buy alcohol from an off-licence without a licence. These are issued by the Police Department to non-Muslims holding a residence visa (and other documentation including a tenancy agreement and salary certificate). They are valid for one year but are easily renewable. Alcohol can only be legally bought from two suppliers, **a+e** and **MMI**.

ATTITUDE & ETIQUETTE

A hugely cosmopolitan city with hundreds of nationalities, Dubai has a well-deserved reputation for being tolerant and relaxed. It is, however, a Muslim state and must be respected as such. Most 'rules' concerning cultural dos and don'ts are basic courtesy and common sense, with particular respect needing to be shown for Islam and the Royal Family.

General guidelines

In formal situations, it's polite to stand when someone enters the room and to offer a handshake to all the men in the room on entering. Only offer your hand to an Arab woman if she does so first. It's courteous to ask Muslim men about their family, but not about their wives. You may find yourself addressed by a title followed by your first name by expat workers – for instance, Mr Tom – and it's not unusual for a woman to be referred to by her husband's name – Mrs Tom, say – so don't take offence.

Although attitudes have relaxed over the years, you should avoid offending locals with public displays of affection and flesh. This is particularly true during Ramadan (when everyone is expected to dress more conservatively) and at the Heritage Village, but in nightclubs you won't find dress codes any different from those in the West. Topless bathing isn't allowed, even on the private beaches, and sometimes women are asked not to wear thongs. Be respectful about taking photographs and always ask for consent. Communication can at times be frustrating, but patience is crucial in a nation where time holds a different significance and civility is paramount. *See also pp24-25* **Local Life**.

For further information, contact the Ministry of Information & Culture on 04 261 5500 or the Sheikh Mohammed Centre for Cultural Understanding on 04 353 6666 or at www.cultures.ae.

In terms of getting by on a day-to-day basis, while the range of personal services can sometimes astound, the all-too-common collapse in communication can also astonish. There's a tendency to be keener to help than actually having the capability of carrying it through, with telephone conversations often leaving you more confused than when you started.

The internet is less harrowing (*see p294*) – there are countless websites that offer straightforward facts and advice for tourists.

BUSINESS

Dubai has been incredibly proactive in its bid to establish itself as the business hub of the UAE. Every effort has been made to welcome new business and its corporate care is the envy of the rest of the world.

Airport business centres

All passengers using Dubai International Airport can use these 24-hour facilities:

Dubai International Hotel Business Centre
04 224 4000, www.dubaiairport.com.

The 24-hour facilities comprise five meeting rooms (capacity six to 18), one conference room (capacity 60), eight workstations, state-of-the-art communication systems, and full secretarial and support services.

Global Link
Departures level, near Gate 16, Terminal 1, Dubai International Airport (04 216 4014, 04 216 4015, www.dubaiairport.com). This business centre provides passengers with six ISD booths, workstations, internet connection, fax and secretarial services.

Conference & exhibition organisers/office hire

Most of the city's hotels provide business facilities/venues with all the necessary support services. Otherwise, the Dubai World Trade Centre and Dubai Chamber of Commerce & Industry are excellent points of contact if you're looking for services and recommendations.

Dubai Chamber of Commerce & Industry
Baniyas Road, on the Creek, Rigga, Deira (04 228 0000, www.dubai chamber.com). **Open** 8am-4pm Mon-Thur, Sun. **Map** p313 K4.
The DCCI exhibition halls and auditoriums are large, flexible spaces developed to accommodate exhibitions, trade and social fairs.

Dubai International Financial Centre
Emirates Towers (04 362 2222, www.difc.ae). **Open** *Registry services* 9am-12.30pm, 3-4.30pm Mon-Thur, Sun. *Government services* 8am-3pm Mon-Thur; 9am-3pm Sun. **Map** p310 H4.
The DIFC supports new initiatives, with the focus on banking services, capital markets, asset management and fund registration, reinsurance, Islamic finance and various back office operations.

Dubai World Trade Centre
Sheikh Zayed Road, near Za'abeel roundabout, Satwa (04 332 1000, www.dwtc.com). **Open** 8am-5pm Mon-Thur, Sun. **Map** p315 G9.
The DWTC incorporates the Dubai International Convention Centre. It comprises nine interconnected, air-conditioned exhibition halls covering 37,000sq m (14,285sq ft), which are available for lease.

Courier companies

Aramex
04 600 54400, www.aramex.com.

DHL
04 800 4004, www.dhl.ae.

FedEx
04 800 33330, 02 183 860, www.fedex.com/ae.

TNT
04 800 4333, www.tnt.com.

Business hours

Most residents in the UAE either have a Friday/Saturday weekend or work a six-day week with only Friday off. Working hours during the day can also vary, with a few firms still operating a split-shift system (normally 8am-noon and 4-8pm), although this is becoming increasingly rare.

Licences

The basic requirement for all business activity in Dubai is a licence (commercial/professional/industrial) issued by the Dubai Department of Economic Development. To apply, contact the department on 04 445 5555, www.dubaided.gov.ae/en.

Sponsors

Companies may be 100 per cent foreign-owned providing a local agent (UAE national) is appointed. These agents will assist in obtaining visas in exchange for a lump sum or a profit-related percentage. The exceptions to this rule are the free zones, where no local sponsor is required.

Translation services

Eman Legal Translation Services
Room 104, 1st Floor, above Golden Fork Restaurant, Nasr Square, Deira (04 224 7066, ets@emirates.net.ae). **Open** 9am-6pm Mon-Wed, Sat, Sun; 9am-2pm Thur. **Map** p313 J3.

Ideal Legal Translation & Secretarial
Room 17, 4th Floor, above Al Ajami Restaurant, Al Ghurair Centre, Al Riwqa Street, Deira (04 222 3699, ideal@emirates.net.ae). **Open** 8am-1pm, 3-7pm Mon-Wed, Sat, Sun; 8am-5pm Thur. **Map** p311 K2.

Lotus Translation Services
Room 411, 4th Floor, Oud Metha Office Building, Oud Metha Street, near Wafi Centre (04 324 4492, www.lotustranslationservices.com). **Open** 8.30am-1.30pm, 2-6pm Mon-Thur, Sun. **Map** p315 G9.

Useful organisations

American Business Council
16th Floor, Dubai World Trade Centre, Sheikh Zayed Road (04 379 1414, www.abcdubai.com). **Open** 8am-5pm Mon-Thur, Sun. **Map** p315 G9.

British Business Group
BBG Office, Conference Centre, British Embassy, Al Seef Road, Bur Dubai (04 397 0303, www.britbiz-uae.com). **Open** 8.30am-5.30pm Mon-Thur, Sun. **Map** p313 J4.

Department of Economic Development
Business Village, near Clock Tower, Deira (04 445 5555, www.dubaided.gov.ae). **Open** 7.30am-2.30pm Mon-Thur, Sun. **Map** p311 K2.

Dubai Chamber of Commerce & Industry
See left.

CONSUMER

Consumers in Dubai can contact the Consumer Protection Division of the Department of Economic Development for information on their rights (www.consumer rights.ae, 04 600 545555). Guidelines for consumers and retailers are available on the website, with plenty of information on how to lodge a complaint should there be any problems with a purchase.

CUSTOMS

There is a duty-free shop in the airport arrivals hall. Each person is permitted to bring into the UAE four litres of alcohol (spirits or wine), 48 cans of beer, 400 cigarettes, 50 cigars and 500g of tobacco.

The following are prohibited in the UAE, and import of these goods will carry a heavy penalty: controlled substances (drugs), firearms and ammunition, pornography (including sex toys), unstrung pearls, pork, raw seafood, and fruit and vegetables from cholera-infected areas.

For further information on what you can and can't bring into the country, call the Dubai Customs hotline on 04 800 80080 or check out www.dxbcustoms.gov.ae.

DISABLED

Generally speaking, Dubai is not disabled-friendly. Although things are improving, many places are still not equipped for wheelchair access. Most hotels have made token efforts, but functionality still plays second fiddle to design, meaning that wheelchair facilities have largely been swept under the carpet. Those that do have some specially adapted rooms include the Burj Al Arab, Crowne Plaza Dubai, Emirates

Towers, Hilton Dubai Creek, Hilton Dubai Jumeirah, Hyatt Regency, Jumeirah Beach Hotel, JW Marriott Dubai, Madinat Jumeirah, Ritz-Carlton Dubai, One&Only Royal Mirage and Sheraton Jumeirah.

The airport and major shopping malls have good access and facilities, and accessible taxis can be booked by calling the RTA taxi booking service (04 208 0808). There are designated disabled parking spaces in nearly all of the city's car parks; to use them you'll need disabled window badges, though many able-bodied drivers fail to respect this.

DRUGS

Dubai has a strict zero tolerance towards drugs. There are harsh penalties for possession of a non-legal substance, and there have been several high-profile cases of expatriates serving time. Drug importation carries the death penalty, although no executions have been carried out in the last few years. But even association with users or importers carries a stiff penalty. Recent court cases suggest anyone caught dealing drugs can expect a lengthy sentence. For more information see the Dubai Police website, www.dubaipolice.gov.ae.

There's a long list of pharmaceutical products the UAE Ministry of Health has classified as narcotics, including tablets readily available over the counter in chemists abroad. For a full list of banned medication, contact the UAE Ministry of Health's Drug Control Department in Dubai (04 230 1000, www.moh.gov.ae).

ELECTRICITY

Domestic supply is 220/240 volts AC, 50Hz. Sockets are suitable for three-pin 13 amp plugs of British standard design; however, it is a good idea to bring an adapter with you just in case. Adapters can also be bought cheaply in local supermarkets. Appliances purchased in the UAE will generally have two-pin plugs.

EMBASSIES & CONSULATES

Australia
Level 25, BurJuman Business Tower, Sheikh Khalifa Bin Zayed Road (04 508 7100, www.austrade.gov.au). **Open** 8.30am-4pm Mon-Thur, Sun. **Map** p313 J5.

Canada
19th Floor, Jumeirah Emirates Tower, Sheikh Zayed Road (04 404 8444, www.canadainternational.gc.ca). **Open** 8-11am Mon, Wed, Thur, Sun. **Map** p310 H4.

New Zealand
Office 6A, Level 6, Jumeirah Emirates Tower, Sheikh Zayed Road (04 331 7500, www.nzte.govt.nz). **Open** 8.30am-5pm Mon-Thur, Sun. **Map** p310 H4.

South Africa
3rd Floor, New Sharaf Building, Khalid Bin Waleed Street, Bur Dubai (04 397 5222, www.dirco.gov.za/dubai). **Open** 8.30am-12.30pm Mon-Thur, Sun. **Map** p313 J5.

United Kingdom
British Embassy Building, Al Seef Road, Bur Dubai (04 309 4444, consular.UAE@fco.gov.uk). **Open** 7.30am-2.30pm Mon-Thur, Sun. **Map** p313 J4.

USA
Corner of Al Seef Road and Sheikh Khalifa Bin Zayed Road, Bur Dubai (04 309 4000, http://dubai.usconsulate.gov). **Open** *by appt only*12.30-3pm Tue-Thur, Sun. **Map** p313 K4.

EMERGENCIES

For **police**, call 999; for **ambulance**, call 998 or 999; and for the **fire brigade**, call 997.

If you dial 999 or 04 282 1111, in an emergency Dubai Police will send a police helicopter, which they guarantee will be with you within eight minutes.

See also p296 **Police**; *see below* **Health** for a list of hospitals.

GAY & LESBIAN

Homosexuality is, in effect, prohibited in the UAE and there are no gay cafés, bars or pubs. Although there is a small gay community in Dubai, it is not centralised around any specific region and there is no official gay presence in the city.

HEALTH

Dubai has well-equipped public and private hospitals. Only emergency care is free of charge, so it's definitely advisable to have medical insurance as well as travel insurance.

For people whose countries have a reciprocal medical agreement with the UAE, further treatments are available. Dubai hospitals are clean and safe.

Accident & emergency

All the hospitals listed in this section have 24-hour accident and emergency departments.

Contraception & abortion

Most pharmacies prescribe contraception over the counter, with relatively few contraceptives requiring prescriptions. It is widely known (although officially illegal) that this includes the morning-after pill. The American Hospital has a Family Planning clinic (04 309 6877), and the Canadian Hospital (04 336 4444) offers consultation.

Abortion is illegal in the UAE unless recommended by a doctor who is concerned about the mother's survival. Written permission is needed from either the husband or guardian.

Dentists

Good dentists are readily available in Dubai, including orthodontists and cosmetic dentists, though prices for treatment can be pretty hefty. Many clinics and hospitals in the city offer dental services.

Doctors

Most big hotels have in-house doctors. Alternatively, you can ring your local embassy for its recommendations (*see left* **Embassies & Consulates**). A handy resource for both tourists and residents is the DHA Dubai Doctors app, which can be used to search for a doctor or clinic (www.dha.gov.ae).

Hospitals

The following are five private hospitals in Dubai that all have Accident & Emergency departments. Note that all private health care must be paid for, including emergency care. Hospitals are required to display price lists for all treatments at reception.

American Hospital Dubai
Off Oud Metha Road, between Lamcy Plaza & Wafi Centre, Al Nasr (04 377 5500, www.ahdubai.com). **Map** p311 J3.

Emirates Hospital
Opposite Jumeirah Beach Park, next to Chili's restaurant, Jumeirah Beach Road, Jumeirah (04 349 6666, www.emirateshospital.ae). **Map** p316 A15.
As well as an A&E facility, the Emirates Hospital has a 24-hour walk-in clinic.

Iranian Hospital
Corner of Al Hudeiba Road & Al Wasl Road, Satwa (04 344 0250, www.ihd.ae). **Map** p314 E9.

Rashid Hospital
Near Maktoum Bridge, Bur Dubai (04 219 2000, www.dha.gov.ae).
Map p311 J2.

Welcare Hospital
Next to Lifco supermarket in Garhoud, Deira (04 282 7788, www.welcarehospital.com).
Map p311 K2.

Insurance

Public hospitals in Dubai will deal with emergencies free of charge. They have good facilities and their procedures are reliable and hygienic.

For non-emergency treatment, medical insurance is often included in travel insurance packages, and it's important to have it unless your country has some kind of reciprocal medical treatment arrangement with the UAE. Although travel insurance typically covers health, it's wise to make sure you have a package that covers all eventualities, especially as you'd need to attend a private hospital or clinic for serious but non-emergency care, where treatment can be expensive.

Pharmacies

There's no shortage of pharmacies in Dubai. Normal opening hours are 8.30am to 1.30pm, 4.30pm to 10.30pm Saturday to Thursday and 4.30pm to 10.30pm Friday, but some open on Friday mornings as well. A system of rotation exists for 24-hour opening, with four chemists holding the fort at any one time for a week each. For a list of the 24-hour pharmacies on duty, check the back of the local newspapers or www.dm.gov.ae. Alternatively, call DM Emergency Offices on 04 800 900 and they will be able to direct you to the nearest pharmacy.

Prescriptions

There is no formal policy of prescription: all you need to know is the name of the drug you need. In rare instances when this isn't the case, pharmacists dispense medicines on receipt of a prescription from a GP.

STDs, HIV & AIDS

To secure residency in Dubai, you have to undergo a blood test and anyone identified as HIV positive is not allowed to stay in the country. Tourists do not have to be tested, but should you become ill and have to be hospitalised, expect to find yourself on the next plane out if tested positive for HIV. Despite there being no official figures, it's widely accepted that there is a genuine problem with sexually transmitted diseases, due in part to the large numbers of prostitutes working in the city.

Sunburn/dehydration

The fierce UAE sun means that heatstroke and heat exhaustion are always a risk, especially in summer. Sunglasses, hats and high-factor sun creams are essential, particularly for children, and the importance of drinking large quantities of water to stave off dehydration cannot be overemphasised.

Vaccinations

No specific immunisations are required for entry to Dubai, but it would be wise to check beforehand – a certificate is sometimes required to prove you are clear of cholera and yellow fever if you are arriving from a high-risk area. Tetanus inoculations are recommended if you are going on a long trip.

There are very few mosquitoes in the towns and cities, and since it's not considered to be a real risk, malaria tablets are rarely prescribed for travel in the UAE.

If you are planning to camp near the mountains or explore wadis in the evening, cover up and use a suitable insect repellent. If in any doubt, consult your doctor before you travel to Dubai. Polio has been virtually eradicated in the UAE and hepatitis is very rare.

ID

ID is necessary for car hire as well as entry into bars and clubs if the bouncers don't think you look over 21. Passports are the most requested type, so have copies made in advance. All UAE residents are issued with an Emirates ID card, which contains biometric data on each individual.

INSURANCE

Although the crime rate in Dubai is exceptionally low, it is still worth insuring yourself before you travel. Travel insurance policies usually cover loss or theft of belongings and medical treatment, but check what is included before you leave, especially if you're intending to take part in activities like desert off-roading and scuba diving.

For car insurance check whether you are covered for the Sultanate of Oman. Since many parts of the UAE have a 'porous' border, you may find yourself driving within Oman without warning (the road to Hatta, for example, will take you through Oman in several places).

Medical insurance is vital, since healthcare in private hospitals can be extremely expensive. Keep all receipts, as you will have to claim them back.

INTERNET

Dubai is leading the way towards electronic government. Not only is the internet often the most efficient way of finding useful information here, but you can now seemingly do everything online, from paying a traffic fine to reporting a lost licence.

The government organisation, Etisalat, controls the server and is the regulator of content. Consequently there is an element of censorship, with pornography, dating and gambling sites blocked, along with a few photography and social networking sites. If the network fails there can be no service at all for hours, although this is uncommon. You can contact Etisalat by dialling 101, or visit www.etisalat.com.

Free Wi-Fi access can be hard to find in Dubai. Most of the major malls have free Wi-Fi, as do some coffee shops, restaurants and hotels. Dubai International Airport and Al Maktoum International Airport offer free Wi-Fi for 30 minutes. Otherwise, Etisalat and du have Wi-Fi hotspots around the city that can be accessed by purchasing a pre-paid card (www.etisalat.ae, www.du.ae).

LANGUAGE

Although Arabic is the UAE's official language, English is widely spoken and understood by nearly everybody. For some basic vocabulary, *see p299*.

LEFT LUGGAGE

There is a left-luggage storage facility at the Dubai International Airport Terminals 1 and 2. Costs are Dhs20 to Dhs25, depending on the size of your bag, for 12 hours.

LEGAL HELP

Dubai has strict laws, severe sentencing, no free legal aid and no equivalent of the Citizens Advice Bureau. Should you require legal help or advice, you should contact your embassy (*see p293* **Embassies & Consulates**).

The government has also set up a Department for Tourist Security (04 800 243), whose purpose is to guide visitors through the labyrinth of the law and to liaise between tourists and the Dubai police.

LIBRARIES

You must be a resident to borrow from Dubai's libraries, but most will be happy for you to browse or use the reading room, where there is usually a broad selection of English-language books. The Dubai Municipality Central Library allows the public to view its collections online, offering title searches, browsing and the capability to reserve books from home. Dubai Municipality has launched its new eLibrary (http://elibrary.dubai.ae), which allows registered members to read hundreds of books, magazines and foreign newspapers online. For information on the city's libraries, visit www.dubaipubliclibrary.ae.

LOST PROPERTY

Theft is extremely rare in Dubai, but there are instances of bag snatching. If you are a victim of crime, contact the nearest police station or report it to the special Tourist Police unit (04 800 4438), necessary for the validation of your travel insurance claims.

If you lose something, most unclaimed items are taken to a general holding unit known as Police Lost & Found, which can be contacted on 04 216 2542.

If you have lost something on a bus or *abra*, call the public transport information line on 04 800 9090 and ask for Lost & Found. This same RTA number can be called if you've left something in a taxi. Be sure to always make a note of the taxi company and registration number, which will be needed when calling the RTA. The airports have a contact number for lost baggage (04 224 5555 for all airlines). Should you lose your passport, report it immediately to the police and contact your embassy (*see p293* **Embassies & Consulates**).

MEDIA

Despite the creation of Dubai Media City (complete with the slogan 'freedom to create'), the media in the UAE is still subject to government censorship, although direct clashes are rare as most organisations operate a policy of self-censorship. This means you'll never see anything that criticises the UAE royal families or the government, and there are no scenes of nudity in any films or TV programmes. Although censorship is becoming more relaxed in some areas (many references to alcohol and images of bikini-clad babes are now allowed), it is unrealistic to expect objective political coverage in local newspapers.

Newspapers & magazines

There are four English language daily newspapers in Dubai: *Gulf News*, *Khaleej Times*, *Gulf Today* (Dhs2-Dhs3) and a free paper *7 Days* (Dubai's equivalent to London's *Metro*). Abu Dhabi's *The National* is also available in Dubai. All publish local and international news. *Gulf News* also publishes a free tabloid, *Xpress*, which comes out on Thursday. *The Times* and *The Sunday Times* are also available, although the Middle East editions are different to the UK version of the newspaper and they avoid subjects sensitive in the region.

The city's magazine sector has become increasingly competitive in recent years and there is now a wealth of magazines published in Dubai. Monthly and weekly entertainment and listings magazines such as *Time Out Dubai* are available, alongside a range of lifestyle magazines including *Emirates Home*, *Viva* and *Identity* (interior decoration), *Ahlan!*, *OK Middle East* and *Grazia*.

There are free tourist magazines available in hotels, although most of them are of dubious quality.

Radio

Dubai has five English-language radio stations. Unfortunately, the quality is generally low, with an over-reliance on chart music, too many advertisements and plenty of unsubtle product placement.

Channel 4 *104.8 FM, www.channel4fm.com.*
Modern chart, dance and R&B music.
City *101.6 FM, www.city1016.ae.*
Part Hindi, part English.
Dubai Eye *103.8 FM, www.dubaieye1038.com.*
Music and talk radio.
Dubai FM *92.0 FM, www.dubai92.com.*
Government-run station that plays older music and contemporary chart.
Radio 1 *100.5 FM, www.radio1uae.com.*
Modern chart, dance and R&B.
Radio 2 *99.3 FM, www.myradio2.ae.*
Easy listening.

Television

The Dubai government runs the English-language channel Dubai One, which shows a mixture of sitcoms, popular series and movies. Most residents and hotels have a satellite package of some form. MBC has a number of channels, including MBC4, which shows the latest TV series from the US. European football, including the English Premier League and Spain's La Liga, is shown on beIN Sports.

MONEY

The national currency is the dirham. At the time of going to press, £1 was equal to Dhs5.49. The US$ has been pegged to the dirham at a fixed rate of Dhs3.6725 since 1980. Bank notes come in denominations of Dhs1,000, Dhs500, Dhs200, Dhs100, Dhs50, Dhs20, Dhs10 and Dhs5. There are Dhs1 coins and then 50, 25 and 10 fils. Small change is notoriously hard to come by, with taxi drivers and shop workers often asking if you have smaller notes, so it's always worth trying to keep a few smaller denominations.

ATMs

Visitors will have no problems finding ATMs in Dubai. These are in every major hotel and mall, and on most of the busier streets. Most credit cards and Cirrus- and Plus-enabled cash cards are accepted. Check with your bank for charges for withdrawing cash overseas.

Banks

Bank opening hours are normally 8am to 1pm Sunday to Thursday and 8am to noon Saturday. Most banks are shut on Fridays.

Bureaux de change

Rates vary and it's worth noting that the airport is the first place you can, but the last place you should, change your money. There are several moneychangers in the city centre (Bur Dubai and Deira) who tend to deal only in cash but whose rates (sometimes without commission) can challenge the banks, particularly with larger sums of money involved. Travellers' cheques are accepted with ID in banks and hotels and other licensed exchange offices affiliated with the issuing bank. There is no separate commission structure but exchange houses make their money on the difference between the rates at which they buy and sell. Below are some reliable bureaux de change in the city:

Al Ansari Exchange
Various branches across Dubai (04 600 54 6000, www.alansari exchange.com).

Al Fardan Exchange
Various branches across Dubai (04 351 3535, www.alfardan exchange.com).

UAE Exchange
Various branches across Dubai (04 600 555 550, 04 250 4265, www.uaeexchange.com).

Credit cards/cheques

All major credit cards are accepted in the larger hotels, restaurants, supermarkets and shops. Acceptance of cheques is less widespread, except for residents who often need to use post-dated cheques to pay their rent. The UAE was slow to jump on the debit card bandwagon, but that has changed in recent years, and you'll find almost every outlet uses chip and pin for debit and credit cards.

Tax

Famous for its absence of direct taxation – meaning thousands of expat workers enjoy tax-free salaries – Dubai does have some 'hidden' taxes, such as the ten per cent municipality tax included in food and hospitality costs, and, for those with a licence, a sales tax on alcohol from off-licences. There is no corporate tax except for oil-producing companies and foreign banks.

OPENING HOURS

The concept of the Saturday/Sunday weekend doesn't apply in the Middle East, since Friday is the holy day for Muslims. The weekend in Dubai is Friday/Saturday, although many workers will have only Friday off.

Unfortunately, there are no clear-cut rules when it comes to opening hours for retail outlets. The most common shopping hours are 10am to 1pm and 4pm to 9pm for stand-alone stores, but shops in malls are open 10am to 10pm and often to midnight on the weekends. The main exception is Friday, when some businesses don't open until 2pm or 4pm.

POLICE

In an emergency, call 999. If you just want information, www.dubai police.gov.ae is a good place to start. If you want to report something confidentially or think you have witnessed something illegal, there is a hotline (Al Ameen Service) on 04 800 4888 or go to www.alameen.ae. For more on emergency contact numbers, *see p293*.

POSTAL SERVICES

The Emirates post is run solely by Empost and works on a PO box system, although a postal delivery service could possibly be implemented with the introduction of the Makani geo-addressing system (*see p291*).

All mail in the UAE is delivered to centrally located post boxes via the Central Post Office. With Dhs250 per year and an email address you can apply for a personal PO box and will be notified by email when you receive registered mail or parcels.

Hotels will handle mail for guests and you can buy stamps at post offices, Emarat petrol stations, many supermarkets and greeting card shops. Shopping malls such as Deira City Centre, Lamcy Plaza and Mall of the Emirates have postal facilities. Delivery takes between two and three days within the UAE and from three to seven days for deliveries to Europe and the USA. The service can be erratic, so don't be surprised if sending something to your home country takes longer than expected.

All postal enquiries can be directed to the Emirates Post call centre on 04 600 599999, 8am to 8pm Saturday to Thursday. Alternatively, phone the Emirates Post Head Office on 04 262 2222, 7.30am to 2.30pm, Saturday to Wednesday.

Central Post Office
Za'abeel Road, Karama (04 337 1500, www.empostuae.com). **Open** 8am-11.30pm Mon-Wed, Sat, Sun; 8am-10pm Thur; 8am-noon Fri.

PROHIBITIONS

The law is very strict with regards to the consumption of alcohol (other than in a licensed venue or a private residence), illegal drugs, gambling and pornography. Israeli nationals are not allowed into the UAE; however, other nationalities can now enter the UAE with an Israeli stamp in their passport.

RELIGION

See also pp18-25 **Today**. Owing to its relative tolerance, Dubai has a variety of Christian churches and Hindu temples. For details of places of worship, see www.yellowpages.ae. The list below is a guide to non-Muslim places of worship:

Anglican

Holy Trinity Church *Umm Hurair 2 Oud Metha (04 337 0247, www.holytrinitychurchdubai.org).* **Map** p311 J3.

Baptist

Emirates Baptist Church International *Villa 7B, Street 69A (opposite Mercato Mall), Jumeirah 1 (04 349 1596, www.ebci.org).* **Map** p316 C11.

Catholic

St Mary's Church *Umm Hurair 2, Oud Metha (04 337 0087, www.saintmarysdubai.org).* **Map** p311 J3.

Evangelical

United Christian Church of Dubai *Jebel Ali Village (04 884 6623, www.uccdubai.com).*

SAFETY & SECURITY

Dubai is one of the safest places in the world to visit. However, bag-snatching and pickpocketing are not unknown, so, as with other countries, be vigilant and don't leave your belongings unattended. The other problem issues tend to be restricted to areas such as money laundering that don't impact on the tourist.

Security is high, and most accommodation blocks and malls are well manned by private guards. Nevertheless, it's always a sensible idea for visitors to follow the normal precautions to safeguard themselves and their valuables during their visit.

STUDY

If you're looking to learn Arabic while in Dubai, two popular options are the Arabic Language Centre and Eton Institute.

Arabic Language Centre
Sheikh Rahsid Tower (Trade Centre Tower), Sheikh Zayed Road (04 331 5600, www.arabiclanguagecentre.com). **Open** 9am-6pm Mon-Thur, Sun. **Map** p315 G9.

Eton Institute
Block 3, Dubai Knowledge Village (04 438 6800, www.etoninstitute.com/ae). **Open** 8am-9pm Mon-Thur, Sun; 10am-6pm Fri; 9am-6pm Sat. **Map** p318 C2.

TELEPHONES

The **international dialling code** for Dubai is 971, followed by the individual emirate's code: 04 for Dubai. Other area codes are Abu Dhabi 02, Ajman 06, Al Ain 03, Fujairah 09, Ras Al Khaimah 07 and Sharjah 06. For mobile phones the code is 050, 055 or 056. Drop the initial '0' of these codes if dialling from abroad.

Operator services can be contacted on 100; directory enquiries are on 181 or 151 for international. Alternatively, consult the *Yellow Pages* online at www.yellowpages.ae, which in many cases can be quicker and less frustrating. To report a fault call 170.

Making a call

Local calls are very inexpensive and direct-dialling is available to 150 countries.

Cheaper rates for international direct calls apply from 9pm to 7am and all day on Fridays and public holidays. Pay phones, both card- and coin-operated, are located throughout the UAE. To make a call within Dubai, dial the seven-digit phone number; for calls to other areas within the UAE, simply dial the area code followed by the seven-digit phone number.

To make an international phone call, dial 00, then the country code (44 for UK; Australia 61; Canada 1; the Republic of Ireland 353; New Zealand 64; South Africa 27; USA 1; France 33; India 91; Pakistan 92; Russia 7), then the area code, omitting the initial 0, followed by the phone number.

Public telephones

There are plenty of public telephones, which accept either cash or phone cards. Phone cards for local and international use are available in two denominations (Dhs25 or Dhs40) from most Etisalat offices, supermarkets, garages and pharmacies. Coin-operated phones take Dhs1 and 50 fils coins.

Mobile telephones

Dubai has one of the world's highest rates of mobile phone usage. A reciprocal agreement exists with over 60 countries allowing GSM international roaming service for other networks in the UAE. There is also a service (Wasel) that enables temporary Etisalat SIM cards (and numbers) lasting 60 days for use during your trip if your network is not covered, or if you do not have a GSM phone. Calls are charged at local rates with good network coverage.

TIME

The UAE is GMT+4 hours, and has no seasonal change of time. So, for instance, if it is noon in London (winter time), it is 4pm in Dubai; after British clocks move forwards for BST, noon is 3pm in Dubai.

TIPPING

Hotels and restaurants usually include a ten to 15 per cent service charge in their bills; if not, adding ten per cent is normal if not obligatory. Unfortunately, this charge usually goes straight to the restaurant and rarely reaches the pockets of the people who served you, so if you're particularly impressed by the standards of service, you will need to tip in addition.

It is common to pay taxi drivers a small tip, rounding up the fare to the nearest Dhs5 being the norm. For other services (supermarket baggers, bag carriers, petrol pump attendants, hotel valets) it is usual to give at least a couple of dirhams.

TOILETS

There are well-kept free public toilets in malls and parks, and most hotels will let you use their facilities free of charge. Petrol stations have conveniences but their condition varies. Toilets in souks and bus stations are usually for men only, and are often unfamiliar to Western visitors – a simple squat toilet set in the floor, with no seat or toilet rolls.

TOURIST INFORMATION

The Department of Tourism & Commerce Marketing (DTCM) has information centres around the city, the most immediately useful being in the airport arrivals lounge. Its one-stop information centres aim to answer any visitor queries, provide maps, tour guides and hotel information, as well as business and conference advice. Most of the larger shopping malls have their own centres providing visitor information. There's also a very handy website (www.visitdubai.com) with plenty of information on what Dubai has to offer.

VISAS & IMMIGRATION

Visa regulations are liable to change, so it is always worth checking with your travel agent or with the UAE embassy in your home country before leaving. Overstaying on your visa can result in detention and fines. Israeli nationals are not permitted to enter the UAE. Your passport must have at least three months (in some cases, six) before expiry for you to be granted admission into the UAE, so check before booking your flight. Nationals of the UK, USA, Canada, Australia and New Zealand do not need to obtain a visa before travelling to Dubai or the UAE; they will receive it upon arrival.

WATER & HYGIENE

The tap water in Dubai comes from desalination plants, and although drinkable, it doesn't taste great. Most people choose to buy their drinking water, which costs only Dhs1-Dhs2 for a litre bottle; but do be wary of the ridiculous mark-ups at certain bars and restaurants. Outside Dubai, avoid drinking water from the tap – you might even want to use bottled water for brushing your teeth.

Standards of food hygiene are extremely high, though caution should be shown at some of the smaller roadside diners. If in doubt, avoid raw salads and shawarmas (meat cooked on a spit and wrapped in flatbread). Outside the city limits, milk is often unpasteurised and should be boiled. Powdered or tinned milk is available, but make sure it is reconstituted with pure water.

WEIGHTS & MEASURES

The UAE uses the metric system, but UK- and US-standard weights and measures are understood.

WHAT TO TAKE

Lightweight summer clothing is ideal in Dubai, with just a wrap, sweater or jacket for cooler winter nights and venues that have fierce air-conditioning. The dress code is generally casual, though guests in the more prestigious hotels such as the Ritz-Carlton and the Royal Mirage do tend to dress more formally in the evening. Bikinis, swimming costumes, shorts and revealing tops should be confined to hotel beach resorts. Bars and clubs are really no different from those in the West, with tans shown off to the max. That said, visitors should dress conservatively when travelling to and from these venues. Visitors can't buy alcohol from off-licences – so be sure to stock up at Dubai Duty Free when you arrive at the airport.

WHEN TO GO

Climate

Straddling the Tropic of Cancer, the UAE is warm and sunny during the winter, and very hot and humid during the summer. Winter daytime temperatures average a very pleasant 24°C, though nights can be relatively cool: perhaps 12-15°C on the coast and less than 5°C in the heart of the desert or high in the mountains. Local north-westerly winds (*shamals*) frequently develop during the winter, bringing cooler windy conditions as well as occasional sandstorms.

Summer temperatures reach the mid-40s, but can be higher inland. Humidity in coastal areas averages between 50 and 60 per cent, reaching over 90 per cent in summer – even the sea offers no relief as the water temperature can reach 37°C. Rainfall in Dubai is sparse and intermittent, on average falling on only five days a year, usually in February or March.

In terms of when to go, you really can't go wrong if you visit any time between November and March, as you're virtually guaranteed beautiful weather every day. June to September can be unbearably hot and humid, although hotel bargain deals can make it an attractive proposition. Also bear in mind when Ramadan is taking place.

Public holidays

There are two kinds of public holiday: those that are fixed in the calendar, and religious days determined by the lunar calendar which vary from year to year. The precise dates are not announced until a day or so before they occur, based on local sightings of phases of the moon.

The fixed dates are as follows:

New Year's Day 1 Jan
Mount Arafat Day 11 Jan
Accession of HH Sheikh Zayed as Ruler of the UAE 6 Aug
UAE National Day 2 Dec

The variable dates are as follows:

Eid Al Adha A three-day feast to mark the end of the haj pilgrimage to Mecca.
Ras al-Sana The start of Islamic New Year.
Mawlid al-Nabi The Prophet Mohammed's birthday.
Lailat al Mi'raj The accession day of the Prophet Mohammed.
Eid Al Fitr Three days marking the end of Ramadan.

WOMEN

The cultural differences between locals and expats in Dubai are obvious, and the traditional advice for women in any big city – catch taxis if you're unsure about the area, don't walk alone at night and so on – should still be heeded, but all women here tend to enjoy a high standard of personal safety.

Wearing revealing clothing in a public place will attract stares, some of simple condemnation and others of a more lascivious nature. That said, physical harassment is rare, as the local police are swift to act against offenders.

Check www.expatwoman.com for advice and information on meeting fellow female expats.

Dubai International Women's Club (DIWC)
Opposite Mercato Mall, Beach Road, Jumeirah (04 344 2389). **Open** 8am-5pm Mon-Thur, Sat, Sun. **Map** p316 C11.
This is a social club with around 150 members, which meets four times a month. The club organises plenty of charity events, in Dubai and overseas.

International Business Women's Group
Jumeirah 1 (www.ibwgdubai.com).
IBWG is an organisation for women in business; it meets monthly to exchange ideas and advice.

WORKING IN DUBAI

If you're considering working in Dubai, it's definitely worth visiting first to get a feel for the place. Dubai has a relatively small business community, so even a week of well-planned networking can be fruitful in terms of making contacts.

There are also several employment agencies and recruitment consultants to help you; try www.yellowpages.ae for a full list of Dubai-based work agencies. Local giant www.bayt.com has earned itself a sound reputation and is worth checking out.

General Directorate of Residency and Foreign Affairs – Dubai
(04 800 5111, 04 313 9999 international, www.dnrd.ae).

LOCAL CLIMATE

Average temperatures and monthly rainfall in Dubai.

	High (°C/°F)	Low (°C/°F)	Max Humidity (%)	Rainfall (mm/in)
Jan	23 / 73	14 / 57	90	12 / 0.5
Feb	24 / 75	15 / 59	89	19 / 0.7
Mar	27 / 81	17 / 63	85	12 / 0.5
Apr	31 / 88	21 / 70	83	4 / 0.1
May	36 / 97	24 / 75	80	0 / 0
June	38 / 100	27 / 81	85	0 / 0
July	39 / 102	29 / 84	80	1 / 0
Aug	39 / 102	30 / 86	82	0 / 0
Sept	38 / 100	27 / 81	85	0 / 0
Oct	34 / 93	23 / 73	87	1 / 0
Nov	30 / 86	19 / 66	86	2 / 0
Dec	25 / 77	16 / 61	88	18 / 0.7

For links to see the latest satellite images of the weather conditions in the Middle East, go to www.uaeinteract.com/uaeint_misc/weather/index.asp.

Further Reference

LANGUAGE

Arabic is the official language of Dubai, and Urdu and Hindi are also widely spoken and understood, but English is the predominant spoken language.

Some basic words and phrases are given below in phonetics. Capitals are not used in Arabic, but are used below to indicate hard sounds. With Arabic possessing so many different dialects and sounds from English, transliterating is never an easy task. We've decided to go for a mainly classical form.

Basic vocabulary

hello marhaba
how are you? kaif il haal?
good morning sabaah il khayr
good evening masaa' il khayr
greetings 'as-salamu 'alaykum
welcome 'ahlan wa sahlan
goodbye ma' 'is-salaama
excuse me afwan
sorry 'aasif
yes na'am
no laa
God willing insha'allah
please *(to a man)* min fadlak
please *(to a woman)* min fadlik
thank you (*very much*) shukran (*jazeelan*)
I don't know lasto adree or laa 'a-arif
who? man?
what? matha?
where? ayina?
why? lematha?
how much? (cost) bekam?
how many? kam?

Numbers

zero sifr
one waahid
two itnain
three talata
four arba'a
five khamsa
six sitta
seven sab'a
eight tamanya
nine tis'a
ten 'ashra

Days & times

Sunday al-ahad
Monday al-itnayn
Tuesday al-talata
Wednesday al-arba'a
Thursday al-khamees
Friday al-jum'a
Saturday al-Sabt
hour sa'aa
day yom
month shahr
year sanah
today al yom
yesterday ams/imbarah
tomorrow bukra

Getting around

airport matar
post office maktab al barid
bank bank
passport jawaz safar
luggage 'aghraad
ticket tath karah
taxi taxi
car say-yarra
city madina
street share'h
road tareeq

BOOKS

For a more detailed list of Arabic authors and bookshops, visit www.uaeinteract.com.

Frauke Heard-Bay *From Trucial States to United Arab Emirates*
In 1971, the seven sheikdoms at the southern end of the Gulf, the Trucial States, formed the state of the United Arab Emirates; it was soon a member of the UN, OPEC and the Arab League. This academic volume examines the historical and social movements that have shaped the present-day UAE.

Denys Johnson-Davies (transl), Roger MA Allen (ed) *Arabic Short Stories*
A charming and insightful set of tales from the Middle East.

Alan Keohane *Bedouin: Nomads of the Desert*
This photographic portrait pays tribute to the tribal customs that survive among those who continue their annual journey across the desert. It's a very timely reminder of the importance of preserving the UAE's ancient traditions.

TE Lawrence *Seven Pillars of Wisdom: A Triumph*
The extraordinary account, by Lawrence of Arabia himself, of the war of the tribes against the Turks.

Edward Said *Reflections on Exile & Other Essays*
Powerfully blending political and aesthetic concerns, Said's writings have revolutionised the field of literary studies.

Freya Stark *A Winter in Arabia: A Journey through Yemen*
There were a number of great travellers and adventurers during the 1930s, but Freya Stark was unusual in being a woman. This is her account of the peoples and tribes of the Yemen.

Wilfred Thesiger *Arabian Sands*
One of the classic travel books. Thesiger recounts the time he spent with the Bedouin, and their travels across the Empty Quarter of Saudi Arabia in the days before 4x4s and air-conditioning.

MAGAZINES

For the top events, meal deals and local listings, be sure to pick up a copy of *Time Out Dubai*. Free listings magazines are also distributed at various malls.

TRAVEL

Dubai Explorer publishes useful maps, including *Off Road Explorer* and *Underwater Explorer*.

UAE Yellow Pages
www.uae-ypages.com
Full of local listings.

WEBSITES

www.timeoutdubai.com
All you need to know about what's happening in the city with extensive event listings.

www.timeoutabudhabi.com
Insiders' glimpses of what's happening when and where.

www.uaeinteract.com
Website of the Ministry of Information & Culture, with information on the UAE.

www.visitdubai.com
General tourist information.

Transport

www.dubaiairport.com
All the news from Dubai International Airport.

www.rta.ae/en
Information on buses, metro, trams and driving.

Index

INDEX

INDEX

Burj Khalifa. *See p80*.

شارع الراس
Al Ras Road
القسائم
13 - 31
PLOTS

Maps

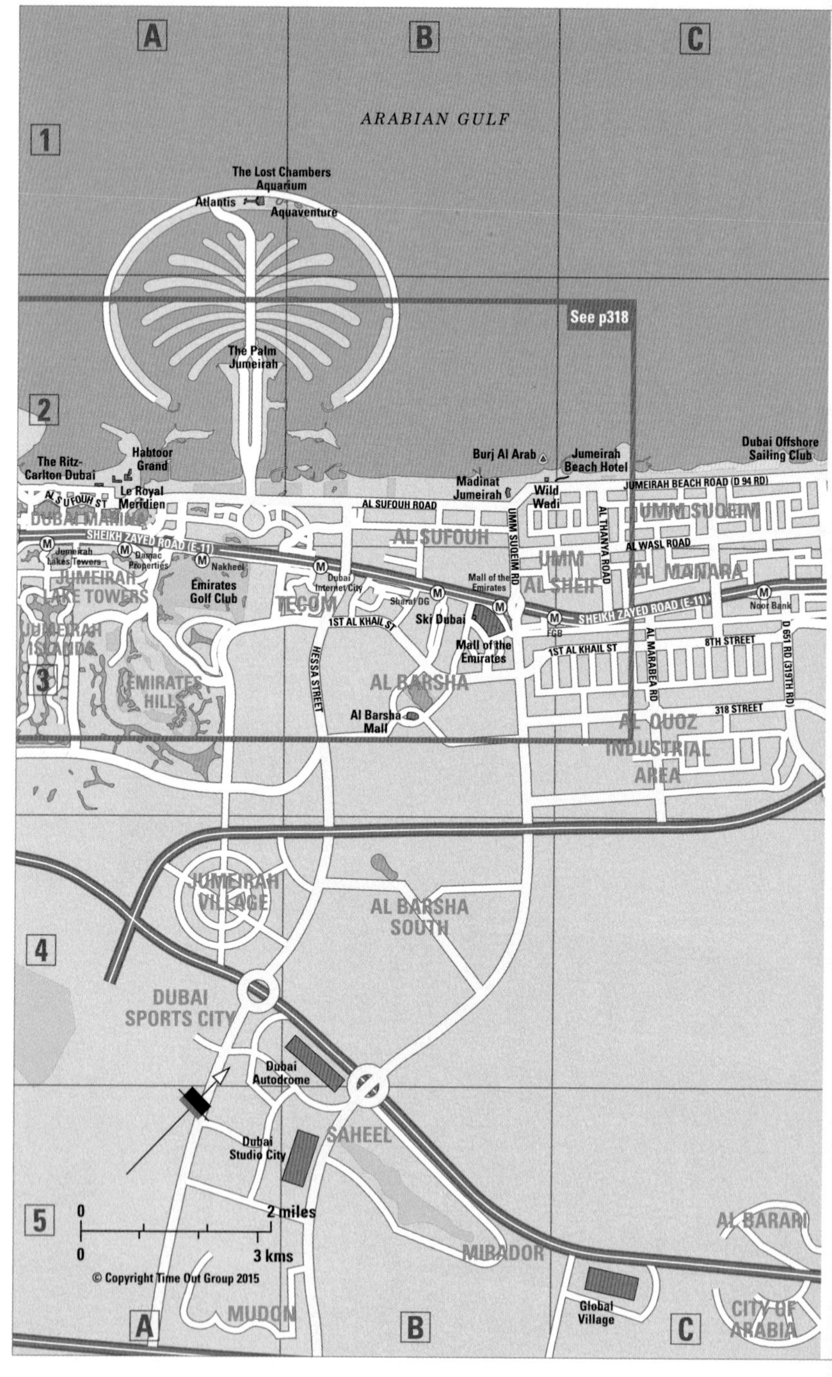
A
B
C
1
2
3
4
5
ARABIAN GULF
The Lost Chambers Aquarium
Atlantis
Aquaventure
The Palm Jumeirah
See p318
The Ritz-Carlton Dubai
Habtoor Grand
Le Royal Meridien
AL SUFOUH ST
DUBAI MARINA
SHEIKH ZAYED ROAD (E-11)
Jumeirah Lakes Towers
Damac Properties
Nakheel
JUMEIRAH LAKE TOWERS
Emirates Golf Club
JUMEIRAH ISLANDS
EMIRATES HILLS
Dubai Internet City
TECOM
AL SUFOUH ROAD
AL SUFOUH
Sharaf DG
1ST AL KHAIL ST
HESSA STREET
Ski Dubai
Mall of the Emirates
AL BARSHA
Al Barsha Mall
Burj Al Arab
Madinat Jumeirah
Jumeirah Beach Hotel
Wild Wadi
UMM SUQEIM RD
UMM AL SHEIF
AL THANYA ROAD
JUMEIRAH BEACH ROAD (D 94 RD)
UMM SUQEIM
AL WASL ROAD
AL MANARA
SHEIKH ZAYED ROAD (E-11)
FGB
Noor Bank
Dubai Offshore Sailing Club
1ST AL KHAIL ST
AL MARABEA RD
8TH STREET
D 651 RD (319TH RD)
318 STREET
AL QUOZ INDUSTRIAL AREA
JUMEIRAH VILLAGE
AL BARSHA SOUTH
DUBAI SPORTS CITY
Dubai Autodrome
Dubai Studio City
SAHEEL
MIRADOR
AL BARARI
Global Village
CITY OF ARABIA
MUDON
0
2 miles
0
3 kms
© Copyright Time Out Group 2015

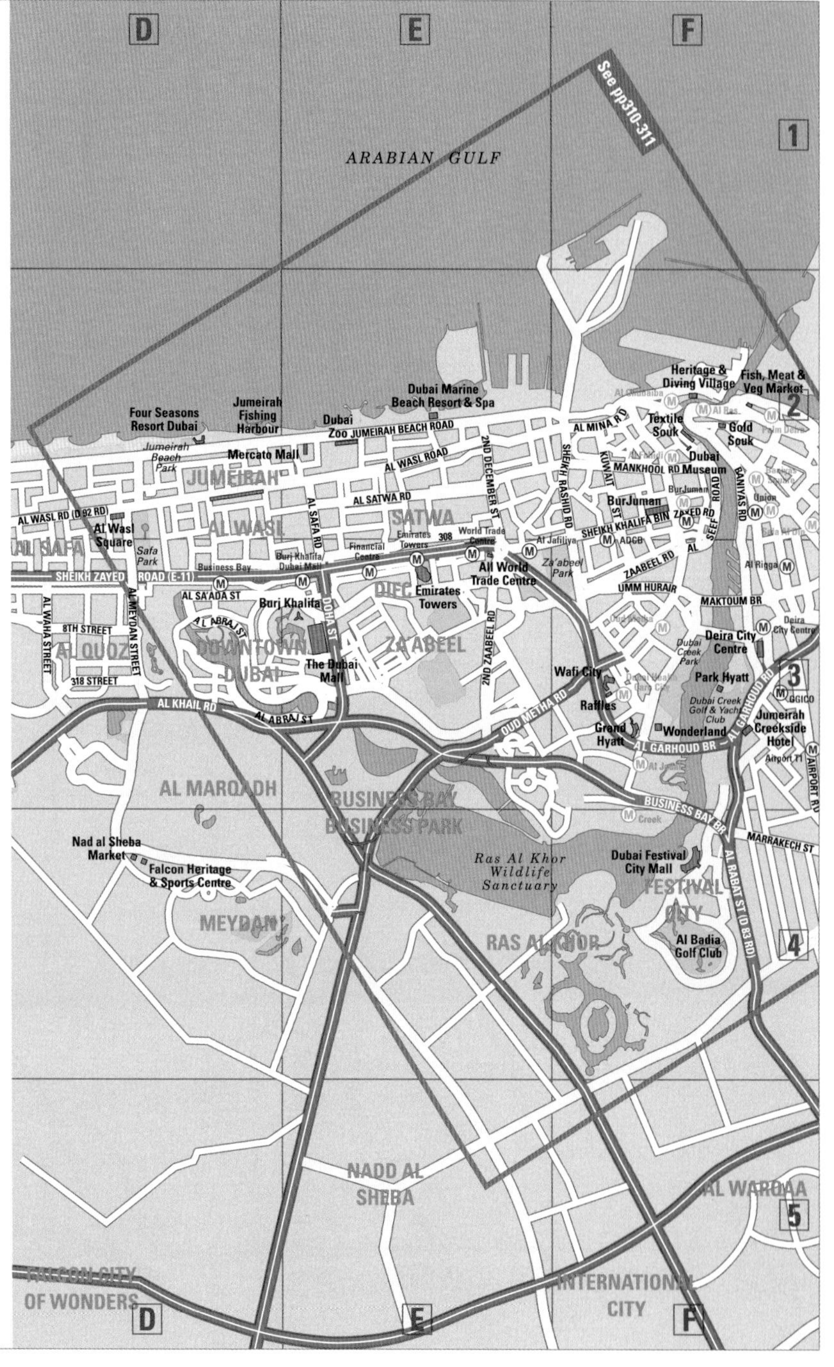

D
E
F
1
2
3
4
5
See pp310-311
ARABIAN GULF
Heritage & Diving Village
Fish, Meat & Veg Market
Dubai Marine Beach Resort & Spa
Four Seasons Resort Dubai
Jumeirah Fishing Harbour
Dubai Zoo
JUMEIRAH BEACH ROAD
AL MINA RD
Textile Souk
Gold Souk
Jumeirah Beach Park
Mercato Mall
AL WASL ROAD
2ND DECEMBER ST
SHEIKH RASHID RD
KUWAIT ST
MANKHOOL RD
Dubai Museum
BANIYAS RD
JUMEIRAH
AL SATWA RD
BurJuman
SHEIKH KHALIFA BIN ZAYED RD
AL SEEF ROAD
AL WASL RD (D 92 RD)
AL SAFA RD
SATWA
Al Wasl Square
AL WASL
Emirates Towers
308
World Trade Centre
Al Jafiliya
ADCB
AL SAFA
Safa Park
Financial Centre
Burj Khalifa/ Dubai Mall
Business Bay
All World Trade Centre
Za'abeel Park
ZAABEEL RD
Al Rigga
SHEIKH ZAYED ROAD (E-11)
UMM HURAIR
AL SA'ADA ST
DIFC
Emirates Towers
AL MEYDAN STREET
AL WAHA STREET
Burj Khalifa
MAKTOUM BR
8TH STREET
AL ABRAJ ST
DOHA ST
2ND ZAABEEL RD
Deira City Centre
AL QUOZ
DOWNTOWN DUBAI
ZA'ABEEL
Dubai Creek Park
318 STREET
The Dubai Mall
Wafi City
Park Hyatt
AL KHAIL RD
OUD METHA RD
Raffles
Dubai Creek Golf & Yacht Club
AL GARHOUD RD
GGICO
AL ABRAJ ST
Grand Hyatt
Wonderland
Jumeirah Creekside Hotel
AL GARHOUD BR
Airport T1
AIRPORT RD
AL MARQADH
BUSINESS BAY BUSINESS PARK
BUSINESS BAY BR
Creek
MARRAKECH ST
Nad al Sheba Market
Falcon Heritage & Sports Centre
Ras Al Khor Wildlife Sanctuary
Dubai Festival City Mall
FESTIVAL CITY
AL RABAT ST (D 83 RD)
MEYDAN
RAS AL KHOR
Al Badia Golf Club
NADD AL SHEBA
AL WARQAA
FALCON CITY OF WONDERS
INTERNATIONAL CITY
MAPS

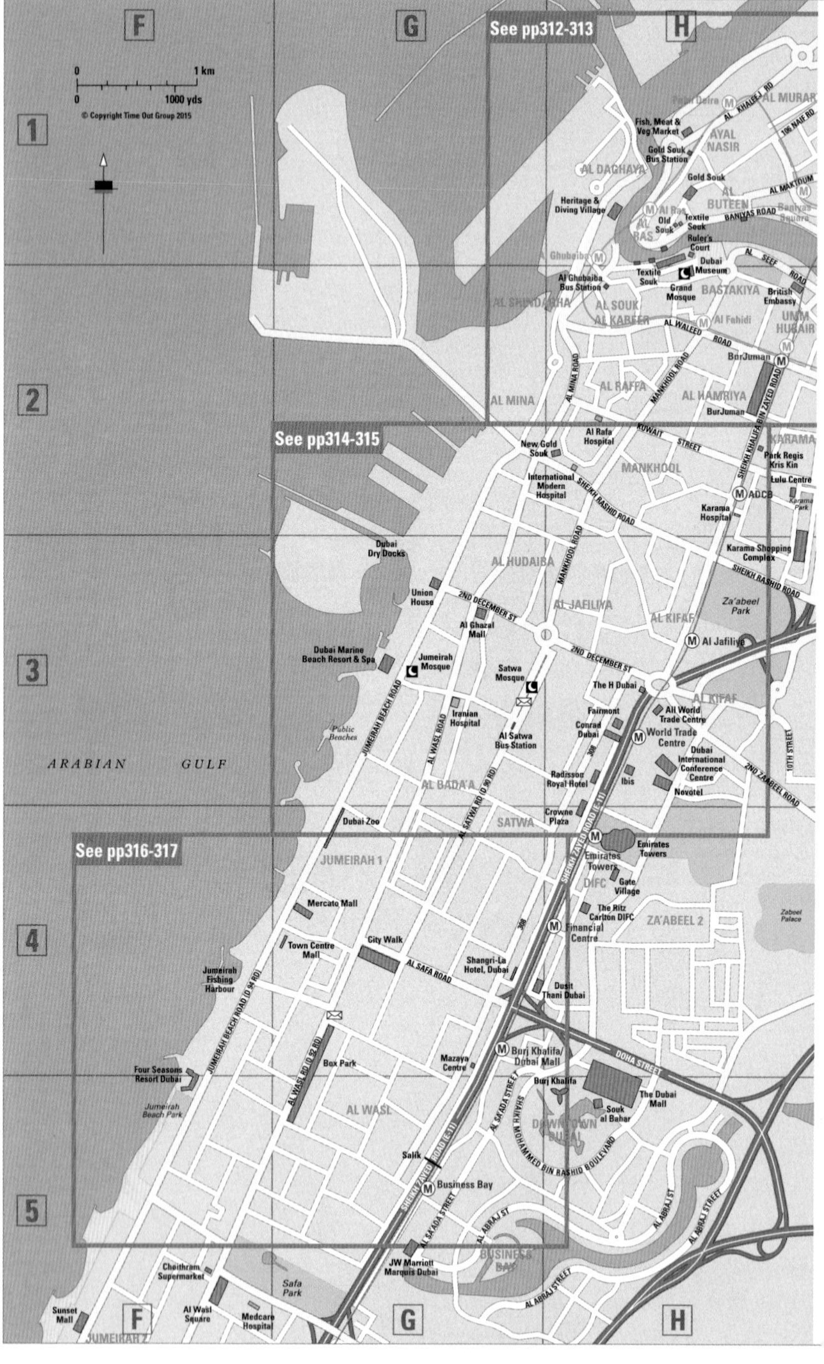
F
G
H
1
2
3
4
5
0
1 km
1000 yds
© Copyright Time Out Group 2015
See pp312-313
See pp314-315
See pp316-317
ARABIAN GULF
AL MURAR
AL KHALEEJ RD
106 NAIF RD
Fish, Meat & Veg Market
AYAL NASIR
Gold Souk Bus Station
AL DAGHAYA
Gold Souk
AL BUTEEN
AL MAKTOUM
Heritage & Diving Village
Al Ras
Old Souk
Textile Souk
BANIYAS ROAD
AL RAS
Ruler's Court
Al Ghubaiba
AL SEEF ROAD
Dubai Museum
Textile Souk
Al Ghubaiba Bus Station
Grand Mosque
BASTAKIYA
British Embassy
AL SHINDAGHA
AL SOUK AL KABEER
AL WALEED ROAD
Al Fahidi
UMM HURAIR
BurJuman
AL MINA ROAD
MANKHOOL ROAD
AL RAFFA
AL HAMRIYA
AL MINA
BurJuman
SHEIKH KHALIFA BIN ZAYED ROAD
Al Rafa Hospital
KUWAIT STREET
KARAMA
New Gold Souk
MANKHOOL
Park Regis Kris Kin
International Modern Hospital
Lulu Centre
SHEIKH RASHID ROAD
ADCB
Karama Hospital
Karama Park
Dubai Dry Docks
MANKHOOL ROAD
AL HUDAIBA
Karama Shopping Complex
SHEIKH RASHID ROAD
Union House
2ND DECEMBER ST
AL JAFILIYA
Za'abeel Park
AL KIFAF
Al Ghazal Mall
Al Jafiliya
Dubai Marine Beach Resort & Spa
Jumeirah Mosque
Satwa Mosque
2ND DECEMBER ST
The H Dubai
AL KIFAF
Fairmont
All World Trade Centre
Iranian Hospital
Conrad Dubai
World Trade Centre
JUMEIRAH BEACH ROAD
AL WASL ROAD
Al Satwa Bus Station
Dubai International Conference Centre
10TH STREET
Public Beaches
308
Radisson Royal Hotel
Ibis
2ND ZA'ABEEL ROAD
AL SATWA RD (D 90 RD)
AL BADA'A
Novotel
Dubai Zoo
Crowne Plaza
SATWA
SHEIKH ZAYED ROAD (E 11)
Emirates Towers
Emirates Towers
JUMEIRAH 1
DIFC
Gate Village
Mercato Mall
The Ritz Carlton DIFC
ZA'ABEEL 2
Zabeel Palace
Financial Centre
Town Centre Mall
City Walk
308
Jumeirah Fishing Harbour
AL SAFA ROAD
Shangri-La Hotel, Dubai
JUMEIRAH BEACH ROAD (D 94 RD)
Dusit Thani Dubai
Burj Khalifa/ Dubai Mall
DOHA STREET
AL WASL RD (D 92 RD)
Box Park
Mazaya Centre
Four Seasons Resort Dubai
Burj Khalifa
AL SA'ADA STREET
The Dubai Mall
Jumeirah Beach Park
Souk al Bahar
SHAIKH MOHAMMED BIN RASHID BOULEVARD
AL WASL
DOWNTOWN DUBAI
Salik
SHEIKH ZAYED ROAD (E 11)
Business Bay
AL ABRAJ ST
AL ABRAJ STREET
AL SA'ADA STREET
AL ABRAJ ST
BUSINESS BAY
Cheithram Supermarket
JW Marriott Marquis Dubai
AL ABRAJ STREET
Safa Park
Sunset Mall
Al Wasl Square
Medcare Hospital
JUMEIRAH 2

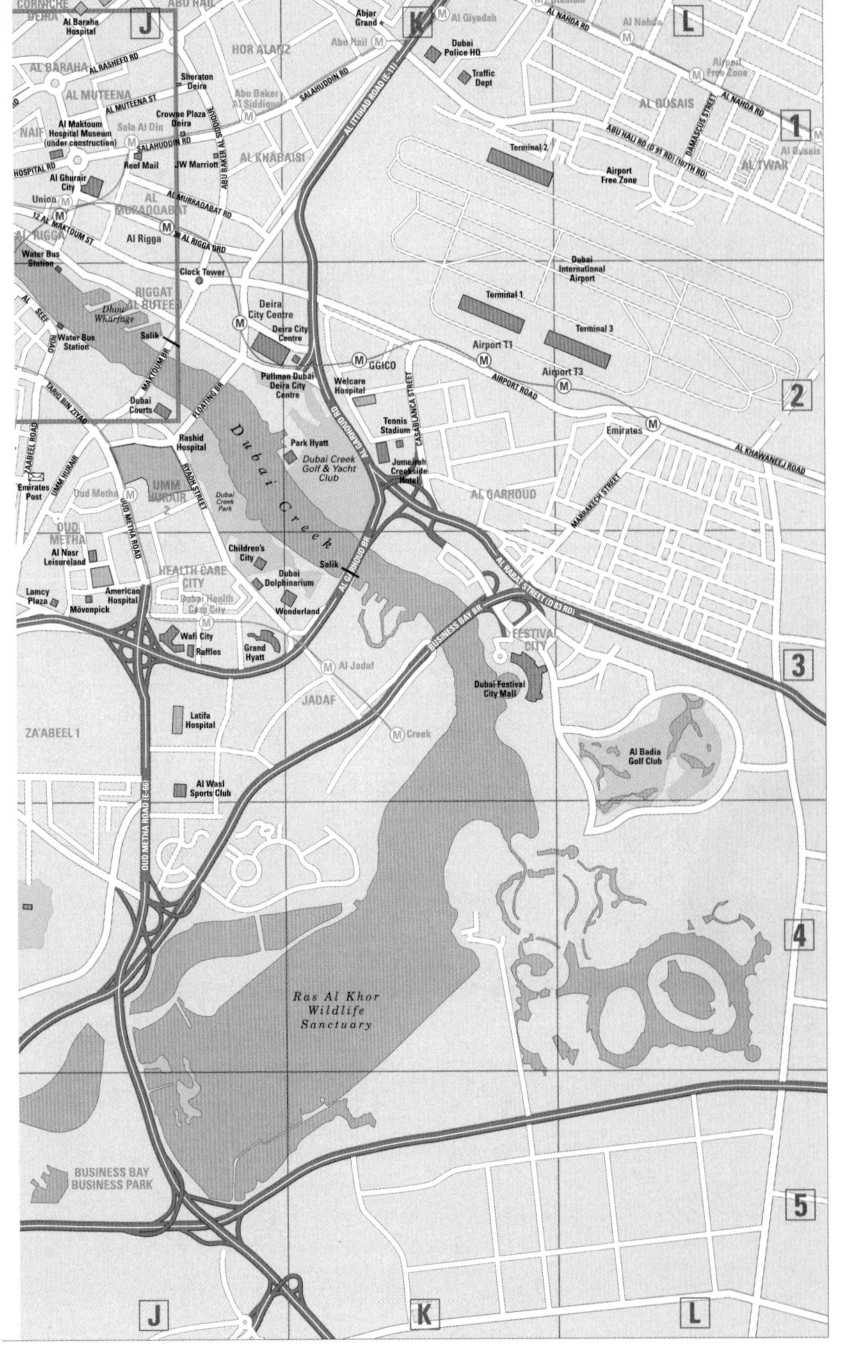

J
K
L
1
2
3
4
5
Abu Hail
Hor Al Anz
Al Baraha
Al Muteena
Naif
Al Khabaisi
Al Muraqqabat
Al Rigga
Al Qusais
Al Twar
Al Garhoud
Umm Hurair 2
Oud Metha
Health Care City
Jadaf
Za'abeel 1
Festival City
Business Bay Business Park
Dubai Creek
Ras Al Khor Wildlife Sanctuary
Dubai International Airport
Terminal 1
Terminal 2
Terminal 3
Airport Free Zone
Deira City Centre
Dubai Creek Golf & Yacht Club
Al Badia Golf Club
Dubai Festival City Mall
Latifa Hospital
Al Wasl Sports Club
Wafi City
Raffles
Grand Hyatt
Wonderland
Dubai Dolphinarium
Children's City
Park Hyatt
Rashid Hospital
Emirates Post
Al Nasr Leisureland
Lamcy Plaza
American Hospital
Mövenpick
Clock Tower
Dubai Courts
Reef Mall
JW Marriott
Crowne Plaza Deira
Sheraton Deira
Al Ghurair City
Al Maktoum Hospital Museum (under construction)
Al Baraha Hospital
Abjar Grand
Dubai Police HQ
Traffic Dept
Welcare Hospital
Tennis Stadium
Jumeirah Creekside Hotel
Pullman Dubai Deira City Centre
Water Bus Station
Dhow Wharfage
Salik
Al Ittihad Road (E-11)
Al Garhoud Rd
Al Garhoud Br
Airport Road
Al Khawaneej Road
Marrakech Street
Casablanca Street
Al Rebat Street (D 83 Rd)
Business Bay Br
Oud Metha Road (E-66)
Oud Metha Road
Riyadh Street
Floating Br
Maktoum Br
Al Nahda Rd
Abu Hail Rd (D 91 Rd) (107th Rd)
Damascus Street
Salahuddin Rd
Abu Baker Al Siddique
Al Muraqqabat Rd
Al Rigga Rd
Al Maktoum St
Al Rasheed Rd
Al Muteena St
Hospital Rd
Tariq Bin Ziyad
Za'abeel Road
Umm Hurair
Al Seef Road
Stadium
Al Qiyadah
Al Nahda
Airport Free Zone
Al Qusais
Abu Hail
Abu Baker Al Siddique
Sala Al Din
Union
Al Rigga
GGICO
Airport T1
Airport T3
Emirates
Oud Metha
Dubai Health Care City
Al Jadaf
Creek

MAPS

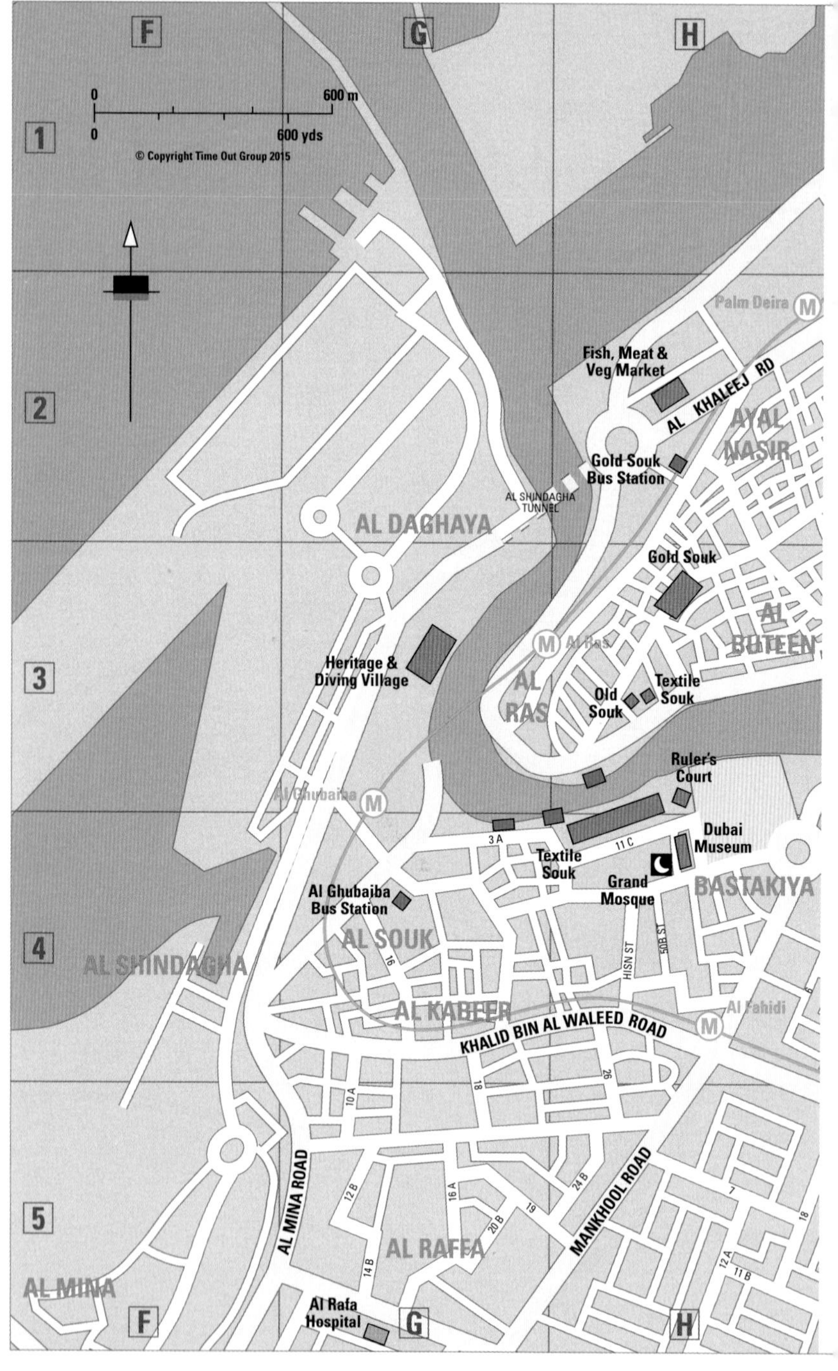

F
G
H
1
2
3
4
5
0
600 m
0
600 yds
© Copyright Time Out Group 2015
Palm Deira
Fish, Meat & Veg Market
AL KHALEEJ RD
AYAL NASIR
Gold Souk Bus Station
AL SHINDAGHA TUNNEL
AL DAGHAYA
Gold Souk
AL BUTEEN
Al Ras
AL RAS
Heritage & Diving Village
Old Souk
Textile Souk
Ruler's Court
Al Ghubaiba
3 A
11 C
Dubai Museum
Textile Souk
Grand Mosque
BASTAKIYA
Al Ghubaiba Bus Station
AL SOUK
HISN ST
50B ST
AL SHINDAGHA
16
AL KABEER
Al Fahidi
KHALID BIN AL WALEED ROAD
18
26
10 A
AL MINA ROAD
12 B
16 A
24 B
MANKHOOL ROAD
19
20 B
7
18
AL RAFFA
14 B
12 A
11 B
AL MINA
Al Rafa Hospital
F
G
H

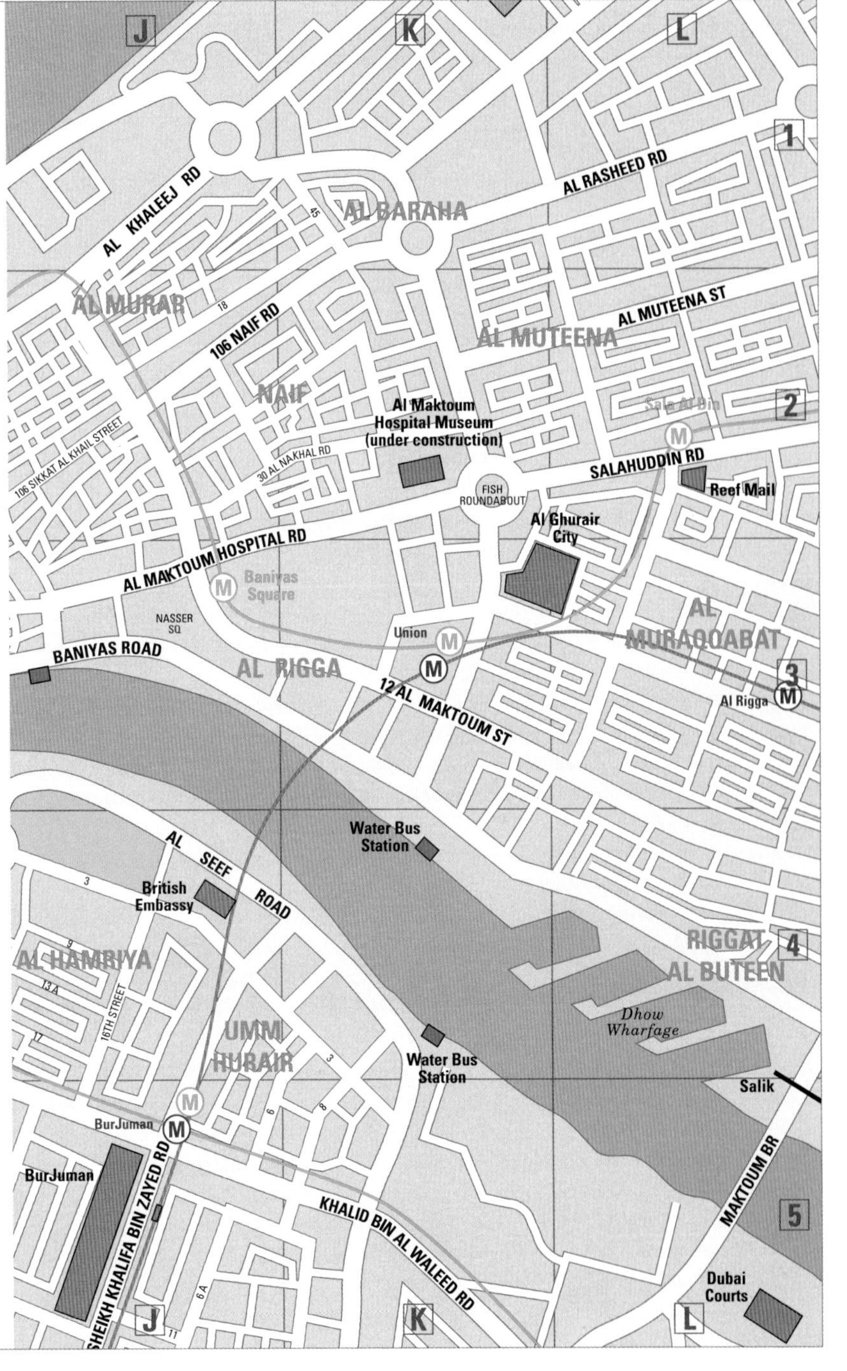
J
K
L
1
2
3
4
5
AL KHALEEJ RD
AL RASHEED RD
AL BARAHA
AL MURAR
106 NAIF RD
AL MUTEENA ST
AL MUTEENA
NAIF
Al Maktoum
Hospital Museum
(under construction)
Sala Al Din
106 SIKKAT AL KHAIL STREET
30 AL NAKHAL RD
SALAHUDDIN RD
FISH
ROUNDABOUT
Reef Mall
Al Ghurair
City
AL MAKTOUM HOSPITAL RD
Baniyas
Square
NASSER
SQ
AL
MURAQQABAT
Union
BANIYAS ROAD
AL RIGGA
12 AL MAKTOUM ST
Al Rigga
Water Bus
Station
AL SEEF ROAD
British
Embassy
AL HAMRIYA
RIGGAT
AL BUTEEN
16TH STREET
UMM
HURAIR
Dhow
Wharfage
Water Bus
Station
Salik
BurJuman
MAKTOUM BR
SHEIKH KHALIFA BIN ZAYED RD
KHALID BIN AL WALEED RD
Dubai
Courts

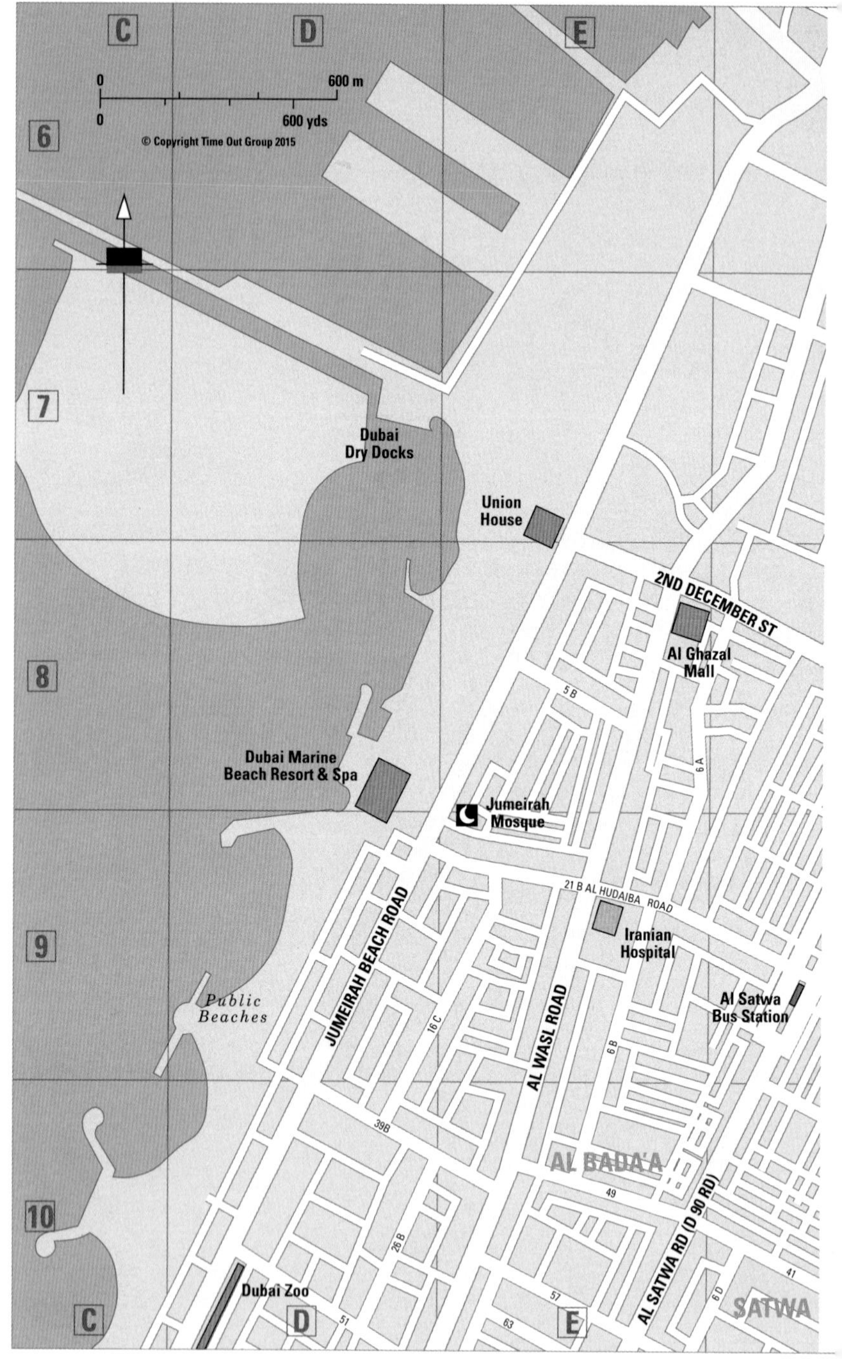
C
D
E
0
600 m
0
600 yds
© Copyright Time Out Group 2015
6
7
8
9
10
Dubai
Dry Docks
Union
House
2ND DECEMBER ST
Al Ghazal
Mall
5 B
6 A
Dubai Marine
Beach Resort & Spa
Jumeirah
Mosque
21 B AL HUDAIBA ROAD
Iranian
Hospital
JUMEIRAH BEACH ROAD
AL WASL ROAD
Al Satwa
Bus Station
Public
Beaches
16 C
6 B
39B
AL BADA'A
49
AL SATWA RD (D 90 RD)
26 B
41
57
6 D
Dubai Zoo
51
63
SATWA
C
D
E

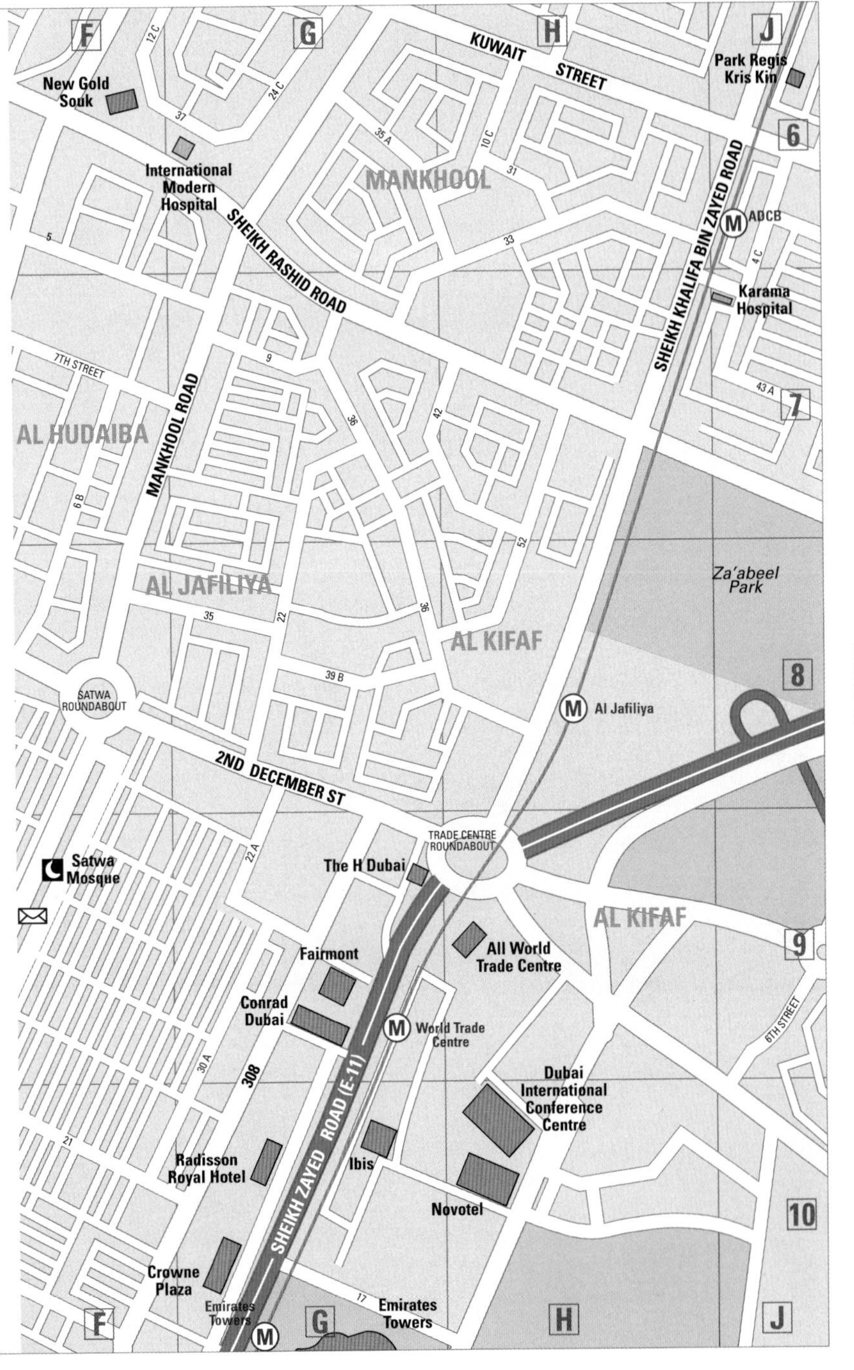
F
G
H
J
KUWAIT STREET
New Gold Souk
Park Regis Kris Kin
6
International Modern Hospital
MANKHOOL
SHEIKH RASHID ROAD
ADCB
SHEIKH KHALIFA BIN ZAYED ROAD
Karama Hospital
7TH STREET
MANKHOOL ROAD
AL HUDAIBA
7
AL JAFILIYA
Za'abeel Park
AL KIFAF
SATWA ROUNDABOUT
Al Jafiliya
8
2ND DECEMBER ST
TRADE CENTRE ROUNDABOUT
Satwa Mosque
The H Dubai
AL KIFAF
9
Fairmont
All World Trade Centre
Conrad Dubai
World Trade Centre
6TH STREET
SHEIKH ZAYED ROAD (E-11)
Dubai International Conference Centre
Radisson Royal Hotel
Ibis
Novotel
10
Crowne Plaza
Emirates Towers
Emirates Towers
F
G
H
J

MAPS

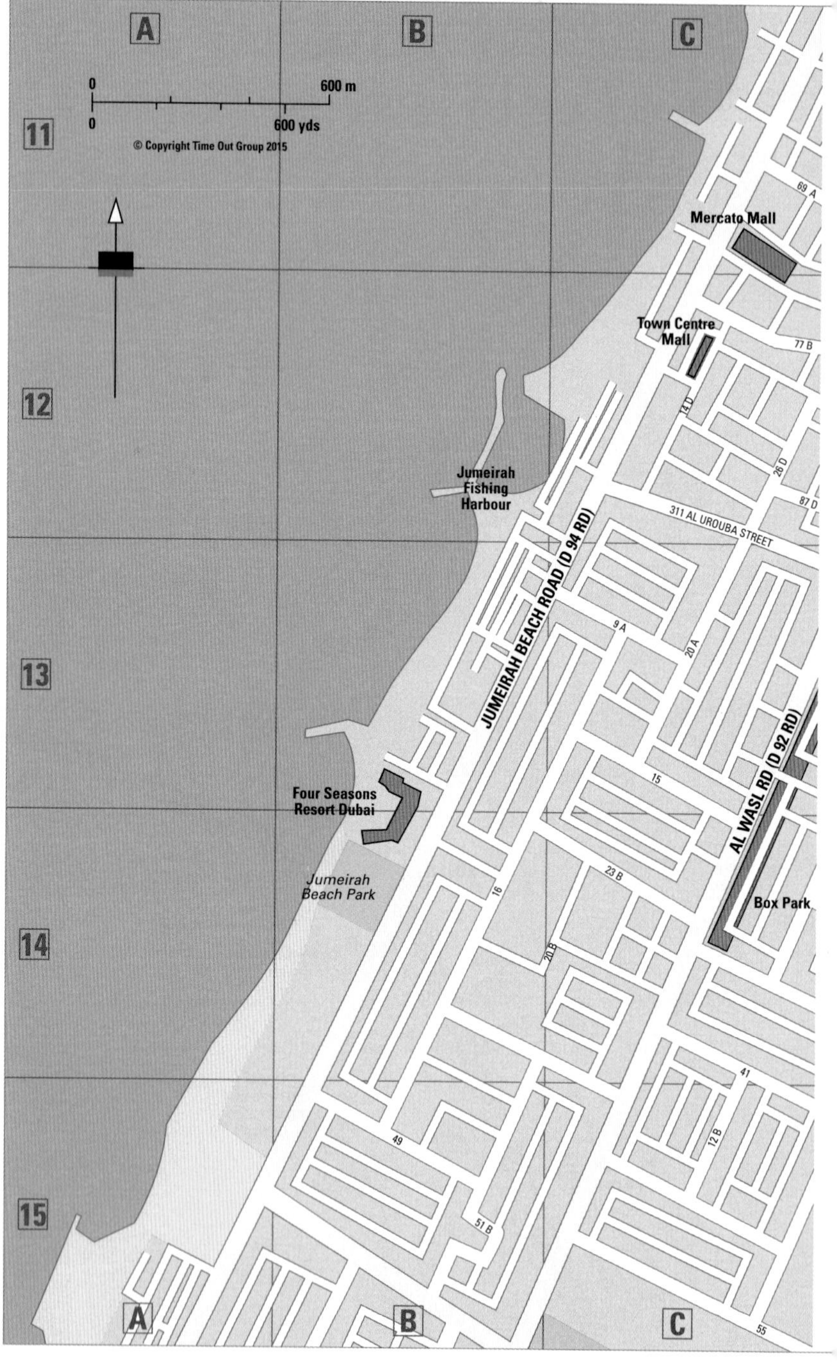
A
B
C
11
12
13
14
15
0
600 m
0
600 yds
© Copyright Time Out Group 2015
Mercato Mall
69 A
Town Centre Mall
77 B
14 D
26 D
87 D
Jumeirah Fishing Harbour
311 AL UROUBA STREET
JUMEIRAH BEACH ROAD (D 94 RD)
9 A
20 A
AL WASL RD (D 92 RD)
15
Four Seasons Resort Dubai
Jumeirah Beach Park
23 B
16
Box Park
20 B
41
12 B
49
51 B
55

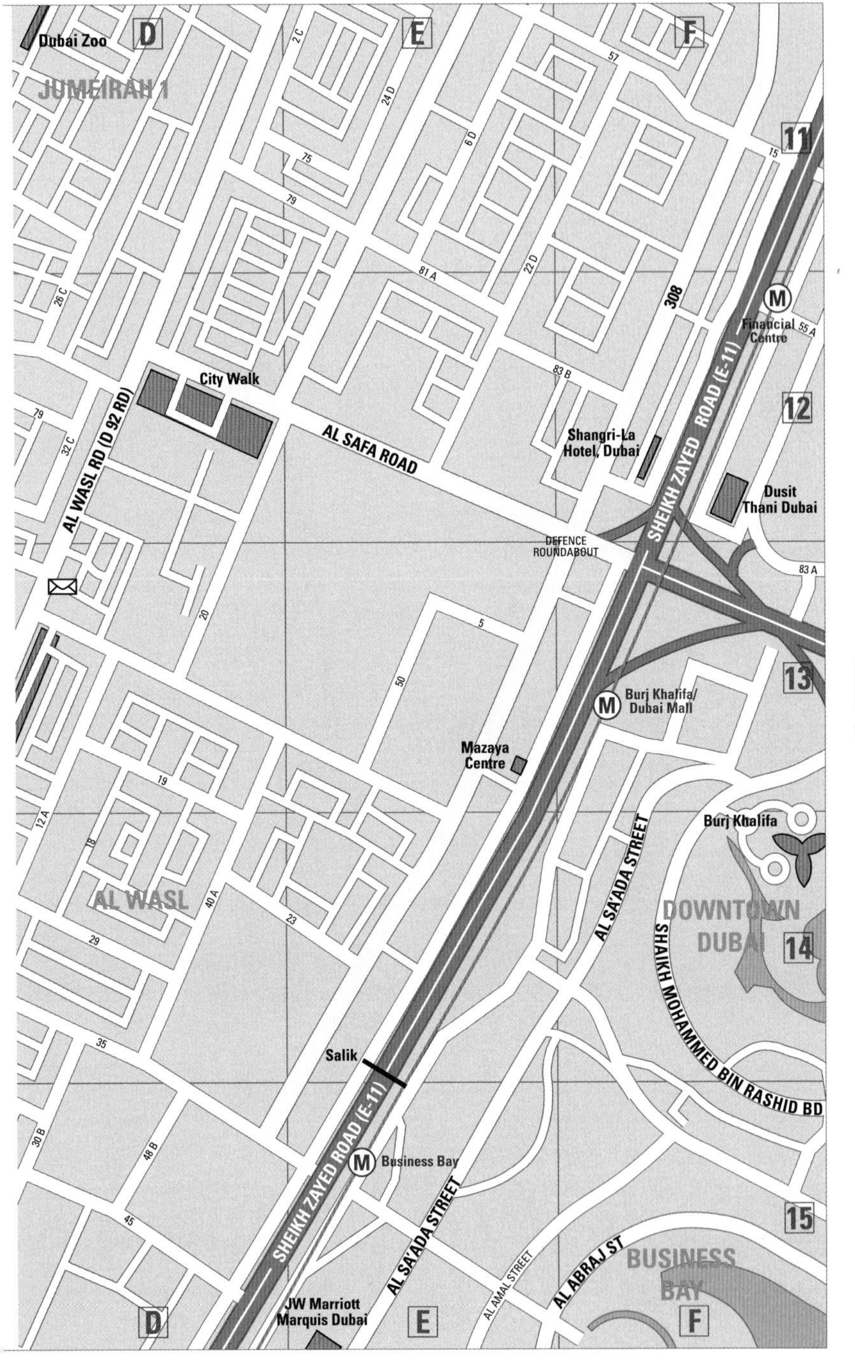

D
E
F
Dubai Zoo
JUMEIRAH 1
2 C
24 D
6 D
57
75
79
15
11
81 A
22 D
308
26 C
Financial Centre
55 A
83 B
City Walk
AL WASL RD (D 92 RD)
79
32 C
AL SAFA ROAD
12
Shangri-La Hotel, Dubai
SHEIKH ZAYED ROAD (E-11)
Dusit Thani Dubai
DEFENCE ROUNDABOUT
83 A
20
5
50
13
Burj Khalifa/ Dubai Mall
Mazaya Centre
19
12 A
18
AL SA'ADA STREET
Burj Khalifa
AL WASL
40 A
23
DOWNTOWN DUBAI
14
29
SHAIKH MOHAMMED BIN RASHID BD
35
Salik
30 B
48 B
Business Bay
45
15
AL SA'ADA STREET
AL AMAL STREET
AL ABRAJ ST
BUSINESS BAY
JW Marriott Marquis Dubai
D
E
F

MAPS

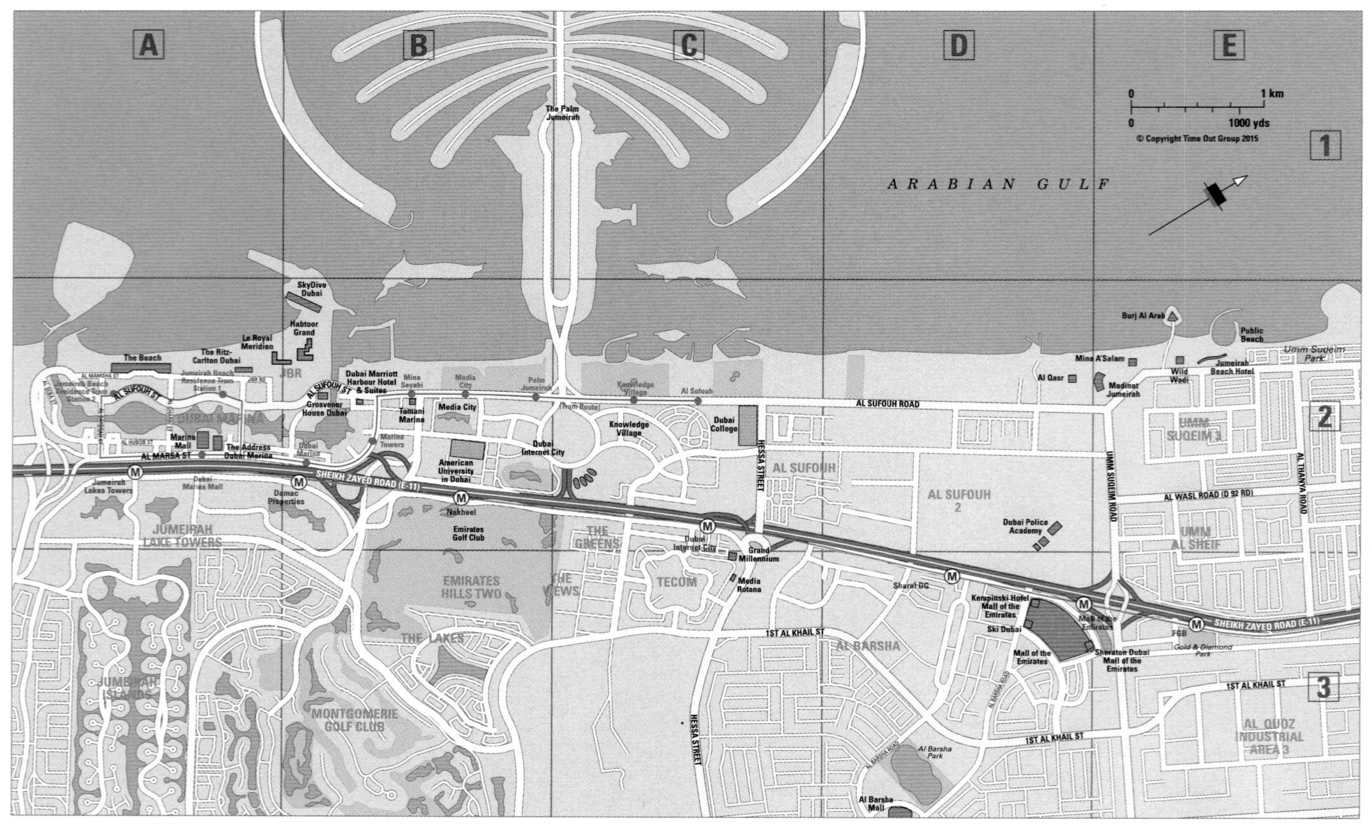
A
B
C
D
E
1
2
3
0
1 km
1000 yds
© Copyright Time Out Group 2015
ARABIAN GULF
The Palm Jumeirah
SkyDive Dubai
Habtoor Grand
Le Royal Meridien
The Ritz-Carlton Dubai
The Beach
JBR
Dubai Marriott Harbour Hotel & Suites
Mina Seyahi
Media City
Palm Jumeirah
Knowledge Village
Al Sufouh
Tram Route
AL SUFOUH ST
Grosvenor House Dubai
DUBAI MARINA
Marina Mall
The Address Dubai Marina
AL MARSA ST
Dubai Marina
Marina Towers
Tamani Marina
Media City
Dubai Internet City
Knowledge Village
Dubai College
AL SUFOUH ROAD
HESSA STREET
AL SUFOUH
AL SUFOUH 2
American University in Dubai
Jumeirah Lakes Towers
Dubai Marina Mall
Damac Properties
SHEIKH ZAYED ROAD (E-11)
Nakheel
Emirates Golf Club
JUMEIRAH LAKE TOWERS
THE GREENS
Grand Millennium
Media Rotana
TECOM
EMIRATES HILLS TWO
THE VIEWS
THE LAKES
JUMEIRAH ISLANDS
MONTGOMERIE GOLF CLUB
1ST AL KHAIL ST
AL BARSHA
Sharaf DG
Dubai Police Academy
Kempinski Hotel Mall of the Emirates
Ski Dubai
Mall of the Emirates
Sheraton Dubai Mall of the Emirates
Al Barsha Park
Al Barsha Mall
Burj Al Arab
Mina A'Salam
Al Qasr
Madinat Jumeirah
Wild Wadi
Jumeirah Beach Hotel
Public Beach
Umm Suqeim Park
UMM SUQEIM 3
UMM SUQEIM ROAD
AL WASL ROAD (D 92 RD)
AL THANYA ROAD
UMM AL SHEIF
FGB
Gold & Diamond Park
AL QUOZ INDUSTRIAL AREA 3

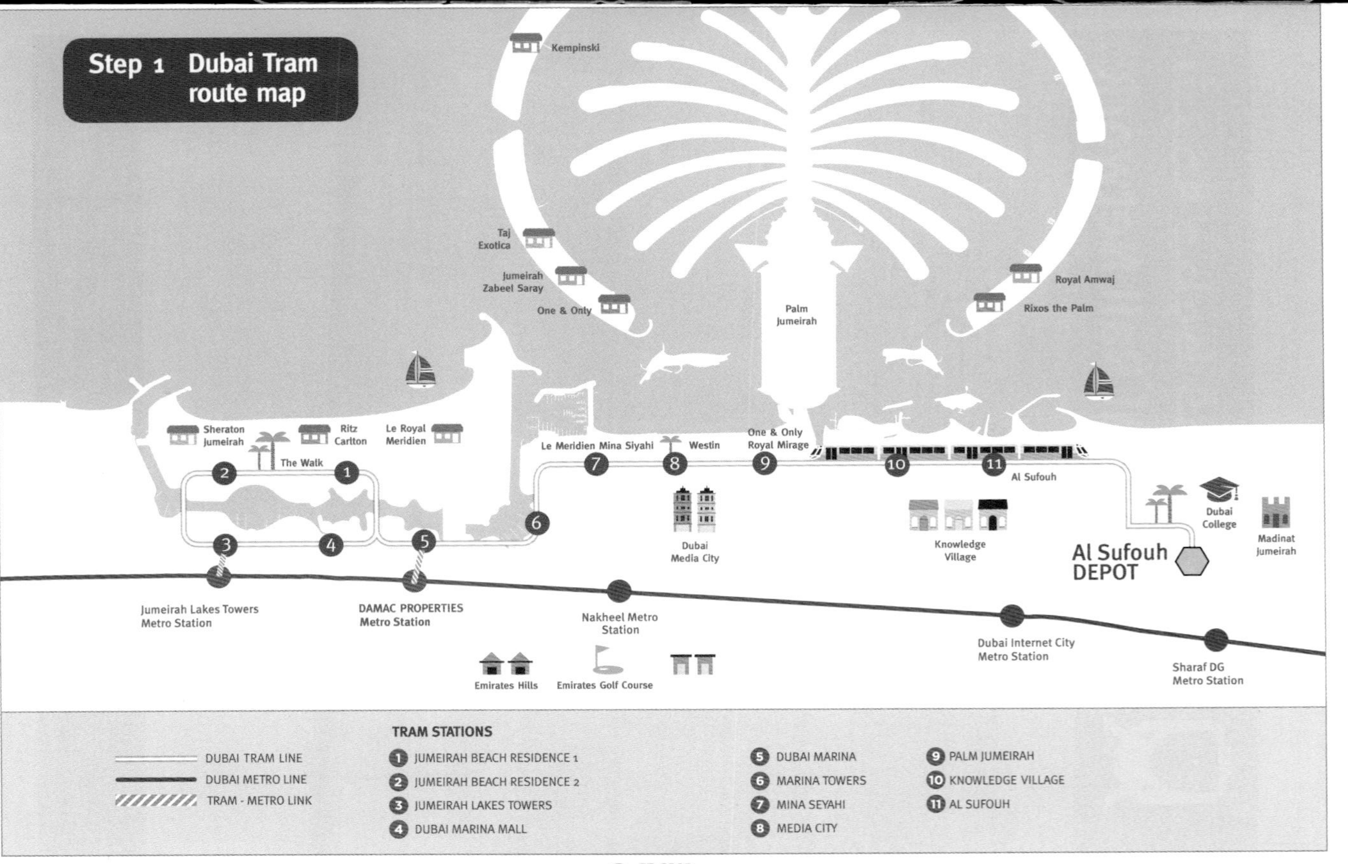
Step 1 Dubai Tram route map
Kempinski
Taj Exotica
Jumeirah Zabeel Saray
One & Only
Palm Jumeirah
Royal Amwaj
Rixos the Palm
Sheraton Jumeirah
The Walk
Ritz Carlton
Le Royal Meridien
Le Meridien Mina Siyahi
Westin
One & Only Royal Mirage
Al Sufouh
Dubai Media City
Knowledge Village
Dubai College
Madinat Jumeirah
Al Sufouh DEPOT
Jumeirah Lakes Towers Metro Station
DAMAC PROPERTIES Metro Station
Nakheel Metro Station
Dubai Internet City Metro Station
Sharaf DG Metro Station
Emirates Hills
Emirates Golf Course
DUBAI TRAM LINE
DUBAI METRO LINE
TRAM - METRO LINK
TRAM STATIONS
1 JUMEIRAH BEACH RESIDENCE 1
2 JUMEIRAH BEACH RESIDENCE 2
3 JUMEIRAH LAKES TOWERS
4 DUBAI MARINA MALL
5 DUBAI MARINA
6 MARINA TOWERS
7 MINA SEYAHI
8 MEDIA CITY
9 PALM JUMEIRAH
10 KNOWLEDGE VILLAGE
11 AL SUFOUH

شبكة خطوط قطارات دبي
Dubai Rail Network

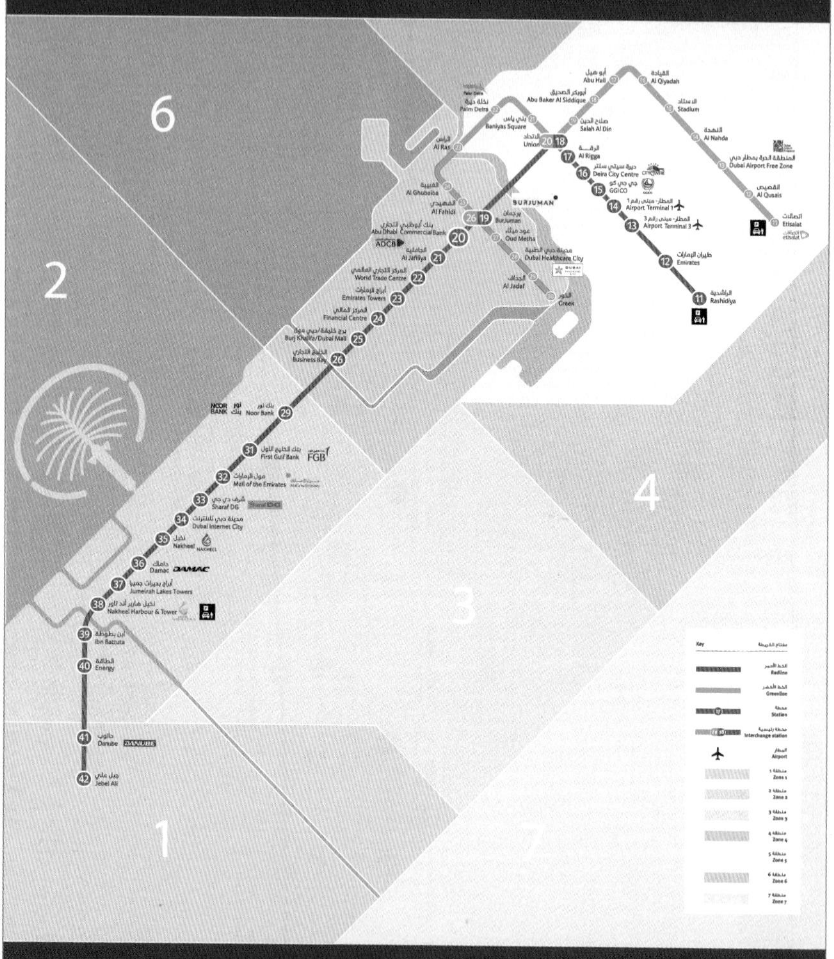

RTA

MAPS